Essentials of
Economics

The McGraw Hill Series Economics

Essentials of
Economics

5th edition

Stanley L. Brue
Pacific Lutheran University

Campbell R. McConnell
University of Nebraska at Lincoln

Sean M. Flynn
Scripps College

With the special assistance of
Randy R. Grant
Linfield University

ESSENTIALS OF ECONOMICS, FIFTH EDITION

Published by McGraw Hill LLC, 1325 Avenue of the Americas, New York, NY 10019. Copyright ©2023 by McGraw Hill LLC. All rights reserved. Printed in the United States of America. Previous editions ©2019, 2014, and 2010. No part of this publication may be reproduced or distributed in any form or by any means, or stored in a database or retrieval system, without the prior written consent of McGraw Hill LLC, including, but not limited to, in any network or other electronic storage or transmission, or broadcast for distance learning.

Some ancillaries, including electronic and print components, may not be available to customers outside the United States.

This book is printed on acid-free paper.

1 2 3 4 5 6 7 8 9 LWI 27 26 25 24 23 22

ISBN 978-1-265-35064-2 (bound edition)
MHID 1-265-35064-7 (bound edition)
ISBN 978-1-265-58606-5 (loose-leaf edition)
MHID 1-265-58606-3 (loose-leaf edition)

Portfolio Manager: *Adam Huenecke*
Lead Product Developer: *Kelly I. Pekelder*
Marketing Manager: *Bobby Pearson*
Content Project Managers: *Melissa Leick, Emily Windelborn*
Buyers: *Rachel Hirschfield/Sue Culbertson*
Designer: *Matt Diamond*
Content Licensing Specialist: *Melissa Homer*
Cover Image: *tantishock/Shutterstock*
Compositor: *Straive*

All credits appearing on page or at the end of the book are considered to be an extension of the copyright page.

Library of Congress Cataloging-in-Publication Data

Names: Brue, Stanley L., 1945- author.
Title: Essentials of economics / Stanley L. Brue, Pacific Lutheran
     University, Campbell R. McConnell, Sean M. Flynn.
Description: 5th Edition. | New York, NY : McGraw Hill LLC, 2022. | Revised
     edition of Essentials of economics, [2019]
Identifiers: LCCN 2021049788 (print) | LCCN 2021049789 (ebook) | ISBN
     9781265350642 (paperback) | ISBN 9781265587352 (ebook)
Subjects: LCSH: Economics.
Classification: LCC HB171 .B778 2022 (print) | LCC HB171 (ebook) | DDC
     330–dc23
LC record available at https://lccn.loc.gov/2021049788
LC ebook record available at https://lccn.loc.gov/2021049789

The Internet addresses listed in the text were accurate at the time of publication. The inclusion of a website does not indicate an endorsement by the authors or McGraw Hill LLC, and McGraw Hill LLC does not guarantee the accuracy of the information presented at these sites.

About the Authors

Stanley L. Brue

Stanley L. Brue did his undergraduate work at Augustana College (South Dakota) and received its Distinguished Achievement Award in 1991. He received his Ph.D. from the University of Nebraska–Lincoln. He is retired from a long career at Pacific Lutheran University, where he was honored as a recipient of the Burlington Northern Faculty Achievement Award. Professor Brue has also received the national Leavey Award for excellence in economic education. He has served as national president and chair of the Board of Trustees of Omicron Delta Epsilon International Economics Honorary. He is coauthor of *Economics,* Twenty-second Edition; *Economic Scenes,* Fifth Edition (Prentice-Hall); *Contemporary Labor Economics,* Eleventh Edition; and *The Evolution of Economic Thought,* Eighth Edition (Cengage). For relaxation, he enjoys international travel, attending sporting events, and going on fishing trips.

Campbell R. McConnell

Campbell R. McConnell earned his Ph.D. from the University of Iowa after receiving degrees from Cornell College and the University of Illinois. He taught at the University of Nebraska–Lincoln from 1953 until his retirement in 1990. He was also coauthor of *Economics,* Twenty-second Edition, *Contemporary Labor Economics*, and *Economics, Brief Edition.* He was a recipient of both the University of Nebraska Distinguished Teaching Award and the James A. Lake Academic Freedom Award and served as president of the Midwest Economics Association. Professor McConnell was awarded an honorary Doctor of Laws degree from Cornell College in 1973 and received its Distinguished Achievement Award in 1994. He was also a jazz expert and aficionado until his passing in 2019.

Sean M. Flynn

Sean M. Flynn did his undergraduate work at the University of Southern California before completing his Ph.D. at U.C. Berkeley, where he served as the Head Graduate Student Instructor for the Department of Economics after receiving the Outstanding Graduate Student Instructor Award. He teaches at Scripps College in Claremont, California, and is also the author of *Economics for Dummies*, Third Edition (Wiley); coauthor of *Economics,* Twenty-second Edition; and *The Cure That Works: How to Have the World's Best Healthcare—at a Quarter of the Price* (Regnery). His research interests include behavioral finance, behavioral economics, and health care economics. An accomplished martial artist, Sean has coached five of his students to national championships and is the author of *Understanding Shodokan Aikido* (Shodokan Press). Other hobbies include running, traveling, and cooking.

IN MEMORIAM

CAMPBELL R. McCONNELL (1928–2019)

We have lost a gracious friend, superb mentor, and legendary coauthor. In 2019 Professor Campbell R. "Mac" McConnell passed away at age 90 in Lincoln, Nebraska. Mac was one of the most significant and influential American economic educators of his generation. Through his best-selling principles textbook, he made introductory economics accessible to millions of students. By way of numerous adaptations and translations of his textbook, he influenced students throughout the world.

Mac was born in Harvey, Illinois, graduated from Cornell College (Iowa), and obtained his Ph.D. from the University of Iowa. He had a long and successful career as a researcher and teacher at the University of Nebraska, publishing peer-reviewed research articles and serving in leadership positions such as President of the Midwest Economic Association. His gift of explaining complex economics simply and thoroughly led him to explore opportunities to extend his educational reach beyond his own classroom. McGraw Hill understood the great potential in his textbook proposal and the first edition of *Economics: Principles, Problems, and Policies* made its debut in 1960. It was an instant hit and by the late 1970s it became the leading seller in the United States, supplanting Paul Samuelson's textbook as the market leader. *Economics* remains the top seller today.

In 1986, Mac and his former student, Stanley Brue, coauthored *Contemporary Labor Economics* and 2 years later Professor Brue joined Mac as a coauthor of *Economics*. Stan, Mac, and McGraw Hill added Sean Flynn as the third coauthor on the authorship team in 2008. The authorship transitions have been planned in advance, with authors working side by side for several editions. These smooth transitions have greatly contributed to the progress of the book and its continuing success.

We (Stan and Sean) are humbled and proud to have worked with Mac and McGraw Hill over these many years. We pledge to instructors and students that we will continue to stress clarity of presentation—in each new chapter, revised paragraph, rephrased explanation, and edited sentence. We believe that our dedication to preserving and improving the quality of the book is absolutely the best way for us to honor and extend Mac's amazing legacy. Mac liked to say that, "*Brevity at the expense of clarity is false economy.*" We will honor him, and his legacy, by always putting clarity first.

We greatly miss our coauthor and long-time friend Campbell R. McConnell.

Stanley L. Brue

Sean M. Flynn

Brief Contents

Contents

Preface

Welcome to the fifth edition of *Essentials of Economics,* a one-semester principles of economics text derived from McConnell-Brue-Flynn *Economics,* the best-selling two-semester economics textbook. Over the years, numerous instructors have requested a short, one-semester version of *Economics* that would cover both microeconomics and macroeconomics. While some other two-semester books simply eliminate chapters, renumber those that remain, and offer the "cut and splice" version as a customized book, this methodology does not fit with our vision of a tightly focused, highly integrated book. We built this text from scratch, incorporating the core content from *Economics* in a format designed specifically for the one-semester course. This book has the clear and careful language and the balanced approach that has made its two-semester counterpart a best-seller, but the pedagogy and topic discussion are much better suited to the needs of the one-semester course.

essentials of
economics

5e

Stanley L. Brue
Campbell R. McConnell
Sean M. Flynn

McGraw Hill

We think *Essentials of Economics* will fit nicely in various one-term courses. It is sufficiently lively and focused for use in principles courses populated primarily by non-business majors. Also, it is suitably analytical and comprehensive for use in combined micro and macro principles courses for business and potential economics majors. Finally, we think this book—if supplemented with appropriate lecture and reading assignments—will work well in refresher courses for students returning to MBA programs.

However the book is used, our goals remain the same:

- Help the student master the principles essential for understanding the economic problem, specific economic issues, and policy alternatives.

- Help the student understand and apply the economic perspective and reason accurately and objectively about economic matters.

- Promote a lasting student interest in economics and the economy.

What's New and Improved?

One of the benefits of writing a successful text is the opportunity to revise—to delete the outdated and install the new, to rewrite misleading or ambiguous statements, to introduce more relevant illustrations, to improve the organizational structure, and to enhance the learning aids. We trust that you will agree that we have used this opportunity wisely and fully.

Improved Efficiency for Instructors

Faculty time is precious. To preserve as much of it as possible for the faculty adopting *Essentials of Economics,* we went sentence by sentence and section by section, pulling out extraneous examples, eliminating unnecessary graphs, and—in some cases—removing entire sections that faculty reported they don't have time to teach. It is our hope that this streamlined presentation frees up faculty time for more advanced classroom activities, including experiments, debates, simulations, and various forms of peer instruction and team-based learning.

Improved Readability for Students

Student time is also precious. The current crop of college students are digital natives and social media pioneers. They are used to Googling for answers, reading things that tend to be no longer than a Tweet, and receiving instant feedback. We have revised our presentation to accommodate their fast-paced, nonlinear learning style. You will find a greater economy of language and an increased focus on key examples, changes that will appeal to the heavy digital consumers as well as traditional students who study the old-fashioned way.

Examples and Illustrations That Resonate with Students

Students absorb economic theory most easily when it resonates with their experiences and is explained with current examples.

Disruptions from the COVID-19 pandemic have been felt throughout the economy, felt as much by our students as anyone. While it has not changed underlying principles, it has provided numerous examples to which students can relate, particularly at the microeconomic level. These have been integrated into topics such as production possibilities, consumer sovereignty, and market failure. In later chapters, the massive shock to the macroeconomy and subsequent policy response is woven into the discussions of business cycle movements and fiscal and monetary policy.

The pandemic isn't the only issue of interest to students, so we include other timely topics such as green-energy subsidies, universal basic income, the $15 minimum wage debate, soaring tuition costs, congestion pricing, and Bitcoin.

Updated End-of-Chapter Questions and Problems

We have updated the end-of-chapter questions, adding new problems to reflect revised and enhanced content, and removing a few that are outdated. The questions are analytic and often ask for free responses, whereas the problems are mainly quantitative. We have aligned the questions and problems with the learning objectives presented at the beginning of the chapters. All of the questions and problems are assignable through McGraw Hill's *Connect,* and many contain additional algorithmic variations and can be automatically graded within the system.

Chapter Changes

Individual chapters contain data updates, revised Learning Objectives, and new examples. In addition to the changes and features listed above, some chapter-specific revisions include:

Chapter 1: Limits, Alternatives, and Choices features a new Applying the Analysis titled, "Is Facebook Free?", another focusing on the pandemic and production possibilities, and a Global Snapshot comparing investment levels in selected countries.

Chapter 2: The Market System and the Circular Flow includes three new Applying the Analysis pieces—on Bitcoin mining, the Korean peninsula at night, and consumer sovereignty in a pandemic.

Chapter 3: Demand, Supply, and Market Equilibrium provides a new Applying the Analysis on market equilibrium, as well as a new Global Snapshot on the price of a loaf of bread in various countries. The Applying the Analysis piece on Uber and dynamic pricing has been moved to the **Chapter Three Appendix: Additional Examples of Supply and Demand**.

Chapter 4: Elasticity of Demand and Supply includes a new Applying the Analysis on "The Southwest Effect," as well as two new Global Snapshots, the first giving income elasticities of the demand for gasoline in selected countries, and the second reporting on cross elasticities between food prices and education spending in various countries.

Chapter 5: Market Failures: Public Goods and Externalities features updated information on the U.S. tax structure, and a new Applying the Analysis on congestion pricing.

Chapter 6: Businesses and Their Costs includes a new Global Snapshot on international differences in manufacturing costs. The presentation has been streamlined by removing the discussion of the business population and the principal-agent problem.

Chapter 7: Pure Competition offers a new Applying the Analysis on the life expectancy of a business to illustrate the frequency of entry and exit of firms.

Chapter 8: Pure Monopoly presents a new Applying the Analysis on France's long history of government salt monopolies.

Chapter 9: Monopolistic Competition and Oligopoly features a new Global Snapshot on restaurants per 100,000 residents in various cities around the world, as well as a new Applying the Analysis piece on product differentiation.

Chapter 10: GDP and Economic Growth contains numerous updates of both domestic and international data.

Chapter 11: Business Cycles, Unemployment, and Inflation incorporates discussion of the pandemic-induced recession that began in February 2020.

Chapter 12: Aggregate Demand and Aggregate Supply features a new Global Snapshot on the size of various countries' GDP gaps.

Chapter 13: Fiscal Policy, Deficits, and Debt includes important updates related to the pandemic recession and the subsequent policy responses, including the CARES Act and the American Rescue Plan.

Chapter 14: Money, Banking, and Financial Institutions is significantly more concise thanks to a shortened discussion of securitization, a streamlined history of the financial crisis, and the elimination of the section on the structure of the post-crisis financial services industry.

Chapter 15: Interest Rates and Monetary Policy features updated coverage of recent U.S. monetary policy, including a new discussion of the Fed's dual mandate to set and pursue targets for both the unemployment rate and inflation rate.

Chapter 16: International Trade and Exchange Rates contains extensive data updates, a streamlined presentation of the arguments in favor of protectionism, and an updated and consolidated discussion of trade pacts, including the USMCA revisions to NAFTA.

Chapter 17: Wage Determination includes an updated presentation of the minimum wage debate, the addition of the demand-enhancement union model, and updated data on occupational employment trends.

Chapter 18: Income Inequality and Poverty features a new discussion of the debate over Universal Basic Income (UBI).

Acknowledgments

We give special thanks to Randy R. Grant of Linfield University who served as the content coordinator for *Essentials of Economics*. Professor Grant modified and seamlessly incorporated appropriate new content and revisions that the authors made in the twenty-second edition of *Economics* into *Essentials*. He also updated the tables and other information in *Essentials of Economics* and made various improvements that he deemed helpful or were suggested to him by the authors, reviewers, and publisher.

We wish to acknowledge William Walstad and Tom Barbiero (the coauthor of the Canadian edition of *Economics*) for their ongoing ideas and insights.

We are greatly indebted to an all-star group of professionals at McGraw Hill—in particular Adam Huenecke, Kelly Pekelder, Melissa Leick, Emily Windelborn, Mark Christianson, and Bobby Pearson for their publishing and marketing expertise. Matt Diamond provided the vibrant interior design and cover.

The fifth edition has benefited from a number of perceptive formal reviews. The reviewers, listed at the end of the preface, were a rich source of suggestions for this revision. To each of you, and others we may have inadvertently overlooked, thank you for your considerable help in improving *Essentials of Economics*.

Stanley L. Brue
Sean M. Flynn
Campbell R. McConnell

Reviewers

Mark Abajian, *San Diego City College*

Rebecca Arnold, *San Diego Mesa College*

Benjamin Artz, *University of Wisconsin, Milwaukee*

Clare Battista, *California Polytechnic State University*

Derek Berry, *Calhoun Community College*

Laura Jean Bhadra, *Northern Virginia Community College, Manassas*

Philip Bohan, *Ventura College*

Kalyan Chakraborty, *Emporia State University*

Jan Christopher, *Delaware State University*

Donald Coffin, *Indiana University Northwest*

Diana Denison, *Red Rocks Community College*

John Allen Deskins, *Creighton University, Omaha*

Caf Dowlah, *Queensborough Community College*

Mariano Escobedo, *Columbus State Community College*

Charles Fairchild, *Northern Virginia Community College, Manassas*

Charles Fraley, *Cincinnati State Tech and Community College*

Amy Gibson, *Christopher Newport University*

John Gibson, *Indiana University Northwest*

Robert Harris, *IUPUI, Indianapolis*

Mark Healy, *William Rainey Harper College*

Melinda Hickman, *Doane College*

Glenn Hsu, *Kishwaukee College*

Scott Hunt, *Columbus State Community College*

John Ifcher, *Santa Clara University*

Vani Kotcherlakota, *University of Nebraska, Kearney*

Marie Kratochvil, *Nassau Community College*

Teresa Laughlin, *Palomar College*

Melissa Lind, *University of Texas, Arlington*

Keith Malone, *University of North Alabama*

Khalid Mehtabdin, *College of Saint Rose*

Jennifer Kelleher Michaels, *Emmanuel College*

Babu Nahata, *University of Louisville*

Jim Payne, *Calhoun Community College*

Michael Petrowsky, *Glendale Community College*

Mitchell Redlo, *Monroe Community College*

Belinda Roman, *Palo Alto College*

Dave St. Clair, *California State University, East Bay*

Courtenay Stone, *Ball State University*

Gary Stone, *Winthrop University*

Anh Le Tran, *Lasell College*

Miao Wang, *Marquette University*

Timothy Wunder, *University of Texas, Arlington*

Connect Tools for Customizing Classes

Our Connect learning platform contains several tools that allow faculty to create and deliver custom content to their students.

Instructor-Authored Homework Problems

McGraw Hill is committed to empowering faculty. One way we do that is by ensuring that instructors can write their own auto-gradable homework questions within our Connect learning platform. These can then be assigned in exactly the same way as our test bank questions and our end-of-chapter questions and problems.

Custom Publishing

Another option for personalization is our "custom pub" program through which we can deliver small print runs of McConnell that include material that faculty have prepared themselves—anything from bullet-pointed lecture notes to privately authored worksheets or reading materials. Those materials can be integrated with McConnell content in any order, thereby allowing faculty total control over course content and reading materials.

Test Builder in Connect

Available within Connect, Test Builder is a cloud-based tool that enables instructors to format tests that can be printed or administered within an LMS. Test Builder offers a modern, streamlined interface for easy content configuration that matches course needs, without requiring a download.

Test Builder allows you to:

- Access all test bank content from a particular title.
- Easily pinpoint the most relevant content through robust filtering options.
- Manipulate the order of questions or scramble questions and/or answers.
- Pin questions to a specific location within a test.
- Determine your preferred treatment of algorithmic questions.
- Choose the layout and spacing.
- Add instructions and configure default settings.

Test Builder provides a secure interface for better protection of content and allows for just-in-time updates to flow directly into assessments.

Remote proctoring and browser-locking capabilities, hosted by Proctorio within Connect, provide control of the assessment environment by enabling security options and verifying the identity of the student.

Seamlessly integrated within Connect, these services allow instructors to control students' assessment experience by restricting browser activity, recording students' activity, and verifying students are doing their own work.

Instant and detailed reporting gives instructors an at-a-glance view of potential academic integrity concerns, thereby avoiding personal bias and supporting evidence-based claims.

Assurance of Learning Ready

Many educational institutions today are focused on the notion of assurance of learning, an important element of many accreditation standards. *Essentials of Economics 5e* is designed specifically to support your assurance of learning initiatives with a simple yet powerful solution.

Each chapter in the book begins with a list of numbered learning objectives, which appear throughout the chapter as well as in the end-of-chapter assignments. Every Test Bank question for *Essentials of Economics 5e* maps to a specific chapter learning objective in the textbook as well as topic area, Bloom's Taxonomy level, and AACSB skill area. You can use our Test Bank software, EZ Test, or Connect Economics to easily search for learning objectives that directly relate to the learning objectives for your course. You can then use the reporting features of EZ Test to aggregate student results in similar fashion, making the collection and presentation of assurance of learning data simple and easy.

AACSB Statement

McGraw Hill is a proud corporate member of AACSB International. Understanding the importance and value of AACSB accreditation, *Essentials of Economics 5e* recognizes the curricula guidelines detailed in the AACSB standards for business accreditation by connecting selected questions in the Test Bank and end-of-chapter material to the general knowledge and skill guidelines in the AACSB standards.

The statements contained in *Essentials of Economics 5e* are provided only as a guide for the users of this textbook. The AACSB leaves content coverage and assessment within the purview of individual schools, the mission of the school, and the faculty. While *Essentials of Economics 5e* and the teaching package make no claim of any specific AACSB qualification or evaluation, we have, within *Essentials of Economics 5e*, labeled selected questions according to the six general knowledge and skills areas.

Instructors: Student Success Starts with You

Tools to enhance your unique voice

Want to build your own course? No problem. Prefer to use an OLC-aligned, prebuilt course? Easy. Want to make changes throughout the semester? Sure. And you'll save time with Connect's auto-grading too.

65%
Less Time Grading

Laptop: McGraw Hill; Woman/dog: George Doyle/Getty Images

Study made personal

Incorporate adaptive study resources like SmartBook® 2.0 into your course and help your students be better prepared in less time. Learn more about the powerful personalized learning experience available in SmartBook 2.0 at **www.mheducation.com/highered/connect/smartbook**

Affordable solutions, added value

Make technology work for you with LMS integration for single sign-on access, mobile access to the digital textbook, and reports to quickly show you how each of your students is doing. And with our Inclusive Access program you can provide all these tools at a discount to your students. Ask your McGraw Hill representative for more information.

Padlock: Jobalou/Getty Images

Solutions for your challenges

A product isn't a solution. Real solutions are affordable, reliable, and come with training and ongoing support when you need it and how you want it. Visit **www.supportateverystep.com** for videos and resources both you and your students can use throughout the semester.

Checkmark: Jobalou/Getty Images

Students: Get Learning that Fits You

Effective tools for efficient studying

Connect is designed to help you be more productive with simple, flexible, intuitive tools that maximize your study time and meet your individual learning needs. Get learning that works for you with Connect.

Study anytime, anywhere

Download the free ReadAnywhere app and access your online eBook, SmartBook 2.0, or Adaptive Learning Assignments when it's convenient, even if you're offline. And since the app automatically syncs with your Connect account, all of your work is available every time you open it. Find out more at **www.mheducation.com/readanywhere**

"I really liked this app—it made it easy to study when you don't have your textbook in front of you."

- Jordan Cunningham,
  Eastern Washington University

Calendar: owattaphotos/Getty Images

Everything you need in one place

Your Connect course has everything you need—whether reading on your digital eBook or completing assignments for class, Connect makes it easy to get your work done.

Learning for everyone

McGraw Hill works directly with Accessibility Services Departments and faculty to meet the learning needs of all students. Please contact your Accessibility Services Office and ask them to email accessibility@mheducation.com, or visit **www.mheducation.com/about/accessibility** for more information.

Top: Jenner Images/Getty Images. Left: Hero Images/Getty Images. Right: Hero Images/Getty Images

Connect Economics Asset Alignment with Bloom's Taxonomy

We Take Students Higher

As a learning science company we create content that supports higher order thinking skills. Within Connect®, we tag assessments accordingly so you can filter your search, assign it, and receive reporting on it. These content asset types can be associated with one or more levels of Bloom's Taxonomy.

The chart below shows a few of the key assignable economics assets with *McGraw Hill Connect* aligned with Bloom's Taxonomy. Take your students higher by assigning a variety of applications, moving them from simple memorization to concept application.

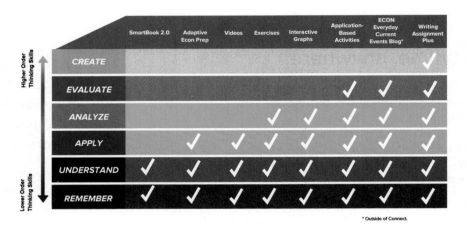

	SmartBook 2.0	Adaptive Econ Prep	Videos	Exercises	Interactive Graphs	Application-Based Activities	ECON Everyday Current Events Blog*	Writing Assignment Plus
CREATE								✓
EVALUATE						✓	✓	✓
ANALYZE			✓	✓	✓	✓	✓	✓
APPLY	✓	✓	✓	✓	✓		✓	✓
UNDERSTAND	✓	✓	✓	✓	✓		✓	✓
REMEMBER	✓	✓	✓	✓	✓	✓	✓	✓

Higher Order Thinking Skills / Lower Order Thinking Skills

* Outside of Connect.

SmartBook 2.0

SmartBook 2.0 provides personalized learning to each student's needs, continually adapts to pinpoint knowledge gaps and focuses learning on concepts requiring additional study. It fosters more productive learning and helps students better prepare for class.

Adaptive Econ Prep

Math and graphing preparedness assignments help students refresh important prerequisite topics necessary to be successful in economics. New Adaptive Econ Prep Tool provides students just-in-time math and graphing remediation that are prerequisite to success in Principles of Economics courses and adapt to each student.

Videos

Tutorial videos provide engaging explanations to help students grasp challenging concepts. Application videos bring economics to life with relevant, real world examples. All videos include closed captioning for accessibility and are assignable with assessment questions for improved retention.

Exercises

Exercises with algorithmic variations provide ample opportunities for students to practice and hone quantitative skills. Graphing Exercises provide opportunities for students to draw, interact with, manipulate, and analyze graphs.

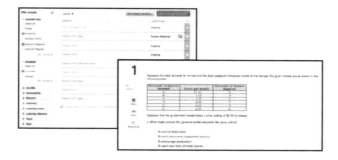

Interactive Graphs

Interactive Graphs provide visual displays of real data and economic concepts for students to manipulate. All graphs are accompanied by assignable assessment questions and feedback to guide students through the experience of learning to read and interpret graphs and data.

Application-Based Activities

Immersive real-life scenarios engage students and put them in the role of everyday economists. Students practice their economic thinking and problem-solving skills as they apply course concepts and see the implications of their decisions as they go. Each activity is designed as a 15-minute experience, unless students eagerly replay for a better outcome.

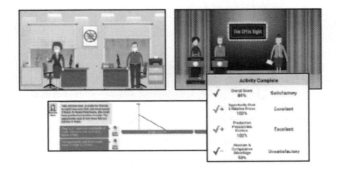

ECON Everyday Current Events Blog

Our ECON Everyday blog saves instructors time bringing current, student-centered content into their course all semester long. Short articles, written for principles-level students, is tagged by topic to bring currency into your course. We also provide discussion questions to help you drive the conversation forward. Visit www.eco neveryday.com and subscribe for updates.

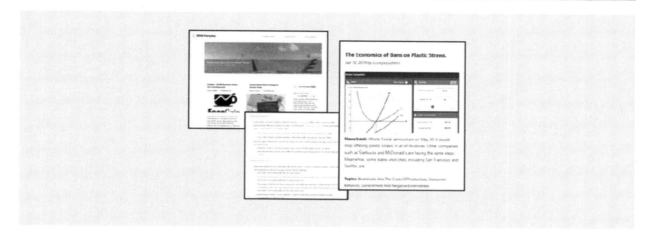

Writing Assignment Plus

Writing Assignment Plus delivers a learning experience that helps students improve their written communication skills and conceptual understanding. Faculty can assign, monitor, grade, and provide feedback on writing projects efficiently. Built-in grammar and writing review helps students improve writing quality while an originality check helps students correct central plagiarism before submission. End result? Improved workplace skills of writing in critical thinking.

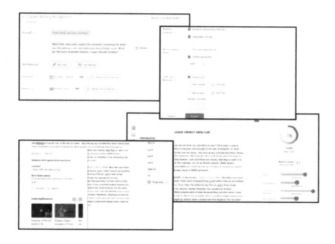

For more information, please visit: www.mheducation.com/highered/economics

To the Student

This book and its ancillaries contain several features designed to help you learn economics:

- *Appendix on graphs* To understand the content in this book, you will need to be comfortable with basic graphical analysis and a few quantitative concepts. The web appendix for Chapter 1 reviews graphing and slopes of curves. Be sure not to skip it.

- *Key terms* Key terms are set in boldface type within the chapters, defined in the margins, listed at the end of each chapter, and again defined in the Glossary toward the end of the book.

- *"Illustrating the Idea" and "Applying the Analysis"* These sections flow logically and smoothly from the content that precedes them. They are part and parcel of the development of the ideas and cannot be skipped. Each "Illustrating the Idea" and "Applying the Analysis" section is followed by a question.

- *Questions and Problems* The end of each chapter features separate sections of Questions and Problems. The Questions are analytic and often ask for free responses, while the Problems are more computational. Each is keyed to a particular learning objective (LO) in the list of LOs at the beginning of the chapter. At the Online Learning Center, there are multiple-choice quizzes and one or more web-based questions for each chapter.

Our two main goals are to help you understand and apply economics and help you improve your analytical skills. An understanding of economics will enable you to comprehend a whole range of economic, social, and political problems that otherwise would seem puzzling and perplexing. Also, your study will enhance reasoning skills that are highly prized in the workplace.

Good luck with your study. We think it will be well worth your time and effort.

CHAPTER ONE
Limits, Alternatives, and Choices

Learning Objectives

LO1.1 Define economics and the features of the economic perspective.
LO1.2 Describe the role of economic theory in economics.
LO1.3 Distinguish microeconomics from macroeconomics.
LO1.4 Explain the individual's economizing problem and illustrate trade-offs, opportunity costs, and attainable combinations with budget lines.
LO1.5 List the categories of scarce resources and explain society's economizing problem.
LO1.6 Apply production possibilities analysis.
LO1.7 (Chapter appendix) Understand graphs, curves, and slopes as they relate to economics.

(An appendix on understanding graphs can be found at the end of this chapter. If you need a quick review of this mathematical tool, you might benefit by reading the appendix first.)

People's wants are numerous and varied. Biologically, people need only air, water, food, clothing, and shelter. But in modern society, people also desire goods and services that provide a more comfortable or affluent standard of living. We want bottled water, soft drinks, and fruit juices, not just water from the creek. We want salads, burgers, and pizzas, not just berries and nuts. We also want flat-panel TVs, Internet service, education, national defense, smartphones, health care, and much more.

Fortunately, society possesses productive resources such as labor and managerial talent, tools and machinery, and land and mineral deposits. These resources, employed in the economic system (or simply the economy), help us produce goods and services that satisfy many of our economic wants. But in reality our economic wants far exceed the productive capacity of our scarce (limited) resources. We are forced to make choices. This unyielding truth underlies the definition of **economics** as the social science concerned with how individuals, institutions, and society make choices under conditions of scarcity.

The Economic Perspective

Economists view things through a particular perspective. This **economic perspective** has several critical and closely interrelated features.

Scarcity and Choice

economics
The study of how people, institutions, and society make economic choices under conditions of scarcity.

economic perspective
A viewpoint that envisions individuals and institutions making rational decisions by comparing the marginal benefits and marginal costs associated with their actions.

scarcity
The limits placed on the amounts and types of *goods* and *services* available for consumption as the result of there being only limited *economic resources* from which to produce output; the fundamental economic constraint that creates *opportunity costs* and that necessitates the use of *marginal analysis (cost-benefit analysis)* to make optimal choices.

opportunity cost
The value of the good, service, or time forgone to obtain something else.

The economic resources needed to make goods are services are in limited supply. This **scarcity** restricts options and demands choices. Because we "can't have it all," we must decide what we will have and what we must forgo.

At the core of economics is the idea that "there is no free lunch." You may be treated to lunch, making it "free" to you, but someone bears a cost (as in the nearby story about Facebook). Scarce inputs involved in creating the lunch include land, equipment, and farm labor. Because society could have used these to produce other things, it sacrifices those other goods and services in making the lunch available. Economists call such sacrifices **opportunity costs:** To obtain more of one thing, society forgoes the opportunity of getting the next best thing that could have been created with those resources.

 APPLYING THE ANALYSIS

Is Facebook Free?

Facebook spends over $20 billion every year updating its platform, running server farms, and paying its employees. It also gives away its product for free to more than 2 billion users. Has Facebook figured out a way to overcome scarcity?

No, it hasn't. Scarcity is permanent. But Facebook *has* figured out a way to more than cover its costs without charging its users a penny. Facebook's trick is to charge advertisers instead. They pay Facebook nearly $40 billion per year to boost content and target ads to specific individuals.

Lesson One: If you are consuming a good or service and not paying for it, the cost is being borne by someone else.

Lesson Two: Companies don't usually give freebies to be nice; they do it as part of their business model. Facebook grants users free access to its platform to make sure that it has as many "eyeballs" as possible to sell to advertisers.

Rvlsoft/Shutterstock

Purposeful Behavior

utility
The want-satisfying power of a good or service; the satisfaction or pleasure a consumer obtains from the consumption of a good or service (or from the consumption of a collection of goods and services).

Economics assumes that human behavior reflects "rational self-interest." Individuals look for and pursue opportunities to increase their **utility:** pleasure, happiness, or satisfaction. They allocate their time, energy, and money to maximize their satisfaction. Because they weigh costs and benefits, their decisions are "purposeful" or "rational," not "random" or "chaotic."

ILLUSTRATING THE IDEA

Did Zuckerberg, Seacrest, and Grande Make Bad Choices?

The importance of opportunity costs in decision making is illustrated by different choices people make with respect to college. Average salaries of college graduates are nearly twice as high as those earned by persons with high school diplomas as their last education completed. For students with both the access to and aptitude for college, "Go to college, stay in college, and earn a degree" is very sound advice.

Yet Facebook founder Mark Zuckerberg and media personality Ryan Seacrest both dropped out of college, while pop singer Ariana Grande never even bothered to start classes. What were they thinking? Unlike most students, Zuckerberg faced enormous opportunity costs for staying in college. He had a vision for his company, and dropping out helped to ensure Facebook's success. Similarly, Seacrest landed a professional DJ job at his local radio station when he was in high school before moving to Hollywood and eventually becoming America's top radio and TV personality. Finishing his college degree might have interrupted the string of successes that made his career possible. And Grande knew that staying on top in the world of pop takes unceasing work. So after her first album became a massive hit, it made sense for her to skip college in order to relentlessly pursue continuing success.

So Zuckerberg, Seacrest, and Grande understood opportunity costs and made their choices accordingly. The size of opportunity costs greatly matters in making individual decisions.

> QUESTION:
>
> Professional athletes sometimes return to college after they retire from professional sports. How does that college decision relate to opportunity costs?

"Purposeful behavior" does not assume that people and institutions are immune from faulty logic and therefore are perfect decision makers. They sometimes make mistakes. Nor does it mean that people's decisions are unaffected by emotion or the decisions of those around them. People sometimes are impulsive or emulative. "Purposeful behavior" simply means that people make decisions with some desired outcome in mind.

Nor is rational self-interest the same as selfishness. Increasing one's own wage, rent, interest, or profit normally requires identifying and satisfying somebody else's want. Also, many people make personal sacrifices to others without expecting any monetary reward. They contribute time and money to charities because they derive pleasure from doing so. Parents help pay for their children's education for the same reason. These self-interested, but unselfish, acts help maximize the givers' satisfaction as much as any personal purchase of goods or services.

Marginal Analysis: Comparing Benefits and Costs

The economic perspective focuses largely on **marginal analysis**—comparisons of marginal benefits and marginal costs. To economists, "marginal" means "extra," "additional," or "a change in." Most choices or decisions involve changes in the existing state of affairs.

marginal analysis
The comparison of marginal ("extra" or "additional") benefits and marginal costs, usually for decision making.

Should you attend school for another year? Should you study an extra hour for an exam? Should a business expand or reduce its output? Should government increase or decrease its funding for a missile defense system?

Each option involves marginal benefits and marginal costs. In making choices rationally, the decision maker must compare those two amounts. Example: You and your partner are shopping for a diamond ring. Should you buy a $\frac{1}{2}$-carat diamond or a 1-carat diamond? The marginal cost of a larger diamond is the added expense beyond the cost of the smaller diamond. The marginal benefit is the perceived greater lifetime pleasure (utility) from the larger stone. If the marginal benefit of the larger diamond exceeds its marginal cost (and you can afford it), buy the larger stone. But if the marginal cost is more than the marginal benefit, you should buy the smaller diamond instead—even if you can afford the larger stone!

In a world of scarcity, the decision to obtain the marginal benefit associated with some specific option always includes the marginal cost of giving up something else. The money spent on the larger diamond means forgoing some other product. An opportunity cost—the value of the next best thing given up—is always present whenever a choice is made.

 APPLYING THE ANALYSIS

Fast-Food Lines

The economic perspective is useful in analyzing all sorts of behaviors. Consider an everyday example: the behavior of fast-food customers. When customers enter the restaurant, they go to the shortest line, believing that line will minimize their time cost of obtaining food. They are acting purposefully; time is limited, and people prefer using it in some way other than standing in a long line.

If one fast-food line is temporarily shorter than other lines, some people will move to that line. These movers apparently view the time saving from the shorter line (marginal benefit) as exceeding the cost of moving from their present line (marginal cost). The line switching tends to equalize line lengths. No further movement of customers between lines occurs once all lines are about equal.

Fast-food customers face another cost-benefit decision when a clerk opens a new station at the counter. Should they move to the new station or stay put? Those who shift to the new line decide that the time saving from the move exceeds the extra cost of physically moving. In so deciding, customers must also consider just how quickly they can get to the new station compared with others who may be contemplating the same move. (Those who hesitate are lost!)

Customers at the fast-food establishment do not have perfect information when they select lines. Thus, not all decisions turn out as expected. For example, you might enter a short line and find someone in front of you is ordering hamburgers and fries for 40 people in the Greyhound bus parked out back (and the employee is a trainee)! Nevertheless, at the time you made your decision, you thought it was optimal.

Finally, customers must decide what food to order when they arrive at the counter. In making their choices, they again compare marginal costs and marginal benefits in attempting to obtain the greatest personal satisfaction for their expenditure.

Economists believe that what is true for the behavior of customers at fast-food restaurants is true for economic behavior in general. Faced with an array of choices, consumers, workers, and businesses rationally compare marginal costs and marginal benefits in making decisions.

> QUESTION:
>
> Have you ever gone to a fast-food restaurant only to observe long lines and then leave? Use the economic perspective to explain your behavior.

Theories, Principles, and Models

Like the other sciences, economics relies on the **scientific method.** That procedure consists of several elements:

scientific method
The procedure for the systematic pursuit of knowledge involving the observation of facts and the formulation and testing of hypotheses to obtain theories, principles, and laws.

* Observing real-world behavior and outcomes.

* Based on those observations, formulating a possible explanation of cause and effect (hypothesis).

* Testing this explanation by comparing the outcomes of specific events to the outcome predicted by the hypothesis.

* Accepting, rejecting, or modifying the hypothesis, based on these comparisons.

* Continuing to test the hypothesis against the facts. As favorable results accumulate, the hypothesis evolves into a *theory.* A very well-tested and widely accepted theory is referred to as a *law* or *principle.* Combinations of such laws or principles are incorporated into *models,* which are simplified representations of how something works, such as a market or segment of the economy.

Theories, principles, and models are "purposeful simplifications." The full scope of economic reality itself is too complex to be understood as a whole. In developing theories, principles, and models, economists remove the clutter and simplify. Despite their simplifications, good theories do a good job of explaining and predicting how individuals and institutions actually behave in producing, exchanging, and consuming goods and services.

There are some other things you should know about economic principles:

* *Generalizations* Economic principles are *generalizations* relating to economic behavior or to the economy itself. Economic principles are expressed as the tendencies of typical or average consumers, workers, or business firms. For example, economists say that consumers buy more of a particular product when its price falls. Economists recognize that some consumers may increase their purchases by a large amount, others by a small amount, and a few not at all. This "price-quantity" principle, however, holds for the typical consumer and for consumers as a group.

* *Other-things-equal assumption* Like other scientists, economists use the *ceteris paribus* or **other-things-equal assumption** to construct their theories. They assume that all variables except those under immediate consideration are held constant for a particular analysis. For example, when considering the relationship between the price of Pepsi and the amount of Pepsi that is purchased, economists do not take into account all the other factors that might influence the amount of Pepsi purchased (e.g., the price of Coca-Cola, and consumer incomes and preferences). Holding other things equal is helpful because the economist can then focus on the relationship between the price of Pepsi and purchases of Pepsi without being confused by changes in other variables.

other-things-equal assumption
The assumption that factors other than those being considered are held constant; *ceteris paribus* assumption.

* *Graphical expression* Many economic models are expressed graphically. Be sure to read the special appendix for this chapter as a review of graphs.

Microeconomics and Macroeconomics

Economists develop economic principles and models at two levels.

Microeconomics

microeconomics
The part of economics concerned with such individual units as a household, a firm, or an industry and with individual markets, specific goods and services, and product and resource prices.

Microeconomics is concerned with decision making by individual consumers, workers, households, and business firms. At this level of analysis, we observe the details of their behavior under a figurative microscope. We measure the price of a specific product, the revenue or income of a particular firm or household, or the expenditures of a specific firm, government entity, or family.

Macroeconomics

macroeconomics
The part of economics concerned with the economy as a whole; with such major aggregates as the household, business, and government sectors; and with measures of the total economy.

Macroeconomics examines the performance and behavior of the economy as a whole. It focuses on economic growth, the business cycle, interest rates, inflation, and the behavior of major economic or aggregates, such as the government, household, and business sectors. An **aggregate** is a collection of specific economic units treated as if they were one unit. Therefore, we might lump together the millions of consumers in the U.S. economy and treat them as if they were one huge unit called "consumers."

aggregate
A collection of specific economic units treated as if they were one. For example, all prices of individual goods and services are combined into a price level, or all the units of output are aggregated into gross domestic product.

In using aggregates, macroeconomics seeks to obtain an overview, or general outline, of the economy and the relationships of its major aggregates. Macroeconomics speaks of such economic measures as total output, total employment, total income, aggregate expenditures, and the general level of prices. Very little attention is given to specific units making up the various aggregates.

PHOTO OP

Micro versus Macro

Figuratively, microeconomics examines the sand, rock, and shells, not the beach; in contrast, macroeconomics examines the beach, not the sand, rocks, and shells.

NPS Photo

Holbox/Shutterstock RF

Individuals' Economic Problem

It is clear from our previous discussion that both individuals and society face an **economic problem**: The need to make choices because economic wants exceed economic means. Let's first build a microeconomic model of the economizing problem faced by an individual.

economic problem
The need for individuals and society to make choices because wants exceed means.

Limited Income

We all have a finite amount of income, even the wealthiest among us. Even Bill Gates must decide how to spend his money! Our income comes in the form of wages, interest, rent, and profit, although we may also receive money from government programs or family members. As **Global Snapshot 1.1** shows, the average income of Americans in 2017 was $58,270. In the poorest nations, it was less than $500.

 GLOBAL SNAPSHOT 1.1

Average Income, Selected Nations

Average income (total income/population) and therefore typical budget constraints vary greatly among nations.

Country	Per Capita Income, 2017*
Switzerland	$80,560
Qatar	61,070
United States	58,270
Singapore	54,530
France	37,970
South Korea	28,380
China	8,690
Mexico	8,610
Iraq	4,770
India	1,820
Madagascar	400
Malawi	320

*U.S. dollars, based on exchange rates.

Source: Organization for Economic Co-operation and Development (OECD), www.compareyourcountry.org.

Unlimited Wants

Most people have virtually unlimited wants. Our wants extend over a wide range of products that provide utility, from *necessities* (food, shelter, clothing) to *luxuries* (perfumes, yachts, sports cars).

Necessities versus Luxuries

Economic wants include both necessities and luxuries. Each type of item provides utility to the buyer.

David Sachs/Getty Images   Ingram Publishing/Superstock RF

Over time, as new and improved products are introduced, economic wants tend to change and multiply. Only recently have people wanted Wi-Fi connections, tablet computers, or flying drones because those products did not exist a few decades ago. Also, the satisfaction of certain wants may trigger others: The acquisition of a Ford Focus or a Honda Civic has been known to whet the appetite for a Lexus or a Mercedes.

Like goods, services also satisfy our wants. Car repair work, legal and accounting advice, and haircuts all satisfy human wants. Actually, we buy many goods, such as automobiles and washing machines, for the services they render.

Most people's desires for goods and services cannot be fully satisfied, though our desires for a particular good or service can be satisfied; over a short period of time, we can surely obtain enough toothpaste or pasta. But our broader desire for more goods and services and higher-quality goods and services seems to be another story.

Because we have only limited income but seemingly insatiable wants, it is in our self-interest to economize: to pick and choose goods and services that maximize our satisfaction, given the limitations we face.

A Budget Line

budget line
A line that shows the different combinations of two products a consumer can purchase with a specific money income, given the products' prices.

We can clarify the economic problem facing consumers by visualizing a **budget line** or *budget constraint,* which is a schedule or curve that shows various combinations of two products a consumer can purchase with a specific money income.

To understand this idea, suppose you received an Amazon gift card as a birthday present. The $120 card is soon to expire. You go online to Amazon.com and confine your purchase decisions to two alternatives: movies and paperback books. Movies are $20 each, and paperback books are $10 each. The table in **Figure 1.1** shows your purchase options.

At one extreme, you might spend all of your $120 "income" on 6 movies at $20 each and have nothing left to spend on books. Or, by giving up 6 movies and thereby gaining $40, you can have 4 movies at $20 each and 4 books at $10 each. And so on to the other extreme, at which you could buy 12 books at $10 each, spending your entire gift card on books with nothing left to spend on movies.

The graph in **Figure 1.1** shows the budget line. Every point on the line represents a possible combination of movies and books, including fractional quantities. The slope of the graphed budget line measures the ratio of the price of books (P_b) to the price of movies (P_m); more precisely, the slope is $P_b/P_m = \$ - 10/\$ + 20 = \frac{1}{2}$. So you must forgo 1 movie (measured on the vertical axis) to buy 2 books (measured on the horizontal axis). This yields a slope of $\frac{1}{2}$ or −0.5.

The budget line illustrates several ideas.

Attainable and Unattainable Combinations All the combinations of movies and books on or inside the budget line are *attainable* from the $120 of money income. You can afford to buy, for example, 3 movies at $20 each and 6 books at $10 each. You also can obviously afford to buy 2 movies and 5 books, thereby using up only $90 of the $120 available on your gift card. But to achieve maximum utility, you will want to spend the full $120. The budget line shows all combinations that cost exactly the full $120.

In contrast, all combinations beyond the budget line are *unattainable*. The $120 limit simply does not allow you to purchase, for example, 5 movies at $20 each and 5 books at $10 each. That $150 expenditure would clearly exceed the $120 limit.

Trade-offs and Opportunity Costs The budget line in **Figure 1.1** illustrates the idea of trade-offs arising from limited income. To obtain more movies, you have to give up some books. For example, to acquire the first movie, you trade off 2 books. So the opportunity cost of the first movie is 2 books. To obtain the second movie, the opportunity cost is also 2 books. The straight-line budget constraint, with its constant slope, indicates **constant opportunity cost.** That is, the opportunity cost of 1 extra movie remains the same (=2 books) as you purchase more movies. Likewise, the opportunity cost of 1 extra book does not change $\left(= \frac{1}{2} \text{ movie} \right)$ as you purchase more books.

constant opportunity cost
An opportunity cost that remains the same for each additional unit as a consumer (or society) shifts purchases (production) from one product to another along a straight-line budget line (production possibilities curve).

FIGURE 1.1

A consumer's budget line. The budget line (or budget constraint) shows all the combinations of any two products that can be purchased, given the prices of the products and the consumer's money income.

The Budget Line: Whole-Unit Combinations of Movies and Paperback Books Attainable with an Income of $120		
Units of Movies (Price = $20)	Units of Books (Price = $10)	Total Expenditure
6	0	$120 = ($120 + $0)
5	2	$120 = ($100 + $20)
4	4	$120 = ($80 + $40)
3	6	$120 = ($60 + $60)
2	8	$120 = ($40 + $80)
1	10	$120 = ($20 + $100)
0	12	$120 = ($0 + $120)

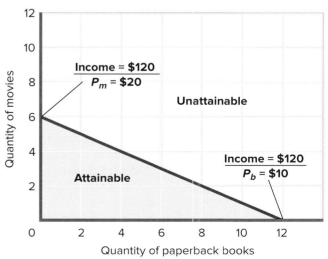

Choice   Limited income forces people to choose what to buy and what to forgo. You will select the combination of movies and paperback books that you think is "best." That is, you will evaluate your marginal benefits and your marginal costs (here, product price) to make choices that maximize your satisfaction. Other people, with the same $120 gift card, would undoubtedly make different choices.

Income Changes   The budget line varies with income. An increase in income shifts the budget line to the right; a decrease in income shifts it to the left. To verify this, recalculate the table in **Figure 1.1**, assuming the card value (income) is (a) $240 and (b) $60, and plot the new budget lines in the graph. No wonder people like to have more income: It shifts their budget lines outward and enables them to buy more goods and services. But even with more income, people will still face spending trade-offs, choices, and opportunity costs.

Society's Economic Problem

Society also faces an economizing problem. Should it devote more of its limited resources to the criminal justice system (police, courts, and prisons) or to education (teachers, books, and schools)? If it decides to devote more resources to both, what other goods and services does it forgo?

Scarce Resources

economic resources
The land, labor, capital, and entrepreneurial ability that are used in the production of goods and services; productive agents; factors of production.

Society has limited or scarce **economic resources,** meaning all natural, human, and manufactured resources that go into the production of goods and services.

Resource Categories

Economists classify economic resources into four general categories.

land
Natural resources ("free gifts of nature") used to produce goods and services.

Land   **Land** includes all natural resources used in the production process. These include forests, mineral and oil deposits, arable land, wind power, sunlight, and water resources.

labor
People's physical and mental talents and efforts that are used to help produce goods and services.

Labor   The **labor** resource consists of the physical actions and mental activities that people contribute to the production of goods and services. The work-related activities of a retail clerk, teacher, professional football player, and nuclear physicist all fall under the general heading "labor."

capital
Human-made resources (buildings, machinery, and equipment) used to produce goods and services; goods that do not directly satisfy human wants; also called *capital goods* and *investment goods.*

Capital   For economists, **capital** (or *capital goods*) includes all manufactured aids used in producing consumer goods and services. Capital includes all factory, storage, transportation, and distribution facilities, as well as tools and machinery. Economists use the term **investment** to describe spending that pays for the production and accumulation of capital goods.

investment
Spending for the production and accumulation of capital and additions to inventories.

  While consumer goods satisfy wants directly, capital goods do so indirectly by aiding the production of consumer goods. For example, large commercial baking ovens (capital goods) help make loaves of bread (consumer goods). Note that the term "capital" as used by economists does not refer to money. Because money produces nothing, economists do not include it as an economic resource.

Economic Resources

Land, labor, capital, and entrepreneurial ability all contribute to producing goods and services.

Monty Rakusen/Cultura/Getty Images; Asiseeit/Getty Images; artiomp/Shutterstock; Helga Esteb/Shutterstock RF

Entrepreneurial Ability   Finally, there is the special human resource, distinct from labor, called **entrepreneurial ability.** It is supplied by entrepreneurs, who perform several important economic functions:

- Entrepreneurs take the initiative in combining resources to produce a good or a service. They are the driving force behind production.

- Entrepreneurs make the strategic business decisions that set the course of an enterprise.

- Entrepreneurs innovate. They commercialize new products, new production techniques, or even new forms of business organization.

- Entrepreneurs bear risk. Because innovation is risky, progress would cease without entrepreneurs who are willing to take on risk by devoting their time, effort, and ability—as well as their own money and the money of others—to commercialize new products and ideas.

Because land, labor, capital, and entrepreneurial ability are combined to produce goods and services, they are called the **factors of production** or simply "inputs."

entrepreneurial ability
The human resource that combines the other resources to produce a product, makes nonroutine decisions, innovates, and bears risks.

factors of production
Economic resources: land, capital, labor, and entrepreneurial ability.

Production Possibilities Model

Society uses its scarce resources to produce goods and services. The alternatives it faces can best be understood through a macroeconomic model of production possibilities. To keep things simple, we assume:

- *Full employment* The economy is employing all of its available resources.

- *Fixed resources* The quantity and quality of the factors of production are fixed.

- *Fixed technology* The state of technology (the methods used to produce output) is constant.

- *Two goods* The economy is producing only two goods: pizzas and industrial robots. Pizzas symbolize **consumer goods,** products that satisfy our wants directly; industrial robots symbolize **capital goods,** products that satisfy our wants indirectly by making possible more efficient production of consumer goods.

consumer goods
Products and services that satisfy human wants directly.

capital goods
Items that are used to produce other goods and therefore do not directly satisfy consumer wants.

Production Possibilities Table

A production possibilities table lists the different combinations of two products that can be produced with a specific set of resources, assuming full employment. **Figure 1.2** contains such a table for a simple economy that is producing pizzas and industrial robots. At alternative *A*, this economy would be devoting all its resources to the production of industrial robots (capital goods); at alternative *E*, all resources would go to pizza production (consumer goods). Those alternatives are unrealistic extremes; an economy typically produces both capital goods and consumer goods, as in *B, C,* and *D*. As we move from alternative *A* to *E*, we increase the production of pizzas at the expense of the production of industrial robots.

Because consumer goods satisfy our wants directly, any movement toward *E* looks tempting. In producing more pizzas, society increases the satisfaction of its current wants. But there is a cost: More pizzas mean fewer industrial robots. This shift of resources to consumer goods catches up with society over time because the stock of capital goods expands more slowly, thereby reducing potential future production. By moving toward alternative *E*, society chooses "more now" at the expense of "much more later."

By moving toward *A*, society chooses to forgo current consumption, thereby freeing up resources that can be used to increase the production of capital goods. By building up its stock of capital this way, society will have greater future production and, therefore, greater future consumption. By moving toward *A*, society is choosing "more later" at the cost of "less now."

Generalization: At any point in time, a fully employed economy must sacrifice some of one good to obtain more of another good. Scarce resources prohibit such an economy from having more of both goods. Having more of one thing means having less of something else.

FIGURE 1.2

The production possibilities curve. Each point on the production possibilities curve represents some maximum combination of two products that can be produced if resources are fully and efficiently employed. When an economy operates on the curve, more industrial robots means fewer pizzas, and vice versa. Limited resources and fixed technology make any combination of industrial robots and pizza lying outside the curve (such as at *W*) unattainable. Points inside the curve are attainable, but they indicate that full employment is not being realized.

Type of Product	Production Alternatives				
	A	C	B	E	D
Pizzas (in hundred thousands)	0	1	2	3	4
Industrial robots (in thousands)	10	9	7	4	0

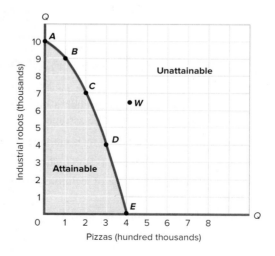

Production Possibilities Curve

The data presented in a production possibilities table can also be shown graphically as a **production possibilities curve.** This curve displays the different combinations of goods and services that society can produce in a fully employed economy, assuming a fixed availability of supplies of resources and fixed technology.

In **Figure 1.2**, each point on the production possibilities curve represents some maximum output of the two products. The curve is a "constraint" because it shows the limit of attainable outputs. Points on the curve are attainable as long as the economy uses all its available resources. Points lying inside the curve are also attainable, but they reflect less total output and therefore are not as desirable as points on the curve. Points lying beyond the production possibilities curve, like *W*, represent a greater output than the output at any point on the curve. Such points, however, are unattainable with the current resources and technology.

production possibilities curve
A curve showing the different combinations of two goods or services that can be produced in a full-employment, full-production economy where the available supplies of resources and technology are fixed.

Law of Increasing Opportunity Costs

Figure 1.2 clearly shows that more pizzas mean fewer industrial robots. The number of units of industrial robots that must be given up to obtain another pizza is the opportunity cost of that unit of pizzas.

In moving from alternative *A* to alternative *B* in the table in **Figure 1.2**, the cost of one additional unit of pizzas is one fewer robot. But when additional units are considered—*B* to *C, C* to *D,* and *D* to *E*—an important economic principle is revealed: For society, the opportunity cost of each additional unit of pizzas is greater than the opportunity cost of the preceding one. When we move from *A* to *B*, just one industrial robot is sacrificed for one more pizza, but in going from *B* to *C,* we sacrifice two industrial robots for one more pizza, then three industrial robots for one more pizza, and finally four for one. Conversely, confirm that as we move from *E* to *A,* the cost of an additional industrial robot (on average) is $\frac{1}{4}, \frac{1}{3}, \frac{1}{2}$, and 1 pizzas, respectively, for the four successive moves.

Our example illustrates the **law of increasing opportunity costs**: As we increase the production of a particular good, the opportunity cost of producing an additional unit rises.

law of increasing opportunity costs
The principle that as the production of a good increases, the opportunity cost of producing an additional unit rises.

Shape of the Curve The law of increasing opportunity costs is reflected in the shape of the production possibilities curve: The curve is bowed out from the origin of the graph. As **Figure 1.2** shows, when the economy moves from *A* to *E*, it must give up successively larger amounts of industrial robots (1, 2, 3, and 4) to acquire equal increments of pizzas (1, 1, 1, and 1). Thus, the slope of the production possibilities curve becomes steeper as we move from *A* to *E*.

Economic Rationale The law of increasing opportunity costs results from the fact that economic resources are not completely adaptable to alternative uses. Many resources are better at producing one type of good than at producing others. Consider land. Some land is highly suited to growing the ingredients necessary for pizza production. But as pizza production expands, society has to start using land that is less suitable for farming. That land is rich in mineral deposits and therefore well suited to producing the materials needed to make industrial robots. That land will be the first land devoted to the production of industrial robots. But as society steps up the production of industrial robots, it must use land that is less and less suited to making robot components.

This lack of perfect flexibility, or interchangeability, of resources causes society's increasing opportunity costs.

Optimal Allocation

Of all the attainable combinations of pizzas and industrial robots on the curve in **Figure 1.2**, which is optimal (best)? That is, which quantities of pizzas and robots will maximize satisfaction?

Recall that economic decisions center on comparisons of marginal benefits (MB) and marginal costs (MC). Any economic activity should be expanded as long as marginal benefit exceeds marginal cost and should be reduced if marginal cost exceeds marginal benefit. The optimal amount of the activity occurs where MB = MC. Society uses the same logic to make its production decision.

Consider pizzas. We already know from the law of increasing opportunity costs that the marginal cost of additional pizzas will rise as more pizzas are produced. At the same time, we need to recognize that the extra or marginal benefits that come from producing and consuming pizzas decline with each additional pizza. Consequently, each additional pizza brings both increasing marginal costs and decreasing marginal benefits.

The optimal quantity of pizza production is indicated in **Figure 1.3** by the intersection of the MB and MC curves: 200,000 units. Why is this amount the optimal quantity? If only 100,000 units of pizzas were produced, the marginal benefit of an extra unit of them would exceed its marginal cost. In money terms, MB is $15, while MC is only $5. When society gains something worth $15 at a marginal cost of only $5, it is better off. In **Figure 1.3**, net gains continue until pizza production has been increased to 200,000.

In contrast, the production of 300,000 pizzas is excessive. There, the MC of an added pizza is $15 and its MB is only $5. This means that one pizza is worth only $5 to society but costs $15 to obtain. This is a losing proposition for society!

So resources are being efficiently allocated to any product when the marginal benefit and marginal cost of its output are equal (MB = MC). Suppose that by applying the above analysis to industrial robots, we find its optimal (MB = MC) quantity is 7,000. This would mean that alternative *C* (200,000 units of pizzas and 7,000 units of industrial robots) on the production possibilities curve in **Figure 1.2** would be optimal for this economy.

FIGURE 1.3

Optimal output: MB = MC. Achieving the optimal output requires the expansion of a good's output until its marginal benefit (MB) and marginal cost (MC) are equal. No resources beyond that point should be allocated to the product. Here, optimal output occurs when 200,000 units of pizzas are produced.

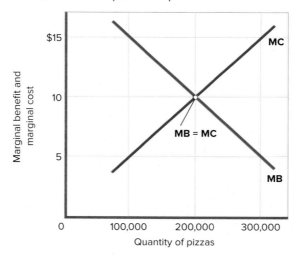

Unemployment, Growth, and the Future

In the depths of the Great Depression of the 1930s, one-quarter of U.S. workers were unemployed and one-third of U.S. production capacity was idle. Subsequent downturns have been much less severe. During the deep 2007–2009 recession, for instance, production fell by a comparably smaller 3.7 percent, and 1 in 10 workers was without a job. The pandemic recession that began in 2020 saw output fall by 33.1 percent and unemployment rise to 14.7 percent in the second quarter, but the third quarter saw output rebound by 31.4 percent and unemployment fall to 7.9 percent.

Almost all nations have experienced widespread unemployment and unused production capacity from business downturns at one time or another. Since the COVID-19 outbreak, most nations around the world have had economic downturns and elevated unemployment.

How do these realities relate to the production possibilities model? Our analysis and conclusions change if we relax the assumption that all available resources are fully employed. The five alternatives in the table of **Figure 1.2** represent maximum outputs; they illustrate the combinations of pizzas and industrial robots that can be produced when the economy is operating at full employment. With unemployment, this economy would produce less than each alternative shown in the table.

Graphically, we represent situations of unemployment by points inside the original production possibilities curve. Point U in **Figure 1.4** is one such point. Here the economy is falling short of the various maximum combinations of pizzas and industrial robots represented by the points on the production possibilities curve. Movement toward full employment would yield a greater output of one or both products.

FIGURE 1.4
Unemployment and the production possibilities curve. Any point inside the production possibilities curve, such as U, represents unemployment or a failure to achieve full employment. The arrows indicate that, by realizing full employment, the economy could operate on the curve. This means it could produce more of one or both products than it is producing at point U.

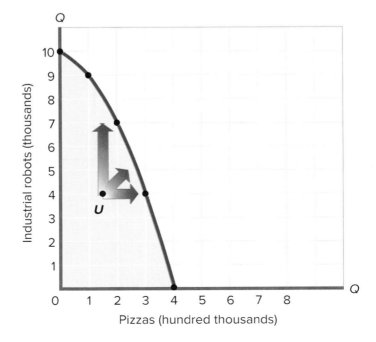

Pizzas (hundred thousands)

A Growing Economy

When we drop the assumptions that the quantity and quality of resources and technology are fixed, the production possibilities curve shifts positions, and the economy's potential maximum output changes.

Increases in Resource Supplies   Although resource supplies are fixed at any specific moment, they change over time. For example, a nation's growing population brings about increases in the supplies of labor and entrepreneurial ability. Also, labor quality usually improves over time. The economy's stock of capital generally increases at a significant, though unsteady, rate. And although some of our energy and mineral resources are being depleted, new sources are also being discovered. The development of irrigation systems, for example, adds to the supply of arable land.

economic growth
(1) An outward shift in the production possibilities curve that results from an increase in resource supplies or quality or an improvement in technology; (2) an increase of real output (gross domestic product) or real output per capita.

The net result of these increased supplies of the factors of production is society's ability to produce more consumer goods and more capital goods. The new production possibilities might look like those in the table in **Figure 1.5**. The greater abundance of resources will result in a greater potential output of one or both products. The economy will have achieved economic growth in the form of expanded potential output. Graphically, the production possibilities curve shifts outward and to the right, as illustrated by the move from the inner curve to curve *A′ B′ C′ D′ E′* in **Figure 1.5**. This sort of shift represents growth of economic capacity, which, when used, means **economic growth**: a larger total output.

FIGURE 1.5

Economic growth and the production possibilities curve. The increase in supplies of resources, the improvements in resource quality, and the technological advances that occur in a dynamic economy move the production possibilities curve outward and to the right, allowing the economy to have larger quantities of both types of goods.

Type of Product	Production Alternatives				
	A′	**B′**	**C′**	**D′**	**E′**
Pizzas (hundred thousands)	0	2	4	6	8
Industrial robots (thousands)	14	12	9	5	0

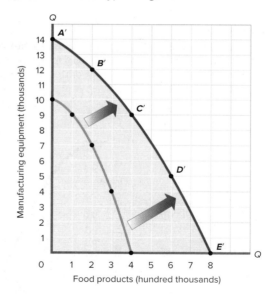

APPLYING THE ANALYSIS

The Economics of Pandemics

Production possibilities analysis is helpful in assessing the costs and benefits of battling a pandemic, including the COVID-19 outbreak that spread globally and brought physical and economic devastation in 2020.

If we categorize all of U.S. production as either "pandemic goods" (such as PPE—personal protective equipment—and research and development of vaccines) or "other goods," we can measure them on the axes of a production possibilities diagram such as that shown in **Figure 1.2**. The opportunity cost of using more resources for pandemic goods is the other goods sacrificed. In a fully employed economy, more pandemic goods are achieved at the opportunity cost of fewer other goods—education, pollution control, personal computers, houses, and so on. The cost of battling the pandemic is the other goods forgone. The benefits of these activities are numerous and diverse, but clearly include the gains from saving lives, minimizing long-term health damage, and reducing economic disruption.

Society must assess the marginal benefit (MB) and marginal cost (MC) of additional pandemic goods to determine their optimal amounts—where to locate on the pandemic goods–other goods production possibilities curve. Although estimating marginal benefits and marginal costs is an imprecise art, the MB-MC framework is a useful way of approaching choices. An optimal allocation of resources requires that society expand the production of pandemic goods until MB = MC.

The experience with COVID-19 increased the perceived marginal benefits of pandemic goods. If we label the horizontal axis in **Figure 1.3** "pandemic goods" and draw in a rightward shift of the MB curve, we see that the optimal quantity of pandemic goods rises. In response to COVID-19, the United States allocated more of its resources to pandemic goods. But the MB-MC analysis also reminds us we can spend too much on pandemics, as well as too little. The United States should not expand pandemic goods beyond the point where MB = MC. If it does, it will be sacrificing other goods of greater value than the pandemic goods obtained.

Pandemics not only force difficult choices, they also reduce the ability of an economy to produce. COVID-19 prompted some communities to impose "shut down orders," closing businesses and causing millions to become unemployed. Even places without shutdown orders saw closures and mass unemployment as concerns over the pandemic kept consumers away from nonessential businesses. This would be represented in **Figure 1.4** by the economy moving from a point on the curve to point *U* inside the curve. Reflecting this, U.S. unemployment rose from 3.5 percent in February 2020, to 14.7 percent in April 2020.

COVID-19 also adversely affected production possibilities through the death or disability of millions of people. **Figure 1.5** represents a growing economy with an outward shifting curve. The loss of labor due to death or disability caused an inward shift of production possibilities. The International Monetary Fund (IMF) estimates that globally the cumulative loss of output from COVID-19 may reach $28 trillion by 2025.

QUESTION:

How might the unemployment effects and inward shift of the production possibilities curve have differed if society had made different choices about the allocation of resources to pandemic versus other goods?

Advances in Technology   Improving technology brings both new and better goods and improved ways of producing them. For now, let's focus on one type of technological advance: improvements in the methods of production—for example, the introduction of computerized systems to manage inventories and schedule production. These advances allow society to produce more goods with available resources. They make possible the production of more industrial robots *and* more pizzas.

APPLYING THE ANALYSIS

Information Technology and Biotechnology

A real-world example of improved technology is the recent surge of new technologies relating to computers, communications, and biotechnology. Technological advances have dropped the prices of computers and greatly increased their speed. Improved software has greatly increased the everyday usefulness of computers. Cellular phones and the Internet have increased communications capacity, enhancing production and improving the efficiency of markets. Advances in biotechnology have resulted in important agricultural and medical discoveries. These and other new and improved technologies have contributed to U.S. economic growth (outward shifts of the nation's production possibilities curve).

> QUESTION:
>
> How have technological advances in medicine helped expand production possibilities in the United States?

Conclusion: Economic growth is the result of (1) increases in supplies of resources, (2) improvements in resource quality, and (3) technological advances. Whereas static, no-growth economies must sacrifice some of one good to obtain more of another, dynamic, growing economies can produce larger quantities of both goods.

Present Choices and Future Possibilities

An economy's current choice of positions on its production possibilities curve helps determine the curve's future location. Let's designate the two axes of the production possibilities curve as "goods for the future" and "goods for the present," as in **Figure 1.6**. Goods for the future are such things as capital goods, research and education, and preventive medicine; they are the ingredients of economic growth. Goods for the present are consumer goods such as food, clothing, and entertainment.

Now suppose there are two hypothetical economies, Presentville and Futureville, that are initially identical in every respect except one: Presentville's current choice of positions on its production possibilities curve (point *P* in **Figure 1.6a**) strongly favors present goods over future goods. Futureville, in contrast, makes a current choice that stresses larger amounts of future goods and smaller amounts of present goods, as shown by point *F* in **Figure 1.6b**.

Now, other things equal, we can expect Futureville's future production possibilities curve to be farther to the right than Presentville's. By currently choosing an output more favorable to technological advances and to increases in the quantity and quality of resources, Futureville will achieve greater economic growth than Presentville. In terms of capital goods, Futureville is choosing to make larger current additions to its "national factory" by devoting more of its current output to capital than does Presentville. The payoff from this choice for Futureville is greater future production capacity and economic growth. The opportunity cost is fewer consumer goods in the present.

Is Futureville's choice thus necessarily "better" than Presentville's? We cannot say. The different outcomes simply reflect different preferences and priorities in the two countries. **Global Snapshot 1.2** indicates that nations differ substantially in how large a fraction of their respective national incomes they choose to devote to purchasing capital goods for the future as opposed to consumption goods for the present.

FIGURE 1.6

Present choices and future locations of production possibilities curves. (a) Presentville's current choice to produce more "present goods" and fewer "future goods," as represented by point *P*, will cause a modest outward shift of the production possibilities curve in the future. (b) Futureville's current choice favoring "future goods," as depicted by point *F*, will result in a greater outward shift of the curve in the future.

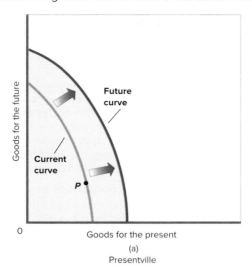

(a)
Presentville

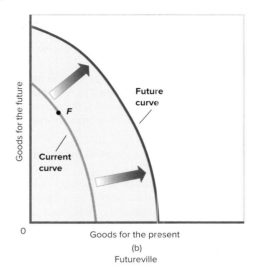

(b)
Futureville

GLOBAL SNAPSHOT 1.2

Gross Fixed Capital Formation as a Percentage of National Income, Selected Nations, 2017

Countries vary widely in the percentage of their respective national incomes that they devote to investments in productive capital ("goods for the future") rather than current consumption. Only the former generates increases in future production capacity and economic growth.

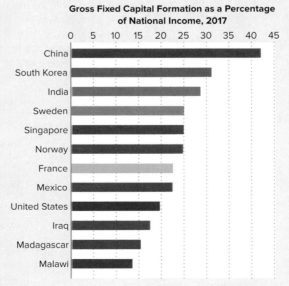

Source: The World Bank, www.worldbank.org.

Summary

LO1.1 Define economics and the features of the economic perspective.

Economics is the social science that studies how people, institutions, and society make choices under conditions of scarcity. Central to economics is the idea of opportunity cost: the value of the next-best good or service forgone to obtain something.

The economic perspective includes three elements: scarcity and choice, purposeful behavior, and marginal analysis. It sees individuals and institutions making rational decisions based on comparisons of marginal costs and marginal benefits.

LO1.2 Describe the role of economic theory in economics.

Economists employ the scientific method, in which they form and test hypotheses of cause-and-effect relationships to generate theories, laws, and principles. Economists often combine theories into representations called models.

LO1.3 Distinguish microeconomics from macroeconomics.

Microeconomics examines the decision making of specific economic units or institutions. Macroeconomics looks at the economy as a whole or its major aggregates.

LO1.4 Explain the individual's economizing problem and illustrate trade-offs, opportunity costs, and attainable combinations with budget lines.

Individuals face an economizing problem. Because their wants exceed their incomes, they must decide what to purchase and what to forgo. Society also faces an economic problem. Societal wants exceed the available resources necessary to fulfill them. Society therefore must decide what to produce and what to forgo.

Graphically, a budget line (or budget constraint) illustrates the economizing problem for individuals. The line shows the various combinations of two products that a consumer can purchase with a specific money income, given the prices of the two products.

LO1.5 List the categories of scarce resources and explain society's economizing problem.

Economic resources are inputs into the production process and can be classified as land, labor, capital, and entrepreneurial ability. Economic resources are also known as factors of production or inputs.

Society's economic problem can be illustrated through production possibilities analysis. Production possibilities tables and curves show the different combinations of goods and services that can be produced in a fully employed economy, assuming that resource quantity, resource quality, and technology are fixed.

LO1.6 Apply production possibilities analysis.

An economy that is fully employed and thus operating on its production possibilities curve must sacrifice the output of some types of goods and services to increase the production of others. The gain of one type of good or service is always accompanied by an opportunity cost in the form of loss of some of the other type.

Because resources are not equally productive in all possible uses, shifting resources from one use to another creates increasing opportunity costs. The production of additional units of one product requires the sacrifice of increasing amounts of the other product.

The optimal point on the production possibilities curve represents the most desirable mix of goods. It requires expanding the production of each good until its marginal benefit (MB) equals its marginal cost (MC).

Over time, technological advances and increases in the quantity and quality of resources enable the economy to produce more of all goods and services—that is, to experience economic growth. Society's choice regarding the mix of consumer goods and capital goods determines the future location of the production possibilities curve and the extent of economic growth.

Terms and Concepts

economics

economic perspective

scarcity

opportunity cost

utility

marginal analysis

scientific method

other-things-equal assumption

microeconomics

macroeconomics

aggregate

economic problem

budget line

constant opportunity cost

economic resources

land

labor

capital

investment

entrepreneurial ability

factors of production

consumer goods

capital goods

production possibilities curve

law of increasing opportunity costs

economic growth

Questions Mc Graw Hill connect

1. Ralph Waldo Emerson once wrote: "Want is a growing giant whom the coat of Have was never large enough to cover." How does this statement relate to the definition of economics? **(LO1)**

2. "Buy 2, get 1 free." Explain why the "1 free" is free to the buyer but not to society. **(LO1)**

3. What is an opportunity cost? How does the idea relate to the definition of economics? Which of the following decisions would entail the greater opportunity cost: allocating a square block in the heart of New York City for a surface parking lot or allocating a square block at the edge of a typical suburb for such a lot? Explain. **(LO1)**

4. What is "utility" and how does it relate to purposeful behavior? **(LO1)**

5. Cite three examples of recent decisions you made in which you, at least implicitly, weighed marginal cost and marginal benefit. **(LO1)**

6. What are the key elements of the scientific method, and how does this method relate to economic principles and laws? **(LO2)**

7. Indicate whether each of the following statements applies to microeconomics or macroeconomics: **(LO3)**

   a. The unemployment rate in the United States was 3.7 percent in December 2018.

   b. A U.S. software firm laid off 15 workers last month and transferred the work to India.

   c. An unexpected freeze in central Florida reduced the citrus crop and caused the price of oranges to rise.

   d. U.S. output, adjusted for inflation, increased by 2.3 percent in 2017.

   e. Last week, Wells Fargo Bank lowered its interest rate on business loans by one-half of 1 percentage point.

   f. The consumer price index rose by 2.2 percent from November 2017 to November 2018.

8. What are economic resources? What categories do economists use to classify them? Why are resources also called factors of production? Why are they called inputs? **(LO5)**

9. Why is money not considered a capital resource in economics? Why is entrepreneurial ability considered a category of economic resource, distinct from labor? What roles do entrepreneurs play in the economy? **(LO5)**

10. Explain the typical shapes of marginal-benefit and marginal-cost curves. How are these curves used to determine the optimal allocation of resources to a particular product? If current output is such that marginal cost exceeds marginal benefit, should more or fewer resources be allocated to this product? Explain. **(LO6)**

11. Explain how (if at all) each of the following events affects the location of a country's production possibilities curve: **(LO6)**

    a. The quality of education increases.

    b. The number of unemployed workers increases.

    c. A new technique improves the efficiency of extracting copper from ore.

    d. A devastating earthquake destroys numerous production facilities.

Problems

1. Potatoes cost Janice $1 per pound, and she has $5.00 that she could possibly spend on potatoes or other items. If she feels that the first pound of potatoes is worth $1.50, the second pound is worth $1.14, the third pound is worth $1.05, and all subsequent pounds are worth $0.30 per pound, how many pounds of potatoes will she purchase? What if she only had $2 to spend? **(LO1)**

2. Pham can work as many or as few hours as she wants at the college bookstore for $12 per hour. But due to her hectic schedule, she has just 15 hours per week that she can spend working at either the bookstore or at other potential jobs. One potential job, at a café, will pay her $15 per hour for up to 6 hours per week. She has another job offer at a garage that will pay her $13 an hour for up to 5 hours per week. And she has a

potential job at a day care center that will pay her $11.50 per hour for as many hours as she can work. If her goal is to maximize the amount of money she can make each week, how many hours will she work at the bookstore? **(LO1)**

3. Suppose you won $15 on a lotto ticket at the local 7-Eleven and decided to spend all the winnings on candy bars and bags of peanuts. Candy bars cost $0.75 each while bags of peanuts cost $1.50 each. **(LO4)**

   a. Construct a table showing the alternative combinations of the two products that are available.

   b. Plot the data in your table as a budget line in a graph. What is the slope of the budget line? What is the opportunity cost of one more candy bar? Of one more bag of peanuts? Do these opportunity costs rise, fall, or remain constant as each additional unit of the product is purchased?

c. Does the budget line tell you which of the available combinations of candy bars and bags of peanuts to buy?

d. Suppose you had won $30 on your ticket, not $15. Show the $30 budget line in your diagram. Has the number of available combinations increased or decreased?

4. Suppose you are on a desert island and possess exactly 20 coconuts. Your neighbor, Friday, is a fisherman, and he is willing to trade 2 fish for every 1 coconut you are willing to give him. Another neighbor, Kwame, is also a fisherman, and he is willing to trade 3 fish for every 1 coconut. **(LO4)**

a. On a single figure, draw budget lines for trading with Friday and for trading with Kwame. (Put coconuts on the vertical axis.)

b. What is the slope of the budget line from trading with Friday?

c. What is the slope of the budget line from trading with Kwame?

d. Which budget line features a larger set of attainable combinations of coconuts and fish?

e. If you are going to trade coconuts for fish, would you rather trade with Friday or Kwame? Why?

5. Below is a production possibilities table for consumer goods (automobiles) and capital goods (forklifts): **(LO5)**

Type of Production	Production Alternatives				
	A	B	C	D	E
Automobiles	0	2	4	6	8
Forklifts	30	27	21	12	0

a. Show these data graphically. Upon what specific assumptions is this production possibilities curve based?

b. If the economy is at point *C*, what is the cost of one more automobile? Of one more forklift? Which characteristic of the production possibilities curve reflects the law of increasing opportunity costs: its shape or its length?

c. If the economy characterized by this production possibilities table and curve were producing 3 automobiles and 20 forklifts, what could you conclude about its use of its available resources?

d. Is production at a point outside the production possibilities curve currently possible? Could a future advance in technology allow production beyond the current production possibilities curve?

6. Referring to the table in problem 5, suppose improvement occurs in the technology of producing forklifts but not in the technology of producing automobiles. Draw the new production possibilities curve. Now assume that a technological advance occurs in producing automobiles but not in producing forklifts. Draw the new production possibilities curve. Now draw a production possibilities curve that reflects technological improvement in the production of both goods. **(LO6)**

7. On average, households in China save 40 percent of their annual income each year, whereas households in the United States save less than 5 percent. Production possibilities are growing at roughly 7 percent annually in China but only 3 percent in the United States. Use graphical analysis of "present goods" versus "future goods" to explain the difference between China's growth rate and the U.S. growth rate. **(LO6)**

CHAPTER ONE APPENDIX
Graphs and Their Meaning

Economists often use graphs to illustrate economic models. By understanding these "pictures," you will more readily comprehend economic relationships.

Construction of a Graph

A graph is a visual representation of the relationship between two variables. The table in **Figure 1** is a hypothetical illustration showing the relationship between income and consumption for the economy as a whole. Because people tend to buy more goods and services when their incomes go up, it is not surprising to find in the table that total consumption in the economy increases as total income increases.

The information in the table is expressed graphically in **Figure 1**. Here is how it is done: We want to show visually how consumption changes as income changes. We therefore represent income on the horizontal axis of the graph and consumption on the vertical axis.

The vertical and horizontal scales of the graph reflect the ranges of values of consumption and income, marked in convenient increments. As you can see, the values on the scales cover all the values in the table.

Because the graph has two dimensions, each point within it represents an income value and its associated consumption value. To find a point that represents one of the five income-consumption combinations in the table, we draw straight lines from the appropriate values on the vertical and horizontal axes. For example, to plot point *c* (the $200 income–$150 consumption point), we draw straight lines up from the horizontal (income) axis at $200 and across from the vertical (consumption) axis at $150. These lines intersect at point *c*, which represents this particular income-consumption combination. You should verify that the other income-consumption combinations shown in the table are properly located in the graph in **Figure 1**.

Finally, by assuming that the same general relationship between income and consumption prevails for all other incomes, we draw a line or smooth curve to connect these points. That line or curve represents the income-consumption relationship.

FIGURE 1

Graphing the direct relationship between consumption and income. Two sets of data that are positively or directly related, such as consumption and income, graph as an upward sloping line.

Income per Week	Consumption per Week	Point
$ 0	$ 50	*a*
100	100	*b*
200	150	*c*
300	150	*d*
400	250	*e*

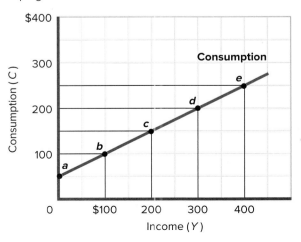

If the curve is a straight line, as in **Figure 1**, we say the relationship is *linear.* (It is permissible, and even customary, to refer to straight lines in graphs as "curves.")

Direct and Inverse Relationships

direct relationship
The relationship between two variables that change in the same direction, for example, product price and quantity supplied.

The line in **Figure 1** slopes upward to the right, so it depicts a **direct relationship** between income and consumption. When two variables have a direct relationship (or positive relationship), they change in the same direction. An increase in consumption is associated with an increase in income; a decrease in consumption accompanies a decrease in income. When two sets of data are positively or directly related, they always graph as an upward sloping line, as in **Figure 1**.

inverse relationship
The relationship between two variables that change in opposite directions, for example, product price and quantity demanded.

In contrast, two sets of data may be inversely related. Consider the table in **Figure 2**, which shows the relationship between the price of basketball tickets and game attendance for Big Time University (BTU). Here we have an **inverse relationship** (or negative relationship) because the two variables change in opposite directions. When ticket prices decrease, attendance increases. When ticket prices increase, attendance decreases. The six data points in the table are plotted in the graph in **Figure 2**. An inverse relationship always graphs as a downward sloping line.

Dependent and Independent Variables

independent variable
The variable causing a change in some other (dependent) variable.

dependent variable
A variable that changes as a consequence of a change in some other (independent) variable; the "effect" or outcome.

Economists seek to determine which variable is the "cause" and which is the "effect." The **independent variable** is the cause or source; it is the variable that changes first. The **dependent variable** is the effect or outcome; it is the variable that changes because of the change in the independent variable. In our income-consumption example, income is the independent variable and consumption the dependent variable. Income causes consumption to be what it is rather than the other way around. Similarly, ticket prices (set in advance of the season and printed on the ticket) determine attendance at BTU basketball games; attendance at games does not determine the printed ticket prices for those games. Ticket price is the independent variable and the quantity of tickets purchased is the dependent variable.

FIGURE 2
Graphing the inverse relationship between ticket prices and game attendance. Two sets of data that are negatively or inversely related, such as ticket price and the attendance at basketball games, graph as a downward sloping line.

Ticket Price	Attendance, Thousands	Point
$50	0	a
40	4	b
30	8	c
20	12	d
10	16	e
0	20	f

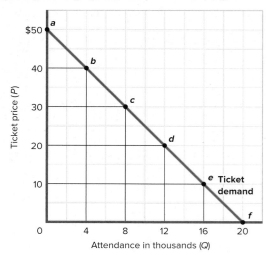

Mathematicians put the independent variable (cause) on the horizontal axis and the dependent variable (effect) on the vertical axis. Economists are less tidy; their graphing of independent and dependent variables is more arbitrary. For example, economists' graphing of the income-consumption relationship is consistent with mathematical convention, but economists historically put price and cost data (which are both cause variables) on the vertical axis, as we did in **Figure 2**. This does not present a problem, but we want you to be aware of this fact to avoid any possible confusion.

Other Things Equal

Our simple two-variable graphs purposely ignore many other factors that might affect the amount of consumption occurring at each income level or the number of people who attend BTU basketball games at each possible ticket price. When economists plot the relationship between any two variables, they employ the *ceteris paribus* (other-things-equal) assumption. Thus, in **Figure 1** all factors other than income that might affect the amount of consumption are presumed to be constant or unchanged. Similarly, in **Figure 2** all factors other than ticket price that might influence attendance at BTU basketball games are assumed constant. In reality, "other things" are not equal; they often change, and when they do, the relationship represented in our two tables and graphs will change. Specifically, the lines we have plotted would *shift* to new locations.

Consider a stock market "crash." The dramatic drop in the value of stocks might cause people to feel less wealthy and therefore less willing to consume at each level of income. The result might be a downward shift of the consumption line. To see this, you should plot a new consumption line in **Figure 1**, assuming that consumption is, say, $20 less at each income level. Note that the relationship remains direct; the line merely shifts downward to reflect less consumption spending at each income level.

Similarly, factors other than ticket prices might affect BTU game attendance. If BTU loses most of its games, attendance at BTU games might be less at each ticket price. To see this, redraw **Figure 2**, assuming that 2,000 fewer fans attend BTU games at each ticket price.

Slope of a Line

Lines can be described in terms of their slopes. The **slope of a straight line** is the ratio of the vertical change (the rise or drop) to the horizontal change (the run) between any two points of the line.

slope of a straight line
The ratio of the vertical change (the rise or fall) to the horizontal change (the run) between any two points on a line.

Positive Slope Between point *b* and point *c* in the graph in **Figure 1**, the rise or vertical change (the change in consumption) is +$50 and the run or horizontal change (the change in income) is +$100. Therefore:

$$\text{Slope} = \frac{\text{vertical change}}{\text{horizontal change}} = \frac{+50}{+100} = \frac{1}{2} = .5$$

Note that our slope of $\frac{1}{2}$ or .5 is positive because consumption and income change in the same direction; that is, consumption and income are directly or positively related.

Negative Slope Between any two of the identified points in the graph of **Figure 2**, say, point *c* and point *d*, the vertical change is −10 (the drop) and the horizontal change is +4 (the run). Therefore:

$$\text{Slope} = \frac{\text{vertical change}}{\text{horizontal change}} = \frac{-10}{+4} = -2\frac{1}{2} = -2.5$$

This slope is negative because ticket price and attendance have an inverse relationship.

Slopes and Marginal Analysis   The concept of slope is important in economics because it reflects marginal changes—those involving 1 more (or 1 fewer) unit. For example, in **Figure 1** the .5 slope shows that $.50 of extra or marginal consumption is associated with each $1 change in income. In this example, people collectively will consume $.50 of any $1 increase in their incomes and reduce their consumption by $.50 for each $1 decline in income. Careful inspection of **Figure 2** reveals that every $1 increase in ticket price for BTU games will decrease game attendance by 400 people and every $1 decrease in ticket price will increase game attendance by 400 people.

Infinite and Zero Slopes   Many variables are unrelated or independent of one another. For example, the quantity of wristwatches purchased is not related to the price of bananas. **Figure 3a**, represents the price of bananas on the vertical axis and the quantity of watches demanded on the horizontal axis. The graph of their relationship is the line parallel to the vertical axis, indicating that the same quantity of watches is purchased no matter what the price of bananas. The slope of such a line is infinite.

Similarly, aggregate consumption is completely unrelated to the nation's divorce rate. **Figure 3b** places consumption on the vertical axis and the divorce rate on the horizontal axis. The line parallel to the horizontal axis represents this lack of relatedness. The slope of horizontal lines is zero.

Slope of a Nonlinear Curve

We now move from the simple world of linear relationships (straight lines) to the somewhat more complex world of nonlinear relationships (curved lines). The slope of a straight line is the same at all its points. The slope of a line representing a nonlinear relationship changes from one point to another. Such lines are always referred to as *curves*.

Consider the downward sloping curve in **Figure 4**. Its slope is negative throughout, but the curve flattens as we move down along it. Thus, its slope constantly changes; the curve has a different slope at each point.

FIGURE 3

Infinite and zero slopes. (a) A line parallel to the vertical axis has an infinite slope. Here, purchases of watches remain the same no matter what happens to the price of bananas. (b) A line parallel to the horizontal axis has a slope of zero. In this case, total consumption remains the same no matter what happens to the divorce rate. In both (a) and (b), the two variables are totally unrelated to one another.

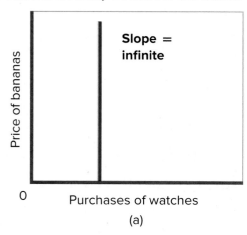

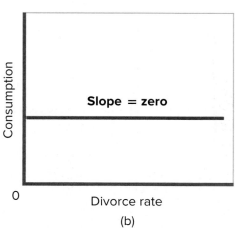

FIGURE 4

Determining the slopes of curves. The slope of a nonlinear curve changes from point to point on the curve. The slope at any point (say, B) can be determined by drawing a straight line that is tangent to that point (line bb) and calculating the slope of that line.

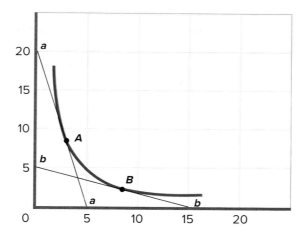

To measure the slope at a specific point, we draw a straight line tangent to the curve at that point. A line is tangent at a point if it touches, but does not intersect, the curve at that point. So line *aa* is tangent to the curve in **Figure 4** at point *A*. The slope of the curve at that point is equal to the slope of the tangent line. Specifically, the total vertical change (drop) in the tangent line *aa* is −20 and the total horizontal change (run) is +5. Because the slope of the tangent line *aa* is −20/+5, or −4, the slope of the curve at point *A* is also −4.

Line *bb* in **Figure 4** is tangent to the curve at point *B*. Using the same procedure, we find the slope at *B* to be −5/+15, or −1/3. Thus, in this flatter part of the curve, the slope is less negative.

Several of the Appendix Problems are of a "workbook" variety, and we urge you to go through them carefully to check your understanding of graphs and slopes.

Appendix Summary

LO1.7 Understand graphs, curves, and slopes as they relate to economics.

1. Graphs are a convenient and revealing way to represent economic relationships.

2. Two variables are positively (or directly) related when their values change in the same direction. The line or curve representing two directly related variables slopes upward.

3. Two variables are negatively (or inversely) related when their values change in opposite directions. The line or curve representing two inversely related variables slopes downward.

4. The value of the dependent variable (the "effect") is determined by the value of the independent variable (the "cause").

5. When the "other factors" that might affect a two-variable relationship are allowed to change,

the graph of the relationship will likely shift to a new location.

6. The slope of a straight line is the ratio of the vertical change to the horizontal change between any two points. The slope of an upward sloping line is positive; the slope of a downward sloping line is negative.

7. The slope of a line or curve is especially relevant for economics because it measures marginal changes.

8. The slope of a horizontal line is zero; the slope of a vertical line is infinite.

9. The slope of a curve at any point is determined by calculating the slope of a straight line tangent to the curve at that point.

Appendix Terms and Concepts

direct relationship

inverse relationship

independent variable

dependent variable

slope of a straight line

Appendix Questions

1. What is an inverse relationship? How does it graph? What is a direct relationship? How does it graph? **(LO7)**

2. Describe the graphical relationship between ticket prices and the number of people choosing to visit amusement parks. Is that relationship consistent with the fact that, historically, park attendance and ticket prices have both risen? Explain. **(LO7)**

3. Look back at **Figure 2**, which shows the inverse relationship between ticket prices and game attendance at Big Time University. (a) Interpret the meaning of the slope. (b) If the slope of the line were steeper, what would that say about the amount by which ticket sales respond to increases in ticket prices? **(LO7)**

Appendix Problems

1. Graph and label as either direct or indirect the relationships you would expect to find between (a) the number of inches of rainfall per month and the sale of umbrellas, (b) the amount of tuition and the level of enrollment at a university, and (c) the popularity of an entertainer and the price of her concert tickets. **(LO7)**

2. Indicate how each of the following might affect the data shown in the table and graph in **Figure 2** of this appendix: **(LO7)**

   a. BTU's athletic director schedules higher-quality opponents.

   b. An NBA team locates in the city where BTU plays.

   c. BTU contracts to have all its home games televised.

3. The following table contains data on the relationship between saving and income. Rearrange these data into a meaningful order and graph them on the accompanying grid. What is the slope of the line? What would you predict saving to be at the $12,500 level of income? **(LO7)**

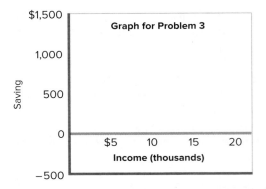

4. Construct a table from the data shown on the graph below. Which is the dependent variable and which is the independent variable? **(LO7)**

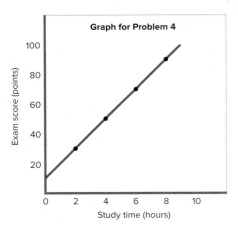

Income per Year	Saving per Year
$15,000	$1,000
0	−500
10,000	500
5,000	0
20,000	1,500

5. Suppose that when the interest rate on loans is 16 percent, businesses find it unprofitable to invest in machinery and equipment. However, when the interest rate is 14 percent, $5 billion worth of investment is profitable. At 12 percent interest, a total of $10 billion is profitable. Similarly, total investment increases by $5 billion for each successive 2-percentage-point decline in the interest rate. Describe the relevant relationship between the interest rate and investment in a table and on a graph. Put the interest rate on the vertical axis and investment on the horizontal axis. **(LO7)**

6. The accompanying graph shows curve *XX'* and tangents to the curve at points *A*, *B*, and *C*. Calculate the slope of the curve at each of these three points. **(LO7)**

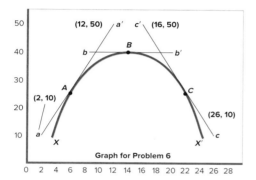

Graph for Problem 6

7. In the accompanying graph, is the slope of curve *AA'* positive or negative? Does the slope increase or decrease as we move along the curve from *A* to *A'*? Answer the same two questions for curve *BB'*. **(LO7)**

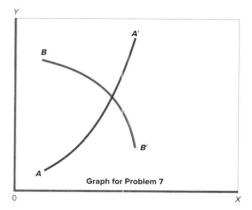

Graph for Problem 7

CHAPTER TWO

The Market System and the Circular Flow

Learning Objectives

LO2.1 Differentiate between a command system and a market system.

LO2.2 List the main characteristics of the market system.

LO2.3 Explain how the market system answers the four fundamental questions.

LO2.4 Discuss how the market system adjusts to change and promotes progress.

LO2.5 Describe the mechanics of the circular flow model.

You are at the mall. Suppose you need to compile a list of all the individual goods and services available for sale there. That task would be daunting and the list would be long! And even though a single shopping mall contains a remarkable quantity and variety of goods, it is only a tiny part of the national economy.

Who decides which goods and services should be produced? How do the producers determine which technology and types of resources to use in producing these goods? Who will obtain these products? What accounts for new and improved products? This chapter answers these questions.

Economic Systems

Every society needs to develop an **economic system**—a particular set of institutional arrangements and a coordinating mechanism—to respond to the economic problem. The economic system has to determine what goods are produced, how they are produced, who gets them, and how to promote technological progress.

Economic systems differ as to (1) who owns the factors of production and (2) the method used to motivate, coordinate, and direct economic activity. There are two general types of economic systems: the command system and the market system.

The Command System

The **command system** is also known as *socialism* or *communism.* In a command system, government owns most property resources, and economic decision making occurs through a central economic plan. A central planning board appointed by the government makes nearly all the major decisions concerning the use of resources, the composition and distribution of output, and the organization of production. The government owns most of the business firms, which produce according to government directives. The central planning board determines production goals for each enterprise and specifies the amount of resources to be allocated to each enterprise so that it can reach its production goals. The division of output between capital and consumer goods is centrally decided, and capital goods are allocated among industries on the basis of the central planning board's long-term priorities.

A pure command economy would rely exclusively on a central plan to allocate the government-owned property resources. But, in reality, even the preeminent command economy—the Soviet Union—tolerated some private ownership and incorporated some markets before its collapse in 1992. Subsequent reforms in Russia and most of the eastern European nations have, to one degree or another, transformed their command economies to capitalistic, market-oriented systems. China's reforms have not gone as far, but they have greatly reduced the reliance on central planning. Although government ownership of resources and capital in China is still extensive, the nation has increasingly relied on free markets to organize and coordinate its economy. North Korea and Cuba are the last remaining examples of largely centrally planned economies. The nearby "Applying the Analysis" discusses the economic differences between North Korea and South Korea—many of them directly attributable to North Korea's nearly complete reliance on the command system and, thus, on dealing poorly with the coordination and incentive problems.

The Market System

The vast majority of the world's economies utilize the **market system,** also known as *capitalism* or the *mixed economy.* The market system is characterized by a mixture of centralized government initiatives and decentralized actions taken by individuals and firms. The precise mixture varies by country, but in each case the system features the private ownership of resources and the use of markets and prices to coordinate and direct economic activity.

In the market system, individuals and businesses seek to achieve their economic goals through their own decisions regarding work, consumption, or production. The system allows for the private ownership of capital, communicates through prices, and coordinates economic activity through *markets*—places where buyers and sellers come together to buy and sell goods, services, and resources. Participants act in their own self-interest, and goods and services are produced and resources are supplied by whoever is willing and able to do so. The result is competition among independently

economic system
A particular set of institutional arrangements and a coordinating mechanism for solving the economizing problem; a method of organizing an economy, of which the market system and the command system are the two general types.

command system
A method of organizing an economy in which property resources are publicly owned and government uses central economic planning to direct and coordinate economic activities; command economy; communism.

market system
All the product and resource markets of a market economy and the relationships among them; a method that allows the prices determined in those markets to allocate the economy's scarce resources and to communicate and coordinate the decisions made by consumers, firms, and resource suppliers.

acting buyers and sellers and an economic system in which decision making is widely dispersed. The market system offers high potential monetary rewards that create powerful incentives for existing firms to innovate and entrepreneurs to pioneer new products and processes.

In *pure* capitalism—or *laissez-faire* capitalism—government's role would be limited to protecting private property and establishing an environment appropriate to the operation of the market system. The term "laissez-faire" means "let it be"—that is, keep government from interfering with the economy. The idea is that such interference will disturb the efficient working of the market system.

But in the capitalism practiced in the United States and most other countries, government plays a substantial role in the economy. It not only sets the rules for economic activity but also promotes economic stability and growth, provides certain goods and services that would otherwise be underproduced or not produced at all, and modifies the distribution of income. The government, however, is not the dominant economic force in deciding what to produce, how to produce it, and who will get it. That force is the market and the individuals participating in it.

 APPLYING THE ANALYSIS

Korea by Night

PlanetObserver/Science Source

After the Second World War, the Korean peninsula was divided into North Korea and South Korea.

North Korea, under the influence of the Soviet Union, established a command economy that emphasized government ownership and central government planning. South Korea, protected by the United States, established a market economy based upon private ownership and the profit motive.

Today, South Korea is far more prosperous, with South Koreans enjoying an average annual income (GDP per capita adjusted for differences in the cost of living) of $39,500 per year versus $1,700 in North Korea. That differential is especially startling when you find out that North Korea was richer and more highly industrialized when the countries were separated in 1953.

South Korea's much greater prosperity shows up dramatically in the accompanying satellite photo of the Korean peninsula at night. The highly electrified South is a sea of light while the North is bathed in darkness save for the lights of its capital city, Pyongyang.

Characteristics of the Market System

Let's examine the key features of the market system.

Private Property

In a market system, private individuals and firms, not the government, own most of the property resources (land and capital). It is this extensive private ownership of capital that gives capitalism its name. This right of **private property,** coupled with the freedom to negotiate binding legal contracts, enables individuals and businesses to obtain, use, and dispose of property resources as they see fit. Property owners' right to designate who will receive their property when they die helps sustain the institution of private property.

Property rights encourage people to cooperate by helping to ensure that only *mutually agreeable* economic transactions take place. In a world without legally enforceable property rights, the strong could simply take whatever they wanted from the weak without compensating them. But in a world of legally enforceable property rights, any person who wants something must pay for it. If someone really wants what you have, they must offer you something that you value in return. That is, the person must offer you a mutually agreeable economic transaction—one that benefits both of you.

Property rights also encourage investment, innovation, exchange, maintenance of property, and economic growth. Nobody would stock a store, build a factory, or clear land for farming if someone else, or the government itself, could take that property away at any moment.

Property rights extend to intellectual property through patents, copyrights, and trademarks. Such long-term protection encourages people to write books, compose music, create social media platforms, and invent new products and production processes without fear that others will steal them and the rewards they may bring.

Property rights facilitate exchange. The title to an automobile or the deed to a cattle ranch assures the buyer that the seller is the legitimate owner. Also, property rights encourage owners to maintain or improve their property so as to preserve or increase its value. Finally, property rights enable people to use their time and resources to produce more goods and services, rather than using them to protect and retain the property they have already produced or acquired.

private property
The right of private persons and firms to obtain, own, control, employ, dispose of, and bequeath land, capital, and other property.

Freedom of Enterprise and Choice

Closely related to private ownership of property is freedom of enterprise and choice.

- **Freedom of enterprise** ensures that entrepreneurs and private businesses are free to obtain and use economic resources to produce their choice of goods and services and to sell them in their chosen markets.

- **Freedom of choice** allows owners to employ or dispose of their property and money as they see fit. It also allows workers to enter any line of work for which they are qualified. Finally, it ensures that consumers are free to buy the goods and services that best satisfy their wants and that their budgets allow.

These choices are free only within legal limitations, however. Illegal choices such as human trafficking and drug trafficking are punished through fines or imprisonment. (**Global Snapshot 2.1** reveals that the degree of economic freedom varies greatly from nation to nation.)

freedom of enterprise
The freedom of firms to obtain economic resources, to use those resources to produce products of the firm's own choosing, and to sell their products in markets of their choice.

freedom of choice
The freedom of owners of property resources to employ or dispose of them as they see fit, of workers to enter any line of work for which they are qualified, and of consumers to spend their incomes in a manner that they think is appropriate.

GLOBAL SNAPSHOT 2.1

Index of Economic Freedom, Selected Economies

The Index of Economic Freedom measures economic freedom using 10 major groupings such as trade policy, property rights, and government intervention, with each category containing more than 50 specific criteria. The index then ranks 180 economies according to their degree of economic freedom. A few selected rankings for 2019 are listed next.

FREE
1 Hong Kong
2 Singapore
3 New Zealand

MOSTLY FREE
12 United States
24 Germany
30 Japan

MODERATELY FREE
36 Botswana
66 Mexico
91 Saudi Arabia

MOSTLY UNFREE
100 China
129 India
150 Brazil

REPRESSED
178 Cuba
179 Venezuela
180 North Korea

Source: The Heritage Foundation, **www.heritage.org.**

Self-Interest

self-interest
The most-advantageous outcome as viewed by each firm, property owner, worker, or consumer.

In the market system, **self-interest** is the motivating force. Self-interest simply means that each economic unit tries to achieve its own particular goal. Entrepreneurs try to maximize profit or minimize loss. Property owners try to get the highest price for the sale or rent of their resources. Workers try to maximize their utility (satisfaction) by finding jobs that offer the best combination of wages, hours, fringe benefits, and working conditions. Consumers try to obtain the products they want at the lowest possible price that provide the most utility. Self-interest provides direction and consistency to what might otherwise be a chaotic economy.

Competition

The market system depends on **competition** among economic units. Very broadly defined, competition requires

- Independently acting sellers and buyers operating in a particular product or resource market.
- Freedom of sellers and buyers to enter or leave markets, on the basis of their economic self-interest.

Competition among buyers and sellers diffuses economic power throughout the economy. When many buyers and sellers act independently in a market, no single buyer or seller is able to dictate the price of the product or resource because others can undercut that price.

In a competitive system, producers can enter or leave an industry; no insurmountable barriers prevent an industry from expanding or contracting. This freedom to expand or contract provides the economy with the flexibility needed to remain efficient over time. Freedom of entry and exit enables the economy to adjust to changes in consumer tastes, technology, and resource availability.

The diffusion of economic power inherent in competition limits the potential abuse of that power. A producer that charges more than the competitive market price will lose sales to other producers. An employer who pays less than the competitive market wage rate will lose workers to other employers. Competition is the key regulatory force in the market system.

competition
The presence in a market of independent buyers and sellers competing with one another along with the freedom of buyers and sellers to enter and leave the market.

Markets and Prices

Markets and prices are key components of the market system. They give the system its ability to coordinate trillions of daily economic decisions. A **market** is an institution or mechanism that brings buyers ("demanders") and sellers ("suppliers") into contact. A market system conveys the decisions made by buyers and sellers of products and resources. The decisions made on each side of the market determine a set of product and resource prices that guide resource owners, entrepreneurs, and consumers as they make and revise their choices and pursue their self-interest.

Just as competition is the regulatory mechanism of the market system, the market system itself is the organizing and coordinating mechanism. It is an elaborate communication network through which innumerable individual free choices are recorded, summarized, and balanced. Those who respond appropriately to market signals are rewarded with greater profit and income; those who do not respond to those signals are penalized.

market
Any institution or mechanism that brings together buyers (demanders) and sellers (suppliers) of a particular good or service.

Technology and Capital Goods

In the market system, the monetary rewards for creating new products or production techniques accrue directly to the innovator. The market system therefore encourages extensive use and rapid development of complex capital goods: tools, machinery, large-scale factories, and facilities for storage, communication, transportation, and marketing.

Advanced technology and capital goods are important because the most direct methods of production are often the least efficient. The only way to avoid that inefficiency is to rely on capital goods. It would be ridiculous for a farmer to undertake production with only bare hands. Huge benefits can be derived from creating and using such capital equipment as plows, tractors, and storage bins. More efficient production means much more output.

Specialization

specialization
The use of the resources of an individual, a firm, a region, or a nation to concentrate production on one or a small number of goods and services.

Market economies rely on **specialization.** Specialization means using the resources of an individual, region, or nation to produce one or a few goods or services rather than the entire range of goods and services. The economic unit then exchanges those goods and services for a wide range of desired products. The majority of consumers produce virtually none of the goods and services they consume, and they consume little or nothing of the items they produce. The person working nine to five installing windows in commercial aircraft may rarely fly. Some dairy farmers sell their milk to the local or regional dairy cooperative and then buy energy drinks at the local grocery store.

division of labor
The separation of the work required to produce a product into a number of different tasks that are performed by different workers; specialization of workers.

Division of Labor   Human specialization—called the **division of labor**—contributes to a society's output in several ways:

- *Specialization makes use of differences in ability* Specialization enables individuals to take advantage of existing differences in their abilities and skills. If LeBron is good at shooting a basketball, while Beyoncé can sing and dance, their talents are most efficiently used if LeBron plays professional basketball and Beyoncé records songs and gives concerts.

- *Specialization fosters learning by doing* Even if two people have identical abilities, specialization may still be advantageous. By devoting time to a single task, people are more likely to develop the skills required and to improve techniques. You learn to be a good lawyer by studying, practicing, and specializing in law.

- *Specialization saves time* By devoting time to a single task, a person avoids the loss of time incurred in shifting from one job to another.

For all these reasons, specialization increases the total output society derives from limited resources.

PHOTO OP

LeBron James and Beyoncé Knowles

It makes economic sense for LeBron James and Beyoncé Knowles to specialize in what they do best.

©Ezra Shaw/Getty Images

©SGranitz/Getty Images

Geographic Specialization Specialization also works on a regional and international basis. Oranges could be grown in Nebraska, but the unsuitability of the land, rainfall, and temperature would make costs very high. And wheat could be grown in Florida, but it would be costly for similar geographical reasons. So Nebraskans produce the wheat for which their resources are best suited, and Floridians produce oranges. By specializing, both economies produce more than is needed locally. Then, very sensibly, Nebraskans and Floridians swap some of their surpluses—wheat for oranges, oranges for wheat.

Similarly, on an international scale, the United States specializes in producing such items as commercial aircraft and software, which it sells abroad in exchange for mobile phones from China, bananas from Honduras, and woven baskets from Thailand. Both human specialization and geographic specialization are needed to achieve efficiency in the use of limited resources.

Use of Money

Any economic system makes extensive use of money. Money performs several functions, but first and foremost it is a **medium of exchange.** It makes trade easier.

Specialization requires exchange. Exchange can, and sometimes does, occur through **barter**—swapping goods for goods, say, wheat for oranges. But barter poses serious problems because it requires a *coincidence of wants* between the buyer and the seller. In our example, we assumed that Nebraskans had excess wheat to trade and wanted oranges. And we assumed that Floridians had excess oranges to trade and wanted wheat. So an exchange occurred. But if such a coincidence of wants is missing, trade is stymied.

Suppose Nebraska has no interest in Florida's oranges but wants potatoes from Idaho. And suppose that Idaho wants Florida's oranges but not Nebraska's wheat. And, to complicate matters, suppose that Florida wants some of Nebraska's wheat but none of Idaho's potatoes. **Figure 2.1** summarizes the situation.

In none of the cases shown in the figure is there a coincidence of wants. Trade by barter clearly would be difficult. Instead, people in each state use **money,** which is simply a convenient social invention to facilitate the exchange of goods and services. To serve as money, an item needs to pass only one test: Sellers must be willing to accept it as payment for their goods and services. Money is socially defined; whatever

medium of exchange
Any item sellers generally accept and buyers generally use to pay for a good or service; money; a convenient means of exchanging goods and services without engaging in barter.

barter
The exchange of one good or service for another good or service.

money
Any item that is generally acceptable to sellers in exchange for goods and services.

FIGURE 2.1

Money facilitates trade when wants do not coincide. The use of money as a medium of exchange permits trade to be accomplished despite a noncoincidence of wants. (1) Nebraska trades the wheat that Florida wants for money from Floridians; (2) Nebraska trades the money it receives from Florida for the potatoes it wants from Idaho; (3) Idaho trades the money it receives from Nebraska for the oranges it wants from Florida.

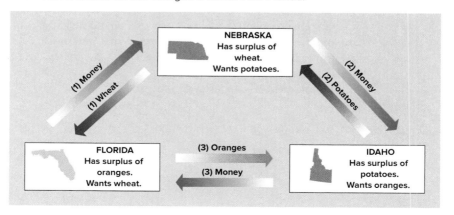

society accepts as a medium of exchange *is* money. Today, most economies use pieces of paper as money in addition to checking account balances and recently, electronic "cryptocurrencies" like Bitcoin.

On a global basis, specialization and exchange are complicated by the fact that different nations have different currencies. But markets in which currencies are bought and sold make it possible for people living in different countries to exchange goods and services without resorting to barter.

Active, but Limited, Government

An active, but limited, government is the final characteristic of modern market systems. Although a market system promotes a high degree of efficiency in the use of its resources, it has certain inherent shortcomings called "market failures." We will discover in Chapter 5 that government can often increase the overall effectiveness of a market system. That said, governments have their own set of shortcomings that can cause misallocations of resources.

Four Fundamental Questions

The key features of the market system help explain how market economies respond to four fundamental questions:

- What goods and services will be produced?
- How will the goods and services be produced?
- Who will get the goods and services?
- How will the system promote progress?

These four questions highlight the economic choices underlying the production possibilities curve discussed in Chapter 1. They reflect the reality of scarce resources in a world of unlimited wants. All economies, whether market or command, must address these four questions.

What Will Be Produced?

How does a market system decide on the specific types and quantities of goods to be produced? The simple answer is this: The goods and services that can be produced at a continuing profit will be produced, while those whose production generates a continuing loss will be discontinued. Profits and losses are the difference between the total revenue (TR) a firm receives from the sale of its products and the total cost (TC) of producing those products.

Continuing economic profit (TR > TC) in an industry results in expanded production and the movement of resources toward that industry. Existing firms grow and new firms enter. Continuing losses (TC > TR) in an industry lead to reduced production and the exit of resources from that industry. Some existing firms shrink; others go out of business. The industry contracts.

In the market system, consumers are sovereign (in command). **Consumer sovereignty** is crucial in determining the types and quantities of goods produced. Consumers spend their income on the goods they are most willing and able to buy. Through these **"dollar votes"** they register their wants in the market. If the dollar votes for a certain product are great enough to create a profit, businesses will produce and sell that product. In contrast, if the dollar votes do not create sufficient revenues to cover costs, businesses will not produce the product. Thus consumers collectively direct resources to industries that are meeting their wants and away from industries that are not meeting their wants.

consumer sovereignty
Determination by consumers of the types and quantities of goods and services that will be produced with the scarce resources of the economy; consumers' direction of production through their dollar votes.

dollar votes
The "votes" that consumers and entrepreneurs cast for the production of consumer and capital goods, respectively, when they purchase those goods in product and resource markets.

APPLYING THE ANALYSIS

Consumer Sovereignty in a Pandemic

As the Coronavirus pandemic unfolded in early 2020, there was a dramatic shift in consumer purchases—significantly changing what was produced in the economy, to the benefit of some industries and the detriment of others.

Hand sanitizer was suddenly in high demand as consumers sought to fight off germs and protect themselves from the virus. Consumers cast so many dollar votes for hand sanitizer and similar goods that producers could not initially keep up with surging demand. The Coronavirus Aid, Relief, and Economic Security (CARES) Act actually authorized distilleries to produce hand sanitizer to try to keep up with and satisfy consumer wants for the product until regular producers could catch up.

In some countries, wearing face masks in public is routine; in the United States, it was extremely rare prior to the pandemic. Whether prompted by government recommendations and edicts, rules imposed by businesses, or simply as a matter of self-protection, mask use became widespread. When it became clear that the pandemic would continue into the foreseeable future, consumers started buying reusable masks, many with clever designs, company and team logos, and a wide variety of styles and colors. Mask manufacturers responded to these dollar votes, causing the value of the global face mask market to rise from $737 million in 2019, to an estimated $22.1 billion in 2021.

While some industries saw a boom in consumer spending, others faced dramatic declines. Tourism and hospitality, including airlines, cruise lines, hotels, and restaurants, all saw significant declines in consumer spending. While some of this decline was mandated by government imposed shutdowns and stay-at-home orders, even in areas where those restrictions were not imposed, consumers stopped casting dollar votes for these goods and services. According to the Organisation for Economic Co-operation and Development (OECD), international tourism fell by 80 percent in 2020. Increases in domestic tourism slightly offset the decline, as some tourists cast their dollar votes at home rather than abroad.

QUESTIONS:

Which of these shifts in consumer spending do you think will last long after the pandemic ends? What spending will return to pre-pandemic "normal?"

Sources: marketsandmarkets.com; OECD.org.

How Will the Goods and Services Be Produced?

What combinations of resources and technologies will be used to produce goods and services? How will the production be organized? The answer: In combinations and ways that minimize the cost per unit of output. Inefficiency drives up costs and lowers profits. As a result, any firm wishing to maximize its profits will make great efforts to minimize production costs. These efforts will include using the right mix of labor and capital. They also mean locating production facilities optimally to hold down production and transportation expenses.

These efforts will be intensified if the firm faces competition, as consumers strongly prefer low prices and will shift their purchases to the firms that can produce a quality product at the lowest possible price. Any firm foolish enough to use higher-cost production methods will go bankrupt as it is undersold by its more efficient competitors who can still make a profit when selling at a lower price. Simply stated: Competition eliminates high-cost producers.

APPLYING THE ANALYSIS

Bitcoin and Cheap Electrons

Bitcoin is an electronic "cryptocurrency" accepted as payment for goods and services by millions of people around the world. It has several novel characteristics, including not being issued by any government and existing and transacting entirely in cyberspace.

The creation of additional Bitcoins (units of Bitcoin currency) is also done entirely electronically, with anyone in the world able to download a free piece of software and start "mining" for Bitcoins by having their computers solve some of the difficult math problems required to maintain the Bitcoin payments system.

Since computers operate on electricity, mining Bitcoins is at its most profitable when Bitcoin miners utilize the least costly electricity. So it should be no surprise that large-scale Bitcoin mining operations have tended to cluster around low-cost sources of electricity, including hydroelectric dams in the United States and geothermal electricity plants in Iceland.

Market forces encourage low-cost production, even for intangible items like Bitcoin.

Valery Bond/123RF

QUESTIONS:

Can you think of other businesses that locate their operations strategically to minimize production or distribution costs? Why are some companies located closer to key inputs and others closer to their customers?

Who Will Get the Output?

The market system helps to determine the distribution of total output in two ways. Generally, any product will be distributed to consumers on the basis of their ability and willingness to pay its existing market price. If the price of some product, say, a small sailboat, is $3,000, then buyers who are willing and able to pay that price will "sail, sail away." Consumers who are unwilling or unable to pay the price will be "sitting on the dock of the bay."

The ability to pay the market prices for sailboats and other products depends on the amount of income that consumers have, along with the prices of, and preferences for, various goods. If consumers have sufficient income and want to spend their money on a particular good, they can have it.

How Will the System Promote Progress?

Society desires economic growth (greater output) and higher standards of living (greater output *per person*). How does the market system promote technological improvements and capital accumulation, which both contribute to a higher standard of living for society?

Technological Advance The market system provides a strong incentive for technological advance. Better products and processes supplant inferior ones. An entrepreneur or firm that introduces a popular new product will gain revenue and economic profit at the expense of rivals.

Technological advance also includes new and improved methods that reduce production or distribution costs. By passing part of its cost reduction on to the consumer through a lower product price, the firm can increase sales and obtain economic profit at the expense of rival firms.

Moreover, the market system promotes the rapid spread of technological advance throughout an industry. Rival firms must follow the lead of the most innovative firm or else suffer immediate losses and eventual failure. In some cases, the result is **creative destruction:** The creation of new products and production methods completely destroys the market positions of firms that are wedded to existing products and older ways of doing business. Example: Compact discs largely demolished vinyl records before MP3 players and then online streaming subsequently supplanted compact discs.

creative destruction
The hypothesis that the creation of new products and production methods simultaneously destroys the market power of existing monopolies.

Capital Accumulation Most technological advances require additional capital goods. The market system provides the resources necessary to produce additional capital through increased dollar votes for those goods. That is, the market system acknowledges dollar voting for capital goods, as well as for consumer goods.

Who counts the dollar votes for capital goods? Answer: Entrepreneurs and business owners. They often use some of their profits to purchase capital goods. They do so because their additional capital may generate even greater profit income in the future if the technological innovation that required the additional capital goods is successful.

"invisible hand"
The tendency of firms and resource suppliers that seek to further their own self-interests in competitive markets to also promote the interest of society.

APPLYING THE ANALYSIS

The "Invisible Hand"

In his 1776 book *The Wealth of Nations,* Adam Smith first noted that the operation of a market system creates a curious unity between private interests and social interests. Firms and resource suppliers, seeking to further their own self-interest and operating within the framework of a highly competitive market system, will simultaneously, as though guided by an **"invisible hand,"** promote the public or social interest. For example, we have seen that in a competitive environment, businesses seek to build new and improved products to increase profits. Those enhanced products increase society's well-being. Businesses also use the least costly combination of resources to produce a specific output because it is in their self-interest. But least-cost production is also clearly in the social interest as well because it "frees up" resources to produce other products or reduce the strain on the environment.

Self-interest, awakened and guided by the competitive market system, is what induces responses appropriate to the changes in society's wants. Businesses seeking to make higher profits and to avoid losses, and resource suppliers pursuing greater monetary rewards, negotiate changes in the allocation of resources and end up with the output that society wants. Competition controls or guides self-interest such that self-interest automatically and quite unintentionally furthers the best interest of society. The invisible hand ensures that when firms maximize their profits, and resource suppliers maximize their incomes, these groups also help maximize society's output and income.

QUESTION:

Are "doing good for others" and "doing well for oneself" conflicting ideas, according to Adam Smith?

 ## APPLYING THE ANALYSIS

The Demise of the Command Systems

Our discussion of how a market system answers the four fundamental questions provides insights on why the command systems of the Soviet Union, eastern Europe, and China (prior to its market reforms) failed. Those systems encountered two insurmountable problems.

The first difficulty was the *coordination problem.* The central planners had to coordinate the millions of individual decisions by consumers, resource suppliers, and businesses. Consider the setting up of a factory to produce tractors. The central planners had to establish a realistic annual production target: for example, 1,000 tractors. They then had to make available all the necessary inputs—labor, machinery, electric power, steel, tires, glass, paint, transportation—for the production and delivery of those 1,000 tractors.

Because the outputs of many industries serve as inputs to other industries, the failure of any single industry to achieve its output target caused a chain reaction of repercussions. For example, if iron mines, for want of machinery or labor or transportation, did not supply the steel industry with the required inputs of iron ore, the steel mills were unable to fulfill the input needs of the many industries that depended on steel. Steel-using industries (such as tractor, automobile, and transportation) were unable to fulfill their planned production goals. Eventually, the chain reaction spread to all firms that used steel as an input, and from there to other input buyers or final consumers.

The coordination problem became more difficult as the economies expanded. Products and production processes grew more sophisticated and the number of industries requiring planning increased. Planning techniques that worked for the simpler economy proved highly inadequate and inefficient for the larger economy. Bottlenecks and production stoppages became the norm, not the exception.

A lack of a reliable success indicator added to the coordination problem in the Soviet Union and China prior to its market reforms. We have seen that market economies rely on profit as a success indicator. Profit depends on consumer demand, production efficiency, and product quality. In contrast, the major success indicator for the command economies usually was a quantitative production target that the central planners assigned. Production costs, product quality, and product mix were secondary considerations. Managers and workers often sacrificed product quality and variety because they were being awarded bonuses for meeting quantitative, not qualitative, targets. If meeting production goals meant sloppy assembly work, so be it.

It was difficult at best for planners to assign quantitative production targets without unintentionally producing distortions in output. If the plan specified a production target for producing nails in terms of *weight* (tons of nails), the enterprise made only large nails. But if its target was specified as a *quantity* (thousands of nails), the producer made all small nails, and lots of them!

The command economies also faced an *incentive problem.* Central planners determined the output mix. When they misjudged how many automobiles, shoes, shirts, and chickens were wanted at the government-determined prices, persistent shortages and surpluses of those products arose. But as long as the managers who oversaw the production of those goods were rewarded for meeting their assigned production goals, they had no incentive to adjust production in response to the shortages and surpluses. And there were no fluctuations in prices and profitability to signal that more or less of certain products was desired. Thus, many products were unavailable or in short supply, while other products were overproduced and sat for months or years in warehouses.

QUESTION:

In market economies, firms rarely worry about the availability of inputs to produce their products, whereas in command economies input availability was a constant concern. Why the difference?

The Circular Flow Model

The dynamic market economy creates continuous, repetitive flows of goods and services, resources, and money. The **circular flow diagram,** shown in **Figure 2.2**, illustrates those flows for a simplified economy in which there is no government. This figure groups the economy's decision makers into *businesses* and *households.* Additionally, we divide this economy's markets into the *resource market* and the *product market.*

circular flow diagram
The flow of resources from households to firms and of products from firms to households. These flows are accompanied by reverse flows of money from firms to households and from households to firms.

Households

The blue rectangle on the right side of the circular flow diagram in **Figure 2.2** represents **households,** defined as one or more persons occupying a housing unit. There are currently about 119 million households in the U.S. economy. Households buy the goods and services that businesses make available in the product market. Households obtain the income needed to buy those products by selling resources in the resource market.

household
An economic unit (of one or more persons) that provides the economy with resources and uses the income received to purchase goods and services that satisfy economic wants.

All the resources in our no-government economy are ultimately owned or provided by households. For instance, the members of one household or another directly provide all of the labor and entrepreneurial ability in the economy. Households also own all of the land and all of the capital in the economy, either directly as personal property, or indirectly as a consequence of owning all of the businesses in the economy (and thereby controlling all of the land and capital owned by businesses). Thus, all of the income in the economy—all wages, rents, interest, and profits—flow to households because they provide the economy's labor, land, capital, and entrepreneurial ability.

Businesses

The blue rectangle on the left side of the circular flow diagram represents **businesses,** which are commercial establishments that attempt to earn profits for their owners by offering goods and services for sale. Businesses sell goods and services in the product market in order to obtain revenue, and they incur costs in the resource markets when they purchase the labor, land, capital, and entrepreneurial ability they need to produce their respective goods and services.

business
A firm that purchases resources and provides goods and services to the economy.

FIGURE 2.2

The circular flow diagram. Products flow from businesses to households through the product market, and resources flow from households to businesses through the resource market. Opposite those real flows are monetary flows. Households receive income from businesses (their costs) through the resource market, and businesses receive revenue from households (their expenditures) through the product market.

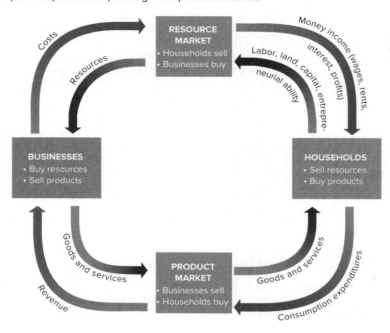

Product Market

product market
A market in which products are sold by firms and bought by households.

The red rectangle at the bottom of the diagram represents the **product market** in which households purchase the goods and services produced by businesses. Households use the income they receive from the sale of resources to buy goods and services. The money that consumers spend on goods and services flows to businesses as revenue.

Resource Market

resource market
A market in which households sell and firms buy resources or the services of resources.

Finally, the red rectangle at the top of the circular flow diagram represents the **resource market** in which households sell resources to businesses. The households sell resources to generate income, and the businesses buy resources to produce goods and services. Productive resources flow from households to businesses, and money flows from businesses to households in the form of wages, rents, interest, and profits.

The circular flow model depicts a complex web of economic activity in which businesses and households are both buyers and sellers. Businesses buy resources and sell products. Households buy products and sell resources. The counterclockwise *real flow* of economic resources and finished products, which is illustrated by the red arrows in **Figure 2.2**, is paid for by the clockwise *money flow* of income and consumption expenditures illustrated by the blue arrows.

PHOTO OP

Resource Markets and Product Markets

The sale of a grove of orange trees would be a transaction in the resource market; the sale of oranges to final consumers would be a transaction in the product market.

©Zu Sanchez Photography/Getty Images RF   ©Renaschild/Getty Images RF

 ## APPLYING THE ANALYSIS

Some Facts About U.S. Businesses

Businesses constitute one part of the private sector. The business population is extremely diverse, ranging from giant corporations such as Walmart, with 2020 revenues of $524 billion and 2.2 million employees, to single-person firms with sales of less than $100 per day. There are three major legal forms of businesses: sole proprietorships, partnerships, and corporations.

A *sole proprietorship* is a business owned and operated by one person. Usually, the proprietor (the owner) personally supervises its operation. In a *partnership,* two or more individuals (the partners) agree to own and operate a business together.

A *corporation* is an independent legal entity that can—on its own behalf—acquire resources, own assets, produce and sell products, incur debts, extend credit, sue and be sued, and otherwise engage in any legal business activity. A corporation sells stocks (ownership shares) to raise funds but is legally distinct and separate from the individual stockholders. The stockholders' legal and financial liability is limited to the loss of the value of their shares. Hired executives and managers operate corporations on a day-to-day basis.

Figure 2.3a shows how the business population is distributed among the three major legal forms. About 72% of firms are sole proprietorships, whereas only 18% are corporations. But as **Figure 2.3b** indicates, corporations account for 82% of total sales revenue (and therefore total output) in the United States. Virtually all the nation's largest business enterprises are corporations. **Global Snapshot 2.2** lists the world's largest corporations.

FIGURE 2.3
The business population and shares of total revenue. (a) Sole proprietorships dominate the business population numerically, but (b) corporations dominate total sales revenue (total output).

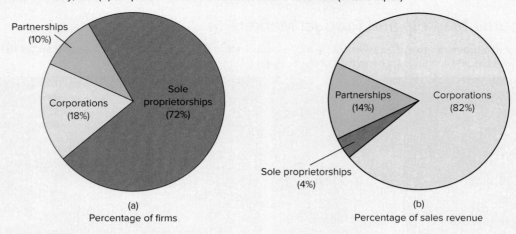

(a)
Percentage of firms

(b)
Percentage of sales revenue

Source: U.S. Census Bureau, www.census.gov.

QUESTION:

Why do you think sole proprietorships and partnerships typically incorporate (become corporations) when they experience rapid and sizable increases in their production, sales, and profits?

GLOBAL SNAPSHOT 2.2

The World's 10 Largest Corporations

Five of the world's 10 largest corporations, based on dollar revenue in 2020, were headquartered in the United States or China. The Netherlands, Saudi Arabia, Germany, Great Britain, and Japan account for the rest of the top 10.

Walmart (USA) $524 billion

Sinopec (China) $407 billion

State Grid (China) $384 billion

China National Petroleum (China) $379 billion

Royal Dutch Shell (Netherlands) $352 billion

Saudi Aramco (Saudi Arabia) $330 billion

Volkswagen (Germany) $283 billion

BP (Britain) $283 billion

Amazon (USA) $281 billion

Toyota Motor (Japan) $275 billion

Source: "Global 500," *Fortune*, **www.fortune.com**. Retrieved February 4, 2021.

APPLYING THE ANALYSIS

Some Facts About U.S. Households

Households constitute the second part of the private sector. The U.S. economy currently has about 119 million households. These households consist of one or more persons occupying a housing unit and are both the ultimate suppliers of all economic resources *and* the major spenders in the economy.

The nation's earned income is apportioned among wages, rents, interest, and profits. *Wages* are paid to labor; *rents* and *interest* are paid to owners of property resources; and *profits* are paid to the owners of corporations and unincorporated businesses.

Figure 2.4a shows the categories of U.S. income earned in 2019. The largest source of income for households is the wages and salaries paid to workers. Notice that the bulk of total U.S. income goes to labor, not to capital. Proprietors' income—the income of doctors, lawyers, small-business owners, farmers, and owners of other unincorporated enterprises—also has a "wage" element. Some of this income is payment for one's own labor, and some of it is profit from one's own business.

FIGURE 2.4

Sources of U.S. income and the composition of spending. (a) Almost 64% of U.S. income is received as wages and salaries. Income to property owners—corporate profit, interest, and rents—accounts for about 25% of total income. (b) Consumers divide their spending among durable goods, nondurable goods, and services. Roughly 64% of consumer spending is for services; the rest is for goods.

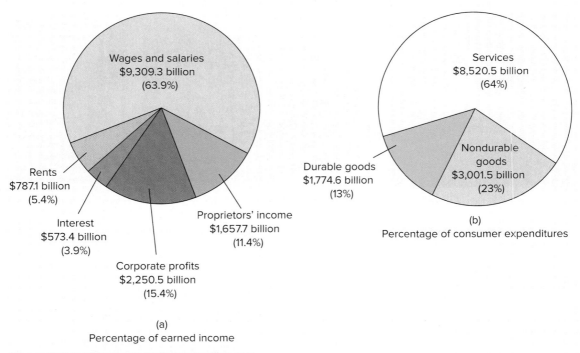

Source: Bureau of Economic Analysis, **www.bea.gov**.

The other three types of income are self-evident: Some households own corporate stock and receive dividend incomes as their share of corporate profits. Many households also own bonds and savings accounts that yield interest income. Some households receive rental income by providing buildings and natural resources (including land) to businesses and other individuals.

U.S. households use their income to buy (spend), save, and pay taxes. **Figure 2.4b** shows how households divide their spending among three broad categories of goods and services: *consumer durables* (goods such as cars, refrigerators, and personal computers that have expected lives of 3 years or longer), *nondurables* (goods such as food, clothing, and gasoline that have lives of less than 3 years), and *services* (the work done by people such as lawyers, physicians, and recreational workers). Observe that approximately 64% of consumer spending is on services. For this reason, the United States is known as a *service-oriented economy*.

> QUESTION:
>
> Over the past several decades, the service share of spending in the United States has increased relative to the goods share. Why do you think that trend has occurred?

PHOTO OP

Durable Goods, Nondurable Goods, and Services

Consumers collectively spend their income on durable goods (such as the washer–dryer combo), nondurable goods (such as the pizza), and services (such as hair care).

©2/Ryan McVay/Ocean/Corbis RF   ©Maren Caruso/Getty Images RF   ©Plush Studios/Blend Images LLC RF

Summary

LO2.1 Differentiate between a command system and a market system.

The market system and the command system are the two broad types of economic systems used to address the economic problem. In the market system (or capitalism), private individuals own most resources, and markets coordinate most economic activity. In the command system (or socialism or communism), government owns most resources, and central planners coordinate most economic activity.

LO2.2 List the main characteristics of the market system.

The market system is characterized by the private ownership of resources, including capital, and the freedom of individuals to engage in economic activities of their choice to advance their material well-being. Self-interest is the driving force of such an economy, and competition functions as a regulatory or control mechanism.

In the market system, markets, prices, and profits organize and make effective the many millions of individual economic decisions that occur daily.

Specialization, use of advanced technology, and the extensive use of capital goods are common features of market systems. By functioning as a medium of exchange, money eliminates the problems of bartering and permits easy trade and greater specialization, both domestically and internationally.

LO2.3 Explain how the market system answers the four fundamental questions.

Every economy faces four fundamental questions: (a) What goods and services will be produced? (b) How will the goods and services be produced? (c) Who will get the goods and services? (d) How will the system promote progress?

The market system produces products whose production and sale yield total revenue sufficient to cover total cost. It does not produce products for which total revenue continuously falls short of total cost. Competition forces firms to use the lowest-cost production techniques.

Economic profit (total revenue minus total cost) indicates that an industry is prosperous and promotes its expansion. Losses signify that an industry is not prosperous and hasten its contraction.

Consumer sovereignty means that both businesses and resource suppliers are subject to consumers' wants. Through their dollar votes, consumers decide on the composition of output.

The prices that a household receives for the resources it supplies to the economy determine that household's income. This income determines the household's claim on the economy's output.

LO2.4 Discuss how the market system adjusts to change and promotes progress.

The market system encourages technological advance and capital accumulation, both of which raise a nation's standard of living.

Competition, the primary mechanism of control in the market economy, promotes a unity of self-interest and social interests. As if directed by an invisible hand, competition harnesses the self-interested motives of businesses and resource suppliers to further the social interest.

LO2.5 Describe the mechanics of the circular flow model.

The circular flow model illustrates the flows of resources and products from households to businesses and from businesses to households, along with the corresponding monetary flows. Businesses are on the buying side of the resource market and the selling side of the product market. Households are on the selling side of the resource market and the buying side of the product market.

Terms and Concepts

economic system

command system

market system

private property

freedom of enterprise

freedom of choice

self-interest

competition

market

specialization

division of labor

medium of exchange

barter

money

consumer sovereignty

dollar votes

creative destruction

"Invisible Hand"

circular flow diagram

household

business

product market

resource market

Questions

1. Contrast how a market system and a command economy try to cope with economic scarcity. **(LO1)**

2. How does self-interest help achieve society's economic goals? Why is there such a wide variety of desired goods and services in a market system? In what way are entrepreneurs and businesses at the helm of the economy but commanded by consumers? **(LO2)**

3. Why are private property, and the protection of property rights, so critical to the success of the market system? How do property rights encourage cooperation? **(LO2)**

4. What are the advantages of using capital in the production process? What is meant by the term "division of labor"? What are the advantages of specialization in the use of human and material resources? Explain why exchange is the necessary consequence of specialization. **(LO2)**

5. What problem does barter entail? Indicate the economic significance of money as a medium of exchange. What is meant by the statement "We want money only to part with it"? **(LO2)**

6. Evaluate and explain the following statements: **(LO2)**

   a. The market system is a profit-and-loss system.

   b. Competition is the disciplinarian of the market economy.

7. In the 1990s, thousands of "dot-com" companies emerged with great fanfare to take advantage of the Internet and new information technologies. A few, like Google, eBay, and Amazon, have generally thrived and prospered, but many others struggled and eventually failed. Explain these varied outcomes in terms of how the market system answers the question "What goods and services will be produced?" **(LO3)**

8. Some large hardware stores, such as Home Depot, boast of carrying as many as 20,000 different products in each store. What motivated the producers of those individual products to make them and offer them for sale? How did the producers decide on the best combinations of resources to use? Who made those resources available, and why? Who decides whether these particular hardware products should continue to be produced and offered for sale? **(LO3)**

9. What is meant by the term "creative destruction"? How does the emergence of self-driving cars relate to this idea? **(LO3)**

10. In a sentence, describe the meaning of the phrase "invisible hand." **(LO4)**

11. Distinguish between the resource market and the product market in the circular flow model. In what way are businesses and households both sellers and buyers in this model? What are the flows in the circular flow model? **(LO5)**

12. What are the three major legal forms of business enterprises? Which form is the most prevalent in terms of numbers? Which form is dominant in terms of total sales revenues? **(LO5)**

13. What are the major forms of household income? Contrast the wage and salary share to the profit share in terms of relative size. Distinguish between a durable consumer good and a nondurable consumer good. How does the combined spending on both types of consumer goods compare to the spending on services? **(LO5)**

Problems

1. Suppose Natasha currently makes $50,000 per year working as a manager at a cable TV company. She then develops two possible entrepreneurial business opportunities. In one, she will quit her job to start an organic soap company. In the other, she will try to develop an Internet-based competitor to the local cable company. For the soap-making opportunity, she anticipates annual revenue of $465,000 and costs for the necessary land, labor, and capital of $395,000 per year. For the Internet opportunity, she anticipates costs for land, labor, and capital of $3,250,000 per year as compared to revenues of $3,275,000 per year. (a) Should she quit her current job to become an entrepreneur? (b) If she does quit her current job, which opportunity should she pursue? **(LO5)**

2. With current technology, suppose a firm is producing 400 loaves of banana bread daily. Also assume that the least-cost combination of resources in producing those loaves is 5 units of labor, 7 units of land, 2 units of capital, and 1 unit of entrepreneurial ability, selling at prices of $40, $60, $60, and $20, respectively. If the firm can sell these 400 loaves at $2 per unit, what is its total revenue? Its total cost? Its profit or loss? Will it continue to produce banana bread? If this firm's situation is typical for the other makers of banana bread, will resources flow toward or away from this bakery good? **(LO3)**

3. Let's put dollar amounts on the flows in the circular flow diagram of **Figure 2.2**. **(LO5)**

   a. Suppose that businesses buy a total of $100 billion of the four resources (labor, land, capital, and entrepreneurial ability) from households. If households receive $60 billion in wages, $10 billion in rent, and $20 billion in interest, how much are households paid for providing entrepreneurial ability?

   b. If households spend $55 billion on goods and $45 billion on services, how much in revenues do businesses receive in the product market?

Demand, Supply, and Market Equilibrium

Learning Objectives

LO3.1 Describe *demand* and explain how it can change.

LO3.2 Describe *supply* and explain how it can change.

LO3.3 Explain how supply and demand interact to determine market equilibrium.

LO3.4 Explain how changes in supply and demand affect equilibrium prices and quantities.

LO3.5 Define government-set prices and explain how they can cause surpluses and shortages.

LO3.6 (Appendix) Use supply and demand analysis to analyze actual economic situations.

The model of supply and demand is the economics profession's greatest contribution to human understanding. It explains the operation of the markets on which we depend for nearly everything that we eat, drink, or consume. The model is so powerful and so widely used that to many people it is economics.

Markets bring together buyers ("demanders") and sellers ("suppliers"). Everyday consumer markets include the corner gas station, Amazon.com, and the local bakery shop. The New York Stock Exchange and the Chicago Board of Trade are markets where buyers and sellers from all over the world exchange stocks, bonds, and commodities. In labor markets, new college graduates "sell" and employers "buy" specific labor services. Ride-sharing apps like Uber and Lyft match people who want to buy rides with people who want to sell rides.

Some markets are local, while others are national or international. Some are highly personal, involving face-to-face contact between demander and supplier; others are faceless, with buyer and seller never seeing or knowing each other. But all competitive markets involve demand and supply, and this chapter discusses how the model works to explain both the *quantities* that are bought and sold in markets, as well as the *prices* at which they trade.

Demand

Demand is a schedule or a curve that shows the various amounts of a product that consumers will purchase at each of a series of possible prices during a specified period of time.[1] The table in **Figure 3.1** is a hypothetical demand schedule for a *single consumer* purchasing a particular product—in this case, lattes. (For simplicity, we will categorize all espresso drinks as "lattes" and assume a highly competitive market.)

The table reveals that, if the price of lattes were $5 each, Joe Java would buy 10 lattes per month; if it were $4, Joe would buy 20 lattes per month; and so forth.

The table does not tell us which of the five possible prices will actually exist in the market. That depends on the interaction between demand and supply. Demand is simply a statement of a buyer's plans, or intentions, with respect to the purchase of a product.

To be meaningful, the quantities demanded at each price must relate to a specific period—a day, a week, a month. Here that period is one month.

demand
A schedule or curve that shows the various amounts of a product that consumers are willing and able to purchase at each of a series of possible prices during a specified period of time.

Law of Demand

Other things equal, as price falls, the quantity demanded rises, and as price rises, the quantity demanded falls. In short, there is an *inverse* relationship between price and quantity demanded. Economists call this inverse relationship the **law of demand.**

The other-things-equal assumption is critical here. Many factors other than the price of the product being considered affect the amount purchased. The quantity of lattes purchased will depend not only on the price of lattes but also on the prices of such substitutes as tea, soda, fruit juice, and bottled water. The law of demand in this case says that fewer lattes will be purchased if the price of lattes rises while the prices of tea, soda, fruit juice, and bottled water all remain constant.

The law of demand is consistent with both common sense and observation. People ordinarily *do* buy more of a product at a low price than at a high price. Price is an obstacle that deters consumers. The higher that obstacle, the less of a product they will buy; the lower the obstacle, the more they will buy. The fact that businesses conduct "clearance sales" to liquidate unsold items firmly supports the law of demand.

law of demand
The principle that, other things equal, an increase in a product's *price* will reduce the quantity of it demanded, and conversely for a decrease in price.

FIGURE 3.1
Joe Java's demand for lattes. Because price and quantity demanded are inversely related, an individual's demand schedule graphs as a downward sloping curve such as *D*. Other things equal, consumers will buy more of a product as its price declines and less of the product as its price rises. (Here and in later figures, *P* stands for price and *Q* stands for quantity demanded or supplied.)

Joe Java's Demand for Lattes	
Price per Latte	**Quantity Demanded per Month**
$5	10
4	20
3	35
2	55
1	80

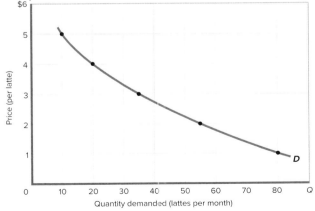

[1] This definition obviously is worded to apply to product markets. To adjust it to apply to resource markets, substitute the word "resource" for "product" and the word "businesses" for "consumers."

The Demand Curve

demand curve
A curve illustrating demand.

The inverse relationship between price and quantity demanded for any product can be represented on a simple graph with *quantity demanded* on the horizontal axis and *price* on the vertical axis. The graph in **Figure 3.1** plots the five price-quantity data points listed in the table and connects the points with a smooth curve, labeled *D*. This is a **demand curve**. Its downward slope reflects the law of demand: People buy more of a product, service, or resource as its price falls.

Market Demand

So far, we have concentrated on just one consumer, Joe Java. But competition requires that more than one buyer be present in each market. By adding the quantities demanded by all consumers at each of the various possible prices, we can get from *individual* demand to *market* demand. If there are just three buyers in the market (Joe Java, Sarah Coffee, and Mike Cappuccino), as represented by the table and graph in **Figure 3.2**, it is relatively easy to determine the total quantity demanded at each price. **Figure 3.2** shows the graphical summing procedure: at each price, we sum horizontally the quantities demanded by Joe, Sarah, and Mike to obtain the total quantity demanded at that price. We then plot the price and the total quantity demanded as one point on the market demand curve.

Competition, of course, ordinarily entails many more than three buyers of a product. For simplicity, we suppose that the table and curve D_1 in **Figure 3.3** show the amounts all the buyers in this market will purchase at each of the five prices.

FIGURE 3.2

Market demand for lattes; three buyers. The market demand curve *D* is the horizontal summation of the individual demand curves (D_1, D_2, and D_3) of all the consumers in the market. At the price of $3, for example, the three individual curves yield a total quantity demanded of 100 lattes.

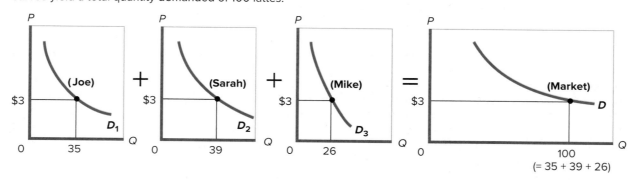

Market Demand for Lattes, Three Buyers							
	Quantity Demanded						Total
Price per Latte	Joe Java		Sarah Coffee		Mike Cappuccino		Quantity Demanded per Month
$5	10	+	12	+	8	=	30
4	20	+	23	+	17	=	60
3	35	+	39	+	26	=	100
2	55	+	60	+	39	=	154
1	80	+	87	+	54	=	221

In constructing a demand curve such as D_1 in **Figure 3.3**, economists assume that price is the most important influence on the amount of any product purchased. But economists know that other factors can and do affect purchases. These factors, called **determinants of demand,** are held constant when a demand curve like D_1 is drawn. When any of these determinants changes, the demand curve will shift to the right or left. For this reason, determinants of demand are sometimes referred to as *demand shifters.*

The basic determinants of demand are (1) consumers' tastes (preferences), (2) the number of consumers in the market, (3) consumers' incomes, (4) the prices of related goods, and (5) consumer expectations.

determinants of demand
Factors other than price that determine the quantities demanded of a good or service.

Changes in Demand

A change in one or more of the determinants of demand will change the demand data (the demand schedule in the table) and therefore the location of the demand curve in **Figure 3.3**. A change in the demand schedule or, graphically, a shift in the demand curve is called a *change in demand.*

If consumers desire to buy more lattes at each possible price, that *increase in demand* is shown as a shift of the demand curve to the right, say, from D_1 to D_2. Conversely, a *decrease in demand* occurs when consumers buy fewer lattes at each possible price. The leftward shift of the demand curve from D_1 to D_3 in **Figure 3.3** shows that situation.

Now let's see how changes in each determinant affect demand.

Tastes A favorable change in consumer tastes (preferences) for a product means more of it will be demanded at each price. Demand will increase; the demand curve will shift rightward. For example, greater concern about the environment has increased the demand for hybrid cars and other "green" technologies. An unfavorable change in consumer preferences will decrease demand, shifting the demand curve to the left. For example, the popularity of plant-based diets has reduced the demand for beef and other meats.

FIGURE 3.3
Changes in the demand for lattes. A change in one or more of the determinants of demand causes a change in demand. An increase in demand is shown as a shift of the demand curve to the right, as from D_1 to D_2. A decrease in demand is shown as a shift of the demand curve to the left, as from D_1 to D_3. These changes in demand are to be distinguished from a change in *quantity demanded,* which is caused by a change in the price of the product, as shown by a movement from, say, point *a* to point *b* on fixed demand curve D_1.

(1) Price per Latte	(2) Total Quantity Demanded per Month
$5	2,000
4	4,000
3	7,000
2	11,000
1	16,000

Market Demand for Lattes (D)

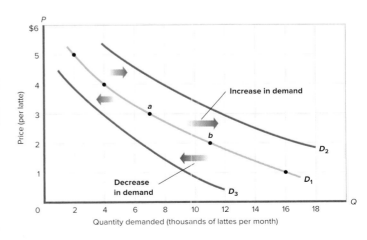

Number of Buyers   An increase in the number of buyers in a market increases product demand. For example, the rising number of older persons in the United States in recent years has increased the demand for motor homes, medical care, and retirement communities. In contrast, out-migration from many small rural communities has reduced their population and thus the demand for housing, home appliances, and auto repair in those towns.

normal good
A good or service whose consumption increases when income increases and falls when income decreases, price remaining constant.

inferior good
A good or service whose consumption declines as income rises, prices held constant.

Income   For most products, a rise in income increases demand. Consumers collectively buy more airplane tickets, HD TVs, and gas grills as their incomes rise. Products whose demand increases or decreases *directly* with changes in income are called *superior goods,* or **normal goods.**

Although most products are normal goods, there are a few exceptions. As incomes increase beyond some point, the demand for used clothing, retread tires, and third-hand automobiles may decrease because the higher incomes enable consumers to buy new versions of these products. Goods whose demand varies *inversely* with money income are called **inferior goods.**

Prices of Related Goods   A change in the price of a related good may either increase or decrease the demand for a product, depending on whether the related good is a substitute or a complement:

substitute goods
Products or services that can be used in place of each other. When the price of one falls, the demand for the other product falls; conversely, when the price of one product rises, the demand for the other product rises.

complementary goods
Products and services that are used together. When the price of one falls, the demand for the other increases (and conversely).

- A **substitute good** is one that can be used in place of another good.
- A **complementary good** is one that is used together with another good.

Beef and chicken are substitute goods or, simply, *substitutes.* When two products are substitutes, an increase in the price of one will increase the demand for the other. For example, when the price of beef rises, consumers will buy less beef and increase their demand for chicken. So it is with other product pairs such as Nikes and Reeboks, Budweiser and Miller beer, or Colgate and Crest toothpaste. They are *substitutes in consumption.*

Because complementary goods (or, simply, *complements*) are used together, they are typically demanded jointly. Examples include computers and software, smartphones and cellular service, and snowboards and lift tickets. If the price of a complement (e.g., lettuce) goes up, the demand for the related good (salad dressing) will decline. Conversely, if the price of a complement (e.g., tuition) falls, the demand for a related good (textbooks) will increase.

The vast majority of goods are unrelated to one another and are called *independent goods.* There is virtually no demand relationship between bacon and golf balls or bananas and wristwatches. A change in the price of one will have virtually no effect on the demand for the other.

Consumer Expectations   Changes in consumer expectations may shift demand. A newly formed expectation of higher future price may cause consumers to buy now in order to "beat" the anticipated price rise, thus increasing current demand. This often happens in "hot" real estate markets; buyers rush in because they think home prices will continue to escalate rapidly. These expectation-driven buyers increase the current demand for houses.

Similarly, changes in expectations concerning future income may prompt consumers to change their current spending. For example, first-round NFL draft choices may splurge on new luxury cars in anticipation of lucrative professional football contracts. Or workers who become fearful of losing their jobs may reduce their demand for, say, vacation travel.

PHOTO OP

Normal versus Inferior Goods

New television sets are normal goods. People buy more of them as their incomes rise. Hand-pushed lawn mowers are inferior goods. As incomes rise, people purchase electric or gas-powered mowers instead.

Robert Daly/Caia Image/Glow Images

Pixtal/Age Fotostock

Changes in Quantity Demanded

A *change in demand* must not be confused with a *change in quantity demanded.* Recall that "demand" is a schedule or curve. So a **change in demand** implies a change in the schedule and a corresponding shift of the curve. A change in demand occurs when a consumer's state of mind about purchasing the product has changed in response to a change in one or more of the determinants of demand. Graphically, a change in demand is a shift of the demand curve to the right (an increase in demand) or to the left (a decrease in demand).

In contrast, a **change in quantity demanded** is a movement from one point to another point—from one price-quantity combination to another—on a fixed demand curve. The cause of such a change is an increase or decrease in the price of the product under consideration. In the table in **Figure 3.3**, for example, a decline in the price of lattes from $5 to $4 will increase the quantity of lattes demanded from 2,000 to 4,000.

In the graph in **Figure 3.3**, the shift of the demand curve D_1 to either D_2 or D_3 is a change in demand. But the movement from point *a* to point *b* on curve D_1 represents a change in quantity demanded: Demand has not changed; it is the entire curve, and it remains fixed in place.

change in demand
A change in the quantity demanded of a good or service at every price; a shift of the demand curve to the left or right.

change in quantity demanded
A movement from one point to another on a demand curve.

PHOTO OP

Substitutes versus Complements

Different brands of soft drinks are substitute goods; goods consumed jointly such as hot dogs and mustard are complementary goods.

Jill Braaten/McGraw Hill Education   Image Source, All rights reserved

Supply

supply
A schedule or curve showing the amounts of a product that sellers (or a seller) will offer for sale at each of a series of possible prices during a specific period.

Supply is a schedule or curve showing the amounts of a product that producers will make available for sale at each of a series of possible prices during a specific period.[2] The table in **Figure 3.4** is a hypothetical supply schedule for Star Buck, a single supplier of lattes. Curve S incorporates the data in the table and is called a *supply curve*. The schedule and curve show the quantities of lattes that will be supplied at various prices, other things equal.

FIGURE 3.4

Star Buck's supply of lattes. Because price and quantity supplied are directly related, the supply curve for an individual producer graphs as an upsloping curve. Other things equal, producers will offer more of a product for sale as its price rises and less of the product for sale as its price falls.

Star Buck's Supply of Lattes	
Price per Latte	Quantity Supplied per Month
$5	60
4	50
3	35
2	20
1	5

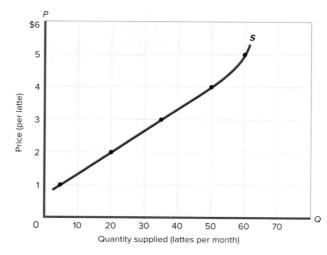

Law of Supply

Figure 3.4 shows that a positive or direct relationship prevails between price and quantity supplied. As price rises, the quantity supplied rises; as price falls, the quantity supplied falls. This relationship is called the **law of supply.** Other things equal, firms will produce and offer for sale more of their product at a high price than at a low price.

Price is an obstacle from the standpoint of the consumer (e.g., Joe Java), who is on the paying end. The higher the price, the less the consumer will buy. The supplier (e.g., Star Buck) is on the receiving end of the product's price. To a supplier, price represents *revenue,* which serves as an incentive to produce and sell more of a product. The higher the price, the greater this incentive and the greater the quantity supplied.

law of supply
The principle that, other things equal, an increase in the *price* of a product will increase the quantity of it supplied, and conversely for a price decrease.

Market Supply

To derive market supply from individual supply, we sum the quantities supplied by each producer at each price. That is, to find the market **supply curve**, we "horizontally add" the supply curves of the individual producers. The price and quantity-supplied data in the table in **Figure 3.5** are for an assumed 200 identical producers in the market, each willing to supply lattes according to the supply schedule shown in **Figure 3.4.** Curve S_1 is a graph of the market supply data. Note that the axes in **Figure 3.5** are the same as those used in our graph of market demand (**Figure 3.3**). The only difference is that we change the label on the horizontal axis from "quantity demanded" to "quantity supplied."

supply curve
A curve illustrating supply.

Determinants of Supply

In constructing a supply curve, we assume that price is the most significant influence on the quantity supplied of any product. But other factors can and do affect supply. The supply curve is drawn on the assumption that these other factors do not change. If one of them does change, a *change in supply* will occur, meaning that the entire supply curve will shift.

FIGURE 3.5
Changes in the supply of lattes. A change in one or more of the determinants of supply causes a change in supply. An increase in supply is shown as a rightward shift of the supply curve, as from S_1 to S_2. A decrease in supply is depicted as a leftward shift of the curve, as from S_1 to S_3. In contrast, a change in the *quantity supplied* is caused by a change in the product's price and is shown by a movement from one point to another, as from *a* to *b* on fixed supply curve S_1.

Market Supply of Lattes (S_1)	
(1) Price per Latte	**(2) Total Quantity Supplied per Month**
$5	12,000
4	10,000
3	7,000
2	4,000
1	1,000

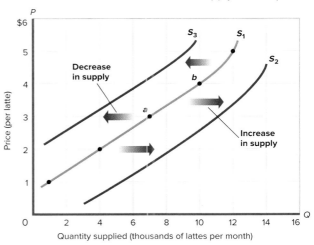

determinants of supply
Factors other than price that determine the quantities supplied of a good or service.

The basic **determinants of supply** are (1) resource prices, (2) technology, (3) taxes and subsidies, (4) prices of other goods, (5) producer expectations, and (6) the number of sellers in the market. A change in any one or more of these determinants of supply, or *supply shifters,* will move the supply curve for a product either right or left. A shift to the *right,* as from S_1 to S_2 in **Figure 3.5**, signifies an *increase* in supply: Producers supply larger quantities of the product at each possible price. A shift to the *left,* as from S_1 to S_3, indicates a *decrease* in supply: Producers offer less output at each price.

Changes in Supply

Let's consider how changes in each of the determinants affect supply. The key idea is that costs are a major factor underlying supply curves; anything that affects costs usually shifts the supply curve.

Resource Prices   The prices of the resources used in the production process help determine a firm's costs of production. Higher *resource* prices raise production costs and, assuming a particular *product* price, squeeze profits. That reduction in profits reduces firms' incentive to supply output at each product price. For example, an increase in the prices of coffee beans and milk will increase the cost of making lattes and reduce their supply.

In contrast, lower *resource* prices reduce production costs and increase profits. So when resource prices fall, firms supply greater output at each product price. For example, a decrease in the prices of sand, gravel, and limestone will increase the supply of concrete.

Technology   Improvements in technology (techniques of production) enable firms to produce units of output with fewer resources. Because resources are costly, using fewer of them lowers production costs and increases supply. Example: Technological advances in producing computer monitors have greatly reduced their cost. Thus, manufacturers will now offer more such monitors than previously at the various prices; the supply of monitors has increased.

Taxes and Subsidies   Businesses treat most taxes as costs. An increase in sales or property taxes will increase production costs and reduce supply. In contrast, subsidies are "taxes in reverse." If the government subsidizes the production of a good, the subsidy in effect lowers the producers' costs and increases supply.

Prices of Other Goods   Firms that produce a particular product, say, soccer balls, can usually use their plant and equipment to produce alternative goods, say, basketballs and volleyballs. The higher prices of these "other goods" may entice soccer ball producers to switch production to those other goods in order to increase profits. This *substitution in production* results in a decrease in the supply of soccer balls. Alternatively, when basketballs and volleyballs decline in price relative to the price of soccer balls, producers of those goods may decide to produce more soccer balls instead.

Producer Expectations   Changes in expectations about the future price of a product may affect the producer's current willingness to supply that product. Farmers anticipating a higher wheat price in the future might withhold some of their current wheat harvest from the market, thereby causing a decrease in the current supply of wheat. In contrast, in many manufacturing industries, new expectations that the price will increase may induce firms to add another shift of workers or expand their production facilities, causing the current supply to increase.

Number of Sellers Other things equal, the larger the number of suppliers, the greater the market supply. As more firms enter an industry, the supply curve shifts to the right. Conversely, the smaller the number of firms in the industry, the less the market supply. This means that as firms leave an industry, the supply curve shifts to the left. Example: The United States and Canada have imposed restrictions on haddock fishing to replenish dwindling stocks. As part of that policy, the U.S. federal government bought the boats of some of the haddock fishers as a way of putting them out of business and decreasing the catch. The result has been a decline in the market supply of haddock.

Changes in Quantity Supplied

The distinction between a *change in supply* and a *change in quantity supplied* parallels the distinction between a change in demand and a change in quantity demanded. Because supply is a schedule or curve, a **change in supply** means a change in the schedule and a shift of the curve. An increase in supply shifts the curve to the right; a decrease in supply shifts it to the left. The cause of a change in supply is a change in one or more of the determinants of supply.

    In contrast, a **change in quantity supplied** is a movement from one point to another on a fixed supply curve. The cause of such a movement is a change in the price of the specific product being considered. In **Figure 3.5**, a decline in the price of lattes from $4 to $3 decreases the quantity of lattes supplied per month from 10,000 to 7,000. This movement from point *b* to point *a* along S_1 is a change in quantity supplied, not a change in supply. Supply is the full schedule of prices and quantities shown, and this schedule does not change when the price of lattes changes.

Market Equilibrium

With our understanding of demand and supply, we can now show how the decisions of Joe Java and other buyers of lattes interact with the decisions of Star Buck and other sellers to determine the equilibrium price and quantity of lattes. In the table in **Figure 3.6**, columns 1 and 2 repeat the market supply of lattes (from **Figure 3.5**), and columns 2 and 3 repeat the market demand for lattes (from **Figure 3.3**). We assume this is a competitive market, so neither buyers nor sellers can set the price.

Equilibrium Price and Quantity

The **equilibrium price** (or *market-clearing price*) is the price where the intentions of buyers and sellers match. It is the price where quantity demanded equals quantity supplied. The table in **Figure 3.6** reveals that at $3, *and only at that price,* the number of lattes that sellers wish to sell (7,000) is identical to the number that consumers want to buy (also 7,000). At $3 and 7,000 lattes, there is neither a shortage nor a surplus of lattes. So 7,000 lattes is the **equilibrium quantity:** the quantity at which the intentions of buyers and sellers match so that the quantity demanded equals quantity supplied.

    Graphically, the equilibrium price is indicated by the intersection of the supply curve and the demand curve in **Figure 3.6**. (The horizontal axis now measures both quantity demanded and quantity supplied.) With neither a shortage nor a surplus at $3, the market is *in equilibrium*, meaning "in balance" or "at rest."

---

change in supply
A change in the quantity supplied of a good or service at every price; a shift of the supply curve to the left or right.

change in quantity supplied
A movement from one point to another on a fixed supply curve.

equilibrium price
The price in a competitive market at which the quantity demanded and the quantity supplied are equal, there is neither a shortage nor a surplus, and there is no tendency for price to rise or fall.

equilibrium quantity
(1) The quantity demanded and supplied at the equilibrium price in a competitive market; (2) the profit-maximizing output of a firm.

FIGURE 3.6

Equilibrium price and quantity. The intersection of the downward sloping demand curve *D* and the upsloping supply curve *S* indicates the equilibrium price and quantity, here $3 and 7,000 lattes. The shortages of lattes at below-equilibrium prices (e.g., 7,000 at $2) drive up price. The higher prices increase the quantity supplied and reduce the quantity demanded until equilibrium is achieved. The surpluses caused by above-equilibrium prices (e.g., 6,000 lattes at $4) push price down. As price drops, the quantity demanded rises and the quantity supplied falls until equilibrium is established. At the equilibrium price and quantity, there are neither shortages nor surpluses of lattes.

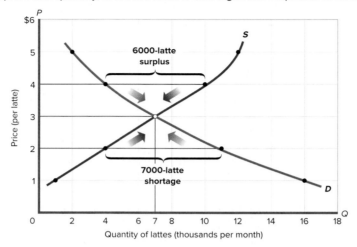

Market Supply of and Demand for Lattes			
(1)	**(2)**	**(3)**	**(4)**
Total Quantity Supplied per Month	**Price per Latte**	**Total Quantity Demanded per Month**	**Surplus (+) or Shortage (−)***
12,000	$5	2,000	+10,000 ↓
10,000	4	4,000	+6,000 ↓
7,000	**3**	**7,000**	**0**
4,000	2	11,000	−7,000 ↑
1,000	1	16,000	−15,000 ↑

*Arrows indicate the effect on price.

surplus
The amount by which the quantity supplied of a product exceeds the quantity demanded at a specific (above-equilibrium) price.

shortage
The amount by which the quantity demanded of a product exceeds the quantity supplied at a particular (below-equilibrium) price.

To better understand the uniqueness of the equilibrium price, let's consider other prices. At any above-equilibrium price, quantity supplied exceeds quantity demanded. For example, at the $4 price, sellers will offer 10,000 lattes, but buyers will purchase only 4,000. The $4 price encourages sellers to offer lots of lattes but discourages many consumers from buying them. The result is a **surplus** or *excess supply* of 6,000 lattes. If latte sellers made them all, they would find themselves with 6,000 unsold lattes.

Surpluses drive prices down. Even if the $4 price existed temporarily, it could not persist. The large surplus would prompt competing sellers to lower the price to encourage buyers to stop in and take the surplus off their hands. As the price fell, the incentive to produce lattes would decline and the incentive for consumers to buy lattes would increase. As shown in **Figure 3.6**, the market would move to its equilibrium at $3.

At any price below the $3 equilibrium price, quantity demanded would exceed quantity supplied. Consider a $2 price, for example. We see in column 4 of the table in **Figure 3.6** that quantity demanded exceeds quantity supplied at that price. The result is a **shortage** or *excess demand* of 7,000 lattes. The $2 price discourages sellers from devoting resources to lattes and encourages consumers to desire more lattes than are available. The $2 price cannot persist as the equilibrium price. Many consumers who want to buy lattes at this price will not obtain them. They will express a willingness to pay more than $2 to get them. Competition among these buyers will drive up the price, eventually to the $3 equilibrium level. Unless disrupted by supply or demand changes, this $3 price of lattes will continue.

Rationing Function of Prices

The *rationing function of prices* refers to the ability of the forces of supply and demand to establish a price at which selling and buying decisions are consistent. In our example, the equilibrium price of $3 clears the market, leaving no burdensome surplus for sellers and no inconvenient shortage for potential buyers. And it is the combination of freely made individual decisions that sets this market-clearing price. In effect, the market outcome says that all buyers who are willing and able to pay $3 for a latte will obtain one; all buyers who cannot or will not pay $3 will go without one. Similarly, all producers who are willing and able to offer a latte for sale at $3 will sell it; all producers who cannot or will not sell for $3 will not sell their product.

APPLYING THE ANALYSIS

Emergent Equilibria

Market equilibrium is a surprising phenomenon. Buyers' demand curves show a *negative* relationship between price and quantity, while sellers' supply curves show a *positive* relationship. Given that contradiction, you would never expect the interaction of demand and supply to lead to the perfectly synchronized outcome of quantity supplied exactly equaling quantity demanded.

Lee Prince/Shutterstock

But that is precisely what happens billions of times per day in markets all over the world. Market equilibrium and market rationing emerge spontaneously from the interactions of buyers and sellers who are simply pursuing their own interests and who are not in any way attempting to coordinate.

Adam Smith tried to explain this miraculous result as the work of an "invisible hand" that guided people's interactions toward a coordinated, socially beneficial outcome.

Nowadays, some economists classify market equilibrium as an "emergent property," or a behavior demonstrated by an entire system that is not found in any of its constituent parts. In the same way that a human brain as a whole is capable of consciousness but its individual neurons are not, so too markets synchronize the actions of individual buyers and sellers without any of them intending to harmonize their activities. Market equilibrium emerges, magically, from a stew of uncoordinated individual actions.

Changes in Demand, Supply, and Equilibrium

We know that prices can and do change in markets. For example, demand might change because of fluctuations in consumer tastes or incomes, changes in expected price, or variations in the prices of related goods. Supply might change in response to changes in resource prices, technology, or taxes. How will such changes in demand and supply affect equilibrium price and quantity?

Changes in Demand

Suppose that the supply of some good (e.g., health care) is constant and demand increases, as shown in **Figure 3.7a**. As a result, the new intersection of the supply and demand curves is at higher values on both the price and the quantity axes. Clearly, an increase in demand raises both equilibrium price and equilibrium quantity. Conversely, a decrease in demand, such as that shown in **Figure 3.7b**, reduces both equilibrium price and equilibrium quantity.

Changes in Supply

What happens if the demand for some good (e.g., smartphones) is constant but supply increases, as in **Figure 3.7c**? The new intersection of supply and demand is located at a lower equilibrium price but at a higher equilibrium quantity. An increase in supply reduces equilibrium price but increases equilibrium quantity. In contrast, if supply decreases, as in **Figure 3.7d**, equilibrium price rises while equilibrium quantity declines.

Complex Cases

When both supply and demand change, the final effect is a combination of the individual effects.

Supply Increase; Demand Decrease What effect will a supply increase and a demand decrease for some good (e.g., apples) have on equilibrium price? Both changes decrease price, so the net result is a price drop greater than that resulting from either change alone.

What happens to equilibrium quantity? Here the effects of the changes in supply and demand are opposed: The increase in supply increases equilibrium quantity, but the decrease in demand reduces it. The direction of the change in equilibrium quantity depends on the relative sizes of the changes in supply and demand. If the increase in supply is larger than the decrease in demand, the equilibrium quantity will increase. But if the decrease in demand is greater than the increase in supply, the equilibrium quantity will decrease.

Supply Decrease; Demand Increase A decrease in supply and an increase in demand for some good (e.g., gasoline) both increase price. Their combined effect is an increase in equilibrium price greater than that caused by either change separately. But their effect on the equilibrium quantity is indeterminate, depending on the relative sizes of the changes in supply and demand. If the decrease in supply is larger than the increase in demand, the equilibrium quantity will decrease. In contrast, if the increase in demand is greater than the decrease in supply, the equilibrium quantity will increase.

FIGURE 3.7

Changes in demand and supply and the effects on price and quantity. The increase in demand from D_1 to D_2 in (a) increases both equilibrium price and equilibrium quantity. The decrease in demand from D_3 to D_4 in (b) decreases both equilibrium price and equilibrium quantity. The increase in supply from S_1 to S_2 in (c) decreases equilibrium price and increases equilibrium quantity. The decrease in supply from S_3 to S_4 in (d) increases equilibrium price and decreases equilibrium quantity. The boxes in the top right summarize the respective changes and outcomes. The upward arrows in the boxes signify increases in equilibrium price *(P)* and equilibrium quantity *(Q)*; the downward arrows signify decreases in these items.

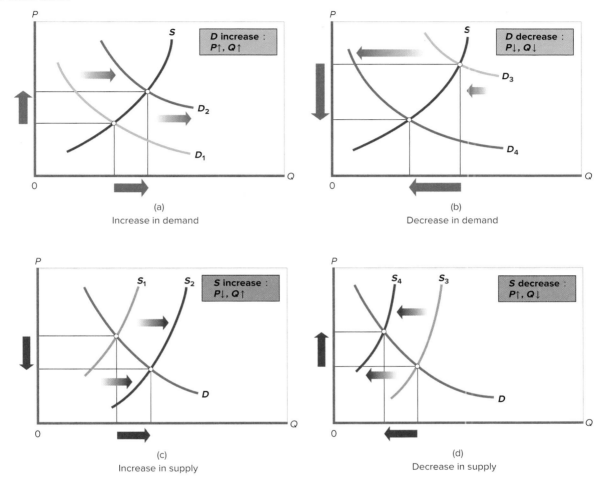

(a)
Increase in demand

(b)
Decrease in demand

(c)
Increase in supply

(d)
Decrease in supply

Supply Increase; Demand Increase   What if supply and demand both increase for some good (e.g., sushi)? A supply increase drops equilibrium price, while a demand increase boosts it. If the increase in supply is greater than the increase in demand, the equilibrium price will fall. If the opposite holds, the equilibrium price will rise.

The effect on equilibrium quantity is certain: The increases in supply and in demand both raise the equilibrium quantity. Therefore, the equilibrium quantity will increase by an amount greater than that caused by either change alone.

Supply Decrease; Demand Decrease   What about decreases in both supply and demand for some good (e.g., new homes)? If the decrease in supply is greater than the decrease in demand, the equilibrium price will rise. If the reverse is true, the equilibrium price will fall. If the two changes are of the same size and cancel out, the price will not change. Because the decreases in supply and demand both reduce equilibrium quantity, we can be sure that the equilibrium quantity will fall.

GLOBAL SNAPSHOT 3.1

Average Price of a Loaf of White Bread, Selected Nations, 2018

The market equilibrium price of a 500-gram (1.1-pound) loaf of white bread differs substantially across countries, reflecting local differences in supply and demand, as well as government interventions like subsidies and price ceilings. All prices are given in U.S. dollars, with currency exchange rates being used to convert foreign prices into U.S. dollar values.

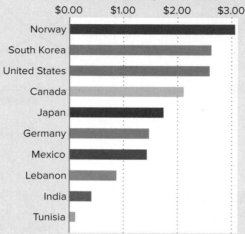

Average Price for a 500g Loaf of White Bread, 2018

Source: Numbeo, www.numbeo.com.

Government-Set Prices

price ceiling
A legally established maximum price for a good or service.

price floor
A legally established minimum price for a good or service.

Prices in most markets are free to rise or fall to their equilibrium levels, no matter how high or low those prices might be. However, government occasionally concludes that supply and demand will produce prices that are unfairly high to buyers or unfairly low to sellers. Government may then place legal limits on how high or low a price or prices may go. Our previous analysis of shortages and surpluses helps us evaluate the wisdom of government-set prices.

APPLYING THE ANALYSIS

Price Ceilings on Gasoline

A **price ceiling** sets the maximum legal price a seller may charge for a product or service. A price at or below the ceiling is legal; a price above it is not. The rationale for establishing price ceilings (or ceiling prices) on specific products is that they purportedly enable consumers to obtain some "essential" good or service that they could not afford at the equilibrium price.

Figure 3.8 shows the effects of price ceilings graphically. Suppose that rapidly rising world income boosts the purchase of automobiles and increases the demand for gasoline so that the equilibrium or market price reaches $5 per gallon. The rapidly rising price of gasoline greatly burdens low- and moderate-income households, who pressure the government to "do something." To keep gasoline prices down, the government imposes a ceiling price of $4 per gallon. To affect the market, a price ceiling must be below the equilibrium price. A ceiling price of $6, for example, would have no effect on the price of gasoline in the current situation.

FIGURE 3.8

A price ceiling. A price ceiling is a maximum legal price, such as $4, that is below the equilibrium price. It results in a persistent product shortage, here shown by the distance between Q_d and Q_s.

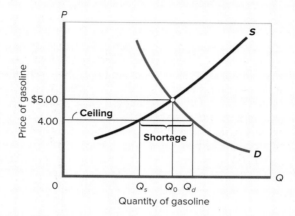

What are the effects of this $4 ceiling price? The rationing ability of the free market is rendered ineffective. Because the $4 ceiling price is below the $5 market-clearing price, there is a lasting shortage of gasoline. The quantity of gasoline demanded at $4 is Q_d, and the quantity supplied is only Q_s; a persistent excess demand or shortage of amount $Q_d - Q_s$ occurs.

The $4 price ceiling prevents the usual market adjustment in which competition among buyers bids up the price, inducing more production and rationing some buyers out of the market. That process would normally continue until the shortage disappeared at the equilibrium price and quantity: $5 and Q_0.

How will sellers apportion the available supply Q_s among buyers, who want the greater amount Q_d? Should they distribute gasoline on a first-come, first-served basis—that is, to those willing and able to get in line the soonest or stay in line the longest? Or should gas stations decide how to distribute? Because an unregulated shortage does not lead to an equitable distribution of gasoline, the government must establish some formal system for rationing it to consumers. One option is to issue ration coupons, which authorize bearers to purchase a fixed amount of gasoline per month. The rationing system might entail first the printing of coupons for Q_s gallons of gasoline, and then the equal distribution of the coupons among consumers so that the families of like sizes across different income levels receive the same number of coupons.

But ration coupons would not prevent a second problem from arising. The demand curve in **Figure 3.8** reveals that many buyers are willing to pay more than the $4 ceiling price. And, of course, it is more profitable for gasoline stations to sell at prices above the ceiling. Thus, despite the laws imposed by the price controls, *secondary markets* arise in which gasoline is illegally bought and sold at prices above the legal limits. Counterfeiting of ration coupons will also be a problem. And because the price of gasoline is now "set by government," the government may face political pressure to set the price even lower.

QUESTION:

Why is it typically difficult to end price ceilings once they have been in place for a long time?

APPLYING THE ANALYSIS

Rent Controls

About 200 cities in the United States, including New York City, Boston, and San Francisco, have at one time or another enacted rent controls—maximum rents established by law—or, more recently, maximum rent increases for existing tenants. Such laws are intended to protect low-income households from escalating rents by making housing more affordable.

What have been the actual economic effects? On the demand side, the below-equilibrium rents attract a larger number of renters. Some are locals seeking to move into their own places after sharing housing with friends or family. Others are outsiders attracted into the area by the artificially lower rents. But a large problem occurs on the supply side. Price controls make it less attractive for landlords to offer housing on the rental market. In the short run, owners may sell their rental units or convert them to condominiums. In the long run, low rents make it unprofitable for owners to repair or renovate their rental units. (Rent controls are one cause of the many abandoned apartment buildings found in some larger cities.) Also, insurance companies, pension funds, and other potential new investors in housing will find it more profitable to invest in office buildings, shopping malls, or motels, where rents are not controlled.

In brief, rent controls distort market signals, and thus resources are misallocated: Too few resources are allocated to rental housing, and too many to alternative uses. Ironically, although rent controls are often legislated to lessen the effects of perceived shortages, controls are in fact a primary cause of such shortages. For that reason, most American cities either have abandoned or are in the process of dismantling rent controls.

QUESTION:
Why does maintenance tend to diminish in rent-controlled apartment buildings relative to maintenance in buildings where owners can charge market-determined rents?

APPLYING THE ANALYSIS

Price Floors on Wheat

A **price floor** is a minimum price fixed by the government. A price at or above the price floor is legal; a price below it is not. Price floors above equilibrium prices are usually invoked when society feels that the market system has not provided a sufficient income for certain groups of resource suppliers or producers. Supported prices for agricultural products and current minimum wages are two examples of price (or wage) floors. Let's look at the former.

Suppose that many farmers have extremely low incomes when the price of wheat is at its equilibrium value of $2 per bushel. The government decides to help out by establishing a legal price floor (or "price support") of $3 per bushel.

What will be the effects? At any price above the equilibrium price, quantity supplied will exceed quantity demanded—that is, there will be a persistent excess supply or surplus of the product. Farmers will be willing to produce and offer for sale more wheat than private buyers are willing to buy. Like a price ceiling, a price floor disrupts the rationing ability of the free market.

Figure 3.9 illustrates the effect of a price floor graphically. Suppose that S and D are the supply and demand curves for wheat. Equilibrium price and quantity are $2 and Q_0, respectively. If the government imposes a price floor of $3, farmers will produce Q_s, but private buyers will purchase only Q_d. The surplus is the excess of Q_s over Q_d.

FIGURE 3.9

A price floor. A price floor is a minimum legal price, such as $3, that results in a persistent product surplus, here shown by the distance between Q_s and Q_d.

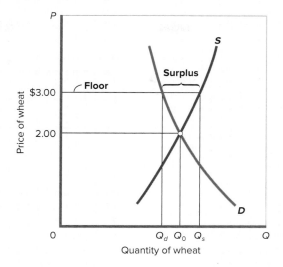

The government may cope with the surplus resulting from a price floor in two ways:

- It can restrict supply (e.g., by instituting acreage allotments by which farmers agree to take a certain amount of land out of production) or increase demand (e.g., by researching new uses for the product involved). These actions may reduce the difference between the equilibrium price and the price floor, and thus reduce the size of the surplus.

- If these efforts are not successful, then the government must purchase the surplus output at the $3 price (thereby subsidizing farmers) and store or otherwise dispose of it.

Price floors such as $3 in **Figure 3.9** not only disrupt the rationing ability of prices but also distort resource allocation. Without the price floor, the $2 equilibrium price of wheat would cause financial losses and force high-cost wheat producers to plant other crops or abandon farming altogether. But the $3 price floor allows them to continue to grow wheat and remain farmers. So society devotes too many scarce resources to wheat production and too few to producing other, more valuable, goods and services. It fails to achieve an optimal allocation of resources.

That's not all. Consumers of wheat-based products pay higher prices because of the price floor. Taxpayers pay higher taxes to finance the government's purchase of the surplus. And the price floor may cause environmental damage by encouraging wheat farmers to bring hilly, erosion-prone "marginal land" into production. The higher price also prompts imports of wheat.

QUESTION:

To maintain price floors on milk, the U.S. government has at times bought out and destroyed entire dairy herds from dairy farmers. What's the economic logic of these actions?

It is easy to see why economists "sound the alarm" when politicians advocate imposing price ceilings or price floors such as price controls, rent controls, interest-rate lids, or agricultural price supports. In all these cases, good intentions lead to bad economic outcomes. Government-controlled prices lead to shortages or surpluses, distort resource allocations, and produce negative side effects.

For additional examples of demand and supply, view the appendix at the end of this chapter. There, you will find examples relating to such diverse products as lettuce, salmon, gasoline, Uber rides, and Olympic tickets. Several of the examples depict simultaneous shifts in demand and supply curves—circumstances that often show up in exam questions!

Summary

LO3.1 Describe *demand* and explain how it can change.

Demand is a schedule or curve representing the buyers' willingness and ability to purchase a particular product at each of various prices in a specific period. The law of demand states that consumers will buy more of a product at a low price than at a high price. So, other things equal, the relationship between price and quantity demanded is negative or inverse; it graphs as a downward sloping curve.

Market demand curves are found by adding horizontally the demand curves of the many individual consumers in the market.

A *change in demand* occurs when there is a change in one or more of the determinants of demand (consumer tastes, the number of buyers in the market, the money incomes of consumers, the prices of related goods, and consumer expectations). A change in demand will shift the market demand curve either or left. A shift to the right is an increase in demand; a shift to the left is a decrease in demand.

A change in demand is different from a *change in the quantity demanded*, the latter being a movement from one point to another point on a fixed demand curve because of a change in the product's price.

LO3.2 Describe *supply* and explain how it can change.

Supply is a schedule or curve showing the amounts of a product that producers are willing to offer in the market at each possible price during a specific period. The law of supply states that, other things equal, producers will offer more of a product at a high price than at a low price. Thus, the relationship between price and quantity supplied is positive or direct; it graphs as an upward sloping curve.

The market supply curve is the horizontal summation of the supply curves of the individual producers of the product.

A *change in supply* occurs when there is a change in one or more of the determinants of supply (resource prices, production techniques, taxes or subsidies, the prices of other goods, producer expectations, or the number of suppliers in the market). A change in supply shifts a product's supply curve. A shift to the right is an increase in supply; a shift to the left is a decrease in supply.

In contrast, a change in the price of the product being considered causes a *change in the quantity supplied*, which is shown as a movement from one point to another point on a fixed supply curve.

LO3.3 Explain how supply and demand interact to determine market equilibrium.

The equilibrium price and quantity are established at the intersection of the supply and demand curves. The interaction of market demand and market supply adjusts the price to the point at which the quantities demanded and supplied are equal. This is the equilibrium price. The corresponding quantity is the equilibrium quantity.

LO3.4 Explain how changes in supply and demand affect equilibrium prices and quantities.

A change in either demand or supply changes the equilibrium price and quantity. Increases in demand raise both equilibrium price and equilibrium quantity; decreases in demand lower both equilibrium price and equilibrium quantity. Increases in supply lower equilibrium price and raise equilibrium quantity; decreases in supply raise equilibrium price and lower equilibrium quantity.

Simultaneous changes in demand and supply affect equilibrium price and quantity in various ways, depending on their direction and relative magnitudes.

LO3.5 Define government-set prices and explain how they can cause product surpluses and shortages.

A price ceiling is a maximum price set by government and is designed to help consumers. Effective price ceilings produce persistent product shortages, and if an equitable distribution of the product is sought, government must ration the product to consumers.

A price floor is a minimum price set by government and is designed to aid producers. Price floors lead to persistent product surpluses; the government must either purchase the product or eliminate the surplus by imposing restrictions on production or increasing private demand.

Legally fixed prices stifle the rationing function of prices and distort the allocation of resources.

Terms and Concepts

demand	inferior good	supply
law of demand	substitute good	law of supply
demand curve	complementary good	supply curve
determinants of demand	change in demand	determinants of supply
normal good	change in quantity demanded	change in supply

change in quantity supplied   surplus   price floor

equilibrium price   shortage

equilibrium quantity   price ceiling

Questions 🔲 connect

1. Explain the law of demand. Why does a demand curve slope downward? How is a market demand curve derived from individual demand curves? **(LO1)**

2. What are the determinants of demand? What happens to the demand curve when any of these determinants changes? Distinguish between a change in demand and a change in the quantity demanded, noting the cause(s) of each. **(LO1)**

3. What effect will each of the following have on the demand for small cars such as the Mini Cooper and Fiat 500? **(LO1)**

   a. Small cars become more fashionable.
   b. The price of large cars rises (with the price of small cars remaining the same).
   c. Income declines and small cars are an inferior good.
   d. Consumers anticipate that the price of small cars will decrease substantially in the near future.
   e. The price of gasoline substantially drops.

4. Explain the law of supply. Why does the supply curve slope upward? How is the market supply curve derived from the supply curves of individual producers? **(LO2)**

5. What are the determinants of supply? What happens to the supply curve when any of these determinants changes? Distinguish between a change in supply and a change in the quantity supplied, noting the cause(s) of each. **(LO2)**

6. What effect will each of the following have on the supply of auto tires? **(LO2)**

   a. A technological advance in the methods of producing tires.
   b. A decline in the number of firms in the tire industry.
   c. An increase in the price of rubber used in the production of tires.
   d. The expectation that the equilibrium price of auto tires will be lower in the future than currently.
   e. A decline in the price of the large tires used for semitrucks and earth-hauling rigs (with no change in the price of auto tires).
   f. The levying of a per-unit tax on each auto tire sold.
   g. The granting of a 50-cent-per-unit subsidy for each auto tire produced.

7. "In the latte market, demand often exceeds supply, and supply sometimes exceeds demand." "The price of a latte rises and falls in response to changes in supply and demand." In which of these two statements are the concepts of supply and demand used correctly? Explain. **(LO4)**

8. In 2001, an outbreak of hoof-and-mouth disease in Europe led to the burning of millions of cattle carcasses. What impact do you think this had on the supply of cattle hides, hide prices, the supply of leather goods, and the price of leather goods? **(LO4)**

9. Critically evaluate: "In comparing the two equilibrium positions in **Figure 3.7b**, I note that a smaller amount is actually demanded at a lower price. This observation refutes the law of demand." **(LO4)**

10. For each stock in the stock market, the number of shares sold daily equals the number of shares purchased. That is, the quantity of each firm's shares demanded equals the quantity supplied. Why, then, do the prices of stock shares change? **(LO4)**

11. Suppose the total demand for wheat and the total supply of wheat per month in the Kansas City grain market are as shown in the following table. Suppose that the government establishes a price ceiling of $3.70 for wheat. What might prompt the government to establish this price ceiling? Explain carefully the main effects. Demonstrate your answer graphically. Next, suppose that the government establishes a price floor of $4.60 for wheat. What will be the main effects of this price floor? Demonstrate your answer graphically. **(LO5)**

Thousands of Bushels Demanded	Price per Bushel	Thousands of Bushels Supplied
85	$3.40	72
80	3.70	73
75	4.00	75
70	4.30	77
65	4.60	79
60	4.90	81

12. What do economists mean when they say "Price floors and ceilings stifle the rationing function of prices and distort resource allocation"? **(LO5)**

Problems

1. Suppose there are three buyers of candy in a market: Tex, Dex, and Rex. The market demand and the individual demands of Tex, Dex, and Rex are shown in the following table. **(LO1)**

   a. Fill in the missing values.

   b. Which buyer demands the least at a price of $5? The most at a price of $7?

   c. Which buyer's quantity demanded increases the most when the price is lowered from $7 to $6?

   d. In which direction would the market demand curve shift if Tex withdrew from the market? What would happen if Dex doubled his purchases at each possible price?

   e. Suppose that at a price of $6, the total quantity demanded increases from 19 to 38. Is this a "change in the quantity demanded" or a "change in demand"? Explain.

Price per Candy	Individual Quantities Demanded			Total Quantity Demanded
	Tex	Dex	Rex	
$8	3 +	1 +	0 =	—
7	8 +	2 +	_ =	12
6	_ +	3 +	4 =	19
5	17 +	_ +	6 =	27
4	23 +	5 +	8 =	—

2. The figure below shows the supply curve for tennis balls, S_1, for Drop Volley Tennis, a producer of tennis equipment. Use the figure and the table below to give your answers to the following questions. **(LO2)**

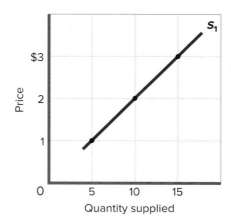

   a. Use the figure to fill in the quantity supplied on supply curve S_1 for each price in the table below.

	S_1	S_2	Change in
Price	Quantity Supplied	Quantity Supplied	Quantity Supplied
$3	_	4	_
2	_	2	_
1	_	0	_

   b. If production costs were to increase, the quantities supplied at each price would be as shown by the third column of the table ("S_2 Quantity Supplied"). Use those data to draw supply curve S_2 on the same graph as supply curve S_1.

   c. In the fourth column of the table, enter the amount by which the quantity supplied at each price changes due to the increase in product costs. (Use positive numbers for increases and negative numbers for decreases.)

   d. Did the increase in production costs cause a "decrease in supply" or a "decrease in quantity supplied"?

3. Refer to the expanded table below from question 11. **(LO3)**

   a. What is the equilibrium price? At what price is there neither a shortage nor a surplus? Fill in the surplus-shortage column and use it to confirm your answers.

   b. Graph the demand for wheat and the supply of wheat. Be sure to label the axes of your graph correctly. Label equilibrium price P and equilibrium quantity Q.

   c. How big is the surplus or shortage at $3.40? At $4.90? How big a surplus or shortage results if the price is 60 cents higher than the equilibrium price? 30 cents lower than the equilibrium price?

Thousands of Bushels Demanded	Price per Bushel	Thousands of Bushels Supplied	Surplus (+) or Shortage (-)
85	$3.40	72	_
80	3.70	73	_
75	4.00	75	_
70	4.30	77	_
65	4.60	79	_
60	4.90	81	_

4. How will each of the following changes in demand and/or supply affect equilibrium price and equilibrium quantity in a competitive market? That is, do price and quantity rise, fall, or remain unchanged, or are the answers indeterminate because they depend on the magnitudes of the shifts? Use supply and demand to verify your answers. **(LO4)**

a. Supply decreases and demand is constant.
b. Demand decreases and supply is constant.
c. Supply increases and demand is constant.
d. Demand increases and supply increases.
e. Demand increases and supply is constant.
f. Supply increases and demand decreases.
g. Demand increases and supply decreases.
h. Demand decreases and supply decreases.

5. Use two market diagrams to explain how an increase in state subsidies to public colleges might affect tuition and enrollments in both public and private colleges. **(LO4)**

6. **ADVANCED ANALYSIS** Assume that demand for a commodity is represented by the equation $P = 10 - .2Q_d$ and supply by the equation $P = 2 + .2Qs$, where Q_d and Q_s are quantity demanded and quantity supplied, respectively, and P is price. Using the equilibrium condition $Q_s = Q_d$, solve the equations to determine equilibrium price and equilibrium quantity. **(LO4)**

7. Suppose that the demand and supply schedules for rental apartments in the city of Gotham are as given in the following table. **(LO5)**

Monthly Rent	Apartments Demanded	Apartments Supplied
$2,500	10,000	15,000
2,000	12,500	12,500
1,500	15,000	10,000
1,000	17,500	7,500
500	20,000	5,000

a. What is the market equilibrium rental price per month and the market equilibrium number of apartments demanded and supplied?

b. If the local government can enforce a rent-control law that sets the maximum monthly rent at $1,500, will there be a surplus or a shortage? Of how many units? And how many units will actually be rented each month?

c. Suppose that a new government is elected that wants to keep out the poor. It declares that the minimum rent that can be charged is $2,500 per month. If the government can enforce that price floor, will there be a surplus or a shortage? Of how many units? And how many units will actually be rented each month?

d. Suppose that the government wishes to decrease the market equilibrium monthly rent by increasing the supply of housing. Assuming that demand remains unchanged, how many additional units of housing would the government need to supply to get the market equilibrium rental price to fall to $1,500 per month? To $1,000 per month? To $500 per month?

CHAPTER THREE APPENDIX
Additional Examples of Supply and Demand

Supply and demand analysis is a powerful tool for understanding equilibrium prices and quantities. The information provided in this chapter is fully sufficient for moving forward in the book, but you may find that additional examples of supply and demand are helpful. This appendix provides several concrete illustrations of changes in supply and demand.

Changes in Supply and Demand

As **Figure 3.7** demonstrates, changes in supply and demand cause changes in price, quantity, or both. The following applications illustrate this fact in several real-world markets. The simplest situations are those in which either supply changes while demand remains constant or demand changes while supply remains constant. Let's consider a simple case first, before looking at more complex applications.

Lettuce   Every now and then we hear on the news that extreme weather has severely reduced the size of some crop. Suppose, for example, that a severe freeze destroys a sizable portion of the lettuce crop. This unfortunate situation implies a significant decline in supply, which we represent as a leftward shift of the supply curve from S_1 to S_2 in **Figure 1**. At each price, consumers desire as much lettuce as before, so the freeze does not affect the demand for lettuce. That is, demand curve D_1 does not shift.

What are the consequences of the reduced supply of lettuce for equilibrium price and quantity? As shown in **Figure 1**, the leftward shift of the supply curve disrupts the previous equilibrium in the market for lettuce and drives the equilibrium price upward from P_1 to P_2. Consumers respond to that price hike by reducing the quantity of lettuce demanded from Q_1 to Q_2. Equilibrium is restored at P_2 and Q_2.

FIGURE 1
The market for lettuce. The decrease in the supply of lettuce, shown here by the shift from S_1 to S_2, increases the equilibrium price of lettuce from P_1 to P_2 and reduces the equilibrium quantity from Q_1 to Q_2.

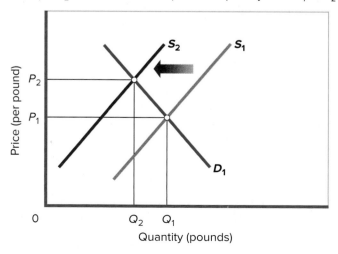

Consumers who are willing and able to pay price P_2 obtain lettuce; consumers unwilling or unable to pay that price do not. Some consumers continue to buy as much lettuce as before, even at the higher price. Others buy some lettuce but not as much as before, and still others opt out of the market completely. The latter two groups use the money they would have spent on lettuce to obtain other products: say, carrots. (Because of our other-things-equal assumption, the prices of other products have not changed.)

Pink Salmon Now let's see what happens when both supply and demand change at the same time. Several decades ago, people who caught salmon earned as much as $1 for each pound of pink salmon—the type of salmon most commonly used for canning. In **Figure 2**, that price is represented as P_1, at the intersection of supply curve S_1 and demand curve D_1. The corresponding quantity of pink salmon is shown as Q_1 pounds.

As time passed, supply and demand changed in the market for pink salmon. On the supply side, improved technology in the form of larger, more efficient fishing boats greatly increased the catch and lowered the cost of obtaining it. Also, high profits at price P_1 encouraged many new fishers to enter the industry. As a result of these changes, the supply of pink salmon greatly increased and the supply curve shifted to the right, as from S_1 to S_2 in **Figure 2**.

Over the same years, the demand for pink salmon declined, as represented by the leftward shift from D_1 to D_2 in **Figure 2**. That decrease was caused by increases in consumer income and reductions of the price of substitute products. As buyers' incomes rose, consumers shifted demand away from canned fish and toward higher-quality fresh or frozen fish, including more-valued chinook, sockeye, and coho salmon. Moreover, the emergence of fish farming, in which salmon are raised in ocean net pens, lowered the prices of these substitute species. That, too, reduced the demand for pink salmon.

The altered supply and demand reduced the price of pink salmon to as low as $.10 per pound, as represented by the drop in price from P_1 to P_2 in **Figure 2**. Both the supply increase and the demand decrease helped reduce the equilibrium price. However, in this particular case, the equilibrium quantity of pink salmon increased, as represented by the move from Q_1 to Q_2. Both shifts reduced the equilibrium price, but equilibrium quantity increased because the increase in supply exceeded the decrease in demand.

FIGURE 2
The market for pink salmon. In the last several decades, the supply of pink salmon has increased and the demand for pink salmon has decreased. As a result, the price of pink salmon has declined, as from P_1 to P_2. Because supply has increased more than demand has decreased, the equilibrium quantity of pink salmon has increased, as from Q_1 to Q_2.

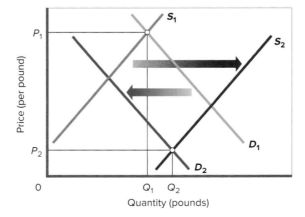

FIGURE 3

The market for gasoline. An increase in the demand for gasoline, as shown by the shift from D_1 to D_2, coupled with a decrease in supply, as shown by the shift from S_1 to S_2, boosts equilibrium price (here from P_1 to P_2). In this case, equilibrium quantity increases from Q_1 to Q_2 because the increase in demand outweighs the decrease in supply.

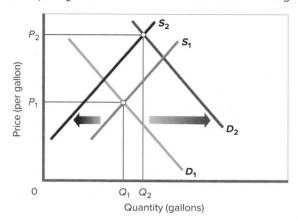

Gasoline   The price of gasoline in the United States has increased rapidly several times during the past several years. For example, the average price of a gallon of gasoline rose from around $1.87 in February 2016 to about $2.99 in May 2018. What caused this 60 percent rise in the price of gasoline? How would we graph this increase?

We begin in **Figure 3** with the price of a gallon of gasoline at P_1, representing the $1.87 price. Simultaneous supply and demand factors disturbed this equilibrium. Supply uncertainties relating to Middle East politics and warfare, and expanded demand for oil by fast-growing countries such as China, pushed up the price of a barrel of oil from $30 per barrel in February 2016 to a bit over $70 per barrel in May 2018. Oil is the main input for producing gasoline, so any sustained rise in its price boosts the per-unit cost of producing gasoline. Such increases in cost decrease the supply of gasoline, as represented by the leftward shift of the supply curve from S_1 to S_2 in **Figure 3**. At times, refinery breakdowns in the United States have also contributed to this reduced supply.

While the supply of gasoline declined between February 2016 and May 2018, the demand for gasoline increased, as depicted by the rightward shift of the demand curve from D_1 to D_2. Incomes in general were rising over this period because the U.S. economy was expanding. Rising incomes raise demand for all normal goods, including gasoline. An increased number of low-gas-mileage SUVs and light trucks on the road also contributed to growing gas demand.

The combined decline in gasoline supply and increase in gasoline demand boosted the price of gasoline from $1.87 to $2.99, as represented by the rise from P_1 to P_2 in **Figure 3**. Because the demand increase outweighed the supply decrease, the equilibrium quantity expanded, here from Q_1 to Q_2.

In other periods, the price of gasoline has *declined* as the demand for gasoline has increased. Test your understanding of the analysis by explaining how such a price decrease could occur.

APPLYING THE ANALYSIS

Uber and Dynamic Pricing

The ride-sharing service known as Uber rose to prominence in 2013 by offering consumers an alternative to government-regulated taxi companies. Uber works via the Internet, matching people who need a ride with people willing to use their own vehicles to provide rides. Both parties can find each other easily and instantly via a mobile phone app and Uber makes its money by taking a percentage of the fare.

Uber is innovative in many ways, including empowering anybody to become a paid driver, breaking up local taxi monopolies, and making it effortless to arrange a quick pickup. But Uber's most interesting feature is dynamic pricing, under which Uber sets equilibrium prices in real time, constantly adjusting fares so as to equalize quantity demanded and quantity supplied. The result is extremely short waiting times for both riders and drivers as Uber will, for instance, set a substantially higher "surge price" in a given location if demand suddenly increases due to, say, a bunch of people leaving a concert all at once and wanting rides. The higher fare encourages more Uber drivers to converge on the area, thereby minimizing wait times for both drivers and passengers.

The short wait times created by Uber's use of dynamic pricing stand in sharp contrast to taxi fares, which are fixed by law and therefore unable to adjust to ongoing changes in supply and demand. On days when demand is low relative to supply, drivers sit idle for long stretches of time. All of that inefficiency and inconvenience is eliminated by Uber's use of market equilibrium prices to equalize the demand and supply of rides.

> QUESTIONS:
>
> How would you expect the introduction of Uber to affect the market for traditional taxi services? Does your answer depend on whether taxi fares (prices) are fixed by law or can move based on changes in demand and supply?

Preset Prices

In this chapter, we saw that an effective government-imposed price ceiling (legal maximum price) causes quantity demanded to exceed quantity supplied—a shortage. An effective government-imposed price floor (legal minimum price) causes quantity supplied to exceed quantity demanded—a surplus.

We now want to establish that shortages and surpluses can occur in markets other than those in which government imposes price floors and ceilings. Such market imbalances happen when sellers set prices in advance of sales, and the prices selected turn out to be below or above equilibrium prices. Consider the following two examples.

Olympic Figure Skating Finals Tickets for the women's figure skating championship at the Olympics are among the world's "hottest tickets." The popularity of this event and the high incomes of buyers translate into tremendous ticket demand. The Olympic officials set the price for the tickets in advance. Invariably, the price, although high, is considerably below the equilibrium price that would equate quantity demanded and quantity supplied. A severe shortage of tickets therefore occurs in this *primary market*—the market involving the official ticket office.

The shortage, in turn, creates a *secondary market* in which buyers bid for tickets held by initial purchasers rather than the original seller. Scalping tickets—selling them above the original ticket price—may be legal or illegal, depending on local laws.

FIGURE 4

The market for tickets to the Olympic women's figure skating finals. The demand curve D and supply curve S for the Olympic women's figure skating finals produce an equilibrium price that is above the P_1 price printed on the ticket. At price P_1, the quantity of tickets demanded, Q_2, greatly exceeds the quantity of tickets available (Q_1). The resulting shortage of ab (= $Q_2 - Q_1$) gives rise to a legal or illegal secondary market.

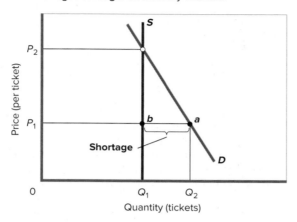

Figure 4 shows how the shortage in the primary ticket market looks in terms of supply and demand analysis. Demand curve D represents the strong demand for tickets, while supply curve S represents the supply of tickets. The supply curve is vertical because a fixed number of tickets are printed to match the capacity of the arena. At the printed ticket price of P_1, the quantity of tickets demanded, Q_2, exceeds the quantity supplied, Q_1. The result is a shortage of ab—the horizontal distance between Q_2 and Q_1 in the primary market.

Olympic Curling Preliminaries Contrast the shortage of tickets for the women's figure skating finals at the Olympics to the surplus of tickets for one of the preliminary curling matches. For the uninitiated, curling is a sport in which participants slide a heavy round object called a "stone" down a lane painted on an ice rink toward a target while teammates called "sweepers" use brooms to alter the course of the stone.

Curling is a popular spectator sport in a few nations, including Canada, but it does not draw many fans in most countries. So the demand for tickets to most of the preliminary curling events is not very strong. We demonstrate this weak demand as D in **Figure 5**. As in our previous example, the supply of tickets is fixed by the size of the arena and is shown as vertical line S.

We represent the printed ticket price as P_1 in **Figure 5**. In this case, the printed price is much higher than the equilibrium price of P_2. At the printed ticket price, quantity supplied is Q_1 and quantity demanded is Q_2. So a surplus of tickets of ba (= $Q_1 - Q_2$) occurs. No ticket scalping results and there are numerous empty seats. Only if the Olympic officials had priced the tickets at the lower price P_2 would the event have been a sellout. (Actually, the Olympic officials try to adjust to demand realities for curling contests by holding them in smaller arenas and by charging less for tickets. Nevertheless, the stands are rarely full for the preliminary contests, which compete against final events in other winter Olympic sports.)

FIGURE 5

The market for tickets to the Olympic curling preliminaries. The demand curve D and supply curve S for the Olympic curling preliminaries produce an equilibrium price below the P_1 price printed on the ticket. At price P_1, the quantity of tickets demanded is less than the quantity of tickets available. The resulting surplus of ba (= $Q_1 - Q_2$) means the event is not sold out.

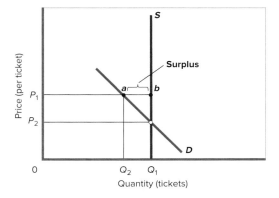

Appendix Summary

LO3.6 Use supply and demand analysis to analyze actual economic situations.

A decrease in the supply of a product increases its equilibrium price and reduces its equilibrium quantity. In contrast, an increase in the demand for a product boosts both its equilibrium price and its equilibrium quantity.

Simultaneous changes in supply and demand affect equilibrium price and quantity in various ways, depending on the relative magnitudes of the changes in supply and demand. Equal increases in supply and demand, for example, leave the equilibrium price unchanged.

Sellers set prices of some items, such as tickets, in advance of the event. These items are sold in the primary market that involves the original seller and buyers. If preset prices turn out to be below the equilibrium prices, shortages occur and scalping in legal or illegal secondary markets arises. The prices in the secondary market then rise above the preset prices. In contrast, surpluses occur when the preset prices happen to exceed the equilibrium prices.

Appendix Questions

1. Why are shortages or surpluses more likely with preset prices (such as those on tickets) than flexible prices (such as those on gasoline)? **(LO6)**

2. Most scalping laws make it illegal to sell—but not to buy—tickets at prices above those printed on the tickets. Assuming that is the case, use supply and demand analysis to explain why the equilibrium ticket price in an illegal secondary market tends to be higher than in a legal secondary market. **(LO6)**

3. Go to the website of the U.S. Energy Information Administration, www.eia.doe.gov, and follow the links to find the current retail price of gasoline. How does the current price of regular gasoline compare with the price a year ago? What must have happened to either supply, demand, or both to explain the observed price change? **(LO6)**

4. Suppose the supply of apples sharply increases because of perfect weather conditions throughout the growing season. Assuming no change in demand, explain the effect on the equilibrium price and quantity of apples. Explain why quantity demanded increases even though demand does not change. **(LO6)**

5. Assume the demand for lumber suddenly rises because of rapid growth in demand for new housing. Assume no change in supply. Why does the equilibrium price of lumber rise? What would happen if the price did not rise under the demand and supply circumstances described? **(LO6)**

6. Suppose both the demand for olives and the supply of olives decline by equal amounts over some time period. Use graphical analysis to show the effect on equilibrium price and quantity. **(LO6)**

7. Assume that both the supply of bottled water and the demand for bottled water rise during the summer but that supply increases more rapidly than demand. What can you conclude about the directions of the impacts on equilibrium price and equilibrium quantity? **(LO6)**

Appendix Problems

1. Demand and supply often shift in the retail market for gasoline. The following are two demand schedules and two supply schedules for gallons of gasoline in the month of May in a small town in Maine. Some of the data are missing. **(LO6)**

Price	Quantities Demanded		Quantities Supplied	
	D_1	D_2	S_1	S_2
$4.00	5,000	7,500	9,000	9,500
___	6,000	8,000	8,000	9,000
2.00	___	8,500	___	8,500
___	___	9,000	5,000	___

a. Use the following facts to fill in the missing data in the table. If demand is D_1 and supply is S_1, the equilibrium quantity is 7,000 gallons per month. When demand is D_2 and supply is S_1, the equilibrium price is $3.00 per gallon. When demand is D_2 and supply is S_1, there is an excess demand of 4,000 gallons per month at a price of $1.00 per gallon. If demand is D_1 and supply is S_2, the equilibrium quantity is 8,000 gallons per month.

b. Compare two equilibriums. In the first, demand is D_1 and supply is S_1. In the second, demand is D_1 and supply is S_2. By how much does the equilibrium quantity change? By how much does the equilibrium price change?

c. If supply falls from S_2 to S_1 while demand declines from D_2 to D_1, does the equilibrium price rise, fall, or stay the same? What if only supply falls? What if only demand falls?

d. Suppose that supply is fixed at S_1 and that demand starts at D_1. By how many gallons per month would demand have to increase at each price level such that the equilibrium price per gallon would be $3.00? $4.00?

2. The following table shows two demand schedules for a given style of men's shoe—that is, how many pairs per month will be demanded at various prices at Stromnord, a men's clothing store.

Price	D_1 Quantity Demanded	D_2 Quantity Demanded
$75	53	13
70	60	15
65	68	18
60	77	22
55	87	27

Suppose that Stromnord has exactly 65 pairs of this style of shoe in inventory at the start of the month of July and will not receive any more pairs of this style until at least August 1. **(LO6)**

a. If demand is D_1, what is the lowest price that Stromnord can charge so that it will not run out of this model of shoe in the month of July? What if demand is D_2?

b. If the price of shoes is set at $75 for both July and August, and demand will be D_2 in July and D_1 in August, how many pairs of shoes should Stromnord order if it wants to end the month of August with exactly zero pairs of shoes in its inventory? What if the price is set at $55 for both months?

3. Use the table below to answer the questions that follow: **(LO6)**

a. If this table reflects the supply of and demand for tickets to a particular World Cup soccer game, what is the stadium capacity?

b. If the preset ticket price is $45, would we expect to see a secondary market for tickets? Would the price of a ticket in the secondary market be higher than, the same as, or lower than the price in the primary (original) market?

c. Suppose for some other World Cup game the quantity of tickets demanded is 20,000 lower at each ticket price than shown in the table. If the ticket price remains $45, would the event be a sellout?

Quantity Demanded, Thousands	Price	Quantity Supplied, Thousands
80	$25	60
75	35	60
70	45	60
65	55	60
60	65	60
55	75	60
50	85	60

CHAPTER FOUR
Elasticity of Demand and Supply

Learning Objectives

LO4.1 Explain and calculate price elasticity of demand.
LO4.2 Explain the usefulness of the total-revenue test.
LO4.3 Explain and calculate price elasticity of supply.
LO4.4 Apply price elasticity of demand and supply to real-world situations.
LO4.5 Explain and apply income elasticity of demand and cross-elasticity of demand.

Why do buyers of some products respond to price increases by substantially reducing their purchases while buyers of other products respond by only slightly cutting back their purchases? Why do price hikes for some goods cause producers to greatly increase their output, while price hikes on other products barely cause any output increase? Why does the demand for some products rise a great deal when household incomes increase while the demand for other products rises just a little? How can we tell whether a given pair of goods are complements, substitutes, or unrelated to each other?

Elasticity extends our understanding of markets by letting us know the degree to which changes in prices and incomes affect supply and demand. Sometimes the responses are substantial, while other times they are minimal or even nonexistent. By knowing what to expect, businesses and the government can do a much better job in deciding what to produce, how much to charge, and, surprisingly, what items to tax.

Price Elasticity of Demand

According to the law of demand, other things equal, consumers will buy more of a product when its price declines and less its price increases. But how much more or less will they buy? The amount varies from product to product and over different price ranges for the same product. It also may vary over time. For example, a firm contemplating a price hike will want to know how consumers will respond. If they remain highly loyal and continue to buy, the firm's revenue will rise. But if consumers defect en masse to other sellers or other products, the firm's revenue will tumble.

price elasticity of demand
The ratio of the percentage change in quantity demanded of a product or resource to the percentage change in its price; a measure of the responsiveness of buyers to a change in the price of a product or resource.

Consumers' responsiveness to a price change is measured by a product's **price elasticity of demand.** For some products (e.g., restaurant meals), consumers are highly responsive to price changes. Modest price changes cause very large changes in the quantity purchased. Economists say that the demand for such products is *relatively elastic* or simply *elastic.*

For other products (e.g., medical care), consumers pay much less attention to price changes. Substantial price changes cause only small changes in the amount purchased. The demand for such products is *relatively inelastic* or simply *inelastic.*

The Price-Elasticity Coefficient and Formula

Economists measure the degree of price elasticity or inelasticity of demand with the coefficient E_d, defined as

$$E_d = \frac{\text{percentage change in quantity demanded of X}}{\text{percentage change in price of X}}$$

The percentage changes in the equation are calculated by dividing the *change* in quantity demanded by the original quantity demanded and by dividing the *change* in price by the original price. So we can restate the formula as

$$E_d = \frac{\text{change in quantity demanded of X}}{\text{original quantity demanded of X}} \div \frac{\text{change in price of X}}{\text{original price of X}}$$

Using Averages   An annoying problem arises in computing the price-elasticity coefficient. A price change from, say, $4 to $5 along a demand curve is a 25 percent (= $1/$4) increase, but the opposite price change from $5 to $4 along the same curve is a 20 percent (= $1/$5) decrease. Which percentage change in price should we use in the denominator to compute the price-elasticity coefficient? And when quantity changes, for example, from 10 to 20, it is a 100 percent (= 10/10) increase. But when quantity falls from 20 to 10 along the identical demand curve, it is a 50 percent (= 10/20) decrease. Should we use 100 percent or 50 percent in the numerator of the elasticity formula? Elasticity should be the same whether price rises or falls!

The simplest solution to the problem is to use the averages of the two prices and the two quantities as the reference points for computing the percentages. That is

$$E_d = \frac{\text{change in quantity}}{\text{sum of quantities}/2} \div \frac{\text{change in price}}{\text{sum of prices}/2}$$

For the same $5-$4 price range, the price reference is $4.50 [= ($5 + $4)/2], and for the same 10-20 quantity range, the quantity reference is 15 units [= (10 + 20)/2]. The percentage change in price is now $1/$4.50, or about 22 percent, and the percentage change in quantity is 10/15, or about 67 percent. So E_d is about 3. This solution eliminates the "up versus down" problem. All the elasticity coefficients that follow are calculated using averages, also known as the *midpoints approach.*

Elimination of Minus Sign Because demand curves slope downward, the price-elasticity coefficient of demand E_d will always be a negative number. For example, if price declines, quantity demanded will increase. This means that the numerator in our formula will be positive and the denominator negative, yielding a negative E_d. For an increase in price, the numerator will be negative but the denominator positive, again yielding a negative E_d.

Economists usually ignore the minus sign and simply present the absolute value of the elasticity coefficient to avoid an ambiguity that might otherwise arise. It can be confusing to say that an E_d of –4 is greater than one of –2. This possible confusion is avoided when we say an E_d of 4 reveals greater elasticity than an E_d of 2. In what follows, we ignore the minus sign in the coefficient of price elasticity of demand and show only the absolute value.

Interpretations of E_d

We can interpret the coefficient of price elasticity of demand as follows.

Elastic Demand Demand is **elastic** if a specific percentage change in price results in a larger percentage change in quantity demanded. In such cases, E_d will be greater than 1. Example: Suppose that a 2 percent decline in the price of cut flowers results in a 4 percent increase in quantity demanded. Then, demand for cut flowers is elastic and

$$E_d = \frac{.04}{.02} = 2$$

Inelastic Demand If a specific percentage change in price produces a smaller percentage change in quantity demanded, demand is **inelastic.** In such cases, E_d will be less than 1. Example: Suppose that a 2 percent decline in the price of tea leads to only a 1 percent increase in quantity demanded. Then, demand is inelastic and

$$E_d = \frac{.01}{.02} = .5$$

Unit Elasticity In some cases, a percentage change in price and the resulting percentage change in quantity demanded are the same. Example: Suppose that a 2 percent drop in the price of chocolate causes a 2 percent increase in quantity demanded. This case is termed **unit elasticity** because E_d is exactly 1, or unity. In this example,

$$E_d = \frac{.02}{.02} = .1$$

Extreme Cases When we say demand is "inelastic," we do not mean that consumers are completely unresponsive to a price change. In that extreme situation, where a price change results in no change whatsoever in the quantity demanded, we say that demand is **perfectly inelastic.** The price-elasticity coefficient is zero because there is no response to a change in price. Approximate examples include an acute diabetic's demand for insulin or a truck driver's demand for gasoline. A line parallel to the vertical axis, such as D_1 in **Figure 4.1a**, shows perfectly inelastic demand graphically.

elastic demand
Product or resource demand whose price elasticity is greater than 1. This means the resulting change in quantity demanded is greater than the percentage change in price.

inelastic demand
Product or resource demand for which the price elasticity of demand is less than 1. This means the resulting percentage change in quantity demanded is less than the percentage change in price.

unit elasticity
Demand or supply for which the elasticity coefficient is equal to 1; means that the percentage change in the quantity demanded or supplied is equal to the percentage change in price.

perfectly inelastic demand
Product or resource demand in which price can be of any amount at a particular quantity of the product or resource demanded; quantity demanded does not respond to a change in price; graphs as a vertical demand curve.

FIGURE 4.1

Perfectly inelastic and elastic demands. Demand curve D_1 in (a) represents perfectly inelastic demand ($E_d = 0$). A price increase will result in no change in quantity demanded. Demand curve D_2 in (b) represents perfectly elastic demand. A price increase will cause quantity demanded to decline from an infinite amount to zero ($E_d = \infty$).

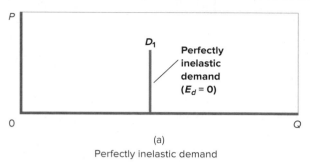

(a)

Perfectly inelastic demand

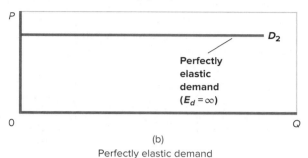

(b)

Perfectly elastic demand

perfectly elastic demand
Product or resource demand in which quantity demanded can be of any amount at a particular product price; graphs as a horizontal demand curve.

Conversely, when we say demand is "elastic," we do not mean that consumers are completely responsive to a price change. In that extreme situation, where a small price reduction causes buyers to increase their purchases from zero to all they can obtain, the elasticity coefficient is infinite ($= \infty$) and we say demand is **perfectly elastic.** A line parallel to the horizontal axis, such as D_2 in **Figure 4.1b**, shows perfectly elastic demand. You will see in **Chapter 7** that perfectly elastic demand applies to firms that sell output in a perfectly competitive market.

PHOTO OP

Elastic versus Inelastic Demand

The demand for expensive leisure activities such as cruise vacations is elastic; the demand for surgery or other nonelective medical care is inelastic.

Ilene MacDonald/Alamy

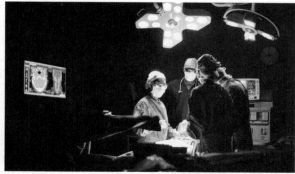

shapecharge/E+/Getty Images

ILLUSTRATING THE IDEA

A Bit of a Stretch

The following analogy might help you remember the distinction between "elastic" and "inelastic." Imagine two objects: (1) an Ace elastic bandage used to wrap injured joints and (2) a relatively firm rubber tie-down used for securing items for transport. The Ace bandage stretches a great deal when pulled with a particular force; the rubber tie-down stretches some, but not a lot.

Similar differences occur for the quantity demanded of various products when their prices change. For some products, a price change causes a substantial "stretch" of quantity demanded. When this stretch in percentage terms exceeds the percentage change in price, demand is elastic. For other products, quantity demanded stretches very little in response to the price change. When this stretch in percentage terms is less than the percentage change in price, demand is inelastic.

In summary:

- Elastic demand displays considerable "quantity stretch" (as with the Ace bandage).
- Inelastic demand displays relatively little "quantity stretch" (as with the rubber tie-down).

And through extension:

- Perfectly elastic demand has infinite quantity stretch.
- Perfectly inelastic demand has zero quantity stretch.

> QUESTION:
> Which do you think has the most quantity stretch, given an equal percentage increase in price—toothpaste or townhouses?

The Total-Revenue Test

Firms want to know the effect of price changes on total revenue and thus on profits (total revenue minus total costs).

Total revenue (TR) is the total amount the seller receives from the sale of a product in a particular time period; it is calculated by multiplying the product price (P) by the quantity demanded and sold (Q). In equation form:

$$TR = P \times Q$$

Graphically, total revenue is represented by the $P \times Q$ rectangle lying below a point on a demand curve. At point a in **Figure 4.2a**, for example, price is $2 and quantity demanded is 10 units. So total revenue is $20 (= $2 × 10), shown by the rectangle composed of the yellow and green areas under the demand curve. We find the area of a rectangle by multiplying one side by the other. Here, one side is "price" ($2) and the other is "quantity demanded" (10 units).

total revenue (TR)
The total number of dollars received by a firm (or firms) from the sale of a product; equal to the total expenditures for the product produced by the firm (or firms); equal to the quantity sold (demanded) multiplied by the price at which it is sold.

FIGURE 4.2

The total-revenue test for price elasticity. (a) Price declines from $2 to $1, and total revenue increases from $20 to $40. So demand is elastic. The gain in revenue (blue area) exceeds the loss of revenue (yellow area). (b) Price declines from $4 to $1, and total revenue falls from $40 to $20. So demand is inelastic. The gain in revenue (blue area) is less than the loss of revenue (yellow area). (c) Price declines from $3 to $1, and total revenue does not change. Demand is unit-elastic. The gain in revenue (blue area) equals the loss of revenue (yellow area).

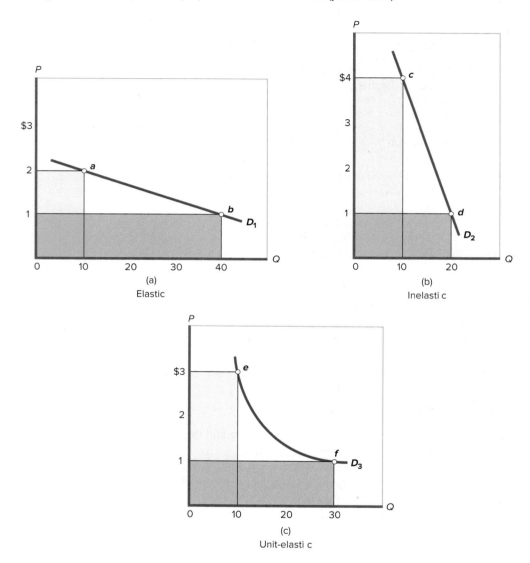

(a)
Elastic

(b)
Inelasti c

(c)
Unit-elasti c

total-revenue test
A test to determine elasticity of demand between any two prices: Demand is elastic if total revenue moves in the opposite direction from price; it is inelastic when it moves in the same direction as price; and it is of unitary elasticity when it does not change when price changes.

Total revenue and the price elasticity of demand are related. In fact, the easiest way to infer whether demand is elastic or inelastic is to employ the **total-revenue test.**

Note what happens to total revenue when price changes. If total revenue changes in the opposite direction from price, demand is elastic. If total revenue changes in the same direction as price, demand is inelastic. If total revenue does not change when price changes, demand is unit-elastic.

Elastic Demand If demand is elastic, a price decrease increases total revenue. Even though a lower price is received per unit, enough additional units are sold to more than make up for the lower price. For example, look at demand curve D_1 in **Figure 4.2a**. At point a, total revenue is $20 (= $2 × 10), shown as the yellow plus green area.

Elastic Demand If the price declines from $2 to $1 (point *b*), the quantity demanded becomes 40 units and total revenue is $40 (= $1 × 40). As a result of the price decline, total revenue increases from $20 to $40. Total revenue has increased in this case because the $1 decline in price applies to 10 units, with a consequent revenue loss of $10 (the yellow area). But 30 more units are sold at $1 each, resulting in a revenue gain of $30 (the blue area). The overall result is a net increase in total revenue of $20 (= $30 − $10).

The analysis is reversible: If demand is elastic, a price increase reduces total revenue. The revenue gained from a higher price per unit will be more than offset by the revenue lost from the lower quantity sold. Other things equal, when price and total revenue move in opposite directions, demand is elastic. E_d is greater than 1, meaning the percentage change in quantity demanded is greater than the percentage change in price.

Inelastic Demand If demand is inelastic, a price decrease will reduce total revenue. The increase in sales does not fully offset the decline in revenue per unit, and total revenue declines. Look at demand curve D_2 in **Figure 4.2b**. At point *c* on the curve, price is $4 and quantity demanded is 10. Thus, total revenue is $40, shown by the combined yellow and green rectangle. If the price drops to $1 (point *d*), total revenue declines to $20. Total revenue has declined because the loss of revenue (the yellow area) from the lower unit price is larger than the gain in revenue (the blue area) from the accompanying increase in sales. Price has fallen, and total revenue has also declined.

Our analysis is again reversible: If demand is inelastic, a price increase will increase total revenue. So, other things equal, when price and total revenue move in the same direction, demand is inelastic. E_d is less than 1, meaning the percentage change in quantity demanded is less than the percentage change in price.

Unit Elasticity In the case of unit elasticity, an increase or a decrease in price leaves total revenue unchanged. The loss in revenue from a lower unit price is exactly offset by the gain in revenue from the accompanying increase in sales. Conversely, the gain in revenue from a higher unit price is exactly offset by the revenue loss associated with the accompanying decline in the amount demanded.

Look at **Figure 4.2c** demand curve D_3. At the $3 price, 10 units will be sold, yielding total revenue of $30. At the lower $1 price, a total of 30 units will be sold, again resulting in $30 of total revenue. The $2 price reduction causes the loss of revenue shown by the yellow area, but this is exactly offset by the revenue gain shown by the blue area. Total revenue does not change.

Other things equal, when price changes and total revenue remains constant, demand is unit-elastic (or unitary). E_d is 1, meaning the percentage change in quantity equals the percentage change in price.

Price Elasticity along a Linear Demand Curve

Although the demand curves depicted in **Figure 4.2** nicely illustrate the total-revenue test for elasticity, it is important to understand that elasticity typically varies along any given demand curve. (The curve in **Figure 4.2c** is exceptional, with elasticity equal to 1 along the entire curve.)

FIGURE 4.3

Price elasticity of demand along a linear demand curve as measured by the elasticity coefficient and the total-revenue test. Demand curve *D* is based on columns (1) and (2) of the table and is labeled to show that the hypothetical weekly demand for movie tickets is elastic at higher price ranges and inelastic at lower price ranges. That fact is confirmed by the elasticity coefficients (column 3), as well as the total-revenue test (columns 4 and 5) in the table.

(1) Total Quantity of Tickets Demanded per Week, Thousands	(2) Price per Ticket	(3) Elasticity Coefficient (E_d)	(4) Total Revenue, (1) × (2)	(5) Total-Revenue Test
1	$8		$ 8000	
		5.00		Elastic
2	7		14,000	
		2.60		Elastic
3	6		18,000	
		1.57		Elastic
4	5		20,000	
		1.00		Unit elastic
5	4		20,000	
		0.64		Inelastic
6	3		18,000	
		0.38		Inelastic
7	2		14,000	
		0.20		Inelastic
8	1		8000	

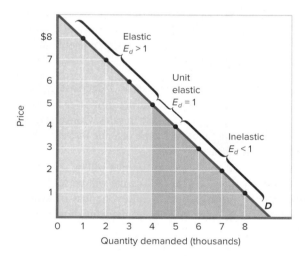

Refer to the table and graph in **Figure 4.3**, which show how elasticity varies over different price ranges of the same demand curve. Plotting the hypothetical data for movie tickets shown in columns 1 and 2 yields demand curve *D* in **Figure 4.3**. That demand curve is linear, but column (3) of the table shows that the price elasticity coefficient declines as price falls. Also, note from column (4) that total revenue first rises as price falls and then eventually declines as price falls further. Column (5) employs the total-revenue test to show that elasticity declines as price falls along a linear demand curve.

The demand curve in **Figure 4.3** illustrates that the slope of a demand curve (its flatness or steepness) is not a sound basis for judging elasticity. The slope of the curve is computed from *absolute* changes in price and quantity, while elasticity involves *relative* or *percentage* changes in price and quantity. The demand curve in **Figure 4.3** is linear, which means its slope is constant throughout. But this linear curve is elastic in its high-price ($8–$5) range and inelastic in its low-price ($4–$1) range.

APPLYING THE ANALYSIS

The Southwest Effect

Southwest Airlines grew from three planes in 1967 to America's largest domestic airline by being committed to low prices and efficiency.

Chris Parypa/Essentials/rypson/iStockphoto

Since its inception, Southwest has also been committed to making air travel so inexpensive that people who could never afford to fly before finally can. That has led to the famous Southwest Effect, whereby ticket prices plunge after Southwest enters a new market and undercuts existing carriers. As just one example, the price of flying from Denver to Phoenix fell by 36.4 percent after Southwest began service out of Denver in 2006.

Those sharp price declines allow us to estimate price elasticity of demand, including for new passengers who could not afford to fly previously. When Southwest entered the market in three California cities, fares dropped by 50 percent while passenger traffic increased 200 percent, implying a highly elastic demand for air travel at those airports. And because "highly elastic demand" implies that "lower prices will increase total revenue," Southwest found those price declines very favorable indeed.

Its higher-cost rivals? Not so much. Nearly the entire increase in passenger traffic, revenue, and profits went to Southwest.

QUESTIONS:

If Southwest continued to lower its prices, would you expect to see further increases in its total revenue? Why or why not?

Determinants of Price Elasticity of Demand

Price elasticity of demand varies by situation. However, the following generalizations are often helpful.

Substitutability Generally, the more substitute goods that are available, the greater is the price elasticity of demand. Mercedes, BMWs, and Lincolns are effective substitutes for Cadillacs, making the demand for Cadillacs elastic. At the other extreme, we saw earlier that the diabetic's demand for insulin is highly inelastic because there simply are no close substitutes.

The elasticity of demand for a product depends on how narrowly the product is defined. Demand for Reebok sneakers is more elastic than is the overall demand for shoes. Many other brands are readily substitutable for Reebok sneakers, but there are few, if any, good substitutes for shoes.

Proportion of Income Other things equal, the higher the price of a product relative to consumers' income, the greater the price elasticity of demand. A 10 percent increase in the price of low-priced pencils or chewing gum amounts to a few more pennies spent from a consumer's income, and quantity demanded will probably decline only slightly. Thus, price elasticity for such low-priced items tends to be low. But a 10 percent increase in the prices of relatively high-priced automobiles or houses means additional expenditures of perhaps $3,000 or $30,000, respectively. These price increases are significant fractions of most families' annual incomes, and quantities demanded will likely diminish significantly. The price elasticities for such items tend to be high.

Luxuries versus Necessities In general, price elasticity of demand is higher for luxury goods than it is for necessities. Electricity is generally regarded as a necessity; it is difficult to get along without it. A price increase will not significantly reduce the amount of lighting and power used in a household. (Note the very low price-elasticity coefficient of these goods in **Table 4.1**.) An extreme case: A person does not decline emergency heart bypass surgery because the physician's fee has just gone up.

In contrast, vacation travel and jewelry are luxuries that can easily be forgone. If the prices of vacation travel and jewelry rise, a consumer need not buy them and will suffer no great hardship without them.

What about the demand for a common product like salt? It is highly inelastic on three counts: Few good substitutes are available; salt is a negligible item in the family budget; and it is a "necessity" rather than a luxury.

Time Generally, product demand is more elastic over longer time periods. Consumers often need time to adjust to changes in prices. For example, consumers may not immediately reduce their purchases very much when the price of beef rises by 10 percent, but in time they may shift to chicken, pork, or fish.

A related consideration is product durability. Studies show that "short-run" demand for gasoline is more inelastic ($E_d = .26$) than is "long-run" demand ($E_d = .58$). In the short run, people are stuck with their present cars and trucks, but with rising gasoline prices they eventually replace them with smaller, more fuel-efficient vehicles.

Table 4.1 shows estimated price-elasticity coefficients for a number of products. Each reflects some combination of the elasticity determinants just discussed.

TABLE 4.1
Selected Price Elasticities of Demand

Product or Service	Coefficient of Price Elasticity of Demand (E_d)	Product or Service	Coefficient of Price Elasticity of Demand (E_d)
Newspapers	.10	Milk	.63
Electricity (household)	.13	Household appliances	.63
Bread	.15	Liquor	.70
Major League Baseball tickets	.23	Movies	.87
Cigarettes	.25	Beer	.90
Telephone service	.26	Shoes	.91
Sugar	.30	Motor vehicles	1.14
Medical care	.31	Beef	1.27
Eggs	.32	China, glassware, tableware	1.54
Legal services	.37	Residential land	1.60
Automobile repair	.40	Restaurant meals	2.27
Clothing	.49	Lamb and mutton	2.65
Gasoline	.58	Fresh peas	2.83

Source: Compiled from numerous studies and sources reporting price elasticity of demand.

 APPLYING THE ANALYSIS

Price Elasticity of Demand and College Tuition

For some goods and services, sellers may find it advantageous to determine differences in price elasticity of demand for different groups of customers and then charge different prices to the different groups. Price increases for groups that have inelastic demand will increase total revenue, as will price decreases for groups that have elastic demand.

It is relatively easy to observe differences between group elasticities. Consider tuition pricing by colleges and universities. Prospective students from low-income families generally have more elastic demand for higher education than similar students from high-income families. Tuition is a much larger proportion of household income for low-income students or families than for their high-income counterparts. Desiring a diverse student body, colleges charge different *net* prices (= tuition *minus* financial aid) to the two groups on the basis of elasticity of demand. High-income students pay full tuition, unless they receive merit-based scholarships. Low-income students receive considerable financial aid in addition to merit-based scholarships and pay a lower *net* price.

Colleges often announce a large tuition increase and immediately cushion the news by emphasizing that they also are increasing financial aid. In effect, the college is increasing the tuition for students with inelastic demand by the full amount and raising the *net* tuition of those with elastic demand by some lesser amount or not at all. Colleges use this strategy to boost revenue to cover rising costs while maintaining affordability for a wide range of students.

QUESTION:
What are some other examples of charging different prices to different groups of customers on the basis of differences in elasticity of demand? (**Hint: Think of price discounts based on age or time of purchase.**)

APPLYING THE ANALYSIS

Decriminalization of Illegal Drugs

In recent years, proposals to legalize drugs have been widely debated. Proponents contend that drugs should be treated like alcohol; they should be made legal for adults and regulated for purity. Legalization, they argue, will reduce drug trafficking significantly by lowering prices and taking the profit out of it. Because addicts' demand is highly inelastic, the amounts consumed at the lower prices would increase only modestly. Addicts' total expenditures for cocaine and heroin would decline, and so would the street crime that finances those expenditures.

Opponents argue that the overall demand for illegal drugs is far more elastic than proponents think. In addition to addicts' inelastic demand, there is another market segment whose demand is relatively elastic. This segment consists of the "dabblers," who use hard drugs when their prices are low but who abstain or substitute (perhaps with alcohol) when drug prices are high. Thus, the lower prices associated with legalization would increase dabblers' consumption. Also, legalization might make drug use more socially acceptable, increasing overall demand.

Marijuana prices in the State of Washington fell by 77 percent in the three years after marijuana was legalized in 2014. Many economists predict that the legalization of cocaine and heroin would reduce street prices by up to 80 percent, as well. According to one important study, such price declines could increase the number of occasional users of heroin by 54 percent and the number of occasional users of cocaine by 33 percent. The total quantity of heroin demanded would rise by an estimated 100 percent, and the quantity of cocaine demanded would rise by 50 percent.* Moreover, many existing and first-time dabblers might become addicts. The overall result, say the opponents of legalization, would be higher social costs, including a possible increase in street crime.

> QUESTION:
> In what ways do drug rehabilitation programs increase the elasticity of demand for illegal drugs?

*Henry Saffer and Frank Chaloupka, "The Demand for Illegal Drugs," *Economic Inquiry,* July 1999, pp. 401–11.

APPLYING THE ANALYSIS

Excise Taxes and Tax Revenue

The government pays attention to elasticity of demand when it selects goods and services to tax. If the government levies a $1 tax on a product and 10,000 units are sold, tax revenue will be $10,000 (= $1 × 10,000 units sold). If the government raises the tax to $1.50, but the higher price that results reduces sales (quantity demanded) to 4,000 because demand is elastic, tax revenue will decline to $6,000 (= $1.50 × 4,000 units sold). Because a higher tax on a product with elastic demand will bring in less tax revenue, legislatures tend to tax products that have inelastic demand, such as liquor, gasoline, and cigarettes.

> QUESTION:
> Under what circumstance might a reduction of an excise tax actually produce more tax revenue?

APPLYING THE ANALYSIS

Large Crop Yields and Farm Income

The demand for most farm products is highly inelastic; E_d is perhaps .20 or .25. As a result, increases in the supply of farm products arising from a good growing season or from increased productivity tend to depress both the prices of farm products and the total revenues (incomes) of farmers. For farmers as a group, the inelastic demand for their products means that large crop yields may be undesirable. For policymakers, it means that achieving the goal of higher total farm income requires that farm output be restricted.

> QUESTION:
> How might government programs that pay farmers to take land out of production in order to achieve conservation goals (such as erosion control and wildlife protection) increase crop prices and farm income?

Price Elasticity of Supply

Price elasticity also applies to supply. If the quantity supplied by producers is relatively responsive to price changes, supply is elastic. If it is relatively insensitive to price changes, supply is inelastic.

We measure the degree of price elasticity or inelasticity of supply with the coefficient E_s, defined almost like E_d except that we substitute "percentage change in quantity supplied" for "percentage change in quantity demanded":

$$E_s = \frac{\text{percentage change in quantity supplied of X}}{\text{percentage change in price of X}}$$

For reasons explained earlier, the averages, or midpoints, of the before and after quantities supplied and the before and after prices are used as reference points for the percentage changes. Suppose an increase in the price of a good from \$4 to \$6 increases the quantity supplied from 10 units to 14 units. The percentage change in price would be 2/5, or 40 percent, and the percentage change in quantity would be 4/12, or 33 percent:

$$E_s = \frac{.33}{.40} = .83$$

In this case, supply is inelastic because the price-elasticity coefficient is less than 1. If E_s is greater than 1, supply is elastic. If it is equal to 1, supply is unit-elastic. Also, E_s is never negative because price and quantity supplied are directly related. Thus, there are no minus signs to drop, as was necessary with price elasticity of demand.

The degree of **price elasticity of supply** depends on how quickly and easily producers can shift resources between alternative uses. The more easily and rapidly producers can shift resources, the greater the price elasticity of supply. Take the case of a producer of surfboards. The producer's response to an increase in the price of surfboards depends on its ability to shift resources from the production of other products such as wakeboards, skateboards, and snowboards (whose prices we assume remain constant) to the production of surfboards. Shifting resources takes time: The more time available, the greater the transferability of resources. So we can expect a greater response, and therefore greater elasticity of supply, the longer a firm has to adjust to a price change.

price elasticity of supply
The ratio of the percentage change in quantity supplied of a product or resource to the percentage change in its price; a measure of the responsiveness of producers to a change in the price of a product or resource.

PHOTO OP

Elastic versus Inelastic Supply

The supply of automobiles is elastic, whereas the supply of Monet paintings is inelastic.

Supergenijalac/Shutterstock

Courtesy National Gallery of Art, Washington

In analyzing the impact of time on elasticity, economists distinguish among the immediate market period, the short run, and the long run.

Price Elasticity of Supply: The Immediate Market Period

immediate market period
A period in which producers of a product are unable to change the quantity produced in response to a change in its price and in which there is a perfectly inelastic supply.

The **immediate market period** is the length of time over which producers are unable to respond to a change in market price with a change in quantity supplied. Suppose a farmer brings to market one truckload of tomatoes that is the entire season's output. The supply curve for the tomatoes is perfectly inelastic (vertical); the farmer will sell the truckload whether the price is high or low. Why? Because the farmer can offer only one truckload of tomatoes even if the price of tomatoes is much higher than anticipated. The farmer might like to offer more tomatoes, but tomatoes cannot be produced overnight. The farmer needs another full growing season to respond to a higher-than-expected price. Similarly, because the product is perishable, the farmer cannot withhold it from the market. If the price is lower than anticipated, the farmer will still sell the entire truckload.

The farmer's costs of production will not enter into this decision to sell. Though the price of tomatoes may fall far short of production costs, the farmer will nevertheless sell everything brought to market to avoid a total loss through spoilage. In the immediate market period, both the supply of tomatoes and the quantity of tomatoes supplied are fixed. The farmer offers only one truckload, no matter how high or low the price.

Figure 4.4a shows the farmer's vertical supply curve during the immediate market period. Supply is perfectly inelastic because the farmer does not have time to respond to a change in demand, say, from D_1 to D_2. The resulting price increase from P_0 to P_m simply determines which buyers get the fixed quantity supplied; it elicits no increase in output.

FIGURE 4.4

Time and the elasticity of supply. The greater the amount of time producers have to adjust to a change in demand, here from D_1 to D_2, the greater will be their output response. In the immediate market period (a), there is insufficient time to change output, and so supply is perfectly inelastic. In the short run (b), plant capacity is fixed, but changing the intensity of its use can alter output; supply is therefore more elastic. In the long run (c), all desired adjustments, including changes in plant capacity, can be made, and supply becomes still more elastic.

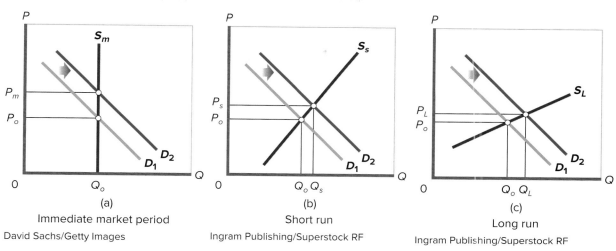

(a)
Immediate market period
David Sachs/Getty Images

(b)
Short run
Ingram Publishing/Superstock RF

(c)
Long run
Ingram Publishing/Superstock RF

However, not all supply curves are perfectly inelastic immediately after a price change. If the product is not perishable and the price rises, producers may choose to increase quantity supplied by drawing down their inventories of unsold, stored goods. This will cause the market supply curve to attain some positive slope. For our tomato farmer, the market period may be a full growing season; for producers of goods that can be inexpensively stored, there may be no immediate market period at all.

Price Elasticity of Supply: The Short Run

The **short run** in microeconomics is a period of time too short to change plant capacity but long enough to use the fixed-size plant more or less intensively. In the short run, our farmer's plant (land and farm machinery) is fixed. But the farmer does have time in the short run to cultivate tomatoes more intensively by applying more labor and more fertilizer and pesticides to the crop. The result is a somewhat greater output in response to increased demand; this greater output is reflected in a more elastic supply of tomatoes, as shown by S_s in **Figure 4.4b**. Note now that the increase in demand from D_1 to D_2 is met by an increase in quantity (from Q_0 to Q_s), so there is a smaller price adjustment (from P_0 to P_s) than would be the case in the immediate market period. The new equilibrium price is therefore lower in the short run than in the immediate market period.

short run
(1) In microeconomics, a period of time in which producers are able to change the quantities of some but not all of the resources they employ; a period in which some resources (usually plant) are fixed and some are variable. (2) In macroeconomics, a period in which nominal wages and other input prices do not change in response to a change in the price level.

Price Elasticity of Supply: The Long Run

The **long run** in microeconomics is a time period long enough for firms to adjust their plant sizes and for new firms to enter (or existing firms to leave) the industry. In the "tomato industry," for example, our farmer has time to acquire additional land and buy more machinery and equipment. Furthermore, other farmers may, over time, be attracted to tomato farming by the increased demand and higher price. Such adjustments create a larger supply response, as represented by the more elastic supply curve S_L in **Figure 4.4c**. The outcome is a smaller price rise (P_0 to P_L) and a larger output increase (Q_0 to Q_L) in response to the increase in demand from D_1 to D_2.

long run
(1) In microeconomics, a period of time long enough to enable producers of a product to change the quantities of all the resources they employ; period in which all resources and costs are variable and no resources or costs are fixed. (2) In macroeconomics, a period sufficiently long for nominal wages and other input prices to change in response to a change in the nation's price level.

There is no total-revenue test for elasticity of supply. Supply shows a positive or direct relationship between price and amount supplied; the supply curve slopes upward. Regardless of the degree of elasticity or inelasticity, price and total revenue always move together.

APPLYING THE ANALYSIS

Antiques and Reproductions

Antiques Roadshow is a popular PBS television program in which people bring antiques for appraisal by experts. Some people are pleased to learn that their old piece of furniture or funky folk art is worth a large amount, say, $30,000 or more.

The high price of an antique results from strong demand and limited, highly inelastic supply. Because a genuine antique can no longer be reproduced, its quantity supplied either does not rise or rises only slightly as its price goes up. The higher price might prompt the discovery of a few more remaining originals and thus add to the quantity available for sale, but this quantity response is usually quite small. So the supply of antiques and other collectibles tends to be inelastic. For one-of-a-kind antiques, the supply is perfectly inelastic.

Factors such as increased population, higher income, and greater enthusiasm for collecting antiques have increased the demand for antiques over time. Because the supply of antiques is limited and inelastic, those increases in demand have greatly boosted the prices of antiques.

Contrast the inelastic supply of original antiques with the elastic supply of modern "made-to-look-old" reproductions. Such faux antiques are quite popular and widely available at furniture stores and knickknack shops. When the demand for reproductions increases, the firms making them simply boost production. Because the supply of reproductions is highly elastic, increased demand raises their prices only slightly.

> QUESTION:
> How does the reluctance to sell antiques add to their inelastic supply?

APPLYING THE ANALYSIS

Volatile Gold Prices

The price of gold is quite volatile, sometimes rocketing upward one period and plummeting downward the next. The main sources of these fluctuations are shifts in demand interacting with highly inelastic supply. Gold production is a costly and time-consuming process of exploration, mining, and refining. Moreover, the physical availability of gold is highly limited. For both reasons, increases in gold prices do not elicit substantial increases in quantity supplied. Conversely, gold mining is costly to shut down, and existing gold bars are expensive to store. Price decreases therefore do not produce large drops in the quantity of gold supplied. In short, the supply of gold is inelastic.

The demand for gold is partly derived from the demand for its uses, such as for jewelry, dental fillings, and coins. But people also demand gold as a speculative financial investment. They increase their demand for gold when they fear economic turmoil that might undermine the value of currency and other types of investments.

They reduce their demand when events settle down. Because of the inelastic supply of gold, even relatively small changes in demand produce relatively large changes in price.

QUESTIONS:
What is the current price of gold? (See www.goldprice.com.) What were the highest and the lowest prices over the last 12 months?

Income Elasticity of Demand

Income elasticity of demand measures the degree to which consumers respond to a change in their incomes by buying more or less of a particular good. The coefficient of income elasticity of demand E_i is determined with the formula

$$E_i = \frac{\text{percentage change in quantity demanded}}{\text{percentage change in income}}$$

income elasticity of demand
The ratio of the percentage change in the quantity demanded of a good to a percentage change in consumer income; measures the responsiveness of consumer purchases to income changes.

Normal Goods

For most goods, the income-elasticity coefficient E_i is positive, meaning that more of them are demanded as income rises. Such goods are called *normal* or *superior goods* (see **Chapter 3**). But the value of E_i varies greatly among normal goods. For example, income elasticity of demand for automobiles is about +3.0, while income elasticity for most farm products is only about +0.2.

Inferior Goods

A negative income-elasticity coefficient designates an inferior good. Cabbages, long-distance bus tickets, and used clothing are likely inferior goods. Consumers decrease their purchases of inferior goods as their incomes rise.

 APPLYING THE ANALYSIS

Which Consumer Products Suffer the Greatest Demand Decreases during Recessions?

Coefficients of income elasticity of demand provide insights into how recessions impact the sales of different consumer products. Recessions are periods of falling real output often characterized by rising unemployment rates, lower profits, falling consumer incomes, and weaker demand for products. In February 2020, the U.S. economy entered its eleventh recession since 1950, precipitated by the COVID-19 outbreak. When recessions occur and incomes fall, coefficients of income elasticity of demand help predict which products will experience more rapid declines in demand than other products.

Products with relatively high income elasticity coefficients—such as automobiles (E_i = +3.0), housing (E_i = +1.5), and restaurant meals (E_i = +1.4)—are generally hit hardest by recessions. Those with low or negative income elasticity coefficients are much less affected. For example, food products (E_i = +.20) respond relatively little to income fluctuations. When incomes drop, purchases of food (and toothpaste and toilet paper) drop little compared to purchases of concert tickets, luxury vacations, and high-definition TVs. Products we view as essential tend to have lower income elasticity coefficients than products we view as luxuries. When our incomes fall, we cannot easily eliminate or postpone the purchase of essential products.

> **QUESTION:**
> Estimates of the income elasticity of air travel range from +1 to +2, indicating that a 10 percent decline in income results in a 10 to 20 percent drop in the demand for airline tickets. Would you expect the drop in demand during a pandemic-induced recession to be the same as during a recession caused by a financial crisis (such as in 2007)? Explain your reasoning.

GLOBAL SNAPSHOT 4.1

Income Elasticity of Demand for Gasoline, Selected Nations

The income elasticity of gasoline demand varies widely across countries, with larger demand responses found in lower-income countries in which driving is a luxury for most of the population.

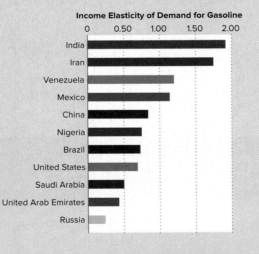

Income Elasticity of Demand for Gasoline

Cross-Elasticity of Demand

cross-elasticity of demand
The ratio of the percentage change in *quantity demanded* of one good to the percentage change in the price of some other good. A positive coefficient indicates the two products are *substitute goods;* a negative coefficient indicates they are *complementary goods.*

Cross-elasticity of demand measures the sensitivity of consumer purchases of one product (say, X) to a change in the price of some other product (say, Y). We calculate the coefficient of cross-elasticity of demand E_{xy} as the percentage change in the consumption of X divided by the percentage change in the price of Y:

$$E_{xy} = \frac{\text{percentage change in quantity demanded of product X}}{\text{percentage change in price of product Y}}$$

Cross-elasticity (or cross-price-elasticity) allows us to quantify and more fully understand substitute and complementary goods, introduced in **Chapter 3**.

Substitute Goods

If cross-elasticity of demand is positive, meaning that sales of X move in the same direction as a change in the price of Y, then X and Y are substitute goods. An example is Evian water (X) and Dasani water (Y). An increase in the price of Dasani causes consumers to buy more Evian, resulting in a positive cross-elasticity. The larger the positive cross-elasticity coefficient, the greater is the substitutability between the two products.

Complementary Goods

When cross-elasticity is negative, we know that X and Y "go together"; an increase in the price of one decreases the demand for the other. So the two are complementary goods. For example, a decrease in the price of digital cameras will increase the number of memory sticks purchased. The larger the negative cross-elasticity coefficient, the greater is the complementarity between the two goods.

Independent Goods

A zero or near-zero cross-elasticity suggests that the two products being considered are unrelated or independent goods. An example is textbooks and plums: We would not expect a change in the price of textbooks to have any effect on purchases of plums, and vice versa.

APPLYING THE ANALYSIS

Using Cross-Elasticity to Make Business and Regulatory Decisions

The cross-elasticity coefficient is important to businesses and government. For example, suppose that Coca-Cola is considering whether or not to lower the price of its Sprite brand. Before making its decision, it wants to know something about the price elasticity of demand for Sprite (will the price cut increase or decrease total revenue?), but it is also interested in knowing if the increased sales of Sprite will come at the expense of its Coke brand. How sensitive are the sales of Coke to a change in the price of Sprite? By how much will the increased sales of Sprite "cannibalize" the sales of Coke? A low cross-elasticity would indicate that Coke and Sprite are weak substitutes for each other and that a lower price for Sprite would have little effect on Coke sales.

Government also uses the idea of cross-elasticity of demand in assessing whether a proposed merger between two large firms will substantially reduce competition and therefore violate the antitrust laws. For example, the cross-elasticity between Coke and Pepsi is high, making them strong substitutes. In addition, Coke and Pepsi together sell about 70 percent of all carbonated cola drinks consumed in the United States. Taken together, the high cross-elasticities and the large market shares suggest that the government would likely block a merger between Coke and Pepsi because the merger would substantially lessen competition. In contrast, the cross-elasticity between cola and gasoline is low or zero. A merger between Coke and Shell Oil Company would have a minimal effect on competition. So government would let that merger happen.

QUESTION:
Prior to the 2007–2009 recession, why did sales of sport-utility vehicles (SUVs) decline dramatically, while sales of hybrid vehicles rose significantly? Relate your answer to cross-elasticity of demand.

GLOBAL SNAPSHOT 4.2

Cross Elasticity of Demand between Education Spending and Increases in the Price of Food, Selected Nations

The amount by which education spending falls when food prices go up is higher in lower-income countries like Tanzania and Vietnam, where family budgets are tighter. The decline in education spending is noticeably smaller in high-income countries like Japan and the United States where budgets are less constrained.

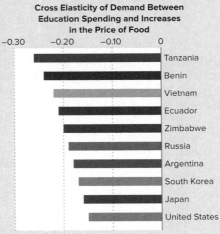

Cross Elasticity of Demand Between Education Spending and Increases in the Price of Food

Source: Economic Research Service, U.S. Department of Agriculture.

Summary

LO4.1 Explain and calculate price elasticity of demand.

Price elasticity of demand measures consumer responsiveness to price changes. If consumers are relatively sensitive to price changes, demand is elastic. If they are relatively unresponsive to price changes, demand is inelastic.

The price-elasticity coefficient E_d measures the degree of elasticity or inelasticity of demand. The coefficient is found by the formula

$$E_d = \frac{\text{percentage change in quantity demanded of X}}{\text{percentage change in price of X}}$$

Economists use the averages of prices and quantities in determining percentage changes in price and quantity. If E_d is greater than 1, demand is elastic. If E_d is less than 1, demand is inelastic. Unit elasticity is a special case in which E_d equals 1.

Perfectly inelastic demand is graphed as a line parallel to the vertical axis; perfectly elastic demand is shown by a line above and parallel to the horizontal axis.

Elasticity varies at different price ranges on a demand curve, tending to be elastic in the upper-left

segment and inelastic in the lower-right segment. Elasticity cannot be judged by the steepness or flatness of a demand curve. The number of available substitutes, the size of an item's price relative to one's budget, whether the product is a luxury or a necessity, and the length of time to adjust are all determinants of elasticity of demand.

LO4.2 Explain the usefulness of the total-revenue test.

If total revenue changes in the opposite direction from price, demand is elastic. If price and total revenue change in the same direction, demand is inelastic. Where demand is of unit elasticity, a change in price leaves total revenue unchanged.

LO4.3 Explain and calculate price elasticity of supply.

The coefficient of price elasticity of supply is found by the formula

$$E_s = \frac{\text{percentage change in quantity supplied of X}}{\text{percentage change in price of X}}$$

The averages of the prices and quantities are used for computing percentage changes. Elasticity of supply depends on the ease of shifting resources between alternative uses, which varies directly with the time producers have to adjust to a price change.

LO4.4 Apply price elasticity of demand and supply to real-world situations.

Price elasticity of demand and supply has numerous private and public sector applications. For example, they inform pricing and output decisions by firms, and government policies regarding the legalization and taxation of goods.

LO4.5 Explain and apply income elasticity of demand and cross-elasticity of demand.

Income elasticity of demand indicates the responsiveness of consumer purchases to a change in income. The coefficient of income elasticity of demand is found by the formula

$$E_i = \frac{\text{percentage change in quantity demanded}}{\text{percentage change in income}}$$

The coefficient is positive for normal goods and negative for inferior goods.

Industries that sell products with high income-elasticity-of-demand coefficients are particularly hard hit by recessions. Those products with low or negative coefficients fare much better.

Cross-elasticity of demand indicates how sensitive the purchase of one product is to changes in the price of another product. The coefficient of cross-elasticity is found by the formula

$$E_{xy} = \frac{\text{percentage change in quantity demanded of product X}}{\text{percentage change in price of product Y}}$$

Positive cross-elasticity of demand identifies substitute goods; negative cross-elasticity identifies complementary goods.

Terms and Concepts

price elasticity of demand	total revenue (TR)	income elasticity of demand
elastic demand	total-revenue test	cross-elasticity of demand
inelastic demand	price elasticity of supply	
unit elasticity	immediate market period	
perfectly inelastic demand	short run	
perfectly elastic demand	long run	

Questions   Mc Graw Hill connect

1. What is the formula for measuring price elasticity of demand? What does it mean (in terms of relative price and quantity changes) if the price-elasticity coefficient is less than 1? Equal to 1? Greater than 1? **(LO1)**

2. Suppose that the total revenue received by a company selling basketballs is $600 when the price is set at $30 per basketball and $600 when the price is set at $20 per basketball. Without using the midpoint formula, can you tell whether demand is elastic, inelastic, or unit-elastic over this price range? **(LO2)**

3. What are the major determinants of price elasticity of demand? Use those determinants and your own reasoning in judging whether demand for each of the following products is probably elastic or inelastic: (a) bottled water; (b) toothpaste; (c) Crest toothpaste; (d) ketchup; (e) diamond bracelets; (f) Microsoft's Windows operating system. **(LO1)**

4. What effect would a rule stating that university students must live in university dormitories have on the price elasticity of demand for dormitory space? How might this rule affect room rates? **(LO1)**

5. Calculate total-revenue data from the demand schedule in Problem 3. Referring to changes in price and total revenue, describe the total-revenue test for elasticity. **(LO2)**

6. How would the following changes in price affect total revenue? That is, would total revenue increase, decrease, or remain unchanged? **(LO2)**
   a. Price falls and demand is inelastic.
   b. Price rises and demand is elastic.
   c. Price rises and supply is elastic.
   d. Price rises and supply is inelastic.
   e. Price rises and demand is inelastic.
   f. Price falls and demand is elastic.
   g. Price falls and demand is of unit elasticity.

7. You are the chairperson of a state tax commission responsible for establishing a program to raise new revenue through excise taxes. Why would elasticity of demand be important to you in determining the products on which the taxes should be levied? **(LO4)**

8. In 2017, Leonardo da Vinci's painting *Salvador Mundi* sold for $450 million. Portray this sale in a demand and supply diagram, and comment on the elasticity of supply. Comedian George Carlin once mused, "If a painting can be forged well enough to fool some experts, why is the original so valuable?" Provide an answer. **(LO4)**

9. The income elasticities of demand for movies, dental services, and clothing have been estimated to be +3.4, +1.0, and +0.5, respectively. Interpret these coefficients. What does a negative income-elasticity coefficient mean? **(LO5)**

10. Suppose the cross-elasticity of demand for products A and B is +3.6, and for products C and D it is −5.4. What can you conclude about how products A and B are related? Products C and D? **(LO5)**

Problems

1. Look at the demand curve in **Figure 4.2a**. Use the midpoint formula and points *a* and *b* to calculate the elasticity of demand for that range of the demand curve. Do the same for the demand curves in **Figures 4.2b** and **4.2c** using, respectively, points *c* and *d* for **Figure 4.2b** and points *e* and *f* for **Figure 4.2c**. **(LO1)**

2. Investigate how demand elasticities are affected by increases in demand. Shift each of the demand curves in **Figures 4.2a**, **4.2b**, and **4.2c** to the right by 10 units. For example, point *a* in **Figure 4.2a** would shift rightward from location (10 units, $2) to (20 units, $2), while point *b* would shift rightward from location (40 units, $1) to (50 units, $1). After making these shifts, apply the midpoint formula to calculate the demand elasticities for the shifted points. Are they larger or smaller than the elasticities you calculated in problem 1 for the original points? In terms of the midpoint formula, what explains the change in elasticities? **(LO1)**

3. Graph the accompanying demand data, and then use the midpoint formula for E_d to determine the price elasticity of demand for each of the four possible $1 price changes. What can you conclude about the relationship between the slope of a curve and its elasticity? **(LO1)**

Product Price	Quantity Demanded
$5	1
4	2
3	3
2	4
1	5

4. Danny "Dimes" Donahue is a neighborhood's 9-year-old entrepreneur. His most recent venture is selling homemade brownies that he bakes himself. At a price of $1.50 each, he sells 100. At a price of $1.00 each, he sells 300. Is demand elastic or inelastic over this price range? *If demand had the same elasticity for a price decline from $1.00 to $0.50 as it does for the decline from $1.50 to $1.00, would cutting the price from $1.00 to $0.50 increase or decrease Danny's total revenue?* **(LO2)**

5. What is the formula for measuring the price elasticity of supply? Suppose the price of apples goes up from $20 to $22 a box. In direct response, Goldsboro Farms supplies 1,200 boxes of apples instead of 1,000 boxes. Compute the

coefficient of price elasticity (midpoint approach) for Goldsboro's supply. Is its supply elastic or inelastic? Explain. **(LO3)**

6. **ADVANCED ANALYSIS** Currently, at a price of $1 each, 100 popsicles are sold per day in the perpetually hot town of Rostin. Consider the elasticity of supply. In the short run, a price increase from $1 to $2 is unit-elastic ($E_s = 1.0$). So, how many popsicles will be sold each day in the short run if the price rises to $2 each? In the long run, a price increase from $1 to $2 has an elasticity of supply of 1.50. How many popsicles will be sold per day in the long run if the price rises to $2 each? (*Hint:* Apply the midpoint approach to the elasticity of supply.) **(LO3)**

7. Ariya likes to play golf. The number of times per year that she plays depends on the price of playing a round of golf, Ariya's income, and the price of other types of entertainment—in particular, how much it costs to go see a movie instead of playing golf. The three demand schedules in the following table show how many rounds of golf per year Ariya will demand at each price under three different scenarios. In scenario D_1, Ariya's income is $50,000 per year and movies cost $9 each. In scenario D_2, Ariya's income is also $50,000 per year, but the price of seeing a movie rises to $11. And in scenario D_3, Ariya's income goes up to $70,000 per year, while movies cost $11. **(LO5)**

	Quantity Demanded		
Price	D_1	D_2	D_3
$50	15	10	15
35	25	15	30
20	40	20	50

a. Using the data under D_1 and D_2, calculate the cross-elasticity of Ariya's demand for golf at all three prices. (To do so, apply the midpoint approach to the cross-elasticity of demand.) Is the cross-elasticity the same at all three prices? Are movies and golf substitute goods, complementary goods, or independent goods?

b. Using the data under D_2 and D_3, calculate the income elasticity of Ariya's demand for golf at all three prices. (To do so, apply the midpoint approach to the income elasticity of demand.) Is the income elasticity the same at all three prices? Is golf an inferior good?

CHAPTER FIVE

Market Failures: Public Goods and Externalities

Learning Objectives

LO5.1   Differentiate between demand-side market failures and supply-side market failures.

LO5.2   Distinguish public goods from private goods, and explain how to determine the optimal quantity of a public good.

LO5.3   Explain how positive and negative externalities cause under- and overallocations of resources, and how they might be corrected.

LO5.4   Describe the differences between the benefits-received and ability-to-pay principles of taxation.

LO5.5   Distinguish between proportional, progressive, and regressive taxes.

Competitive markets usually do a remarkable job of allocating society's scarce resources to their highest-valued uses. But markets have certain limitations. In some circumstances, economically desirable goods are not produced at all. In other situations, they are either overproduced or underproduced. This chapter examines **market failure,** which occurs when the competitive market system (1) does not allocate any resources whatsoever to the production of certain goods or (2) either underallocates or overallocates resources to the production of certain goods.

Where private markets fail, an economic role for government may arise. In this chapter, we examine that role as it relates to public goods and externalities—situations where market failures lead to suboptimal outcomes that the government may improve upon through taxation, spending, and regulation. We conclude the chapter by noting potential government inefficiencies that can hinder government's economic efforts.

Market Failures in Competitive Markets[1]

market failure
The inability of a market to bring about the allocation of resources that best satisfies the wants of society; in particular, the overallocation or underallocation of resources to the production of a particular good or service because of spillovers or informational problems or because markets do not provide desired public goods.

demand-side market failures
Underallocations of resources that occur when private demand curves understate consumers' full willingness to pay for a good or service.

supply-side market failures
Overallocations of resources that occur when private supply curves understate the full cost of producing a good or service.

Competitive markets usually produce an assignment of resources that is "right" from an economic perspective. Unfortunately, the presence of robust competition involving many buyers and many sellers may not be enough to guarantee that a market will allocate resources correctly. Market failures sometimes happen in competitive markets. The focus of this chapter is to explain how and why such market failures can arise and how they might be corrected.

Fortunately, the broad picture is simple. Market failures in competitive markets fall into just two categories:

- **Demand-side market failures** happen when demand curves do not reflect consumers' full willingness to pay for a good or service.

- **Supply-side market failures** occur when supply curves do not reflect the full cost of producing a good or service.

Demand-Side Market Failures

Demand-side market failures arise because it is sometimes impossible to charge consumers what they are willing to pay for a product. Consider outdoor fireworks displays. People enjoy fireworks and would be *willing* to pay to see a fireworks display if the only way to see it was to have to pay. But because such displays are outdoors and in public, people don't actually *have* to pay to see the display because there is no way to exclude those who haven't paid from also enjoying the show. Private firms will therefore be unwilling to produce outdoor fireworks displays, because it will be nearly impossible for them to raise enough revenue to cover production costs.

Supply-Side Market Failures

Supply-side market failures arise when a firm does not have to pay the full cost of producing its output. Consider a coal-burning power plant. The firm running the plant will have to pay for all of the land, labor, capital, and entrepreneurship that it uses to generate electricity by burning coal. But if the firm is not charged for the smoke it releases into the atmosphere, it will fail to pay another set of costs—the costs that its pollution imposes on other people. These include future harm from climate change, toxins that affect wildlife, and possible damage to agricultural crops downwind.

Market failures arise because it is not possible for the market to correctly weigh costs and benefits in situations where some of the costs are completely unaccounted for. The coal-burning power plant produces more electricity and generates more pollution than it would if it had to pay for each ton of smoke it released into the atmosphere. The extra units produced are units of output for which the costs are *greater than* the benefits. Obviously, these units should not be produced.

---

[1] Other market failures arise when there are not enough buyers or sellers to ensure competition. In those situations, the lack of competition allows either buyers or sellers to restrict purchases or sales below optimal levels for their own benefit. As an example, a monopoly—a firm that is the only producer in its industry—can restrict the amount of output it supplies in order to drive up the market price and thereby increase its own profit.

Efficiently Functioning Markets

The best way to understand market failure is to first understand how properly functioning competitive markets achieve economic efficiency.

A competitive market not only makes private goods available to consumers but also allocates society's resources efficiently to the particular product. Competition forces producers to use the best technology and right mix of productive resources. Otherwise, lower-cost producers will drive them out of business. The result is **productive efficiency:** the production of any particular good in the least costly way. When society produces, say, bottled water at the lowest achievable per-unit cost, it is expending the smallest amount of resources to produce that product and therefore makes available the largest amount of resources to produce other desired goods. Suppose society has only $100 worth of resources available. If it can produce a bottle of water using only $1 of those resources, then it will have available $99 of resources to produce other goods. This is clearly better than producing the bottle of water for $5 and having only $95 of resources available for alternative uses.

Competitive markets also produce **allocative efficiency:** the *particular mix* of goods and services most highly valued by society (minimum-cost production assumed). For example, society wants high-quality mineral water to be used for bottled water, not for gigantic blocks of refrigeration ice. It wants MP3 players (such as iPods), not phonographs and 45-rpm records. Moreover, society does not want to devote all its resources to bottled water and MP3 players. It wants to assign some resources to automobiles and personal computers. Competitive markets make those proper assignments, as we will demonstrate.

Two conditions must hold if a competitive market is to produce efficient outcomes:

- The market demand curve must reflect the full willingness to pay of every person receiving benefits from the product being sold in the market.

- The market supply curve must reflect all of the costs of production, including those that may fall onto persons not directly involved in production of the product being sold in the market.

If these conditions hold, then the market will produce only units for which benefits are at least equal to costs.

productive efficiency
The production of a good in the least costly way; occurs when production takes place at the output at which average total cost is a minimum and marginal product per dollar's worth of input is the same for all inputs.

allocative efficiency
The apportionment of resources among firms and industries to obtain the production of the products most wanted by society (consumers); the output of each product at which its marginal cost and price or marginal benefit are equal.

Private and Public Goods

Demand-side market failures arise in competitive markets when demand curves fail to reflect consumers' full willingness to pay for a good or service. In such situations, markets fail to produce all of the units for which there are net benefits because demand curves underreport how much consumers are willing and able to pay. This underreporting problem reaches its most extreme form in the case of a public good: Markets may fail to produce *any* of the public good because its demand curve may reflect *none* of its consumers' willingness to pay.

To understand public goods, we first need to understand the characteristics that define private goods.

Private Goods Characteristics

The market system produces a wide range **private goods,** the goods offered for sale in stores and on the Internet. Examples include automobiles, clothing, restaurant meals, household appliances, and video games. Private goods have two characteristics: rivalry and excludability.

private good
A good or service that is individually consumed and that can be profitably provided by privately owned firms because they can exclude nonpayers from receiving the benefits.

- *Rivalry* (in consumption) means that when one person consumes a product, it is not available for another person to consume. When Garcia purchases and drinks a bottle of mineral water, it is not available for Johnson to purchase and consume.
- *Excludability* means that sellers can prevent people who do not pay for a product from obtaining its benefits. Only people who are willing and able to pay the market price for bottles of water can obtain these drinks and the benefits they confer.

Profitable Provision

Consumers fully express their personal demands for private goods in the market. If Garcia likes bottled mineral water, that fact will be known by Garcia's desire to purchase the product. Other things equal, the higher the price of bottled water, the fewer bottles Garcia will buy. This is simply *individual* demand, as described in **Chapter 3**.

The *market* demand for a private good is the horizontal summation of the individual demand schedules (review **Figure 3.2**). Suppose there are just two consumers in the market for bottled water and the price is $1 per bottle. If Garcia will purchase three bottles and Johnson will buy two, the market demand will reflect that consumers demand five bottles at the $1 price. Similar summations of quantities demanded at other prices will generate the market demand schedule and curve.

Suppose the equilibrium price of bottled water is $1. Garcia and Johnson will buy a total of five bottles, and the sellers will obtain total revenue of $5 (= $1 × 5). If the sellers' cost per bottle is $0.80, their total cost will be $4 (= $0.80 × 5). So sellers charging $1 per bottle will obtain $5 of total revenue, incur $4 of total cost, and earn $1 of profit on the five bottles sold.

Because firms can profitably "tap market demand" for private goods, they will produce and offer them for sale. Consumers demand private goods, and profit-seeking suppliers produce goods to satisfy the demand. Consumers willing to pay the market price obtain the goods; nonpayers go without. A competitive market not only makes private goods available to consumers but also allocates society's resources efficiently to the particular product. There is neither underproduction nor overproduction of the product.

Public Goods Characteristics

public good
A good or service that is characterized by nonrivalry and nonexcludability; a good or service with these characteristics provided by government.

Public goods are the opposite of private goods. Public goods are distinguished by nonrivalry and nonexcludability.

- *Nonrivalry* (in consumption) means that one person's consumption of a good does not preclude consumption of the good by others. Everyone can simultaneously obtain the benefit from a public good such as a global positioning system, national defense, street lighting, and environmental protection.
- *Nonexcludability* means there is no effective way of excluding individuals from the benefit of the good once it comes into existence. You cannot keep someone from benefiting from GPS, national defense, street lighting, and a cleaner environment.

free-rider problem
The inability of potential providers of an economically desirable good or service to obtain payment from those who benefit because of nonexcludability.

These two characteristics create a **free-rider problem.** Once a producer has provided a public good, everyone, including nonpayers, can obtain the benefit. Because most people do not voluntarily pay for something they can obtain for free, most people become free riders. Free riders would be willing to pay for the public good if producers could somehow force them to pay—but nonexcludability means there is no way for producers to withhold the good from the free riders without also denying it to the few who do pay. Free riding means that the willingness to pay of the free riders is not expressed in the market. From producers' viewpoints, free riding reduces demand. The more free riding, the less demand. And if all consumers free ride, demand will collapse to zero.

PHOTO OP

Private versus Public Goods

Apples, distinguished by rivalry (in consumption) and excludability, are examples of private goods. In contrast, streetlights, distinguished by nonrivalry (in consumption) and nonexcludability, are examples of public goods.

Marc Bruxelle/123RF

milan noga/Shutterstock

The low or even zero demand caused by free riding makes it virtually impossible for private firms to profitably provide public goods. With little or no demand, firms cannot effectively "tap market demand" for revenues and profits. As a result, they will not produce public goods. Society will therefore suffer efficiency losses because goods for which marginal benefits exceed marginal costs are not produced. Thus, if society wants a public good to be produced, it must turn to nonmarket provision by entities that do not have to worry about profitability.

One option is private philanthropy. But many public goods, such as national defense and universal public education, are too expensive for private philanthropy. So society often looks to government to provide public goods.

Government-provided public goods will still be nonexcludable, so the government won't have any better luck preventing free riding. But the government doesn't have to worry about profitability because it can finance the provision of the public good through taxation. It can therefore provide the public good even when private firms can't.

Examples of public goods include national defense, outdoor firework displays, public art displays, and public concerts. All of these goods or services show both nonrivalry and nonexcludability.

For the large majority of public goods, private provision is unprofitable. As a result, there are only two main ways for a public good to be provided: private philanthropy or government provision. For many less expensive or less important public goods, such as fireworks displays or public art, society may feel comfortable relying on private philanthropy. But when it comes to public goods like national defense, people normally look to the government. This leads to an important question: How can a government determine the optimal amount of a public good to provide?

ILLUSTRATING THE IDEA

Art for Art's Sake

fightbegin/123RF

Suppose an enterprising sculptor creates a piece of art costing $600 and, with permission, places it in the town square. Also, suppose that Jack gets $300 of enjoyment from the art and Diane gets $400. Sensing this enjoyment and hoping to make a profit, the sculptor approaches Jack for a donation equal to his satisfaction. Jack falsely says that, unfortunately, he does not particularly like the piece. The sculptor then tries Diane, hoping to get $400 or so. Same deal: Diane professes not to like the piece either. Jack and Diane have become free riders. Although feeling a bit guilty, both reason that it makes no sense to pay for something when anyone can receive the benefits without paying for them. The artist is a quick learner; he vows never to try anything like that again.

> **QUESTION:**
>
> What is the rationale for government funding for art placed in town squares and other public spaces?

Optimal Quantity of a Public Good If consumers need not reveal their true demand for a public good in the marketplace, how can society determine the optimal amount of that good? The answer is that the government has to try to estimate the demand for a public good through surveys or public votes. It can then compare the marginal benefit of an added unit of the good against the government's marginal cost of providing it. Adhering to the MB = MC rule, it can provide the "right" amount of the public good.

Measuring Demand Suppose that Garcia and Johnson are the only two people in the society and that their marginal willingness to pay for a public good, national defense, is as shown in **Table 5.1**. Economists might have discovered these schedules through a survey asking hypothetical questions about how much each citizen was willing to pay for various types and amounts of public goods rather than go without them.

TABLE 5.1
Optimal Quantity of a Public Good, Two Individuals

(1) Quantity of Public Good	(2) Garcia's Willingness to Pay (Price)		(3) Johnson's Willingness to Pay (Price)		(4) Collective Willingness to Pay (Price)	(5) Marginal Cost
1	$4	+	$5	=	$9	$3
2	3	+	4	=	7	4
3	2	+	3	=	5	5
4	1	+	2	=	3	6
5	0	+	1	=	1	7

Notice that the schedules in the first four columns of **Table 5.1** are price-quantity schedules, meaning they are demand schedules. Rather than depicting demand in the usual way—the quantity of a product someone is willing to buy at each possible price—these schedules show the price someone is willing to pay for the extra unit of each possible quantity. That is, Garcia is willing to pay $4 for the first unit of the public good, $3 for the second, $2 for the third, and so on.

Suppose the government produces 1 unit of this public good. Because of nonrivalry, Garcia's consumption of the good does not preclude Johnson from also consuming it, and vice versa. So both people consume the good, and neither volunteers to pay for it. But from **Table 5.1** we can find the amount these two people would be willing to pay, together, rather than do without this 1 unit of the good. Columns 1 and 2 show that Garcia would be willing to pay $4 for the first unit of the public good, whereas columns 1 and 3 reveal that Johnson would be willing to pay $5 for it. Garcia and Johnson therefore are jointly willing to pay $9 (= $4 + $5) for this first unit.

For the second unit of the public good, the collective price they are willing to pay is $7 (= $3 from Garcia + $4 from Johnson); for the third unit they would pay $5 (= $2 + $3); and so on. By finding the collective willingness to pay for each additional unit (column 4), we can construct a collective demand schedule (a willingness-to-pay schedule) for the public good. Here we are *not* adding the quantities demanded at each possible price, as with the market demand for a private good. Instead, we are adding the prices that people are willing to pay for the last unit of the public good at each possible quantity demanded.

What does it mean in columns 1 and 4 of **Table 5.1** that, for example, Garcia and Johnson are collectively willing to pay $7 for the second unit of the public good? It means they jointly expect to receive $7 of extra benefit or utility from that unit. Column 4, in effect, reveals the collective marginal benefit of each unit of the public good.

Comparing Marginal Benefit and Marginal Cost

Now let's suppose the marginal cost of providing the public good is as shown in column 5 of **Table 5.1**. As explained in **Chapter 1**, marginal cost tends to rise as more of a good is produced. In view of the marginal-cost data shown, how much of the good should government provide? The optimal amount occurs at the quantity where marginal benefit equals marginal cost. In **Table 5.1**, that quantity is 3 units, where the collective willingness to pay for the third unit—the $5 marginal benefit—just matches that unit's $5 marginal cost. As we saw in **Chapter 1**, equating marginal benefit and marginal cost efficiently allocates society's scarce resources.

cost-benefit analysis
A comparison of the marginal costs of a government project or program with the marginal benefits to decide whether or not to employ resources in that project or program and to what extent.

APPLYING THE ANALYSIS

Cost-Benefit Analysis

The preceding example suggests a practical means, called **cost-benefit analysis,** for deciding whether to provide a particular public good and how much of it to provide. Let's go through an extended example that applies cost-benefit analysis to an infrastructure project.

Suppose the federal government is contemplating a highway construction plan. Because the economy's resources are limited, any decision to use more resources in the public sector will mean fewer resources for the private sector. There will be an opportunity cost as well as a benefit. The cost is the loss of satisfaction resulting from the accompanying decline in the production of private goods; the benefit is the extra satisfaction resulting from the output of more public goods. Should the needed resources be shifted from the private to the public sector? The answer is yes if the benefit from the new highways exceeds the cost of having fewer private goods. The answer is no if the cost of the forgone private goods is greater than the benefit associated with the new highways.

Roads and highways can be run privately, as excludability is possible with toll booths. However, the U.S. federal highway system is almost entirely nonexclusive because anyone with a car can get on and off most federal highways without restriction. Federal highways therefore satisfy one characteristic of a public good: nonexcludability. Highways are also nonrival; unless a highway is already extremely crowded, one person's driving on the highway does not preclude another person's driving on the highway. Thus, the federal highway system is effectively a public good. This leads us to ask: Should the federal government expand the federal highway system? If so, what is the proper size or scope for the overall project?

Table 5.2 lists four increasingly ambitious and increasingly costly highway projects: widening existing two-lane highways; building new two-lane highways; building new four-lane highways; and building new six-lane highways. The extent to which government should undertake highway construction depends on the costs and benefits. The costs are largely the costs of constructing and maintaining the highways; the benefits are improved flows of people and goods throughout the nation.

TABLE 5.2
Cost-Benefit Analysis for a National Highway Construction Project (in Billions)

(1) Plan	(2) Total Cost of Project	(3) Marginal Cost	(4) Total Benefit	(5) Marginal Benefit	(6) Net Benefit (4) − (2)
No new construction	$ 0		$ 0		$ 0
		$ 4		$ 5	
A: Widen existing highways	4		5		1
		6		8	
B: New 2-lane highways	10		13		3
		8		10	
C: New 4-lane highways	18		23		5
		10		3	
D: New 6-lane highways	28		26		−2

The table shows that total benefit (column 4) exceeds total cost (column 2) for plans A, B, and C, indicating that some highway construction is economically justifiable. We see this directly in column 6, where total costs (column 2) are subtracted from total benefits (column 4). Net benefits are positive for plans A, B, and C. Plan D is not economically justifiable because net benefits are negative.

But the question of optimal size or scope for this project remains. Comparing the marginal cost (the change in total cost) and the marginal benefit (the change in total benefit) relating to each plan determines the answer. The guideline is well known to you from previous discussions: Increase an activity, project, or output as long as the marginal benefit (column 5) exceeds the marginal cost (column 3). Stop the activity at, or as close as possible to, the point at which the marginal benefit equals the marginal cost. Do not undertake a project for which marginal cost exceeds marginal benefit.

Applying those rules, we see that plans A, B, and C should all be undertaken because marginal benefit exceeds marginal cost for all of them. But the federal government should stop there because Plan D's marginal cost ($10 billion) exceeds its marginal benefit ($3 billion). Plan C is closest to the theoretical optimum because its marginal benefit ($10 billion) still exceeds marginal cost ($8 billion) while coming closest to the MB = MC ideal.

This marginal-cost–marginal-benefit rule tells us which plan provides the maximum excess of total benefits over total costs or, in other words, the plan that provides society with the maximum net benefit. You can confirm directly in column 6 that the maximum net benefit ($5 billion) is associated with plan C.

QUESTION:

Do you think it is generally easier to measure the costs of public goods or their benefits? Explain your reasoning.

Externalities

In addition to providing public goods, governments also can improve the allocation of resources in the economy by correcting for market failures caused by externalities. An *externality* occurs when some of the costs or the benefits of a good or service are passed onto or "spill over" to someone other than the immediate buyer or seller. These spillovers are called externalities because they accrue to some third party that is external to the market transaction.

Negative Externalities

Negative externalities (or *spillover costs*) occur when producers or suppliers impose costs on third parties who are not directly involved in a market transaction. Environmental pollution is an example. Consider the costs of breathing polluted air that are imposed on third parties living downwind of smoke-spewing factories. Because polluting firms do not take account of such costs, they oversupply the products they make, producing units for which total costs (including those that fall on third parties) exceed total benefits.

negative externalities
Spillover production or consumption costs imposed on third parties without compensation to them.

Figure 5.1a illustrates how negative externalities affect the allocation of resources. When producers shift some of their costs onto the community as external costs, producers' marginal costs are lower than they would be if they had to pay for these costs. So their supply curves do not include or "capture" all the costs legitimately associated with the production of their goods. A polluting producer's supply curve such as S in **Figure 5.1a** therefore understates the total cost of production. The polluters' supply curve lies to the right of (below) the total-cost supply curve S_t, which includes the spillover costs. Through polluting and thus transferring cost to society, the firm enjoys lower production costs than it would if it had to pay for those negative externalities. By dumping those costs onto others, it produces more at each price than it would if it had to account for all costs. That is why supply curve S lies to the right of supply curve S_p.

The resource allocation outcome is shown in **Figure 5.1a**, where equilibrium output Q_e is larger than the optimal output Q_o. Resources are *overallocated* to the production of this commodity; too many units of it are produced. In fact, there is a net loss to society for every unit from Q_o to Q_e. That net loss occurs because, for each of those units, the supply curve that accounts for all costs, S_t, lies above the demand curve. Therefore, marginal cost (MC) exceeds marginal benefit (MB) for those units. The resources that went into producing those units should have been used elsewhere in the economy to produce other things.

FIGURE 5.1

Negative externalities and positive externalities. (a) With negative externalities borne by society, the producers' supply curve *S* is to the right of (below) the total-cost supply curve *S_t*. Consequently, the equilibrium output *Q_e* is greater than the optimal output *Q_o*. (b) When positive externalities accrue to society, the market demand curve *D* is to the left of (below) the total-benefit demand curve *D_t*. As a result, the equilibrium output *Q_e* is less than the optimal output *Q_o*.

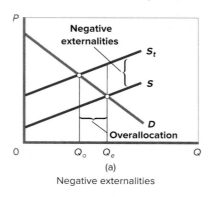

(a)
Negative externalities

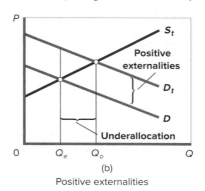

(b)
Positive externalities

Positive Externalities

positive externalities
Spillover production or consumption benefits conferred on third parties without compensation from them.

Positive externalities (or *spillover benefits*) occur when people who are not directly involved in a market transaction receive benefits from the transaction without having to pay for them. Immunization against deadly viruses directly benefits the immediate consumer of those vaccines. But it also results in widespread substantial positive externalities to the entire community. Education benefits consumers through increased income and job access. But education also benefits society through a more versatile and more productive labor force, on the one hand, and smaller outlays for crime prevention, law enforcement, and welfare programs, on the other.

Figure 5.1b shows the impact of positive externalities on resource allocation. When spillover benefits occur, the market demand curve *D* lies to the left of (below) the total-benefits demand curve, *D_t*. That is, *D* does not include the positive externalities of the product, whereas *D_t* does. Consider inoculations against a communicable disease. When someone gets vaccinated against a disease, they benefit not only themselves (because they can no longer contract the disease) but also everyone else around them (because they will not infect others in the future). These other people would presumably be willing to pay some positive amount of money for the benefit they receive when someone else is vaccinated. But because there is no way to make them pay, the market demand curve *D* reflects only the direct, private benefits to the vaccinated person. It does not reflect the positive externalities—the spillover benefits—to those around the vaccinated person, which are included in *D_t*.

Coase theorem
The idea, first stated by economist Ronald Coase, that externality problems may be resolved through private negotiations of the affected parties.

The outcome, as shown in **Figure 5.1b**, is that the equilibrium output *Q_e* is less than the optimal output *Q_o*. The market fails to produce enough vaccinations, and resources are *underallocated* to this product. The underproduction implies that society is missing out on potential net benefits. For every unit from *Q_e* to *Q_o*, the demand curve that accounts for all benefits, *D_t*, lies above the supply curve that accounts for all costs—including the opportunity cost of producing other products with the resources that were used to produce these units. Therefore, MB exceeds MC for each of these units and society should redeploy some of its resources away from the production of other things in order to produce these units that generate positive net benefits.

Economists have explored several approaches to the problems of negative and positive externalities. Sometimes, private parties work out their own solutions to externality problems; other times, government intervention is warranted.

PHOTO OP

Positive and Negative Consumption Externalities

Homeowners create positive externalities when they put up nice holiday lighting displays. Not only does the homeowner benefit from consuming the sight, but so do people who pass by the house. In contrast, when people smoke in public, it creates a negative externality. This takes the form of secondhand smoke, imposing health costs on nonsmokers and those with respiratory problems.

Kenneth Sponsler/Shutterstock

ONOKY – Fabrice LEROUGE/Getty Images

ILLUSTRATING THE IDEA

Beekeepers and the Coase Theorem

Economist Ronald Coase received the Nobel Prize for his so-called **Coase theorem,** which pointed out that private individuals could often negotiate their own mutually agreeable solutions to externality problems without the need for government interventions like pollution taxes.

This is a very important insight because it means that we shouldn't automatically call for government intervention every time we see an externality problem. Consider the positive externalities that bees provide by pollinating farmers' crops. Should we assume that beekeeping will be underprovided unless the government intervenes with, for instance, subsidies to encourage more hives and hence more pollination?

As it turns out, no. Research has shown that farmers and beekeepers long ago used private bargaining to develop customs and payment systems that avoid free riding by farmers and encourage beekeepers to keep the optimal number of hives. Free riding is avoided by the custom that all farmers in an area simultaneously hire beekeepers to provide bees to pollinate their crops. And farmers always pay the beekeepers for their pollination services because if they didn't, then no beekeeper would ever work with them in the future—a situation that would lead to massively reduced crop yields due to a lack of pollination.

The "Fable of the Bees" is a good reminder that it is a fallacy to assume that the government must always get involved to remedy externalities. In many cases, the private sector can solve both positive and negative externality problems on its own.

QUESTIONS:

Suppose that in a town a large number of home gardeners need pollination services for their fruit and vegetable crops, but none can individually afford to pay a professional beekeeper. How might that affect the contracting of beekeepers? Would it suggest a possible role for government?

Government Intervention

Government intervention may achieve economic efficiency when externalities affect large numbers of people or when community interests are at stake. Government can counter the overproduction caused by negative externalities with direct controls or Pigovian taxes (discussed below). And governments can counter underproduction caused by positive externalities with subsidies or government provision.

Direct Controls   The most direct way to reduce negative externalities from a certain activity is to pass legislation limiting that activity. Such direct controls force the offending firms to incur the actual costs of the offending activity. Historically, direct controls in the form of uniform emission standards—limits on allowable pollution—have dominated U.S. air pollution policy. Similarly, clean-water legislation limits the amounts of heavy metals, detergents, and other pollutants that firms can discharge into rivers and bays. Toxic-waste laws dictate special procedures and dump sites for disposing of contaminated soil and solvents. Violating these laws means fines and, in some cases, imprisonment.

Direct controls raise the marginal cost of production because polluting firms must operate and maintain pollution-control equipment. The supply curve S in **Figure 5.2b**, which does not reflect external costs, shifts leftward (upward) to the total-cost supply curve, S_t. Product price increases, equilibrium output falls from Q_e to Q_o, and the initial overallocation of resources shown in **Figure 5.2a** is corrected.

Pigovian tax
A tax or charge levied on the production of a product that generates *negative externalities*. If set correctly, the tax will precisely offset the overallocation (overproduction) generated by the negative externality.

Pigovian Taxes   Another way to approach negative externalities is for government to levy taxes or charges on the related good. These targeted tax assessments are often called **Pigovian taxes**, in honor of A.C. Pigou, the first economist to study externalities. Example: The government has placed a tax on CFCs, which deplete the stratospheric ozone layer protecting Earth from excessive solar ultraviolet radiation. Facing this tax, manufacturers must decide whether to pay the tax or expend additional funds to purchase or develop substitute products. In either case, the tax raises the marginal cost of producing CFCs, shifting the private supply curve for this product leftward (upward).

FIGURE 5.2
Correcting for negative externalities. (a) Negative externalities (spillover costs) result in an overallocation of resources. (b) Government can correct this overallocation in two ways: (1) using direct controls, which would shift the supply curve from S to S_t and reduce output from Q_e to Q_o, or (2) imposing a Pigovian tax T, which would also shift the supply curve from S to S_t, eliminating the overallocation of resources.

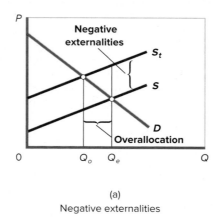

(a)
Negative externalities

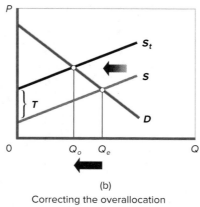

(b)
Correcting the overallocation
of resources via direct controls
or via a tax

In **Figure 5.2b**, a tax equal to T per unit increases the firm's marginal cost, shifting the supply curve from S to S_t. The equilibrium price rises, and the equilibrium output declines from Q_e to the economically efficient level Q_o. The tax thus eliminates the initial overallocation of resources associated with the negative externality.

Subsidies and Government Provision Where spillover benefits (positive externalities) are large and diffuse, as in our earlier example of inoculations, government has three options for correcting the underallocation of resources:

- *Subsidies to buyers* **Figure 5.3a** replicates the supply-demand situation for positive externalities. Government could correct the underallocation of resources to inoculations by subsidizing consumers of the product. It could give each person in the United States a discount coupon to be used to obtain inoculations for themselves and their children. The coupon would reduce the "price" to the person by, say, 50 percent. As shown in **Figure 5.3b**, this program would shift the demand curve for inoculations from too-low, D, to the appropriate D_t. The number of inoculations would rise from Q_e to the economically optimal Q_o, eliminating the underallocation of resources shown in **Figure 5.3a**.

- *Subsidies to producers* A subsidy to producers is a tax in reverse. Taxes are payments *to* the government that increase producers' costs. Subsidies are payments *from* the government that decrease producers' costs. As **Figure 5.3c** shows, a subsidy of U per inoculation to physicians and medical clinics would reduce their marginal costs and shift their supply curve rightward from S_t to S_t'. The output of inoculations would increase from Q_e to the optimal level Q_o, correcting the underallocation of resources shown in **Figure 5.3a**.

- *Government provision* Finally, where positive externalities are extremely large, the government may decide to provide the product for free to everyone. The U.S. government largely eradicated the crippling disease polio by administering free vaccines to all children. India ended smallpox by paying people in rural areas to come to public clinics to have their children vaccinated.

FIGURE 5.3
Correcting for positive externalities. (a) Positive externalities (spillover benefits) result in an underallocation of resources. (b) Government can correct this underallocation through a subsidy to consumers, which shifts market demand from D to D_t and increases output from Q_e to Q_o. (c) Alternatively, government can eliminate the underallocation by giving producers a subsidy of U, which shifts their supply curve from S_t to S_t', increasing output from Q_e to Q_o.

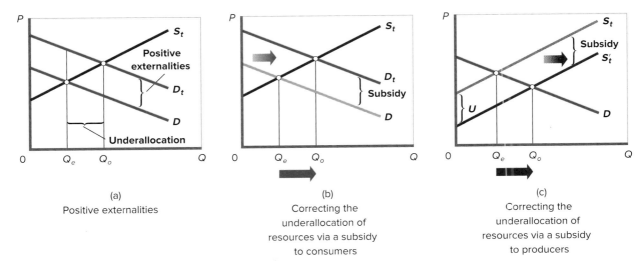

(a)
Positive externalities

(b)
Correcting the underallocation of resources via a subsidy to consumers

(c)
Correcting the underallocation of resources via a subsidy to producers

quasi-public good
A good or service to which exclud-ability could apply but that has such a large spillover benefit that govern-ment sponsors its production to pre-vent an underallocation of resources.

Quasi-Public Goods Government provides many goods that could be produced and delivered in such a way that exclusion would be possible. Such goods, called **quasi-public goods,** include education, streets and highways, police and fire protection, libraries and museums, preventive medicine, and sewage disposal. They could all be priced and provided by private firms through the market system because the free-rider problem would be minimal. But, because spillover benefits extend well beyond the individual buyer, the market system may underproduce them. Therefore, government often provides quasi-public goods to avoid the underallocation of resources that would otherwise occur.

APPLYING THE ANALYSIS

Congestion Pricing

Driving is costly. The private costs include paying for gas and the opportunity cost of the time drivers spend in traffic getting to their destinations. But there are external costs, too.

Stefano Carnevali/Shutterstock

If you are the only person driving down a highway, there is no way for you to impose a negative externality on other drivers. But if traffic is moderate or heavy, your entering a roadway imposes an additional amount of congestion on other drivers. That additional crowding slows traffic down, raising time and gasoline costs for you and everyone else. And the problem is mutual, because the presence of the other drivers imposes a negative congestion externality on you, too.

One solution is to charge people for using the roadway, as with toll roads and the paid express lanes now found in many major cities. The fees that are assessed raise the direct private cost of driving to you and other drivers. But that higher private cost will discourage some people from driving, especially at peak hours. If the tolls are set correctly, drivers will collectively save more in reduced congestion costs than they pay in tolling fees. In the case of highways that have paid express lanes running in parallel with free lanes, drivers will sort themselves according to their opportunity costs and their willingness and ability to pay. Those with low oppor-tunity costs for time will prefer to endure heavier traffic in the free lanes even if they have the ability to pay for the express lanes. But those who have a high opportunity cost for time will prefer to pay for the express lanes whenever they can afford to do so.

QUESTIONS:

What are some other ways that cities try to alleviate congestion? Given that congestion in most cities happens only at certain times, in what ways is congestion pricing a better alternative to some of those other approaches?

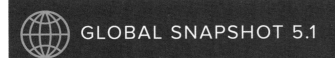

GLOBAL SNAPSHOT 5.1

Percentage of CO$_2$ Emissions Taxed, Selected Nations, 2015

Countries vary widely in the percentage of their total carbon dioxide (CO$_2$) emissions that they tax at a price of \$35 per ton or higher. The percentages vary across countries due to both differences in the tax rate per ton and differences in which industries (agricultural, industrial, transportation, etc.) are subject to CO$_2$ taxes in each country.

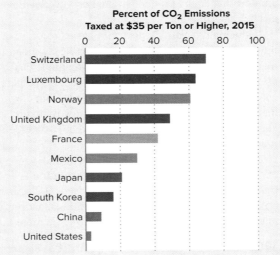

Percent of CO$_2$ Emissions Taxed at \$35 per Ton or Higher, 2015

Source: compareyourcountry.org, Organisation for Economic Co-operation and Development (OECD).

Table 5.3 lists several methods for correcting externalities, including those we have discussed thus far.

TABLE 5.3
Methods for Dealing with Externalities

Problem	Resource Allocation Outcome	Ways to Correct
Negative externalities (spillover costs)	Overproduction of output and therefore overallocation of resources	Private bargaining Liability rules and lawsuits Tax on producers Direct controls Market for externality rights
Positive externalities (spillover benefits)	Underproduction of output and therefore underallocation of resources	Private bargaining Subsidy to consumers Subsidy to producers Government provision

Society's Optimal Amount of Externality Reduction

Negative externalities such as pollution reduce the utility of those affected. These spillovers are not economic goods but economic "bads." If something is bad, shouldn't society eliminate it? Why should society allow firms to discharge *any* impure waste into public waterways or to emit *any* pollution into the air?

Economists answer these questions by pointing out that reducing pollution and negative externalities is not free. There are costs as well as benefits to reducing pollution. As a result, the correct question to ask is not, "Do we pollute a lot or pollute zero?" That is an all-or-nothing question that ignores marginal costs and marginal benefits. Instead, the correct question is, "What is the optimal amount to clean up—the amount that equalizes the marginal cost of cleaning up with the marginal benefit of a cleaner environment?"

Reducing a negative externality has a "price." Society must decide how much of a reduction it wants to "buy." High costs may mean that totally eliminating pollution might not be desirable, even if it is technologically feasible. Because of the law of diminishing returns, cleaning up the second 10 percent of pollutants from an industrial smokestack normally is more costly than cleaning up the first 10 percent. Eliminating the third 10 percent is more costly than cleaning up the second 10 percent, and so on. Therefore, cleaning up the last 10 percent of pollutants is the most costly reduction of all.

The marginal cost (MC) to the firm and hence to society—the opportunity cost of the extra resources used—rises as pollution is reduced more and more. At some point, MC may rise so high that it exceeds society's marginal benefit (MB) of further pollution abatement (reduction). Additional actions to reduce pollution will therefore lower society's well-being; total cost will rise more than total benefit.

MC, MB, and Equilibrium Quantity   **Figure 5.4** shows both the upward sloping marginal-cost curve, MC, for pollution reduction and the downward sloping marginal-benefit curve, MB, for pollution reduction. MB slopes downward because of the law of diminishing marginal utility: The more pollution reduction society accomplishes, the lower the utility (and benefit) of the next unit of pollution reduction.

FIGURE 5.4
Society's optimal amount of pollution abatement. The optimal amount of externality reduction—in this case, pollution abatement—occurs at Q_1, where society's marginal cost MC and marginal benefit MB of reducing the spillover are equal.

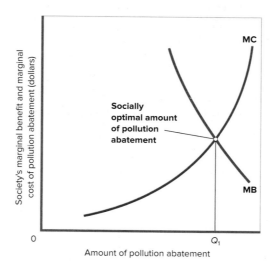

The **optimal reduction of an externality** occurs when society's marginal cost and marginal benefit of reducing that externality are equal (MC = MB). In **Figure 5.4**, this optimal amount of pollution abatement is Q_1 units. When MB exceeds MC, additional abatement moves society toward economic efficiency; the added benefit of cleaner air or water exceeds the benefit of any alternative use of the required resources. When MC exceeds MB, additional abatement reduces economic efficiency; there would be greater benefits from using resources in some other way than to further reduce pollution.

In reality, it is difficult to measure the marginal costs and benefits of pollution control. **Figure 5.4** demonstrates that some pollution may be economically efficient. This is so not because pollution is desirable but because beyond some level of control, further abatement may reduce society's net well-being. For example, it would cost the government billions of dollars to clean up every last piece of litter in America. Thus, it would be better to tolerate some trash blowing around if the money saved by picking up less trash would yield larger net benefits when spent on other things.

Shifts of the MB and MC Curves The locations of the marginal-cost and marginal-benefit curves in **Figure 5.4** are not forever fixed. They can, and probably do, shift over time. For example, suppose that the technology of pollution-control equipment improved noticeably. We would expect the cost of pollution abatement to fall, society's MC curve to shift rightward, and the optimal level of abatement to rise. Or suppose society were to decide it wanted cleaner air and water because of new information about the adverse health effects of pollution. The MB curve in **Figure 5.4** would shift rightward and the optimal level of pollution control would increase beyond Q_1. Test your understanding of these statements by drawing the new MC and MB curves in **Figure 5.4**.

> **optimal reduction of an externality** The reduction of a negative externality such as pollution to a level at which the marginal benefit and marginal cost of reduction are equal.

Financing the Public Sector: Taxation

How are resources reallocated from the production of private goods to the production of public goods (and quasi-public goods)? How are government programs to deal with externalities funded? If the resources of the economy are fully employed, government must free up resources from the production of private goods and make them available for producing public and quasi-public goods. It does so by reducing the demand for private goods. And it does that by levying taxes on households and businesses, taking some of their income out of the circular flow. With lower incomes, and therefore reduced purchasing power, households and businesses must curtail their spending.

As a result, the private demand for goods and services declines, as does the private demand for resources. So by diverting purchasing power from private spenders to government, taxes remove resources from private use.

Government then spends the tax proceeds to provide public and quasi-public goods and services. Taxation releases resources from the production of private consumer goods (food, clothing, television sets) and private investment goods (printing presses, boxcars, warehouses). Government shifts those resources to the production of public and quasi-public goods (post offices, submarines, parks), changing the composition of the economy's total output.

Apportioning the Tax Burden

Once government has decided on the total tax revenue it needs to finance its activities, including the provision of public and quasi-public goods, it must determine how to apportion the tax burden among the citizens. (By "tax burden," we mean the total cost of taxes imposed on society.) This apportionment question affects each of us. The overall level of taxes is important, but the average citizen is much more concerned with their share of taxes.

Benefits Received versus Ability to Pay

Two basic philosophies coexist on how the economy's tax burden should be assigned.

benefits-received principle
The idea that those who receive the benefits of goods and services provided by government should pay the taxes required to finance them.

Benefits Received The **benefits-received principle** of taxation asserts that households and businesses should purchase government goods and services in the same way they buy other commodities. Those who benefit most from government-supplied goods or services should pay the taxes necessary to finance them. A few public goods are financed on this basis. For example, money collected as gasoline taxes is typically used to finance highway construction and repairs. Thus, people who benefit from good roads pay the cost of those roads. Difficulties immediately arise, however, when we consider widespread application of the benefits-received principle:

- How will the government determine the benefits that individual households and businesses receive from national defense, education, the court system, and police and fire protection? Recall that public goods are characterized by nonrivalry and nonexcludability. Thus, benefits from public goods are especially widespread and diffuse. Even in the seemingly straightforward case of highway financing, it is difficult to measure benefits. Good roads benefit the owners of cars in different degrees. But others also benefit. For example, businesses benefit because good roads bring them workers and customers.

- The benefits-received principle cannot logically apply to income redistribution programs. It would be absurd to ask poor families to pay the taxes needed to finance their welfare payments. It would also be self-defeating to tax only unemployed workers to finance the unemployment compensation payments they receive.

ability-to-pay principle
The idea that those who have greater income (or wealth) should pay a greater proportion of it as taxes than those who have less income (or wealth).

Ability to Pay The **ability-to-pay principle** asserts that the tax burden should be apportioned according to taxpayers' income and wealth. In practice, this principle means that individuals and businesses with larger incomes should pay more taxes in both absolute and relative terms than those with smaller incomes.

In justifying the ability-to-pay principle, proponents contend that each additional dollar of income received by a household yields a smaller amount of satisfaction or marginal utility when it is spent. Because consumers act rationally, the first dollars of income received in any time period will be spent on high-urgency goods that yield the greatest marginal utility. Successive dollars of income will be spent on less urgently needed goods and finally for trivial goods and services. Thus, a dollar taken through taxes from a poor person whose income is only a few dollars represents a greater utility sacrifice than a dollar taken through taxes from a rich person who has many dollars. To balance the sacrifices that taxes impose on people of different incomes, the tax burden should fall mostly or entirely on those with higher incomes.

Application problems arise here too. Although we might agree that the household earning $100,000 per year has a greater ability to pay taxes than a household receiving $10,000, we don't know exactly how much more ability to pay the first family has. Should the wealthier family pay the same percentage of its larger income, and hence a larger absolute amount, as taxes? Or should it be made to pay a larger fraction of its income as taxes? And how much larger should that fraction be? Who is to decide?

There is no scientific way of making utility comparisons among individuals and thus of measuring someone's relative ability to pay taxes. In practice, the solution hinges on guesswork, expediency, the tax views of the political party in power, and how urgently the government needs revenue.

Progressive, Proportional, and Regressive Taxes

Any discussion of taxation leads ultimately to the question of tax rates. The **marginal tax rate** is the rate paid on each additional dollar of income (or purchases). The **average tax rate** is the total tax paid as a percentage of income.

Taxes are classified as progressive, regressive, or proportional taxes, depending on the relationship between average tax rates and taxpayer incomes. We focus on incomes because all taxes, whether on income, a product, a building, or a parcel of land, are ultimately paid out of someone's income.

- A tax is **progressive** if its average rate increases as income increases. Such a tax claims not only a larger absolute (dollar) amount but also a larger percentage of income as income increases.

- A tax is **regressive** if its average rate declines as income increases. Such a tax takes a smaller proportion of income as income increases. A regressive tax may or may not take a larger absolute amount of income as income increases. (You may want to derive an example to substantiate this conclusion.)

- A tax is **proportional** if its average rate remains the same regardless of the size of income. Proportional income taxes are often called *flat taxes* or *flat-rate taxes* because their average rates do not vary with (are flat with respect to) income levels.

We can illustrate these ideas with the personal income tax. Suppose tax rates are such that a household pays 10 percent of its income in taxes regardless of the size of its income. This income tax is *proportional.* Now suppose that a household with an annual taxable income of less than $10,000 pays 5 percent in income taxes; a household with an income of $10,000 to $20,000 pays 10 percent; one with a $20,000 to $30,000 income pays 15 percent; and so forth. This income tax is progressive. Finally, suppose the rate declines as taxable income rises: You pay 15 percent if you earn less than $10,000; 10 percent if you earn $10,000 to $20,000; 5 percent if you earn $20,000 to $30,000; and so forth. This income tax is *regressive.*

In general, progressive taxes are those that fall relatively more heavily on people with high incomes; regressive taxes are those that fall relatively more heavily on the poor.

Tax Progressivity in the United States

The progressivity or regressivity of taxes varies by type of tax in the United States. As shown in **Table 5.4**, the federal *personal income tax* is progressive, with marginal tax rates (column 2) ranging from 10 to 37 percent in 2019. Rules that allow deductions for interest on home mortgages and property taxes tend to make the tax less progressive than these marginal rates suggest. Nevertheless, average tax rates (column 4) rise with income.

At first thought, a *general sales tax* with, for example, a 5 percent rate, would seem to be proportional. But, in fact, it is regressive with respect to income. A larger portion of a low-income person's income is exposed to the tax than is the case for a high-income person; the rich pay no tax on the part of income that is saved, whereas the poor are unable to save. Example: "Low-income" Schmidt has an income of $15,000 and spends it all. "High-income" Lopez has an income of $300,000 but spends only $200,000 and saves the rest. Assuming a 5 percent sales tax applies to all expenditures of each individual, we find that Schmidt pays $750 (= 5 percent of $15,000) in sales taxes and Lopez pays $10,000 (= 5 percent of $200,000). But Schmidt pays $750/$15,000, or 5 percent of income as sales taxes, while Lopez pays $10,000/$300,000, or 3.3 percent of income. The general sales tax therefore is regressive.

marginal tax rate
The tax rate paid on an additional dollar of income.

average tax rate
Total tax paid divided by total (taxable) income, as a percentage.

progressive tax
A tax whose average tax rate increases as the taxpayer's income increases and decreases as the taxpayer's income decreases.

regressive tax
A tax whose average tax rate decreases as the taxpayer's income increases and increases as the taxpayer's income decreases.

proportional tax
A tax whose average tax rate remains constant as the taxpayer's income increases or decreases.

TABLE 5.4
Federal Personal Income Tax Rates, 2019*

(1) Total Taxable Income	(2) Marginal Tax Rate, %	(3) Total Tax on Highest Income in Bracket	(4) Average Tax Rate on Highest Income in Bracket, % (3) ÷ (1)
$0–$19,400	10.0	$ 1,940	10
$19,401–$78,950	12.0	9,086	12
$78,951–$168,400	22.0	28,765	17
$168,401–$321,450	24.0	65,496	20
$321,451–$408,200	32.0	93,256	23
$408,201–$612,350	35.0	164,708	27
Over $612,351	37.0		

* For a married couple filing a joint return.

The *federal corporate income tax* is essentially a proportional tax with a flat 21 percent tax rate. In the short run, the corporate owners (shareholders) bear the tax through lower dividends and share values. In the long run, workers may bear some of the tax because it reduces the return on investment and therefore slows capital accumulation. It also causes corporations to relocate to other countries that have lower tax rates. With less capital per worker, U.S. labor productivity may decline and wages may fall. To the extent this happens, the corporate income tax may be somewhat regressive.

Payroll taxes (Social Security and Medicare) are regressive because the Social Security tax applies to only a fixed amount of income. For example, in 2019 the Social Security tax rate on employees was 6.2 percent, but only of the first $132,900 of a person's wage income. The Medicare tax was 1.45 percent of all wage income. Consider a person with $132,900 in wage income. They would pay $10,166.85, or 7.65 percent (6.2 percent + 1.45 percent) of their income in payroll taxes. Someone with twice that wage income, or $265,800, would pay $12,093.90 (= $10,166.85 on the first $132,900 + $1,927.05 on the second $132,900), which is only 4.55 percent of their wage income. Thus, the average payroll tax falls as income rises, confirming that the payroll tax is regressive.

But payroll taxes are even more regressive than suggested by this example because they only apply to wage and salary income. People earning high incomes tend to derive a higher percentage of their total incomes from nonwage sources like rents and dividends than do people who have incomes below the $132,900 cap on which Social Security taxes are paid. Thus, if our individual with $265,800 of wage income also received $265,800 of nonwage income, the $12,093.90 of payroll taxes would be only 2.3 percent of their total income of $531,600.

Most economists conclude that *property taxes* on buildings are regressive for the same reasons as are sales taxes. First, property owners add the tax to the rents they charge tenants. Second, property taxes, as a percentage of income, are higher for low-income families than for high-income families because the poor must spend a larger proportion of their incomes for housing.

Is the overall U.S. tax structure—federal, state, and local taxes combined—progressive, proportional, or regressive? This question is difficult to answer. Estimates of the distribution of the total tax burden depend on the extent to which the various taxes are shifted to others, and who bears the ultimate burden is subject to dispute. But most economists who study taxes conclude the following:

- The federal tax system is progressive. In 2015, the 20 percent of households with the lowest income paid an effective tax rate (on federal income, payroll, and excise taxes) of 1.5 percent. The 20 percent with the highest income paid a 26.7 percent rate; the top 1 percent paid 33.3 percent.

- The state and local tax structures are largely regressive. As a percentage of income, property taxes and sales taxes fall as income rises. Also, state income taxes are generally less progressive than the federal income tax.

- The overall U.S. tax system is slightly progressive. Higher-income people carry a slightly larger tax burden, as a percentage of their income, than do lower-income people.

- The overall U.S. tax system is more progressive than that of other rich countries. A study by the Organisation for Economic Co-operation and Development (OECD) concluded that the U.S. tax system is the most progressive among OECD nations and therefore more progressive than those of Canada, Japan, France, Sweden, Korea, Australia, and dozens of other rich industrialized nations.

Government's Role in the Economy

Along with providing public goods and correcting externalities, government's economic role includes setting the rules and regulations for the economy, redistributing income when desirable, and taking macroeconomic actions to stabilize the economy.

Market failures can be used to justify government interventions in the economy. The inability of private-sector firms to break even when attempting to provide public goods and the over- and underproduction problems caused by positive and negative externalities mean that government can play important role if society's resources are to be efficiently allocated to the goods and services that people most highly desire.

Correcting for market failures is not, however, an easy task. To begin with, government officials must correctly identify the existence and cause of any given market failure. That alone may be difficult, time-consuming, and costly. Even if a market failure is correctly identified and diagnosed, government may fail to take appropriate corrective action due to the fact that government undertakes its economic role in the context of politics.

To serve the public, politicians need to get elected. To stay elected, officials (presidents, senators, representatives, mayors, council members, school board members) need to satisfy their particular constituencies. At best, the political realities complicate government's role in the economy; at worst, they produce undesirable economic outcomes.

In the political context, overregulation can occur in some cases; underregulation in others. Some public and quasi-public goods are produced not because their benefits exceed their costs, but because their benefits accrue to firms located in states served by powerful elected officials. Inefficiency can creep into government activities because of the lack of a profit incentive to hold down costs. Policies to correct negative externalities can be politically blocked by the very parties that are producing the spillovers. Income can be redistributed to such an extent that incentives to work, save, and invest suffer. In short, the economic role of government, although critical to a well-functioning economy, is not always perfectly carried out.

Economists use the term "government failure" to describe economically inefficient outcomes caused by shortcomings in the public sector.

Summary

LO5.1 Differentiate between demand-side market failures and supply-side market failures.

A market failure happens when the market produces an equilibrium level of output that either overallocates or underallocates resources to the product traded in the market. In competitive markets, market failures can be divided into two types: Demand-side market failures occur when demand curves do not reflect consumers' full willingness to pay; supply-side market failures occur when supply curves do not reflect all production costs, including those that may be borne by third parties.

Properly functioning competitive markets ensure that private goods are (a) available, (b) produced in the least costly way, and (c) produced and sold in the "right" amounts.

LO5.2 Distinguish public goods from private goods, and explain how to determine the optimal quantity of a public good.

Private goods are characterized by rivalry (in consumption) and excludability. One person's purchase and consumption of a private good precludes others from also buying and consuming it. Producers can exclude nonpayers (free riders) from receiving the benefits. In contrast, public goods are characterized by nonrivalry (in consumption) and nonexcludability. Public goods are not profitable to private firms because nonpayers (free riders) can obtain and consume those goods without paying. Government can, however, provide desirable public goods, financing them through taxation.

The collective demand schedule for a public good is found by summing the prices that each individual is willing to pay for an additional unit. The optimal quantity of a public good occurs where the society's willingness to pay for the last unit—the marginal benefit of the good—equals the marginal cost of the good.

LO5.3 Explain how positive and negative externalities cause under- and overallocations of resources, and how they might be corrected.

Externalities cause the equilibrium output of goods to vary from society's optimal output. Negative externalities (spillover costs) result in an overallocation of resources to a product. Positive externalities (spillover benefits) involve an underallocation of resources to a product.

Direct controls and Pigovian taxes can improve resource allocation in situations where negative externalities affect many people and community resources. Both direct controls (e.g., smokestack emission standards) and Pigovian taxes (e.g., taxes on firms producing toxic chemicals) increase production costs and hence product price. As product price rises, the externality and overallocation of resources are reduced because less of the output is produced.

Government can correct the underallocation of resources in a market either by subsidizing consumers (which increases market demand) or by subsidizing producers (which increases market supply). Such subsidies increase the equilibrium output, reducing or eliminating the positive externality and consequent underallocation of resources.

The Coase theorem suggests that private bargaining can solve externality problems. Thus, government intervention is not always needed to deal with externality problems.

The socially optimal amount of externality abatement occurs where society's marginal cost and marginal benefit of reducing the externality are equal. With pollution, for example, this optimal amount of pollution abatement is likely to be less than a 100 percent reduction. Changes in technology or changes in society's attitudes toward pollution can affect the optimal amount of pollution abatement.

LO5.4 Describe the differences between the benefits-received and ability-to-pay principles of taxation.

Government reallocates resources from the private sector to the public sector through taxation, which decreases after-tax income and therefore reduces the demand for private goods. Government then uses the tax revenues to finance the provision of public and quasi-public goods.

The benefits-received principle of taxation states that those who receive the benefits of goods and services provided by government should pay the taxes required to finance them. The ability-to-pay principle states that those who have greater income should be taxed more, absolutely and relatively, than those who have less income.

LO5.5 Distinguish between proportional, progressive, and regressive taxes.

The federal income tax is progressive (average tax rate rises as income rises). The corporate income tax is roughly proportional (average tax rate remains constant as income rises). General sales, excise, payroll, and property taxes are regressive (average tax rate falls as income rises). Overall, the U.S. tax system is slightly progressive.

Market failures present government with opportunities to improve the allocation of society's resources and thereby enhance society's total well-being. But even when government correctly identifies the existence and cause of a market failure, political pressures may make it difficult or impossible for government officials to implement a proper solution.

Terms and Concepts

market failure	cost-benefit analysis	benefits-received principle
demand-side market failures	negative externalities	ability-to-pay principle
supply-side market failures	positive externalities	marginal tax rate
productive efficiency	Coase theorem	average tax rate
allocative efficiency	Pigovian tax	progressive tax
private good	quasi-public good	regressive tax
public good	optimal reduction of an	proportional tax
free-rider problem	externality	

Questions

1. Explain the two causes of market failures. Given their definitions, could a market be affected by both types of market failures simultaneously? **(LO1)**

2. What are the two characteristics of public goods? Explain the significance of each for public provision as opposed to private provision. What is the free-rider problem as it relates to public goods? **(LO2)**

3. Draw a production possibilities curve with public goods on the vertical axis and private goods on the horizontal axis. Assuming the economy is initially operating on the curve, indicate how the production of public goods might be increased. How might the output of public goods be increased if the economy is initially operating at a point inside the curve? **(LO2)**

4. Use the distinction between the characteristics of private and public goods to determine whether the following should be produced through the market system or provided by government: (a) French fries, (b) airport screening, (c) court systems, (d) mail delivery, and (e) medical care. Explain your answers. **(LO2)**

5. What divergences arise between equilibrium output and efficient output when (a) negative externalities and (b) positive externalities are present? How might government correct these divergences? Cite an example (other than the text examples) of an external cost and an external benefit. **(LO3)**

6. Why are spillover costs and spillover benefits also called negative and positive externalities? Show graphically how a tax can correct for a negative externality and how a subsidy to producers can correct for a positive externality. How does a subsidy to consumers differ from a subsidy to producers in correcting for a positive externality? **(LO3)**

7. An apple grower's orchard provides nectar to a neighbor's bees, while the beekeeper's bees help the apple grower by pollinating his apple blossoms. Use **Figure 5.1b** to explain why this situation of dual positive externalities might lead to an underallocation of resources to both apple growing and beekeeping. How might this underallocation get resolved via the means suggested by the Coase theorem? **(LO3)**

8. The LoJack car recovery system allows the police to track stolen cars. As a result, they not only recover 90 percent of LoJack-equipped cars that are stolen, but also arrest many auto thieves and shut down many "chop shops" that rip apart stolen vehicles to get their parts. Thus, LoJack provides both private benefits and positive externalities. Should the government consider subsidizing LoJack purchases? **(LO3)**

9. Use marginal-cost–marginal-benefit analysis to determine if the following statement is true or false: "The optimal amount of pollution abatement for some substances, say, dirty water from storm drains, is very low; the optimal amount of abatement for other substances, say, cyanide poison, is close to 100 percent." **(LO3)**

10. Explain why zoning laws, which allow certain land uses only in specific locations, might be justified in dealing with negative externalities. Explain why in areas where buildings sit close together, tax breaks to property owners for installing extra fire prevention equipment might be justified in view of positive externalities. **(LO3)**

11. Distinguish between the benefits-received and the ability-to-pay principles of taxation. Which philosophy is more evident in our present tax structure? Justify your answer. To which principle of taxation do you subscribe? Why? **(LO4)**

12. What is meant by a progressive tax? A regressive tax? A proportional tax? Comment on the progressivity or regressivity of each of the following taxes, indicating in each case where you think the tax incidence lies: (a) the federal personal income tax, (b) a 4 percent state general

sales tax, (c) a federal excise tax on automobile tires, (d) a municipal property tax on real estate, (e) the federal corporate income tax, (f) the portion of the payroll tax levied on employers. **(LO5)**

13. Is it possible for a country with a regressive tax system to have a tax-spending system that transfers resources from the rich to the poor? **(LO5)**

Problems

1. The accompanying table shows the total costs and total benefits, in billions of U.S. dollars, for four different antipollution programs of increasing scope. Use cost-benefit analysis to determine which program should be undertaken. **(LO2)**

Program	Total Cost	Total Benefit
A	$ 100	$200
B	280	350
C	480	470
D	1,240	580

2. On the basis of the three individual demand schedules in the following table, and assuming these three people are the only ones in the society, determine (a) the market demand schedule on the assumption that the good is a private good and (b) the collective demand schedule on the assumption that the good is a public good. **(LO2)**

P	$Q_d\ (D_1)$	$Q_d\ (D_2)$	$Q_d\ (D_3)$
$8	0	1	0
7	0	2	0
6	0	3	1
5	1	4	2
4	2	5	3
3	3	6	4
2	4	7	5
1	5	8	6

3. Use your demand schedule for a public good, determined in problem 2, and the following supply schedule to ascertain the optimal quantity of this public good. **(LO2)**

P	Q_s
$19	10
16	8
13	6
10	4
7	2
4	1

4. Look at the following tables, which show, respectively, buyers' willingness to pay for and sellers' willingness to accept, bags of oranges. For the following questions, assume that the equilibrium price and quantity will depend on the indicated changes in supply and demand. Assume that the only market participants are those listed by name in the two tables. **(LO3)**

Person	Maximum Price Willing to Pay	Actual Price (Equilibrium Price)
Bob	$13	$8
Barb	12	8
Bill	11	8
Bart	10	8
Brent	9	8
Betty	8	8

Person	Minimum Acceptable Price	Actual Price (Equilibrium Price)
Carlos	$3	$8
Courtney	4	8
Chuck	5	8
Cindy	6	8
Craig	7	8
Chad	8	8

a. What are the equilibrium price and quantity for the data displayed in the two tables?

b. What if, instead of bags of oranges, the data in the two tables dealt with a public good like fireworks displays? If all the buyers free ride, what will be the quantity supplied by private sellers?

c. Assume we are back to talking about bags of oranges (a private good), but that the government has decided that tossed orange peels impose a negative externality on the public that must be rectified by imposing a $2-per-bag tax on sellers. What are the new equilibrium price and quantity? If the new equilibrium quantity is the optimal quantity, by how many bags were oranges being overproduced before?

5. Suppose a tax is such that an individual with an income of $10,000 pays $2,000 of tax, a person with an income of $20,000 pays $3,000 of tax, a person with an income of $30,000 pays $4,000 of tax, and so forth. What is each person's average tax rate? Is this tax regressive, proportional, or progressive? **(LO5)**

6. Suppose in Fiscalville there is no tax on the first $10,000 of income, but there is a 20 percent tax on earnings between $10,000 and $20,000 and a 30 percent tax on income between $20,000 and $30,000. Any income above $30,000 is taxed at 40 percent. If your income is $50,000, how much will you pay in taxes? Determine your marginal and average tax rates. Is Fiscalville's income tax progressive? **(LO5)**

7. For tax purposes, "gross income" is all the money a person receives in a given year from any source. But income taxes are levied on "taxable income" rather than on gross income. The difference between the two is the result of many exemptions and deductions. To see how they work, suppose you made $60,000 last year in wages, earned $10,000 from investments, and received a $5,000 gift from your grandmother. Also, assume that you are a single parent with one small child living with you. **(LO5)**

    a. What is your gross income?

    b. Gifts of up to $15,000 per year from any person are not counted as taxable income. Given that exemption, what is your taxable income?

    c. Next, assume you paid $700 in interest on your student loans last year, put $2,000 into a health savings account (HSA), and deposited $4,000 into an individual retirement account (IRA). These expenditures are all *tax exempt*, meaning that any money spent on them reduces taxable income dollar for dollar. Knowing that fact, now what is your taxable income?

    d. Next, you can either take the so-called *standard deduction* or apply for itemized deductions (which involve a lot of tedious paperwork). You opt for the standard deduction that allows you, as head of your household, to exempt another $18,350 from your taxable income. Taking that into account, what is your taxable income?

    e. Apply the tax rates shown in **Table 5.4** to your taxable income. How much federal income tax will you owe? What marginal tax rate applies to your last dollar of taxable income?

    f. As the parent of a dependent child, you qualify for the government's $2,000-per-child "tax credit." Like all tax credits, this $2,000 credit "pays" for $2,000 of whatever amount of tax you owe. Given this credit, how much money will you actually have to pay in taxes? Using that actual amount, what is your average tax rate relative to your taxable income? What is your average tax rate relative to your gross income?

Product Markets

CHAPTER SIX
Businesses and Their Costs

Learning Objectives

LO6.1   Explain why economic costs include both explicit costs and implicit costs.

LO6.2   Relate the law of diminishing returns to a firm's short-run production costs.

LO6.3   Distinguish between fixed and variable costs and among total, average, and marginal costs.

LO6.4   Use economies of scale to link a firm's size and its average costs in the long run.

LO6.5   Give business examples of short-run costs, economies of scale, and minimum efficient scale.

In market economies, a wide variety of businesses produce an even greater variety of goods and services. Each of those businesses needs economic resources in order to produce its product. In obtaining and using resources, a business makes monetary payments to resource owners (e.g., workers) and incurs opportunity costs when using resources that it already owns (e.g., entrepreneurial talent). Those payments and opportunity costs constitute the firm's *costs of production,* which we discuss in this chapter. In the chapters that follow, we bring demand, product price, and revenue into the analysis and explain how businesses compare revenues and costs to decide how much to produce and how much to charge.

Economic Costs

economic cost
A payment that must be made to obtain and retain the services of a resource; the income a firm must provide to a resource supplier to attract the resource away from an alternative use; equal to the quantity of other products that cannot be produced when resources are instead used to make a particular product.

Because resources are scarce, firms wanting a particular resource have to bid it away from other firms. For this reason, economists define an **economic cost** as the payment that must be made to obtain and retain the services of a resource. It is the income the firm must provide to resource suppliers to attract resources away from alternative uses.

This section explains how firms incorporate opportunity costs to calculate economic costs. If you need a refresher on opportunity costs, see Chapter 1.

Explicit and Implicit Costs

All resources used by the firm have an opportunity cost. This is true both for the resources that a firm purchases from outsiders, as well as for the resources it already owns. As a result, *all* of the resources a firm uses have economic costs. Economists refer to these two types of economic costs as *explicit costs* and *implicit costs*:

explicit cost
The monetary payment a firm must make to an outsider to obtain a resource.

- A firm's **explicit costs** are the monetary payments it makes to purchase resources from others. Because these costs involve an obvious cash transaction, they are called explicit costs. Remember that explicit costs are opportunity costs because every purchase of outside resources necessarily involves forgoing the best alternatives that could have been purchased with the money.

implicit cost
The monetary income a firm sacrifices when it uses a resource it owns rather than supplying the resource in the market; equal to what the resource could have earned in the best-paying alternative employment; includes a normal profit.

- A firm's **implicit costs** are the opportunity costs of using the resources it already owns rather than selling those resources to outsiders for cash. Because these costs are present but not obvious, they are called implicit costs.

A firm's economic costs are the sum of its explicit costs and its implicit costs:

$$\text{Economic costs} = \text{Explicit costs} + \text{Implicit costs}$$

Accounting Profit and Normal Profit

Suppose that after considering many potential business ventures, you decide to open a retail T-shirt shop. As explained in Chapter 2, you will be providing two different economic resources to your new enterprise: labor and entrepreneurial ability. Your labor includes the routine tasks that help run the business—things like answering customer e-mails, taking inventory, and sweeping the floor. Providing entrepreneurial ability includes any nonroutine tasks involved with organizing the business and directing its strategy—things like deciding on whether to include children's clothing in your product mix and how to brand your store.

You begin providing entrepreneurial ability by making some initial organizational decisions. You decide to work full time at your new business, so you quit your old job that paid you $22,000 per year. Then, you invest $20,000 of savings that has been earning $1,000 per year interest. You decide that your new firm will occupy a small retail space that you own but had previously rented out for $5,000 per year. Finally, you decide to hire one clerk, whom you will pay $18,000 per year.

After a year in business, you total up your accounts and find the following:

Total sales revenue	$ 120,000
Cost of T-shirts	$40,000
Clerk's salary	18,000
Utilities	5,000
Total (explicit) costs	63,000
Accounting profit	$ 57,000

These numbers look very good. You are happy with your $57,000 **accounting profit,** the profit number that accountants calculate by subtracting total explicit costs from total sales revenue. This is the profit (or "net income") that appears on your accounting statement and that you report to the government for tax purposes.

accounting profit
The total revenue of a firm less its explicit costs.

But don't celebrate yet! Your $57,000 accounting profit overstates the economic success of your business because it ignores your implicit costs. The true measure of success is doing as well as you possibly can—that is, making more money in your new venture selling T-shirts than you could pursuing any other business venture.

To determine whether you are achieving that goal, you must take into account *all* of your opportunity costs—both your implicit costs as well as your explicit costs. To make these calculations, let's continue with our example.

By providing your own financial capital, retail space, and labor, you incurred three different implicit costs during the year: $1,000 of forgone interest, $5,000 of forgone rent, and $22,000 of forgone wages. There is also another implicit cost you must account for—how much income you chose to forgo by applying your entrepreneurial abilities to your retail T-shirt venture rather than to another venture. But what dollar value should we place on the profits that you might have made if you had provided your entrepreneurial ability to another venture?

The answer is given by estimating a **normal profit,** the typical (or "normal") amount of accounting profit that you would most likely have earned in other ventures. Let's assume that with your particular set of skills and talents, your entrepreneurial abilities would have yielded a normal profit of $5,000 in other potential ventures. Knowing that value, we can take all of your implicit costs into account and subtract them from your accounting profit:

normal profit
The payment made by a firm to obtain and retain entrepreneurial ability; the minimum income entrepreneurial ability must receive to induce it to perform entrepreneurial functions for a firm.

Accounting profit	$57,000
Forgone interest	$ 1,000
Forgone rent	5,000
Forgone wages	22,000
Forgone entrepreneurial income	5,000
Total implicit costs	33,000
Economic profit	$24,000

After subtracting your $33,000 of implicit costs from your accounting profit of $57,000, we are left with an *economic profit* of $24,000.

Economic Profit

Please distinguish clearly between accounting profit and economic profit. Accounting profit is the result of subtracting only explicit costs from revenue: *Accounting Profit = Revenue - Explicit Costs.* By contrast, **economic profit** accounts for all of your economic costs—both explicit costs and implicit costs: *Economic Profit = Revenue - Explicit Costs - Implicit Costs.*

economic profit
The total revenue of a firm less its economic costs (which include both explicit costs and implicit costs); also called *pure profit* and *above-normal profit.*

By subtracting all your economic costs from your revenue, you determine how your current business venture compares with your best alternative business venture. In our example, the fact that you are generating an economic profit of $24,000 means you are making $24,000 more than you could expect to make in your best alternative business venture.

By contrast, suppose that your T-shirt business had done poorly, so that this year your firm generated an economic loss (a negative economic profit) of $8,000. In that case, you did worse in your current venture than you could have done in your best alternative venture. As a result, you would wish to switch to that alternative.

From these examples, we see that there is an important behavioral threshold at $0 of economic profit. If a firm is breaking even (i.e., earning exactly $0 of economic profit), then its entrepreneurs know that they are doing exactly as well as they could expect to do in their best alternative business venture. They are earning enough to cover all their explicit and implicit costs, including the normal profit they could expect to earn in other business ventures. Thus, they have no incentive to change. By contrast, those achieving positive economic profits know they are doing better than they could in alternative ventures and will want to continue doing what they are doing or maybe even expand their business. Those with an economic loss know they can do better by switching to something else.

For these reasons, economists focus on economic profits rather than accounting profits. Simply put, economic profits allocate resources to their best use. Entrepreneurs running economic losses close their businesses, thereby liberating the land, labor, capital, and entrepreneurial ability they had been using. These resources are freed up for use by firms that generate positive economic profits or at least break even. Resources thus flow from producing goods and services with lower net benefits toward producing goods and services with higher net benefits. Allocative efficiency increases as profit signals lead firms to produce more of what consumers want the most.

Figure 6.1 summarizes the relationships among the various cost and profit concepts that we have just discussed. To test yourself, enter the cost data from our example in the appropriate blocks.

Short Run and Long Run

When the demand for a firm's product changes, the firm's profitability may depend on how quickly it can adjust its use of resources. It can easily and quickly adjust the quantities employed of hourly labor, raw materials, fuel, and power. It needs much more time, however, to adjust its *plant capacity*—the size of the factory building, the amount of machinery and equipment, and other capital resources. In some heavy industries such as aircraft manufacturing, a firm may need several years to alter plant capacity. Because of these differences in adjustment time, economists find it useful to distinguish between two conceptual periods: the short run and the long run.

FIGURE 6.1
Economic profit versus accounting profit. Economic profit is equal to total revenue less economic costs. Economic costs are the sum of explicit and implicit costs and include a normal profit to the entrepreneur. Accounting profit is equal to total revenue less accounting (explicit) costs.

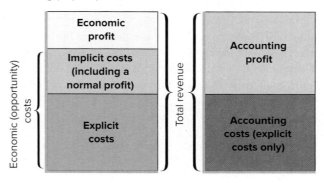

Short Run: Fixed Plant In microeconomics, the **short run** is a period too brief for a firm to alter its plant capacity, yet long enough to permit a change in the degree to which the plant's current capacity is used. The firm's plant capacity is fixed in the short run. However, the firm can vary its output by applying larger or smaller amounts of labor, materials, and other resources to that plant. That is, it can use its existing plant capacity more or less intensively in the short run.

Long Run: Variable Plant In microeconomics, the **long run** is a period long enough for a firm to adjust the quantities of all the resources it employs, including plant capacity. From the industry's viewpoint, the long run also includes enough time for existing firms to leave the industry or for new firms to enter the industry. While the short run is a "fixed-plant" period, the long run is a "variable-plant" period.

If Boeing hires 1,000 extra workers for one of its commercial airline plants or adds an entire shift of workers, we are speaking of the short run. If it adds a new production facility and installs more equipment, we are referring to the long run. The first situation is a *short-run adjustment;* the second *is a long-run adjustment.*

The short run and the long run are conceptual periods rather than calendar time periods. As indicated in the Photo Op, light-manufacturing industries can accomplish changes in plant capacity almost overnight. But for heavy industry the long run is a different matter. A firm may require several years to construct a new facility.

short run
(1) In microeconomics, a period of time in which producers are able to change the quantities of some but not all of the resources they employ; a period in which some resources (usually plant) are fixed and some are variable. (2) In macroeconomics, a period in which nominal wages and other input prices do not change in response to a change in the price level.

long run
(1) In microeconomics, a period of time long enough to enable producers of a product to change the quantities of all the resources they employ; period in which all resources and costs are variable and no resources or costs are fixed. (2) In macroeconomics, a period sufficiently long for nominal wages and other input prices to change in response to a change in the nation's price level.

PHOTO OP

Long-Run Adjustments by Firms

An apparel manufacturer can make long-run adjustments to add production capacity in a matter of days by leasing another building and ordering and installing extra sewing machines. In contrast, an oil firm may need 2 to 3 years to construct a new refinery to increase its production capacity.

©Roberto Westbrookk/Blend Images RF

©Steve Allen/Brand X Pictures/Alamy Images RF

Short-Run Production Relationships

A firm's cost to produce a specific output depends on both the prices and the quantities of those resources (inputs) needed to produce that output. Resource supply and demand determine resource prices. The technological aspects of production, specifically the relationships between inputs and output, determine the quantities of resources needed. Here we focus on the *labor*-output relationship, given a fixed plant capacity. But before examining that relationship, we need to define three terms:

total product (TP)
The total output of a particular good or service produced by a firm (or a group of firms or the entire economy).

marginal product (MP)
The additional output produced when 1 additional unit of a resource is employed (the quantity of all other resources employed remaining constant); equal to the change in total product divided by the change in the quantity of a resource employed.

average product (AP)
The total output produced per unit of a resource employed (total product divided by the quantity of that employed resource).

- **Total product (TP)** is the total quantity, or total output, of a particular good or service produced.

- **Marginal product (MP)** is the extra output or added product associated with adding one more unit of a variable resource, in this case labor, to the production process.

$$\text{Marginal product} = \frac{\text{change in total product}}{\text{change in labor input}}$$

- **Average product (AP)**, also called *labor productivity,* is output per unit of labor input:

$$\text{Average product} = \frac{\text{total product}}{\text{units of labor}}$$

In the short run, a firm for a time can increase its output by adding units of labor to its fixed plant. But by how much will output rise when it adds the labor? Why do we say "for a time"?

Law of Diminishing Returns

law of diminishing returns
The principle that as successive increments of a variable resource are added to a fixed resource, the marginal product of the variable resource will eventually decrease.

The answers are provided in general terms by the **law of diminishing returns.** This law assumes that technology is fixed and thus production techniques do not change. Consequently, as successive units of a variable resource (say, labor) are added to a fixed resource (say, capital or land), beyond some point the extra, or marginal, product of each additional unit of the variable resource will decline. For example, if additional workers are hired to work with a constant amount of capital equipment, output will eventually rise by smaller and smaller amounts as more workers are hired.

Relevancy for Firms

The law of diminishing returns is highly relevant for production within firms. As successive units of a variable input (say, labor) to a fixed input (say, capital), the marginal product of labor eventually declines. Diminishing returns will occur sooner or later. Total product eventually will rise at a diminishing rate, reach a maximum, and then decline.

Suppose a farmer has a fixed resource—80 acres of land—planted in corn. If the farmer does not cultivate the cornfields (clear the weeds) at all, the yield will be 40 bushels per acre. Cultivating the land once may cause output to rise to 50 bushels per acre. A second cultivation may increase output to 57 bushels per acre, a third to 61, and a fourth to 63. Succeeding cultivations will add less and less to the land's yield. If this were not so, the world's needs for corn could be fulfilled by extremely intense cultivation of this single 80-acre plot of land. Indeed, if diminishing returns did not occur, the world could be fed out of a flowerpot.

ILLUSTRATING THE IDEA

Diminishing Returns from Study

The following noneconomic example of a relationship between "inputs" and "output" may help you better understand the idea. Suppose for an individual that

> Total course learning = f(intelligence, quality of course materials, instructor effectiveness, class time, and study time)

where f means "function of" or "depends on." So this relationship supposes that total course learning depends on intelligence (however defined), the quality of course materials such as the textbook, the effectiveness of the instructor, the amount of class time, and the amount of personal study time outside the class.

For analytical purposes, let's assume that one's intelligence, the quality of course materials, the effectiveness of the instructor, and the amount of class time are *fixed*—meaning they do not change over the length of the course. Now let's add units of study time per day over the length of the course to "produce" greater course learning. The first hour of study time per day increases total course learning. Will the second hour enhance course learning by as much as the first? By how much will the third, fourth, fifth, . . . or fifteenth hour of study per day contribute to total course learning relative to the *immediately previous hour*?

We think you will agree that eventually diminishing returns to course learning will set in as successive hours of study are added each day. At some point, the marginal product of an extra hour of study time will decline and, at some further point, become zero.

> QUESTION:
> Given diminishing returns to study time, why devote any extra time to study?

The law of diminishing returns also holds true in nonagricultural industries. Assume a wood shop is manufacturing furniture frames. It has a specific amount of equipment such as lathes, planers, saws, and sanders. If this shop hired just one or two workers, total output and productivity (output per worker) would be very low. Machines would stand idle much of the time. In short, the plant would be under-staffed, and production would be inefficient because there would be too much capital relative to the amount of labor.

The shop could eliminate those difficulties by hiring more workers. Then, the equipment would be more fully used, and workers could specialize in doing a single job. As more workers were added, production would become more efficient and the marginal product of each succeeding worker would rise.

But the rise will not continue indefinitely. Beyond a certain point, adding more workers will cause overcrowding. Workers will have to wait in line to use the machinery. Total output will increase at a diminishing rate because, given the fixed size of the plant, each worker will have less capital equipment to work with as more labor is hired. The marginal product of additional workers will decline because there will be more labor in proportion to the fixed amount of capital. Eventually, adding more workers would cause so much congestion that marginal product would become negative and total product would decline. At the extreme, the addition of more and more labor would exhaust all the standing room, and total product would fall to zero.

The law of diminishing returns assumes that all units of labor are of equal quality. Each successive worker is presumed to have the same innate ability, motor coordination, education, and work experience. Marginal product ultimately diminishes, but not because success workers are less skilled or less energetic. It declines because the firm is using more workers relative to the amount of plant and equipment available.

Tabular and Graphical Representations

The table in **Figure 6.2** illustrates the law of diminishing returns. Column 2 shows the total product, or total output, resulting from combining each level of a variable input (labor) in column 1 with a fixed amount of capital.

Column 3 shows the marginal product (MP), the change in total product associated with each additional unit of labor. With no labor input, total product is zero; a plant with no workers will produce no output. The first three units of labor generate increasing marginal returns, with marginal products of 10, 15, and 20 units, respectively. Beginning with the fourth unit of labor, marginal product diminishes continuously, becoming zero with the seventh unit of labor and negative with the eighth.

Average product, or output per labor unit, is shown in column 4. It is calculated by dividing total product (column 2) by the number of labor units needed to produce it (column 1). At 5 units of labor, for example, AP is 14 (= 70/5).

Figure 6.2 also shows the diminishing-returns data graphically and further clarifies the relationships between total, marginal, and average products. Note first in **Figure 6.2a** that total product, TP, goes through three phases: It rises initially at an increasing rate; then it increases, but at a diminishing rate; finally, after reaching a maximum, it declines.

Marginal product—shown by the MP curve in **Figure 6.2b**—is the slope of the total-product curve. Marginal product measures the change in total product associated with each additional unit of labor. Thus, the three phases of total product are also reflected in marginal product. Where total product is increasing at an increasing rate, marginal product is rising. Here, extra units of labor are adding larger and larger amounts to total product. Where total product is increasing but at a decreasing rate, marginal product is positive but falling. Each additional unit of labor adds less to total product than did the previous unit. When total product is at a maximum, marginal product is zero. When total product declines, marginal product becomes negative.

Average product, AP (**Figure 6.2b**), displays the same tendencies as marginal product. It increases, reaches a maximum, and then decreases as more and more units of labor are added to the fixed plant. But note the relationship between marginal product and average product: Where marginal product exceeds average product, average product rises. And where marginal product is less than average product, average product declines. It follows that marginal product intersects average product where average product is at a maximum.

FIGURE 6.2

The law of diminishing returns. (a) As a variable resource (labor) is added to fixed amounts of other resources (land or capital), the total product that results will eventually increase by diminishing amounts, reach a maximum, and then decline. (b) Marginal product is the change in total product associated with each new unit of labor. Average product is simply output per labor unit. Note that marginal product intersects average product at the maximum average product.

(1) Units of the Variable Resource (Labor)	(2) Total Product (TP)	(3) Marginal Product (MP), Change in (2)/ Change in (1)		(4) Average Product (AP), (2)/(1)
0	0			—
1	10	10 ⎫ Increasing		10.00
2	25	15 ⎬ marginal		12.50
3	45	20 ⎭ returns		15.00
4	60	15 ⎫ Diminishing		15.00
5	70	10 ⎬ marginal		14.00
6	75	5 ⎭ returns		12.50
7	75	0 ⎫ Negative		10.71
8	70	−5 ⎬ marginal returns		8.75

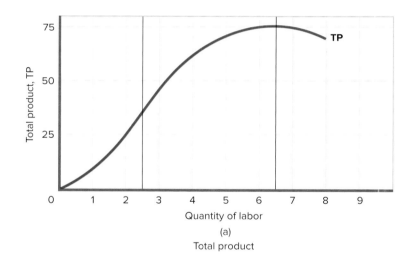

(a)
Total product

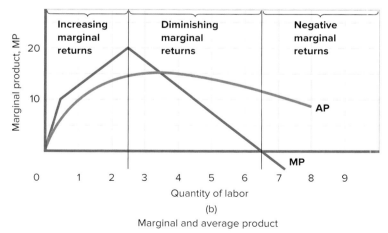

(b)
Marginal and average product

ILLUSTRATING THE IDEA

Exam Scores

The relationship between "marginal" and "average" shown in **Figure 6.2b** is a mathematical necessity. If you add to a total a number larger than the current average of that total, the average must rise. If you add to a total a number smaller than the current average of that total, the average must fall. You raise your average examination grade only when your score on an additional (marginal) examination is greater than the average of all your past scores. You lower your average when your grade on an additional exam is below your current average. In our production example, when the amount an extra worker adds to total product exceeds the average product of all workers currently employed, average product will rise. Conversely, when the amount an extra worker adds to total product is less than the current average product, average product will decrease.

QUESTIONS:

Suppose your average exam score for the first three exams is 80 and you receive a 92 on your fourth exam. What is your marginal score? What is your new average score? Why did your average go up?

Short-Run Production Costs

Production information such as that in **Figure 6.2** must be coupled with resource prices to determine the total and per-unit costs of producing various levels of output. We know that in the short run, resources associated with the firm's plant are fixed. Other resources, however, are variable in the short run. As a result, short-run costs can be either fixed or variable.

Fixed, Variable, and Total Costs

Let's see what distinguishes fixed costs, variable costs, and total costs from one another.

fixed cost
Any cost that in total does not change when the firm changes its output; the cost of fixed resources.

Fixed Costs   **Fixed costs** are costs that do not vary with changes in output. Fixed costs are associated with the very existence of a firm's plant and therefore must be paid even if its output is zero. Rental payments, interest on a firm's debts, and insurance premiums are generally fixed costs; they do not change even if a firm produces more. In column 2 of **Figure 6.3**'s table, we assume that the firm's total fixed cost is $100. By definition, this fixed cost is incurred at all levels of output, including zero. The firm cannot avoid paying fixed costs in the short run.

variable cost
A cost that in total increases when the firm increases its output and decreases when the firm reduces its output.

Variable Costs   **Variable costs** change with the level of output. They include payments for materials, fuel, power, transportation services, most labor, and similar variable resources. In column 3 of the table in **Figure 6.3**, we find that the total of variable costs changes directly with output.

FIGURE 6.3

A firm's cost curves. Average fixed cost (AFC) falls as a given amount of fixed costs is apportioned over a larger and larger output. Average variable cost (AVC) initially falls because of increasing marginal returns but then rises because of diminishing marginal returns. The marginal-cost (MC) curve eventually rises because of diminishing returns and cuts through the average-total-cost (ATC) curve and the AVC curve at their minimum points.

Total-Cost Data				Average-Cost Data			Marginal Cost
(1)	(2)	(3)	(4)	(5)	(6)	(7)	(8)
				Average Fixed	Average Variable	Average Total Cost	
Total Product (Q)	Total Fixed Cost (TFC)	Total Variable Cost (TVC)	Total Cost (TC) $TC = TFC + TVC$	Cost (AFC) $AFC = \dfrac{TFC}{Q}$	Cost (AVC) $AVC = \dfrac{TVC}{Q}$	(ATC) $ATC = \dfrac{TC}{Q}$	Marginal Cost (MC) $MC = \dfrac{\text{change in TC}}{\text{change in Q}}$
0	$100	$ 0	$ 100				
1	100	90	190	$100.00	$90.00	$190.00	$ 90
2	100	170	270	50.00	85.00	135.00	80
3	100	240	340	33.33	80.00	113.33	70
4	100	300	400	25.00	75.00	100.00	60
5	100	370	470	20.00	74.00	94.00	70
6	100	450	550	16.67	75.00	91.67	80
7	100	540	640	14.29	77.14	91.43	90
8	100	650	750	12.50	81.25	93.75	110
9	100	780	880	11.11	86.67	97.78	130
10	100	930	1030	10.00	93.00	103.00	150

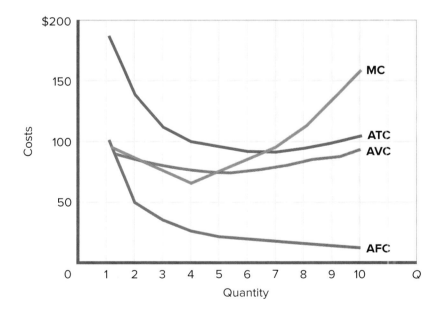

APPLYING THE ANALYSIS

Sunk Costs

It is a deep-seated human tendency to drag past costs—so-called sunk costs—into marginal-benefit, marginal-cost calculations. Doing so is known as the *sunk cost fallacy.*

As an example of this error, suppose a family on vacation stops at a roadside stand to buy some apples. After driving a bit, they discover that the apples are mushy and gross. Would it be logical for a parent to insist that everyone eat the apples "because we paid a premium price for them?" Absolutely not. In making a new decision, you should ignore all costs that are not affected by that new decision. The prior bad decision (in retrospect) to buy the apples should not dictate a subsequent decision for which marginal benefit is less than marginal cost.

Consider a business example. Suppose a firm spends $1 million on R&D to bring out a new product, only to discover that the product sells very poorly. Should the firm continue to produce the product at a loss even when there is no realistic hope for future success? Obviously, it should not. In making this decision, the firm realizes that the amount it has spent in developing the product is irrelevant; it should stop production of the product and cut its losses.

The emotional tendency that drives the sunk cost fallacy is the desire to "get one's money's worth" out of a past expenditure. But giving in to that emotion can lead to "throwing good money after bad." Both individuals and firms should ignore all sunk costs and focus solely on those that depend on the decision at hand.

> QUESTION:
>
> Which is a sunk cost rather than simply a recurring fixed cost: (1) a prior expenditure on a business computer that is now outdated or (2) a current monthly payment on an equipment lease that runs for 6 more months? Explain.

total cost
The sum of fixed cost and variable cost.

Total Cost **Total cost** is the sum of total fixed cost and total variable cost at each level of output.

$$TC = TFC + TVC$$

TC is shown in column 4 of the table in **Figure 6.3**. At zero units of output, total cost is equal to the firm's fixed cost. Then, for each unit of the 10 units of production, total cost increases by the same amount as variable cost.

The distinction between fixed and variable costs is significant to the business manager. Variable costs can be controlled or altered in the short run by changing production levels. Fixed costs are beyond the business manager's current control; they are incurred in the short run and must be paid regardless of output level.

Per-Unit, or Average, Costs

Producers are certainly interested in their total costs, but they are equally concerned with per-unit, or average, costs. In particular, average-cost data are more meaningful for making comparisons with product price, which is always stated on a per-unit basis. Average fixed cost, average variable cost, and average total cost are shown in columns 5 to 7 of the table in **Figure 6.3**.

AFC **Average fixed cost (AFC)** for any output level is found by dividing total fixed cost (TFC) by that output (Q). That is,

$$AFC = \frac{TFC}{Q}$$

average fixed cost (AFC)
A firm's total fixed cost divided by output (the quantity of product produced).

Because the total fixed cost is, by definition, the same regardless of output, AFC must decline as output increases. As output rises, the total fixed cost is spread over a larger and larger output. When output is just one unit in **Figure 6.3**'s table, TFC and AFC are the same at $100. But at two units of output, the total fixed cost of $100 becomes $50 of AFC or fixed cost per unit; then it becomes $33.33 per unit as $100 is spread over three units, and $25 per unit when spread over four units. This process is sometimes referred to as "spreading the overhead." **Figure 6.3** shows that AFC graphs as a continuously declining curve as total output increases.

AVC **Average variable cost (AVC)** for any output level is calculated by dividing total variable cost (TVC) by that quantity of output (Q):

$$AVC = \frac{TVC}{Q}$$

average variable cost (AVC)
A firm's total variable cost divided by output (the quantity of product produced).

Due to increasing and then diminishing returns, AVC declines initially, reaches a minimum, and then increases again. A graph of AVC is a U-shaped or saucer-shaped curve, as **Figure 6.3** shows.

Because total variable cost reflects the law of diminishing returns, so must AVC, which is derived from total variable cost. Because marginal returns increase initially, it takes fewer and fewer additional variable resources to produce each of the first four units of output. As a result, variable cost per unit declines. AVC hits a minimum with the fifth unit of output, and beyond that point AVC rises because diminishing returns require more and more variable resources to produce each additional unit of output.

Production is relatively inefficient—and therefore costly—at low levels of output. Because the firm's fixed plan is understaffed, average variable cost is relatively high. As output expands, however, greater specialization and better use of the firm's capital equipment yield more efficiency, and variable cost per unit of output declines. As still more variable resources are added, a point is reached where crowding causes diminishing returns to set in. Once diminishing returns start, each additional unit of input does not increase output by as much as preceding units did, which means that AVC eventually increases.

ATC **Average total cost (ATC)** for any output level is found by dividing total cost (TC) by that output (Q) or by adding AFC and AVC at that output:

$$ATC = \frac{TC}{Q} = \frac{TFC}{Q} + \frac{TVC}{Q} = AFC + AVC$$

average total cost (ATC)
A firm's total cost divided by output (the quantity of product produced); equal to average fixed cost plus average variable cost.

Graphically, ATC can be found by adding vertically the AFC and AVC curves, as in **Figure 6.3**. Thus, the vertical distance between the ATC and AVC curves measures AFC at any level of output.

Marginal Cost

One final and very crucial cost concept remains: **Marginal cost (MC)** is the extra, or additional, cost of producing one more unit of output. MC can be determined for each added unit of output by noting the change in total cost entailed by that unit's production:

$$MC = \frac{\text{change in TC}}{\text{change in } Q}$$

marginal cost (MC)
The extra (additional) cost of producing 1 more unit of output; equal to the change in total cost divided by the change in output (and, in the short run, to the change in total variable cost divided by the change in output).

Calculations In column 4 of **Figure 6.3**'s table, production of the first unit of output increases total cost from $100 to $190. Therefore, the additional, or marginal, cost of that first unit is $90 (column 8). The marginal cost of the second unit is $80 (= $270 – $190); the MC of the third is $70 (= $340 – $270); and so forth. The MC for each of the 10 units of output is shown in column 8.

MC can also be calculated from the TVC column because the only difference between total cost and total variable cost is the constant amount of fixed costs ($100). Thus, the change in total cost and the change in total variable cost accompanying each additional unit of output are always the same.

Marginal Decisions The firm can control marginal costs directly and immediately. Specifically, MC designates all the cost incurred in producing the last unit of output. Thus, it also designates the cost that can be "saved" by not producing that last unit. Average-cost figures do not provide this information. For example, suppose the firm is undecided whether to produce three or four units of output. At four units, the table in **Figure 6.3** indicates that ATC is $100. But the firm does not increase its total costs by $100 by producing the fourth unit, nor does it save $100 by not producing that unit. Rather, the change in costs involved here is only the $60 in marginal cost, as column 8 in the table reveals.

A firm's decisions as to what output level to produce are typically marginal decisions—that is, decisions to produce a few more or a few less units. Marginal cost is the change in costs when one more or one fewer unit of output is produced. When coupled with marginal revenue (which, as you will see in Chapter 7, is the change in revenue from one more or one fewer unit of output), marginal cost allows a firm to determine if it is profitable to expand or contract its production. The analysis in the next three chapters focuses on those marginal calculations.

Graphical Portrayal Marginal cost is shown graphically in **Figure 6.3**. Marginal cost at first declines sharply, reaches a minimum, and then rises rather abruptly. This reflects the fact that total variable cost, and therefore total cost, increase first by decreasing amounts and then by increasing amounts.

Relation of MC to AVC and ATC **Figure 6.3** shows that the marginal-cost curve MC intersects both the AVC and the ATC curves at their respective minimum points. As noted earlier, this marginal-average relationship is a mathematical necessity. When the amount (the marginal cost) added to total cost is less than the current average total cost, ATC will fall. Conversely, when the marginal cost exceeds ATC, ATC will rise. This means, in **Figure 6.3**, that as long as MC lies below ATC, ATC will fall, and whenever MC lies above ATC, ATC will rise. Therefore, at the point of intersection where MC equals ATC, ATC has just ceased to fall but has not yet begun to rise. This, by definition, is the minimum point on the ATC curve. The marginal-cost curve intersects the average-total-cost curve at the ATC curve's minimum point.

Marginal cost can be defined as the addition either to total cost or to total variable cost resulting from one more unit of output; thus, this same rationale explains why the MC curve also crosses the AVC curve at the AVC curve's minimum point. No such relationship exists between the MC curve and the average-fixed-cost curve because the two are not related; marginal cost includes only those costs that change with output, and fixed costs by definition are those that are independent of output.

Global Snapshot 6.1 demonstrates that manufacturing costs vary substantially across countries. Despite the wide variation, higher cost countries can still compete by specializing their manufacturing efforts on products with higher selling prices.

APPLYING THE ANALYSIS

Rising Gasoline Prices

Changes in supply and demand often lead to rapid increases in the price of gasoline. Because gasoline is used to power most motor vehicles, including those used by businesses, increases in the price of gasoline lead to increases in firms' short-run variable costs, marginal costs, and average total costs. In terms of our analysis, their AVC, MC, and ATC curves all shift upward when an increase in the price of gasoline increases their production costs.

The extent of these upward shifts depends upon the relative importance of gasoline as a variable input in the various firms' individual production processes. Package-delivery companies like FedEx that use a lot of gasoline-powered vehicles will see substantial upward shifts, while software companies like Symantec and Microsoft, which deliver many of their products through Internet downloads, may see only small upward shifts.

> QUESTION:
>
> If rising gasoline prices increase the cost for delivery to firms such as FedEx, how would that affect the cost curves for Internet retailers such as Amazon that ship a lot of packages?

GLOBAL SNAPSHOT 6.1

Relative Manufacturing Costs, Selected Nations, 2018

Total costs per unit of output vary substantially from country to country in the manufacturing sector, as you can see in this figure in which U.S. manufacturing costs are assigned an index value of 100 and average manufacturing costs in other countries are presented relative to that index value. Switzerland, for instance, has production costs that are on average about 20 percent higher than those found in the United States, while Indonesia has production costs that are about 18 percent lower than those found in the United States.

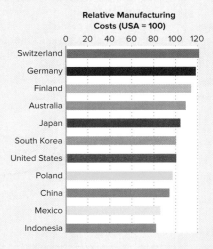

Source: Boston Consulting Group.

Long-Run Production Costs

In the long run, an industry and its individual firms can undertake all desired resource adjustments. That is, they can change the amount of all inputs used. The firm can alter its plant capacity; it can build a larger plant or revert to a smaller plant than that assumed in **Figures 6.2** and **6.3**. The industry also can change its overall capacity; the long run allows sufficient time for new firms to enter or for existing firms to leave an industry. We will discuss the impact of the entry and exit of firms to and from an industry in the next chapter; here we are concerned only with changes in plant capacity made by a single firm. Let's couch our analysis in terms of average total cost (ATC), making no distinction between fixed and variable costs because all resources, and therefore all costs, are variable in the long run.

Firm Size and Costs

Suppose a manufacturer with a single plant begins on a small scale and, as the result of successful operations, expands to successively larger plant sizes with larger output capacities. What happens to average total cost as this occurs? For a time, successively larger plants will reduce average total cost. However, eventually the building of a still larger plant may cause ATC to rise.

Figure 6.4 illustrates this situation for five possible plant sizes. ATC-1 is the short-run average-total-cost curve for the smallest of the five plants, and ATC-5, the curve for the largest. Constructing larger plants will lower the minimum average total costs through plant size 3. But then larger plants will mean higher minimum average total costs.

The Long-Run Cost Curve

The vertical lines perpendicular to the output axis in **Figure 6.4** indicate the outputs at which the firm should change plant size to realize the lowest attainable average total costs of production. These are the outputs at which the per-unit costs for a larger plant drop below those for the current, smaller plant. For all outputs up to 20 units,

FIGURE 6.4

The long-run average-total-cost curve: five possible plant sizes. The long-run average-total-cost curve is made up of segments of the short-run cost curves (ATC-1, ATC-2, etc.) of the various-size plants from which the firm might choose. Each point on the bumpy planning curve shows the lowest unit cost attainable for any output when the firm has had time to make all desired changes in its plant size.

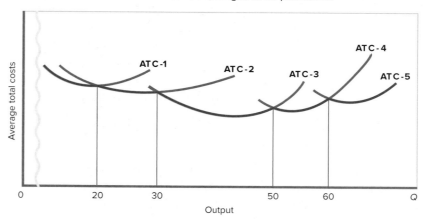

the lowest average total costs are attainable with plant size 1. However, if the firm's volume of sales expands beyond 20 units but less than 30, it can achieve lower per-unit costs by constructing a larger plant, size 2. Although total cost will be higher at the expanded levels of production, the cost per unit of output will be less. For any output between 30 and 50 units, plant size 3 will yield the lowest average total costs. From 50 to 60 units of output, the firm must build the size-4 plant to achieve the lowest unit costs. Lowest average total costs for any output over 60 units require construction of the still larger plant, size 5.

Tracing these adjustments, we find that the long-run ATC curve for the enterprise is made up of segments of the short-run ATC curves for the various plant sizes that can be constructed. The long-run ATC curve shows the lowest average total cost at which *any output level* can be produced after the firm has had time to make all appropriate adjustments in its plant size. In **Figure 6.4**, the blue, bumpy curve is the firm's long-run ATC curve or, as it is often called, the firm's *planning curve.*

In most lines of production, the choice of plant size is much wider than in our illustration. In many industries, the number of possible plant sizes is virtually unlimited, and in time, quite small changes in the volume of output will lead to changes in plant size. Graphically, this implies an unlimited number of short-run ATC curves, one for each output level, as suggested by **Figure 6.5**. Then, rather than being made up of segments of short-run ATC curves as in **Figure 6.4**, the long-run ATC curve is made up of all the points of tangency of the unlimited number of short-run ATC curves from which the long-run ATC curve is derived. Therefore, the planning curve is smooth rather than bumpy. Each point on it tells us the minimum ATC of producing the corresponding level of output.

FIGURE 6.5

The long-run average-total-cost curve: unlimited number of plant sizes. If the number of possible plant sizes is very large, the long-run average-total-cost curve approximates a smooth curve. Economies of scale, followed by diseconomies of scale, cause the curve to be U-shaped.

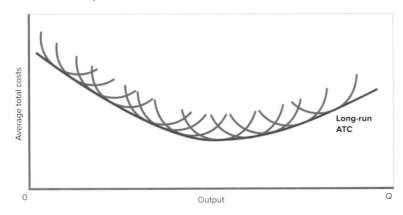

Economies and Diseconomies of Scale

We have assumed that, for a time, larger and larger plant sizes will lead to lower unit costs but that, beyond some point, successively larger plants will mean higher average total costs. That is, we have assumed the long-run ATC curve is U-shaped. But why should this be? It turns out that the U shape is caused by economies and diseconomies of large-scale production, as we explain in a moment. But before we do, please understand that the U shape of the long-run average-total-cost curve *cannot* be the result of rising resource prices or the law of diminishing returns. First, our discussion assumes that resource prices are constant. Second, the law of diminishing returns does not apply to production in the long run. This is true because the law of diminishing returns only deals with situations in which a productive resource or input is held constant. Under our definition of "long run," all resources and inputs are variable.

economies of scale
Reductions in the average total cost of producing a product as the firm expands the size of plant (its output) in the long run; the economies of mass production.

Economies of Scale   **Economies of scale,** or *economies of mass production,* explain the downward sloping part of the long-run ATC curve, as indicated in **Figure 6.6,** graphs (a), (b), and (c). As plant size increases, a number of factors will for a time lead to lower average costs of production.

FIGURE 6.6
Various possible long-run average-total-cost curves. (a) Economies of scale are rather rapidly obtained as plant size rises, and diseconomies of scale are not encountered until a considerably large scale of output has been achieved. Thus, long-run average total cost is constant over a wide range of output. (b) Economies of scale are extensive, and diseconomies of scale occur only at very large outputs. Average total cost therefore declines over a broad range of output. (c) Economies of scale are exhausted quickly, followed immediately by diseconomies of scale. Minimum ATC thus occurs at a relatively low output.

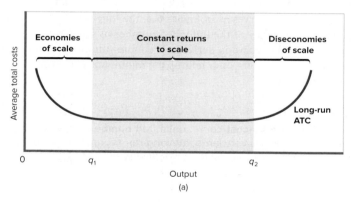

(a)

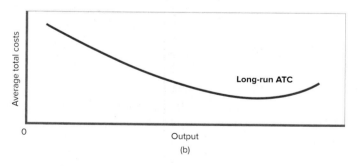

(b)

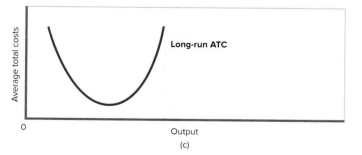

(c)

Labor Specialization Increased specialization in the use of labor becomes more achievable as a plant increases in size. Hiring more workers means jobs can be divided and subdivided. Each worker may now have just one task to perform instead of five or six. Workers can work full time on the tasks for which they have special skills. By contrast, skilled machinists in a small plant may spend half their time performing unskilled tasks, leading to higher production costs.

Further, by working at fewer tasks, workers become even more proficient at those tasks. The jack-of-all-trades doing five or six jobs is not likely to be efficient in any of them. Concentrating on one task, the same worker may become highly efficient.

Finally, greater labor specialization eliminates the loss of time that occurs whenever a worker shifts from one task to another.

Managerial Specialization Large-scale production also means better use of, and greater specialization in, management. A supervisor who can handle 20 workers is underused in a small plant that employs only 10 people. The production staff could be doubled with no increase in supervisory costs.

Small firms cannot use management specialists to best advantage. For example, a sales specialist working in a small plant has to spend some time on functions outside their area of expertise—marketing, personnel, and finance. A larger scale of operations allows the sales specialist to supervise marketing full time, while other specialists perform other managerial functions. Greater efficiency and lower unit costs are the net result.

Efficient Capital Small firms often cannot afford the most efficient equipment. In many lines of production, such machinery is available only in very large and extremely expensive units. Furthermore, effective use of the equipment demands a high volume of production, and that again requires large-scale producers.

In the automobile industry, the most efficient fabrication method employs robotics and elaborate assembly-line equipment. Effective use of this equipment demands an annual output of several thousand automobiles. Only very-large-scale producers can afford to purchase and use this equipment efficiently. The small-scale producer is faced with a dilemma. To fabricate automobiles using other equipment is inefficient and therefore more costly per unit. But so, too, is buying and underutilizing the equipment used by the large manufacturers. Because it cannot spread the high equipment cost over very many units of output, the small-scale producer will be stuck with high costs per unit of output.

Other Factors Many products entail design and development costs, as well as other "start-up" costs, which must be incurred regardless of projected sales. These costs decline per unit as output is increased. Similarly, advertising costs decline per auto, per computer, per stereo system, and per box of detergent as more units are produced and sold. Also, the firm's production and marketing expertise usually rises as it produces and sells more output. This *learning by doing* is a further source of economies of scale.

All these factors contribute to lower average total costs for the firm that is able to expand its scale of operations. Where economies of scale are possible, an increase in all resources of, say, 10 percent will cause a more-than-proportionate increase in output of, say, 20 percent. The result will be a decline in ATC.

In many U.S. manufacturing industries, economies of scale have been of great significance. Firms that have expanded their scale of operations to obtain economies of mass production have survived and flourished. Those unable to expand have become relatively high-cost producers, doomed to struggle to survive.

PHOTO OP

Economies of Scale

Economies of scale are extensive in the automobile industry, where the capital required is large and expensive and many workers are needed to perform the numerous, highly specialized tasks. Economies of scale in copying keys are exhausted at low levels of output; production usually occurs in small shops, the capital involved is relatively small and inexpensive, and a small number of workers (often only one) perform all of the labor and managerial functions of the business. There would be little, if any, cost advantage to establishing a key copying "factory" with hundreds of stations.

©RainerPlendl/Getty Images RF

©Image Source RF

APPLYING THE ANALYSIS

The Verson Stamping Machine

In 1996, Verson (a U.S. firm located in Chicago) introduced a 49-foot-tall metal-stamping machine that is the size of a house and weighs as much as 12 locomotives. This $30 million machine, which cuts and sculpts raw sheets of steel into automobile hoods and fenders, enables automakers to make new parts in just 5 minutes compared with 8 hours for older stamping presses. A single machine is designed to make 5 million auto parts per year. So, to achieve the cost saving from the machine, an auto manufacturer must have sufficient auto production to use all these parts. By allowing the use of this cost-saving piece of equipment, large firm size achieves economies of scale.

> QUESTION:
>
> Do you see any potential problems for a company that relies too heavily on just a few large machines for fabricating millions of its critical product parts?

Diseconomies of Scale In time, the expansion of a firm may lead to diseconomies and therefore higher average total costs.

The main factor causing **diseconomies of scale** is the difficulty of efficiently controlling and coordinating a firm's operations as it becomes a large-scale producer. In a small plant, a single key executive may make all the basic decisions for the plant's operation. Because of the firm's small size, the executive is close to the production line, understands the firm's operations, and can make efficient decisions because the small plant size requires only a relatively small amount of information to be examined and understood in optimizing production.

This neat picture changes as a firm grows. One person cannot assemble, digest, and understand all the information essential to decision making on a large scale. Authority must be delegated to many vice presidents, second vice presidents, and so forth. This expansion of the management hierarchy leads to problems of communication and cooperation, bureaucratic red tape, and the possibility that decisions will not be coordinated. At the same time, each new manager must be paid a salary. Thus, declining efficiency in making and executing decisions goes hand-in-hand with rising average total costs as bureaucracy expands beyond a certain point.

Also, in massive production facilities, workers may feel alienated from their employers and care little about working efficiently. Opportunities to shirk, by avoiding work in favor of on-the-job leisure, may be greater in large plants than in small ones. Countering worker alienation and shirking may require additional worker supervision, which increases costs.

Where diseconomies of scale are operative, an increase in all inputs of, say, 10 percent will cause a less-than-proportionate increase in output of, say, 5 percent. As a consequence, ATC will increase. The rising portion of the long-run cost curves in **Figure 6.6** illustrates diseconomies of scale.

Constant Returns to Scale In some industries, there may exist a rather wide range of output between the output at which economies of scale end and the output at which diseconomies of scale begin. That is, there may be a range of **constant returns to scale** over which long-run average cost does not change. The q_1q_2 output range of **Figure 6.6a** is an example. Here, a given percentage increase in all inputs of, say, 10 percent will cause a proportionate 10 percent increase in output. Thus, in this range ATC is constant.

Minimum Efficient Scale and Industry Structure

Economies and diseconomies of scale are an important determinant of an industry's structure. Here, we introduce the concept of **minimum efficient scale (MES),** which is the lowest level of output at which a firm can minimize long-run average costs. In **Figure 6.6a**, that level occurs at q_1 units of output. Because of the extended range of constant returns to scale, firms producing substantially greater outputs could also realize the minimum attainable long-run average costs. Specifically, firms within the q_1q_2 range would be equally efficient. So we would not be surprised to find an industry with such cost conditions to be populated by firms of quite different sizes. The apparel, banking, furniture, snowboard, wood products, food processing, and small-appliance industries are examples. With an extended range of constant returns to scale, relatively large and relatively small firms can coexist in an industry and be equally successful.

Compare this with **Figure 6.6b**, where economies of scale continue over a wide range of outputs, and diseconomies of scale appear only at very high levels of output. This pattern of declining long-run average total cost occurs in the automobile, aluminum, steel, and other heavy industries. The same pattern holds in several of the

diseconomies of scale
Increases in the average total cost of producing a product as the firm expands the size of its plant (its output) in the long run.

constant returns to scale
No changes in the average total cost of producing a product as the firm expands the size of its operations (output) in the long run.

minimum efficient scale (MES)
The lowest level of output at which a firm can minimize long-run average total cost.

new industries related to information technology—for example, computer microchips, operating system software, and Internet service provision. Given consumer demand, efficient production will be achieved with a few large-scale producers. Small firms cannot realize the minimum efficient scale and will not be able to compete.

Where economies of scale are few and diseconomies come into play quickly, the minimum efficient size occurs at a low level of output, as shown in **Figure 6.6c**. In such industries, a particular level of consumer demand will support a large number of relatively small producers. Many retail trades and some types of farming fall into this category. So do certain kinds of light manufacturing, such as the baking, clothing, and shoe industries. Fairly small firms are more efficient than larger-scale producers would be if they were present in such industries.

Our point here is that the shape of the long-run average-total-cost curve is determined by technology, as well as the economies and diseconomies of scale that result. The shape of the long-run ATC curve, in turn, can be significant in determining whether an industry is populated by a relatively large number of small firms or is dominated by a few large producers, or lies somewhere in between.

But we must be cautious in our assessment because industry structure does not depend on cost conditions alone. Government policies, the geographic size of markets, managerial strategy and skill, and other factors must be considered in explaining the structure of a particular industry.

APPLYING THE ANALYSIS

Aircraft Assembly Plants versus Concrete Plants

Why are there only two plants in the United States (both operated by Boeing) that produce large commercial aircraft but thousands of plants (owned by hundreds of firms) that produce ready-mix concrete? The simple answer is that MES is radically different in the two industries. First, economies of scale are extensive in assembling large commercial aircraft, but only very modest in mixing concrete. Manufacturing airplanes is a complex process that requires huge facilities, thousands of workers, and very expensive, specialized machinery. Economies of scale extend to huge plant sizes. But mixing Portland cement, sand, gravel, and water to produce concrete requires only a handful of workers and relatively inexpensive equipment. Economies of scale are exhausted at a relatively small size.

The differing MESs also derive from vast differences in the size of geographic markets. The market for commercial airplanes is global, and aircraft manufacturers can deliver new airplanes anywhere in the world by flying them there. In contrast, the geographic market for a concrete plant is roughly the 50-mile radius within which the concrete can be delivered before it "sets up." So thousands of small concrete plants locate close to their customers in hundreds of small and large cities in the United States.

> QUESTION:
>
> Speculate as to why the MES of firms in the Portland cement industry is considerably larger than the MES of single ready-mix concrete plants.

Summary

LO6.1 Explain why economic costs include both explicit costs and implicit costs.

The economic cost of using a resource to produce a good or service is the value or worth that resource in its best alternative use. Economic costs include explicit costs, which flow to resources owned and supplied by others, and implicit costs, which are the opportunity costs of using resources that are already owned. One implicit cost is a normal profit to the entrepreneur. Economic profit occurs when total revenue exceeds total cost (= explicit costs + implicit costs, including a normal profit).

In the short run, a firm's plant capacity is fixed. The firm can use its plant more or less intensively by adding or subtracting units of variable resources, but it does not have sufficient time in the short run to alter plant size.

LO6.2 Relate the law of diminishing returns to a firm's short-run production costs.

The law of diminishing returns describes what happens to output as a fixed plant is used more intensively. As successive units of a variable resource, such as labor, are added to a fixed plant, beyond some point the marginal product associated with each additional unit of a resource declines.

LO6.3 Distinguish between fixed and variable costs and among total, average, and marginal costs.

Costs can be classified as variable or fixed in the short run. Fixed costs are independent of the level of output; variable costs vary with output. The total cost of any output is the sum of fixed and variable costs at that output.

Average fixed, average variable, and average total costs are fixed, variable, and total costs per unit of output. Average fixed cost declines continuously as output increases because a fixed sum is being spread over a larger and larger number of units of production. A graph of average variable cost is U-shaped, reflecting increasing returns followed by diminishing returns. Average total cost is the sum of average fixed and average variable costs; its graph is also U-shaped.

Marginal cost is the extra, or additional, cost of producing one more unit of output. It is the amount by which total cost and total variable cost change when one more unit of output is produced. Graphically, the MC curve intersects the ATC and AVC curves at their minimum points.

Lower resource prices shift cost curves downward, as does technological progress. Higher input prices shift cost curves upward.

LO6.4 Use economies of scale to link a firm's size and its average costs in the long run.

The long run is a period of time sufficiently long for a firm to vary the amounts of all resources used, including plant size. In the long run, all costs are variable. The long-run ATC, or planning, curve is composed of segments of the short-run ATC curves, and it represents the various plant sizes a firm can construct in the long run.

The long-run ATC curve is generally U-shaped. Economies of scale are first encountered as a small firm expands. Greater specialization in the use of labor and management, use of the most efficient equipment, and the spreading of start-up costs across more units of output all contribute to economies of scale. As the firm continues to grow, it will encounter diseconomies of scale stemming from the managerial complexities that accompany large-scale production. The output ranges over which economies and diseconomies of scale occur in an industry are often an important determinant of that industry's structure.

A firm's minimum efficient scale (MES) is the lowest level of output at which it can minimize its long-run average cost. In some industries, MES occurs at such low levels of output that numerous firms can populate the industry. In other industries, MES occurs at such high output levels that only a few firms can exist in the long run.

LO6.5 Give business examples of short-run costs, economies of scale, and minimum efficient scale.

Rising gasoline prices increase (shift upward) the AVC, ATC, and MC cost curves of firms like FedEx that use gasoline as an input in their production process.

The automobile and airline industries exhibit significant economies of scale, characterized by huge facilities, thousands of workers, and expensive, specialized equipment used, such as the Verson stamping machine. Other production processes, such as ready-mix concrete require only a few workers and relatively inexpensive equipment, so economies of scale are exhausted quickly.

Terms and Concepts

economic cost	total product (TP)	average variable cost (AVC)
explicit cost	marginal product (MP)	average total cost (ATC)
implicit cost	average product (AP)	marginal cost (MC)
accounting profit	law of diminishing returns	economies of scale
normal profit	fixed cost	diseconomies of scale
economic profit	variable cost	constant returns to scale
short run	total cost	minimum efficient scale (MES)
long run	average fixed cost (AFC)	

Questions

1. Distinguish between explicit and implicit costs, giving examples of each. What are some explicit and implicit costs of attending college? **(LO1)**

2. Distinguish between accounting profit, economic profit, and normal profit. Which type of profit determines how entrepreneurs allocate resources between different business ventures? Explain. **(LO1)**

3. Complete the following table by calculating marginal product and average product. **(LO2)**

Inputs of Labor	Total Product	Marginal Product	Average Product
0	0		
1	15	_____	_____
2	34	_____	_____
3	51	_____	_____
4	65	_____	_____
5	74	_____	_____
6	80	_____	_____
7	83	_____	_____
8	82	_____	_____

Plot the total, marginal, and average products and explain in detail the relationship between each pair of curves. Explain why marginal product first rises, then declines, and ultimately becomes negative. What bearing does the law of diminishing returns have on short-run costs? Be specific.

4. Why can the distinction between fixed costs and variable costs be made in the short run? Classify the following as fixed or variable costs: advertising expenditures, fuel, interest on company-issued bonds, shipping charges, payments for raw materials, real estate taxes, executive salaries, insurance premiums, wage payments, sales taxes, and rental payments on leased office machinery. "There are no fixed costs in the long run; all costs are variable." Explain. **(LO3)**

5. A firm has fixed costs of $60 and variable costs as indicated in the table. **(LO3)** Complete the table and check your calculations by referring to **problem 4** at the end of Chapter 7.

   a. Graph the AFC, ATC, and MC curves. Why does the AFC curve slope continuously downward? Why does the MC curve eventually slope upward? Why does the MC curve intersect both the AVC and the ATC curve at their minimum points?

   b. Explain how the location of each curve graphed in question 5a would be altered if (1) total fixed cost is $100 rather than $60 and (2) total variable cost is $10 less at each level of output.

Total Product	Total Fixed Cost	Total Variable Cost	Total Cost	Average Fixed Cost	Average Variable Cost	Average Total Cost	Marginal Cost
0	$_____	$ 0	$___			$_____	
1	_____	45	___	$_____	$_____	_____	$_____
2	_____	85	___	_____	_____	_____	_____
3	_____	120	___	_____	_____	_____	_____
4	_____	150	___	_____	_____	_____	_____
5	_____	185	___	_____	_____	_____	_____
6	_____	225	___	_____	_____	_____	_____
7	_____	270	___	_____	_____	_____	_____
8	_____	325	___	_____	_____	_____	_____
9	_____	390	___	_____	_____	_____	_____
10	_____	465	___	_____	_____	_____	_____

6. Indicate how each of the following would shift the (1) MC curve, (2) AVC curve, (3) AFC curve, and (4) ATC curve of a manufacturing firm. In each case, specify the direction of the shift. **(LO3)**

a.   A reduction in business property taxes.

b.   An increase in the hourly wage rates of production workers.

c.   A decrease in the price of electricity.

d.   An increase in insurance rates on plant and equipment.

e.   An increase in transportation costs.

7. Suppose a firm has only three possible plant-size options, represented by the ATC curves shown in the figure. What plant size will the firm choose in producing (a) 50, (b) 130, (c) 160, and (d) 250 units of output? Draw the firm's long-run average-cost curve on the diagram and describe this curve. **(LO4)**

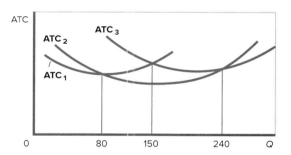

8. Use the concepts of economies and diseconomies of scale to explain the shape of a firm's long-run ATC curve. What does "minimum efficient scale" mean? What bearing can the shape of the long-run ATC curve have on the structure of an industry? **(LO4)**

Problems

1. Gomez runs a small pottery firm. He hires one helper at $12,000 per year, pays annual rent of $5,000 for his shop, and spends $20,000 per year on materials. He has $40,000 of his own funds invested in equipment (pottery wheels, kilns, and so forth) that could earn him $4,000 per year if alternatively invested. He has been offered $15,000 per year to work as a potter for a competitor. He estimates his entrepreneurial talents are worth $3,000 per year. Total annual revenue from pottery sales is $72,000. Calculate the accounting profit and the economic profit for Gomez's pottery firm. **(LO1)**

2. Imagine you have some workers and some handheld computers that you can use to take inventory at a warehouse. There are diminishing returns to taking inventory. If one worker uses one computer, he can inventory 100 items per hour. Two workers sharing a computer can together inventory 150 items per hour. Three workers sharing a computer can together inventory 160 items per hour. And four or more workers sharing a computer can together inventory fewer than 160 items per hour. Computers cost $100 each and you must pay each worker $25 per hour. If you assign one worker per computer, what is the cost of inventorying a single item? What is the cost if you assign two workers per computer? Three? How many workers per computer should you assign if you wish to minimize the cost of inventorying a single item? **(LO2)**

3. You are a newspaper publisher. You are in the middle of a one-year rental contract for your factory that requires you to pay $500,000 per month, and you have contractual salary obligations of $1 million per month that you can't get out of. You also have a marginal printing cost of $0.25 per paper, as well as a marginal delivery cost of $0.10 per paper. If sales fall by 20 percent from 1 million papers per month to 800,000 papers per month, what happens to the AFC per paper, the MC per paper, and the minimum amount you must charge to break even on these costs? **(LO3)**

4. There are economies of scale in ranching, especially with regard to fencing land. Suppose that barbed-wire fencing costs $10,000 per mile to set up. How much would it cost to fence a single property whose area is one square mile if that property also happens to be perfectly square, with sides that are each one mile long? How much would it cost to fence exactly four such properties, which together would contain four square miles of area? Now consider how much it would cost to fence in four square miles of ranch land if, instead, it comes as a single large square that is two miles long on each side. Which is more costly—fencing in the four, one-square-mile properties or the single four-square-mile property? **(LO4)**

CHAPTER SEVEN

Pure Competition

Learning Objectives

LO7.1 Summarize the main characteristics of the four basic market models.
LO7.2 List the conditions required for purely competitive markets.
LO7.3 Describe how purely competitive firms maximize profits or minimize losses.
LO7.4 Explain why a competitive firm's marginal cost curve is also its supply curve.
LO7.5 Describe how profits and losses drive the long-run adjustment process of pure competition.
LO7.6 Explain the differences between constant-cost, increasing-cost, and decreasing-cost industries.
LO7.7 Show how long-run equilibrium in pure competition produces an efficient allocation of resources.

A firm analyzes revenues and costs to decide what price to charge and how much to produce. A firm's decisions concerning price and production depend greatly on the industry in which it operates. At one extreme are industries in which a single producer dominates the market; at the other extreme are industries in which thousands of firms each produce a tiny fraction of market supply.

Because we cannot examine each industry individually, we focus on four basic *models* of market structure. Together, these models help us understand how price and output are determined in product markets. They will help us evaluate those markets' efficiency or inefficiency and assess public policies (such as antitrust policy) relating to certain firms and industries.

Four Market Models

Economists group industries into four distinct market structures based on the number of firms in the industry, whether those firms produce a standardized or differentiated product, how easy it is for firms to enter the industry, and how much control firms have over the price of their products.

These are the four models:

- *Pure competition* involves a very large number of firms producing a standardized product (i.e., a product like cotton for which each producer's output is virtually identical to that of every other producer). New firms can enter or exit the industry very easily. Firms must accept the market price.

- *Monopolistic competition* is characterized by a relatively large number of sellers producing differentiated products (clothing, furniture, books). Present in this model is widespread *nonprice competition,* a selling strategy in which firms try to distinguish their products on attributes like design and workmanship (an approach called *product differentiation*). Both entry into and exit from monopolistically competitive industries is quite easy. Monopolistically competitive firms possess some, but not much, control over selling prices.

- *Oligopoly* involves only a few sellers of a standardized (steel) or differentiated (cars) product, so each firm is affected by its rivals' decisions and must take those decisions into account in determining its own price and output.

PHOTO OP

Standardized versus Differentiated Products

Wheat is an example of a standardized product, whereas Dove shampoo is an example of a differentiated product.

Glow Images   Kolonko/Shutterstock

- *Pure monopoly* is a market structure in which one firm (e.g., a local electric utility) is the sole seller of a product or service. Because the entry of additional firms is blocked, one firm constitutes the entire industry. The monopoly firm produces a single unique product and has full control over that product's price.

Pure Competition: Characteristics and Occurrence

Although pure competition is somewhat rare in the real world, this market model is highly relevant to several industries. In particular, we can learn much about markets for agricultural goods, fish products, foreign exchange, basic metals, and stock shares by studying the pure-competition model. Also, pure competition is a meaningful starting point for any discussion of how prices and output are determined. Moreover, the operation of a purely competitive economy provides a norm for evaluating the efficiency of the real-world economy.

Let's look more closely at the characteristics of **pure competition:**

- *Very large numbers* A basic feature of a purely competitive market is the presence of a large number of independently acting sellers, often offering their products in large national or international markets. Examples include the markets for farm commodities, the stock market, and the foreign exchange market.

pure competition
A market structure in which a very large number of firms sell a standardized product, into which entry is very easy, in which the individual seller has no control over the product price, and in which there is no nonprice competition; a market characterized by a very large number of buyers and sellers.

- *Standardized product* Purely competitive firms produce a standardized (identical or homogeneous) product. As long as the price is the same, consumers are indifferent about which seller to buy the product from. Buyers view the products of firms B, C, and D as perfect substitutes for the product of firm A. Because purely competitive firms sell standardized products, they make no attempt to differentiate their products and do not engage in other forms of nonprice competition.

- *"Price takers"* In a purely competitive market, individual firms do not exert control over product price. Each firm produces such a small fraction of total output that increasing or decreasing its output will not perceptibly influence total supply or, therefore, product price. In short, the competitive firm is a **price taker:** It cannot change market price; it can only adjust to it. Thus the individual competitive producer is at the mercy of the market. Charging a price higher than the market price would be futile. Consumers will not buy from firm A at $2.05 when its 9,999 competitors are selling an identical product at $2 per unit. Conversely, because firm A can sell as much as it chooses at $2 per unit, it has no reason to charge a lower price, say, $1.95. Doing this would shrink its profit.

price taker
A seller (or buyer) that is unable to affect the price at which a product or resource sells by changing the amount it sells (or buys).

- *Free entry and exit* New firms can freely enter, and existing firms can freely leave purely competitive industries. No significant legal, technological, financial, or other obstacles prohibit new firms from selling their output in a competitive market.

Demand as Seen by a Purely Competitive Seller

To develop a model of pure competition, let's now examine demand from a purely competitive seller's viewpoint and see how it affects revenue. This seller might be a wheat farmer, a stockbroker, a contract clothing manufacturer, or some other pure competitor. Because each purely competitive firm offers only a negligible fraction of total market supply, it must accept the price predetermined by the market. Pure competitors are price takers, not price makers.

Perfectly Elastic Demand

The demand schedule faced by the *individual firm* in a purely competitive industry is perfectly elastic at the market price, as **Figure 7.1** shows. According to column 1 of the table in **Figure 7.1**, the market price is $131. The firm represented cannot obtain a higher price by restricting its output, nor does it need to lower its price to increase its sales volume. Columns 1 and 2 show that the firm can produce and sell as many or as few units as it likes at the market price of $131.

We are *not* saying that *market* demand is perfectly elastic in a competitive market. Rather, market demand graphs as a downward sloping curve. An entire industry (all firms producing a particular product) *can* affect price by changing industry output. For example, all firms, acting independently but simultaneously, can increase price by reducing output. But the individual competitive firm cannot do that because its output is such a small fraction of its industry's total output. For the individual competitive firm, the market price is therefore a fixed value at which it can sell as many or as few units as it cares to. Graphically, this implies that the individual competitive firm's demand curve will plot as a horizontal line such as *D* in **Figure 7.1**.

Average, Total, and Marginal Revenue

average revenue (AR)
Total revenue from the sale of a product divided by the quantity of the product sold (demanded); equal to the price at which the product is sold when all units of the product are sold at the same price.

total revenue (TR)
The total number of dollars received by a firm (or firms) from the sale of a product; equal to the total expenditures for the product produced by the firm (or firms); equal to the quantity sold (demanded) multiplied by the price at which it is sold.

marginal revenue (MR)
The change in total revenue that results from the sale of 1 additional unit of a firm's product; equal to the change in total revenue divided by the change in the quantity of the product sold.

The firm's demand schedule is also its average-revenue schedule. To say that all buyers must pay $131 per unit is to say that the revenue per unit, or **average revenue (AR)**, received by the seller is $131. Price and average revenue are the same thing.

The **total revenue (TR)** for each sales level is found by multiplying price by the corresponding quantity the firm can sell. (Column 1 multiplied by column 2 in the table in **Figure 7.1** yields column 3.) In this case, total revenue increases by a constant amount, $131, for each additional unit of sales. Each unit sold adds exactly its constant price to total revenue.

When a firm is pondering a change in its output, it will consider how its total revenue will change as a result. **Marginal revenue (MR)** is the change in total revenue (or the extra revenue) that results from selling one more unit of output. In column 3 of the table in **Figure 7.1**, total revenue is zero when zero units are sold. The first unit of output sold increases total revenue from zero to $131, so marginal revenue for that unit is $131. The second unit sold increases total revenue from $131 to $262, and marginal revenue is again $131. Note in column 4 that marginal revenue is a constant $131, as is price. *In pure competition, marginal revenue and price are equal.*

Figure 7.1 shows the purely competitive firm's TR, demand, MR, and AR curves. Total revenue (TR) is a straight line that slopes upward to the right. Its slope is constant because each extra unit of sales increases TR by $131. The demand curve (*D*) is horizontal, indicating perfect price elasticity. The MR curve coincides with the demand curve because the product price (and hence MR) is constant. The AR curve equals price and therefore also coincides with the demand curve.

FIGURE 7.1

A purely competitive firm's demand and revenue curves. The demand curve (*D*) of a purely competitive firm is a horizontal line (perfectly elastic) because the firm can sell as much output as it wants at the market price (here, $131). Because each additional unit sold increases total revenue by the amount of the price, the firm's total-revenue curve (TR) is a straight upward-sloping line and its marginal-revenue curve (MR) coincides with the firm's demand curve. The average-revenue curve (AR) also coincides with the demand curve.

Firm's Demand Schedule		Firm's Revenue Data	
(1) Product Price (*P*) (Average Revenue)	**(2)** Quantity Demanded (*Q*)	**(3)** Total Revenue (TR), (1) × (2)	**(4)** Marginal Revenue (MR)
$131	0	$ 0	
131	1	131	$131
131	2	262	131
131	3	393	131
131	4	524	131
131	5	655	131
131	6	786	131
131	7	917	131
131	8	1048	131
131	9	1179	131
131	10	1310	131

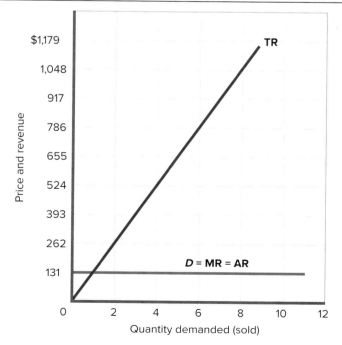

Profit Maximization in the Short Run

Because the purely competitive firm is a price taker, it cannot attempt to maximize its profit by raising or lowering the price it charges. With its price set by supply and demand in the overall market, the only variable that the firm can control is its output. Thus, the purely competitive firm attempts to maximize its economic profit (or minimize its economic loss) by adjusting its *output*. In the short run, the firm has a fixed plant. Thus it can adjust its output only through changes in the amount of variable resources (materials, labor) it uses. It adjusts its variable resources to achieve the output level that maximizes its profit.

To find the profit-maximizing output, the firm compares the amounts that each *additional* unit of output would add to total revenue and to total cost. In other words, the firm compares the *marginal revenue* (MR) and the *marginal cost* (MC) of each successive unit of output. Assuming that producing is preferable to shutting down, the firm should produce any unit of output whose marginal revenue exceeds its marginal cost because the firm will gain more in revenue from selling that unit than it would add to its costs by producing it. Conversely, if the marginal cost of a unit of output exceeds its marginal revenue, the firm should not produce that unit. Producing it would add more to costs than to revenue, and profit would decline or loss would increase.

In the initial stages of production, where output is relatively low, marginal revenue will usually (but not always) exceed marginal cost (MR > MC). So it is profitable to produce through this range of output. At later stages of production, where output is relatively high, rising marginal costs will exceed marginal revenue (MR < MC). Obviously, a profit-maximizing firm will want to avoid output levels in that range. Separating these two production ranges is a unique point at which marginal revenue equals marginal cost (MR = MC). This point is the key to the output-determining rule: *As long as producing is preferable to shutting down, the firm will maximize profit or minimize loss in the short run by producing the quantity of output at which marginal revenue equals marginal cost (MR = MR)*. This profit-maximizing guide is known as the **MR = MC rule.**

Keep in mind these features of the MR = MC rule:

MR = MC rule
The principle that a firm will maximize its profit (or minimize its losses) by producing the output at which marginal revenue and marginal cost are equal, provided product price is equal to or greater than average variable cost.

- For most sets of MR and MC data, MR and MC will be precisely equal at a fractional level of output. In such instances, the firm should produce the last complete unit of output for which MR exceeds MC.

- The rule applies only if producing is preferable to shutting down. If marginal revenue does not equal or exceed average variable cost, the firm will shut down rather than produce the amount of output.

- The rule is an accurate guide to profit maximization for all firms, whether they are purely competitive, monopolistic, monopolistically competitive, or oligopolistic.

- We can restate the rule as *P* = MC when applied to a purely competitive firm. Because the demand schedule faced by a competitive seller is perfectly elastic at the going market price, product price and marginal revenue are equal. So under pure competition (and only under pure competition), we may substitute *P* for MR in the rule: *When producing is preferable to shutting down, the purely competitive firm should produce at that point where price equals marginal cost (P = MC)*.

Now let's apply the MR = MC rule or, because we are considering pure competition, the *P* = MC rule.

Profit-Maximizing Case

The first five columns in the table in **Figure 7.2** include the AFC, AVC, ATC, and MC data derived for our product in Chapter 6. We will compare the marginal-cost data of column 5 with price (equals marginal revenue) for each unit of output. Suppose first that the market price, and therefore marginal revenue, is $131, as shown in column 6.

FIGURE 7.2

Short-run profit maximizing for a purely competitive firm. The MR = MC output enables the purely competitive firm to maximize profits or to minimize losses. In this case, MR (= P in pure competition) and MC are equal at an output Q of 9 units. There, P exceeds the average total cost A = $97.78, so the firm realizes an economic profit of P − A per unit. The total economic profit is represented by the green rectangle and is 9 × (P − A).

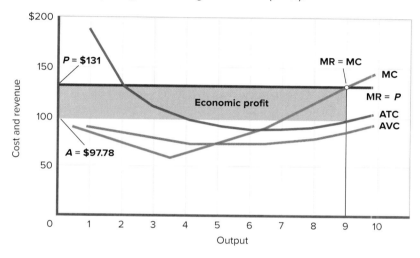

(1)	(2)	(3)	(4)	(5)	(6)	(7)
Total Product (Output)	Average Fixed Cost (AFC)	Average Variable Cost (AVC)	Average Total Cost (ATC)	Marginal Cost (MC)	$131 Price = Marginal Revenue (MR)	Total Economic Profit (+) or Loss (−)
0						$−100
1	$100.00	$90.00	$190.00	$ 90	$131	−59
2	50.00	85.00	135.00	80	131	−8
3	33.33	80.00	113.33	70	131	+53
4	25.00	75.00	100.00	60	131	+124
5	20.00	74.00	94.00	70	131	+185
6	16.67	75.00	91.67	80	131	+236
7	14.29	77.14	91.43	90	131	+277
8	12.50	81.25	93.75	110	131	+298
9	11.11	86.67	97.78	130	131	+299
10	10.00	93.00	103.00	150	131	+280

What is the profit-maximizing output? Every unit of output up to and including the ninth unit represents greater marginal revenue than marginal cost. Each of the first 9 units therefore adds to the firm's profit and should be produced. The tenth unit, however, should not be produced. It would add more to cost ($150) than to revenue ($131).

The economic profit realized by producing 9 units can be calculated by subtracting total cost from total revenue. Multiplying price ($131) by output (9) yields total revenue of $1,179. From the ATC data in column 4, we see that ATC is $97.78 at 9 units of output. Multiplying $97.78 by 9 gives us a total cost of $880.[1] The difference of $299 (= $1,179 − $880) is the economic profit. Clearly, this firm will prefer to operate rather than shut down.

Perhaps an easier way to calculate the economic profit is to use this simple equation, in which A is average total cost:

$$\text{Profit} = (P - A) \times Q$$

By subtracting the average total cost ($97.78) from the product price ($131), we obtain a per-unit profit of $33.22. Multiplying that amount by 9 units of output, we determine that the profit is $299 (rounded). Take some time now to verify the numbers in column 7. You will find that any output other than that which adheres to the MR = MC rule will yield either profits below $299 or losses.

Figure 7.2 also shows price (= MR) and marginal cost graphically. Price equals marginal cost at the profit-maximizing output of 9 units. There the per-unit economic profit is $P - A$, where P is the market price and A is the average total cost for an output of 9 units. The total economic profit is $9 \times (P - A)$, shown by the green rectangular area.

Loss-Minimizing Case

Now let's assume that the market price is $81 rather than $131. Should the firm still produce? If so, how much? And what will be the resulting profit or loss?

The first five columns of the table in **Figure 7.3** are the same as the first five columns of the table in **Figure 7.2**. Column 6 shows the new price (equal to MR), $81. Comparing columns 5 and 6, notice that the first unit of output adds $90 to total cost but only $81 to total revenue. One might conclude: "Don't produce—close down!" But that would be hasty. Remember that in the very early stages of production, marginal product is low, making marginal cost unusually high. The price–marginal cost relationship improves with increased production. For units 2 through 6, price exceeds marginal cost. Each of these 5 units adds more to revenue than to cost, and as shown in column 7, they decrease the total loss. Together, they more than compensate for the "loss" taken on the first unit. Beyond 6 units, however, MC exceeds MR (= P). The firm should therefore produce 6 units. In general, the profit-seeking producer should always compare marginal revenue (or price under pure competition) with the rising portion of the marginal-cost schedule or curve.

Will production be profitable? No, because at 6 units of output the average total cost of $91.67 exceeds the price of $81 by $10.67 per unit. If we multiply that by the 6 units of output, we find the firm's total loss is $64. Alternatively, comparing the total revenue of $486 (= 6 × $81) with the total cost of $550 (= 6 × $91.67), we see again that the firm's loss is $64.

Then why produce? Because this loss is less than the firm's $100 of fixed costs, which is the $100 loss the firm would incur in the short run by closing down. The firm receives enough revenue per unit ($81) to cover its average variable costs of $75 and also provide $6 per unit, or a total of $36, to apply against fixed costs. Therefore, the firm's loss is only $64 (= $100 − $36), not $100.

---

[1] Most of the unit-cost data are rounded figures from the total-cost figures presented in the previous chapter. Therefore, economic profits calculated from the unit-cost figures will typically vary by a few cents from the profits determined by subtracting actual total cost from total revenue. Here we simply ignore the few-cents differentials.

The graph in **Figure 7.3** illustrates this loss-minimizing case. Wherever price P exceeds AVC but is less than ATC, the firm can pay part, but not all, of its fixed costs by producing. The loss is minimized by producing the output at which MC = MR (here, 6 units). At that output, each unit contributes $P - V$ to covering fixed cost, where V is the AVC at 6 units of output. The per-unit loss is $A - P = \$10.67$, and the total loss is $6 \times (A - P)$, or 64, as shown by the red area.

FIGURE 7.3

Short-run loss minimization for a purely competitive firm. If price P exceeds the minimum AVC (here, 74 at $Q = 5$) but is less than ATC, the MR = MC output (here, 6 units) will permit the firm to minimize its losses. In this instance, the loss is $A - P$ per unit, where A is the average total cost at 6 units of output. The total loss is shown by the red area and is equal to $6 \times (A - P)$.

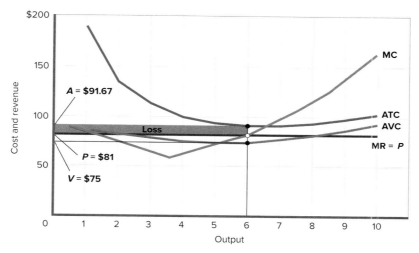

(1)	(2)	(3)	(4)	(5)	(6)	(7)
Total Product (Output)	Average Fixed Cost (AFC)	Average Variable Cost (AVC)	Average Total Cost (ATC)	Marginal Cost (MC)	$81 Price = Marginal Revenue (MR)	Profit (+) or Loss (−), $81 Price
0						$−100
1	$100.00	$90.00	$190.00	$ 90	$81	−109
2	50.00	85.00	135.00	80	81	−108
3	33.33	80.00	113.33	70	81	− 97
4	25.00	75.00	100.00	60	81	− 76
5	20.00	74.00	94.00	70	81	− 65
6	**16.67**	**75.00**	**91.67**	**80**	**81**	**−64**
7	14.29	77.14	91.43	90	81	− 73
8	12.50	81.25	93.75	110	81	−102
9	11.11	86.67	97.78	130	81	−151
10	10.00	93.00	103.00	150	81	−220

Shutdown Case

Suppose now that the market price is only $71. Should the firm produce? No, because at every output level the firm's average variable cost is greater than the price (compare columns 3 and 6 of the table in **Figure 7.4**). The smallest loss the firm can incur by producing is greater than the $100 fixed cost it will lose by shutting down (as shown by column 7). The best action is to shut down.

FIGURE 7.4
The short-run shutdown case for a purely competitive firm. If price P (here, $71) falls below the minimum AVC (here, $74 at Q = 5), the competitive firm will minimize its losses in the short run by shutting down. There is no level of output at which the firm can produce and realize a loss smaller than its total fixed cost.

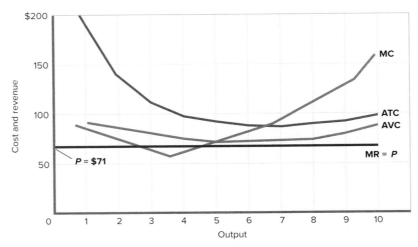

(1)	(2)	(3)	(4)	(5)	(6)	(7)
	Average	Average	Average		$71 Price =	
Total	Fixed	Variable	Total	Marginal	Marginal	Profit (+)
Product	Cost	Cost	Cost	Cost	Revenue	or Loss (−),
(Output)	(AFC)	(AVC)	(ATC)	(MC)	(MR)	$81 Price
0						**$−100**
				$ 90	$71	
1	$100.00	$90.00	$190.00			−119
				80	71	
2	50.00	85.00	135.00			−128
				70	71	
3	33.33	80.00	113.33			−127
				60	71	
4	25.00	75.00	100.00			−116
				70	71	
5	20.00	74.00	94.00			−115
				80	71	
6	16.67	75.00	91.67			−124
				90	71	
7	14.29	77.14	91.43			−143
				110	71	
8	12.50	81.25	93.75			−182
				130	71	
9	11.11	86.67	97.78			−241
				150	71	
10	10.00	93.00	103.00			−320

You can see this shutdown situation in the graph in **Figure 7.4**, where the MR = P line lies below AVC at all points. Price comes closest to covering average variable costs at the MR (= P) = MC output of 5 units. But even here, price or revenue per unit would fall short of average variable cost by $3 (= $74 − $71). By producing at the MR (= P) = MC output, the firm would lose its $100 worth of fixed cost plus 15 (= $3 of variable cost on each of the 5 units), for a total loss of $115. This compares unfavorably with the $100 fixed-cost loss the firm would incur by shutting down and producing no output. So it will make sense for the firm to shut down rather than produce at a $71 price—or at any price less than the minimum average variable cost of $74.

The shutdown case reminds us of the qualifier to our MR (= P) = MC rule. A competitive firm maximizes profit or minimizes loss in the short run by producing that output at which MR (= P) = MC, *provided that market price exceeds minimum average variable cost.*

APPLYING THE ANALYSIS

The Still There Motel

Have you ever driven by a poorly maintained business facility and wondered why the owner does not either fix up the property or go out of business? The somewhat surprising reason is that it may be unprofitable to improve the facility yet profitable to continue for a time to operate the business as it deteriorates. Seeing why will aid your understanding of the "stay open or shut down" decision facing firms experiencing declining demand.

Consider the Still There Motel on Old Highway North, Anytown, USA. The owner built the motel on the basis of traffic patterns and competition existing several decades ago. But as interstate highways were built, the motel found itself located on a relatively untraveled stretch of road. Also, it faced severe competition from "chain" motels located much closer to the interstate highway.

As demand and revenue fell, Still There moved from profitability to loss ($P <$ ATC). But at first its room rates and annual revenue were sufficient to cover its total variable costs and contribute some to the payment of fixed costs such as insurance and property taxes ($P >$ AVC). By staying open, Still There lost less than it would have if it shut down. But since its total revenue did not cover its total costs (or $P <$ ATC), the owner realized that something must be done in the long run. So the owner decided to lower average total costs by reducing annual maintenance. In effect, the owner opted to allow the motel to deteriorate as a way of regaining temporary profitability.

This renewed profitability of Still There cannot last, because in time no further reduction in maintenance costs will be possible. The further deterioration of the motel structure will produce even lower room rates, and therefore even less total revenue. The owner of Still There knows that sooner or later total revenue will again fall below total cost (or P will again fall below ATC), even with an annual maintenance expense of zero. When that occurs, the owner will close down the business, tear down the structure, and sell the vacant property. But, in the meantime, the motel is still there—open, deteriorating, and profitable.

QUESTION:

Why might even a well-maintained, profitable motel shut down in the long run if the land on which it is located becomes extremely valuable due to surrounding economic development?

Marginal Cost and Short-Run Supply

In the preceding section, we selected three different prices and asked what quantity the profit-seeking competitive firm, faced with certain costs, would choose to offer in the market at each price. This set of product prices and corresponding quantities supplied constitutes part of the supply schedule for the competitive firm.

Table 7.1 summarizes the supply schedule data for those three prices ($131, $81, and $71) and four others. This table confirms the direct relationship between product price and quantity supplied that we identified in **Chapter 3**. Note first that the firm will not produce at price $61 or $71 because both are less than the $74 minimum AVC. Then, note that quantity supplied increases as price increases. Observe finally that economic profit is higher at higher prices.

Generalized Depiction

Figure 7.5 displays the ATC, AVC, and MC curves, along with several marginal-revenue lines drawn at possible market prices. Let's observe quantity supplied at each of these prices:

- Price P_1 is below the firm's minimum average variable cost, so at this price the firm won't operate at all. Quantity supplied will be zero, as it will be at all other prices below P_2.

- Price P_2 is just equal to the minimum average variable cost. The firm will supply Q_2 units of output (where $MR_2 = MC$) and just cover its total variable cost. Its loss will equal its total fixed cost. (Actually, the firm will be indifferent as to shutting down or supplying Q_2 units of output, but we assume it produces.)

- At price P_3, the firm will supply Q_3 units of output to minimize its short-run losses. At any other price between P_2 and P_4, the firm will minimize its losses by producing and supplying the quantity at which $MR = MC$.

- The firm will just break even at price P_4. There it will supply Q_4 units of output (where $MR_4 = MC$), earning a normal profit but not an economic profit. Total revenue will just cover total cost, including a normal profit, because the revenue per unit ($MR_4 = P_4$) and the total cost per unit (ATC) are the same.

- At price P_5, the firm will realize an economic profit by producing and supplying Q_5 units of output. In fact, at any price above P_4, the firm will obtain economic profit by producing to the point where $MR (= P) = MC$.

TABLE 7.1

The Supply Schedule of a Competitive Firm Confronted with the Cost Data in the Table in Figure 7.2

Price	Quantity Supplied	Maximum Profit (+) or Minimum loss (−)
$151	10	$+480
131	9	+299
111	8	+138
91	7	−3
81	6	−64
71	0	−100
61	0	−100

FIGURE 7.5

The *P* = MC rule and the competitive firm's short-run supply curve. Application of the *P* = MC rule, as modified by the shutdown case, reveals that the (solid) segment of the firm's MC curve that lies above AVC is the firm's short-run supply curve.

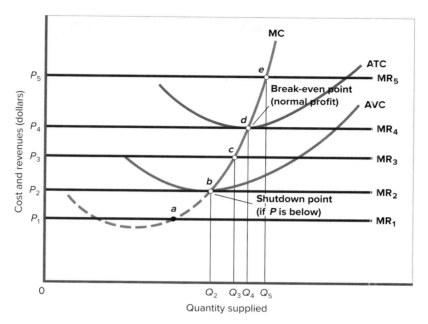

Note that each of the MR (= *P*) = MC intersection points labeled *b, c, d,* and *e* in **Figure 7.5** indicates a possible product price (on the vertical axis) and the corresponding quantity that the firm would supply at that price (on the horizontal axis). Thus, these points are on the upward sloping supply curve of the competitive firm. Note, too, that quantity supplied would be zero at any price below the minimum average variable cost (AVC). *We can conclude that the portion of the firm's marginal-cost curve lying above its average-variable-cost curve is its short-run supply curve.* In **Figure 7.5,** the solid segment of the marginal-cost curve MC *is* this firm's **short-run supply curve.** It tells us the amount of output the firm will supply at each price in a series of prices.

Table 7.2 summarizes the MR = MC approach to determining the competitive firm's profit-maximizing output level.

short-run supply curve
A supply curve that shows the quantity of a product a firm in a purely competitive industry will offer to sell at various prices in the short run; the portion of the firm's short-run marginal cost curve that lies above its average-variable-cost curve.

TABLE 7.2

Output Determination in Pure Competition in the Short Run

Question	Answer
Should this firm produce?	Yes, if price is equal to, or greater than, minimum average variable cost. This means that the firm is profitable or that its losses are less than its fixed cost.
What quantity should this firm produce?	Produce where MR (= *P*) = MC; there, profit is maximized (TR exceeds TC by a maximum amount) or loss is minimized.
Will production result in economic profit?	Yes, if price exceeds average total cost (so that TR exceeds TC). No, if average total cost exceeds price (so that TC exceeds TR).

Firm and Industry: Equilibrium Price

We have established the competitive firm's short-run supply curve by applying the MR (= P) = MC rule. But which of the various possible prices will actually be the market equilibrium price?

We know that the market equilibrium price will be the price at which the total quantity supplied of the product equals the total quantity demanded. So to determine the equilibrium price, we first need to obtain a total supply schedule and a total demand schedule. We find the total supply schedule by assuming a particular number of firms in the industry and supposing that each firm has the same individual supply schedule as the firm represented in **Figure 7.5**. Then, we sum the quantities supplied at each price level to obtain the total (or market) supply schedule. Columns 1 and 3 in **Table 7.3** repeat the supply schedule for the individual competitive firm, as derived in **Table 7.1**. Suppose 1,000 firms compete in this industry, all having the same total and unit costs as the single firm we discussed. We can calculate the market supply schedule (columns 2 and 3) by multiplying the quantity-supplied figures of the single firm (column 1) by 1,000.

Market Price and Profits   To determine the equilibrium price and output, we must compare the total-supply data with total-demand data. Let's assume that total demand is shown in columns 3 and 4 in **Table 7.3**. By comparing the total quantity supplied and the total quantity demanded at the seven possible prices, we determine that the equilibrium price is $111 and the equilibrium quantity is 8,000 units for the industry—8 units for each of the 1,000 identical firms.

Will these conditions of market supply and demand make this a profitable or unprofitable industry? Multiplying product price ($111) by output (8 units), we find that the total revenue of each firm is $888. The total cost is $750, found by looking at column 4 of the table in **Figure 6.3**. The $138 difference is the economic profit of each firm. For the industry, total economic profit is $138,000. This, then, is a profitable industry.

Another way of calculating economic profit is to determine per-unit profit by subtracting average total cost ($93.75) from product price ($111) and multiplying the difference (per-unit profit of $17.25) by the firm's equilibrium level of output (8). Again we obtain an economic profit of $138 per firm and $138,000 for the industry.

TABLE 7.3
Firm and Market Supply and Market Demand

(1) Quantity Supplied, Single Firm	(2) Total Quantity Supplied, 1,000 Firms	(3) Product Price	(4) Total Quantity Demanded
10	10,000	$151	4,000
9	9,000	131	6,000
8	**8,000**	**111**	**8,000**
7	7,000	91	9,000
6	6,000	81	11,000
0	0	71	13,000
0	0	61	16,000

Figure 7.6 shows this analysis graphically. The individual supply curves of each of the 1,000 identical firms—one of which is shown as s = MC in **Figure 7.6a**—are summed horizontally to get the total-supply curve S = ΣMC's of **Figure 7.6b**. With total-demand curve D, it yields the equilibrium price $111 and an equilibrium quantity (for the industry) of 8,000 units. This equilibrium price is given and unalterable to the individual firm; that is, each firm's demand curve is perfectly elastic at the equilibrium price, as indicated by d in **Figure 7.6a**. Because the individual firm is a price taker, the marginal-revenue curve coincides with the firm's demand curve d. This $111 price exceeds the average total cost at the firm's equilibrium MR = MC output of 8 units, so the firm earns an economic profit represented by the green area in **Figure 7.6a**.

Assuming no changes in costs or market demand, these diagrams reveal a genuine equilibrium in the short run. No shortages or surpluses occur in the market to cause price or total quantity to change. Nor can any firm in the industry increase its profit by altering its output. Note, however, that higher unit and marginal costs, on the one hand, or weaker market demand on the other, could change the situation to losses ($P <$ ATC) or even to shutdown ($P <$ AVC).

Firm versus Industry   **Figure 7.6** underscores a point made earlier: Product price is a given fact to the *individual* competitive firm, but the supply plans of all competitive producers as *a group* are a basic determinant of product price. There is no inconsistency here. Although one firm, supplying a negligible fraction of total supply, cannot affect price, the sum of the supply curves of all the firms in the industry constitutes the market supply curve, and that curve does have an important bearing on equilibrium price. The individual firms are *price takers*. Their collective supply is a *price maker*.

FIGURE 7.6

Short-run competitive equilibrium for (a) a firm and (b) the industry. The horizontal sum of the 1,000 firms' individual supply curves (s) determines the industry (market) supply curve (S). Given industry (market) demand (D), the short-run equilibrium price and output for the industry are $111 and 8,000 units. Taking the equilibrium price as given, the individual firm establishes its profit-maximizing output at 8 units and, in this case, realizes the economic profit represented by the green area.

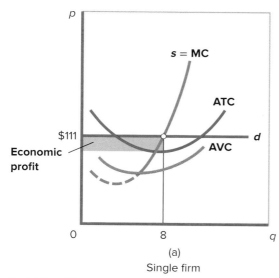

(a)
Single firm

David Sachs/Getty Images

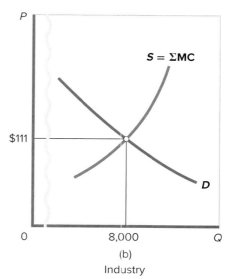

(b)
Industry

Ingram Publishing/Superstock RF

Profit Maximization in the Long Run

The entry and exit of firms in our market models can only take place in the long run. In the short run, the industry is composed of a specific number of firms, each with a fixed plant size. Firms may shut down in the sense that they can produce zero units of output in the short run, but they do not have sufficient time to liquidate their assets and go out of business.

In the long run, by contrast, the firms already in an industry have sufficient time to either expand or contract their capacities. The number of firms in the industry may increase or decrease as new firms enter or existing firms leave.

The length of time constituting the long run varies substantially by industry, however, so do not think in terms of a specific number of years, months, or days. Instead, focus your attention on the incentives provided by profits and losses. The time horizons are far less important than the process by which profits and losses guide business managers toward the efficient use of resources.

Assumptions

We make three simplifying assumptions, none of which alters our conclusions:

- *Entry and exit only* The only long-run adjustment in our graphical analysis is caused by the entry or exit of firms. Moreover, we ignore all short-run adjustments in order to concentrate on the effects of the long-run adjustments.
- *Identical costs* All firms in the industry have identical cost curves. This assumption lets us discuss an "average," or "representative," firm, knowing that all other firms in the industry are similarly affected by any long-run adjustments.
- *Constant-cost industry* The industry is a constant-cost industry. This means that the entry and exit of firms do not affect resource prices or, consequently, the individual firms' ATC curves.

Goal of Our Analysis

The basic conclusion we seek to explain is this: After all long-run adjustments are completed in a purely competitive industry, product price will be exactly equal to, and production will occur at, each firm's minimum average total cost.

This conclusion follows from two basic facts: (1) Firms seek profits and shun losses and (2) under pure competition, firms are free to enter and leave an industry. If market price initially exceeds minimum average total costs, the resulting economic profits will attract new firms to the industry. But this industry expansion will increase supply until price decreases to minimum average total cost. Conversely, if price is initially less than minimum average total cost, the resulting loss will cause firms to leave the industry. As they leave, total supply will decline, increasing the price to minimum average total cost.

Long-Run Equilibrium

Consider the average firm in a purely competitive industry that is initially in long-run equilibrium. This firm is represented in **Figure 7.7a**, where MR = MC and price and minimum average total cost are equal at $50. Economic profit here is zero; the industry is in equilibrium or "at rest" because there is no tendency for firms to enter or to leave. The existing firms are earning normal profits, which means that their accounting profits are equal to the profits that the firms' owners can expect to receive on average in alternative business ventures. The $50 market price is determined in **Figure 7.7b** by market or industry demand D_1 and supply S_1. (S_1 is a short-run supply curve; we will develop the long-run industry supply curve in our discussion.)

FIGURE 7.7

Temporary profits and the reestablishment of long-run equilibrium in (a) a representative firm and (b) the industry.
A favorable shift in demand (D_1 to D_2) will upset the original industry equilibrium and produce economic profits. But those profits will entice new firms to enter the industry, increasing supply (S_1 to S_2) and lowering product price until economic profits are once again zero.

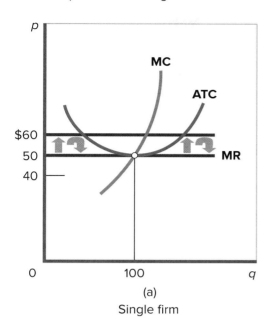
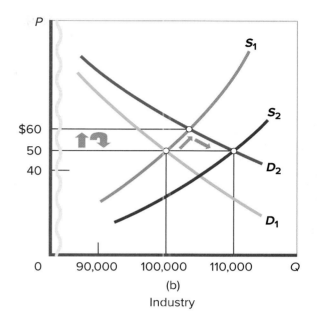

(a)
Single firm

(b)
Industry

As shown on the quantity axes of the two graphs, equilibrium output in the industry is 100,000, while equilibrium output for the single firm is 100. If all firms in the industry are identical, there must be 1,000 firms (=100,000/100).

Entry Eliminates Economic Profits Let's upset the long-run equilibrium in **Figure 7.7** and see what happens. Suppose a change in consumer tastes increases product demand from D_1 to D_2. Price will rise to $60, as determined at the intersection of D_2 and S_1, and the firm's marginal-revenue curve will shift upward to $60. This $60 price exceeds the firm's average total cost of $50 at output 100, creating an economic profit of $10 per unit. This economic profit will lure new firms into the industry. Some entrants will be newly created firms; others will shift from less-prosperous industries.

As firms enter, the market supply of the product increases, pushing the product price below $60. Economic profits persist, and entry continues until short-run supply increases to S_2. Market price falls to $50, as does marginal revenue for the firm. Price and minimum average total cost are again equal at $50. The economic profits caused by the boost in demand have been eliminated, and, as a result, the previous incentive for more firms to enter the industry has disappeared because the remaining firms are earning only a normal profit (zero economic profit). Entry ceases and a new long-run equilibrium is reached.

As **Figures 7.7a** and **7.7b** show, total quantity supplied is now 110,000 units and each firm is producing 100 units. Now 1,100 firms rather than the original 1,000 populate the industry. Economic profits have attracted 100 more firms.

Exit Eliminates Losses Now let's consider a shift in the opposite direction. We begin in **Figure 7.8b** with curves S_1 and D_1 setting the same initial long-run equilibrium situation as in our previous analysis, including the $50 price.

FIGURE 7.8

Temporary losses and the reestablishment of long-run equilibrium in (a) a representative firm and (b) the industry.
An unfavorable shift in demand (D_1 to D_3) will upset the original industry equilibrium and produce losses. But those losses will cause firms to leave the industry, decreasing supply (S_1 to S_3) and increasing product price until all losses have disappeared.

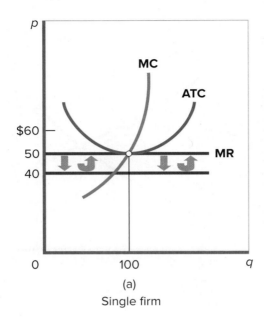
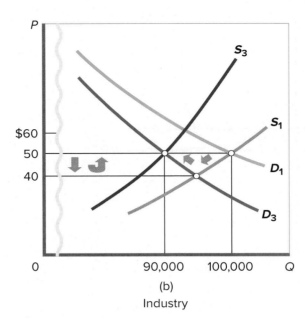

(a)
Single firm

(b)
Industry

Suppose consumer demand declines from D_1 to D_3. This forces the market price and marginal revenue down to $40, making production unprofitable at the minimum ATC of $50. In time, the resulting economic losses will induce firms to leave the industry. Their owners will seek a normal profit elsewhere rather than accept the below-normal profits (losses) now confronting them. As this exodus of firms proceeds, industry supply decreases, pushing the price up from $40 toward $50. Losses continue and more firms leave the industry until the supply curve shifts to S_3. Price is again $50, just equal to the minimum average total cost. Losses have been eliminated, and the remaining firms are earning only a normal profit (zero economic profit). Because this is no better or worse than entrepreneurs could expect to earn in other business ventures, there is no longer any incentive to exit the industry. Long-run equilibrium is restored.

In **Figures 7.8a** and **7.8b**, total quantity supplied is now 90,000 units, and each firm is producing 100 units. Only 900 firms, not the original 1,000, populate the industry. Losses have forced 100 firms out.

You may have noted that we have sidestepped the question of which firms will leave the industry when losses occur by assuming that all firms have identical cost curves. In the real world, of course, managerial talents differ. Even if resource prices and technology are the same for all firms, less skillfully managed firms tend to incur higher costs and therefore are the first to leave an industry when demand declines. Similarly, firms with less-productive labor forces or higher transportation costs will be higher-cost producers and likely candidates to quit an industry when demand decreases.

APPLYING THE ANALYSIS

Running a Company Is Hard Business

The life expectancy of a U.S. business is just 10.2 years. About 9.5 percent of U.S. firms go out of business each year. In addition, 22 percent of new start-up firms go bankrupt within 2 years, 53 percent within 5 years, and nearly 65 percent within 10 years.

Wendell and Carolyn/Getty Images

These numbers testify to the ability of competition to quickly dispose of firms that have high production costs or unpopular products. In a competitive environment, such firms quickly prove unprofitable and are shut down by their owners.

Balancing out the dying firms are start-ups that hope to use the resources freed up by the closed firms to deliver better products or lower costs. In a typical year, more than 650,000 new businesses are started in the United States. Most of these new firms will themselves eventually fall victim to creative destruction and the pressures of competition, but one of them may just be the next SpaceX, Starbucks, or Amazon.

> QUESTIONS:
>
> What factors might affect the life expectancy of a new business? What types of businesses might last longer, on average? Which would fail quicker?

Long-Run Supply for a Constant-Cost Industry

Although our analysis has dealt with the long run, we have noted that the market supply curves in **Figures 7.7b** and **7.8b** are short-run curves. What then is the character of the **long-run supply curve** of a competitive industry? Our analysis points us toward an answer. The crucial factor here is the effect, if any, that changes in the number of firms in the industry will have on costs of the individual firms in the industry.

Our analysis thus far has assumed that the industry under discussion is a **constant-cost industry** in which industry expansion or contraction does not affect resource prices and therefore production costs. Graphically, constant costs mean that firms' entry or exit does not shift individual firms' long-run ATC curves. This is the case when the industry's demand for resources is small in relation to the total demand for those resources. Then the industry can expand or contract without significantly affecting resource prices and costs.

long-run supply curve
A curve showing the prices at which a purely competitive industry will make various quantities of the product available in the long run.

constant-cost industry
An industry in which expansion by the entry of new firms has no effect on the prices firms in the industry must pay for resources and thus no effect on production costs.

What does the long-run supply curve of a constant-cost industry look like? The answer is contained in our previous analysis. There we saw that the entry and exit of firms changes industry output but always brings the product price back to its original level, where it is just equal to the constant minimum ATC. Specifically, we discovered that the industry would supply 90,000, 100,000, or 110,000 units of output, all at a price of $50 per unit. In other words, the long-run supply curve of a constant-cost industry is perfectly elastic.

Figure 7.9a demonstrates this graphically. Suppose industry demand is originally D_1, industry output is Q_1 (100,000 units), and product price is P_1 ($50). This situation, from **Figure 7.7**, is one of long-run equilibrium. We saw that when demand increases to D_2, upsetting this equilibrium, the resulting economic profits attract new firms. Because this is a constant-cost industry, entry continues and industry output expands until the price is driven back down to the level of the unchanged minimum ATC. This is at price P_2 ($50) and output Q_2 (110,000).

From **Figure 7.8**, we saw that a decline in market demand from D_1 to D_3 causes an exit of firms and ultimately restores equilibrium at price P_3 ($50) and output Q_3 (90,000 units). The points Z_1, Z_2, and Z_3 in **Figure 7.9a** represent these three price-quantity combinations. A line or curve connecting all such points shows the various price-quantity combinations that firms would produce if they had enough time to make all desired adjustments to changes in demand. This line or curve is the industry's long-run supply curve. In a constant-cost industry, this curve (straight line) is horizontal, as in **Figure 7.9a**, thus representing perfectly elastic supply.

FIGURE 7.9

Long-run supply: constant-cost industry versus increasing-cost industry.

(a) In a constant-cost industry, the entry of firms does not affect resource prices or, therefore, unit costs. So an increase in demand (D_1 to D_2) or a decrease in demand (D_1 to D_3) causes a change in industry output (Q_1 to Q_2 or Q_1 to Q_3) but no alteration in price ($50). Thus the long-run industry supply curve (S) is horizontal through points Z_3, Z_1, and Z_2. (b) In an increasing-cost industry, the entry of new firms in response to an increase in demand (D_3 to D_1 to D_2) will bid up resource prices and thereby increase unit costs. As a result, an increased industry output (Q_3 to Q_1 to Q_2) will be forthcoming only at higher prices ($45 to $50 to $55). The long-run industry supply curve (S) therefore slopes upward through points Y_3, Y_1, and Y_2.

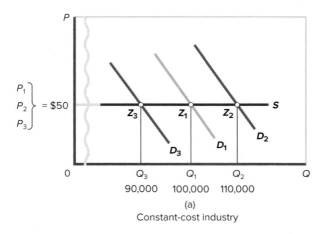

(a)
Constant-cost industry

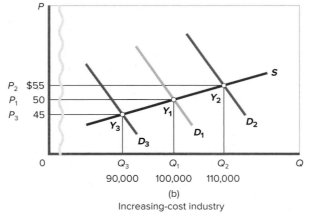

(b)
Increasing-cost industry

Long-Run Supply for an Increasing-Cost Industry

Constant-cost industries are a special case. Most industries are **increasing-cost industries,** in which firms' ATC curves shift upward as the industry expands and downward as the industry contracts. The construction and medical care industries are examples.

Usually, the entry of new firms will increase resource prices, particularly in industries using specialized resources whose long-run supplies do not readily increase in response to increases in resource demand. Higher resource prices result in higher long-run average total costs for all firms in the industry. These higher costs shift each firm's long-run ATC curve upward.

Thus, when an increase in product demand results in economic profits and attracts new firms to an increasing-cost industry, a two-way squeeze works to eliminate those profits. As before, the entry of new firms increases market supply and lowers the market price. But now each firm's ATC curve also shifts upward. The overall result is a higher-than-original equilibrium price. The industry produces a larger output at a higher product price because the industry expansion has increased resource prices and the minimum average total cost.

Because more output will be supplied at a higher price, the long-run industry supply curve is upward sloping. Instead of supplying 90,000, 100,000, or 110,000 units at the same price of $50, an increasing-cost industry might supply 90,000 units at $45, 100,000 units at $50, and 110,000 units at $55. A higher price is required to induce more production because costs per unit of output increase as production rises.

Figure 7.9b nicely illustrates the situation. Original market demand is D_1 and industry price and output are P_1 ($50) and Q_1 (100,000 units), respectively, at equilibrium point Y_1. An increase in demand to D_2 upsets this equilibrium and leads to economic profits. New firms enter the industry, increasing both market supply and production costs of individual firms. A new price is established at point Y_2, where P_2 is $55 and Q_2 is 110,000 units.

Conversely, a decline in demand from D_1 to D_3 makes production unprofitable and causes firms to leave the industry. The resulting decline in resource prices reduces the minimum average total cost of production for firms that stay. A new equilibrium price is established at some level below the original price, say, at point Y_3, where P_3 is $45 and Q_3 is 90,000 units. Connecting these three equilibrium positions, we derive the upward sloping long-run supply curve S in **Figure 7.9b**.

increasing-cost industry
An industry in which expansion through the entry of new firms raises the prices firms in the industry must pay for resources and therefore increases their production costs.

Long-Run Supply for a Decreasing-Cost Industry

In **decreasing-cost industries,** firms experience lower costs as their industry expands. The personal computer industry is an example. As demand for personal computers increased, new manufacturers of computers entered the industry and greatly increased the resource demand for the components used to build them (e.g., memory chips, hard drives, monitors, and operating software). The expanded production of the components enabled the producers of those items to achieve substantial economies of scale. The decreased production costs of the components reduced their prices, which greatly lowered the computer manufacturers' average costs of production. The supply of personal computers increased by more than demand, and the price of personal computers declined. Although not shown in **Figure 7.9**, the long-run supply curve of a decreasing-cost industry is *downward sloping.*

decreasing-cost industry
An industry in which expansion through the entry of firms lowers the prices that firms in the industry must pay for resources and therefore decreases their production costs.

PHOTO OP

Increasing-Cost versus Decreasing-Cost Industries

Mining is an example of an increasing-cost industry, whereas electronics is an example of a decreasing-cost industry.

rozpedowski/iStock/Getty Images

Henrik Jonsson/Getty Images

Unfortunately, the industries that show decreasing costs when output expands also show increasing costs if output contracts. A decline in demand (say from foreign competition) makes production unprofitable and causes firms to leave the industry. Firms that remain face a greater minimum average total cost of production, implying a higher long-run equilibrium price in the market.

Pure Competition and Efficiency

Our final goal in this chapter is to examine the efficiency characteristics of individual firms and the market after long-run adjustments in pure competition. Assuming a constant- or increasing-cost industry, the final long-run equilibrium positions of all firms have the same basic efficiency characteristics. As shown in **Figure 7.10**, price (and marginal revenue) will settle where it is equal to minimum average total cost: P (and MR) = minimum ATC. Moreover, because the MC curve intersects the ATC curve at its minimum point, marginal cost and average total cost are equal: MC = minimum ATC. So in long-run equilibrium, a multiple equality occurs: P (and MR) = MC = minimum ATC. Thus, in long-run equilibrium, each firm produces at the output level that is associated with this triple equality.[2]

The triple equality tells us two important things about long-run equilibrium. First, although a competitive firm may realize economic profit or loss in the short run, it will earn only a normal profit by producing in accordance with the MR (= P) = MC rule in the long run. Second, the triple equality tells us that in long-run equilibrium, the profit-maximizing decision that leads each firm to produce the quantity at which P = MC also implies that each firm will produce at the output level that is associated with the minimum point on each identical firm's ATC curve.

These conclusions are important because they suggest that pure competition leads to the most efficient possible use of society's resources. Indeed, subject only to Chapter 5's qualifications relating to public goods and externalities, an idealized purely competitive market economy composed of constant- or increasing-cost industries will generate both productive efficiency and allocative efficiency.

---

[2] This triple equality does not hold for decreasing-cost industries because MC always remains below ATC if average costs are decreasing. We will discuss this situation of "natural monopoly" in Chapter 8.

FIGURE 7.10

Long-run equilibrium of a competitive firm. The equality of price (*P*), marginal cost (MC), and minimum average total cost (ATC) at output Q_f indicates that the firm is achieving productive efficiency and allocative efficiency. It is using the most efficient technology, charging the lowest price, and producing the greatest output consistent with its costs. It is receiving only a normal profit, which is incorporated into the ATC curve. The equality of price and marginal cost indicates that society allocated its scarce resources in accordance with consumer preferences.

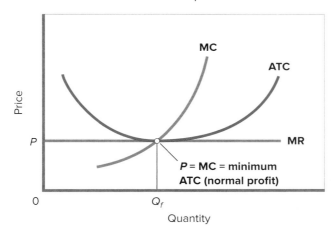

Productive Efficiency: *P* = Minimum ATC

Productive efficiency requires that goods be produced in the least costly way. In the long run, pure competition forces firms to produce at the minimum average total cost of production and to charge a price that is just consistent with that cost. Firms that do not use the best-available (least-cost) production methods and combinations of inputs will not survive.

To see why, let's suppose that **Figure 7.10** represents pure competition in the cucumber industry. In the final equilibrium position shown in **Figure 7.10**, suppose each firm in the cucumber industry is producing 100 units (say, pickup truckloads) of output by using $5,000 (equal to average total cost of $50 × 100 units) worth of resources. If any firm produced that same amount of output at any higher total cost, say $7,000, it would be wasting resources because all of the other firms in the industry are able to produce that same amount of output using only $5,000 worth of resources. Society would be faced with a net loss of $2,000 worth of alternative products. But this cannot occur in pure competition; this firm would incur a loss of $2,000, requiring it to either reduce its costs or go out of business.

Note, too, that consumers benefit from productive efficiency by paying the lowest product price possible under the prevailing technology and cost conditions. And the firm receives only a normal profit, which is part of its economic costs and thus incorporated in its ATC curve.

Allocative Efficiency: *P* = MC

Long-run equilibrium in pure competition guarantees productive efficiency, with output produced in the least-cost way. But productive efficiency by itself does not guarantee that anyone will want to buy the items that are being produced. For all we know, consumers might prefer to redirect the resources used to produce those items toward producing other products.

Fortunately, long-run equilibrium in pure competition also guarantees *allocative efficiency*, so we can be certain that society's scarce resources are directed toward producing the goods and services that people most want to consume. Stated formally, allocative efficiency occurs when it is impossible to produce any net gains for society by altering the combination of goods and services that are produced from society's limited supply of resources. There are two critical elements here:

- The money price of any product is society's measure of the relative worth of an additional unit of that product—for example, cucumbers. So the price of a unit of cucumbers is the marginal benefit derived from that unit of the product.
- Similarly, recalling the idea of opportunity cost, we see that the marginal cost of an additional unit of a product measures the value, or relative worth, of the other goods sacrificed to obtain it. In producing cucumbers, resources are drawn away from producing other goods. The marginal cost of producing a unit of cucumbers measures society's sacrifice of those other products.

Efficient Allocation   In pure competition, when profit-motivated firms produce each good or service to the point where price (marginal benefit) and marginal cost are equal, society's resources are being allocated efficiently. Each item is being produced to the point at which the value of the last unit is equal to the value of the alternative goods sacrificed by its production. Altering the production of cucumbers would reduce consumer satisfaction. Producing cucumbers beyond the $P = MC$ point in **Figure 7.10** would sacrifice alternative goods whose value to society exceeds that of the extra cucumbers. Producing cucumbers short of the $P = MC$ point would sacrifice cucumbers that society values more than the alternative goods its resources could produce.

Dynamic Adjustments   Another attribute of purely competitive markets is their ability to restore efficiency when disrupted by changes in the economy. A change in consumer tastes, resource supplies, or technology will automatically set in motion the appropriate realignments of resources. For example, suppose that cucumbers and pickles become dramatically more popular. First, the price of cucumbers will increase, and so, at current output, the price of cucumbers will exceed their marginal cost. At this point, efficiency will be lost, but the higher price will create economic profits in the cucumber industry and stimulate its expansion. The profitability of cucumbers will permit the industry to bid resources away from now less-pressing uses, say, watermelons. Expansion of the industry will end only when the price of cucumbers and their marginal cost are equal—that is, when allocative efficiency has been restored.

Similarly, a change in the supply of a particular resource—for example, the field laborers who pick cucumbers—or in a production technique will upset an existing price–marginal-cost equality by either raising or lowering marginal cost. The resulting inequality of MC and P will cause business managers, in either pursuing profit or avoiding loss, to reallocate resources until price once again equals marginal cost. In so doing, they will correct any inefficiency in the allocation of resources that the original change may have temporarily imposed on the economy.

"Invisible Hand" Revisited   The highly efficient allocation of resources that a purely competitive economy promotes comes about because businesses and resource suppliers seek to further their self-interest. For private goods with no externalities (Chapter 5), the "invisible hand" (Chapter 2) is at work. The competitive system not only maximizes profits for individual producers but at the same time creates a pattern of resource allocation that maximizes consumer satisfaction. The invisible hand thus organizes the private interests of producers in a way that is fully in sync with society's interest in using scarce resources efficiently. Striving for profit produces highly desirable economic outcomes.

Summary

LO7.1 Summarize the main characteristics of the four basic market models.

Economists group industries into four models based on their market structures: (a) pure competition, (b) monopolistic competition, (c) oligopoly, and (d) pure monopoly.

LO7.2 List the conditions required for purely competitive markets.

A purely competitive industry consists of a large number of independent firms producing a standardized product. Pure competition assumes that firms and resources are mobile among different industries. Firms can freely enter or exit a purely competitive industry.

LO7.3 Describe how purely competitive firms maximize profits or minimize losses.

In a competitive industry, no single firm can influence market price. This means that the firm's demand curve is perfectly elastic and price equals both marginal revenue and average revenue.

Provided price exceeds minimum average variable cost, a competitive firm maximizes profit or minimizes loss in the short run by producing the output at which price or marginal revenue equals marginal cost.

If price is less than minimum average variable cost, a competitive firm minimizes its loss by shutting down. If price is greater than average variable cost but is less than average total cost, a competitive firm minimizes its loss by producing the $P = MC$ amount of output. If price also exceeds average total cost, the firm maximizes its economic profit at the $P = MC$ amount of output.

LO7.4 Explain why a competitive firm's marginal cost curve is also its supply curve.

Applying the MR ($= P$) $= MC$ rule at various possible market prices leads to the conclusion that the segment of the firm's short-run marginal-cost curve that lies above the firm's average-variable-cost curve is its short-run supply curve.

LO7.5 Describe how profits and losses drive the long-run adjustment process of pure competition.

In the long run, the market price of a product will equal the minimum average total cost of production. At a higher price, economic profits would entice firms to enter the industry until those profits had been competed away. At a lower price, losses would force firms to exit the industry until the product price rose to equal average total cost.

LO7.6 Explain the differences between constant-cost, increasing-cost, and decreasing-cost industries.

The long-run supply curve is horizontal for a constant-cost industry, upward sloping for an increasing-cost industry, and downward sloping for a decreasing-cost industry.

LO7.7 Show how long-run equilibrium in pure competition produces an efficient allocation of resources.

The long-run equality of price and minimum average total cost means that competitive firms will use the most efficient known technology and charge the lowest price consistent with their production costs. That is, purely competitive firms will achieve productive efficiency.

The long-run equality of price and marginal cost implies that resources will be allocated in accordance with consumer tastes. Allocative efficiency will occur. The competitive price system will reallocate resources in response to a change in consumer tastes, in technology, or in resource supplies and will thereby maintain allocative efficiency over time.

Terms and Concepts

pure competition

price taker

average revenue (AR)

total revenue (TR)

marginal revenue (MR)

MR = MC rule

short-run supply curve

long-run supply curve

constant-cost industry

increasing-cost industry

decreasing-cost industry

Questions   **Mc Graw Hill** connect

1. Briefly state the basic characteristics of pure competition, pure monopoly, monopolistic competition, and oligopoly. Into which of these market classifications does each of the following most accurately fit? (a) a supermarket in your hometown; (b) the steel industry; (c) a Kansas wheat farm; (d) the commercial bank in which you or your family has an account; (e) the automobile industry. In each case, justify your classification. **(LO1)**

2. Use the following demand schedule to determine total revenue and marginal revenue for each possible level of sales: **(LO2)**

Product Price	Quantity Demanded	Total Revenue	Marginal Revenue
$2	0	$_____	
2	1	_____	$_____
2	2	_____	_____
2	3	_____	_____
2	4	_____	_____
2	5	_____	_____

   a. What can you conclude about the structure of the industry in which this firm is operating? Explain.

   b. Graph this firm's demand, TR, and MR curves.

   c. Why do the demand and MR curves coincide?

   d. "Marginal revenue is the change in total revenue associated with additional units of output." Explain verbally and graphically, using the data in the table.

3. "Even if a firm is losing money, it may be better to stay in business in the short run." Is this statement ever true? If so, under what condition(s)? **(LO3)**

4. Why is the equality of marginal revenue and marginal cost essential for profit maximization in all market structures? Explain why price can be substituted for marginal revenue in the MR = MC rule when an industry is purely competitive. **(LO3)**

5. "That segment of a competitive firm's marginal-cost curve that lies above its AVC curve constitutes the firm's short-run supply curve." Explain using a graph and words. **(LO4)**

6. Using diagrams for both the industry and a representative firm, illustrate competitive long-run equilibrium. Assuming constant costs, employ these diagrams to show how (a) an increase and (b) a decrease in market demand will upset that long-run equilibrium. Trace graphically and describe verbally the adjustment processes by which long-run equilibrium is restored. Now rework your analysis for increasing- and decreasing-cost industries, and compare the three long-run supply curves. **(LO5, LO6)**

7. In long-run equilibrium, P = minimum ATC = MC. Of what significance for economic efficiency is the equality of P and minimum ATC? The equality of P and MC? Distinguish between productive efficiency and allocative efficiency in your answer. **(LO7)**

8. Suppose that purely competitive firms producing cashews discover that P exceeds MC. Is their combined output of cashews too little, too much, or just right to achieve allocative efficiency? In the long run, what will happen to the supply of cashews and the price of cashews? **(LO7)**

Problems

1. A purely competitive firm finds that the market price for its product is $20. It has a fixed cost of $100 and a variable cost of $10 per unit for the first 50 units and then $25 per unit for all successive units. Does price exceed average variable cost for the first 50 units? For the first 100 units? What is the marginal cost per unit for the first 50 units? The marginal cost for units 51 and higher? What output level will yield the largest possible profit for this purely competitive firm? **(LO3)**

2. A purely competitive wheat farmer can sell any wheat he grows for $10 per bushel. His five acres of land show diminishing returns because some are better suited for wheat production than others. The first acre can produce 1,000 bushels of wheat, the second acre 900, the third 800, and so on. Draw a table with multiple columns to help you answer the following questions. How many bushels will each of the farmer's five acres produce? How much revenue will each acre

generate? What are the TR and MR for each acre? If the marginal cost of planting and harvesting an acre is $7,000 per acre for each of the five acres, how many acres should the farmer plant and harvest? **(LO3)**

3. Karen runs a print shop that makes posters for large companies. It is a very competitive business. The market price is currently $1 per poster. She has fixed costs of $250. Her variable costs are $1,000 for the first thousand posters, $800 for the second thousand, and then $750 for each additional thousand posters. What is her AFC per poster (not per thousand!) if she prints 1,000 posters? 2,000? 10,000? What is her ATC per poster if she prints 1,000? 2,000? 10,000? If the market price fell to 70 cents per poster, would there be *any* output level at which Karen would *not* shut down production immediately? **(LO3)**

4. Assume that the cost data in the table below are for a purely competitive producer: **(LO3)**

   a. At a product price of $56, will this firm produce in the short run? If it is preferable to produce, what will be the profit-maximizing or loss-minimizing output? What economic profit or loss will the firm realize per unit of output?

Total Product	Average Fixed Cost	Average Variable Cost	Average Total Cost	Marginal Cost
0				
1	$60.00	$45.00	$105.00	$45
2	30.00	42.50	72.50	40
3	20.00	40.00	60.00	35
4	15.00	37.50	52.50	30
5	12.00	37.00	49.00	35
6	10.00	37.50	47.50	40
7	8.57	38.57	47.14	45
8	7.50	40.63	48.13	55
9	6.67	43.33	50.00	65
10	6.00	46.50	52.50	75

   b. Answer the questions in part *a* assuming product price is $41.

   c. Answer the questions in part *a* assuming product price is $32.

d. In the following table, complete the short-run supply schedule for the firm (columns 1 and 2) and indicate the profit or loss incurred at each output (column 3).

(1) Price	(2) Quantity Supplied, Single Firm	(3) Profit (+) or Loss (−)	(4) Quantity Supplied, 1500 Firms
$26	_____	$_____	_____
32	_____	_____	_____
38	_____	_____	_____
41	_____	_____	_____
46	_____	_____	_____
56	_____	_____	_____
66	_____	_____	_____

e. Now assume that there are 1,500 identical firms in this competitive industry; that is, there are 1,500 firms, each of which has the cost data shown in the table above. Complete the industry supply schedule (column 4).

f. Suppose the market demand data for the product are as follows:

Price	Total Quantity Demanded
$26	17,000
32	15,000
38	13,500
41	12,000
46	10,500
56	9500
66	8000

What is the equilibrium price? What is the equilibrium output for the industry? For each firm? What will profit or loss be per unit? Per firm? Will this industry expand or contract in the long run?

CHAPTER EIGHT

Pure Monopoly

Learning Objectives

LO8.1 List the characteristics of pure monopoly and discuss the barriers to entry that relate to monopoly.

LO8.2 Explain how a pure monopoly sets its profit-maximizing output and price.

LO8.3 Discuss the economic effects of monopoly.

LO8.4 Describe why a monopolist might charge different prices in different markets.

LO8.5 Identify the antitrust laws that are used to deal with monopoly.

We turn now from pure competition to pure monopoly. You deal with monopolies—or near-monopolies—more often than you might think. When you purchase certain prescription drugs, you are buying monopolized products. When you make a local telephone call, turn on your lights, or subscribe to cable TV, you may be patronizing a monopoly, depending on your location.

What exactly is pure monopoly, and what conditions enable it to arise and survive? How does a pure monopolist determine its profit-maximizing price and output? Does a pure monopolist achieve the efficiency associated with pure competition? If not, what should the government do about it? A model of pure monopoly will help us answer these questions.

An Introduction to Pure Monopoly

Pure monopoly exists when a single firm is the sole producer of a product for which there are no close substitutes. A pure monopoly has these characteristics:

- *Single seller* In a pure, or absolute, monopoly, a single firm is the sole producer of a specific good or the sole supplier of a service; the firm and the industry are synonymous.
- *No close substitutes* A pure monopoly's product is unique in that there are no close substitutes. The consumer who chooses not to buy the monopolized product must do without it.
- *Price maker* The pure monopolist controls the total quantity supplied and thus has considerable control over price; it is a *price maker.* (Unlike a pure competitor, which has no such control and therefore is a *price taker.*) The pure monopolist confronts the usual downward sloping product demand curve. It can change its product price by changing the quantity of the product it produces. The monopolist will use this power whenever it is advantageous to do so.
- *Blocked entry* A pure monopolist has no immediate competition because certain barriers keep potential competitors from entering the industry. Those barriers may be economic, technological, legal, or of some other type.
- *Nonprice competition* The product produced by a pure monopolist may be either standardized (as with natural gas and electricity) or differentiated (as with the Windows operating system or Frisbees). Monopolists that have standardized products engage mainly in public relations advertising, while those with differentiated products sometimes advertise their products' attributes.

pure monopoly
A market structure in which one firm sells a unique product, into which entry is blocked, in which the single firm has considerable control over product price, and in which nonprice competition may or may not be found.

Examples of *pure* monopoly are relatively rare, but there are many examples of less pure forms. In many cities, government-owned or government-regulated public utilities—natural gas and electric companies, the water company, and the cable TV company—are all monopolies or virtually so.

There are also many "near-monopolies" in which a single firm has the bulk of sales in a specific market. Intel, for example, produces 80 percent of the central microprocessors used in personal computers. Illumina produces 90 percent of the world's gene-sequencing machines. Google's smartphone operating system, Android, is installed on 86 percent of the world's cell phones.

Professional sports teams are, in a sense, monopolies because they are the sole suppliers of specific services in large geographic areas. With a few exceptions, a single major-league team in each sport serves each large American city. If you want to see a live major-league baseball game in St. Louis or Seattle, you must patronize the Cardinals or the Mariners, respectively. Other geographic monopolies exist. For example, a small town may be served by only one airline or railroad. In a small, extremely isolated community, the local barber shop, dry cleaner, or grocery store may approximate a monopoly.

Nonetheless, there is almost always some competition. Satellite television is a substitute for cable, and amateur softball is a substitute for professional baseball. The Linux operating system can substitute for Windows. But such substitutes are typically either more costly or in some way less appealing.

Barriers to Entry

The factors that prohibit firms from entering an industry are called **barriers to entry.** In pure monopoly, strong barriers to entry effectively block all potential competition. Somewhat weaker barriers may permit *oligopoly,* a market structure dominated by a few firms. Still weaker barriers may permit the entry of a fairly large number of competing firms, giving rise to *monopolistic competition.* And the absence of any

barrier to entry
Anything that artificially prevents the entry of firms into an industry.

effective entry barriers permits the entry of a very large number of firms, which provide the basis of pure competition. So barriers to entry are pertinent not only to the extreme case of pure monopoly but also to other market structures in which there are monopoly-like characteristics or monopoly-like behavior.

We will now discuss the four most prominent barriers to entry.

Economies of Scale

Modern technology in some industries is such that economies of scale—declining average total cost with added firm size—are extensive. In such cases, a firm's long-run average-cost schedule will decline over a wide range of output. Given market demand, only a few large firms or, in the extreme, only a single large firm can achieve low average total costs.

If a pure monopoly exists in such an industry, economies of scale will serve as an entry barrier and will protect the monopolist from competition. New firms that try to enter the industry as small-scale producers cannot realize the cost economies of the monopolist. They will be undercut and forced out of business by the monopolist, which can sell at a much lower price and still make a profit because of its lower per-unit cost associated with its economies of scale. A new firm might try to start out big—that is, to enter the industry as a large-scale producer—so as to achieve the necessary economies of scale. But the massive expense of the plant facilities along with customer loyalty to the existing product would make the entry highly risky. Therefore, the new and untried enterprise would find it difficult to secure financing for its venture. In most cases, the financial obstacles and risks to "starting big" are prohibitive. This explains why efforts to enter such industries as computer operating software, commercial aircraft, and household laundry equipment are so rare.

natural monopoly
An industry in which economies of scale are so great that a single firm can produce the product at a lower average total cost than would be possible if more than one firm produced the product.

A monopoly firm is referred to as a **natural monopoly** if the market demand curve cuts the long-run ATC curve where average total costs are still declining. If a natural monopoly were to set its price where market demand intersects long-run ATC, its price would be lower than if the industry were more competitive. But it will probably set a higher price. As with any monopolist, a natural monopolist may, instead, set its price far above ATC and obtain substantial economic profit. In that event, the lowest-unit-cost advantage of a natural monopolist would accrue to the monopolist as profit and not as lower prices to consumers.

Legal Barriers to Entry: Patents and Licenses

Government also creates legal barriers to entry by awarding patents and licenses.

Patents   A *patent* is the exclusive right of inventors to use, or to allow others to use, their inventions. Patents and patent laws aim to protect the inventor from rivals who would use the invention without having shared in the effort and expense of developing it. At the same time, patents provide inventors with a monopoly position for the life of the patent. The world's nations have agreed on a uniform patent length of 20 years from the time of application. Patents have figured prominently in the growth of modern-day giants such as IBM, Pfizer, Intel, Xerox, Amazon, and DuPont.

Research and development (R&D) is what leads to most patentable inventions and products. Firms that gain monopoly power through their own research or by purchasing the patents of others can use patents to strengthen their market position. The profit from one patent can finance the research required to develop new patentable products. In the pharmaceutical industry, patents on prescription drugs have produced large monopoly profits that have helped finance the discovery of new patentable medicines. So monopoly power achieved through patents may well be self-sustaining, even though patents eventually expire and generic drugs then compete with the original brand.

Licenses Government may also limit entry into an industry or occupation through *licensing*. At the national level, the Federal Communications Commission licenses only so many radio and television stations in each geographic area. In a few instances, the government might license *itself* to provide some product and thereby create a public monopoly. For example, in some states only state-owned retail outlets can sell liquor. Similarly, many states have "licensed" themselves to run lotteries.

Ownership or Control of Essential Resources

A monopolist can use private property as an obstacle to potential rivals. For example, a firm that owns or controls a resource essential to the production process can prohibit the entry of rival firms. At one time, the International Nickel Company of Canada (now called Vale Canada Limited) controlled 90 percent of the world's known nickel reserves. A local firm may own all the nearby deposits of sand and gravel. And it is very difficult for new sports leagues to be created because existing professional sports leagues have contracts with the best players and have long-term leases on the major stadiums and arenas.

Pricing and Other Strategic Barriers to Entry

Even if a firm is not protected from entry by, say, extensive economies of scale or ownership of essential resources, entry may effectively be blocked by the way the monopolist responds to attempts by rivals to enter the industry. Confronted with a new entrant, the monopolist may "create an entry barrier" by slashing its price, stepping up its advertising, or taking other strategic actions to make it difficult for the entrant to succeed.

Examples of entry deterrence: In 2005, Dentsply, the dominant American maker of false teeth (80 percent market share) was found to have unlawfully precluded independent distributors of false teeth from carrying competing brands. That prevented several foreign competitors from entering the U.S. market and competing against Dentsply. As another example, in 2015, American Express was found guilty of an unlawful restraint of trade because it prohibited any merchant who had signed up to accept American Express credit cards from promoting rival credit cards—such as Visa and MasterCard—to their customers.

Monopoly Demand

Now that we have explained the sources of monopoly, we want to build a model of pure monopoly so we can analyze monopoly price and output decisions. Let's start with three assumptions:

- Patents, economies of scale, or resource ownership secure our firm's monopoly.
- No unit of government regulates the firm.
- The firm is a single-price monopolist; it charges the same price for all units of output.

The crucial difference between a pure monopolist and a purely competitive seller lies on the demand side of the market. The purely competitive seller faces a perfectly elastic demand at the price determined by market supply and demand. It is a price taker that can sell as much or as little as it wants at the going market price. Each additional unit sold will add the amount of the constant product price to the firm's total revenue. Therefore marginal revenue for the competitive seller is constant and equal to product price. (Review **Figure 7.1** for price, marginal-revenue, and total-revenue relationships for the purely competitive firm.)

The demand curve for the monopolist (or for any imperfectly competitive seller) is quite different from that of the pure competitor. Because the pure monopolist *is* the industry, its demand curve is *the market demand curve*. And because market demand is not perfectly elastic, the monopolist's demand curve is downward sloping. Columns 1 and 2 in the table in **Figure 8.1** illustrate this fact. Note that quantity demanded increases as price decreases.

In **Chapter 7**, we drew separate demand curves for the purely competitive industry and for a single firm in such an industry. But only a single demand curve is needed in pure monopoly because the firm and the industry are one and the same. We have graphed part of the monopolist's demand data in the table in **Figure 8.1** as demand curve *D* in **Figure 8.1a**. This is the monopolist's demand curve *and* the market demand curve. The downward slope of the demand curve has two important implications.

Marginal Revenue Is Less than Price

With a fixed downward sloping demand curve, the pure monopolist can increase sales only by charging a lower price. Consequently, marginal revenue is less than price (average revenue) for every unit of output except the first. Why? The lower price of the extra unit of output also applies to all prior units of output. The monopolist could have sold these prior units at a higher price if it had not produced and sold the extra output. Each additional unit of output sold increases total revenue by an amount equal to its own price less the sum of the price cuts that apply to all prior units of output.

Figure 8.1a confirms this point. There, we have highlighted two price-quantity combinations from the monopolist's demand curve. The monopolist can sell 1 more unit at $132 than it can at $142 and that way obtain $132 of extra revenue (the blue area). But to sell that fourth unit for $132, the monopolist must also sell the first 3 units at $132 rather than $142. The $10 reduction in revenue on 3 units results in a $30 revenue loss (the red area). The net difference in total revenue from selling a fourth unit is $102: the $132 gain from the fourth unit minus the $30 forgone on the first 3 units. This net gain (marginal revenue) of $102 from the fourth unit is clearly less than the $132 price of the fourth unit.

Column 4 in the table shows that marginal revenue is always less than the corresponding product price in column 2, except for the first unit of output. **Figure 8.1b** shows the relationship between the monopolist's demand curve and marginal-revenue curve. For this figure, we extended the demand and marginal-revenue data of columns 1, 2, and 4 in the table, assuming that each successive $10 price cut elicits 1 additional unit of sales. That is, the monopolist can sell 11 units at $62, 12 units at $52, and so on. Note that the monopolist's MR curve lies below the demand curve, indicating that marginal revenue is less than price at every output quantity except the very first unit.

The Monopolist Is a Price Maker

All imperfect competitors, whether pure monopolists, oligopolists, or monopolistic competitors, face downward sloping demand curves. As a result, any change in quantity produced causes a movement along their respective demand curves and a change in the price they can charge. Firms with downward sloping demand curves are thus *price makers*. By controlling output, they can "make the price." From columns 1 and 2 in the table in **Figure 8.1**, we find that the monopolist can charge a price of $72 if it produces and offers for sale 10 units, a price of $82 if it produces and offers for sale 9 units, and so forth.

FIGURE 8.1

Demand, price, and marginal revenue in pure monopoly. (a) A pure monopolist (or any other imperfect competitor) must set a lower price in order to sell more output. Here, by charging $132 rather than $142, the monopolist sells an extra unit (the fourth unit) and gains $132 from that sale. But from this gain $30 is subtracted, which reflects the $10 less the monopolist received for each of the first 3 units. Thus, the marginal revenue of the fourth unit is $102 (= $132 − $30), considerably less than its $132 price. (b) Because a monopolist must lower the price on all units sold in order to increase its sales, its marginal-revenue curve (MR) lies below its downward sloping demand curve (D).

	Revenue Data		
(1) Quantity of Output	**(2)** Price (Average Revenue)	**(3)** Total Revenue, (1) × (2)	**(4)** Marginal Revenue
0	$172	$ 0	
1	162	162	─$162
2	152	304	─ 142
3	142	426	─ 122
4	132	528	─ 102
5	122	610	─ 82
6	112	672	─ 62
7	102	714	─ 42
8	92	736	─ 22
9	82	738	─ 2
10	72	720	─ −18

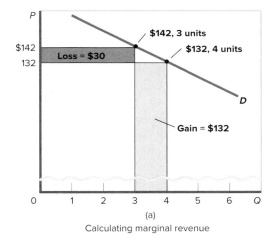

(a)
Calculating marginal revenue

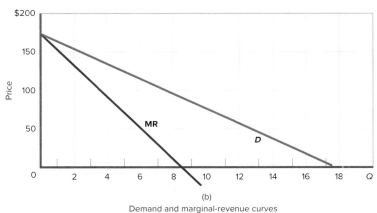

(b)
Demand and marginal-revenue curves

Output and Price Determination

At what specific price-quantity combination will a profit-maximizing monopolist choose to operate? To answer this question, we must add production costs to our analysis.

Cost Data

On the cost side, we will assume that the monopolist hires resources competitively. It also employs the same technology and therefore has the same cost structure as the purely competitive firms that we studied in **Chapter 7**. By using the same cost data we developed in **Chapter 6** and applied to the competitive firm in **Chapter 7**, we will be able to directly compare the price and output decisions of a pure monopoly with those of a pure competitor. Columns 5 through 7 in the table in **Figure 8.2** restate the pertinent cost data from the table in **Figure 7.2**.

MR = MC Rule

A monopolist seeking to maximize total profit will employ the same rationale as a profit-seeking firm in a competitive industry. If producing is preferable to shutting down, it will produce the output at which marginal revenue equals marginal cost (MR = MC).

A comparison of columns 4 and 7 in the table in **Figure 8.2** indicates that the profit-maximizing output is 5 units because the fifth unit is the last unit of output whose marginal revenue exceeds its marginal cost. What price will the monopolist charge? The demand schedule shown as columns 1 and 2 in the table indicates there is only one price at which 5 units can be sold: $122.

Figure 8.2 graphs the demand, MR, ATC, and MC data from the table. The profit-maximizing output occurs at 5 units of output (Q_m), where the marginal-revenue (MR) and marginal-cost (MC) curves intersect. There, MR = MC.

To find the price the monopolist will charge, we extend a vertical line from Q_m up to the demand curve D. The unique price P_m at which Q_m units can be sold is $122. In this case, $122 is the profit-maximizing price. So the monopolist sets the quantity at Q_m to charge its profit-maximizing price of $122.

Columns 2 and 5 of the table show that at 5 units of output, the product price ($122) exceeds the average total cost ($94). The monopolist thus obtains an economic profit of $28 per unit, and the total economic profit is then $140 (= 5 units × $28). In the graph in **Figure 8.2**, per-unit profit is $P_m − A$, where A is the average total cost of producing Q_m units. Total economic profit (the green rectangle) is found by multiplying this per-unit profit by the profit-maximizing output Q_m.

Misconceptions Concerning Monopoly Pricing

Our analysis exposes three fallacies concerning monopoly behavior.

Not Highest Price   Because a monopolist can manipulate output and price, people often believe it will charge the highest price possible. That is incorrect. There are many prices above P_m in **Figure 8.2**, but the monopolist shuns them because they yield a smaller-than-maximum total profit. The monopolist seeks maximum total profit, not maximum price.

FIGURE 8.2

Profit maximization by a pure monopolist. The pure monopolist maximizes profit by producing the MR = MC output, here Q_m = 5 units. Then, as seen from the demand curve, it will charge price P_m = \$122. Average total cost is A = \$94, so per-unit profit is $P_m - A$ and total profit is 5 × ($P_m - A$). Total economic profit is thus \$140, as shown by the green rectangle.

	Revenue Data				Cost Data		
(1)	(2)	(3)	(4)	(5)	(6)	(7)	(8)
Quantity of Output	Price (Average Revenue)	Total Revenue, (1) × (2)	Marginal Revenue	Average Total Cost	Total Cost, (1) × (5)	Marginal Cost	Profit (+) or Loss (−)
0	\$172	\$ 0			\$ 100		\$−100
1	162	162 ⌐——\$162		\$190.00	190 ⌐——\$ 90		− 28
2	152	304 ⌐—— 142		135.00	270 ⌐—— 80		+ 34
3	142	426 ⌐—— 122		113.33	340 ⌐—— 70		+ 86
4	132	528 ⌐—— 102		100.00	400 ⌐—— 60		+ 128
5	**122**	**610** ⌐—— **82**		**94.00**	**470** ⌐—— **70**		**+140**
6	112	672 ⌐—— 62		91.67	550 ⌐—— 80		+ 122
7	102	714 ⌐—— 42		91.43	640 ⌐—— 90		+ 74
8	92	736 ⌐—— 22		93.75	750 ⌐—— 110		− 14
9	82	738 ⌐—— 2		97.78	880 ⌐—— 130		− 142
10	72	720 ⌐—— −18		103.00	1030 ⌐—— 150		− 310

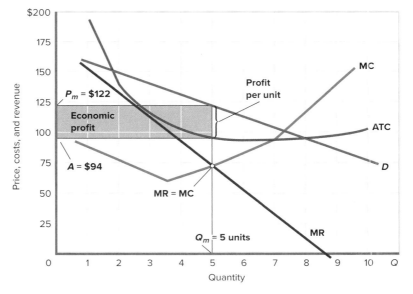

Total, Not Unit, Profit The monopolist seeks maximum *total* profit, not maximum *unit* profit. In **Figure 8.2**, a careful comparison of the vertical distance between ATC and price at various possible outputs indicates that per-unit profit is greater at a point slightly to the left of the profit-maximizing output Q_m. This is seen in the table, where the per-unit profit at 4 units of output is \$32 (= \$132 − \$100) compared with \$28 (= \$122 − \$94) at the profit-maximizing output of 5 units. Here, the monopolist accepts a lower-than-maximum per-unit profit because additional sales more than compensate for the lower unit profit. A profit-seeking monopolist would rather sell 5 units at a profit of \$28 per unit (for a total profit of \$140) than 4 units at a profit of \$32 per unit (for a total profit of only \$128).

Possibility of Losses The likelihood of economic profit is greater for a pure monopolist than for a pure competitor. In the long run, the pure competitor is destined to have only a normal profit, whereas barriers to entry mean that any economic profit realized by the monopolist can persist. In pure monopoly, there are no new entrants to increase supply, drive down price, and eliminate economic profit.

But pure monopoly does not guarantee profit. Despite dominance in its market (as, say, a seller of home sewing machines), a monopoly enterprise can suffer a loss because of weak demand and relatively high costs. If the demand and cost situation faced by the monopolist is far less favorable than that in **Figure 8.2**, the monopolist can incur losses. Like the pure competitor, the monopolist will not persist in operating at a loss. Faced with continuing losses, in the long run the firm's owners will move their resources to alternative industries that offer better profit opportunities. Like any firm, a monopolist must obtain a minimum of a normal profit in the long run or it will go out of business.

 ## APPLYING THE ANALYSIS

Salt Monopolies

Starting in the 1300s, the French government claimed for itself a monopoly over the sale of salt, which was a valuable commodity at the time, especially in inland areas away from the ocean. But as the centuries passed, the French monarchy found it convenient and profitable to auction off the monopoly right to sell salt.

Vincent Ting/Moment Open/Getty Images

The contract would be for a fixed number years and the winner of the auction would attempt to make more money selling salt as a monopolist than he paid to win the auction. The government liked that it got paid a large lump sum in advance. It was also freed of the costs of hiring tens of thousands of government tax collectors; collection costs fell entirely on the auction winner.

How high would bids go? That depended on profit estimates. If a bidder thought he could make a monopoly profit of 50 million francs selling salt, he would be willing to bid up to 50 million francs to become the monopolist. The most aggressive bidders were the people who thought they could squeeze out the largest profit.

Economic Effects of Monopoly

Let's now evaluate pure monopoly from the standpoint of society as a whole. Our reference for this evaluation will be the outcome of long-run efficiency in a purely competitive market, identified by the triple equality $P = MC = $ minimum ATC.

Price, Output, and Efficiency

Figure 8.3 graphically contrasts the price, output, and efficiency outcomes of pure monopoly and a purely competitive *industry*. The $S = MC$ curve in **Figure 8.3a** reminds us that the market supply curve S for a purely competitive industry is the horizontal sum of the MC curves of all the firms in the industry. Suppose there are 1,000 such firms. Comparing their combined supply curve S with market demand D, we see that the purely competitive price and output are P_c and Q_c.

Recall that this price-output combination results in both productive efficiency and allocative efficiency. *Productive efficiency* is achieved because free entry and exit force firms to operate where ATC is at a minimum. The sum of the minimum-ATC outputs of the 1,000 pure competitors is the industry output: here, Q_c. Product price is at the lowest level consistent with minimum average total cost. The *allocative efficiency* of pure competition results because production occurs up to that output at which price (the measure of a product's value or marginal benefit to society) equals marginal cost (the worth of the alternative products forgone by society in producing any given commodity). In short: $P = MC = $ minimum ATC.

FIGURE 8.3

Inefficiency of pure monopoly relative to a purely competitive industry. (a) In a purely competitive industry, entry and exit of firms ensure that price (P_c) equals marginal cost (MC) and that the minimum average-total-cost output (Q_c) is produced. Both productive efficiency ($P = $ minimum ATC) and allocative efficiency ($P = $ MC) are obtained. (b) In pure monopoly, the MR curve lies below the demand curve. The monopolist maximizes profit at output Q_m, where MR = MC, and charges price P_m. Thus, output is lower (Q_m rather than Q_c) and price is higher (P_m rather than P_c) than they would be in a purely competitive industry. Monopoly is inefficient because output is less than that required for achieving minimum ATC (here, at Q_c) and because the monopolist's price exceeds MC.

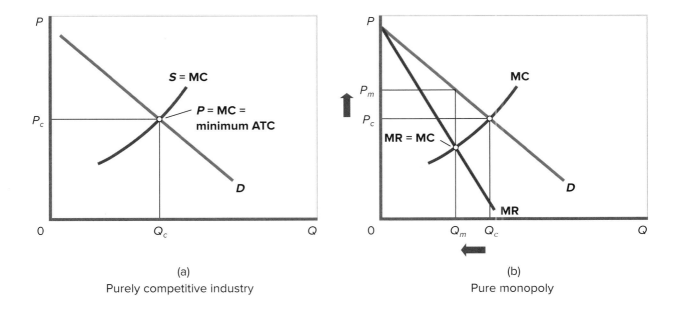

(a)
Purely competitive industry

(b)
Pure monopoly

Now let's suppose that this industry becomes a pure monopoly (**Figure 8.3b**) as a result of one firm acquiring all its competitors. We also assume that no changes in costs or market demand result from this dramatic change in the industry structure. One thousand competing firms have become a single pure monopolist.

The competitive market supply curve S has become the marginal-cost curve (MC) of the monopolist, the summation of the individual marginal-cost curves of its many branch plants. (Because the monopolist does not have a supply curve, we have removed the S label.) The important change, however, is on the demand side. From the viewpoint of each of the 1,000 individual competitive firms, demand was perfectly elastic, and marginal revenue was therefore equal to the market equilibrium price P_c. Thus each competitive firm equated its marginal revenue of P_c dollars per unit with its individual marginal cost curve to maximize profits. But market demand and individual demand are the same to the pure monopolist. The firm is the industry, and thus the monopolist sees the downward sloping demand curve D shown in **Figure 8.3b**.

For the monopolist, marginal revenue is less than price, and graphically the MR curve lies below demand curve D. In using the MR = MC rule, the monopolist selects output Q_m and price P_m. The monopolist finds it profitable to sell a smaller output at a higher price than do the competitive producers.

Monopoly yields neither productive nor allocative efficiency. Note that the monopolist's output Q_m is less than Q_c, the output at which average total cost is lowest. In addition, the monopoly price P_m is higher than the competitive price P_c that we know in long-run equilibrium in pure competition equals minimum average total cost. Thus, the monopoly price exceeds minimum average total cost, which means that the monopoly will not be productively efficient.

The monopolist's underproduction also implies allocative inefficiency. At the monopoly output level Q_m, the monopoly price P_m that consumers are willing to pay exceeds the marginal cost of production. Consumers therefore value additional units of this product more highly than they do the alternative products that could be produced from the resources that would be necessary to make more units of the monopolist's product.

Also note that for every unit between Q_m and Q_c, marginal benefit exceeds marginal cost because the demand curve lies above the supply curve. By choosing not to produce these units, the monopolist reduces allocative efficiency because the resources that should have been used to make these units will be redirected instead toward producing items that bring lower net benefits to society. In monopoly, then

- P exceeds MC.
- P exceeds minimum ATC.

Income Transfer

In general, a monopoly transfers income from consumers to the owners of the monopoly. The owners received the income as revenue. Because a monopoly has market power, it can charge a higher price than would a purely competitive firm with the same costs. So the monopoly in effect levies a "private tax" on consumers. This private tax can often generate substantial economic profits that can persist because entry to the industry is blocked.

Cost Complications

Given identical costs, a purely monopolistic industry will charge a higher price, produce a smaller output, and allocate economic resources less efficiently than a purely competitive industry. These inferior results are rooted in the entry barriers characterizing monopoly.

But we must recognize that costs may not be the same for purely competitive and monopolistic producers. The unit cost incurred by a monopolist may be either larger or smaller than that incurred by a purely competitive firm. Costs may differ for four reasons: (1) economies of scale, (2) a factor called "X-inefficiency," (3) the need for monopoly-preserving expenditures, and (4) the "very long run" perspective, which allows for technological advance.

Economies of Scale Where economies of scale are extensive, market demand may not be sufficient to support a large number of competing firms, each producing at minimum efficient scale (MES). In such cases, an industry of one or two firms would have a lower average total cost than would the same industry made up of numerous competitive firms. At the extreme, only a single firm—a natural monopoly—might be able to achieve the lowest long-run average total cost.

Some firms relating to new information technologies—for example, computer software, Internet service, and wireless communications—have displayed extensive economies of scale. As these firms have grown, their long-run average total costs have declined because of greater use of specialized inputs, the spreading of product development costs, and learning by doing. *Simultaneous consumption* and *network effects* have also reduced costs.

A product's ability to satisfy a large number of consumers at the same time is called **simultaneous consumption.** Lenovo needs to produce a laptop for each customer, but Microsoft needs to produce its Windows program only once. Then, at very low marginal cost, Microsoft delivers its program by disk or Internet to millions of consumers. Music producers and video game makers have similarly low costs when delivering their products to additional consumers. Because their marginal costs are so low, their average total cost of output declines as more customers are added and the fixed costs of product development are spread over more and more users.

Network effects are present if the value of a product to each user, including existing users, increases as the total number of users rises. Good examples are computer software, smartphones, and social media like Facebook where users provide the content. The greater the number of persons connected to the system, the greater are the benefits of the product to each person.

Such network effects may drive a market toward monopoly because consumers tend to choose standard products that everyone else is using. The focused demand for these products permits their producers to grow rapidly and thus achieve economies of scale. Smaller firms get acquired or go out of business.

Even if natural monopoly develops, the monopolist is unlikely to pass cost reductions along to consumers as price reductions. So, with perhaps a handful of exceptions, economies of scale do not change the general conclusion that monopoly industries are inefficient relative to competitive industries.

X-Inefficiency In constructing all the average-total-cost curves used in this book, we have assumed that the firm uses the most efficient existing technology. This assumption is only natural because firms cannot maximize profits unless they are minimizing costs. **X-inefficiency** occurs when a firm produces output at a higher cost than is necessary to produce it. For example, in **Figure 8.2** the ATC and MC curves might be located above those shown, indicating higher costs at each level of output.

Why does X-inefficiency occur? Managers may have goals, such as expanding their power, avoiding business risk, or giving jobs to incompetent relatives, that conflict with cost minimization. X-inefficiency may also arise when a firm's workers are poorly motivated or ineffectively supervised. And a firm may simply become lethargic, relying on rules of thumb in decision making rather than careful calculations of costs and revenues.

simultaneous consumption
A product's ability to satisfy a large number of consumers at the same time.

network effects
Increases in the value of a product to each user, including existing users, as the total number of users rises.

X-inefficiency
The production of output, whatever its level, at higher than the lowest average (and total) cost.

Presumably, monopolistic firms tend more toward X-inefficiency than competitive producers do. Firms in competitive industries are continually under pressure from rivals, forcing them to be internally efficient to survive. But monopolists are sheltered from such competitive forces by entry barriers, and that lack of pressure may lead to X-inefficiency.

rent-seeking behavior
The actions by persons, firms, or unions to gain special benefits from government at the taxpayers' or someone else's expense.

Rent-Seeking Expenditures   **Rent-seeking behavior** is any activity designed to transfer income or wealth to a particular firm or resource supplier at someone else's, or even society's, expense. We have seen that a monopolist can obtain an economic profit even in the long run. Therefore, it is no surprise that a firm may go to great expense to acquire or maintain a monopoly granted by government through legislation or an exclusive license. Such rent-seeking expenditures add nothing to the firm's output, but they clearly increase its costs. Taken alone, rent-seeking implies that monopoly involves higher costs and less efficiency than suggested in **Figure 8.3b**.

Technological Advance   In the very long run, firms can reduce their costs through the discovery and implementation of new technology. If monopolists are more likely than competitive producers to develop more efficient production techniques over time, then the inefficiency of monopoly might be overstated. In general, economists believe that a pure monopolist will not be technologically progressive. Although its economic profit provides ample means to finance research and development, it has little incentive to implement new techniques (or products). The absence of competitors means that there is no external pressure for technological advance. Because of its sheltered market position, the pure monopolist can afford to be complacent and lethargic. There is no major penalty for not being innovative.

One caveat: Research and technological advance may be one of the monopolist's barriers to entry. Thus, the monopolist may continue to seek technological advance to avoid falling prey to new rivals. In this case, technological advance is essential to maintaining the monopoly.

APPLYING THE ANALYSIS

Monopoly Power in the Internet Age

In the early 1990s, when the Internet was young, many analysts predicted that it would foster pure competition across a wide range of activities. Because the Internet allowed any user to publish text and images that could be read for free by any other user, they assumed that the Internet would create a level playing field for all types of media, communications, and commerce.

These predictions turned out to be wrong. One mistake was in not understanding that in a world awash in information, finding what you want becomes a huge problem. When the Internet started, there was no directory and there were no search engines. So it was nearly impossible to find what you were looking for.

Google solved that problem by creating the first effective search engine. Thanks to Google, people could easily locate what they were looking for. But this meant that anyone wishing to be found was now dependent on Google or some other search engine to be found.

If you were an advertiser, you would want to spend your money placing keyword ads on the most popular search engine so your ads would reach as many potential customers as possible. And if you were a customer who found ads helpful in finding what you were looking for, you would also want to utilize the most popular search engine so you could be exposed to the greatest number of helpful ads. Thus, Google quickly came to dominate search as the result of network effects.

Network effects created a barrier to entry that protects Google from competitors because both those searching for information and those wanting to provide it have an interest in sticking with whatever search engine has the most users. There are in fact many smaller search engines, but few want to use them much because almost nobody else is using them. Consequently, Google controls about 92 percent of the U.S. search market and receives a majority of the revenue generated by search ads.

The network effects that help Google dominate search also drive the dominance of firms such as Facebook and Amazon. Facebook is a well-run website with lots of interesting things to do, but most people come back for the wall posts and other content generated by fellow users. If there were no fellow users, there would be little content and little reason to visit the site. That makes it hard for smaller social-networking sites to compete with Facebook. As a result, Facebook has come to dominate social media. With over a billion users, it enjoys the largest network effect and grows even bigger thanks to already being big.

The early predictions that the Internet would create a level playing field for all types of media, communications, and commerce have also been doomed by economies of scale. Consider Amazon. To the public, Amazon is the world's largest online retailer, with over $386 billion in annual sales in 2020. But behind the scenes, its success is driven by two activities that each enjoy massive economies of scale: data and logistics.

In terms of data, Amazon runs some of the world's largest server farms. These giant buildings are stacked top to bottom with tens of thousands of networked computers that store customer data, process payments, and keep track of inventory. The cost of building and running these server farms runs into the billions of dollars each year—including massive electricity bills. But because a larger server farm generates a lower cost per sale than a smaller server farm, Amazon enjoys economies of scale that allow it to undersell any rival operating on a smaller scale with smaller server farms.

The story with logistics is much the same. Amazon operates dozens of massive distribution warehouses that benefit from economies of scale because a warehouse that is twice as big costs less than twice as much to operate.

We should note, however, that Google, Facebook, and Amazon are not full-on monopolies, something we'll explore in Chapter 9. Each faces robust competition. While network effects and economies of scale benefit them greatly, those factors are not strong enough to guarantee them permanent dominance or even large profits.

QUESTION:

Does *simultaneous consumption* also help explain the ability of Google and Facebook to achieve economies of scale? Explain. Use **Figure 6.6** to demonstrate how economies of scale give Google, Facebook, and Amazon an advantage over smaller competitors.

Price Discrimination

We have assumed that the monopolist charges a single price to all buyers. But under certain conditions, the monopolist can increase its profit by charging different prices to different buyers. In so doing, the monopolist is engaging in **price discrimination,** the practice of selling a specific product at more than one price when the price differences are not justified by cost differences. Price discrimination can take three forms:

price discrimination
The selling of a product to different buyers at different prices when the price differences are not justified by differences in cost.

- Charging each customer in a single market the maximum price they are willing to pay.

- Charging each customer one price for the first set of units purchased and a lower price for subsequent units purchased.

- Charging some customers one price and other customers another price.

Conditions

Price discrimination is possible when the following conditions are met:

- *Monopoly power* The seller must be a monopolist or, at least, must possess some degree of monopoly power; that is, some ability to control output and price.

- *Market segregation* At relatively low cost to itself, the seller must be able to segregate buyers into distinct classes, each with a different willingness or ability to pay for the product. This separation of buyers is usually based on different price elasticities of demand.

- *No resale* The original purchaser cannot resell the product or service. This condition suggests that service industries such as the transportation industry or legal and medical services, where resale is impossible, are candidates for price discrimination.

Examples

Price discrimination is common in the U.S. economy. For example, airlines charge high fares to business travelers, whose demand for travel is inelastic, and offer lower highly restricted, nonrefundable fares to attract vacationers and others whose demands are more elastic.

Movie theaters and golf courses vary their charges on the basis of time (e.g., higher evening and weekend rates) and age (e.g., lower rates for children and senior discounts). Railroads vary the rate charged per ton-mile of freight according to the market value of the product being shipped. The shipper of 10 tons of television sets or refrigerators pays more than the shipper of 10 tons of gravel or coal.

Discount coupons, redeemable at purchase, are a form of price discrimination. They enable firms to give price discounts to their most price-sensitive customers who have elastic demand. Less price-sensitive consumers who have less elastic demand are not as likely to take the time to clip and redeem coupons. The firm thus makes a larger profit than if it had used a single-price, no-coupon strategy.

Finally, price discrimination often occurs in international trade. A Russian aluminum producer, for example, might sell aluminum for less in the United States than in Russia. In the United States, this seller faces an elastic demand because several substitute suppliers are available. But in Russia, where the manufacturer dominates the market and trade barriers impede imports, consumers have fewer choices and thus demand is less elastic.

Graphical Analysis

Figure 8.4 demonstrates graphically the most frequently seen form of price discrimination. The two graphs represent a single pure monopolist selling its product, say, software, in two segregated parts of the market. For example, one segment might be small-business customers and the other students. Student versions of the software are identical to the versions sold to businesses but are available (one per person) only to customers with a student ID. Presumably, students have a lower ability to pay for the software and are charged a discounted price.

The demand curve D_b, in **Figure 8.4a**, represents the relatively inelastic demand for the product by business customers. The demand curve D_s, in **Figure 8.4b**, reflects students' more elastic demand. The marginal revenue curves (MR_b and MR_s) lie below their respective demand curves, reflecting the demand–marginal revenue relationship previously described.

FIGURE 8.4

Price discrimination to different groups of buyers. The price-discriminating monopolist represented here maximizes its total profit by dividing the market into two segments based on differences in elasticity of demand. It then produces and sells the MR = MC output in each market segment. (For visual clarity, average total cost (ATC) is assumed to be constant. Therefore, MC equals ATC at all output levels.) (a) The firm charges a higher price (here, P_b) to customers who have a less elastic demand curve and (b) a lower price (here, P_s) to customers with a more elastic demand. The price discriminator's total profit (the sum of the two green rectangles) exceeds the profit that would have occurred if the monopolist had charge the same price to all customers.

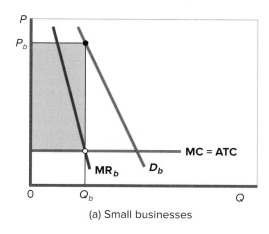

(a) Small businesses

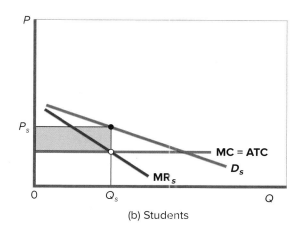

(b) Students

For visual clarity, we have assumed that average total cost (ATC) is constant. Therefore, marginal cost (MC) equals average total cost (ATC) at all quantities of output. These costs are the same for both versions of the software and therefore appear as the single straight line labeled "MC = ATC."

What price will the pure monopolist charge to each set of customers? Using the MR = MC rule for profit maximization, the firm will offer Q_b units of the software for sale to small businesses. It can sell that profit-maximizing output by charging price P_b. Again using the MR = MC rule, the monopolist will offer Q_s units of software to students. To sell those Q_s units, the firm will charge students the lower price P_s.

Price discrimination increases profit. The numbers (not shown) behind the curves in **Figure 8.4** would reveal that the sum of the two profit rectangles shown in green exceeds the single profit rectangle the firm would obtain from a single monopoly price. How do consumers fare? In this case, students clearly benefit by paying a lower price than they would if the firm charged a single monopoly price; in contrast, the price discrimination results in a higher price for business customers. Therefore, compared to the single-price situation, students buy more of the software and small businesses buy less. Such price discrimination is widespread in the economy and is illegal only when it is part of a firm's strategy to lessen or eliminate competition.

APPLYING THE ANALYSIS

Price Discrimination at the Ballpark

Professional baseball teams earn substantial revenues through ticket sales. To maximize profit, they offer significantly lower ticket prices for children (whose demand is elastic) than for adults (whose demand is inelastic). This discount may be as much as 50 percent.

If this type of price discrimination increases revenue and profit, why don't teams also price-discriminate at the concession stands? Why don't they offer half-price hot dogs, soft drinks, peanuts, and Cracker Jack to children? The answer involves the three requirements for successful price discrimination. All three requirements are met for game tickets: (1) The team has monopoly power; (2) it can segregate ticket buyers by age group, with each group having a different elasticity of demand; and (3) children cannot resell their discounted tickets to adults.

It's a different situation at the concession stands. Specifically, the third condition is *not* met. If the team had dual prices, it could not prevent the exchange or "resale" of the concession goods from children to adults. Many adults would send children to buy food and soft drinks for them: "Here's some money, Billy. Go buy *10* hot dogs for all of us." In this case, price discrimination would reduce, not increase, team profit. Thus, children and adults are charged the same high prices at the concession stands.

> QUESTION:
>
> Why are the prices for concessions at the games quite high compared to prices for the same or similar items at the local convenience store?

Monopoly and Antitrust Policy

Monopoly is a legitimate concern. Monopolists can charge higher-than-competitive prices that result in an underallocation of resources to the monopolized product. They can stifle innovation, engage in rent-seeking behavior, and foster X-inefficiency. Even when their costs are low because of economies of scale, there is no guarantee that the price they charge will reflect those low costs. The cost savings may simply accrue to the monopoly as greater economic profit.

Not Widespread

Fortunately, however, monopoly is not widespread in the United States. Barriers to entry are seldom completely successful. Although research and technological advances may strengthen the market position of a monopoly, technology may also undermine monopoly power. Over time, the creation of new technologies may work to destroy monopoly positions. For example, the development of courier delivery, fax machines, and e-mail has eroded the monopoly power of the U.S. Postal Service. Cable television monopolies are now challenged by satellite TV and by new technologies that transmit audio and video over the Internet.

Patents eventually expire, and even before they do, the development of new and distinct substitutable products often circumvents existing patent advantages. New sources of monopolized resources sometimes are found, and competition from foreign firms may emerge (see **Global Snapshot 8.1**). If a monopoly is sufficiently fearful of future competition from new products, it may keep its prices relatively low so as to discourage rivals from developing such products. If so, consumers may pay nearly competitive prices even though competition is currently lacking.

GLOBAL SNAPSHOT 8.1

Competition from Foreign Multinational Corporations

Competition from foreign multinational corporations diminishes the market power of firms in the United States. Here are just a few of the hundreds of foreign multinational corporations that compete strongly with U.S. firms in certain American markets.

Company (Country)	Main Products
Bayer (Germany)	chemicals
Volkswagen (Germany)	automobiles
Michelin (France)	tires
Lenovo (China)	electronics
Nestlé (Switzerland)	food products
Trafigura Group (Singapore)	commodities trading
Panasonic (Japan)	electronics
Petrobras (Brazil)	gasoline
Royal Dutch Shell (Netherlands)	gasoline
Samsung (South Korea)	electronics
Toyota (Japan)	automobiles

Source: Compiled from the Fortune 500 listing of the world's largest firms, "FORTUNE Global 500," 2016, www.fortune.com.

Antitrust Policy

So what, if anything, should government do about monopoly? Economists agree that government needs to examine monopoly on a case-by-case basis. If the monopoly appears to be unsustainable over a long period of time, say, because of emerging new technology, society can simply choose to ignore it. In contrast, the government may want to file charges against a monopoly under the antitrust laws if the monopoly was achieved through anticompetitive actions, creates substantial economic inefficiency, and appears to be long-lasting. (Monopolies were once called "trusts.") The relevant antitrust law is the Sherman Act of 1890, which has two main provisions:

- **Section 1** "Every contract, combination in the form of a trust or otherwise, or conspiracy, in restraint of trade or commerce among the several States, or with foreign nations is declared to be illegal."[1]

- **Section 2** "Every person who shall monopolize, or attempt to monopolize, or combine or conspire with any person or persons, to monopolize any part of the trade or commerce among the several States, or with foreign nations, shall be deemed guilty of a felony . . ." (as later amended from "misdemeanor").[2]

[1] Fifty-first Congress of the United States of America.
[2] Fifty-first Congress of the United States of America.

rule of reason
The rule stated and applied in the U.S. Steel case that only combinations and contracts unreasonably restraining trade are subject to actions under the antitrust laws and that size and possession of monopoly power are not illegal.

In the 1911 Standard Oil case, the Supreme Court found Standard Oil guilty of monopolizing the petroleum industry through a series of abusive and anticompetitive actions. The Court's remedy was to divide Standard Oil into several competing firms. But the Standard Oil case left open an important question: Is every monopoly in violation of Section 2 of the Sherman Act or just those created or maintained by anticompetitive actions?

In the 1920 U.S. Steel case, the courts established a **rule of reason** interpretation of Section 2, saying that it is not illegal to be a monopoly. Only monopolies that "unreasonably" restrain trade violate Section 2 of the Sherman Act and are subject to antitrust action. Size alone was not an offense. Although U.S. Steel clearly possessed monopoly power, it was innocent of "monopolizing" because it had not resorted to illegal acts against competitors in obtaining and then maintaining its monopoly power. Unlike Standard Oil, which was a "bad trust," U.S. Steel was a "good trust" and therefore not in violation of the law. The rule of reason was attacked and once reversed by the courts, but today it is the accepted legal interpretation of the Sherman Act's monopoly provisions.

Today, the U.S. Department of Justice, the Federal Trade Commission, injured private parties, or state attorney generals can file antitrust suits against alleged violators of the Sherman Act. The courts can issue injunctions to prohibit anticompetitive practices (a behavioral remedy) or, if necessary, break up monopolists into competing firms (a structural remedy). Courts also can fine and imprison violators. Also, parties injured by monopolies can sue for *treble damages*—an award of three times the amount of the monetary injury done to them. In some cases, these damages have summed to millions or even billions of dollars.

The largest and most significant monopoly case of recent times is the Microsoft case, which is the subject of the application that follows.

APPLYING THE ANALYSIS

United States v. Microsoft

In May 1998, the U.S. Justice Department, 19 individual states, and the District of Columbia (hereafter, "the government") filed antitrust charges against Microsoft under the Sherman Antitrust Act. The government charged that Microsoft had violated Section 2 of the act through a series of unlawful actions designed to maintain its "Windows" monopoly. It also charged that some of that conduct violated Section 1 of the Sherman Act, which prohibits actions that restrain trade or commerce.

Microsoft denied the charges, arguing it had achieved its success through product innovation and lawful business practices. Microsoft contended it should not be penalized for its superior foresight, business acumen, and technological prowess. It also insisted that its monopoly was highly transitory because of rapid technological advance.

In June 2000, the district court ruled that the relevant market was software used to operate Intel-compatible personal computers (PCs). Microsoft's 95 percent share of that market clearly gave it monopoly power. The court pointed out, however, that being a monopoly is not illegal. The violation of the Sherman Act occurred because Microsoft used anticompetitive means to maintain its monopoly power.

According to the court, Microsoft feared that the success of Netscape's Navigator, which allowed people to browse the Internet, might allow Netscape to expand its software to include a competitive PC operating system—software that would threaten the Windows monopoly. It also feared that Sun's Internet applications of its Java programming language might eventually threaten Microsoft's Windows monopoly.

To counter these and similar threats, Microsoft illegally signed contracts with PC makers that required them to feature its Internet Explorer on the PC desktop and penalized companies that promoted software products that competed with Microsoft products. Moreover, it gave friendly companies coding that linked Windows to software applications and withheld such coding from companies featuring Netscape. Finally, under license from Sun, Microsoft developed Windows-related Java software that made Sun's own software incompatible with Windows.

The district court ordered Microsoft to split into two competing companies, one initially selling the Windows operating system and the other initially selling Microsoft applications (such as Word, Hotmail, MSN, Power-Point, and Internet Explorer). Both companies would be free to develop new products that compete with each other, and both could derive those products from the intellectual property embodied in the common products existing at the time of divestiture.

In late 2000, Microsoft appealed the district court decision to a U.S. court of appeals. In 2001, the higher court affirmed that Microsoft illegally maintained its monopoly, but tossed out the district court's decision to break up Microsoft. It agreed with Microsoft that the company was denied due process during the penalty phase of the trial and concluded that the district court judge had displayed an appearance of bias by holding extensive interviews with the press. The appeals court sent the remedial phase of the case to a new district court judge to determine appropriate remedies. The appeals court also raised issues relating to the wisdom of a structural remedy.

At the urging of the new district court judge, the federal government and Microsoft negotiated a proposed settlement. With minor modification, the settlement became the final court order in 2002. The breakup was rescinded and replaced with a behavioral remedy. It (1) prevents Microsoft from retaliating against any firm that is developing, selling, or using software that competes with Microsoft Windows or Internet Explorer or is shipping a personal computer that includes both Windows and a non-Microsoft operating system; (2) requires Microsoft to establish uniform royalty and licensing terms for computer manufacturers wanting to include Windows on their PCs; (3) requires that manufacturers be allowed to remove Microsoft icons and replace them with other icons on the Windows desktop; and (4) calls for Microsoft to provide technical information to other companies so those firms can develop programs that work as well with Windows as Microsoft's own products.

Microsoft's actions and conviction have indirectly resulted in billions of dollars of fines and payouts by Microsoft. Main examples: To AOL Time Warner (Netscape), $750 million; to the European Commission, $600 million in 2004 and $1.35 billion in 2008; to Sun Microsystems, $1.6 billion; to Novell, $536 million; to Brust.com, $60 million; to Gateway, $150 million; to interTrust, $440 million; to RealNetworks, $761 million; and to IBM, $850 million.

QUESTION:

Why is the 2002 Microsoft settlement a behavioral remedy rather than a structural remedy?

Sources: *United States v. Microsoft* (District Court Conclusions of Law), April 2000; *United States v. Microsoft* (court of appeals), June 2001; *United States v. Microsoft* (Final Judgment), November 2002; and Reuters and Associated Press news services.

Summary

LO8.1 List the characteristics of pure monopoly and discuss the barriers to entry that relate to monopoly.

A pure monopolist is the sole producer of a good or service for which there are no close substitutes.

The existence of pure monopoly is explained by barriers to entry in the form of (a) economies of scale, (b) patents and licenses, (c) ownership or control of essential resources, and (d) pricing and other strategic behavior.

LO8.2 Explain how a pure monopoly sets its profit-maximizing output and price.

The pure monopolist's market situation differs from that of a competitive firm in that the monopolist's demand curve is downward sloping, causing the MR curve to lie below the demand curve. Like the competitive seller, the pure monopolist will maximize profit by equating marginal revenue and marginal cost. Barriers to entry may permit a monopolist to acquire economic profit even in the long run. However, (a) the monopolist does not charge "the highest price possible"; (b) the price that yields maximum total profit to the monopolist rarely coincides with the price that yields maximum unit profit; and (c) high costs and weak demand may prevent the monopolist from realizing any profit at all.

LO8.3 Discuss the economic effects of monopoly.
With the same costs, the pure monopolist will find it profitable to restrict output and charge a higher price than would sellers in a purely competitive industry. This restriction of output causes resources to be misallocated because price exceeds marginal cost in monopolized markets.

Monopoly transfers income from consumers to monopolists because monopolists can charge a higher price than would a purely competitive firm with the same costs. Monopolists in effect levy a "private tax" on consumers and, if demand is strong enough, obtain substantial economic profits.

Monopolists and competitive producers may not face the same costs. On the one hand, economies of scale may make lower unit costs available to monopolists but not to competitors. Also, pure monopoly may be more likely than pure competition to reduce costs via technological advance because of the monopolist's ability to realize economic profit, which can be used to finance research. On the other hand, X-inefficiency—the failure to produce with the least costly combination of inputs—is more common among monopolists than among competitive firms. Also, monopolists may make costly expenditures to maintain monopoly privileges that are conferred by government. Finally, the blocked entry of rival firms weakens the monopolist's incentive to be technologically progressive.

LO8.4 Describe why a monopolist might charge different prices in different markets.
A monopolist can increase its profit by price discriminating provided (a) it has monopoly pricing power, (b) it can segregate buyers on the basis of elasticities of demand, and (c) its product or service cannot be readily transferred between the segregated markets.

LO8.5 Identify the antitrust laws that are used to deal with monopoly.
The cornerstone of U.S. antitrust law is the Sherman Act of 1890, particularly Section 2. According to the rule of reason, possession of monopoly power is not illegal. But monopoly that is unreasonably gained or unreasonably maintained is a violation of the law.

If a company is found guilty of violating the Sherman Act, the government can either break up the monopoly into competing firms (a structural remedy) or prohibit it from engaging in specific anticompetitive business practices (a behavioral remedy).

Terms and Concepts

pure monopoly	simultaneous consumption	rent-seeking behavior
barrier to entry	network effects	price discrimination
natural monopoly	X-inefficiency	rule of reason

Questions

1. "No firm is completely sheltered from rivals; all firms compete for consumer dollars. Therefore, pure monopoly does not exist." Do you agree? Explain. How might you use the concept of cross-elasticity of demand to judge whether monopoly exists? **(LO1)**

2. Discuss the major barriers to entry into an industry. Explain how each barrier can foster monopoly. Which barriers, if any, do you feel give rise to monopoly that is socially justifiable? **(LO1)**

3. How does the demand curve faced by a purely monopolistic seller differ from that confronting a purely competitive firm? Why does it differ? Of what significance is the difference? Why is the pure monopolist's demand curve typically not perfectly inelastic? **(LO2)**

4. Use the following demand schedule to calculate total revenue and marginal revenue at each quantity. Plot the demand and MR curves, and explain the relationships between them. Explain why the marginal revenue of the fourth unit of output is $3.50, even though its price is $5. Use Chapter 4's total-revenue test for price elasticity to designate the elastic and inelastic segments of your graphed demand curve. What generalization can you make as to the relationship between marginal revenue and the elasticity of demand? Suppose the marginal cost of successive units of output was zero. What output would the single-price monopolist produce, and what price would it charge? **(LO2)**

Price (P)	Quantity Demanded (Q)	Price (P)	Quantity Demanded (Q)
$7.00	0	$4.50	5
6.50	1	4.00	6
6.00	2	3.50	7
5.50	3	3.00	8
5.00	4	2.50	9

5. Assume a monopolistic publisher has agreed to pay an author 10 percent of the total revenue from the sales of a text. Will the author and the publisher want to charge the same price for the text? Explain. **(LO2)**

6. Assume that a pure monopolist and a purely competitive firm have the same unit costs. Contrast the two with respect to (a) price, (b) output, (c) profits, (d) allocation of resources, and (e) impact on income transfers. Because both monopolists and competitive firms follow the MR = MC rule in maximizing profits, how do you account for the different results? Why might the costs of a purely competitive firm and those of a monopolist be different? What are the implications of such a cost difference? **(LO3)**

7. Critically evaluate and explain each statement: **(LO3)**

    a. Because they can control product price, monopolists are always assured of profitable production by simply charging the highest price consumers will pay.

b. The pure monopolist seeks the output that will yield the greatest per-unit profit.

c. An excess of price over marginal cost is the market's way of signaling the need for more production of a good.

d. The more profitable a firm, the greater its monopoly power.

e. The monopolist has a pricing policy; the competitive producer does not.

f. With respect to resource allocation, the interests of the seller and of society coincide in a purely competitive market but conflict in a monopolized market.

8. U.S. pharmaceutical companies charge different prices for prescription drugs to buyers in different nations, depending on elasticity of demand and government-imposed price ceilings. Explain why these companies, for profit reasons, oppose laws allowing re-importation of drugs to the United States. **(LO4)**

9. Why have firms such as Google, Facebook, and Amazon gained monopoly power in search, social media, and online retail, respectively, despite potential competitors having virtually unrestricted access to the internet? What economic concepts explain their ability to monopolize these markets? **(LO1)**

10. Under what law and on what basis did the federal district court find Microsoft guilty of violating the antitrust laws? What was the initial district court's remedy? How did Microsoft fare with its appeal to the court of appeals? Was the final remedy in the case a structural remedy or a behavioral remedy? **(LO5)**

Problems

1. Assume that the most efficient production technology available for making vitamins has the cost structure given in the following table. Note that output is measured as the number of bottles of vitamins produced per day and that costs include a normal profit. **(LO1)**

Output	TC	MC
25,000	$100,000	$0.50
50,000	150,000	1.00
75,000	187,500	2.50
100,000	275,500	3.00

    a. What is ATC per unit for each level of output listed in the table?

b. Are there economies of scale in production? (Answer yes or no.)

c. Suppose that the market price for a bottle of vitamins is $2.50. At that price the total market quantity demanded is 75,000,000 bottles. How many firms will be in this industry?

d. Suppose that, instead, the market quantity demanded at a price of $2.50 is only 75,000. How many firms will be in this industry?

e. Review your answers to parts b, c, and d. Does the level of demand determine this industry's market structure?

2. A new production technology for making vitamins is invented by a college professor who decides not to patent it. Thus, it is available for anybody to

copy and put into use. The TC per bottle for production up to 100,000 bottles per day is given in the following table. **(LO1)**

Output	TC
25,000	$50,000
50,000	70,000
75,000	75,000
100,000	80,000

a. What is ATC for each level of output listed in the table?

b. Suppose that for each 25,000-bottle-per-day increase in production above 100,000 bottles per day, TC increases by $5,000 (so that, for instance, 125,000 bottles per day would generate total costs of $85,000, while 150,000 bottles per day would generate total costs of $90,000). Is this a decreasing-cost industry?

c. Suppose that the price of a bottle of vitamins is $1.33. At that price the total quantity demanded by consumers is 75,000,000 bottles. How many firms will there be in this industry?

d. Suppose that, instead, the market quantity demanded at a price of $1.33 is only 75,000. How many firms will be in this industry?

e. Review your answers to parts b, c, and d. Does the level of demand determine this industry's market structure?

f. Compare your answer to part d of this problem with your answer to part d of problem 1. Do both production technologies show constant returns to scale?

3. Suppose a pure monopolist faces the following demand schedule and the same cost data as the competitive producer discussed in problem 4 at the end of **Chapter 7**. Calculate the missing TR and MR amounts, and determine the profit-maximizing price and profit-maximizing output for this monopolist. What is the monopolist's profit? Verify your answer graphically and by comparing total revenue and total cost. **(LO2)**

Price	Quantity Demanded	Total Revenue	Marginal Revenue
$115	0	$___	
100	1	___	$___
83	2	___	___
71	3	___	___
63	4	___	___
55	5	___	___
48	6	___	___
42	7	___	___
37	8	___	___
33	9	___	___
29	10	___	___

4. Suppose that a price-discriminating monopolist has segregated its market into two groups of buyers. The first group is described by the demand and revenue data that you developed for problem 3. The demand and revenue data for the second group of buyers is shown in the following table. Assume that MC is $13 in both markets and MC = ATC at all output levels. What price will the firm charge in each market? Based solely on these two prices, which market has the higher price elasticity of demand? What will be this monopolist's total economic profit? **(LO4)**

Price	Quantity Demanded	Total Revenue	Marginal Revenue
$71	0	$ 0	
63	1	63	$63
55	2	110	47
48	3	144	34
42	4	168	24
37	5	185	17
33	6	198	13
29	7	203	5

CHAPTER NINE

Monopolistic Competition and Oligopoly

Learning Objectives

LO9.1   List the characteristics of monopolistic competition.
LO9.2   Explain why monopolistic competitors earn only a normal profit in the long run.
LO9.3   Describe the characteristics of oligopoly.
LO9.4   Discuss how game theory relates to oligopoly.
LO9.5   Relate why the demand curve of an oligopolist may be kinked.
LO9.6   Compare the incentives and obstacles to collusion among oligopolists.
LO9.7   Contrast the positive and potential negative effects of advertising.
LO9.8   Discuss the efficiency of oligopoly.

In the United States, most industries have a market structure that falls somewhere between the two poles of pure competition and pure monopoly. That is, most real-world industries have fewer than the large number of producers required for pure competition but more than the single producer that defines pure monopoly. In addition, most firms have both differentiated rather than standardized products, as well as some discretion over the prices they charge. Finally, entry to most real-world industries ranges from easy to very difficult, but is rarely completely blocked.

This chapter examines two models that more closely approximate these widespread industry structures. You will discover that *monopolistic competition* mixes a small amount of monopoly power with a large amount of competition. *Oligopoly*, in contrast, blends a large amount of monopoly power with considerable rivalry among existing firms.

PHOTO OP

Monopolistic Competition versus Oligopoly

Furniture is produced in a monopolistically competitive industry, whereas refrigerators are produced in an oligopolistic industry.

Stockernumber2/iStock/Getty Images

Ryan McVay/Getty Images

Monopolistic Competition

Monopolistic competition is characterized by a fairly large number of firms—say, 25, 35, 60, or 70—not by the hundreds or thousands of firms in pure competition. Consequently, monopolistic competition involves:

- *Small market shares* Each firm has a comparatively small percentage of the total market and consequently has limited control over market price.
- *No collusion* The presence of a relatively large number of firms ensures that collusion (coordination) by a group of firms to restrict output and set prices is unlikely.
- *Independent action* There is no interdependence among firms; each can determine its own pricing policy without considering rival firms' possible reactions of rival firms. A single firm may realize a modest increase in sales by cutting its price, but that action's effect on competitors' sales will be nearly imperceptible and will probably trigger no response.

Differentiated Products

product differentiation
A strategy in which one firm's product is distinguished from competing products by means of its design, related services, quality, location, or other attributes (except price).

Unlike pure competition, in which there is a standardized product, monopolistic competition features **product differentiation.** Monopolistically competitive firms produce variations of a particular product. Their products have slightly different physical characteristics, offer varying degrees of customer service, provide varying amounts of locational convenience, or proclaim special qualities, real or imagined.

Product Attributes   Product differentiation may entail physical or qualitative differences in the products themselves. Real differences in functional features, materials, design, and workmanship are vital aspects of product differentiation. Personal computers, for example, differ in terms of storage capacity, speed, and quality of graphic displays. Most cities have a variety of retail stores selling clothes that differ greatly in styling, materials, and quality of work. Similarly, one pizza place may feature its thin-crust Neapolitan-style pizza, while another may tout its thick-crust Chicago-style pizza.

Service   Service and the conditions surrounding the sale of a product are forms of product differentiation, too. One shoe store may stress its clerks' fashion knowledge and helpfulness. A competitor may leave trying on shoes and carrying them to the register to its customers but offer lower prices. Customers may prefer one-day over three-day dry cleaning of equal quality. A store's prestige appeal, the firm's reputation for servicing or exchanging its products, and the credit it makes available are all service aspects of product differentiation.

Location   Products may also be differentiated through the location and accessibility of the stores that sell them. Small convenience stores manage to compete with large supermarkets, even though these mini-marts sell fewer products and charge higher prices. They compete mainly on the basis of location—being close to customers and situated on busy streets. A motel's proximity to an interstate highway gives it a locational advantage that may allow it to charge a higher room rate than other motels in less convenient locations.

Brand Names and Packaging   Product differentiation may also be created through the use of brand names and trademarks, packaging, and celebrity connections. Most aspirin tablets are very much alike, but many headache sufferers believe that one brand—for example, Bayer, Anacin, or Bufferin—is superior and worth a higher price than a generic substitute. A celebrity's name associated with watches, perfume, or athletic shoes may enhance those products' appeal for some buyers. Packaging that touts "natural spring" bottled water may attract additional customers.

Some Control over Price   Monopolistic competitors have some control over their product prices because of product differentiation. If consumers prefer the products of specific sellers, then within limits they will pay more to satisfy their preferences. Sellers and buyers are not linked randomly, as in a purely competitive market. But the monopolistic competitor's control over price is quite limited because there are numerous potential substitutes for its product.

Easy Entry and Exit

Entry into monopolistically competitive industries is relatively easy. Because monopolistic competitors are typically small firms, both absolutely and relatively, economies of scale are few and capital requirements are low. However, financial barriers may result from the need to develop and advertise a product that differs from rivals' products. Some firms may have trade secrets relating to their products or hold trademarks on their brand names, making it difficult and costly for other firms to imitate them.

Exit from monopolistically competitive industries is relatively easy. Nothing prevents an unprofitable monopolistic competitor from holding a going-out-of-business sale and shutting down.

Advertising

The expense and effort involved in product differentiation would be wasted if consumers are not aware of product differences. Thus, monopolistic competitors advertise their products, often heavily. The goal of product differentiation and advertising—so-called **nonprice competition**—is to make price less of a factor in consumer purchases and to make product differences a greater factor. If successful, the firm's demand will shift to the right *and* become less elastic.

nonprice competition
Competition based on distinguishing one's product by means of product differentiation and then advertising the distinguished product to consumers.

Monopolistically Competitive Industries

Several manufacturing industries approximate monopolistic competition. Examples of manufactured goods produced in monopolistically competitive industries are jewelry, asphalt, wood pallets, commercial signs, leather goods, plastic pipes, textile bags, and kitchen cabinets. In addition, many retail establishments in metropolitan areas are monopolistically competitive, including grocery stores, gasoline stations, hair salons, dry cleaners, clothing stores, and restaurants (see **Global Snapshot 9.1**). Also, many providers of professional services such as medical care, legal assistance, real estate sales, and basic bookkeeping are monopolistic competitors.

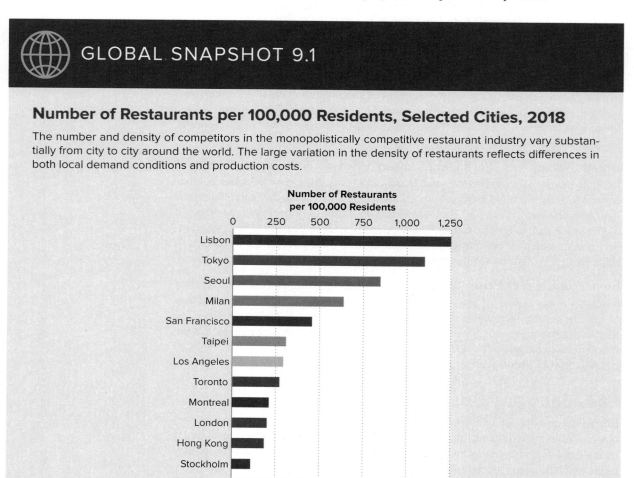

GLOBAL SNAPSHOT 9.1

Number of Restaurants per 100,000 Residents, Selected Cities, 2018

The number and density of competitors in the monopolistically competitive restaurant industry vary substantially from city to city around the world. The large variation in the density of restaurants reflects differences in both local demand conditions and production costs.

Source: World Cities Culture Forum.

Price and Output in Monopolistic Competition

How does a monopolistically competitive firm decide on its price and output? Initially, we assume that each firm in the industry is producing a specific differentiated product and engaging in a particular amount of advertising.

The Firm's Demand Curve

Our explanation is based on **Figure 9.1**, which shows that the demand curve faced by a monopolistically competitive seller is highly, but not perfectly, elastic. It is precisely this feature that distinguishes monopolistic competition from both pure monopoly and pure competition. The monopolistic competitor's demand is more elastic than the demand faced by a pure monopolist because the monopolistically competitive seller competes with many other firms producing close substitutes. The pure monopolist has no rivals at all. Yet, for two reasons, the monopolistic competitor's demand is not perfectly elastic like that of the pure competitor. First, the monopolistic competitor has fewer rivals; second, its products are differentiated, so they are not perfect substitutes.

The price elasticity of demand faced by the monopolistically competitive firm depends on the number of rivals and the degree of product differentiation. The more rivals and the weaker the product differentiation, the greater the price elasticity of each seller's demand—that is, the closer monopolistic competition will be to pure competition.

FIGURE 9.1

A monopolistically competitive firm: short run and long run. The monopolistic competitor maximizes profit or minimizes loss by producing the output at which MR = MC. The economic profit shown in (a) will induce new firms to enter, eventually eliminating economic profit. The loss shown in (b) will cause an exit of firms until normal profit is restored. After such entry and exit, the price will settle in (c) to where it just equals average total cost at the MR = MC output. At this price P_3 and output Q_3, the monopolistic competitor earns only a normal profit, and the industry is in long-run equilibrium.

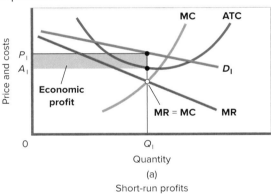

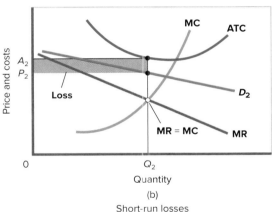

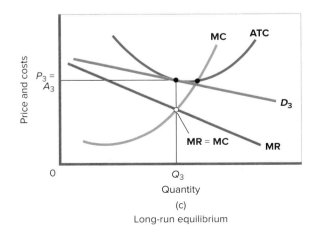

The Short Run: Profit or Loss

In the short run, monopolistically competitive firms maximize profit or minimize loss using exactly the same strategy as pure competitors and monopolists: They produce the level of output at which marginal revenue equals marginal cost (MR = MC). Thus, the monopolistically competitive firm in **Figure 9.1a** produces output Q_1, where MR = MC. As shown by demand curve D_1, it then charges price P_1. It realizes an economic profit, shown by the green area [$= (P_1 - A_1) \times Q_1$].

But with less favorable demand or costs, the firm may incur a loss in the short run. We show this possibility in **Figure 9.1b**, where the firm's best strategy is to minimize its loss. It does so by producing output Q_2 (where MR = MC) and, as determined by demand curve D_2, by charging price P_2. Because price P_2 is less than average total cost A_2, the firm incurs a per-unit loss of $A_2 - P_2$, and a total loss represented as the red area [$= (A_2 - P_2) \times Q_2$].

The Long Run: Only a Normal Profit

In the long run, firms will enter a profitable monopolistically competitive industry and leave an unprofitable one. Therefore, a monopolistic competitor will earn only a normal profit in the long run or, in other words, will only break even. (Remember that the cost curves include both explicit and implicit costs, including a normal profit.)

Profits: Firms Enter   In the case of short-run profit (**Figure 9.1a**), economic profits attract new rivals because entry to the industry is relatively easy. As new firms enter, the demand curve faced by the typical firm shifts to the left (falls) because each firm has a smaller share of total demand and now faces a larger number of close-substitute products. This decline in the firm's demand reduces its economic profit. When entry of new firms has reduced demand to the extent that the demand curve is tangent to the average-total-cost curve at the profit-maximizing output, the firm is just making a normal profit. This situation is graphed in **Figure 9.1c**, where demand is D_3 and the firm's long-run equilibrium output is Q_3. Any greater or lesser output will entail an average total cost that exceeds product price P_3, meaning a loss for the firm. At the tangency point between the demand curve and ATC, total revenue equals total costs. With the economic profit gone, there is no further incentive for additional firms to enter.

Losses: Firms Leave   When the industry suffers short-run losses, as in **Figure 9.1b**, some firms will exit in the long run. Faced with fewer substitute products and an expanded share of total demand, the surviving firms will see their demand curves shift to the right (rise), as to D_3. Their losses will disappear and give way to normal profits (**Figure 9.1c**).

Monopolistic Competition and Efficiency

Economic efficiency requires each firm to produce the amount of output at which $P = MC = $ minimum ATC. The equality of price and minimum average total cost yields *productive efficiency.* The good is being produced in the least costly way, and the price is just sufficient to cover average total cost, including a normal profit. The equality of price and marginal cost yields *allocative efficiency.* The right amount of output is being produced, and thus the right amount of scarce resources is devoted to this specific use.

How efficient is monopolistic competition, as measured against this triple equality? In particular, do monopolistically competitive firms produce the efficient output level associated with $P = MC$ = minimum ATC?

Neither Productive nor Allocative Efficiency

In monopolistic competition, neither productive nor allocative efficiency occurs in long-run equilibrium. **Figure 9.2** enlarges part of **Figure 9.1c** and clearly shows this. Note that the profit-maximizing price P_3 slightly exceeds the lowest average total cost, A_4. In producing the profit-maximizing output Q_3, the firm's average total cost therefore is slightly higher than optimal from society's perspective—productive efficiency is not achieved. Also note that the profit-maximizing price P_3 exceeds marginal cost (here M_3), meaning that monopolistic competition causes an underallocation of resources. Society values each unit of output between Q_3 and Q_4 more highly than the goods it would have to forgo to produce those units. Thus, to a modest extent, monopolistic competition also fails the allocative-efficiency test. Consumers pay a higher-than-competitive price and obtain a less-than-optimal output. Indeed, monopolistic competitors must charge a higher-than-competitive price in the long run in order to achieve a normal profit.

FIGURE 9.2
The inefficiency of monopolistic competition. In long-run equilibrium, a monopolistic competitor achieves neither productive nor allocative efficiency. Productive efficiency is not realized because production occurs where the average total cost A_3 exceeds the minimum average total cost A_4. Allocative efficiency is not achieved because the product price P_3 exceeds the marginal cost M_3. The results are an underallocation of resources and excess production capacity of $Q_4 - Q_3$.

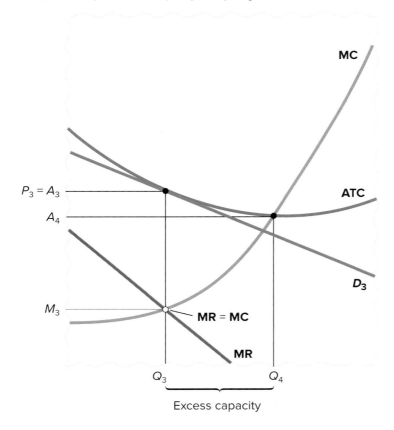

Excess Capacity

In monopolistic competition, the gap between the minimum-ATC output and the profit-maximizing output identifies **excess capacity:** plant and equipment that are underused because firms are producing less than the minimum-ATC output. This gap is shown as the distance between Q_4 and Q_3 in **Figure 9.2**. Note in the figure that the minimum ATC is at the intersection of price A_4 and quantity Q_4, where MC intersects ATC. If each monopolistic competitor could profitably produce at this point on its ATC curve, the lower average total cost would enable a lower price than P_3. More importantly, if each firm produced at Q_4 rather than at Q_3, fewer firms would be needed to produce the industry output. But because monopolistically competitive firms produce at Q_3 in long-run equilibrium, monopolistically competitive industries are overpopulated with firms, each operating below its optimal capacity. For example, in most cities there is an abundance of small motels and restaurants that operate well below half capacity.

Product Variety and Improvement

But monopolistic competition also has two notable virtues. It promotes product variety and product improvement. A monopolistic competitor is rarely satisfied with the situation portrayed in **Figure 9.1c** because it means only a normal profit. Instead, it may try to regain its economic profit through further product differentiation and better advertising. By developing or improving its product, it may be able to re-create, at least for a while, the profit outcome of **Figure 9.1a**.

The product variety and product improvement that accompany the drive to maintain or regain economic profit in monopolistic competition are benefits for society. That benefit may offset the cost of the inefficiency associated with monopolistic competition. Consumers have a wide diversity of tastes: Some like regular fries, others like curly fries; some like contemporary furniture, others prefer traditional furniture. If a product is differentiated, then at any time the consumer can choose from a wide range of types, styles, and brands. Compared with pure competition, this variety provides an advantage to the consumer. The range of choice is widened, and producers more fully meet the wide variation in consumer tastes.

The product improvement promoted by monopolistic competition further differentiates products and expands choices. And a successful product improvement by one firm obligates rivals to imitate or improve on that firm's temporary market advantage or else lose business. So society benefits from better products.

 APPLYING THE ANALYSIS

The Spice of Life

The Wendy's hamburger chain debuted a humorous TV commercial in 1987. The commercial depicted a Soviet communist fashion show. A woman walks down the runway in a drab grey factory uniform. The emcee shouts out, "Day wear!" Then she marches down the runway again in the same uniform but holding a flashlight. The emcee shouts out, "Evening wear!" She then marches out in the same uniform again but holding an inflatable beach ball. "Swimwear!"

Chuck Nacke/Alamy Stock Photo

Communist central planners didn't care about product differentiation. They typically made one design of a given product to be able to mass produce it at the lowest possible cost. The result was a society of painful sameness.

The Wendy's TV commercial hammered home a single idea—that we should embrace the fact that the food produced by Wendy's was different from that produced by its main rivals, McDonald's and Burger King. Unlike the communist central planning of the old Soviet Union, the free-market system of the United States allows for huge amounts of product differentiation. If "variety is the spice of life," American capitalism is extremely well seasoned.

Source: Wendy's, "Soviet Fashion Show," 1987.

Oligopoly

An **oligopoly** is a market dominated by a few large producers of a homogeneous or differentiated product. Because of their "fewness," oligopolists have considerable control over their prices, but each must consider the possible reaction of rivals to its own pricing, output, and advertising decisions.

oligopoly
A market structure in which a few firms sell either a standardized or a differentiated product, into which entry is difficult, in which the firm has limited control over product price because of mutual interdependence (except when there is collusion among firms), and in which there is typically nonprice competition.

A Few Large Producers

The phrase "a few large producers" is necessarily vague because the market model of oligopoly covers much ground. Oligopoly encompasses the U.S. aluminum industry, in which three huge firms dominate an entire national market, and the situation in which four or five much smaller auto-parts stores enjoy roughly equal shares of the market in a medium-size town. Generally, however, terms such as "Big Three," "Big Four," and "Big Six," refer to an oligopolistic industry. Examples of U.S. industries that are oligopolies are tires, beer, cigarettes, copper, greeting cards, light bulbs, aircraft, motor vehicles, gypsum products, and breakfast cereals. There are numerous others.

Homogeneous or Differentiated Products

An oligopoly may be either a **homogeneous oligopoly** or a **differentiated oligopoly,** depending on whether the firms in the oligopoly produce standardized (homogeneous) or differentiated products. Many industrial products (steel, zinc, copper, lead, cement) are standardized. In contrast, many consumer goods industries (automobiles, household appliances, electronic equipment, breakfast cereals, and many sporting goods) are differentiated oligopolies. These differentiated oligopolies typically engage in considerable nonprice competition supported by heavy advertising.

homogeneous oligopoly
An oligopoly in which the firms produce a standardized product.

differentiated oligopoly
An oligopoly in which the firms produce a differentiated product.

Control over Price, but Mutual Interdependence

strategic behavior
Self-interested economic actions that take into account the expected reactions of others.

mutual interdependence
A situation in which a change in price strategy (or in some other strategy) by one firm will affect the sales and profits of another firm (or other firms). Any firm that makes such a change can expect the other rivals to react to the change.

Because oligopolistic industries have only a few firms, each firm is a "price maker"; like the monopolist, it can set its price and output levels to maximize its profit. But unlike the monopolist, which has no rivals, the oligopolist must consider how its rivals will react to any change in its price, output, product characteristics, or advertising. Oligopoly is thus characterized by *strategic behavior* and *mutual interdependence.* By **strategic behavior,** we mean self-interested behavior that takes into account the reactions of others. Firms develop and implement price, quality, location, service, and advertising strategies to "grow their business" and expand their profits. But because rivals are few, there is **mutual interdependence,** in which each firm's profit depends not just on its own price and sales strategies but also on those of the other firms in its highly concentrated industry. Therefore, oligopolistic firms base their decisions on how they think rivals will react. Examples: In deciding whether to increase the price of its cosmetics, L'Oréal will try to predict the response of the other major producers, such as Clinique. In deciding on its advertising strategy, Burger King will take into consideration how McDonald's might react.

 ILLUSTRATING THE IDEA

Creative Strategic Behavior

The following story, written tongue in cheek, illustrates a localized market that exhibits some characteristics of oligopoly, including strategic behavior.

Sofia Martinez's Native American Arts and Crafts store is located in the center of a small tourist town that borders on a national park. In its early days, Sofia had a mini-monopoly. Business was brisk, and prices and profits were high.

To Sofia's annoyance, two "copycat" shops opened adjacent to her store, one on either side of her shop. Worse yet, the competitors named their shops to take advantage of Sofia's advertising. One was "Native Arts and Crafts"; the other, "Indian Arts and Crafts." These new sellers drew business away from Sofia's store, forcing her to lower her prices. The three side-by-side stores in the small, isolated town constituted a localized oligopoly for Native American arts and crafts.

Sofia began to think strategically about ways to boost profit. She decided to distinguish her shop from those on either side by offering a greater mix of high-quality, expensive products and a lesser mix of inexpensive souvenir items. The tactic worked for a while, but the other stores eventually imitated her product mix.

Then, one of the competitors next door escalated the rivalry by hanging up a large sign proclaiming "We Sell for Less!" Shortly thereafter, the other shop put up a large sign stating "We Won't Be Undersold!"

Not to be outdone, Sofia painted a colorful sign of her own and hung it above her door. It read "Main Entrance."

QUESTION:

How do you think the two rivals will react to Sofia's strategy?

Entry Barriers

The same barriers to entry that create pure monopoly also contribute to the creation of oligopoly. Economies of scale are important entry barriers in the aircraft, rubber, and copper industries. In those industries, three or four firms might each have sufficient sales to achieve economies of scale, but new firms would have such a small market share that they could not do so. They would then be high-cost producers, and as such they could not survive. A closely related barrier is the large expenditure for capital—the cost of obtaining necessary plant and equipment—required for entering certain industries. The jet engine, automobile, commercial aircraft, and petroleum-refining industries, for example, are all characterized by very high capital requirements.

The ownership and control of raw materials help explain why oligopoly exists in many mining industries, including gold, silver, and copper. Patents have served as entry barriers in the computer, chemicals, consumer electronics, and pharmaceutical industries. Oligopolists can also prevent the entry of new competitors through preemptive and retaliatory pricing and advertising strategies.

Mergers

Some oligopolies have emerged mainly through the growth of the dominant firms in a given industry (examples: breakfast cereals, chewing gum, candy bars). For other industries, mergers have been the route to oligopoly (examples: steel, airlines, banking, and entertainment). The merging, or combining, of two or more firms may substantially increase their market share, which in turn may help the new firm achieve greater economies of scale.

Another motive underlying the "urge to merge" is the desire for monopoly power. The larger firm that results from a merger has greater control over market supply and thus the price of its product. Also, because it is a larger buyer of inputs, it may be able to demand and obtain lower prices (costs) on its production inputs.

Oligopoly Behavior: A Game-Theory Overview

Oligopoly pricing behavior has the characteristics of certain games of strategy, such as poker, chess, and bridge. The best strategy for one player will depend on the opponent's strategy, and vice versa. Players (and oligopolists) must pattern their actions according to their rivals' actions and expected reactions. The study of how people or firms behave in strategic situations is called **game theory.**

game theory
A means of analyzing the business behavior of oligopolists that uses the theory of strategy associated with games such as chess and bridge.

 ILLUSTRATING THE IDEA

The Prisoner's Dilemma

A classic example of game theory is the *prisoner's dilemma game,* in which two people—let's call them Betty and Al—have committed a diamond heist and are detained by the police as prime suspects. Unbeknownst to the two, the evidence against them is weak, so the police try to convict the criminals by getting one or both of them to confess to the crime. The police place Betty and Al in separate holding cells and offer each the same deal: Confess to the crime and receive a lighter prison sentence.

The prisoners face the same dilemma. Each may be inclined to remain silent and hope that their partner will, too. But the offer made by the police means that it will be in the other person's best interest to confess so that they can be sure of a shorter sentence. Fearful that the other person will confess, both confess, even though they each would be better off saying nothing. The "confess–confess" outcome can occur when two oligopolists escalate their advertising budgets to high levels, even though both would earn higher profits at agreed-upon lower levels. In politics, it occurs when two candidates engage in negative advertising, despite claiming that, in principle, they are opposed to its use.

> QUESTION:
> How might the prisoners' strategies or decisions be affected if the general prison population tends to punish those who are known to "rat out" (confess against) their partners?

Now let's look at a more detailed prisoner's dilemma game, using the tools of game theory to analyze the pricing behavior of oligopolists. We assume that a *duopoly,* or two-firm oligopoly, is producing athletic shoes. Each of the two firms—for example, RareAir and Uptown—has a choice of two pricing strategies: price high or price low. Each firm's profit will depend on the strategy it chooses *and* the strategy its rival chooses.

There are four possible combinations of strategies for the two firms, as shown by the lettered cells in **Figure 9.3.** For example, cell C represents a low-price strategy for Uptown, along with a high-price strategy for RareAir. **Figure 9.3** is called a *payoff matrix* because each cell shows the payoff (profit) to each firm that would result from each combination of strategies. Cell C shows that if Uptown adopts a low-price strategy and RareAir a high-price strategy, then Uptown will earn $15 million (yellow portion) and RareAir will earn $6 million (blue portion).

FIGURE 9.3

Profit payoff (in millions) for a two-firm oligopoly. Each firm has two possible pricing strategies. RareAir's strategies are shown in the top margin, and Uptown's in the left margin. Each lettered cell of this four-cell payoff matrix represents one combination of a RareAir strategy and an Uptown strategy and shows the profit that combination would earn for each firm. Assuming no collusion, the outcome of this game is cell D, with both parties using low-price strategies and earning $8 million in profits.

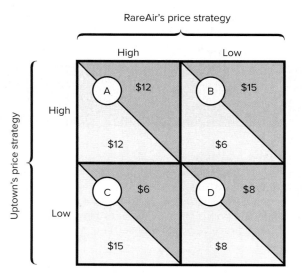

Mutual Interdependence Revisited

The data in **Figure 9.3** are hypothetical, but their relationships are typical of real situations. Recall that oligopolistic firms can increase their profits, and influence their rivals' profits, by changing their pricing strategies. Each firm's profit depends on its own pricing strategy and that of its rivals. This mutual interdependence of oligopolists is the most obvious aspect of **Figure 9.3**. If Uptown adopts a high-price strategy, its profit will be $12 million, provided that RareAir also employs a high-price strategy (cell A). But if RareAir uses a low-price strategy against Uptown's high-price strategy (cell B), RareAir will increase its market share and boost its profit from $12 million to $15 million. RareAir's higher profit will come at the expense of Uptown, whose profit will fall from $12 million to $6 million. Uptown's high-price strategy is a good strategy *only if* RareAir *also* employs a high-price strategy. Thus, we see that neither firm has independent control of its profitability. Its profit is mutually interdependent with the actions taken by its rival.

Collusion

Figure 9.3 also implies that oligopolists often can benefit from **collusion**—that is, cooperation with rivals. To see the benefits of collusion, note that the best outcome for both firms is cell A, where each would obtain a profit of $12 million. But that is possible only if both firms can successfully collude and commit to having both of them pursue the high-price strategy. Without collusion, the profit incentives of the prisoner's dilemma situation will cause both firms to end up in cell D, with each firm making only $8 million per year.

To see why the mutually beneficial equilibrium at cell A will break down without collusion, note that both RareAir or Uptown can see from the payouts in **Figure 9.3** that each of them could increase its own profit by switching to a low-price strategy. For RareAir, switching from the high-price strategy to the low-price strategy would move the game to cell B. If that were to happen, RareAir's profit would increase from $12 million (cell A) to a substantially higher—and therefore quite tempting—$15 million (cell B). If there is no collusion to keep RareAir from switching strategies, RareAir will "follow the money" and switch to the low-price strategy. However, Uptown faces the same incentives to switch from a high-price to a low-price strategy. The net result is that, absent collusion, both firms will pursue a low-price strategy and end up at cell D.

How can oligopolists avoid the low-profit outcome of cell D? By colluding, rather than setting prices competitively or independently. In our example, the two firms could agree to establish and maintain a high-price policy, in which case each firm's profit would increase from $8 million (cell D) to $12 million (cell A).

Incentive to Cheat

The payoff matrix also explains why an oligopolist will be strongly tempted to cheat on a collusive agreement. Suppose Uptown and RareAir agree to maintain high-price policies, with each earning $12 million in profit (cell A). Both are tempted to cheat on this collusive pricing agreement because either firm can increase its profit to $15 million by lowering its price. That implies that the collusive agreement will be "unstable" because it contradicts each firm's profit motive. Both firms will probably cheat, and the game will settle back to cell D, with each firm using the low-price strategy. The lesson? Collusion agreements are often fragile, so that we mostly see oligopoly industries in which there is a substantial amount of low-price, competitive behavior.

collusion
A situation in which firms act together and in agreement (collude) to fix prices, divide a market, or otherwise restrict competition.

Kinked-Demand Model

Our game-theory discussion is helpful in understanding more traditional, graphical oligopoly models. We begin by examining a model in which rivals do not overtly collude to fix a common price. Such collusion is, in fact, illegal in the United States. Specifically, Section 1 of the Sherman Act of 1890 outlaws conspiracies to restrain trade. In antitrust law, these violations are known as **per se violations;** they are "in and of themselves" illegal, and therefore not subject to the rule of reason (**Chapter 8**). To gain a conviction, the government needs to show only that there was a conspiracy to fix prices, rig bids, or divide up markets, not that the conspiracy succeeded or caused serious damage to other parties.

Kinked-Demand Curve

Imagine an oligopolistic industry made up of three hypothetical firms (Arch, King's, and Dave's), each having about one-third of the total market for a differentiated product. Assume that these firms act independently, meaning they compete against each other and do not collude.

Now the question is, "What does the firm's demand curve look like?" Mutual interdependence and the uncertainty about rivals' reactions make this question hard to answer. The location and shape of an oligopolist's demand curve depend on how the firm's rivals will react to a price change.

Let's focus on Arch's demand curve, understanding that the analysis is applicable to each firm. Assume that the going price for Arch's product is P_0 and its current sales are Q_0, as shown in **Figure 9.4**. Suppose Arch is considering a price increase. If Arch raises its price above P_0 and its rivals ignore the price increase, Arch will lose sales significantly to its two rivals, who will be underpricing it. If that is the case, the demand and marginal-revenue curves faced by Arch will resemble the straight lines D_2 and MR_2 in **Figure 9.4**. Demand, in this case, is quite elastic: Arch's total revenue will fall. Because of product differentiation, however, Arch's sales and total revenue will not fall to zero when it raises its price; some of Arch's customers will pay the higher price because they have a strong preference for Arch's product.

What if Arch lowers its price? If Arch cuts its price, its sales will increase only modestly because its rivals will also cut prices to prevent Arch from gaining an advantage over them. Arch's sales will increase only modestly. The small increase in sales that Arch (and its two rivals) will realize is at the expense of other industries; Arch will gain no sales from King's and Dave's. So Arch's demand and marginal-revenue curves below price P_0 will look like the straight lines labeled D_1 and MR_1 in **Figure 9.4**.

Graphically, the D_2e "rivals ignore" segment of Arch's demand curve seems relevant for price increases, and the D_1e "rivals match" segment of demand seems relevant for price cuts. It is logical, then, or at least a reasonable assumption, that the noncollusive oligopolist faces the **kinked-demand curve** D_2eD_1, as shown in **Figure 9.4**. Demand is highly elastic above the going price P_0, but much less elastic or even inelastic below that price.

Note also that if rivals match a price cut but ignore an increase, the marginal-revenue curve of the oligopolist also will have an odd shape. It, too, will be made up of two segments: the left-hand marginal-revenue curve MR_2f in **Figure 9.4** and the right-hand marginal-revenue curve MR_1g. Because of the sharp difference in elasticity of demand above and below the going price, there is a gap, or what we can simply treat as a vertical segment, in the marginal-revenue curve. This gap is the dashed segment fg in the combined marginal-revenue curve MR_2fgMR_1.

FIGURE 9.4

The kinked-demand curve. In all likelihood, an oligopolist's rivals will ignore a price increase above the going price P_0 but follow a price cut below P_0. This causes the oligopolist's demand curve (D_2eD_1) to be kinked at e (price P_0) and the marginal-revenue curve to have a vertical break, or gap (fg). The firm will be highly reluctant to raise or lower its price. Moreover, any shift in marginal costs between MC_1 and MC_2 will cut the vertical (dashed) segment of the marginal-revenue curve and produce no change in price P_0 or output Q_0.

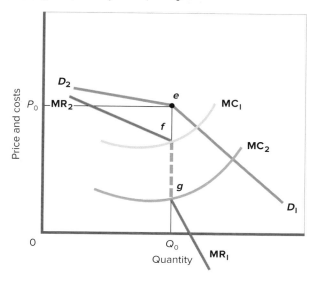

Price Inflexibility

This analysis helps explain why prices are generally stable in noncollusive oligopolistic industries. There are both demand and cost reasons.

On the demand side, the kinked-demand curve gives each oligopolist reason to believe that any change in price will be for the worse. If it raises its price, many of its customers will desert it. If it lowers its price, its sales at best will increase very modestly because rivals will match the lower price. Even if a price cut increases the oligopolist's total revenue somewhat, its costs may increase by a greater amount, depending on demand elasticity. For instance, if its demand is inelastic to the right of Q_0, as it may well be, then the firm's profit will surely fall. A price decrease in the inelastic region lowers the firm's total revenue, and the production of a larger output increases its total costs.

On the cost side, the broken marginal-revenue curve suggests that even if an oligopolist's costs change substantially, the firm may have no reason to change its price. In particular, all positions of the marginal-cost curve between MC_1 and MC_2 in **Figure 9.4** will result in the firm's deciding on exactly the same price and output. For all those positions, MR equals MC at output Q_0; at that output, it will charge price P_0.

Price Leadership

The uncertainties of the reactions of rivals create a major problem for oligopolists. There are times when wages and other input prices rise beyond the marginal costs associated with MC_1 in **Figure 9.4**. If no oligopolist dares raise its price, profits for all rivals will be severely squeezed. In many industries, a pattern of price leadership has emerged to handle these situations. **Price leadership** entails an implicit understanding by which oligopolists can coordinate prices without engaging in outright collusion based on formal agreements and secret meetings. Rather, a practice evolves whereby the "dominant firm"—usually the largest or most efficient in the industry—initiates price changes and all other firms more or less automatically follow the leader. Many

price leadership
An informal method that firms in an oligopoly may employ to set the price of their product: One firm (the leader) is the first to announce a change in price, and the other firms (the followers) soon announce identical or similar changes.

industries, including farm machinery, cement, copper, newsprint, glass containers, steel, beer, fertilizer, cigarettes, and tin, practice, or have in the recent past practiced, price leadership.

An examination of price leadership in a variety of industries suggests that the price leader is likely to observe the following tactics.

- *Infrequent price changes* Because price changes always carry the risk that rivals will not follow the lead, price adjustments are made only infrequently. The price leader does not respond to minuscule day-to-day changes in costs and demand. Price is changed only when cost and demand conditions have been altered significantly and on an industrywide basis as the result of, for example, industrywide wage increases, an increase in excise taxes, or an increase in the price of some basic input such as energy. In the automobile industry, price adjustments traditionally have been made when new models are introduced each fall.

- *Communications* The price leader often communicates impending price adjustments to the industry through speeches by major executives, trade publication interviews, or press releases. By publicizing "the need to raise prices," the price leader seeks agreement among its competitors regarding the actual increase.

- *Limit pricing* Price leaders do not always choose the price that maximizes short-run profits for the industry because the industry may want to discourage new firms from entering. If the cost advantages (economies of scale) of existing firms are a major barrier to entry, new entrants could surmount that barrier if the price leader and the other firms set product prices high enough. So, in order to discourage new competitors and to maintain the current oligopolistic structure of the industry, the price leader may keep the price below the short-run profit-maximizing level. The strategy of establishing a price that blocks the entry of new firms is called *limit pricing*.

APPLYING THE ANALYSIS

Breakdowns in Price Leadership: Price Wars

Despite attempts to maintain orderly price leadership, price wars occasionally break out in oligopolistic industries. Sometimes price wars result from attempts to establish new price leaders; other times, they result from attempts to "steal" business from rivals.

Consider the breakfast cereal industry, in which Kellogg traditionally had been the price leader. General Mills countered Kellogg's leadership in 1995 by reducing the prices of its cereals by 11 percent. In 1996, Post, another rival, responded with a 20 percent price cut, which Kellogg then followed. Not to be outdone, Post reduced its prices by another 11 percent.

As another example, in October 2009, with the holiday shopping season just getting under way, Walmart cut its price on 10 highly anticipated new books to just $10 each. Within hours, Amazon.com matched the price cut. Walmart then retaliated by cutting its price for the books to just $9 each. Amazon.com matched that reduction—at which point Walmart went to $8.99! Then, out of nowhere, Target jumped in at $8.98, a price that Amazon.com and Walmart immediately matched. And that is where the price finally came to rest—at a level so low that each company was losing money on each book it sold.

Most price wars eventually run their course. After a period of low or negative profits, they again yield price leadership to one of the industry's dominant firms. That firm then begins to raise prices back to their previous levels, and the other firms willingly follow suit.

> QUESTION:
>
> How might a low-cost price leader "enforce" its leadership through implied threats to rivals?

Collusion

The disadvantages and uncertainties of kinked-demand oligopolies and price leadership make collusion tempting. By controlling price through collusion, oligopolists may be able to reduce uncertainty, increase profits, and perhaps even prohibit the entry of new rivals. Collusion may assume a variety of forms. The most comprehensive form is the **cartel,** a group of producers that typically creates a formal written agreement specifying how much each member will produce and charge. Output must be controlled—the market must be divided up—in order to maintain the agreed-upon price. The collusion is *overt,* or open to view.

cartel
A formal agreement among firms (or countries) in an industry to set the price of a product and establish the outputs of the individual firms (or countries) or to divide the market for the product geographically.

Joint-Profit Maximization

To see the benefits of a cartel or other form of collusion, assume there are three hypothetical oligopolistic firms (Gypsum, Sheetrock, and GSR) producing, in this instance, gypsum drywall panels for finishing interior walls. Suppose all three firms produce a homogeneous product and have identical cost, demand, and marginal-revenue curves. **Figure 9.5** represents the position of each of our three oligopolistic firms.

FIGURE 9.5
Collusion and the tendency toward joint-profit maximization. If oligopolistic firms face identical or highly similar demand and cost conditions, they may collude to limit their joint output and set a single, common price. Thus, each firm acts as if it were a pure monopolist, setting output at Q_0 and charging price P_0. This price and output combination maximizes each firm's profit (green area) and thus the joint profits of all.

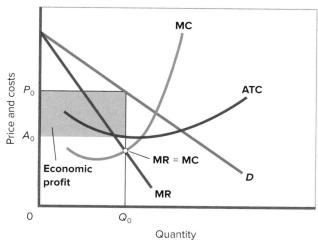

What price and output combination should, say, Gypsum select? If Gypsum were a pure monopolist, the answer would be clear: Establish output at Q_0, where marginal revenue equals marginal cost, charge the corresponding price P_0, and enjoy the maximum profit attainable. However, Gypsum does have two rivals selling identical products, and if Gypsum's assumption that its rivals will match its price of P_0 proves to be incorrect, the consequences could be disastrous for Gypsum. Specifically, if Sheetrock and GSR actually charge prices below P_0, then Gypsum's demand curve D will shift sharply to the left as its potential customers turn to its rivals, which are now selling the same product at a lower price. Of course, Gypsum can retaliate by cutting its price too, but this will move all three firms down their demand curves, lowering their profits. It may even drive them to a point where average total cost exceeds price and losses are incurred.

So the question becomes, "Will Sheetrock and GSR want to charge a price below P_0?" Under our assumptions, and recognizing that Gypsum has little choice except to match any price they may set below P_0, the answer is no. Faced with the same demand and cost circumstances, Sheetrock and GSR will find it in their interest to produce Q_0 and charge P_0. This is a curious situation; each firm finds it most profitable to charge the same price, P_0, but only if its rivals actually do so! How can the three firms ensure the price P_0 and quantity Q_0 solution in which each is keenly interested? How can they avoid the less profitable outcomes associated with either higher or lower prices?

The answer is evident: They can collude. They can get together, talk it over, and agree to charge the same price, P_0. In addition to reducing the possibility of price wars, this will give each firm the maximum profit. For society, the result will be the same as would occur if the industry were a pure monopoly composed of three identical plants.

 ## APPLYING THE ANALYSIS

Cartels and Collusion

Undoubtedly, the most significant international cartel is the Organization of Petroleum Exporting Countries (OPEC), comprising 13 oil-producing nations (Algeria, Angola, Congo, Equatorial Guinea, Gabon, Iran, Iraq, Kuwait, Libya, Nigeria, Saudi Arabia, UAE, and Venezuela). OPEC produces about 40 percent of the world's oil and supplies about 60 percent of all oil traded internationally. OPEC has, in some cases, been able to drastically alter oil prices by increasing or decreasing supply. In the late 1990s, for instance, it caused oil prices to rise from $11 per barrel to $34 per barrel over a 15-month period.

That being said, most increases in the price of oil are not caused by OPEC. Between 2005 and 2008, for example, oil prices went from $40 per barrel to $140 per barrel due to rapidly rising demand from China and supply uncertainties related to armed conflict in the Middle East. But as the recession that began in December 2007 took hold, demand slumped and oil prices collapsed back down to about $40 per barrel. OPEC was largely a non-factor in this rise and fall in the price of oil. But in those cases where OPEC can effectively enforce its production agreements, there is little doubt it can hold the price of oil substantially above the marginal cost of production.

Cartels are illegal in the United States, hence any collusion that exists is covert or secret. Yet we find numerous examples of collusion, as shown by evidence from antitrust (antimonopoly) cases. In 2011, U.S.-based Whirlpool, Japan-headquartered Panasonic, the Danish firm Danfoss, and the Italian company Appliance Components were fined over $200 million for attempting to run an international cartel that could rig the worldwide prices of refrigerator components. In 2012, several Japanese autoparts makers pleaded guilty to rigging the bids that they submitted to a major carmaker. The conspirators employed measures to keep their conduct secret, including using code names and instructing participants to destroy evidence of collusion.

There are many other examples of price-fixing: ConAgra and Hormel agreed to pay more than $21 million to settle their roles in a nationwide price-fixing case involving catfish. The U.S. Justice Department fined UCAR International $110 million for scheming with rivals to fix prices and divide the world market for graphite electrodes used in steel mills. The auction houses Sotheby's and Christy's were found guilty of conspiring over a six-year period to set the same commission rates for sellers at auctions. Bayer AG pleaded guilty to, and was fined $66 million for, taking part in a conspiracy to divide up the market and set prices for chemicals used in rubber manufacturing.

QUESTIONS:

In what way might mergers be an alternative to illegal collusion? In view of your answer, why is it important to enforce laws that outlaw mergers that substantially reduce competition?

Obstacles to Collusion

Normally, cartels and similar collusive arrangements are difficult to establish and maintain. There are several barriers to collusion beyond antitrust laws.

Demand and Cost Differences When oligopolists face different costs and demand curves, it is difficult for them to agree on a price. This is particularly the case in industries where products are differentiated and change frequently. Even with highly standardized products, firms usually have somewhat different market shares and operate with differing degrees of productive efficiency. Thus, it is unlikely that even homogeneous oligopolists would have the same demand and cost curves.

In either case, differences in costs and demand mean that the profit-maximizing price will differ among firms; no single price will be readily acceptable to all, as we assumed was true in **Figure 9.5**. So price collusion depends on compromises and concessions that are not always easy to obtain and hence act as an obstacle to collusion.

Number of Firms Other things equal, the larger the number of firms, the more difficult it is to create a cartel or some other form of price collusion. Agreement on price by three or four producers that control an entire market may be relatively easy to accomplish. But such agreement is more difficult to achieve where there are, say, 10 firms, each with roughly 10 percent of the market, or where the Big Three have 70 percent of the market, while a competitive fringe of 8 or 10 smaller firms battles for the remainder.

Cheating As the *prisoner's dilemma game* makes clear, collusive oligopolists are tempted to engage in secret price-cutting to increase sales and profit. The difficulty with such cheating is that buyers who are paying a high price for a product may become aware of the lower-priced sales and demand similar treatment. Or buyers receiving a price concession from one producer may use the concession as a wedge to get even larger price concessions from a rival producer. Buyers' attempts to play producers against one another may precipitate price wars among the producers. Although secret price concessions are potentially profitable, they threaten collusive oligopolies over time. Collusion is more likely to succeed when cheating is easy to detect and punish. Then, the conspirators are less likely to cheat on the price agreement.

Recession Long-lasting recession usually serves as an enemy of collusion because slumping markets increase average total cost. In technical terms, as the oligopolists' demand and marginal-revenue curves shift to the left in **Figure 9.5** in response to a recession, each firm moves leftward and upward to a higher operating point on its average-total-cost curve. Firms find they have substantial excess production capacity, sales are down, unit costs are up, and profits are being squeezed. Under such conditions, businesses may feel they can avoid serious profit reductions (or even losses) by cutting price and thus gaining sales at the expense of rivals.

Potential Entry   The greater prices and profits that result from collusion may attract new entrants, including foreign firms. Since that would increase market supply and reduce prices and profits, successful collusion requires that colluding oligopolists block the entry of new producers.

Oligopoly and Advertising

Oligopolists would rather not compete on the basis of price and may become involved in price collusion. Thus, each firm's share of the total market is typically determined through product development and advertising, for two reasons:

- Product development and advertising campaigns are less easily duplicated than price cuts. A firm's rivals can quickly and easily match price cuts to cancel any potential gain in sales derived from that strategy. In contrast, product improvements and successful advertising can produce more permanent gains in market share because they cannot be duplicated as quickly and completely as price reductions.
- Oligopolists have sufficient financial resources to engage in product development and advertising. For most oligopolists, the economic profits earned in the past can help finance current advertising and product development.

In 2018, U.S. firms spent an estimated $163 billion on advertising in the United States. *Advertising is prevalent in both monopolistic competition and oligopoly.* **Table 9.1** lists the 10 leading U.S. advertisers in 2018.

Advertising may affect prices, competition, and efficiency both positively and negatively, depending on the circumstances. We focus here on advertising by oligopolists, but the analysis is equally applicable to advertising by monopolistic competitors.

TABLE 9.1
The Largest U.S. Advertisers, 2018

Company	Advertising Spending (in millions of $)
Comcast	$6,122
AT&T	5,362
Amazon	4,470
Procter & Gamble	4,305
General Motors	3,139
Disney	3,132
Charter	3,042
Alphabet (Google)	2,960
American Express	2,798
Verizon	2,682

Source: *Advertising Age*, **www.adage.com**.

Positive Effects of Advertising

To make rational (efficient) decisions, consumers need information about product characteristics and prices. Media advertising may be a low-cost means for consumers to obtain that information. Suppose you are in the market for a high-quality camera. If there were no advertising describing and promoting high-quality cameras, you would have to spend several days visiting stores to determine the availability, prices, and features of various brands. This search entails both direct costs (gasoline, parking fees) and indirect costs (the value of your time). By providing information about the available options, advertising reduces these direct and indirect costs.

By providing information about various competing goods, advertising also reduces monopoly power. In fact, advertising is frequently used to introduce new products designed to compete with existing brands. Could Toyota and Honda have so strongly challenged U.S. auto producers without advertising? Could FedEx have sliced market share away from UPS and the U.S. Postal Service without advertising?

Viewed this way, advertising is an efficiency-enhancing activity. It is a relatively inexpensive means of providing useful information to consumers and thus lowering their search costs. By enhancing competition, advertising results in greater economic efficiency. By facilitating the introduction of new products, advertising speeds up technological progress. By increasing sales and output, advertising can reduce long-run average total cost by enabling firms to obtain economies of scale.

Potential Negative Effects of Advertising

Not all the effects of advertising are positive, of course. Much advertising is designed simply to manipulate or persuade consumers—that is, to alter their preferences in favor of the advertiser's product. A television commercial that indicates that a popular personality drinks a particular brand of soft drink—and therefore you should too—conveys little or no information to consumers about price or quality. In addition, advertising is sometimes based on misleading and extravagant claims that confuse consumers rather than enlighten them. Indeed, in some cases, advertising sometimes persuades consumers to pay high prices for much-acclaimed but inferior products, forgoing better but unadvertised products selling at lower prices. Example: *Consumer Reports* has found that heavily advertised premium motor oils provide no better engine performance and longevity than do cheaper brands.

Firms often establish substantial brand-name loyalty and thus achieve monopoly power via their advertising (see **Global Snapshot 9.2**). As a consequence, they are able to increase their sales, expand their market shares, and enjoy greater profits. Larger profits permit still more advertising and further enlargement of the firm's market share and profit. In time, consumers may lose the advantages of competitive markets and face the disadvantages of monopolized markets. Moreover, new entrants to the industry need to incur large advertising costs in order to establish their products in the marketplace; thus, advertising costs may be a barrier to entry.

Advertising can also be self-canceling. The advertising campaign of one fast-food hamburger chain may be offset by equally costly campaigns waged by rivals, so each firm's demand remains unchanged. Few, if any, extra burgers will be purchased, and each firm's market share will stay the same. But because of the advertising, every firm will experience higher costs. That, in turn, will either reduce profits or, if there is successful price leadership, cause their product prices to rise.

When advertising either leads to increased monopoly power or is self-canceling, economic inefficiency results.

GLOBAL SNAPSHOT 9.2

The World's Top 10 Brand Names

Here are the world's top 10 brands, based on four criteria: the brand's market share within its category, the brand's world appeal across age groups and nationalities, the loyalty of customers to the brand, and the ability of the brand to "stretch" to products beyond the original product.

World's Top 10 Brands

Apple
Google
Amazon
Microsoft
Coca-Cola
Samsung
Toyota
Mercedes-Benz
McDonald's
Disney

Source: Best Global Brands, 2019: Iconic Moves, Interbrand, www.interbrand.com

Oligopoly and Efficiency

Is oligopoly an efficient market structure from society's standpoint? How do the oligopolist's price and output decisions measure up to the triple equality P = MC = minimum ATC that occurs in pure competition?

Inefficiency

Based on evidence that many oligopolists sustain sizable economic profits year after year, many economists believe that the outcome of some oligopolistic markets is approximately as shown in **Figure 9.5**. In that case, the oligopolist's production occurs where price exceeds marginal cost and average total cost. Moreover, production is below the output at which average total cost is minimized. In this view, neither productive efficiency (P = minimum ATC) nor allocative efficiency (P = MC) is likely to occur under oligopoly.

A few observers assert that oligopoly is actually less desirable than pure monopoly because government usually regulates pure monopoly in the United States to guard against abuses of monopoly power. Informal collusion among oligopolists may yield price and output results similar to those under pure monopoly yet give the outward appearance of competition involving independent firms.

We should note, however, three qualifications to this view:

- **Increased foreign competition** In recent decades, foreign competition has increased rivalry in a number of oligopolistic industries—steel, automobiles, video games, electric shavers, outboard motors, and copy machines, for example. This has helped to break down such cozy arrangements as price leadership and to stimulate much more competitive pricing.

- **Limit pricing** Recall that some oligopolists may purposely keep prices below the short-run profit-maximizing level in order to bolster entry barriers. Thus, consumers and society may get some of the benefits of competition—prices closer to marginal cost and minimum average total cost—even without the competition that free entry would provide.

- **Technological advance** Over time, oligopolistic industries may foster more rapid product development and greater improvement of production techniques than purely competitive industries would. Oligopolists have large economic profits from which they can fund expensive research and development (R&D). Moreover, barriers to entry may give the oligopolist some assurance that it will reap the rewards of successful R&D. Thus, the short-run economic inefficiencies created by oligopolists may be partly or wholly offset by the oligopolists' contributions to better products, lower prices, and lower costs over time.

APPLYING THE ANALYSIS

Internet Oligopolies

The Internet only became accessible to the average person in the mid-1990s. Over the past 10 years, it has evolved into a medium dominated by a few major firms. Chief among them are Google, Facebook, and Amazon. Other major players include Microsoft and Apple.

A key characteristic of each of these firms is that it holds a near-monopoly in a particular part of the tech business. Google dominates search. Facebook holds sway in social networking. Amazon rules the roost in online shopping. Microsoft holds a near-monopoly on PC operating systems and business-productivity software. And Apple became the world's most valuable company in 2012 by way of being the planet's most profitable manufacturer of computers, mobile phones, and tablets—all of which run on Apple's own operating software.

But instead of just trying to maintain dominance in its own sector, each of these Internet titans has used the profits generated by its own near-monopoly to try to steal business from one or more of the other titans. The result has been intense oligopolistic competition between a few well-funded rivals.

Consider search. Google's 63 percent share of the search market creates massive amounts of advertising revenue for Google. In fact, Google's 2018 ad revenues of over $100 billion exceeded the ad revenues received by all U.S. magazines and newspapers combined. So it may not be surprising that Microsoft created its Bing search engine to compete with Google. As of late 2018, Bing held 24 percent of the search market. Along with Yahoo, which held 12 percent, Bing maintains competitive pressure on Google, forcing ad rates lower. They, in fact, fell by nearly 30 percent in 2018.

Facebook is by far the largest social networking website, with more than 2.4 billion regular users. But in 2011, Google succeeded in creating a large enough social network to challenge Facebook. Google did so by encouraging the users of its various free services—such as Gmail and YouTube—to join the Google+ social network. By late 2012, Google+ had 500 million total users and 235 million regular users—enough to compete credibly with Facebook. Unfortunately for Google, growth later stalled and Google opted to shut down most of Google+ in 2018 after a major data breach.

Google+ was important to Google because Facebook had been encouraging advertisers to switch from using Google search ads to using Facebook banner ads that could be targeted at specific types of Facebook users (such as, "25–30-year-old males with pets living in Pittsburgh"). Google was able to counter by offering its own social network on which advertisers could place those sorts of targeted ads.

Google has also challenged Apple by releasing its very popular Android operating system for mobile devices to compete with the iOS operating system that Apple uses on its iPhones and iPads. By doing so, Google reduced the threat that Apple could at some point in the future substantially reduce Google's search revenues by directing searches done on Apple devices to a proprietary search engine of Apple's own design.

Apple's dominance in smartphones and tablets has also been challenged by some of the other Internet titans. In addition to licensing the Android operating system to any manufacturer who wants to use it on their own cell phones or tablets, Google launched its own line of Nexus mobile devices to compete with Apple's iPhone and iPad. Also seeking to challenge Apple in mobile devices, Microsoft updated its Windows operating system to handle phones and tablets, launched its Surface line of tablets to compete with the iPad, and attempted to compete with the iPhone by marketing its own Windows Phone, which failed in the marketplace.

These are just a few examples of oligopoly competition resulting from Internet titans branching out of their own dominant sectors to compete with each other, and there's a simple reason for their aggressive competition. When a near-monopoly already dominates its own sector, its only chance for major profit growth is to invade a rival's sector.

QUESTION:

Can you think of other industries where firms branch into new areas to offset dominance by potential competitors?

Summary

LO9.1 List the characteristics of monopolistic competition.

The distinguishing features of monopolistic competition are (a) enough firms in the industry to ensure that each firm has only limited control over price, mutual interdependence is absent, and collusion is nearly impossible; (b) products are characterized by real or perceived differences so that economic rivalry entails both price and nonprice competition; and (c) entry to the industry is relatively easy. Many aspects of retailing, and some manufacturing industries in which economies of scale are few, approximate monopolistic competition.

LO9.2 Explain why monopolistic competitors earn only a normal profit in the long run.

Monopolistically competitive firms may earn economic profits or incur losses in the short run. The easy entry and exit of firms result in only normal profits in the long run.

The long-run equilibrium position of the monopolistically competitive producer is less efficient than that of the pure competitor. Under monopolistic competition, price exceeds marginal cost, indicating an underallocation of resources to the product. Price also exceeds minimum average total cost, indicating that consumers do not get the product at the lowest price that cost conditions might allow.

Nonprice competition allows monopolistically competitive firms to offset the long-run tendency for economic profit to fall to zero. Through product differentiation, product development, and advertising, a firm may strive to increase the demand for its product in order to exceed the added cost of such nonprice competition. Consumers benefit from the wide diversity of product choices that monopolistic competition provides.

LO9.3 Describe the characteristics of oligopoly.

Oligopolistic industries are characterized by the presence of few large producers, each having a significant fraction of the market. Firms thus situated engage in strategic behavior and are mutually interdependent: The behavior of any one firm directly affects, and is affected by, the actions of rivals. Products may be either virtually uniform or significantly differentiated. Various barriers to entry, including economies of scale, underlie and maintain oligopoly.

LO9.4 Discuss how game theory relates to oligopoly.

Game theory (a) shows the interdependence of oligopolists' pricing policies, (b) reveals oligopolists' tendency to collude, and (c) explains oligopolists' temptation to cheat on collusive arrangements.

LO9.5 Relate why the demand curve of an oligopolist may be kinked.

A kinked-demand curve may face non-collusive oligopoly firms. This curve and the accompanying MR curve help explain the price rigidity that often characterizes oligopolies.

LO9.6 Compare the incentives and obstacles to collusion among oligopolists.

Price leadership is an informal means of collusion whereby one firm, usually the largest or most efficient, initiates price changes, while the industry's other firms follow the leader.

Collusion between oligopoly firms can lead to higher profits. But demand and cost differences, a larger number of firms, cheating through secret price concessions, recessions, and antitrust laws are all obstacles to collusive oligopoly.

LO9.7 Contrast the positive and potential negative effects of advertising.

Market shares in oligopolistic industries are usually determined on the basis of product development and advertising. Oligopolists emphasize nonprice competition because (a) advertising and product variations are less easy for rivals to match and (b) oligopolists frequently have ample resources to finance nonprice competition.

Advertising may affect prices, competition, and efficiency either positively or negatively. Positives: Advertising can provide consumers with low-cost information about competing products, help introduce new competing products into concentrated industries, and generally reduce monopoly power and its inefficiencies. Negatives: Advertising can promote monopoly power via persuasion and the creation of entry barriers. Moreover, it can be self-canceling when rivals engage in advertising, causing price boosts and creating inefficiency while accomplishing little else.

LO9.8 Discuss the efficiency of oligopoly.

Oligopolistic markets generate neither productive nor allocative efficiency, but oligopoly may be superior to pure competition in promoting research and development, as well as technological progress.

Terms and Concepts

monopolistic competition	homogeneous oligopoly	collusion
product differentiation	differentiated oligopoly	per se violations
nonprice competition	strategic behavior	kinked-demand curve
excess capacity	mutual interdependence	price leadership
oligopoly	game theory	cartel

Questions

1. How does monopolistic competition differ from pure competition in its basic characteristics? From pure monopoly? Explain fully what product differentiation may involve. Explain how the entry of firms into their industry affects the demand curve facing a monopolistic competitor and its economic profit. **(LO1)**

2. Compare the elasticity of the monopolistic competitor's demand with that of a pure competitor and a pure monopolist. Assuming identical long-run costs, compare graphically the prices and outputs that would result in the long run under pure competition and under monopolistic competition. Contrast the two market structures in terms of productive and allocative efficiency. Explain the following statement: "Monopolistically competitive industries are characterized by too many firms, each of which produces too little." **(LO2)**

3. "Monopolistic competition is monopolistic up to the point at which consumers become willing to buy close-substitute products and competitive beyond that point." Explain. **(LO1, LO2)**

4. "Competition in quality and service may be just as effective as price competition in giving buyers more for their money." Do you agree? Why or why not? Explain why monopolistically competitive firms frequently prefer nonprice competition to price competition. **(LO2)**

5. Why do oligopolies exist? List five or six oligopolists whose products you own or regularly purchase. What distinguishes oligopoly from monopolistic competition? **(LO3)**

6. Explain the general meaning of the following profit payoff matrix for oligopolists X and Y. All profit figures are in thousands. **(LO4)**

X's possible prices

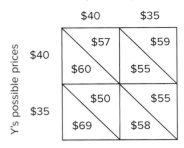

a. Use the payoff matrix to explain the mutual interdependence that characterizes oligopolistic industries.

b. Assuming no collusion between X and Y, what is the likely pricing outcome?

c. In view of your answer to part b, explain why price collusion is mutually profitable. Why might there be a temptation to cheat on the collusive agreement?

7. **ADVANCED ANALYSIS** Construct a game-theory payoff matrix involving two firms and their decisions on high versus low advertising budgets and the effects of each on profits. Show a circumstance in which both firms select high advertising budgets even though both would be more profitable with low advertising budgets. Why won't they unilaterally cut their advertising budgets? **(LO4, LO7)**

8. What assumptions about a rival's response to price changes underlie the kinked-demand curve for oligopolists? Why is there a gap in the oligopolist's marginal-revenue curve? How does the kinked-demand curve explain price rigidity in oligopoly? **(LO5)**

9. Why might price collusion occur in oligopolistic industries? Assess the economic desirability of collusive pricing. What are the main obstacles to collusion? Speculate as to why price leadership is legal in the United States, whereas price-fixing is not. **(LO6)**

10. Why is there so much advertising in monopolistic competition and oligopoly? How does such advertising help consumers and promote efficiency? How does advertising promote inefficiency? **(LO7, LO8)**

11. Why have tech firms with near-monopolies in their own sectors sought to compete with tech firms that have extremely strong, near-monopoly positions in other sectors? **(LO4)**

Problems

1. Assume that in short-run equilibrium, a particular monopolistically competitive firm charges $12 for each unit of its output and sells 52 units of output per day. How much revenue will it take in each day? If its average total cost (ATC) for those 52 units is $10, will the firm (a) earn a short-run economic profit, (b) break even with only a normal profit, or (c) suffer an economic loss? If a profit or loss, what will be the amount? Next, suppose that entry or exit occurs in this monopolistic industry and establishes a long-run equilibrium. If the firm's daily output remains at 52 units, what price will it be able to charge? What will be its economic profit? **(LO2)**

2. Suppose that a monopolistically competitive restaurant is currently serving 230 meals per day (the output where MR = MC). At that output level, ATC per meal is $10, and consumers are willing to pay $12 per meal. What is this firm's profit or loss? Will there be entry or exit? Will this restaurant's demand curve shift left or right? In long-run equilibrium, suppose that this restaurant charges $11 per meal for 180 meals and that the marginal cost of the 180th meal is $8. What is the firm's profit? **(LO2)**

3. Suppose that an oligopolist is charging $21 per unit of output and selling 31 units each day. What is its daily total revenue? Also suppose that previously it had lowered its price from $21 to $19, rivals matched the price cut, and the firm's sales increased from 31 to 32 units. It also previously raised its price from $21 to $23, rivals ignored the price hike, and the firm's daily total revenue came in at $482. Which of the following is most logical to conclude? The firm's demand curve is (a) inelastic over the $21 to $23 price range, (b) elastic over the $19 to $21 price range, (c) a linear (straight) downsloping line, or (d) a curve with a kink in it? **(LO5)**

CHAPTER TEN

GDP and Economic Growth

Learning Objectives

LO10.1   Define and measure gross domestic product (GDP).

LO10.2   Describe how economists distinguish between nominal GDP and real GDP.

LO10.3   Explain two ways to measure economic growth.

LO10.4   Identify the supply, demand, and efficiency forces that lead to economic growth.

LO10.5   Describe the specific factors accounting for U.S. economic growth.

LO10.6   Explain how U.S. productivity growth has fluctuated since 1973.

LO10.7   Discuss whether economic growth is desirable and sustainable.

Macroeconomics focuses on national economies while seeking answers to large-scale economic questions, including: Why are some countries really rich while others are poor? Why do all countries—even the richest—go through alternating boom and bust periods? Can governments do anything to improve living standards or fight recessions?

This chapter explains how economists measure the overall (aggregate) production of goods and services in the economy. We then examine factors that expand that output and improve a society's standard of living. We explore not only the main sources of economic growth, but also consider the question of whether economic growth is desirable.

Gross Domestic Product

National income accounting measures the economy's overall performance. The Bureau of Economic Analysis (BEA), an agency of the U.S. Commerce Department, compiles the **national income and product accounts (NIPA)** for the U.S. economy. This accounting helps economists and policymakers:

- Assess the economy's health by monitoring production and employment levels.
- Track the economy's long-run growth trajectory.
- Adjust economic policies to safeguard and improve the economy's health.

national income and product accounts (NIPA)
The national accounts that measure overall production and income of the economy and other related aggregates for the nation as a whole.

The primary measure of an economy's performance is its *aggregate output,* or total output, of goods and services. There are several ways to measure aggregate output. The one favored by the BEA is **gross domestic product (GDP):** the total market value of all final goods and services produced within a country's borders during a specific period of time, typically a year.

gross domestic product (GDP)
The total market value of all final goods and services produced annually within the boundaries of the United States, whether by U.S.- or foreign-supplied resources.

> GDP includes only the value of final goods and services produced within a nation's boundaries. The value of cars produced at a Japanese-owned Toyota factory in Ohio count as part of U.S. GDP (because the factory is located in the United States), but the value of trucks produced at an American-owned Ford factory in Canada would not (because the factory lies outside the borders of the United States). What matters for GDP is where the final output is produced, not who makes or consumes it.[1]

A Monetary Measure

If the economy produces three sofas and two computers in year 1 and two sofas and three computers in year 2, in which year is output greater? We can't answer that question until we attach a price tag to each of the two products to indicate how society evaluates their relative worth.

That's what GDP does. It is a *monetary measure.* Such a measure allows us to compare the relative values of the vast number of goods and services produced in different years. Consider **Table 10.1**, where the price of sofas is $500 and the price of computers is $2,000. The market value (dollar value) of the economy's output in year 1 is $5,500, while the monetary value of the economy's output in year 2 is $7,000. Aggregate output has increased by $1,500.

By measuring GDP in the common unit of dollars, it is easy to see that aggregate output has increased. Using dollars as the common unit of measurement for calculating GDP has an additional benefit. Because people put higher values on things they like, we can infer that higher levels of GDP imply higher levels of satisfaction, all other things equal. It is for this reason that policymakers are concerned with how to increase GDP.

TABLE 10.1
Comparing Heterogeneous Output by Using Money Prices

Year	Annual Output	Market Value
1	3 sofas and 2 computers	3 at $500 + 2 at $2,000 = $5,500
2	2 sofas and 3 computers	2 at $500 + 3 at $2,000 = $7,000

[1] In contrast to GDP, U.S. gross national product (GNP) consists of the total value of all the final goods and services produced by American-supplied resources, whether those goods and services are produced within the borders of the United States or abroad. The United States switched from GNP to GDP accounting in 1992 to match the type of accounting used by other countries worldwide.

Avoiding Multiple Counting

To measure aggregate output accurately, all goods and services produced in a particular year must be counted once and only once. Because most products go through a series of production stages before they reach the market, some of their components are bought and sold many times. To avoid counting those components each time, GDP includes only the market value of *final goods* and ignores *intermediate goods* altogether.

intermediate goods
Products that are purchased for resale or further processing or manufacturing.

final goods and services
Goods and services that have been purchased for final use and not for resale or further processing or manufacturing.

Intermediate goods are goods and services that are purchased for resale or for further processing or manufacturing. **Final goods** are products that are purchased by their end users. Crude oil is an intermediate good; gasoline used for personal transportation is a final good. Steel beams are intermediate goods; completed high-rise apartments are final goods. A loaf of bread purchased by a family for a camping trip is counted in GDP (because the family is the end user), while an identical loaf purchased by a sandwich shop is not counted in GDP (because the sandwich shop will use the loaf of bread as an input to the production of its final product, sandwiches).

Including the value of intermediate goods in calculating GDP would amount to *multiple counting,* and that would distort the value of GDP. For example, suppose that among other inputs an automobile manufacturer uses $4,000 of steel, $2,000 of glass, and $1,000 of tires in producing a new automobile that sells for $20,000. The $20,000 final good already includes the $7,000 of steel, glass, and tires. We would be greatly overstating GDP if we added the $7,000 of components to the $20,000 price of the auto and obtained $27,000 of output.

PHOTO OP

Intermediate versus Final Goods

Lumber is an intermediate good, while a new townhouse is a final good.

Juanmonino/E+/Getty Images   jhorrocks/E+/Getty Images

Excluding Secondhand Sales and Financial Transactions

Secondhand sales contribute nothing to current production and therefore are excluded from GDP. Suppose you sell your 2012 Ford Mustang to a friend. That transaction will not be counted in this year's GDP because it generates no current production.

Likewise, purely financial transactions are excluded from GDP. These include:

- *Public transfer payments*, such as Social Security and welfare payments that the government makes directly to households. Because the recipients contribute nothing to current production in return, including such payments in GDP would overstate this year's output.

- *Private transfer payments*, such as cash that parents give children for allowance money or gifts. They produce no output; they simply transfer funds from one private individual to another and consequently do not enter into GDP.

- *Stock and bond market transactions*, which simply transfer pieces of paper representing company ownership (stocks) or loans (bonds). Payments for the services provided by a stockbroker are included, however, because their services are currently provided and are thus part of the economy's current output of goods and services.

PHOTO OP

New Goods versus Secondhand Goods

The goods offered for sale at a shopping mall are new goods. Therefore, they are included in current GDP. In contrast, many of the goods sold through eBay are secondhand items and thus not part of current GDP.

Elnur/Shutterstock   John Flournoy/McGraw Hill Education

Measuring GDP

The simplest way to measure GDP is using the *expenditures approach,* where we add up all the spending on final goods and services that has taken place throughout the year. National income accountants use precise definitions for the four categories of spending.

Personal Consumption Expenditures (*C*)

personal consumption expenditures
The expenditures of households for durable and nondurable consumer goods and services.

The symbol *C* designates the **personal consumption expenditures** component of GDP. That term covers all expenditures by households on *durable goods*—goods that have expected lives of more than three years (automobiles, refrigerators, cameras), *nondurable goods* (food, clothing, gasoline), and *services* (of lawyers, doctors, mechanics). Of total U.S. household consumption expenditures, approximately 10 percent is spent on durable goods, 30 percent on nondurable goods, and 60 percent on services.

Gross Private Domestic Investment (*I_g*)

gross private domestic investment
Expenditures for newly produced capital goods (such as machinery, equipment, tools, and buildings) and for additions to inventories.

The following items fall in the category of **gross private domestic investment:**

- Final purchases of plant, machinery, and equipment of business enterprises.
- Residential construction.
- Expenditures on the *research and development* (R&D) of new productive technologies.
- Money spent on the creation of new works of art, music, writing, film, and software.
- Changes in inventories.

Investment—or, more correctly, *economic investment*—refers to activities that increase the nation's stock of capital, the human-made resources that help to produce goods and services. Those human-created resources can be divided into two broad categories that we can informally refer to as "tools" and "recipes."

Tools are tangible physical objects used to produce goods and services. Recipes are the intangible methods, techniques, and management practices necessary to produce goods and services. A well-stocked kitchen requires both cooking equipment (tools) and an understanding of how to cook (recipes). A productive economy requires both tangible physical capital (factories, wireless networks, infrastructure) and intangible intellectual capital (knowing when to plant, understanding how to fly a plane, comprehending the best way to organize a factory).

The first two items fall into the tools category. Final purchases of plant, machinery, and equipment increase the amount of physical capital available to produce future output. Residential construction generates a future flow of output—housing services—that will keep people productive by keeping them healthy and sheltered.

The next two items fall into the recipes category. R&D increases the intangible stock of methods and techniques that we can use to produce output. The creation of new works of art, music, writing, and film increases the flow of entertainment and educational services, while improving software increases the productivity of everything from smartphones to self-driving cars.

Increases in inventories (unsold goods) are considered to be an investment because they represent "unconsumed output," or output available for future consumption when it is sold out of inventory. For economists, all new output that is not consumed is, by definition, capital. An increase in inventories is an addition (although temporary) to the stock of capital goods.

Positive and Negative Changes in Inventories We need to look at changes in inventories more closely. Inventories can either increase or decrease over some period. Suppose inventories rose by $10 billion between December 31, 2023, and December 31, 2024. Therefore, in 2024 the economy produced $10 billion more output than people purchased. We want to count all output produced in 2024 as part of that year's GDP, even though some of it remained unsold at the end of the year. We do so by including the $10 billion increase in inventories as part of 2024 investment. That way, the expenditures in 2024 will correctly measure the output produced that year.

Alternatively, suppose inventories fell by $10 billion in 2024. This "drawing down of inventories" means that the economy sold $10 billion more of output in 2024 than it produced that year. It did so by selling goods produced in prior years—goods already counted as GDP in those years. Unless corrected, expenditures in 2024 will overstate GDP for 2024. So in 2024 we consider the $10 billion decline in inventories as "negative investment" and subtract it from total investment that year.

Noninvestment Transactions So much for what investment *is.* You also need to know what it *isn't.* Economists and NIPA accountants distinguish between *economic investment* and *financial investment.* Economic investment involves the creation of new productive capital, either new tools or new recipes. By contrast, financial investments, like buying stocks and bonds, merely transfer the ownership of existing assets; they do not produce new capital goods. Therefore, such transactions (so-called financial investments) are not included as investments in the GDP accounts.

Gross Investment When we speak of *gross private domestic investment,* the words "private" and "domestic" mean that we are speaking of investment spending by private businesses, not by government, and that the investment is taking place inside the country, not abroad.

The word "gross" means that we are referring to *all* investment goods—both those that replace machinery, equipment, and buildings that were used up (worn out or made obsolete) in producing the current year's output as well as any net additions to the economy's stock of capital. In contrast, *net private domestic investment* takes the economy's gross investment and subtracts out the amount of capital used up (depreciated) over the course of the year.

The symbol I represents private domestic investment spending, along with the subscript g to signify gross investment.

Government Purchases (G)

The third category of expenditures in the national income accounts is **government purchases,** officially labeled "government consumption expenditures and gross investment." These expenditures have three components: (1) expenditures for goods and services that government consumes in providing public services; (2) expenditures for *publicly owned capital* such as schools and highways, which have long lifetimes; and (3) government expenditures on R&D and other activities that increase the economy's stock of know-how.

government purchases
Expenditures by government for goods and services that government consumes in providing public goods and for public capital that has a long lifetime; the expenditures of all governments in the economy for those final goods and services.

These purchases include all government expenditures (federal, state, and local) on final goods and all direct purchases of resources, including labor. They do *not* include government transfer payments because, as we have seen, such payments merely transfer money to certain households and generate no production. The symbol G signifies government purchases.

Net Exports (X_n)

International trade transactions are a significant item in national income accounting. But when calculating U.S. GDP, we must keep in mind that we want to total up only those expenditures used to purchase goods and services produced *within the borders of the United States.* Thus, we must add in the value of exports, X, because the money that foreigners spend purchasing U.S. exports is by definition spending on goods and services produced within the United States.

Don't be confused by the fact that it is foreigners who buy up our exports. The definition of GDP does not specify *who* is buying U.S.-made goods and services—only that the goods and services they buy are made within U.S. borders. Thus, foreign spending on our exports must be included in GDP.

At this point, you might incorrectly think that GDP should be equal to the sum of $C + I_g + G + X$. But C, I_g, and G include not only expenditures on *domestically produced* goods and services, but also goods and services produced outside of the United States. So to correctly count gross domestic product, we must subtract the spending that goes to imports, M. That subtraction yields the correct formula for calculating gross domestic product:

$$GDP = C + I_g + G + X - M$$

net exports
Exports minus imports.

Accountants simplify this formula for GDP by defining **net exports,** X_n, to be equal to exports minus imports:

$$\text{Net exports } (X_n) = \text{exports } (X) - \text{imports } (M)$$

Using this definition of net exports, the formula for gross domestic product simplifies to

$$GDP = C + I_g + G + X_n$$

In 2019, Americans spent $611 billion more on imports than foreigners spent on U.S. exports. That is, net exports in 2019 were a *minus* $611 billion.

Adding It Up: GDP = $C + I_g + G + X_n$

Taken together, these four categories of expenditures provide a measure of the market value of a given year's total output—its GDP. For the United States in 2019 (in billions),

$$GDP = \$14{,}545 + 3{,}751 + 3{,}748 - 611 = \$21{,}433 \text{ billion (or } \$21.433 \text{ trillion)}$$

Global Snapshot 10.1 lists the GDPs of several countries in U.S. dollars, for 2017.

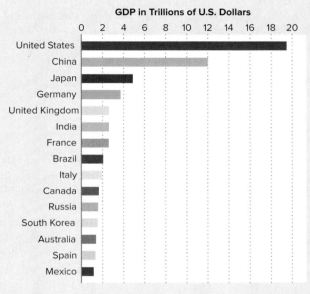

GLOBAL SNAPSHOT 10.1

Comparative GDPs in Trillions of U.S. Dollars, Selected Nations, 2017

The United States, China, and Japan have the world's highest GDPs when local, domestic-currency GDPs are converted into U.S. dollars using international exchange rates.

GDP in Trillions of U.S. Dollars

United States
China
Japan
Germany
United Kingdom
India
France
Brazil
Italy
Canada
Russia
South Korea
Australia
Spain
Mexico

Source: The World Bank Group.

Nominal GDP versus Real GDP

Recall that GDP is a measure of the market or money value of all final goods and services produced by the economy in a given year. We use money or nominal values as a common denominator to sum that heterogeneous output into a meaningful total. But that creates a problem: How can we compare the market values of GDP from year to year if the value of money itself changes in response to inflation?

As an example of what can go wrong, consider the fact that the same McDonald's hamburger that sold for 18 cents in 1967 cost $1.19 in 2019. The hamburger was the same in both years and the utility that people got from it was the same, but its nominal GDP value was over six times higher in 2019 because the price had increased from 18 cents to $1.19.

The way around this problem is to *deflate* GDP when prices rise and to *inflate* GDP when prices fall. This is accomplished by choosing a reference year and then using the output prices that prevailed in that reference year to value the quantities of output produced in other years.

A GDP based on the prices that prevailed when the output was produced is called *unadjusted GDP*, or **nominal GDP.** A GDP that has been deflated or inflated to reflect changes in the price level is called *adjusted GDP*, or **real GDP.**

nominal GDP
Gross domestic product measured in terms of the price level at the time of the measurement; GDP that is unadjusted for inflation.

real GDP
Gross domestic product measured in terms of the price level in a base period (i.e., GDP that is adjusted for inflation).

To see how real GDP can be found, let's imagine an economy produces only one good, pizza, in the amounts indicated in **Table 10.2** for years 1, 2, 3, 4, and 5. Suppose that we measure each year's nominal GDP (= the money value of the pizzas produced each year) by gathering price and output data directly from the financial reports of the economy's pizza business in various years.

TABLE 10.2
Calculating Real GDP (Base Year = Year 1)

	(1)	(2)	(3)	(4)
Year	Units of Output	Price of Pizza per Unit	Unadjusted, or Nominal, GDP, (1) × (2)	Adjusted, or Real, GDP
1	5	$ 10	$ 50	$50
2	7	20	140	70
3	8	25	200	80
4	10	30	___	___
5	11	28	___	___

We can then determine the unadjusted, or nominal, GDP in each year by multiplying the number of units of output by the price per unit. Nominal GDP—here, the market value of pizza—is shown for each year in column 3.

We can also determine adjusted, or real, GDP from the data in **Table 10.2**. We want to know the market value of outputs in successive years *if the base-year price ($10) had prevailed*. (Note that any of the years in the table could have been selected as the base year). In year 2, the 7 units of pizza would have a value of $70 (= 7 units × $10) at the year-1 price. As column 4 shows, that $70 worth of output is year 2's real GDP. Similarly, we can determine the real GDP for year 3 by multiplying the 8 units of output that year by the $10 price in the base year. You should check your understanding of nominal versus real GDP by completing columns 3 and 4, where we purposely left the last rows blank.

Let's return to the real economy. In 2019, nominal GDP in the United States was $21,433 billion and real GDP was $19,092 billion, using a base year of 2012. In the language of economics, "GDP in 2019 was $19,092 billion in 2012 prices." The fact that nominal GDP exceeded real GDP in 2019 tells us that, on average, prices were higher in 2019 than in 2012.

APPLYING THE ANALYSIS

The Underground Economy

Real GDP is a reasonably accurate and highly useful measure of how well or how poorly the economy is performing. But some production never shows up in GDP, which measures only the *market value* of output. Embedded in the U.S. economy is a flourishing, productive underground sector. Some of the people who conduct business there are gamblers, smugglers, prostitutes, "fences" of stolen goods, drug producers, and drug dealers. They have good reason to conceal their economic activities.

Most participants in the underground economy, however, engage in perfectly legal activities but choose illegally not to report their full incomes to the Internal Revenue Service (IRS). A barista at a coffee shop may report just a portion of the tips received from customers. Storekeepers may report only a portion of their sales receipts. Workers who want to hold on to their unemployment compensation benefits may take an "off-the-books" or "cash-only" job. A brick mason may agree to rebuild a neighbor's fireplace in exchange for the neighbor's repairing the mason's boat engine. None of these transactions show up in GDP.

Global Snapshot 10.2 shows estimates of how big the underground economy was in various countries in 2015. The value of underground transactions in the United States amounted to about 7 percent of the recorded GDP in the United States in 2015, which means that U.S. GDP in 2015 was understated by about $1.3 trillion.

QUESTIONS:

How would the decriminalization of drugs instantly increase a nation's real GDP? What might be the downside of the decriminalization of drugs for growth of real GDP over time?

GLOBAL SNAPSHOT 10.2

The Underground Economy as a Percentage of GDP, Selected Nations, 2015

Underground economies vary in size worldwide. Three factors that help explain the variation are (1) the extent and complexity of regulation, (2) the type and degree of taxation, and (3) the effectiveness of law enforcement.

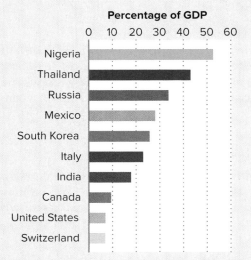

Source: Medina, Leandro, and Friedrich Schneider. *Shadow Economies Around the World: What Did We Learn Over the Last 20 Years?* International Monetary Fund (IMF). 2018.

Economic Growth

economic growth
(1) An outward shift in the production possibilities curve that results from an increase in resource supplies or quality or an improvement in technology; (2) an increase of real output (gross domestic product) or real output per capita.

Economists define and measure **economic growth** as either:

- An increase in *real GDP* over some time period.
- An increase in *real GDP per capita* over some time period.

For the first definition, for example, real GDP in the United States (measured in constant 2012 dollars) was $18,687.8 billion in 2018 and $19,091.7 in 2019. To the real (inflation-adjusted) U.S. economic growth rate for 2019 was 2.2 percent $\{ = [(19,091.7 - 18,687.8) / 18,687.8)] \times 100 \}$.

real GDP per capita
Real output (GDP) divided by population.

Real GDP per capita (or *output per person*) is found by dividing real GDP by the size of the population. Real GDP per capita grew from $57,377 (=$18,687.8 billion divided by 325.7 million) in 2018, to $58,171 (=$19,091.7 billion divided by 328.2 million). So the growth rate of real GDP per capita for 2019 was 1.4 percent $\{ = [(58,171 - 57,377) / 57,377)] \times 100 \}$.

For measuring expansion of military potential or political preeminence, the growth of real GDP is more useful. Unless specified otherwise, growth rates reported in the news and by international agencies use this definition of economic growth. For comparing living standards, however, the second definition is superior. While China's GDP in 2017 was $12,238 billion compared with Denmark's $306 billion, Denmark's real GDP per capita was $56,308 compared with China's $8,827.

Growth as a Goal

Economic growth is a widely held economic goal. The expansion of total output relative to population results in rising real wages and incomes and thus higher standards of living. An economy that is experiencing economic growth is better able to meet people's wants and resolve socioeconomic problems. Rising real wages and income provide more opportunities to individuals and families—a vacation trip, a personal computer, tuition—without sacrificing other opportunities and pleasures. A growing economy can undertake new programs to alleviate poverty, cultivate the arts, and protect the environment without impairing existing levels of consumption, investment, and public goods production.

In short, *growth lessens the burden of scarcity.* Unlike a static economy, a growing economy can consume more today while increasing its capacity to produce more in the future. By easing the burden of scarcity—by relaxing society's constraints on production—economic growth helps a nation attain its economic goals and undertake new endeavors.

Arithmetic of Growth

The mathematical approximation called the *rule of 70* shows the effect of compounding of economic growth rates over time. According to the rule of 70, we can find the number of years it will take for some measure to double by dividing the number 70 by the measure's annual percentage growth rate. For real GDP:

$$\text{Approximate number of years required to double real GDP} = \frac{70}{\text{annual percentage rate of growth}}$$

Examples: A 3 percent annual rate of growth will double real GDP in about 23 (= 70/3) years. Growth of 8 percent per year will double it in about 9 (= 70/8) years.

ILLUSTRATING THE IDEA

Growth Rates Matter!

Small absolute differences in rates of economic growth add up to substantial differences in real GDP and standards of living. Consider three hypothetical countries—Slogo, Sumgo, and Speedo. Suppose that in 2024 these countries have identical levels of real GDP ($6 trillion), population (200 million), and real GDP per capita ($30,000). Also, assume that annual real GDP growth is 2 percent in Slogo, 3 percent in Sumgo, and 4 percent in Speedo.

How will these alternative growth rates affect real GDP and real GDP per capita over a long period, say, a 70-year span? By 2094, the 2, 3, and 4 percent growth rates would boost real GDP from $6 trillion to $24 trillion in Slogo, to $47 trillion in Sumgo, and to $93 trillion in Speedo.

For illustration, let's assume that each country experienced an average annual population growth of 1 percent over the 70 years. Then, in 2094, real GDP per capita would be about $60,000 in Slogo, $118,000 in Sumgo, and $233,000 in Speedo.

No wonder economists pay so much attention to small changes in the rate of economic growth. For the United States, with a current real GDP of about $19 trillion, the difference between a 3 percent and a 4 percent rate of growth is about $19 billion of output each year. For a poor country, a difference of one-half of a percentage point in the rate of growth may mean the difference between starvation and mere hunger. Economic growth rates matter!

> QUESTION:
> Why would gaps in GDP per capita for Slogo and Speedo be even more dramatic if population growth was faster in Slogo than in Speedo?

Growth in the United States

Table 10.3 gives an overview of economic growth in the United States over past periods. Column 2 reveals strong growth as measured by increases in real GDP. Note that real GDP increased more than sevenfold between 1950 and 2019. But the U.S. population also increased over these years. Nevertheless, in column 4 we find that real GDP per capita rose more than threefold.

TABLE 10.3
Real GDP and per Capita Real GDP, Selected Years, 1950–2019

(1)	(2)	(3)	(4)
Year	Real GDP, Billions of 2012 $	Population, Millions	Real Per Capita GDP, 2012 $ (2) ÷ (3)
1950	$ 2,290	152	$ 15,066
1960	3,260	181	18,011
1970	4,951	205	24,151
1980	6,759	228	29,645
1990	9,366	250	37,464
2000	13,131	282	46,564
2010	15,599	309	50,482
2019	19,092	328	58,207

Sources: Bureau of Economic Analysis, www.bea.gov, and U.S. Census Bureau, www.census.gov.

How quickly has U.S. GDP grown since 1950? Real GDP grew at an annual rate of about 3.1 percent while real GDP per capita increased about 2 percent per year.

Over the past two centuries, most countries have experienced growth in living standards, as measured by GDP per capita. However, the experience has not been uniform, with substantial variation in growth rates over time. As reflected in **Global Snapshot 10.3**, since 1820, U.S. growth rates exceeded those of Japan and western Europe. These nations, in turn, significantly outperformed the rest of the world, especially from 1950 to 2000. The result has been widening gaps in living standards around the world.

GLOBAL SNAPSHOT 10.3

The Divergence in Living Standards, 1820–2000

Income levels around the world were very similar in 1820. But they are now very different because certain areas, including the United States and western Europe, began experiencing modern economic growth much earlier than other areas.

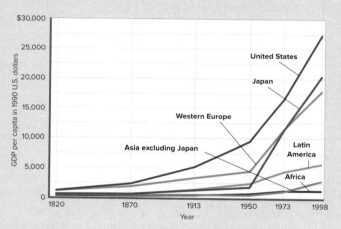

Source: Angus Maddison, *The World Economy: A Millennial Perspective* (Paris: OECD, 2001), p. 264.

Determinants of Growth

There are six main determinants of economic growth. We can group them as supply, demand, and efficiency factors.

Supply Factors

Four of the determinants of economic growth relate to relaxing the physical and technical limits that constrain economic expansion. They are:

- Increases in the quantity and quality of natural resources.
- Increases in the quantity and quality of human resources.
- Increases in the supply (or stock) of capital goods.
- Improvements in technology.

Any increases or improvements in these *supply factors* will increase an economy's *potential* GDP. The remaining two factors are necessary for that potential to be fulfilled.

Demand Factor

The fifth determinant of economic growth is the *demand factor:*

* To achieve the higher production potential created when the supply factors increase or improve, households, businesses, and government must expand their *purchases* of goods and services so as to provide a market for all the new potential output.

When this demand condition is met, there will be no unplanned increases in inventories, and resources will remain fully employed. Economic growth requires increases in total spending to realize the output gains made available by increased production capacity.

Efficiency Factor

The sixth determinant of economic growth is the *efficiency factor:*

* An economy must achieve economic efficiency in addition to full employment if it is to maximize the amount of satisfaction or utility that can be derived from its scarce resources.

To maximize well-being, the economy must use its resources in the least costly way (productive efficiency) to produce the specific mix of goods and services that maximizes people's utility (allocative efficiency). The ability to expand production, together with the full use of available resources, is not sufficient for achieving welfare-maximizing growth. Those resources must be used efficiently, as well.

The supply, demand, and efficiency factors in economic growth are related. Unemployment caused by insufficient total spending (the demand factor) may lower the rate of new capital accumulation (a supply factor) and delay expenditures on research (also a supply factor). Conversely, low spending on investment (a supply factor) may cause insufficient spending (the demand factor) and unemployment. Widespread inefficiency in the use of resources (the efficiency factor) may translate into higher costs of goods and services and thus lower profits, which in turn may slow innovation and reduce the accumulation of capital (supply factors).

Production Possibilities Analysis

To put the six factors affecting the rate of economic growth into better perspective, let's use the production possibilities analysis introduced in **Chapter 1**.

Growth and Production Possibilities

Recall that a curve like *AB* in **Figure 10.1** is a production possibilities curve. It indicates the various *maximum* combinations of products an economy can produce with its fixed quantity and quality of natural, human, and capital resources and its stock of technological knowledge. An improvement in any of the supply factors will push the production possibilities curve outward, as from *AB* to *CD*.

But the demand factor reminds us that an increase in total spending is needed to move the economy from a point like *a* on curve *AB* to any of the points on the higher curve *CD*. And the efficiency factor reminds us that we need least-cost production and an optimal location on *CD* for the resources to make their maximum possible contribution to total output. Recall from **Chapter 1** that this "best allocation" is determined by expanding production of each good until its marginal benefit equals its marginal cost. Here, we assume that this optimal combination of capital and consumer goods occurs at point *b*.

FIGURE 10.1

Economic growth and the production possibilities curve. Economic growth is made possible by the four supply factors that shift the production possibilities curve outward, as from *AB* to *CD*. Economic growth is realized when the demand factor and the efficiency factor move the economy from points such as *a* and *c* that are inside *CD* to the optimal output point, assumed to be point *b* in this figure.

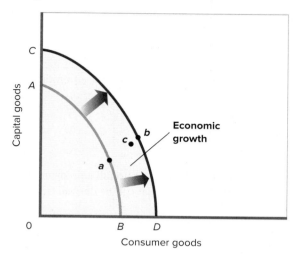

Example: The net increase in the size of the U.S. labor force in recent years has been 1.5 million to 2 million workers per year. That increase raises the economy's production capacity. But obtaining the extra output that these added workers could produce depends on their success in finding jobs. It also depends on whether jobs are available in firms and industries where the workers' talents are fully and optimally used. Society does not want new labor-force entrants to be unemployed. Nor does it want pediatricians working as plumbers, or pediatricians producing services for which marginal costs exceed marginal benefits.

Normally, increases in total spending match increases in production capacity, and the economy moves from a point on the previous production possibilities curve to a point on the expanded curve. Moreover, the competitive market system tends to drive the economy toward productive and allocative efficiency. Occasionally, however, the economy may end up at some point such as *c* in **Figure 10.1**. That outcome occurred in the United States during the severe recession of 2007–2009. Real output fell far below the real output that the economy could have produced if it had achieved full employment and operated on its production possibilities curve.

Labor and Productivity

labor productivity
Total output divided by the quantity of labor employed to produce it; the average product of labor or output per hour of work.

Society can increase its real output and income in two fundamental ways: (1) by increasing its inputs of resources and (2) by raising the productivity of those inputs. **Figure 10.2** concentrates on the input of *labor* and provides a useful framework for discussing the role of supply factors in growth. A nation's real GDP in any year depends on the input of labor (measured in hours of work) multiplied by **labor productivity** (measured as real output per hour of work):

$$\text{Real GDP} = \text{hours of work} \times \text{labor productivity}$$

From this perspective, a nation's economic growth from one year to the next depends on its increase in labor inputs (if any) and its increase in labor productivity (if any).

FIGURE 10.2
The supply determinants of real output. Real GDP is usefully viewed as the product of the quantity of labor inputs (hours of work) multiplied by labor productivity.

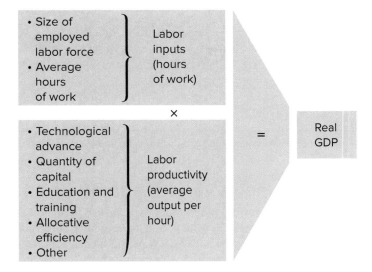

Illustration: Assume that the hypothetical economy of Ziam has 10 workers in year 1, each working 2,000 hours per year (= 50 weeks at 40 hours per week). The total input of labor therefore is 20,000 hours. If productivity (average real output per hour of work) is $10, then real GDP in Ziam will be $200,000 (= 20,000 × $10). If work hours rise to 20,200 and labor productivity rises to $10.40, Ziam's real GDP will increase to $210,080 in year 2. Ziam's rate of economic growth will be about 5 percent [= ($210,080 − $200,000)/$200,000] for the year.

Hours of Work What determines the number of hours worked each year? As shown in **Figure 10.2**, the hours of labor input depend on the size of the employed labor force and the length of the average workweek. Labor-force size depends on the size of the working-age population and the **labor-force participation rate**—the percentage of the working-age population actually in the labor force. The length of the average workweek is governed by legal and institutional considerations and by collective bargaining agreements between unions and employers.

labor-force participation rate
The percentage of the working-age population that is actually in the labor force.

Labor Productivity **Figure 10.2** tells us that labor productivity is determined by technological progress, the quantity of capital goods available to workers, the quality of labor inputs, and the efficiency with which inputs are allocated, combined, and managed. Productivity rises when the health, training, education, and motivation of workers improve; when workers have more and better machinery and natural resources to work with; when production is better organized and managed; and when labor is reallocated from less efficient industries to more efficient industries.

Accounting for Growth

The President's Council of Economic Advisers uses a system called **growth account-ing** to assess the relative importance of the supply-side elements that contribute to changes in real GDP. This system groups these elements into two main categories:

growth accounting
The bookkeeping of the supply-side elements that contribute to changes in real GDP over some specific time period.

- Increases in hours of work.
- Increases in labor productivity.

TABLE 10.4
Accounting for the Growth of U.S. Real GDP, 1953–2017 Plus Projection from 2018 to 2029 (Average Annual Percentage Changes)

Item	Actual				Projected
	1953 Q2 to 1973 Q4	1973 Q4 to 1995 Q2	1995 Q2 to 2007 Q3	2007 Q3 to 2017 Q3	2018 Q4 to 2029 Q4
Increase in real GDP	3.6	2.8	3.2	1.6	3.0
Increase in quantity of labor	1.1	1.3	0.5	0.4	0.4
Increase in labor productivity	2.5	1.5	2.7	1.2	2.6

Sources: Derived from *Economic Report of the President, 2008* and *2019*; U.S. Bureau of Economic Analysis; and U.S. Bureau of Labor Statistics.

Labor Inputs versus Labor Productivity

Table 10.4 provides the relevant data for five periods. The symbol "Q" in the table stands for "quarter" of the year. The beginning points for the first four periods are business-cycle peaks, and the last period includes future projections by the Council of Economic Advisers. The table clearly shows that increases in the quantity of labor and increases in labor productivity are both important sources of economic growth. Between 1953 and 2018, the labor force increased from 63 million to 163 million workers. Over that period, the average length of the workweek remained relatively stable. Falling birth rates slowed the growth of the native population, but increased immigration partly offset that slowdown. Of particular significance was a surge of women's participation in the labor force. Partly as a result, U.S. labor-force growth averaged about 1.5 million workers per year over the past 65 years.

The growth of labor productivity has also been important to economic growth. In fact, productivity growth has usually been more significant than labor force growth. For example, between 2007 and 2018, labor inputs increased by just 0.4 percent per year. As a result, 75 percent of the 1.6 percent average annual growth rate of GDP over that time period was due to increases in labor productivity. The final column of **Table 10.4** indicates that this trend will intensify; productivity growth is projected to account for 87 percent of the growth of real GDP between 2018 and 2029.

Because increases in labor productivity are so important to economic growth, economists investigate and assess the relative importance of the factors that contribute to productivity growth. There are five factors that appear to explain changes in productivity growth rates: technological advance, the amount of capital per worker, education and training, economies of scale, and resource allocation. We will examine each factor in turn, noting how much each factor contributes to productivity growth.

Technological Advance

The largest contributor to productivity growth is technological advance, which is thought to account for about 40 percent of productivity growth. As Nobel Laureate Paul Romer stated, "Human history teaches us that economic growth springs from better recipes, not just from more cooking."

Technological advance includes not only innovative production techniques but new managerial methods and new forms of business organization that improve the production process. Technological advance is generated by the discovery of new knowledge, which allows resources to be combined in improved ways that increase output. Once discovered and implemented, new knowledge soon becomes available to entrepreneurs and firms at relatively low cost. Technological advance therefore eventually spreads through the entire economy, boosting productivity and economic growth.

Technological advance and capital formation (investment) are closely related because technological advance usually promotes investment in new machinery and equipment. In fact, technological advance is often *embodied* within new capital (e.g., new computers and autonomous drones).

Technological advance has been both rapid and profound. Gas and diesel engines, conveyor belts, and assembly lines are significant developments of the past. So, too, are fuel-efficient commercial aircraft, integrated microcircuits, personal computers, and containerized shipping. More recently, technological advance has exploded, particularly in the areas of computers, wireless communications, artificial intelligence, and the Internet. Other fertile areas of recent innovation are medicine and biotechnology.

Quantity of Capital

A second major contributor to productivity growth is increased capital, which explains roughly 30 percent of productivity growth. More and better plant and equipment make workers more productive. And a nation acquires more capital by saving some of its income and using that savings to invest in plant and equipment.

Although some capital substitutes for labor, most capital is complementary to labor—it makes labor more productive. A key determinant of labor productivity is the amount of capital goods available *per worker*. If both the aggregate stock of capital goods and the size of the labor force increase over a given period, the individual worker is not necessarily better equipped and productivity will not necessarily rise. Fortunately, the quantity of capital equipment available per U.S. worker has increased greatly over time. (In 2017, it was about $139,000 per worker.)

U.S. public investment in **infrastructure** (highways and bridges, public transit systems, water and sewage systems, airports, industrial parks, educational facilities, and so on) has also grown over the years. This publicly owned capital complements private capital. Investments in new highways promote private investment in new factories and retail stores along their routes.

infrastructure
The capital goods usually provided by the public sector for the use of its citizens and firms (e.g., highways, bridges, transit systems, wastewater treatment facilities, municipal water systems, and airports).

Private investment in infrastructure also plays a large role in economic growth. One example is the tremendous growth of private capital relating to communications systems over the years.

Education and Training

Ben Franklin once said, "He that hath a trade hath an estate," meaning that education and training contribute to a worker's stock of **human capital**—the knowledge and skills that make a worker productive. Investment in human capital includes not only formal education but also on-the-job training. Like investment in physical capital, investment in human capital is an important means of increasing labor productivity and earnings. An estimated 15 percent of productivity growth derives from investments in people's education and skills.

human capital
The accumulation of knowledge and skills that make a worker productive.

One measure of a nation's quality of labor is its level of educational attainment. **Figure 10.3** shows large gains in educational attainment over the past several decades. In 1960, only 44 percent of the U.S. population age 25 or older had at least a high school education; and only 8 percent had a college or post-college education. By 2018, those numbers had increased to over 90 and 35 percent, respectively. More people are receiving an education than ever before.

PHOTO OP

Public and Private Investment in Infrastructure

Both public infrastructure investments (such as highways and bridges) and private infrastructure investments (such as wireless communications systems) have increased the nation's stock of private and public capital and helped expand real GDP.

Shutterstock/Ammar Yasir Photography

DreamPictures/Shannon Faulk/Blend Images

But all is not upbeat with education in the United States. Many observers think that the quality of education in the United States has declined. For example, U.S. students in science and mathematics perform poorly on tests on those subjects relative to students in many other nations. The United States has been producing fewer engineers and scientists, a problem that may trace back to inadequate training in math and science in elementary, middle, and high schools. For these reasons, much recent public policy discussion and legislation have been directed toward improving the quality of the U.S. education and training system.

FIGURE 10.3

Changes in the educational attainment of the U.S. adult population. The percentage of the U.S. adult population, age 25 or more, completing high school and college (bachelor's degree or higher) has been rising over recent decades.

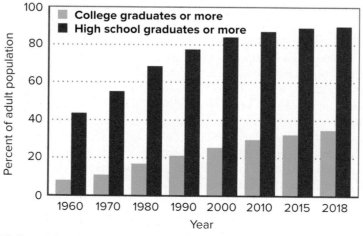

Source: U.S. Census Bureau, www.census.gov.

Economies of Scale and Resource Allocation

Economies of scale and improved resource allocation are a fourth and fifth source of productivity growth, and together they explain about 15 percent of productivity growth.

Economies of Scale Reductions in per-unit production costs that result from increases in output levels are called **economies of scale.** Markets have increased in size over time, allowing firms to increase output levels and thereby achieve production advantages associated with greater size. As firms expand their size and output, they are able to use larger, more productive equipment and employ methods of manufacturing and delivery that increase productivity. They also are better able to recoup substantial investments in developing new products and production methods.

economies of scale
Reductions in the average total cost of producing a product as the firm expands the size of plant (its output) in the long run; the economies of mass production.

Examples: A large manufacturer of autos can use elaborate assembly lines with computerization and robotics, while smaller producers must settle for less-advanced technologies using more labor inputs. Large pharmaceutical firms greatly reduce the average amount of labor (researchers, production workers) needed to produce each pill as they increase the number of pills produced. Accordingly, economies of scale result in greater real GDP and account for about 7 percent of all productivity growth.

Improved Resource Allocation Thanks to improved resource allocation, workers have moved from low-productivity employment to high-productivity employment. Historically, many workers shifted from agriculture, where labor productivity is low, to manufacturing, where it is high. More recently, labor has shifted away from some manufacturing industries to even higher-productivity industries such as computer software, business consulting, and pharmaceuticals. As a result of such shifts, the average productivity of U.S. workers has increased.

Also, discrimination in education and the labor market has historically deterred some women and minorities from entering high-productivity jobs. With the decline of such discrimination over time, many members of those groups have shifted from lower-productivity jobs to higher-productivity jobs. The result has been higher overall labor productivity and higher real GDP.

Finally, tariffs, import quotas, and other barriers to international trade tend to relegate resources to relatively unproductive pursuits. The long-run movement toward liberalized international trade through international agreements has improved the allocation of resources, increased labor productivity, and expanded real output, both here and abroad. Improved resource allocation accounts for about 8 percent of all productivity growth.

Institutional Structures That Promote Growth

Economic historians have identified several institutional structures that promote and sustain modern economic growth. Some institutions increase the savings and investment that are needed to fund the construction and maintenance of the factories and infrastructure required to run modern economies. Other institutions promote the development of new technologies. Still others act to ensure that resources flow efficiently to their most productive uses. These growth-promoting institutional structures include

- *Strong property rights* Strong property rights are essential for rapid and sustained economic growth. People will not invest if they believe that thieves, bandits, or a rapacious and tyrannical government will steal their investments or their expected returns.

- *Patents and copyrights* Before patents and copyrights were first issued and enforced, inventors and authors usually saw their ideas stolen before they could profit from them. By giving inventors and authors the exclusive right to market and sell their creations, patents and copyrights give a strong financial incentive to invent and create.

- *Efficient financial institutions* These institutions channel household savings toward the businesses, entrepreneurs, and inventors that do most of society's investing and inventing. Banks, along with stock and bond markets, appear to be crucial to modern economic growth.

- *Literacy and widespread education* Without highly educated scientists and inventors, new technologies do not get developed. And without a highly educated workforce, it is impossible to put those technologies to productive use.

- *Free trade* Free trade promotes economic growth by allowing countries to specialize. With specialization, various types of output are produced in the countries where they can be made at the lowest opportunity cost. Free trade also promotes the rapid spread of new ideas so that innovations made in one country quickly spread to other countries.

- *A competitive market system* Under a market system, prices and profits serve as the signals that tell firms what and how much to make. Rich leader countries vary substantially in terms of how much government regulation they impose on markets, but in all cases, firms have substantial autonomy to follow market signals in determining their production and investment decisions.

Other Factors

Several other difficult-to-measure factors also influence a nation's capacity for economic growth. The overall social-cultural-political environment of the United States, for example, has encouraged economic growth. The United States has had a stable political system characterized by democratic principles, internal order, the right of property ownership, the legal status of enterprise, and the enforcement of contracts. Economic freedom and political freedom have been "growth-friendly."

In addition, there are virtually no social or moral taboos on production and material progress in the United States. The nation's social philosophy has embraced wealth creation as an attainable and desirable goal, and the inventor, innovator, and businessperson are accorded high degrees of prestige and respect. Finally, Americans have a positive attitude toward work and risk taking, resulting in an ample supply of willing workers and innovative entrepreneurs. A flow of enterprising immigrants has greatly augmented that supply.

Recent Fluctuations in Average Productivity Growth

Figure 10.4 shows the growth of labor productivity (as measured by changes in the index of labor productivity for the full business sector) in the United States from 1973 to 2018, along with separate trend lines for 1973–1995, 1995–2010, and 2010–2018. Labor productivity in the business sector grew by an average of only 1.5 percent yearly over the 1973–1995 period. But productivity growth nearly doubled to 2.8 percent per year between 1995 and 2010 before plummeting to just 0.7 percent per year between 2010 and 2018.

FIGURE 10.4

Growth of labor productivity in the United States, 1973–2018. U.S. labor productivity (here, for the business sector) increased at an average annual rate of only 1.5 percent from 1973 to 1995. But between 1995 and 2010, it rose at an annual rate of 2.8 percent before decreasing to just 0.7 percent per year between 2010 and 2018.

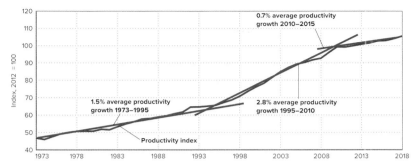

Source: U.S. Bureau of Labor Statistics, www.bls.gov.

Robust productivity growth is important because real output, real income, and real wages are linked to labor productivity. To see why this is the case, imagine you are alone on an uninhabited island. The number of fish you can catch or the coconuts you can pick per hour—your productivity—is your real wage (or real income) per hour. By *increasing* your productivity, you can improve your standard of living because greater output per hour means there are more fish and coconuts (goods) available to consume.

So it is for the economy as a whole: Over long periods, the economy's labor productivity determines its average real hourly wage. Thus, productivity growth is the economy's main route for improving living standards.

Reasons for the Rise in the Average Rate of Productivity Growth Between 1995 and 2010

Why did productivity growth increase rapidly between 1995 and 2010?

The Microchip and Information Technology The core element of the productivity speedup between 1995 and 2010 was an explosion of entrepreneurship and innovation based on the microprocessor, or *microchip,* which bundles transistors on a piece of silicon. Some observers liken the invention of the microchip to that of electricity, the automobile, air travel, the telephone, and television in importance and scope.

The microchip has found its way into thousands of applications. It has helped create a wide array of new products and services and new ways of doing business. Its immediate results were the pocket calculator, the bar-code scanner, the personal computer, and more powerful business computers. The miniaturization of electronic circuits also advanced the development of many other products, including cell phones, the global positioning system, Doppler radar, and gene sequencing equipment.

Perhaps of greatest significance, the widespread availability of personal and laptop computers stimulated the desire to tie them together. That desire promoted rapid development of the Internet and its many manifestations, such as business-to-household and business-to-business electronic commerce *(e-commerce).* The combination of the computer, fiber optic cable, wireless technology, and the Internet constitutes a spectacular advance in **information technology,** which now connects almost all parts of the world.

information technology
New and more efficient methods of delivering and receiving information through use of computers, fax machines, wireless phones, and the Internet.

start-up (firm)
A new firm focused on creating and introducing a particular new product or employing a specific new production or distribution method.

increasing returns
An increase in a firm's output by a larger percentage than the percentage increase in its inputs.

New Firms and Increasing Returns

Hundreds of new **start-up firms** advanced various aspects of the new information technology. Many of these firms created more "hype" than goods and services and quickly fell by the wayside. But a number of firms flourished, including Intel (microchips); Apple and Dell (personal computers); Microsoft and Oracle (computer software); Cisco Systems (Internet switching systems); Yahoo and Google (Internet search engines); and eBay, PayPal, and Amazon.com (electronic commerce). There are scores more! Most of these firms were either nonexistent or just a small blip on the radar 30 years ago. Today, each of them has a large annual revenue and employs thousands of workers.

Many of the successful information technology start-ups enjoyed **increasing returns,** which is what happens when a given percentage increase in the amount of inputs used by a firm leads to a larger percentage increase in the amount of outputs produced by the firm.

As an illustration, suppose that a company called Techco decides to double the size of its operations to meet the growing demand for its services.

- After doubling its plant and equipment and doubling its workforce, say, from 100 workers to 200 workers, it finds that its total output has tripled from 8,000 units to 24,000 units.

- Techco has experienced increasing returns; its output has increased by 200 percent, while its inputs have increased by only 100 percent.

- Techco's labor productivity has gone up from 80 units per worker (= 8,000 units/ 100 workers) to 120 units per worker (= 24,000 units/200 workers).

Increasing returns boost labor productivity and lower per-unit production costs. Because these cost reductions result from increases in output levels, they are examples of *economies of scale.*

Both emerging firms as well as established firms can exploit several different sources of increasing returns and economies of scale:

- *More specialized inputs* Firms can use more specialized and thus more productive capital and workers as they expand their operations. A growing e-commerce business, for example, can purchase highly specialized inventory management systems and hire specialized personnel such as accountants, marketing managers, and system maintenance experts.

- *Spreading of development costs* Firms can spread high product development costs over greater output. For example, suppose that a new software product costs $100,000 to develop and only $2 per unit to manufacture and sell. If the firm sells 1,000 units of the software, its cost per unit will be $102 [= ($100,000 + $2,000)/1,000], but if it sells 500,000 units, that cost will drop to only $2.20 [= ($100,000 + $1 million)/500,000].

- *Simultaneous consumption* Many technology products and services are able to satisfy large numbers of customers at the same time. Unlike a gallon of gas that needs to be produced for each buyer, a software program needs to be produced only once. It can then be made available at very low expense to thousands or even millions of buyers. The same is true of books delivered to electronic reading devices, movies distributed on DVDs, and information disseminated through the Internet.

- *Network effects* The domestic and global expansion of the Internet, wireless networks, and social media produced enormous network effects that magnified the value of output well beyond the cost of the inputs. **Network effects** occur when a product's value to each user increases as more users use it. To see the power of network effects, imagine that you are the only one in the world with an Instagram account. That would be pointless, as the whole point is to share content and connect with people. But if there were a few thousand people also using Instagram, you would be able to derive significant benefits from your account. The larger the network of people using the service, the more beneficial it becomes to each individual user. Since the Internet was the largest network ever created, it's not surprising that it generated the largest network effects ever seen and, along with them, extremely large economies of scale.

network effects
Increases in the value of a product to each user, including existing users, as the total number of users rises.

- *Learning by doing* Finally, the start-ups that produce new products or pioneer new ways of doing business experience increasing returns through **learning by doing.** Tasks that initially may have taken firms hours may take them only minutes once the methods are perfected.

learning by doing
Achieving greater productivity and lower average total cost through gains in knowledge and skill that accompany repetition of a task; a source of economies of scale.

Whatever the particular source of increasing returns, the result is higher productivity, which tends to reduce the per-unit cost of producing and delivering products.

Global Competition As with today's economy, the economy between 1995 and 2010 was characterized not only by information technology and increasing returns but also by heightened global competition. The market liberalization in China and the collapse of the socialist economies in the early 1990s, led to a reawakening of capitalism throughout the world. New information technologies "shrank the globe" and made it imperative for all firms to lower their costs and innovate in order to remain competitive. Free-trade zones such as NAFTA and the European Union (EU), along with trade liberalization through the World Trade Organization (WTO), increased international competition by removing trade barriers. The larger geographic markets, in turn, enabled firms to expand beyond their national borders. Countries had to compete if they wanted to grow.

Implications for Economic Growth

Other things equal, stronger productivity growth and heightened global competition allowed the economy to achieve a higher rate of economic growth during the 1995 to 2010 period. A glance back at **Figure 10.1** will help make this point. Suppose the shift of the production possibilities curve from *AB* to *CD* reflects annual changes in potential output levels before the increase in growth rates observed during the 1995 to 2010 period. Then, the higher growth rates of that period would be depicted by a *larger* outward shift of the economy's production possibilities from *AB* to a curve beyond *CD*. When coupled with economic efficiency and increased total spending, the economy's real GDP was able to rise by even more than what is shown.

PHOTO OP

Key Elements of the Rise in U.S. Productivity

A combination of information technology, emerging new firms, and globalization helps explain the speedup in U.S. productivity growth between 1995 and 2010.

Glow Images   Alex Segre/Alamy Stock Photo   Ingram Publishing/SuperStock

The Recent Productivity Slowdown

It is not clear whether the dramatic slowdown in productivity growth that took place after the Great Recession is permanent or transitory. Some economists have argued that the high productivity growth rates observed between 1995 and 2010 were a one-time anomaly due to the information technology revolution. But even if information technology caused an unusual burst of growth for 15 years, it is still surprising that post-2010 productivity growth rates have been so very low—much lower in fact than the rates that prevailed before the information technology revolution.

Several possible explanations have been put forward to explain why productivity growth rates have fallen so low. One possible culprit is the high debt levels that accumulated before the Great Recession. Under this hypothesis, individuals and firms are now too busy paying down debts to make productive investments. At the same time, entrepreneurs who might be able to improve productivity may be unable to obtain loans because banks are reluctant to lend after having made so many bad loans prior to the Great Recession.

Overcapacity may be another possible explanation for the productivity slowdown. During the boom that preceded the Great Recession, worldwide productive capacity increased massively as many new factories were built. But the additional capacity may have been excessive relative to consumer demand. If so, firms would have been reluctant to install newer, more productive equipment or build newer, more productive factories because they already had more than enough production capacity. Under this hypothesis, productivity stagnated because producers continued to rely on aging machinery and equipment.

Another possible explanation points to the fact that many recent products—especially Internet apps—do not generate much of a measurable effect on GDP. Consider Facebook, YouTube, and Instagram. They are for the most part totally free to consumers. So measured output will hardly increase even if billions of people are using them. That being said, measured output isn't everything. The new products are undoubtedly generating a huge amount of consumer satisfaction; we just can't see those benefits in the GDP and productivity statistics.

Finally, it is also possible that technological progress itself may have stalled. Under this hypothesis, productivity growth will remain slow until invention and innovation speed up again.

While the future of productivity growth is uncertain, the United States remains competitive (see **Global Snapshot 10.4**), which bodes well for its long-term growth prospects.

GLOBAL SNAPSHOT 10.4

Global Competitiveness Index

The Global Competitiveness Index, published annually by the World Economic Forum, measures each country's potential for economic growth. The index uses various factors—such as innovativeness, the capability to transfer technology among sectors, the efficiency of the financial system, rates of investment, and the degree of integration with the rest of the world—to measure a country's ability to achieve economic growth over time. Here is the top 10 list for 2017–2018.

Country	Global Competitiveness Ranking, 2017–2018
Switzerland	1
United States	2
Singapore	3
Netherlands	4
Germany	5
Hong Kong	6
Sweden	7
United Kingdom	8
Japan	9
Finland	10

Source: Schwab, Klaus. The Global Competitiveness Report 2017–2018. World Economic Forum, 2017, www.weforum.org.

Is Growth Desirable and Sustainable?

Economists usually take for granted that economic growth is desirable and sustainable. But not everyone agrees.

The Antigrowth View

Critics of growth say industrialization and growth result in pollution, climate change, species extinction, and other environmental problems. These adverse negative externalities occur because inputs in the production process reenter the environment as some form of waste. The more rapid our growth and the higher our standard of living, the more waste the environment must absorb—or attempt to absorb. In an already wealthy society, further growth usually means satisfying increasingly trivial wants at the cost of mounting threats to the ecological system.

Critics of growth also argue that there is little compelling evidence that economic growth has solved social problems such as poverty, homelessness, and discrimination. Consider poverty: In the antigrowth view, U.S. poverty is a problem of distribution, not production. Solving the problem requires a firm commitment to redistribute wealth and income, not further increases in output.

Antigrowth sentiment also says that while growth may permit us to "make a better living," it does not give us "the good life." We may be producing more and enjoying less, focused too much on materialism and not enough on families, friendship, and community. Growth means zero work–life balance, employee burnout, and worker alienation. In addition, the changing technology at the core of growth poses new anxieties and new sources of insecurity for workers. Both experienced and entry-level workers face the prospect of having their hard-earned skills and experience rendered obsolete by an onrushing technology. High-growth economies are high-stress economies, which may impair our physical and mental health.

Finally, critics of high rates of growth doubt that they are sustainable. The Earth has finite amounts of natural resources available, and they are being consumed at alarming rates. Higher rates of economic growth simply speed up the degradation and exhaustion of the Earth's resources. In this view, slower economic growth that is sustainable is preferable to faster growth.

In Defense of Economic Growth

Those who support economic growth believe that it is the path to the greater material abundance and higher living standards desired by the vast majority of people. Growth also enables society to improve the nation's infrastructure, enhance the care of the sick and elderly, provide greater access for the disabled, and provide more police and fire protection.

Economic growth may also be the only realistic way to reduce poverty, because there is only limited political support for greater redistribution of income. Proponents of growth argue that the best way to improve the economic position of the poor is to increase household incomes through higher productivity and faster economic growth. Also, a no-growth policy among industrial nations might severely limit growth in poor nations. Foreign investment and development assistance in those nations would fall, keeping the world's poor in poverty longer.

Economic growth has not made labor more unpleasant or hazardous, as critics suggest. New machinery is usually less taxing and less dangerous than the machinery it replaces. Air-conditioned workplaces are more pleasant than steamy workshops. Furthermore, there is no guarantee that an end to economic growth will reduce materialism or worker alienation. The loudest protests against materialism are heard in those nations and groups that now enjoy the highest levels of material abundance! The high standard of living that growth provides has increased our leisure and given us more time for reflection and self-fulfillment.

Economic growth need not threaten the environment, say growth proponents. Pollution is not so much a by-product of growth as it is a "problem of the commons." Much of the environment—streams, lakes, oceans, and the air—is treated as common property, with insufficient or no restrictions on its use. The commons have become our dumping grounds; we have overused and debased them. Environmental pollution is a case of negative externalities, and correcting this problem involves regulatory legislation, Pigovian taxes, or market-based incentives. In addition, economic growth has allowed economies to preserve wilderness, create national parks and monuments, and clean up hazardous waste, while still enabling rising household incomes.

Is growth sustainable? Yes, say the proponents of growth. If we were depleting natural resources faster than their discovery, we would see the prices of those resources rise. That has not been the case for most natural resources; in fact, the prices of most of them have declined. And if one natural resource becomes too expensive, another resource will be substituted for it. Moreover, say growth advocates, economic growth has to do with the expansion and application of human knowledge and information, not of extractable natural resources. In this view, economic growth—and solving any problems it may create—is limited only by human imagination.

Summary

LO10.1 Define and measure gross domestic product (GDP).

Gross domestic product (GDP) is the market value of all final goods and services produced within a nation's borders in a year. Final goods are purchased by end users, whereas intermediate goods are those purchased for resale or for further processing. Intermediate goods, nonproduction transactions, and secondhand sales are excluded in calculating GDP.

GDP is determined by adding consumer purchases of goods and services, gross investment spending by businesses, government purchases, and net exports: $GDP = C + I_g + G + X_n$.

LO10.2 Describe how economists distinguish between nominal GDP and real GDP.

Nominal (current-dollar) GDP measures each year's output valued in terms of the prices prevailing in that year. Real (constant-dollar) GDP measures each year's output in terms of the prevailing prices in a selected base year. Because real GDP is adjusted for price-level changes, differences in real GDP are due only to differences in output.

LO10.3 Explain two ways to measure economic growth.

Economic growth is measured either as an increase of real GDP over time or as an increase in real GDP per capita over time. Real GDP has grown at an average annual rate of about 3.1 percent since 1950; real GDP per capita has grown at roughly 2.0 percent annually over that same time period.

LO10.4 Identify the supply, demand, and efficiency forces that lead to economic growth.

The determinants of economic growth include four supply factors (changes in the quantity and quality of natural resources, changes in the quantity and quality of human resources, changes in the stock of capital goods, and improvements in technology), one demand factor (changes in total spending), and one efficiency factor (changes in how well an economy achieves allocative and productive efficiency).

The growth of a nation's capacity to produce output is shown graphically by an outward shift of its production possibilities curve. Growth is realized when total spending rises sufficiently to match the growth of production capacity.

LO10.5 Describe the specific factors accounting for U.S. economic growth.

U.S. real GDP has grown partly because of increased inputs of labor and primarily because of increases in the productivity of labor. The increases in productivity have resulted mainly from technological progress, increases in the quantity of capital per worker, improvements in the quality of labor, exploitation of economies of scale, and improvements in the allocation of labor across different industries.

LO10.6 Explain how U.S. productivity growth has fluctuated since 1973.

Over long time periods, the growth of labor productivity underlies an economy's growth of real wages and its standard of living. Productivity rose by 1.5 percent annually between 1973 and 1995, 2.8 percent annually between 1995 and 2010, and just 0.7 percent annually from 2010 to 2018.

The 1995–2010 increase in the average rate of productivity growth was based on (a) rapid technological change in the form of the microchip and information technology, (b) increasing returns and lower per-unit costs, and (c) heightened global competition that holds down prices.

The main sources of increasing returns are (a) the use of more specialized inputs as firms grow, (b) the spreading of development costs, (c) simultaneous consumption by consumers, (d) network effects, and (e) learning by doing. Increasing returns mean higher productivity and lower per-unit production costs.

Possible explanations for the slow productivity growth after the Great Recession of 2007–2009 include high debt levels, overcapacity, the rise of "free" Internet products, and a slowdown in technological innovation.

LO10.7 Discuss whether economic growth is desirable and sustainable.

Critics of rapid growth say that it degrades the environment, increases human stress, and depletes the Earth's finite supply of natural resources. Defenders of rapid growth say that it is the primary path to the high and rising living standards that most people desire, that it need not debase the environment, and that there are no indications that we are running out of resources. Defenders argue that there are no natural limits to sustainable, environmentally friendly growth because growth is based on the expansion and application of human knowledge, which is limited only by human imagination.

Terms and Concepts

national income and product accounts (NIPA)

gross domestic product (GDP)

intermediate goods

final goods and services

personal consumption expenditures (C)

gross private domestic investment (I_g)

government purchases (G)

net exports (X_n)

nominal GDP

real GDP

economic growth

real GDP per capita

labor productivity

labor-force participation rate

growth accounting

infrastructure

human capital

economies of scale

information technology

start-up (firm)

increasing returns

network effects

learning by doing

Questions   Mc Graw Hill connect

1. Why do national income accountants compare the market value of the total outputs in various years rather than actual physical volumes of production? What problem is posed by any comparison over time of the market values of various total outputs? How is this problem resolved? **(LO1)**

2. Why do economists include only final goods and services when measuring GDP? Why don't they include the value of the stocks and bonds bought and sold? Why don't they include the value of the used furniture bought and sold? **(LO1)**

3. Provide three examples of each: consumer durable goods, consumer nondurable goods, and services. **(LO1)**

4. Why are changes in inventories included as part of investment spending? Suppose inventories decline by $1 billion during 2022. How would this $1 billion decrease affect the size of gross private domestic investment and gross domestic product in 2022? Explain. **(LO1)**

5. Define net exports. How are net exports determined? Explain why net exports might be a negative amount. **(LO1)**

6. Which of the following are included in this year's GDP? Which are excluded? Explain your answers. **(LO1)**

   a. Interest received on an AT&T corporate bond.

   b. Social Security payments received by a retired factory worker.

   c. Unpaid services of a family member who painted the family home.

   d. Income of a dentist from the dental services they provided.

   e. A monthly allowance that a college student receives from home.

   f. Money received by Josh when he resells his nearly brand-new Honda automobile to Kim.

   g. The publication and sale of a new college textbook.

   h. An increase in leisure resulting from a 2-hour decrease in the workweek, with no reduction in pay.

   i. A $2 billion increase in business inventories.

   j. The purchase of 100 shares of Alphabet (the parent company of Google) stock.

7. What are the four supply factors of economic growth? What is the demand factor? What is the efficiency factor? Illustrate these factors in terms of the production possibilities curve. **(LO4)**

8. What is growth accounting? To what extent have increases in U.S. real GDP resulted from more labor inputs? From greater labor productivity? Rearrange the following contributors to the growth of real GDP in order of their quantitative importance: economies of scale, quantity of capital per worker, improved resource allocation, education and training, technological advance. **(LO5)**

9. True or false? If false, explain why. **(LO5)**

   a. Technological advance, which to date has played a relatively small role in U.S. economic growth, is destined to play a more important role in the future.

   b. Many public capital goods are complementary to private capital goods.

   c. Immigration has slowed economic growth in the United States.

10. Explain why there is such a close relationship between changes in a nation's rate of productivity growth and changes in its average real hourly wage. **(LO6)**

11. Relate each of the following to the 1995–2010 increase in the productivity growth rate: **(LO6)**

    a. information technology

    b. increasing returns

c. network effects

d. global competition

12. Provide three examples of products or services that can be simultaneously consumed by many people. Explain why labor productivity greatly

rises as the firm sells more units of the product or service. Explain why the higher level of sales greatly reduces the per-unit cost of the product. **(LO6)**

Problems

1. Suppose that annual output in year 1 in a three-good economy is 3 quarts of ice cream, 1 bottle of shampoo, and 3 jars of peanut butter. In year 2, the output mix changes to 5 quarts of ice cream, 2 bottles of shampoo, and 2 jars of peanut butter. If the prices in both years are $4 per quart for ice cream, $3 per bottle of shampoo, and $2 per jar of peanut butter, what was the economy's GDP in year 1? What was its GDP in year 2? **(LO1)**

2. If in some country personal consumption expenditures in a specific year are $50 billion, purchases of stocks and bonds are $30 billion, net exports are −$10 billion, government purchases are $20 billion, sales of secondhand items are $8 billion, and gross investment is $25 billion, what is the country's GDP for the year? **(LO1)**

3. Assume that a grower of flower bulbs sells its annual output of bulbs to an Internet retailer for $70,000. The retailer, in turn, brings in $160,000 from selling the bulbs directly to final customers. What amount would these two transactions add to personal consumption expenditures and thus to GDP during the year? **(LO1)**

4. Using the following NIPA data, compute GDP. All figures are in billions of U.S. dollars. **(LO1)**

Personal consumption expenditures	$245
Wages and salaries	223
Imports	18
Corporate profits	42
Depreciation	28
Gross private domestic investment	86
Government purchases	82
Exports	9

5. Suppose that in 1994 the total output in a single-good economy was 7,000 buckets of chicken. Also, suppose that in 1994 each bucket of chicken was priced at $10. Finally, assume that in 2015 the price per bucket of chicken was $16 and that 22,000 buckets were produced. Determine real GDP for 1994 and 2015, in 1994 prices. **(LO2)**

6. Suppose an economy's real GDP is $30,000 in year 1 and $31,200 in year 2. What is the growth rate of its real GDP? Assume that population is 100 in year 1 and 102 in year 2. What is the growth rate of GDP per capita? **(LO3)**

7. What annual growth rate is needed for a country to double its output in seven years? In 35 years? In 70 years? In 140 years? **(LO3)**

8. Assume that a leader country has real GDP per capita of $40,000, whereas a follower country has real GDP per capita of $20,000. Next, suppose that the growth of real GDP per capita falls to 0 percent in the leader country and rises to 7 percent in the follower country. If these rates continue for long periods of time, how many years will it take for the follower country to catch up to the living standard of the leader country? **(LO3)**

9. Suppose that work hours in New Zombie are 200 in year 1 and productivity is $8 per hour worked. What is New Zombie's real GDP? If work hours increase to 210 in year 2 and productivity rises to $10 per hour, what is New Zombie's rate of economic growth? **(LO5)**

CHAPTER ELEVEN

Business Cycles, Unemployment, and Inflation

Learning Objectives

LO11.1   Describe the phases of the business cycle.

LO11.2   Measure unemployment and inflation.

LO11.3   Describe the types of unemployment and inflation and explain their economic impacts.

The United States has experienced remarkable economic growth over time. But this growth has not been smooth, steady, or predictable from year to year. At various times, the United States has experienced recessions, high unemployment rates, or high inflation rates. For example, U.S. unemployment rose by eight million workers and the unemployment rate increased from 4.7 percent to 10.1 percent during the Great Recession of 2007–2009. In 2020, in the early months of the COVID-19 pandemic, U.S. real GDP plummeted at an annual rate of 31.4 percent in the second quarter, then rebounded at an annual rate of 33.4 percent in the third quarter. Other nations also have suffered high unemployment and inflation. For example, the Greek unemployment rate exceeded 25 percent in 2015, and Venezuela's inflation rate soared to 1.4 *million* percent in 2018!

In this chapter, we examine the concepts, terminology, and facts relating to macroeconomic instability. Specifically, we discuss the business cycle, unemployment, and inflation.

Business Cycles

In the United States, real GDP grows by about 3 percent per year, *on average*. So the long-run growth trend is up, as illustrated by the upward sloping line labeled "Growth Trend" in **Figure 11.1**. There is, however, a lot of variation around the average growth trend, with growth interrupted by periods of economic instability usually associated with *business cycles*. **Business cycles** are alternating rises and declines in the level of economic activity over periods of years. Individual cycles (one "up" followed by one "down") vary substantially in duration and intensity.

business cycles
Recurring increases and decreases in the level of economic activity over periods of years; a cycle consists of peak, recession, trough, and expansion phases.

FIGURE 11.1

The business cycle. Economists distinguish two primary phases of the business cycle (recessions and expansions); the duration and strength of each phase may vary.

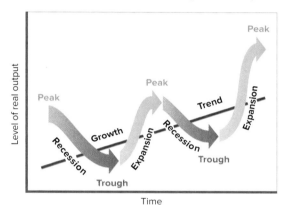

Figure **11.1** shows the two primary phases of a generalized business cycle, recessions and expansions ("peaks" and "troughs" are merely turning points). A **recession** is a period of decline in total output, income, and employment that lasts at least six months. Along with a decline in real GDP, unemployment increases significantly. **Table 11.1** documents the 10 recessions in the United States that occurred from 1950 through 2009. The 11th recession began in February 2020, precipitated by the COVID-19 outbreak.

recession
A period of declining real GDP, accompanied by lower real income and higher unemployment.

TABLE 11.1
U.S. Recessions since 1950

Period	Duration, Months	Depth (Decline in Real Output)
1953–54	10	−2.6%
1957–58	8	−3.7
1960–61	10	−1.1
1969–70	11	−0.2
1973–75	16	−3.2
1980	6	−2.2
1981–82	16	−2.9
1990–91	8	−1.4
2001	8	−0.4
2007–2009	18	−4.3

Source: National Bureau of Economic Research (NBER), www.nber.org.

expansion
The phase of the business cycle in which output, income, and business activity rise.

A recession eventually reaches a *trough* ("bottoms out") and then is followed by recovery and **expansion,** a period in which real GDP, income, and employment rise. At some point, full employment is again achieved, usually signifying that the cycle has reached a *peak.* If spending then expands more rapidly than does production capacity, prices of nearly all goods and services will rise. In other words, inflation will occur.

The Business Cycle Dating Committee of the National Bureau of Economic Research (NBER)—a nonprofit economic research organization—declares the start and end of recessions in the United States. Citing evidence of declining real output and falling employment, the NBER officially declared that the 2007–2009 recession—the so-called Great Recession—began in December 2007. The NBER subsequently declared that this recession ended in June 2009, 18 months after it began. According to the NBER, the expansionary phase that began in June 2009 lasted 128 months, reaching its peak in February 2020.

Causes of Business Cycles

A key question in macroeconomics is why the economy experiences business cycle fluctuations rather than slow, smooth growth. In terms of **Figure 11.1**, why does output move up and down rather than just staying on the smooth growth trend line?

shocks
Sudden, unexpected changes in *demand* (or *aggregate demand*) or *supply* (or *aggregate supply*).

The most prominent theory is that business cycle fluctuations are driven by **shocks**—situations in which individuals and firms were expecting one thing to happen but then something else occurred. For instance, consider a situation in which a firm decides to build a high-speed railroad that will shuttle passengers between Los Angeles and Las Vegas. The firm expects it to be very popular and make a handsome profit. But what if the railroad turns out to be unpopular and loses money? The firm must figure out how to respond. Should it go out of business? Change the service it provides? Spend millions on a massive advertising campaign? These sorts of decisions are necessitated by the shock and surprise of having to deal with an unexpected situation.

demand shocks
Sudden, unexpected change in *aggregate demand.*

supply shocks
Sudden, unexpected changes in *aggregate supply.*

Economies experience both demand shocks and supply shocks. **Demand shocks** are unexpected changes in the demand for goods and services. **Supply shocks** are unexpected changes in the supply of goods and services. Note that the word *shock* reveals only that something unexpected has happened. It does not tell us whether what has happened is unexpectedly good or unexpectedly bad. For this reason, economists use more specific terms. For instance, a *positive demand shock* refers to a situation in which demand is higher than expected, while a *negative demand shock* refers to a situation in which demand is lower than expected.

Economists believe that most short-run fluctuations in GDP and the business cycles are the result of demand shocks. Supply shocks do happen in some cases, and are important, but most of our focus will be on demand shocks. Subsequent chapters will further address how shocks affect the economy, and how government policy may help the economy adjust to them.

But why are demand shocks such a big problem? Why would we have to consider calling in the government for help? Why can't firms deal with shocks on their own?

inflexible prices
Product prices that remain in place (at least for a while) even though supply or demand has changed; stuck prices or sticky prices.

The answer to these questions is that the prices of many goods and services are inflexible (slow to change, also known as "sticky" or **inflexible prices**) in the short run. This implies that price changes do not quickly equalize the quantities demanded of such goods and services with their respective quantities supplied. Instead, because prices are inflexible, the economy is forced to respond in the short run to demand shocks primarily through changes in output and employment rather than through changes in prices.

Economists cite several possible general sources of shocks that can cause business cycles.

- *Irregular innovation* Significant new products or production methods, such as those associated with railroads, automobiles, computers, and the Internet, can rapidly spread through the economy, sparking sizable increases in investment, consumption, output, and employment. After the economy has largely absorbed the new innovation, the economy may for a time slow down or possibly decline. Because such innovations occur irregularly and unexpectedly, they may contribute to the variability of economic activity.

- *Productivity changes* When productivity—output per unit of input—unexpectedly increases, the economy booms; when productivity unexpectedly decreases, the economy recedes. These changes in productivity can result from unexpected changes in resource availability (of, say, oil or agricultural commodities) or from unexpected changes in the general rate of technological advances.

- *Monetary factors* Some economists see business cycles as purely monetary phenomena. When a nation's central bank shocks the economy by creating more money than people were expecting, an inflationary boom in output occurs. By contrast, printing less money than people were expecting triggers an output decline and, eventually, a decrease in the price level.

- *Political events* Unexpected political events, such as peace treaties, new wars, or terrorist attacks, can create economic opportunities or strains. In adjusting to these shocks, the economy may experience upswings or downswings.

- *Financial instability* Unexpected financial bubbles (rapid asset price increases) or bursts (abrupt asset price decreases) can spill over to the general economy. They may expand or contract lending, and they may boost or erode the confidence of consumers and businesses. Booms and busts in the rest of the economy may follow.

- *Random events* Natural disasters, global disease outbreaks, and other random events can cause unexpected changes with widespread economic consequences. Loss of life and property resources may reduce productive capacity or encourage new innovations as nations and communities respond. Spending may rise or fall depending on how consumers and business choose and are able to react to the events.

The severe recession of 2007–2009 was precipitated by a combination of excessive money and a financial frenzy that led to overvalued real estate and unsustainable mortgage debt. Institutions bundled this debt into new securities ("derivatives") that were sold to financial investors. Some of the investors, in turn, bought insurance against losses that might arise from the securities. As real estate prices plummeted and mortgage defaults unexpectedly rocketed, the securitization and insurance structure buckled and nearly collapsed. Credit markets froze, pessimism prevailed, and spending by businesses and households declined.

The recession that began in February 2020 was sparked by the COVID-19 outbreak and the subsequent responses of consumers, firms, and policymakers. Households and businesses significantly curtailed spending, some by choice and some because of shutdown orders. As many non-essential businesses shuttered, production dropped significantly, as did the incomes of workers as millions were suddenly unemployed. Shutdowns in some industries created supply chain problems in others, further fueling the massive drop in output. Some firms, however, thrived as a result of the pandemic, including providers of online shopping and delivery services, manufacturers of personal protective equipment (PPE such as masks and face shields), and pharmaceutical companies rushing to produce vaccines and treatments for COVID-19.

Whatever the source of economic shocks, most economists agree that unexpected changes in the level of total spending cause the majority of cyclical fluctuations. If total spending unexpectedly sinks and firms cannot lower prices, firms will sell fewer units of output (because with prices fixed, lower spending implies fewer items purchased). Slower sales cause firms to cut back on production. As they do, GDP falls. And because fewer workers are needed to produce less output, employment also falls. The economy contracts and enters a recession.

By contrast, if the level of spending unexpectedly rises, then output, employment, and incomes rise. With prices sticky, the increased spending means that consumers buy more goods and services (because, with prices fixed, more spending means more items purchased). Firms respond by increasing output, which increases GDP. And because firms need to hire more workers to produce the larger volume of output, employment also increases. The economy booms and enjoys an expansion. Eventually, as time passes and prices become more flexible, prices also rise due to the increased spending.

Cyclical Impact: Durables and Nondurables

Although the business cycle is felt throughout the economy, it affects different sectors in different ways and to different degrees.

Firms and industries producing *capital goods* (e.g., housing, commercial buildings, and heavy equipment) and *consumer durables* (e.g., automobiles, personal computers, and refrigerators) are affected most by the business cycle. Within limits, firms can postpone the purchase of capital goods. When a recession strikes, firms patch up their old equipment and make do rather than replace the old equipment. As a result, investment in capital goods declines sharply. The pattern is much the same for consumer durables such as cars and refrigerators. When recession occurs and households must trim their budgets, they often defer their purchases of these goods. Households repair their old cars and appliances rather than buy new ones, and the firms producing these products suffer. (However, producers of capital goods and consumer durables also benefit most from expansions.)

In contrast, *service* industries and industries that produce *nondurable consumer goods* are somewhat insulated from the recession's most severe effects. People find it difficult to cut back on needed medical and legal services, for example. And a recession actually helps some service firms, such as pawnbrokers and law firms that specialize in bankruptcies. Nor are the purchases of many nondurable goods such as food and clothing easy to postpone. As a result, purchases of nondurables will decline, but not so much as will purchases of capital goods and consumer durables.

 APPLYING THE ANALYSIS

Stock Prices and Macroeconomic Instability

Every day, the individual stocks (ownership shares) of thousands of corporations are bought and sold in the stock market. The owners of the individual stocks receive dividends—a portion of the firm's profit. Supply and demand in the stock market determine the price of each firm's stock, with individual stock prices generally rising and falling in concert with the collective expectations for each firm's profits. Greater profits normally result in higher dividends to the stock owners, and, in anticipation of higher dividends, people are willing to pay a higher price for the stock.

The media closely monitor and report stock market averages such as the Dow Jones Industrial Average (DJIA)—the weighted-average price of the stocks of 30 major U.S. industrial firms. It is common for these price averages to change over time or even to rise or fall sharply during a single day. On "Black Monday," October 19, 1987, the DJIA fell by 20 percent. In contrast, the stock market averages rose spectacularly in 1998 and 1999, with the DJIA rising 16 and 25 percent in those two years. In 2002, the DJIA fell 17 percent. In 2003, it rose by 25 percent. In the last three months of 2008, the DJIA plummeted by 34 percent, the steepest decline since the 1930s. Falling oil prices, economic slowdown in China, and uncertainty about monetary policy caused the DJIA to decline slightly in 2015, but it rebounded sharply in 2016, gaining over 23 percent from the previous year.

The volatility of the stock market raises this question: Do changes in stock price averages and thus stock market wealth cause macroeconomic instability? Linkages between the stock market and the economy might lead us to answer "yes." Consider a sharp increase in stock prices. Feeling wealthier, stock owners respond by increasing their spending (the *wealth effect*). Firms react by increasing their purchases of new capital goods because they can finance such purchases through issuing new shares of high-valued stock (the *investment effect*). Of course, sharp declines in stock prices would produce the opposite results.

Studies find that changes in stock prices do affect consumption and investment but that these consumption and investment impacts are relatively weak. For example, a 10 percent sustained increase in stock market values in one year is associated with a 4 percent increase in consumption spending over the next three years. The investment response is even weaker. So typical day-to-day and year-to-year changes in stock market values have little impact on the macroeconomy.

In contrast, *stock market bubbles* can be detrimental to an economy. Such bubbles are huge run-ups of overall stock prices, caused by excessive optimism and frenzied buying. The rising stock values are unsupported by realistic prospects of the future strength of the economy and the firms operating in it. Rather than slowly decompress, such bubbles may burst and cause harm to the economy. The free fall of stock values, if long-lasting, causes reverse wealth effects. The stock market crash also may create an overall pessimism about the economy that undermines consumption and investment spending even further. Indeed, the plunge of the stock market in 2007 and 2008 contributed to the severe recession of 2007–2009 by stressing financial institutions and creating a tremendous amount of pessimism about the direction of the economy.

QUESTION:

Suppose that your college savings fund of $100,000, all invested in stocks, was reduced in value to $25,000 because of a stock market crash. Explain how that would affect your spending for college (including your choice of school) and spending for other goods and services.

Unemployment

Two problems that arise over the course of the business cycle are unemployment and inflation. Let's look at unemployment first.

Measurement of Unemployment

The U.S. Bureau of Labor Statistics (BLS) conducts a nationwide random survey of some 60,000 households each month to determine who is employed and who is not. It asks which members of the household are working, unemployed and looking for work, not looking for work, and so on. From the answers, it determines the nation's unemployment rate.

Figure 11.2 helps explain the mathematics. It divides the total U.S. population into four groups. One group is made up of people less than 16 years of age and people who are institutionalized, for example, in psychological hospitals or correctional institutions. These people are assumed to be unemployable due to their circumstances. A second group, "Not in labor force," is composed of noninstitutionalized people 16 years of age or older who are neither employed nor seeking work. They include stay-at-home parents, full-time students, and retirees. The third and fourth groups combined form the **labor force,** which constituted about 50 percent of the total

labor force
Persons 16 years of age and older who are not in institutions and who are employed or are unemployed and seeking work.

unemployment rate
The percentage of the labor force unemployed at any time.

population in 2018. The labor force consists of people who are employed—those who both want and have a job—and the unemployed, those without a job but who want a job *and* are actively seeking work. The **unemployment rate** is the percentage of the labor force unemployed:

$$\text{Unemployment rate} = \frac{\text{unemployed}}{\text{labor force}} \times 100$$

The statistics underlying the rounded numbers in **Figure 11.2** show that in 2018 the unemployment rate averaged

$$\frac{6,300,000}{163,200,000} \times 100 = 3.9\%$$

FIGURE 11.2

The labor force, employment, and unemployment, 2018. The labor force consists of persons 16 years of age or older who are not in institutions and who are (1) employed or (2) unemployed but seeking employment.

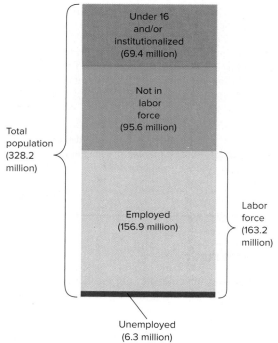

Source: Bureau of Labor Statistics, www.bls.gov (civilian labor force data, which excludes military employment).

Types of Unemployment

There are three types of unemployment: frictional, structural, and cyclical.

Frictional Unemployment At any moment, some workers are "between jobs." Some of them are moving voluntarily from one job to another. Others have been fired and are seeking reemployment. Still others have been laid off because they work seasonal jobs and the season just changed. In addition to those between jobs, many young workers will be searching for their first jobs.

As these unemployed people find jobs or are called back from temporary layoffs, other job seekers and laid-off workers replace them in the "unemployment pool." While the pool itself persists because newly unemployed workers are always flowing into it, most workers do not stay in the unemployment pool for very long. Indeed, when the economy is strong, most unemployed workers find new jobs within a couple of months. We should be careful not to confuse the permanence of the pool itself with the false idea that the pool's membership is permanent, too. That being said, there *are* workers who do remain unemployed and in the unemployment pool for many months or even several years.

Economists use the term **frictional unemployment,** or *search unemployment,* for workers who are unemployed as they actively search for a job. The word "frictional" reflects the fact that the labor market does not operate perfectly and instantaneously (without friction) in matching workers and jobs.

frictional unemployment
A type of unemployment caused by workers voluntarily changing jobs and by temporary layoffs; unemployed workers between jobs.

Frictional unemployment is inevitable and, at least in part, desirable. Many people who are between jobs are moving from low-paying, low-productivity jobs to higher-paying, higher-productivity positions. Their new jobs mean greater income for the workers, a better allocation of labor resources, and a larger real GDP for the economy.

Structural Unemployment Frictional unemployment blurs into **structural unemployment.** Changes over time in consumer demand and in technology alter the "structure" of the total demand for labor, both occupationally and geographically.

structural unemployment
Unemployment of workers whose skills are not demanded by employers, who lack sufficient skill to obtain employment, or who cannot easily move to locations where jobs are available.

Occupationally, the demand for certain skills (e.g., sewing clothes or working on farms) may decline or even vanish. The demand for other skills (e.g., designing software or maintaining computer networks) will intensify. Structural unemployment occurs because the composition of the labor force does not respond immediately or completely to the new structure of job opportunities. Workers whose skills and experience have become obsolete or unneeded thus find that they have no marketable talents. They are structurally unemployed until they develop skills that employers want.

Geographically, the demand for labor also changes over time. An example is the migration of industry and thus of employment opportunities from the Snowbelt to the Sunbelt over the past few decades. Another example is the *offshoring* of jobs that occurs when the demand for a particular type of labor shifts from domestic firms to foreign firms. As job opportunities shift from one place to another, some workers become structurally unemployed.

The distinction between frictional and structural unemployment is hazy. The key difference is that *frictionally* unemployed workers have marketable skills and either live in areas where jobs exist or are able to move to areas that have job opportunities. *Structurally* unemployed workers find it hard to obtain new jobs without retraining or additional education. Frictional unemployment is short-term; structural unemployment is more likely to be long-term and consequently more serious.

Cyclical Unemployment Unemployment caused by a decline in total spending is called **cyclical unemployment.** It typically begins in the recession phase of the business cycle. As the demand for goods and services decreases, employment falls and unemployment rises. The 25 percent unemployment rate in 1933 reflected mainly cyclical unemployment, as did significant parts of the 9.7 percent unemployment rate in 1982, the 7.5 percent rate in 1992, the 9.3 percent rate in 2009, and the 14.8 percent rate in April 2020.

cyclical unemployment
A type of unemployment caused by insufficient total spending (or by insufficient aggregate demand).

Cyclical unemployment is a very serious problem when it occurs. To understand its costs, we need to define "full employment."

APPLYING THE ANALYSIS

Downwardly Sticky Wages and Unemployment

© JGI/Jamie Grill/Getty Images RF

Labor markets have an important quirk that helps to explain why unemployment goes up so much during a recession.

The quirk is that wages are flexible upward but sticky downward.

On the one hand, workers are perfectly happy to accept wage increases. So when the economy is booming and firms start bidding for the limited supply of labor, wages rise— often quite rapidly.

On the other hand, workers deeply resent pay cuts. So if the economy goes into a recession and firms need to reduce labor costs, managers almost never cut wages because doing so would only lead to disgruntled employees, low productivity, and—in extreme cases—workers stealing supplies or actively sabotaging their own firms.

Instead, managers usually opt for layoffs. The workers who are let go obviously don't like being unemployed. But those who remain get to keep their old wages. As a result, they keep on being as productive and cooperative as they were before.

The preference that managers show for layoffs over wage cuts results in downwardly sticky wages and an informal price floor that help to explain why unemployment goes up so much during a recession. The problem is that when the demand for labor falls during a recession, the informal price floor prevents wages from falling. As a result, there is no way for falling wages to help entice at least some firms to hire a few more workers. Thus, when a recession hits, employment falls more precipitously than it would have if wages had been downwardly flexible.

Definition of Full Employment

potential output
The real output (GDP) an economy can produce when it fully employs its available resources.

Because frictional and structural unemployment are largely unavoidable in a dynamic economy, *full employment* is something less than 100 percent employment of the labor force. Economists say that the economy is "fully employed" when it is experiencing only frictional and structural unemployment. That is, full employment occurs when there is no cyclical unemployment. Most economists believe that the economy is fully employed when the unemployment rate is between 4 and 5 percent. The level of real GDP that occurs when labor and other inputs are "fully employed" is called **potential output** (or *potential GDP*).

Economic Cost of Unemployment

The basic economic cost of unemployment is forgone output. When the economy fails to create enough jobs for all who have the necessary skills and are willing to work, potential production is irretrievably lost. The presence of cyclical unemployment means that society is operating at some point inside its production possibilities curve. Economists call this sacrifice of output a **GDP gap**—the difference between actual and potential GDP. That is:

$$\text{GDP gap} = \text{actual GDP} - \text{potential GDP}$$

GDP gap
Actual gross domestic product minus potential output; may be either a positive amount (a positive GDP gap) or a negative amount (a negative GDP gap).

The GDP gap can be either a negative number (actual GDP is less than potential GDP) or a positive number (actual GDP exceeds potential GDP). There is a close correlation between the actual unemployment rate and the GDP gap. The higher the unemployment rate, the greater is the negative GDP gap.

Society's cost of unemployment—its forgone output—translates to forgone income for individuals. This loss of income is borne unequally. Some groups have higher unemployment rates than others and bear the brunt of rising rates during recessions. For instance, workers in lower-skilled occupations (e.g., laborers) have higher unemployment rates than workers in higher-skilled occupations (e.g., professionals). Lower-skilled workers have more and longer spells of structural unemployment than higher-skilled workers. They also are less likely to be self-employed than are higher-skilled workers. Manufacturing, construction, and mining workers tend to be particularly hard-hit, but businesses generally retain most of their higher-skilled workers, in whom they have invested the expense of training.

Less-educated workers, on average, have higher unemployment rates than workers with more education. Less education is usually associated with lower-skilled, less- permanent jobs; more time between jobs; and jobs that are more vulnerable to cyclical layoff.

The unemployment rates for men and women normally are very similar. But during the 2007–2009 recession, the unemployment rate for men significantly exceeded that for women. In 2020, women initially suffered more unemployment during the pandemic, but toward the end of the year the rates for men and women were similar.

Teenagers have much higher unemployment rates than adults. Teenagers have lower skill levels, quit their jobs more frequently, are more frequently fired, and have less geographic mobility than adults. Many unemployed teenagers are new in the labor market, searching for their first jobs. The unemployment rate for teenagers rises dramatically during recessions; in the early days of the pandemic, the teenage unemployment rate exceeded 32 percent.

Finally, the overall unemployment rate for African Americans and Hispanics is higher than that for whites and Asians. The causes of the higher rates include lower rates of educational attainment, greater concentration in lower-skilled occupations, and discrimination in the labor market. In general, the unemployment rate for African Americans is twice that of whites, with male African American teenagers having among the highest unemployment rates of any demographic group.

Inflation

Inflation is a rise in the general level of prices. When inflation occurs, each dollar of income buys fewer goods and services than before. Inflation reduces the "purchasing power" of money. But inflation does not mean that *all* prices are rising. Even during periods of rapid inflation, some prices may be relatively constant and others may even fall. For example, although the United States experienced high rates of inflation in the 1970s and early 1980s, the prices of video recorders, digital watches, and personal computers declined.

inflation
A rise in the general level of prices in an economy.

Measurement of Inflation

Consumer Price Index (CPI)
An index that measures the prices of a fixed "market basket" of some 300 goods and services bought by a "typical" consumer.

The **Consumer Price Index (CPI)** is the main measure of inflation in the United States. Compiled by the Bureau of Labor Statistics (BLS), the government uses this index to report inflation rates each month and each year. It also uses the CPI to adjust Social Security benefits and income tax brackets for inflation. The CPI reports the price of a "market basket" of some 300 consumer goods and services that are purchased by typical urban consumers.

The composition of the market basket for the CPI is based on spending patterns of urban consumers in a specific period, presently 2013-2014. The BLS updates the composition of the market basket every few years so it reflects the most recent patterns of consumer purchases and captures current inflation. The BLS arbitrarily sets the CPI equal to 100 for 1982–1984. So the CPI for any particular year is found as follows:

$$CPI = \frac{\text{price of the most recent market basket in the particular year}}{\text{price of the same market basket in 1982–1984}}$$

The inflation rate is equal to the percentage growth of the CPI from one year to the next. For example, the CPI rose from 245.1 in 2017 to 251.1 in 2018. So the rate of inflation for 2018 was 2.4 percent.

$$\text{Rate of inflation} = \frac{251.1 - 245.1}{245.1} \times 100 = 2.4\%$$

deflation
A decline in the economy's price level.

In rare cases, the CPI declines from one year to the next. For example, the CPI fell from 215.3 in 2008 to 214.5 in 2009. The rate of inflation for 2009 therefore was −0.4 percent. A decline in the price level is called **deflation.**

In **Chapter 10**, we discussed the *rule of 70,* which tells us that we can find the number of years it will take for some measure to double, assuming that it grows at a constant annual percentage rate. To do so, we divide the number 70 by the annual percentage growth rate. Inflation is the growth rate of the price level, so a 3 percent annual inflation rate will double the price level in about 23 (= 70/3) years.

Facts of Inflation

Figure 11.3 shows December-to-December rates of annual inflation in the United States between 1960 and 2018. Observe that inflation reached double-digit rates in the 1970s and early 1980s before declining. It remained muted during the 10-year period following the Great Recession of 2007–2009.

FIGURE 11.3

Annual inflation rates in the United States, 1960–2018 (December-to-December changes in the CPI). Since 1960, the major periods of rapid inflation in the United States were in the 1970s and 1980s.

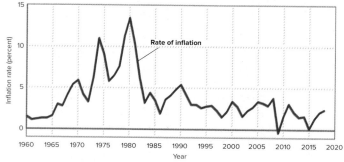

Source: Bureau of Labor Statistics, www.bls.gov.

In recent years, U.S. inflation has been neither unusually high nor unusually low relative to inflation in several other industrial countries (see **Global Snapshot 11.1**). By contrast, some other nations (not shown) have had double-digit or even higher annual rates of inflation in recent years. In 2017, for example, the annual inflation rate in Ukraine was 14 percent; Argentina, 25 percent; Libya, 33 percent; Yemen, 53 percent; and Venezuela, 1.4 *million* percent.

GLOBAL SNAPSHOT 11.1

Inflation Rates in Five Industrial Nations, 2008–2018

Inflation rates in the United States in recent years were neither extraordinarily high nor extraordinarily low relative to rates in other industrial nations.

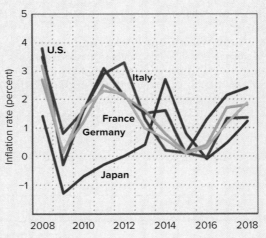

Source: International Monetary Fund, www.imf.org.

Types of Inflation

Nearly all prices in the economy are set by supply and demand. So if the overall price level is rising, we need to look for an explanation in terms of supply and demand. Reflecting this, economists distinguish between two types of inflation: *demand-pull inflation* and *cost-push inflation.*

Demand-Pull Inflation   Usually, increases in the price level are caused by an excess of total spending beyond the economy's capacity to produce. Where inflation is rapid and sustained, the cause invariably is an overissuance of money by the central bank (the Federal Reserve in the United States). When resources are already fully employed, the business sector cannot respond to excess demand by expanding output. So the excess demand bids up the prices of the limited output, producing **demand-pull inflation.** The essence of this type of inflation is "too much spending chasing too few goods."

demand-pull inflation
Increases in the price level (inflation) resulting from an excess of demand over output at the existing price level, caused by an increase in aggregate demand.

ILLUSTRATING THE IDEA

Clipping Coins

Some interesting early episodes of demand-pull inflation occurred in Europe from the ninth to fifteenth centuries under feudalism. In that economic system, *lords* (or *princes*) ruled individual fiefdoms, and their *vassals* (or *peasants*) worked the fields. The peasants initially paid parts of their harvest as taxes to the princes. Later, when the princes began issuing "coins of the realm," peasants began paying their taxes with gold coins.

Some princes soon discovered a way to transfer purchasing power from their vassals to themselves without explicitly increasing taxes. As coins came into the treasury, princes clipped off parts of the gold coins, making them slightly smaller. From the clippings they minted new coins and used them to buy more goods for themselves.

This practice of clipping coins was a subtle form of taxation. The quantity of goods being produced in the fiefdom remained the same, but the number of gold coins increased. With "too much money chasing too few goods," inflation occurred. Each gold coin earned by the peasants therefore had less purchasing power than previously because prices were higher. The increase of the money supply shifted purchasing power away from the peasants and toward the princes just as surely as if the princes had increased taxation of the peasants.

In more recent eras, some dictators have simply printed money to buy more goods for themselves, their relatives, and their key loyalists. These dictators, too, have levied hidden taxes on their population by creating inflation.

The moral of the story is quite simple: A society that values price-level stability should not entrust the control of its money supply to people who benefit from inflation.

> **QUESTION:**
>
> Why might a government with a huge foreign debt be tempted to increase its domestic money supply and cause inflation?

Cost-Push Inflation Inflation may also arise on the supply, or cost, side of the economy. During some periods in U.S. economic history, including the mid-1970s, the price level increased even though total spending was not excessive. These were periods when output and employment were both *declining* (evidence that total spending was not excessive), while the general price level was *rising.*

cost-push inflation
Increases in the price level (inflation) resulting from an increase in resource costs (e.g., raw-material prices) and hence in per-unit production costs; inflation caused by reductions in aggregate supply.

The theory of **cost-push inflation** explains rising prices in terms of factors that raise per-unit (average) production costs at each level of output. Rising per-unit production costs squeeze profits and reduce the economy's supply of goods and services. In this scenario, costs are *pushing* the price level upward, whereas in demand-pull inflation, demand is *pulling* it upward.

The major source of cost-push inflation has been *supply shocks.* Specifically, abrupt increases in the costs of raw materials or energy inputs have, on occasion, driven up per-unit production costs and thus product prices. The rocketing prices of imported oil in 1973–1974 and again in 1979–1980 are good illustrations. As energy prices surged upward during these periods, the costs of producing and transporting virtually every product in the economy rose, and so cost-push inflation ensued.

Redistribution Effects of Inflation

Inflation redistributes real income. This redistribution helps some people and hurts others, while leaving many people largely unaffected. Who gets hurt? Who benefits? Before we can answer, we need some terminology.

There is a difference between money (nominal) income and real income. **Nominal income** is the number of dollars received as wages, rent, interest, or profit. **Real income** measures the amount of goods and services nominal income can buy; it is the purchasing power of nominal income, or income adjusted for inflation, and it is calculated as follows:

$$\text{Real income} = \frac{\text{nominal income}}{\text{price index (in hundredths)}}$$

Inflation need not alter an economy's overall real income—its total purchasing power. The above equation makes it clear that real income will remain the same when nominal income rises at the same percentage rate as the price index.

But when inflation occurs, not everyone's nominal income rises at the same pace as the price level. Therein lies the potential for redistribution of real income. If the change in the price level differs from the change in a person's nominal income, their real income will be affected. The following approximation (shown by the $\cong$ sign) tells us roughly how much real income will change:

$$\begin{matrix} \text{Percentage} \\ \text{change in} \\ \text{real income} \end{matrix} \cong \begin{matrix} \text{Percentage} \\ \text{change in} \\ \text{nominal income} \end{matrix} - \begin{matrix} \text{Percentage} \\ \text{change in} \\ \text{price level} \end{matrix}$$

For example, suppose that the price level rises by 6 percent in some period. If Jamal's nominal income rises by 6 percent, his real income will *remain unchanged.* But if his nominal income instead rises by 10 percent, his real income will *increase* by about 4 percent. And if Jamal's nominal income rises by only 2 percent, his real income will *decline* by about 4 percent.

The redistribution effects of inflation depend on whether or not it is expected. With fully expected or *anticipated inflation,* an income receiver may be able to avoid or lessen the adverse effects of inflation on real income. The generalizations that follow assume *unanticipated inflation*—inflation whose full extent was not expected.

Who Is Hurt by Inflation?

Unanticipated inflation hurts fixed-income recipients, savers, and creditors. It redistributes real income away from them and toward others.

Fixed-Income Receivers People whose nominal incomes are fixed see their real incomes fall when inflation occurs. The classic case is the elderly couple living on a private pension or annuity that provides a fixed amount of nominal income each month. They may have retired in, say, 1998, on what appeared to be an adequate pension. However, by 2018, they would have discovered that inflation had cut the annual purchasing power of that pension—their real income—by one-third.

Similarly, rental property owners who receive lease payments of fixed dollar amounts will be hurt by inflation as they receive dollars of declining value over time. Likewise, public sector workers whose incomes are based on fixed pay schedules may see a decrease in purchasing power. The fixed "steps" (the upward yearly increases) in their pay schedules may not keep up with inflation. Minimum-wage workers and families living on fixed welfare incomes are also hurt by inflation.

nominal income
The number of dollars received by an individual or group for supplying resources during some period of time; income that is not adjusted for inflation.

real income
The amount of goods and services that can be purchased with nominal income during some period of time; nominal income adjusted for inflation.

Savers Unanticipated inflation hurts savers. As prices rise, the real value, or purchasing power, of accumulated savings deteriorates. Paper assets such as savings accounts, insurance policies, and annuities that once were adequate to meet rainy-day contingencies or provide for a comfortable retirement decline in real value. The simple case is the person who hoards cash. A $1,000 cash balance lost one-third its real value between 1995 and 2015. Of course, most forms of savings earn interest. But the value of savings will still decline if the inflation rate exceeds the interest rate.

Creditors Unanticipated inflation harms creditors (lenders). Suppose Chase Bank lends Cala $1,000, to be repaid in two years. If in that time the price level doubles, the $1,000 that Cala repays will possess only half the purchasing power of the $1,000 borrowed. As prices go up, the purchasing power of the dollar goes down. So the borrower pays back less-valuable dollars than those received from the lender. The owners of Chase Bank suffer a loss of real income.

Who Is Unaffected or Helped by Inflation?

Some people are unaffected by inflation, and others are actually helped by it. For the second group, inflation redistributes real income toward them and away from others.

Flexible-Income Receivers People who have flexible nominal incomes may escape inflation's harm or even benefit from it. For example, individuals who derive their incomes solely from Social Security are largely unaffected by inflation because Social Security payments are *indexed* to the CPI. Benefits automatically increase when the CPI increases, preventing inflation from eroding their purchasing power. Some union workers also get automatic *cost-of-living adjustments (COLAs)* in their pay when the CPI rises, although such increases rarely equal the full percentage rise in inflation.

Some flexible-income receivers are helped by unanticipated inflation. The strong product demand and labor shortages implied by rapid demand-pull inflation may cause some nominal incomes to spurt ahead of the price level, thereby enhancing real incomes. As an example, property owners faced with an inflation-induced real estate boom may be able to boost rents more rapidly than the rate of inflation. Also, some business owners may benefit from inflation. If product prices rise faster than their resource prices, business revenues will increase more rapidly than costs.

Debtors Unanticipated inflation benefits debtors (borrowers). In our earlier example, Chase Bank's loss of real income from inflation is Cala's gain of real income. Debtor Cala borrows "dear" dollars but, because of inflation, pays back the principal and interest with "cheap" dollars whose purchasing power has been eroded by inflation. Real income is redistributed away from the owners of Chase Bank toward borrowers such as Cala.

Anticipated Inflation

The redistribution effects of inflation are less severe or eliminated altogether if people anticipate inflation and can adjust their nominal incomes to reflect expected increases in the price level. The prolonged inflation that began in the late 1960s prompted many labor unions in the 1970s to insist on labor contracts that provided cost-of-living adjustments.

Similarly, if inflation is anticipated, the redistribution of income from lender to borrower may be altered. Suppose a lender (perhaps a bank) and a borrower (a household) both agree that 5 percent is a fair rate of interest on a one-year loan provided the price level is constant. But assume that inflation has been occurring and is expected to be 6 percent over the next year. The lender will neutralize inflation by charging

11 percent, the 5 percent rate plus an *inflation premium* of 6 percent, the amount of the anticipated inflation.

Our example reveals the difference between the real rate of interest and the nominal rate of interest. The **real interest rate** is the percentage increase in *purchasing power* that the borrower pays the lender. In our example, the real interest rate is 5 percent. The **nominal interest rate** is the percentage increase in *money* that the borrower pays the lender, including that resulting from the built-in expectation of inflation, if any. In equation form:

Nominal interest rate = real interest rate + inflation premium
(the expected rate of inflation)

As illustrated in **Figure 11.4**, the nominal interest rate in our example is 11 percent.

real interest rate
The interest rate expressed in dollars of constant value (adjusted for inflation) and equal to the nominal interest rate less the expected rate of inflation.

nominal interest rate
The interest rate expressed in terms of annual amounts currently charged for interest and not adjusted for inflation.

FIGURE 11.4
The inflation premium and nominal and real interest rates. The inflation premium—the expected rate of inflation—gets built into the nominal interest rate. Here, the nominal interest rate of 11 percent comprises the real interest rate of 5 percent plus the inflation premium of 6 percent.

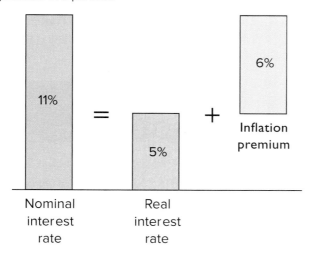

Does Inflation Affect Output?

Thus far, our discussion has focused on how inflation redistributes a given level of total real income. But inflation also may affect an economy's level of real output (and thus its level of real income).

Cost-Push Inflation and Real Output

Recall that abrupt and unexpected increases in prices of key resources such as oil can drive up overall production costs and generate cost-push inflation. As prices rise, the quantity of goods and services demanded falls. Firms respond by producing less output, and unemployment goes up.

Demand-Pull Inflation and Real Output

Economists do not fully agree on the effects of mild inflation (less than 3 percent) on real output.

Some economists believe that even low levels of inflation reduce real output because inflation diverts time and effort toward activities designed to hedge against inflation. For example:

- Businesses incur the cost of changing thousands of prices on their shelves and in their computers simply to keep up with inflation.
- Households and businesses spend considerable time and effort obtaining the information they need to distinguish between real and nominal prices, wages, and interest rates.

These economists argue that without inflation, more time and effort would be spent producing valuable goods and services. Proponents of "zero inflation" bolster their case by pointing to cross-country studies indicating that lower inflation rates are associated with higher rates of economic growth. Even mild inflation, say these economists, is detrimental to economic growth.

Other economists note that full employment and economic growth depend on strong levels of total spending. They argue that strong spending creates high profits, strong demand for labor, and a powerful incentive for firms to expand their plants and equipment. In this view, the mild inflation that is a by-product of strong spending is a small price to pay for full employment and continued economic growth. Defenders of mild inflation argue that it is much better for an economy to err on the side of strong spending, full employment, economic growth, and mild inflation than on the side of weak spending, unemployment, recession, and deflation.

 APPLYING THE ANALYSIS

The Specter of Deflation

Inflation rates typically rise during the expansion phase of the business cycle as demand increases faster than supply throughout the economy. But when the peak is past and the recession phase of the business cycle begins, the inflation rate will tend to decline as unemployment rises and the demand for goods and services declines. In some cases, the decrease in demand may be so precipitous that deflation (a falling price level) becomes a possibility.

Economists fear deflation because it can lead to a wave of bankruptcies among firms that owe money. With prices falling, firms have a hard time making enough revenue to pay back their loans. If enough bankruptcies occur, deflation may accelerate as workers are laid off and demand decreases even more. The downward spiral may be further exacerbated if consumers delay purchases in anticipation of lower future prices. After all, why buy something today if its price is expected to be substantially lower in a month?

To prevent the downward spiral of deflation, central banks use monetary policy to try to always maintain a positive inflation rate. They are almost always successful, so that deflation hardly ever takes hold, even after severe recessions like the Great Recession of 2007–2009. That's good news, because with inflation always at least a little bit positive, a downward deflationary spiral can't get started.

QUESTION:

Consumers prefer and seek out lower prices. Why is it good for consumers to have prices of *some* goods lower, but not to have a lower price level overall?

APPLYING THE ANALYSIS

Hyperinflation

All economists agree that *hyperinflation,* defined as extraordinarily rapid inflation, can have a devastating impact on real output and employment.

- As prices shoot up during hyperinflation, normal economic relationships are disrupted. Business owners do not know what to charge for their products. Consumers do not know what to pay.
- Production declines because businesses, anticipating further price increases, find that it makes more financial sense to hoard (rather than use) materials and to stockpile (rather than sell) finished products. Why sell today when the same product will fetch more money tomorrow?
- Investment declines as savers refuse to extend loans to businesses, knowing that the loans will be repaid with rapidly depreciating money.
- Many people give up on money altogether and revert to barter, causing production and exchange to drop further as people spend hours every day trading and bartering instead of working and producing.
- The net result is economic collapse and, often, political chaos.

Andrey_Popov/Shutterstock

Examples of hyperinflation are Germany after the First World War and Japan after the Second World War. In Germany, "prices increased so rapidly that waiters changed the prices on the menu several times during the course of a lunch. Sometimes customers had to pay double the price listed on the menu when they ordered."[*] In postwar Japan, in 1947 "fishermen and farmers...used scales to weigh currency and change, rather than bothering to count it."[†]

Hyperinflations are always caused by governments instituting highly imprudent expansions of the money supply. The rocketing money supply produces frenzied total spending and severe demand-pull inflation. Zimbabwe's 14.9 billion percent in 2008 is just the worse recent example. Venezuela in 2018 and several dozen other countries over the last century have caused inflation rates of 1 million percent per year or more.

QUESTION:

How would you alter your present spending plans if you were quite certain that the prices of everything were going to double in the coming week?

---

[*] Theodore Morgan, *Income and Employment*, 2nd ed. (Englewood Cliffs, N.J.: Prentice-Hall, 1952), p. 361.

[†] Raburn M. Williams, *Inflation! Money, Jobs, and Politicians* (Arlington Heights, IL: AHM Publishing, 1980), p. 2.

Summary

LO11.1 Describe the phases of the business cycle.
Business cycles are recurring ups and downs in economic activity. Their two primary phases are expansions and recessions.

LO11.2 Measure unemployment and inflation.
The U.S. Bureau of Labor Statistics (BLS) surveys 60,000 households each month and categorizes respondents based on whether they are employed, unemployed, or not in the labor force. To be unemployed, one must be without a job and actively seeking work. The BLS calculates the unemployment rate as the percentage of the labor force that is unemployed.

Inflation is a rise in the general price level and is measured in the United States by the Consumer Price Index (CPI). When inflation occurs, each dollar of income will buy fewer goods and services than before. That is, inflation reduces the purchasing power of money. Deflation is a decline in the general price level.

LO11.3 Describe the types of unemployment and inflation and explain their economic impacts.
Economists distinguish between frictional, structural, and cyclical unemployment. The rate of unemployment at full employment consists of frictional and structural unemployment and is currently between 4 and 5 percent.

The economic cost of unemployment, as measured by the negative GDP gap, consists of the goods and services forgone by society when its resources are involuntarily idle.

Economists identify both demand-pull and cost-push (supply-side) inflation. Demand-pull inflation results from an excess of total spending relative to the economy's capacity to produce. The main source of cost-push inflation is abrupt and rapid increases in the prices of key resources. These supply shocks push up per-unit production costs and ultimately raise the prices of consumer goods.

Unanticipated inflation arbitrarily redistributes real income at the expense of fixed-income receivers, creditors, and savers. If inflation is anticipated, individuals and businesses may be able to take steps to lessen or eliminate adverse redistribution effects.

Cost-push inflation reduces real output and employment. Proponents of zero inflation argue that even mild demand-pull inflation (1 to 3 percent) reduces the economy's real output. Other economists say that mild inflation may be a necessary by-product of the high and growing spending that produces high levels of output, full employment, and economic growth.

Deflation occurs when falling demand for goods and services is significant enough to reduce the price level. The falling prices encourage buyers to postpone purchases, reduce business revenue, weaken firms' ability to repay debts, and can spark a wave of bankruptcies that worsen a recession.

Hyperinflation, caused by highly imprudent expansions of the money supply, may undermine the monetary system and severely decrease real output.

Terms and Concepts

business cycles	unemployment rate	deflation
recession	frictional unemployment	demand-pull inflation
expansion	structural unemployment	cost-push inflation
shocks	cyclical unemployment	nominal income
demand shocks	potential output	real income
supply shocks	GDP gap	real interest rate
inflexible prices	inflation	nominal interest rate
labor force	Consumer Price Index (CPI)	

Questions

1. What are the two primary phases of the business cycle? What tends to happen to real GDP, unemployment, and inflation during these phases? **(LO1)**

2. How many recessions has the United States experienced since 1950? Which ones were the longest in duration? Which ones were the most severe in terms of declines in real output? **(LO1)**

3. Even though the United States has an unemployment compensation program that provides income for those out of work, why should we worry about unemployment? **(LO3)**

4. What are the three types of unemployment? Unemployment is seen by some as undesirable. Are all three types of unemployment undesirable? Explain. **(LO3)**

5. What is the Consumer Price Index (CPI), and how is it determined each month? What effect does inflation have on the purchasing power of a dollar? How does it explain differences between nominal and real interest rates? How does deflation differ from inflation? **(LO2)**

6. Distinguish between demand-pull inflation and cost-push inflation. Which of the two types is more likely to be associated with a negative GDP gap? Which is more likely to be associated with a positive GDP gap, in which actual GDP exceeds potential GDP? **(LO3)**

7. How does unanticipated inflation hurt creditors and help borrowers? How can anticipating the inflation make these effects less severe? **(LO3)**

8. How might falling prices that occur during deflation ultimately hurt consumers? **(LO3)**

9. Explain how hyperinflation might lead to a severe decline in total output. **(LO3)**

Problems

1. Suppose that a country's annual growth rates were 5, 3, 4, −1, −2, 2, 3, 4, 6, and 3 in yearly sequence over a 10-year period. What was the country's trend rate of growth over this period? Which set of years most clearly demonstrates an expansionary phase of the business cycle? Which set of years best illustrates a recessionary phase of the business cycle? **(LO1)**

2. Assume the following data for a country: total population, 500; population under 16 years of age or institutionalized, 120; not in labor force, 150; unemployed, 23; part-time workers looking for full-time jobs, 10. What is the size of the labor force? What is the official unemployment rate? **(LO2)**

3. If the CPI was 110 last year and is 121 this year, what is this year's rate of inflation? In contrast, suppose that the CPI was 110 last year and is 108 this year. What is this year's rate of inflation? What term do economists use to describe this second outcome? **(LO3)**

4. How long would it take for the price level to double if inflation persisted at (a) 2 percent per year, (b) 5 percent per year, and (c) 10 percent per year? **(LO3)**

5. If your nominal income rises by 5.3 percent and the price level rises by 3.8 percent in some year, by what percentage will your real income (approximately) increase? If your nominal income rises by 2.8 percent and your real income rises by 1.1 percent in some year, what is the (approximate) inflation rate? **(LO3)**

6. Suppose that the nominal rate of interest is 4 percent and the inflation premium is 2 percent. What is the real interest rate? Alternatively, assume that the real interest rate is 1 percent and the nominal interest rate is 6 percent. What is the inflation premium? **(LO3)**

7. If the inflation premium is 2 percent and the nominal interest rate is 1 percent, what is the real interest rate? What is the real interest rate if the inflation premium is 3 percent while the nominal interest rate is 0.5 percent? **(LO3)**

CHAPTER TWELVE
Aggregate Demand and Aggregate Supply

Learning Objectives

LO12.1 Define aggregate demand (AD) and explain the factors that cause it to change.

LO12.2 Define aggregate supply (AS) and explain the factors that cause it to change.

LO12.3 Explain how AD and AS determine an economy's equilibrium price level and real GDP.

LO12.4 Use the AD–AS model to explain periods of demand-pull inflation, cost-push inflation, and recession.

During the recession of 2007–2009, the economic terms *aggregate demand* and *aggregate supply* moved from the obscurity of economic journals to the spotlight of national newspapers, websites, and television.

The media and public asked: Why had aggregate demand declined, producing the deepest recession and highest rate of unemployment since 1982? Would the federal government's $787 billion stimulus package increase aggregate demand and reduce unemployment as intended? Would a resurgence of oil prices and other energy prices reduce aggregate supply, choking off an economic expansion?

Aggregate demand and aggregate supply are the featured elements of the **aggregate demand–aggregate supply model (AD–AS model),** the focus of this chapter. The AD–AS model enables us to analyze change in real GDP and the price level simultaneously. The model therefore provides keen insights on inflation, recession, unemployment, and economic growth. In later chapters, we will see that the AD–AS model easily depicts fiscal and monetary policies such as those used in 2008 and 2009 to try to halt the downward slide of the economy and promote its recovery.

Aggregate Demand

Aggregate demand is a schedule or curve that shows the quantities of a nation's output (real GDP) that buyers collectively want to purchase at each possible price level. These buyers include the nation's households, businesses, and government along with consumers located abroad (households, businesses, and governments in other nations).

There is an inverse, or negative, relationship between the economy's overall price level (as measured by the GDP price index) and the amount of real output that is demanded by households, businesses, and governments: When the price level rises, the quantity of real GDP demanded falls; when the price level falls, the quantity of real GDP demanded rises.

Figure 12.1 shows the inverse relationship between the price level and real GDP. The downward slope of the AD curve reflects the fact that higher U.S. price levels discourage domestic buyers (households and businesses) and foreign buyers from purchasing U.S. real GDP. Lower price levels encourage them to buy more U.S. real output.

aggregate demand–aggregate supply (AD–AS) model
The macroeconomic model that uses aggregate demand and aggregate supply to determine and explain the price level and the real domestic output.

aggregate demand
The real amounts of domestic output that domestic consumers, businesses, governments and foreign buyers collectively will desire to purchase at each possible price level.

FIGURE 12.1

The aggregate demand curve. The downward-sloping aggregate demand curve AD indicates an inverse (or negative) relationship between the price level and the amount of real output purchased.

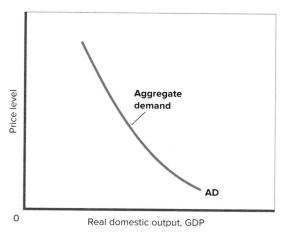

Changes in Aggregate Demand

Other things equal, a change in the price level will change the amount of total spending and therefore change the amount of real GDP demanded by the economy. Movements along a fixed aggregate demand curve represent changes in the amount of real GDP demanded that occur in response to a change in the price level. However, if one or more of those "other things" change, the entire aggregate demand curve will shift. We call these other things **determinants of aggregate demand.** When they change, they shift the AD curve. These AD shifters are listed in **Table 12.1**, at the bottom of **Figure 12.2**. In that figure, the rightward shift of the curve from AD_1 to AD_2 shows an increase in aggregate demand. The leftward shift from AD_1 to AD_3 shows a decrease in aggregate demand. Notice that the categories of spending are the same as those in the national income and product accounts (**Chapter 10**). To provide a clear understanding of these AD shifters, we need to elaborate on them.

determinants of aggregate demand
Factors such as consumption spending, investment, government spending, and net exports that, if they change, shift the aggregate demand curve.

TABLE 12.1

Determinants of Aggregate Demand: Factors That Shift the Aggregate Demand Curve

1. Change in consumer spending
   a. Consumer wealth
   b. Household borrowing
   c. Consumer expectations
   d. Personal taxes
2. Change in investment spending
   a. Interest rates
   b. Expected returns
      • Expected future business conditions
      • Technology
      • Degree of excess capacity
      • Business taxes
3. Change in government spending
4. Change in net export spending
   a. National income abroad
   b. Exchange rates

FIGURE 12.2

Changes in aggregate demand. A change in one or more of the listed determinants of aggregate demand will shift the aggregate demand curve. The rightward shift from AD_1 to AD_2 represents an increase in aggregate demand; the leftward shift from AD_1 to AD_3 shows a decrease in aggregate demand.

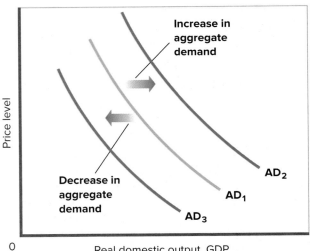

Consumer Spending

If consumers decide to buy more output at each price level, the aggregate demand curve shifts to the right, as from AD_1 to AD_2 in **Figure 12.2**. If they decide to buy less output, the aggregate demand curve will shift to the left, as from AD_1 to AD_3.

Several factors other than a change in the price level may change consumer spending and therefore shift the aggregate demand curve. As the table in **Figure 12.2** shows, those factors are real consumer wealth, household borrowing, consumer expectations, and personal taxes.

Consumer Wealth Consumer wealth is the total dollar value of all assets owned by consumers in the economy, less the dollar value of their liabilities (debts). Assets include stocks, bonds, and real estate. Liabilities include mortgages, student loans, and credit card balances.

Consumer wealth sometimes changes suddenly and unexpectedly due to surprising changes in asset values. An unforeseen increase in the stock market is a good example. The increase in wealth prompts pleasantly surprised consumers to save less and buy more. The resulting increase in consumer spending—the so-called *wealth effect*—shifts the aggregate demand curve to the right. In contrast, an unexpected decline in asset values will cause an unanticipated reduction in consumer wealth at each price level. As consumers tighten their belts in response to the bad news, a "reverse wealth effect" sets in. Unpleasantly surprised consumers increase savings and reduce consumption, thereby shifting the aggregate demand curve to the left.

Household Borrowing Consumers can increase their consumption spending by borrowing. Doing so shifts the aggregate demand curve to the right. By contrast, a decrease in borrowing for consumption purposes shifts the aggregate demand curve to the left. The aggregate demand curve also will shift to the left if consumers increase their savings to pay off their debts. With more money flowing to debt repayment, consumption expenditures decline and the AD curve shifts left.

Consumer Expectations Changes in expectations about the future may alter consumer spending. When people expect their future real incomes to rise, they tend to spend more of their current incomes. Thus, current consumption spending increases (current saving falls), and the aggregate demand curve shifts to the right. Similarly, a widely held expectation of surging inflation in the near future may increase aggregate demand today because consumers will want to buy products before their prices escalate. Conversely, expectations of lower future income or lower future prices may reduce current consumption and shift the aggregate demand curve to the left.

Personal Taxes A reduction in personal income tax rates raises take-home income and increases consumer purchases at each possible price level. Tax cuts shift the aggregate demand curve to the right. Tax increases reduce consumption spending and shift the curve to the left.

APPLYING THE ANALYSIS

What Wealth Effect?

The consumption component of aggregate demand is usually relatively stable even during rather extraordinary times. Between March 2000 and July 2002, the U.S. stock market lost a staggering $3.7 trillion of value (yes, trillion). Yet consumption spending was greater at the end of that period than at the beginning. How can that be? Why didn't a negative wealth effect reduce consumption?

There are a number of reasons. Of greatest importance, the amount of consumption spending in the economy depends mainly on the *flow* of income, not the *stock* of wealth. At the time, disposable income (after-tax income) in the United States was nearly $9 trillion annually, and consumers spent a large portion of it. Even though there was a mild recession in 2001, disposable income and consumption spending were both greater in July 2002 than in March 2000. Second, the federal government cut personal income tax rates during this period, and that bolstered consumption spending. Third, household wealth did not fall by the full amount of the $3.7 trillion stock market loss because the value of houses increased dramatically over this period. Finally, lower interest rates during this period enabled many households to refinance their mortgages, reduce monthly loan payments, and increase their current consumption. For all these offsetting reasons, the consumption component of aggregate demand held up in the face of the extraordinary loss of stock market value.

The 2007–2009 recession tells a somewhat different story, with consumption falling, but not enough to definitively establish the presence of a wealth effect. Between losses in both the housing and stock markets, U.S. household wealth decreased by about $14 trillion from June 2007 to March 2009, and economic contraction began in December 2007. However, in part because of federal government policies to stimulate spending, household disposable income did not fall until the second half of 2008, reaching a low point in early 2009 and then beginning a slow but steady increase. Consumption spending followed a similar pattern, declining in the latter part of 2008 and bottoming out in the first quarter of 2009. While most economists agree that wealth losses from the housing and financial market crises contributed to lower consumption (or, at the very least, slower growth in consumption spending), the reductions in household expenditures appear to have been far less substantial than one might have anticipated.

QUESTION:

Which do you think will decrease consumption more: a 10 percent decrease in after-tax income or a 10 percent decrease in stock market values? Explain.

Investment Spending

Investment spending (the purchase of capital goods) is a second major determinant of aggregate demand. Increases in investment spending at each price level boost aggregate demand, and decreases in investment spending reduce it.

The investment decision is a marginal benefit–marginal cost decision. The marginal benefit of the investment is a stream of higher profits that is expected to result from the investment. In percentage terms, economists call these higher profits (net of new operation expenses) the *expected return on the investment, r*. For example, suppose the owner of a small cabinetmaking shop is considering whether to invest in a new sanding machine that costs $1,000, expands output, and has a useful life of only one year. (Extending the life of the machine beyond one year complicates the economic calculation but does not change the fundamental analysis.) Suppose the net expected revenue from the machine (i.e., after such operating costs as power, lumber, labor, and certain taxes have been subtracted) is $1,100. Then the expected net revenue is sufficient to cover the initial $1,000 cost of the machine and leave a profit of $100. Comparing this $100 to the $1,000 initial cost of the machine, we find that the expected rate of return, *r*, on the investment is 10 percent (= $100/$1,000).

It is important to note that the return just discussed is an *expected* rate of return, not a *guaranteed* rate of return. Investment involves risk, so the investment may or may not pay off as anticipated. Moreover, investment faces diminishing returns. As more of it occurs, the best investment projects are completed and the subsequent projects produce lower expected rates of return. So, the expected return, r, tends to fall as firms undertake more and more investment.

The marginal cost of the investment to a firm is reflected in either the explicit costs of borrowing money from others or the implicit cost of using its own retained earnings to make the investment. In percentage terms, and adjusted for expected inflation, this cost is the real interest rate, i.

The business firm compares the real interest rate (marginal cost) with the expected return on investment (marginal benefit). If the expected rate of return (e.g., 6 percent) exceeds the interest rate (say, 5 percent), the investment is undertaken. The firm expects the investment to be profitable. But if the interest rate (e.g., 7 percent) exceeds the expected rate of return (6 percent), the investment will not be undertaken. The firm expects the investment to be unprofitable. The profit-maximizing firm will undertake all investments that it thinks will be profitable. That means it will invest up to the point where $r = i$ in order to exhaust all investment possibilities for which r exceeds i.

So real interest rates and expected returns are the two main determinants of investment spending.

Real Interest Rates   Other things equal, increases in real interest rates will raise borrowing costs, lower investment spending, and reduce aggregate demand. Declines in interest rates will have the opposite effects. As we will discover later, a nation's central bank—the Federal Reserve in the United States—can take monetary actions to increase and decrease interest rates. When it takes those actions, it shifts the nation's aggregate demand curve.

Expected Returns   Higher expected returns on investment projects will increase the demand for capital goods and shift the aggregate demand curve to the right. Alternatively, declines in expected returns will decrease investment and shift the curve to the left. Expected returns are influenced by several factors:

- *Future business conditions* If firms are optimistic about future business conditions, they are more likely to forecast high rates of return on current investment and therefore may invest more today. In contrast, if they think the economy will deteriorate in the future, they will forecast low rates of return and perhaps invest less today.

- *Technology* New and improved technologies enhance expected returns on investment and thus increase aggregate demand. For example, recent advances in microbiology have motivated pharmaceutical companies to establish new labs and production facilities.

- *Changes in excess capacity* A rise in excess capacity—unused capital—reduces the expected return on new investment and hence decreases aggregate demand. Other things equal, firms operating factories at well below capacity have little incentive to build new factories. But when firms discover that their excess capacity is dwindling or has completely disappeared, their expected returns on new investment in factories and capital equipment rise. Thus, they increase their investment spending, and aggregate demand curve shifts to the right.

- *Business taxes* An increase in business taxes will reduce after-tax profits from capital investment and lower expected returns. As a result, investment and aggregate demand will decline. A decrease in business taxes has the opposite effect.

The variability of interest rates and expected returns makes investment highly volatile. Unlike consumption, investment spending rises and falls often, independent of changes in total income. Investment, in fact, is the least stable component of aggregate demand.

Global Snapshot 12.1 compares investment spending relative to GDP for several nations in 2018.

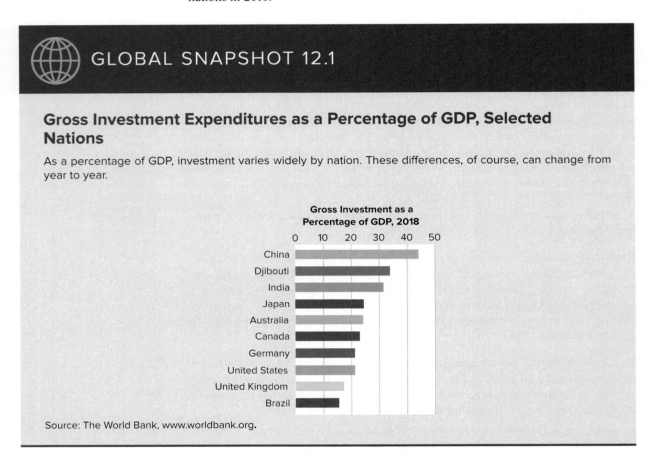

GLOBAL SNAPSHOT 12.1

Gross Investment Expenditures as a Percentage of GDP, Selected Nations

As a percentage of GDP, investment varies widely by nation. These differences, of course, can change from year to year.

Gross Investment as a Percentage of GDP, 2018

Source: The World Bank, www.worldbank.org.

Government Spending

Government purchases are the third determinant of aggregate demand. An increase in government purchases (e.g., more transportation projects) shifts the aggregate demand curve to the right, as long as tax collections and interest rates do not change as a result. In contrast, a reduction in government spending (e.g., less military equipment) shifts the curve to the left.

Net Export Spending

The final determinant of aggregate demand is net export spending. Other things equal, higher U.S. *exports* mean an increased foreign demand for U.S. goods. So a rise in net exports (higher exports relative to imports) shifts the aggregate demand curve to the right. In contrast, a decrease in U.S. net exports shifts the aggregate demand curve leftward.

What might cause net exports to change, other than the price level? Two possibilities are changes in national income abroad and changes in exchange rates.

National Income Abroad   Rising national income abroad encourages foreigners to buy more products, some of which are made in the United States. U.S. net exports thus rise, and the U.S. aggregate demand curve shifts to the right. Declines in national income abroad do the opposite: They reduce U.S. net exports and shift the U.S. aggregate demand curve to the left.

Exchange Rates   Changes in the dollar's **exchange rate**—the price of foreign currencies in terms of the U.S. dollar—may affect U.S. net exports and therefore aggregate demand. Suppose the dollar *depreciates* (declines in value) in terms of the euro (meaning the euro *appreciates* in terms of the dollar). The new, relatively lower value of dollars and higher value of euros enable European consumers to obtain more dollars with each euro. From the perspective of Europeans, U.S. goods are now less expensive; it takes fewer euros to obtain them. So European consumers buy more U.S. goods, and U.S. exports rise. But U.S. consumers can now obtain fewer euros for each dollar. Because they must pay more dollars to buy European goods, Americans reduce their imports. U.S. exports rise, and U.S. imports fall. Conclusion: Dollar depreciation increases net exports (imports go down; exports go up) and therefore increases aggregate demand.

exchange rate
The rate of exchange of one nation's currency for another nation's currency.

Dollar appreciation has the opposite effects: Net exports fall (imports go up; exports go down) and aggregate demand declines.

As shown in **Global Snapshot 12.2**, net exports vary greatly among the major industrial nations.

GLOBAL SNAPSHOT 12.2

Net Exports of Goods and Services, Selected Nations, 2019

Some nations, such as Germany and China, have positive net exports; other countries, such as the United States and the United Kingdom, have negative net exports.

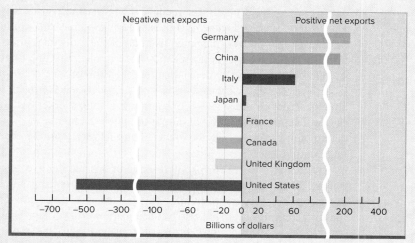

Source: The World Bank **data.worldbank.org.**

Aggregate Supply

aggregate supply
A schedule or curve showing the total quantity of goods and services supplied (produced) at different price levels.

Aggregate supply is a schedule or curve showing the relationship between a nation's price level and the amount of real domestic output that firms produce. This relationship varies depending on the time horizon and how quickly output prices and input prices can change. We will define three time horizons:

- In the *immediate short run*, both input prices and output prices are fixed.
- In the *short run*, input prices are fixed, but output prices can vary.
- In the *long run*, both input prices and output prices can vary.

In **Chapter 11**, we introduced the concept of inflexible (or "sticky") prices. The relationship between the price level and total output is different in each of the three time horizons because input prices are stickier than output prices. Although both become more flexible as time passes, output prices usually adjust more rapidly.

Aggregate Supply in the Immediate Short Run

Depending on the type of firm, the immediate short run can last anywhere from a few days to a few months. It lasts as long as *both* input prices and output prices stay fixed. Input prices are fixed in both the immediate short run and the short run by contractual agreements. In particular, 75 percent of the average firm's costs are wages and salaries—and these are almost always fixed by labor contracts for months or years at a time. As a result, they are usually fixed much longer than output prices, which can begin to change within a few days or a few months depending upon the type of firm.

That said, output prices are also typically fixed in the immediate short run. Firms set fixed prices for their customers and then agree to supply whatever quantity demanded results at those fixed prices. For instance, once an appliance manufacturer sets its annual prices for refrigerators, stoves, and microwaves, it is obligated to supply as many appliances customers want to buy at those prices. Similarly, a catalog company is obliged to sell however much customers want to buy of its products at the prices listed in its current catalog—and it is obligated to supply those quantities demanded until it sends out its next catalog.

immediate-short-run aggregate supply curve
An aggregate supply curve for which real output, but not the price level, changes when the aggregate demand curve shifts; a horizontal aggregate supply curve that implies an inflexible price level.

With output prices fixed and firms selling however much customers want to purchase at those fixed prices, the **immediate-short-run aggregate supply curve** (AS_{ISR}) is a horizontal line, as **Figure 12.3** shows. The AS_{ISR} curve is horizontal at the overall price level P_1, which is calculated from all of the individual prices set by the various firms in the economy. Its horizontal shape implies that the total amount of output supplied in the economy depends directly on the volume of spending that results at price level P_1. If total spending is low at price level P_1, firms will supply a small amount to match the low level of spending. If total spending is high at price level P_1, they will supply a high level of output to match the high level of spending. The resulting amount of output may be higher than or lower than the economy's full-employment output level Q_f.

Notice, however, that firms will respond in this manner to changes in total spending only as long as output prices remain fixed. As soon as firms are able to change their product prices, they can respond to changes in aggregate spending not only by increasing or decreasing output but also by raising or lowering prices. This is the situation that leads to the upward sloping short-run aggregate supply curve that we discuss next.

Aggregate Supply in the Short Run

In macroeconomics, the short run begins after the immediate short run ends. More specifically, the short run is the period of time during which output prices are flexible but input prices are either totally fixed or highly inflexible.

FIGURE 12.3

Aggregate supply in the immediate short run. In the immediate short run, the aggregate supply curve AS$_{ISR}$ is horizontal at the economy's current price level, P_1. With output prices fixed, firms collectively supply the level of output demanded at those prices.

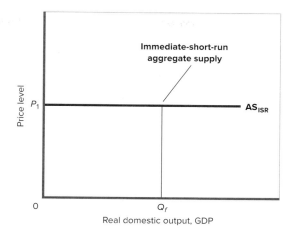

Some input prices are more flexible than others. Consider gasoline, an input for delivery firms like UPS. Because gasoline prices are quite flexible, UPS will have at least one very flexible input price. In contrast, wages at UPS are set by five-year labor contracts negotiated with its drivers' union, the Teamsters. Because wages are the firm's largest and most important input cost, UPS faces overall input prices that are inflexible for several years at a time. Thus, its "short run"—the period in which it can change its shipping prices but not its substantially fixed input prices—is actually quite long. Keep this example in mind as we derive the short-run aggregate supply for the entire economy. Its applicability does not depend on some arbitrary definition of how long the "short run" should be. Instead, the short run for which the model is relevant is any period of time during which output prices are flexible, but input prices are fixed or nearly fixed.

As **Figure 12.4** shows, the **short-run aggregate supply curve** (AS) slopes upward because, with input prices fixed, changes in the price level will raise or lower firms' real profits. Consider an economy that has only a single multiproduct firm called Sahara, whose owners must receive a real profit of $20 in order to produce the full-employment output of 100 units. Assume the owner's only input (aside from entrepreneurial talent) is 10 units of hired labor at $8 per worker, for a total wage cost of $80. Also, assume that the 100 units of output sell for $1 per unit, so total revenue is $100. Sahara's nominal profit is $20 (= $100 − $80), and using the $1 price to designate the base-price index of 100, its real profit is also $20 (= $20/1.00). Well and good; the full-employment output is produced.

Next, consider what will happen if the price of Sahara's output doubles. The doubling of the price level boosts total revenue from $100 to $200, but because we are discussing the short run during which input prices are fixed, the $8 nominal wage for each of the 10 workers remains unchanged so that total costs stay at $80. Nominal profit rises from $20 (= $100 − $80) to $120 (= $200 − $80). Dividing that $120 profit by the new price index of 200 (= 2.0 in hundredths), we find that Sahara's real profit is now $60. The rise in the real reward from $20 to $60 prompts the firm (economy) to produce more output. Conversely, price-level declines reduce real profits and cause the firm (economy) to reduce its output. So, in the short run, there is a direct, or positive, relationship between the price level and real output. When the price level rises, real output rises, and when the price level falls, real output falls. The result is an upward-sloping short-run aggregate supply curve.

short-run aggregate supply curve
An aggregate supply curve relevant to a time period in which input prices (particularly nominal wages) do not change in response to changes in the price level.

FIGURE 12.4

The aggregate supply curve (short run). The upward-sloping aggregate supply curve AS indicates a direct (or positive) relationship between the price level and the amount of real output that firms will offer for sale. The AS curve is relatively flat below the full-employment output because unemployed resources and unused capacity allow firms to respond to price-level rises with large increases in real output. It is relatively steep beyond the full-employment output because resource shortages and capacity limitations make it difficult to expand real output as the price level rises.

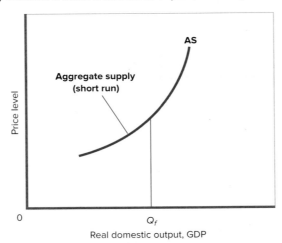

Notice, however, that the upslope of the short-run aggregate supply curve is not constant. It is flatter at outputs below the full-employment output level Q_f and steeper at outputs above it. The reason lies in the lower per-unit production costs that underlie the short-run aggregate supply curve.

As the economy expands in the short run, per-unit production costs generally rise because of reduced efficiency. But the extent of that rise depends on where the economy is operating relative to its capacity. When the economy is operating below its full-employment output, it has large amounts of unused machinery and equipment and large numbers of unemployed workers. Firms can put these idle human and capital resources back to work with little upward pressure on per-unit production costs. And as output expands, few if any shortages of inputs will arise to raise per-unit production costs. Thus, the slope of the short-run aggregate supply curve increases only slowly at output levels below the full-employment output level Q_f.

In contrast, when the economy is operating beyond Q_f, the vast majority of its available resources are already employed. Adding more workers to a relatively fixed number of highly used capital resources such as plant and equipment creates congestion in the workplace and reduces the average efficiency of workers. Adding more capital, given the limited number of available workers, leaves equipment idle and reduces the efficiency of capital. Adding more land resources when capital and labor are highly constrained reduces the efficiency of land resources. Under these circumstances, total input costs rise more rapidly than total output. The result is rapidly rising per-unit production costs that give the short-run aggregate supply curve its rapidly increasing slope at output levels beyond Q_f.

Aggregate Supply in the Long Run

In macroeconomics, the long run is the time horizon over which both input prices and output prices are flexible. It begins after the short run ends. Depending on the type of firm and industry, the long run may last from a couple of weeks to several years. But for the economy as a whole, it is the time horizon over which all output and input prices—including wage rates—are fully flexible.

FIGURE 12.5

Aggregate supply in the long run. The long-run aggregate supply curve (AS$_{LR}$) is vertical at the full-employment level of real GDP (Q_f) because in the long run wages and other input prices rise and fall to match changes in the price level. So price-level changes do not affect firms' profits, and thus they create no incentive for firms to alter their output.

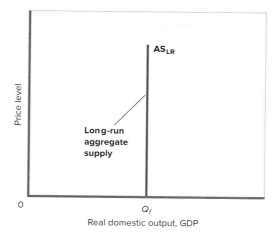

The **long-run aggregate supply curve** AS$_{LR}$ is vertical at the economy's full-employment output Q_f, as shown in **Figure 12.5**. The vertical curve means that in the long run the economy will produce the full employment output level no matter what the price level is. How can this be? Shouldn't higher prices cause firms to increase output? The explanation lies in the fact that in the long run, when both input prices and output prices are flexible, profit levels always adjust so as to give firms exactly the right profit incentive to produce exactly the full-employment output level, Q_f.

To see why, look back at the short-run aggregate supply curve (AS) in **Figure 12.4**. Suppose that the economy starts out producing at the full-employment output level Q_f and that the price level at that moment has an index value of $P = 100$. Now suppose that output prices double, so that the price index goes to $P = 200$. We previously demonstrated for our single-firm economy that this doubling of the price level will cause profits to rise in the short run and that the higher profits would motivate the firm to increase output.

This outcome, however, is dependent on the fact that input prices are fixed in the short run. Consider what will happen in the long run when they are free to change. Firms can produce beyond the full-employment output level only by running factories and businesses at extremely high rates. This creates a great deal of demand for the economy's limited supply of productive resources. In particular, labor is in great demand because the only way to produce beyond full employment is to have employees work overtime.

As time passes and input prices are free to change, the high level of resource demand will start to raise input prices. In particular, overworked employees will demand and receive raises as employers scramble to deal with the labor shortages that arise when the economy is producing above its full-employment output level. As input prices increase, firm profits begin to fall. As they decline, so does the motive firms have to produce more than the full-employment output level.

This process of rising input prices and falling profits continues until the rise in input prices exactly matches the initial change in output prices (in our example, they both double). When that happens, firm profits in real terms return to their original level so that firms are once again motivated to produce at exactly the full-employment output level. This adjustment process means that in the long run, the economy will produce at full employment regardless of the price level (in our example, at either

long-run aggregate supply curve
The aggregate supply curve associated with a time period in which input prices (especially nominal wages) are fully responsive to changes in the price level.

$P = 100$ or $P = 200$). Thus, the long-run aggregate supply curve (AS_{LR}) is vertical above the full-employment output level. Every possible price level on the vertical axis is associated with the economy producing at the full-employment output level in the long run.

Focusing on the Short Run

The immediate-short-run aggregate supply curve, the short-run aggregate supply curve, and the long-run aggregate supply curve are all important. Each curve is appropriate to situations that match their respective assumptions about the flexibility of input and output prices. But our focus in the rest of this chapter and the chapters that immediately follow will be on short-run aggregate supply curves such as the AS curve shown in **Figure 12.4**. Unless explicitly stated otherwise, all references to "aggregate supply" are to short-run aggregate supply and the short-run aggregate supply curve, AS.

We emphasize the short-run aggregate supply curve because real-world economies typically manifest simultaneous changes in both their price levels and their levels of real output. The upward-sloping short-run AS curve is the only version of aggregate supply that can handle simultaneous movements in both of these variables. By contrast, the price level is fixed in the immediate short run (**Figure 12.3**) and output is fixed in the long run (**Figure 12.5**). This renders these versions of aggregate supply unhelpful when it comes to understanding business cycles and macroeconomic policy. To analyze those issues correctly, we must employ the short-run aggregate supply curve, AS.

Changes in Aggregate Supply

An aggregate supply curve identifies the relationship between the price level and real output, other things equal. But when other things change, the curve shifts. The rightward shift of the curve from AS_1 to AS_2 in **Figure 12.6** represents an increase in aggregate supply, indicating that firms are willing to produce and sell more real output at each price level. The leftward shift of the curve from AS_1 to AS_3 represents a decrease in aggregate supply. At each price level, firms produce less output than before.

FIGURE 12.6
Changes in aggregate supply. A change in one or more of the determinants of aggregate supply listed in **Table 12.2** will shift the aggregate supply curve. The rightward shift of the aggregate supply curve from AS_1 to AS_2 represents an increase in aggregate supply; the leftward shift of the curve from AS_1 to AS_3 shows a decrease in aggregate supply.

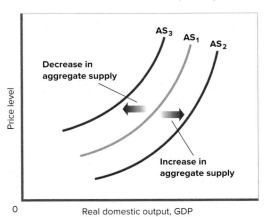

Table 12.2 lists the "other things" that shift the aggregate supply curve. Called the **determinants of aggregate supply,** they collectively position the aggregate supply curve and shift the curve when they change. Changes in these determinants raise or lower per-unit production costs *at each price level.* These changes in per-unit production costs affect profits, leading firms to alter the amount of output they are willing to produce *at each price level.* Changes that increase profits cause firms to produce more, while changes that decrease profits cause firms to produce less.

As an example, firms may collectively offer $9 trillion of real output at a price level of 1.0 (100 in index value) when the supply shifters are all at particular values, but then only $8.8 trillion at the same price level if one or more shifters change. The point is that when one of the determinants listed in **Figure 12.6** changes, the aggregate supply curve shifts to the right or left. Changes that reduce per-unit production costs shift the aggregate supply curve to the right, as from AS_1 to AS_2, while changes that increase per-unit production costs shift it to the left, as from AS_1 to AS_3.

determinants of aggregate supply
Factors such as input prices, productivity, and the legal-institutional environment that, if they change, shift the aggregate supply curve.

TABLE 12.2

Determinants of Aggregate Supply: Factors That Shift the Aggregate Supply Curve
1. Change in input prices
a. Domestic resource prices
b. Prices of imported resources
2. Change in productivity
3. Change in legal-institutional environment
a. Business taxes
b. Government regulations

The three aggregate supply determinants listed in **Table 12.2** require more discussion.

Input Prices

Input or resource prices—to be distinguished from the output prices that make up the price level—are a major ingredient of per-unit production costs and therefore a key determinant of aggregate supply. These resources can be either domestic or imported.

Domestic Resource Prices As stated earlier, wages and salaries make up about 75 percent of all business costs. Other things equal, decreases in wages increase profits by reducing per-unit production costs. So when wages fall, the aggregate supply curve shifts to the right. By contrast, increases in wages reduce profits by raising per-unit production costs. So when wages rise, aggregate supply shifts to the left. Examples:

* Labor supply increases because of substantial immigration. Wages and per-unit production costs fall, shifting the AS curve to the right.
* Labor supply decreases because a rapid increase in pension income causes many older workers to opt for early retirement. Wage rates and per-unit production costs rise, shifting the AS curve to the left.

Similarly, the aggregate supply curve shifts when the prices of land and capital inputs change. Examples:

* The price of machinery and equipment falls because of declines in the prices of steel and electronic components. Per-unit production costs decline, and the AS curve shifts to the right.
* The supply of available land resources expands through discoveries of mineral deposits or technical innovations that transform "nonresources" (say, vast desert lands) into valuable resources (productive lands). The price of land declines, per-unit production costs fall, and the AS curve shifts to the right.

Prices of Imported Resources Resources imported from abroad (such as oil, tin, and copper) affect U.S. aggregate supply because added supplies of resources—whether domestic or imported—typically reduce resource prices and, consequently, per-unit production costs. Other things equal, a decrease in the price of imported resources will raise U.S. profits and increase U.S. aggregate supply. Conversely, an increase in the price of imported resources will lower U.S. profits and reduce U.S. aggregate supply, other things equal.

A good example of the major effect that changing resource prices can have on aggregate supply is the oil price hikes of the 1970s. At that time, the members of the Organization of Petroleum Exporting Countries (OPEC) worked in concert to decrease oil production in order to raise the price of oil. The tenfold increase in the price of oil that OPEC achieved during the 1970s drove per-unit production costs up and jolted the U.S. aggregate supply curve leftward.

Exchange-rate fluctuations may also alter the price of imported resources. Suppose that the dollar appreciates, enabling U.S. firms to obtain more foreign currency with each dollar. Domestic producers will now face a lower *dollar* price of imported resources. U.S. firms will respond by increasing their imports of foreign resources. By substituting cheap foreign resources for more expensive domestic resources, firms will lower their per-unit production costs at each level of output. Falling per-unit production costs will shift the U.S. aggregate supply curve to the right.

A depreciation of the dollar will have the opposite set of effects and shifts the aggregate supply curve to the left.

Productivity

productivity
A measure of average output or real output per unit of input. For example, the productivity of labor is determined by dividing real output by hours of work.

The second major determinant of aggregate supply is **productivity,** which measures how much output can be produced from any given set of inputs. Mathematically, productivity is defined as average real output, or of real output per unit of input:

$$\text{Productivity} = \frac{\text{total output}}{\text{total inputs}}$$

With no change in resource prices, increases in productivity affect aggregate supply by reducing the per-unit production cost of output. This cost is determined by dividing the total cost of production by the dollar amount of output. For example, if the total cost of production is $20 billion and total output is $40 billion, per-unit production cost is $0.50. If productivity rises such that output increases from $40 billion to $60 billion, the per-unit production cost will fall from $0.50 (= $20/$40) to $0.33 (= $20/$60).

By reducing per-unit production costs, increases in productivity shift the aggregate supply curve to the right. The main source of productivity advance is improved production technology, often embodied within new plant and equipment that replaces old plant and equipment. Other sources of productivity increases are a better-educated and better-trained workforce, improved forms of business enterprises, and the reallocation of labor resources from lower-productivity to higher-productivity uses.

Decreases in productivity are rare. But when they occur, they increase per-unit production costs and therefore reduce aggregate supply (shift the AS curve to the left).

Legal-Institutional Environment

Changes in the legal-institutional setting in which businesses operate are the final determinant of aggregate supply. Such changes may alter the per-unit costs of output and, in doing so, shift the aggregate supply curve. Two changes of this type are (1) changes in business taxes and subsidies, and (2) changes in the extent of regulation.

Business Taxes and Subsidies   Higher business taxes, such as sales, excise, and payroll taxes, increase per-unit costs and reduce short-run aggregate supply. Higher business taxes shift aggregate supply to the left.

Similarly, a business subsidy—a payment or tax break by government to producers—lowers production costs and increases short-run aggregate supply. For example, the federal government subsidizes firms that blend ethanol (derived from corn) with gasoline to increase the U.S. gasoline supply. This reduces the per-unit production cost of making blended gasoline. To the extent that this and other subsidies are successful, the aggregate supply curve shifts rightward.

Government Regulation   It is usually costly for businesses to comply with government regulations. More regulation therefore tends to increase per-unit production costs and shift the aggregate supply curve to the left. "Supply-side" proponents of deregulation of the economy have argued forcefully that, by increasing efficiency and reducing the paperwork associated with complex regulations, deregulation will reduce per-unit costs and shift the aggregate supply curve to the right. Other economists are less certain. Deregulation that results in accounting manipulations, monopolization, and business failures is likely to shift the AS curve to the left rather than to the right.

Equilibrium Price Level and Real GDP

Of all the possible combinations of price levels and levels of real GDP, which combination will the economy gravitate toward, at least in the short run? **Figure 12.7** and its accompanying table (**Table 12.3**) provide the answer. Equilibrium occurs at the price level that equalizes the amounts of real output demanded and supplied. The intersection of the aggregate demand curve AD and the aggregate supply curve AS establishes the economy's **equilibrium price level** and **equilibrium real output.** Aggregate demand and aggregate supply *jointly* establish the price level and level of real GDP.

equilibrium price level
The price level at which the aggregate demand curve intersects the aggregate supply curve.

equilibrium real output
The gross domestic product at which the total quantity of final goods and services purchased (aggregate expenditures) is equal to the total quantity of final goods and services produced (the real domestic output); the real domestic output at which the aggregate demand curve intersects the aggregate supply curve.

FIGURE 12.7

The equilibrium price level and equilibrium real GDP. The intersection of the aggregate demand curve and the aggregate supply curve determines the economy's equilibrium price level. At the equilibrium price level of 100 (in index-value terms), the $510 billion of real output demanded matches the $510 billion of real output supplied. So equilibrium real GDP is $510 billion.

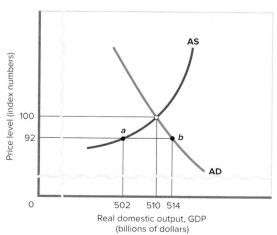

TABLE 12.3

Real Output Demanded (Billions)	Price Level (Index Number)	Real Output Supplied (Billions)
$506	108	$513
508	104	512
510	**100**	**510**
512	96	507
514	92	502

In **Figure 12.7**, the equilibrium price level and level of real output are 100 and $510 billion, respectively. To illustrate why those values constitute an equilibrium, suppose the price level is 92 rather than 100. We see from **Table 12.3** that the lower price level will encourage businesses to produce real output of $502 billion. This is shown by point *a* on the AS curve in the graph. But, as revealed by the table and point *b* on the aggregate demand curve, buyers will want to purchase $514 billion of real output at price level 92. There will consequently be a $12 billion (=$514 billion demanded − $502 billion supplied shortage of real output).

This shortage will not persist. Competition among buyers to purchase the limited ($502 billion) supply of real output will eliminate the shortage and drive the price level up from 92 to 100. The rise in the price level from 92 to 100 encourages producers to increase their real output from $502 billion to $510 billion and causes buyers to scale back their purchases from $514 billion to $510 billion. When equality occurs between the amounts of real output produced and purchased, as it does at price level 100, the economy will achieve equilibrium (here, at $510 billion of real GDP). Note that although the equilibrium price level happens to be 100 in our example, nothing special is implied by that. Any price level can be an equilibrium price level.

Changes in Equilibrium

Aggregate demand and aggregate supply typically change from one period to the next. If aggregate demand and aggregate supply increase proportionately over time, real GDP will expand and neither demand-pull inflation nor cyclical unemployment will occur. But we know from our discussion of the business cycle that macroeconomic stability is not always certain. A number of less-desirable situations can confront the economy. Let's apply the model to several such situations. For simplicity, we will use *P* and *Q* symbols, rather than actual numbers. Remember that these symbols represent price index values and amounts of real GDP.

 APPLYING THE ANALYSIS

Demand-Pull Inflation

Suppose the economy is operating at its full-employment output and businesses and government increase their spending—actions that shift the aggregate demand curve to the right. Our list of determinants of aggregate demand (**Table 12.1**) provides several reasons why this shift might occur. Perhaps firms boost their investment spending because they anticipate higher future profits from investments in new capital. Perhaps government increases spending to expand national defense.

As shown by the rise in the price level from P_1 to P_2 in **Figure 12.8**, the increase in aggregate demand beyond the full-employment level of output moves the economy from *a* to *b* and causes inflation. This is *demand-pull inflation* because the price level is being pulled up by the increase in aggregate demand. Also, observe that the increase in demand expands real output from the full-employment level Q_f to Q_1. The distance between Q_1 and Q_f is a positive, or "inflationary," *GDP gap:* Actual GDP exceeds potential GDP.

FIGURE 12.8

Demand-pull inflation. The increase of aggregate demand from AD_1 to AD_2 moves the economy from *a* to *b*, causing demand-pull inflation of P_1 to P_2. It also causes a positive GDP gap of Q_1 minus Q_f.

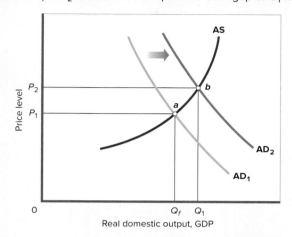

A classic American example of demand-pull inflation occurred in the late 1960s. The escalation of the war in Vietnam resulted in a 40 percent increase in defense spending between 1965 and 1967 and another 15 percent increase in 1968. The rise in government spending, imposed on an already growing economy, shifted the economy's aggregate demand curve to the right, producing the worst inflation in two decades. Actual GDP exceeded potential GDP, thereby creating an inflationary GDP gap. Inflation jumped from 1.6 percent in 1965 to 5.7 percent by 1970.

A more recent example of demand-pull inflation occurred in the late 1980s. As aggregate demand expanded beyond its full-employment level between 1986 and 1990, the price level rose at an increasing rate. Specifically, the annual rate of inflation increased from 1.9 percent in 1986 to 3.6 percent in 1987 to 4.1 percent in 1988 to 4.8 percent in 1989. In terms of **Figure 12.8**, the aggregate demand curve moved rightward from year to year, raising the price level and the size of the positive GDP gap. The gap closed and the rate of inflation fell as the expansion gave way to the recession of 1990–1991.

QUESTION:

How is the upward slope of the aggregate supply curve important in explaining demand-pull inflation?

APPLYING THE ANALYSIS

Cost-Push Inflation

Suppose that a major terrorist attack on oil facilities severely disrupts world oil supplies and drives up oil prices by, say, 300 percent. Higher energy prices will spread through the economy, driving up production and distribution costs on a wide variety of goods and services. The U.S. aggregate supply curve would shift to the left, say, from AS_1 to AS_2 in **Figure 12.9**. The resulting increase in the price level would be *cost-push inflation*.

FIGURE 12.9
Cost-push inflation. A leftward shift of aggregate supply from AS_1 to AS_2 moves the economy from a to b, raises the price level from P_1 to P_2, and produces cost-push inflation. Real output declines and a negative GDP gap (of Q_1 minus Q_f) occurs.

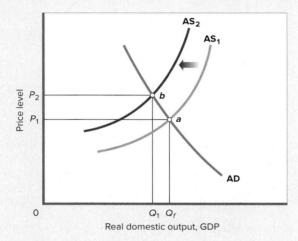

The effects of a leftward shift in aggregate supply are doubly bad. Along with the rising price level (the cost-push inflation), a recession (the negative GDP gap) occurs. That is exactly what happened in the United States in the mid-1970s when OPEC showed production rates and the price of crude oil rocketed upward.

Back in the 1970s, oil expenditures were about 10 percent of U.S. GDP compared to only 3 percent today. So the U.S. economy is now less vulnerable to cost-push inflation arising from oil shocks. That said, it is not immune from such shocks. A substantial supply shock caused by soaring oil prices would almost certainly cause U.S. aggregate supply to shift to the left by enough to again generate a decrease in output accompanied by significant cost-push inflation.

> QUESTION:
>
> Which is costlier to an economy in terms of lost real output, an equal degree of demand-pull inflation or cost-push inflation?

PHOTO OP

Demand-Pull versus Cost-Push Inflation

A boom in investment spending, such as that for new construction, can cause demand-pull inflation. Soaring prices of key resources, such as oil, can cause cost-push inflation.

instamatics/E+/Getty Images   Brian Kanof/McGraw Hill Education

Downward Price-Level Inflexibility

We have just seen examples where, despite what we have learned about price "stickiness," the price level is readily flexible upward. But in the U.S. economy, deflation (a decline in the price level) rarely occurs even though the rate of inflation rises and falls. Why is the price level "sticky" or inflexible, particularly on the downside? Economists have offered several possible reasons for this:

- **Fear of price wars** Some oligopolists may be concerned that if they reduce their prices, rivals not only will match their price cuts but may retaliate by making even deeper cuts. An initial price cut may touch off an unwanted *price war:* successively deeper and deeper rounds of price cuts. In such a situation, all the firms end up with far less profit or higher losses than would be the case if they had simply maintained their prices. For this reason, each firm may resist making the initial price cut, choosing instead to reduce production and lay off workers.

- **Menu costs** Firms that think a recession will be relatively short-lived may hesitate to cut their prices. One reason is what economists call *menu costs,* named after their most obvious example: the cost of printing new menus when a restaurant decides to change its prices. But lowering prices also creates other costs. There are the costs of (1) estimating the magnitude and duration of the shift in demand to determine whether prices should be lowered, (2) repricing items held in inventory, (3) printing and mailing new catalogs, and (4) communicating new prices to customers, perhaps through advertising. When menu costs are present, firms may choose to avoid them by retaining current prices. They may wait to see if the decline in aggregate demand is permanent.

- **Wage contracts** It usually is not profitable for firms to cut their product prices if they cannot also cut their wage rates. Wages are usually inflexible downward because large parts of the labor force work under contracts prohibiting wage cuts for the duration of the contract. (It is not uncommon for collective bargaining agreements in major industries to run for three years.) Similarly, the wages and salaries of nonunion workers are usually adjusted once a year, rather than quarterly or monthly.

- *Morale, effort, and productivity* Downward wage inflexibility is reinforced by the reluctance of many employers to reduce wage rates. If worker productivity (output per hour of work) remains constant, lower wages *do* reduce labor costs per unit of output. But lower wages might impair worker morale and work effort, thereby reducing productivity. Considered alone, lower productivity raises labor costs per unit of output because less output is produced. If the higher labor costs resulting from reduced productivity exceed the cost savings from the lower wage, then wage cuts increase rather than reduce labor costs per unit of output. In such situations, firms resist lowering wages when faced with a decline in aggregate demand.

- *Minimum wage* The minimum wage imposes a legal floor under the wages of the least skilled workers. Firms paying those wages cannot reduce that wage rate when aggregate demand declines.

Conclusion: In the United States, the price level readily rises but only reluctantly falls.

 ILLUSTRATING THE IDEA

The Ratchet Effect

Yevhenii Orlov/Shutterstock

A *ratchet analogy* is a good way to think about the asymmetry of price-level changes. A ratchet is a tool or mechanism such as a winch, car jack, or socket wrench that cranks a wheel forward but does not allow it to go backward. Properly set, each allows the operator to move an object (boat, car, or nut) in one direction while preventing it from moving in the opposite direction.

The price level, wage rates, and per-unit production costs readily rise when aggregate demand increases along the aggregate supply curve. In the United States, the price level has increased in every year but two since 1950.

But the price level, wage rates, and per-unit production costs are inflexible downward when aggregate demand declines. The U.S. price level has fallen in only two years (1955 and 2009) since 1950, even though aggregate demand and real output have declined in a number of years.

In terms of our analogy, increases in aggregate demand ratchet the U.S. price level upward. Once in place, the higher price level remains until it is ratcheted up again. The higher price level tends to remain even with declines in aggregate demand. Inflation rates *do* rise and fall in the United States, but the price level mainly rises.

QUESTIONS:

Does the ratchet analogy also apply to changes in real GDP? Why or why not?

APPLYING THE ANALYSIS

Recession and Cyclical Unemployment

Decreases in aggregate demand result in recession and cyclical unemployment. For example, suppose that investment spending sharply declines. In **Figure 12.10**, we show the resulting decline in aggregate demand as a leftward shift from AD_1 to AD_2.

FIGURE 12.10

A recession. If the price level is downwardly inflexible at P_1, a decline of aggregate demand from AD_1 to AD_2 will move the economy from a to b and reduce real GDP from Q_f to Q_1. Idle production capacity, cyclical unemployment, and a negative GDP gap (of Q_1 minus Q_f) will result.

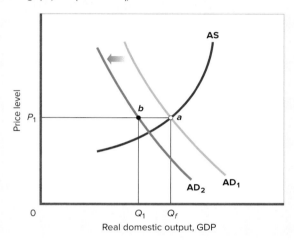

With the price level inflexible downward at P_1, the decline in aggregate demand moves the economy from a to b and reduces real output from Q_f to Q_1. The distance between Q_1 and Q_f measures the negative GDP gap—the amount by which actual output falls short of potential output. Because fewer workers are needed to produce the lower output, *cyclical unemployment* arises.

All recent demand-caused recessions in the United States have mimicked the "GDP gap but no deflation" scenario shown in **Figure 12.10**. Consider the recession of 2007–2009, which resulted from chaos in the financial markets that quickly led to significant declines in spending by businesses and households. Aggregate demand declined dramatically, with actual GDP falling short of potential GDP by $1 trillion in 2009. At the same time, however, the price level barely budged, falling by only three-tenths of 1 percent in 2008 and in fact rising during 2009 as government stimulus efforts (lower taxes and higher spending) kicked in.

QUESTION:

How can a decline in expected investment returns on the construction of new houses, condominiums, and office buildings contribute to a recession?

GLOBAL SNAPSHOT 12.3

Size of GDP Gaps, Selected Countries, 2017

The GDP gap between potential output and actual output can be expressed as a percentage of potential output. In 2017, these percentage GDP gaps varied widely across developed nations, reflecting different local circumstances as well as differences in what stage of the business cycle each country was at. Please note that inflation was positive in every country, including those with negative GDP gaps.

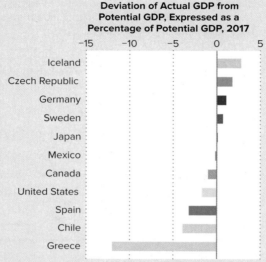

Deviation of Actual GDP from Potential GDP, Expressed as a Percentage of Potential GDP, 2017

Source: Organisation for Economic Co-operation and Development (OECD).

The Multiplier Effect

Before leaving the topic of aggregate demand and aggregate supply, we need to supply two additional insights. First, shifts in the aggregate demand curves such as those in **Figures 12.8** and **12.10** embody an "initial change" in spending, say, an increase in investment, followed by successive rounds of additional spending by businesses and households that are on the receiving end of the prior spending. Our shifts from one AD curve to another AD curve simply show the final results.

Assuming an economy has room to expand—so that increases in spending do not lead to increases in prices—there is a direct (positive) relationship between changes in spending and change in real GDP. But there is more to this relationship between these two aggregates. For example, an initial change in investment spending can change output and income by an amount larger than the initial spending change. That surprising result is called the *multiplier effect*. The **multiplier** measures how much larger the final change in GDP will be; it is the ratio of a change in GDP to the initial change in spending (in this case, investment). Stated algebraically,

multiplier
The ratio of a change in the equilibrium GDP to the change in *investment* or in any other component of aggregate expenditures or *aggregate demand;* the number by which a change in any such component must be multiplied to find the resulting change in the equilibrium GDP.

$$\text{Multiplier} = \frac{\text{change in real GDP}}{\text{initial change in spending}}$$

By rearranging this equation, we can also say that

Change in real GDP = multiplier × initial change in spending

So if investment in an economy rises by $30 billion and aggregate demand and real GDP increase by $90 billion as a result, we know from the first equation that the multiplier is 3 (=$90/30).

Note these two points about the multiplier:

- The initial change in spending is often associated with investment spending because of investment's volatility. But changes in consumption spending (unrelated to change in income), government purchases, and net exports also lead to the multiplier effect.

- The multiplier works in both directions. An increase in initial spending may create a "multiplied" increase in GDP, while an initial decrease will create a multiplied decrease in GDP.

The multiplier effect follows from the fact that the economy supports repetitive, continuous flows of expenditures and income, as we saw in the circular flow model in **Chapter 2**. Through this process, dollars spent by Smith are received as income by Chin, who spends a portion that Gonzales receives as income, and so on. Because a portion of new income is saved (not spent), the amount of new spending in each successive round declines, eventually bringing the multiplier process to an end.

Self-Correction?

The second insight is a caution: There is some evidence that the price level and average level of wages are becoming more flexible downward in the United States. Intense international competition and the declining power of unions in the United States seem to be undermining the ability of firms and workers to resist price and wage cuts when faced with falling aggregate demand. This increased flexibility of some prices and wages may be one reason the recession of 2001 was relatively mild. The U.S. auto manufacturers, for example, maintained output in the face of falling demand by offering zero-interest loans on auto purchases. This, in effect, was a disguised price cut.

In theory, fully flexible downward prices and wages would automatically "self-correct" a recession. Reduced aggregate demand, with its accompanying negative GDP gap and greater unemployment, would reduce the price level and level of (nominal) wages. In **Figure 12.10**, the lower wages would reduce per-unit production costs and shift the AS curve rightward. Eventually, the economy would return to its full-employment output, but at a considerably lower price level than before. That is, the economy would move back to its long-run aggregate supply curve, like the one shown in **Figure 12.5**.

In reality, the government and monetary authorities have been reluctant to wait for these slow and uncertain "corrections." Instead, they focus on trying to move the aggregate demand curve to its prerecession location. For example, toward the end of 2007, crises in the housing and credit markets precipitated a recession, prompting the Fed to begin a series of interest rate cuts to try to boost spending. In February 2008, the federal government passed a tax rebate package, which it followed in February 2009 with $787 billion in spending increases and tax cuts, also in an effort to support aggregate demand and deal with the recession. The recession officially ended in June 2009, and the economy slowly recovered, reaching its next peak in the business cycle in February 2020.

In March 2020, much of the economy shut down or scaled back significantly due to the COVID-19 pandemic. Output dropped by 31.4 percent in the second quarter of 2020. The Fed responded quickly by lowering interest rates and Congress passed legislation to provide relief to struggling households and businesses. Policymakers chose not to wait for the economy to self-correct, and the combination of policy action and much of the economy reopening saw output rebound with 33.4 percent growth in the third quarter. Despite the strong third-quarter performance, significant unemployment and below-potential real GDP continued on into 2021. Unwilling to wait for the economy to fully recover on its own, the Fed kept interest rates low and the government provided additional support in the form of stimulus checks and extended unemployment benefits to households and loans and subsidies to businesses.

We will examine stabilization policies such as these in the chapters that follow.

Summary

LO12.1 Define aggregate demand (AD) and explain the factors that cause it to change.

The aggregate demand–aggregate supply model (AD–AS model) enables analysis of simultaneous changes of real GDP and the price level.

The aggregate demand curve shows the level of real output that the economy will purchase at each price level. It slopes downward because higher price levels dissuade U.S. businesses and households, along with foreign buyers, from purchasing as much output as before.

The determinants of aggregate demand consist of spending by domestic consumers, businesses, and government and by foreign buyers. Changes in the factors listed in **Table 12.1** alter the spending by these groups and shift the aggregate demand curve.

LO12.2 Define aggregate supply (AS) and explain the factors that cause it to change.

The aggregate supply curve shows the levels of real output that businesses will produce at various possible price levels. The slope of the aggregate supply curve depends upon the flexibility of input and output prices.

The *immediate-short-run aggregate supply curve* assumes that both input prices and output prices are fixed. With output prices fixed, the aggregate supply curve is a horizontal line at the current price level. The *short-run aggregate supply curve* assumes nominal wages and other input prices remain fixed while output prices vary. The aggregate supply curve generally slopes upward because per-unit production costs, and hence the prices that firms must receive, rise as real output expands. The aggregate supply curve is relatively steep to the right of the full-employment output level and relatively flat to the left of it. The *long-run aggregate supply curve* assumes that nominal wages and other input prices fully match any change in the price level. The curve is vertical at the full-employment output level.

Because the short-run aggregate supply curve is the only version of aggregate supply that can handle simultaneous changes in the price level and real output, it serves well as the core aggregate supply curve for analyzing the business cycle and economic policy.

Table 12.2 lists the determinants of aggregate supply: input prices, productivity, and the legal-institutional environment. A change in any one of these factors will change per-unit production costs at each level of output and shift the aggregate supply curve.

LO12.3 Explain how AD and AS determine an economy's equilibrium price level and real GDP.

The intersection of the aggregate demand and aggregate supply curves determines an economy's equilibrium price level and real GDP. At the intersection, the quantity of real GDP demanded equals the quantity of real GDP supplied.

LO12.4 Use the AD–AS model to explain periods of demand-pull inflation, cost-push inflation, and recession.

Increases in aggregate demand to the right of the full-employment output cause inflation and positive GDP gaps (actual GDP exceeds potential GDP).

Leftward shifts of the aggregate supply curve reflect increases in per-unit production costs at each level of output and cause cost-push inflation, with accompanying negative GDP gaps.

Shifts of the aggregate demand curve to the left of the full-employment output cause recession, negative GDP gaps, and cyclical unemployment. The price level may not fall during U.S. recessions because of downwardly inflexible prices and wages. This inflexibility results from fear of price wars, menu costs, wage contracts, morale concerns, and minimum wages.

When an economy has room to expand, changes in spending (consumption, investment, government purchases, and net exports) will lead to larger changes in GDP through the multiplier effect.

In theory, price and wage flexibility would allow the economy automatically to self-correct from a recession. In reality, downward price and wage flexibility make the process slow and uncertain. Recessions usually prompt the federal government and the Federal Reserve to take actions to try to increase aggregate demand.

Terms and Concepts

aggregate demand–aggregate supply (AD–AS) model

aggregate demand

determinants of aggregate demand

exchange rate

aggregate supply

immediate-short-run aggregate supply curve

short-run aggregate supply curve

long-run aggregate supply curve

determinants of aggregate supply

productivity

equilibrium price level

equilibrium real output

multiplier

Questions

1. What is the general relationship between a country's price level and the quantity of its domestic output (real GDP) demanded? Who are the buyers of U.S. real GDP? **(LO1)**

2. What assumptions cause the immediate-short-run aggregate supply curve to be horizontal? Why is the long-run aggregate supply curve vertical? Explain the shape of the short-run aggregate supply curve. Why is the short-run curve relatively flat to the left of the full-employment output and relatively steep to the right? **(LO2)**

3. What effects would each of the following have on aggregate demand or aggregate supply, other things equal? In each case, use a diagram to show the expected effects on the equilibrium price level and the level of real output, assuming that the price level is flexible both upward and downward. **(LO3)**

   a. A widespread fear by consumers of an impending economic depression.

   b. A new national tax on producers based on the value added between the costs of the inputs and the revenue received from their output.

   c. A reduction in interest rates.

   d. A major increase in spending for health care by the federal government.

   e. The general expectation of coming rapid inflation.

   f. The complete disintegration of OPEC, causing oil prices to fall by one-half.

   g. A 10 percent across-the-board reduction in personal income tax rates.

   h. A sizable increase in labor productivity (with no change in nominal wages).

   i. A 12 percent increase in nominal wages (with no change in productivity).

   j. An increase in exports that exceeds an increase in imports (not due to tariffs).

4. Assume that (a) the price level is flexible upward but not downward and (b) the economy is currently operating at its full-employment output. Other things equal, how will each of the following affect the equilibrium price level and equilibrium level of real output in the short run? **(LO3)**

   a. An increase in aggregate demand.

   b. A decrease in aggregate supply, with no change in aggregate demand.

   c. Equal increases in aggregate demand and aggregate supply.

   d. A decrease in aggregate demand.

   e. An increase in aggregate demand that exceeds an increase in aggregate supply.

5. Why does a reduction in aggregate demand tend to reduce real output, rather than the price level? **(LO4)**

6. Explain the following statement: "Unemployment can be caused by a decrease of aggregate demand or a decrease of aggregate supply." In each case, specify the price-level outcomes. **(LO4)**

7. In early 2001, investment spending sharply declined in the United States. In the two months following the September 11, 2001, attacks on the United States, consumption also declined. Use AD–AS analysis to show the two impacts on real GDP. **(LO4)**

8. Using the concept of the multiplier, explain why mass layoffs by large companies such as Boeing or General Motors are a concern to the citizens and leaders where those firms are located. **(LO4)**

Problems

1. Suppose that consumer spending initially rises by $5 billion for every 1 percent rise in household wealth and that investment spending initially rises by $20 billion for every 1 percentage point fall in the real interest rate. Also assume that the economy's multiplier is 4. If household wealth falls by 5 percent because of declining house values, and the real interest rate falls by 2 percentage points, in what direction and by how much will the aggregate demand curve initially shift at each price level? In what direction and by how much will it eventually shift? **(LO1)**

2. Answer the following questions on the basis of the three sets of data below for the country of North Vaudeville: **(LO2)**

    a. Which set of data illustrates aggregate supply in the immediate short run in North Vaudeville? The short run? The long run?
    b. Assuming no change in hours of work, if real output per hour of work increases by 10 percent, what will be the new levels of real GDP in the right column of A? Do the new data reflect an increase in aggregate supply or do they indicate a decrease in aggregate supply?

(A)		(B)		(C)	
Price Level	Real GDP	Price Level	Real GDP	Price Level	Real GDP
110	275	100	200	110	225
100	250	100	225	100	225
95	225	100	250	95	225
90	200	100	275	90	225

3. Suppose that the aggregate demand and aggregate supply schedules for a hypothetical economy are as shown in the following table. **(LO3)**

Amount of Real GDP Demanded, Billions	Price Level (Price Index)	Amount of Real GDP Supplied, Billions
$100	300	$450
200	250	400
300	200	300
400	150	200
500	100	100

    a. Use the preceding data to graph the aggregate demand and aggregate supply curves. What is the equilibrium price level and the equilibrium level of real output in this hypothetical economy? Is the equilibrium real output also necessarily the full-employment real output?

    b. If the price level in this economy is 150, will quantity demanded equal, exceed, or fall short of quantity supplied? By what amount? If the price level is 250, will quantity demanded equal, exceed, or fall short of quantity supplied? By what amount?

    c. Suppose that buyers desire to purchase $200 billion of extra real output at each price level. Sketch in the new aggregate demand curve as AD₁. What is the new equilibrium price level and level of real output?

4. Suppose that the following table shows an economy's relationship between real output and the inputs needed to produce that output:**(LO3)**

Input Quantity	Real GDP
150.0	$400
112.5	300
75.0	200

    a. What is productivity in this economy?
    b. What is the per-unit cost of production if the price of each input unit is $2?
    c. Assume that the input price increases from $2 to $3 with no accompanying change in productivity. What is the new per-unit cost of production? In what direction would the $1 increase in input price push the economy's aggregate supply curve? What effect would this shift of aggregate supply have on the price level and the level of real output?
    d. Suppose that the increase in input price does not occur but, instead, that productivity increases by 100 percent. What would be the new per-unit cost of production? What effect would this change in per-unit production cost have on the economy's aggregate supply curve? What effect would this shift of aggregate supply have on the price level and the level of real output?

5. Refer to the data in the table that accompanies problem 2. Suppose that the present equilibrium price level and level of real GDP are 100 and $225, and that data set B represents the relevant aggregate supply schedule for the economy. **(LO4)**

    a. What must be the current amount of real output demanded at the 100 price level?
    b. If the amount of output demanded declined by $25 at the 100 price level shown in B, what would be the new equilibrium real GDP? In business cycle terminology, what would economists call this change in real GDP?

CHAPTER THIRTEEN

Fiscal Policy, Deficits, and Debt

Learning Objectives

LO13.1 Identify the purposes, tools, and limitations of fiscal policy.
LO13.2 Explain how built-in stabilizers moderate business cycles.
LO13.3 Describe how the cyclically adjusted budget reveals the status of U.S. fiscal policy.
LO13.4 Discuss the problems that governments may encounter in enacting and applying fiscal policy.
LO13.5 Discuss the size, composition, and consequences of the U.S. public debt.
LO13.6 Explain why there is a long-run fiscal imbalance in the Social Security system.

In the previous chapter, we saw that an excessive increase in aggregate demand can cause demand-pull inflation and that a significant decline in aggregate demand can cause recession and cyclical unemployment. For those reasons, the federal government sometimes tries to "stimulate the economy" or "rein in inflation." Such countercyclical **fiscal policy** consists of deliberate changes in government spending and tax collections designed to achieve full employment, control inflation, and encourage economic growth. (The adjective "fiscal" simply means "financial.")

We begin this chapter by examining the logic behind fiscal policy, its current status, and its limitations. Then, we examine two related topics: the U.S. public debt and the Social Security funding problem.

Fiscal Policy and the AD–AS Model

fiscal policy
Changes in government spending and tax collections designed to achieve a full-employment and noninflationary domestic output; also called *discretionary fiscal policy*.

Fiscal policy consists of changes in government spending and tax collections designed to achieve full employment, price stability, and economic growth. Fiscal policy can be either *discretionary* or *nondiscretionary*. Discretionary fiscal policy refers to changes in government spending and taxes that are *at the option* of the federal government. They do not occur automatically. The current congress must pass a discretionary spending or tax bill and the president must sign it into law. Nondiscretionary fiscal policy refers to changes in spending and taxes that occur automatically, or passively, without the need for congressional action. They occur as the result of spending and tax provisions put into law by earlier congresses.

Council of Economic Advisers (CEA)
A group of three persons that advises and assists the president of the United States on economic matters (including the preparation of the annual *Economic Report of the President*).

Discretionary fiscal policy is often initiated on the advice of the president's **Council of Economic Advisers (CEA),** a group of three economists who provide expertise and assistance on economic matters. Various congressional committees have final say, however, on the contents of any discretionary spending or tax bill that is sent to the president.

Expansionary Fiscal Policy

expansionary fiscal policy
An increase in government purchases of goods and services, a decrease in net taxes, or some combination of the two, for the purpose of increasing aggregate demand and expanding real output.

When a recession occurs, the government may initiate an **expansionary fiscal policy** designed to increase aggregate demand and therefore raise real GDP. Consider **Figure 13.1**, where lower profit expectations cause a sharp decline in investment spending that shifts the economy's aggregate demand curve to the left from AD_1 to AD_2. (Disregard the arrow for now.)

FIGURE 13.1

Expansionary fiscal policy. Expansionary fiscal policy uses increases in government spending, tax cuts, or a combination of both to increase aggregate demand and push the economy out of recession. Here, this policy increases aggregate demand from AD_2 to AD_1, increases real GDP from $490 billion to $510 billion, and restores full employment.

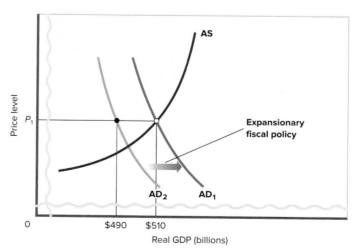

Suppose the economy's potential or full-employment output is $510 billion in **Figure 13.1**. If the price level is inflexible downward at P_1, the aggregate demand curve slides leftward at that price level and reduces real GDP to $490 billion. The result is a GDP gap of negative $20 billion (= $490 billion − $510 billion) arises. Unemployment increases because fewer workers are needed to produce the reduced output. In short, the economy depicted is suffering both recession and cyclical unemployment.

What fiscal policy should the federal government use to stimulate the economy? It has three main options: (1) increase government spending, (2) reduce taxes, or (3) use some combination of the two. If the federal budget is balanced at the outset, expansionary fiscal policy will create a government **budget deficit**—government spending in excess of tax revenues.

Increased Government Spending To increase aggregate demand, the federal government can increase its spending. For example, it might boost spending on highways, education, and health care. Other things equal, a sufficient increase in government spending will shift an economy's aggregate demand curve to the right, as from AD_2 to AD_1 in **Figure 13.1**. Observe that real output rises to $510 billion, up $20 billion from its recessionary level of $490 billion. Firms increase their employment to the full-employment level, output increases, and the negative GDP gap disappears.

Tax Reductions Alternatively, the government could reduce taxes to shift the aggregate demand curve rightward, as from AD_2 to AD_1. Suppose the government cuts personal income taxes, which increases disposable income. Households will spend a large part of that income and save the rest. The part spent—the new consumption spending—will increase aggregate demand. In **Figure 13.1**, this increase in aggregate demand from AD_2 to AD_1 expands real GDP by $20 billion, eliminating the negative GDP gap. Employment increases accordingly, and the unemployment rate falls.

A tax cut must be larger than an increase in government spending to achieve the same rightward shift of the aggregate demand curve. This is because households save part of the higher after-tax income provided by the tax cut. Only the part of the tax cut that increases consumption spending shifts the aggregate demand curve to the right.

Combined Government Spending Increases and Tax Reductions The government may combine spending increases and tax cuts to produce the desired initial increase in spending and the eventual increase in aggregate demand and real GDP. In the economy depicted in **Figure 13.1**, there is some combination of greater government spending and lower taxes (increased consumption spending) that will shift the aggregate demand curve from AD_2 to AD_1 and remove the negative GDP gap.

Contractionary Fiscal Policy

When demand-pull inflation occurs, a restrictive or **contractionary fiscal policy** may help control it. Take a look at **Figure 13.2**, where the full-employment level of real GDP is $510 billion. Suppose a sharp increase in investment and net export spending shifts the aggregate demand curve from AD_3 to AD_4. The outcomes are demand-pull inflation, as shown by the rise of the price level from P_1 to P_2, and a positive GDP gap of $12 billion (= $522 billion − $510 billion).

If the government decides on fiscal policy to control this inflation, its options are the opposite of those used to combat recession. It can (1) decrease government spending, (2) raise taxes, or (3) use some combination of those two policies. When the economy faces demand-pull inflation, fiscal policy should move toward a government **budget surplus**—tax revenues in excess of government spending.

Decreased Government Spending To control demand-pull inflation, the government can decrease aggregate demand by reducing government spending. In **Figure 13.2**, this spending cut shifts the aggregate demand curve leftward from AD_4 to AD_3. The policy would work fine if prices were downwardly flexible. The economy's equilibrium output would move back to the full-employment level of $510 billion and the price level would return to P_1.

budget deficit
The amount by which the expenditures of the federal government exceed its revenues in any year.

contractionary fiscal policy
A decrease in government purchases for goods and services, an increase in net taxes, or some combination of the two, for the purpose of decreasing aggregate demand and thus controlling inflation.

budget surplus
The amount by which the revenues of the federal government exceed its expenditures in any year.

FIGURE 13.2

Contractionary fiscal policy. Contractionary fiscal policy uses decreases in government spending, increases in taxes, or a combination of both to reduce aggregate demand and slow or eliminate demand-pull inflation. Here, this policy shifts the aggregate demand curve from AD_4 to AD_3, removes the upward pressure on the price level, and halts the demand-pull inflation. Note, however, that even though the inflation is stopped, the presence of inflexible ("sticky") prices may prevent the price level from falling to P_1.

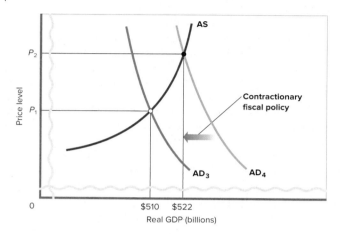

But this scenario is unlikely to happen as neatly as **Figure 13.2** suggests. Increases in aggregate demand tend to ratchet the price level upward, but declines in aggregate demand do not seem to push the price level downward. So stopping inflation is a matter of halting the rise of the price level, not trying to lower it to the previous level. Demand-pull inflation usually is experienced as a continual rightward shifting of the aggregate demand curve. Contractionary fiscal policy is designed to stop a further shift, not to restore a lower price level. Successful fiscal policy eliminates a continuing positive (and thus inflationary) GDP gap and prevents the price level from continuing its inflationary rise. Nevertheless, **Figure 13.2** displays the basic principle: Reductions in government expenditures can be used as a fiscal policy action to tame demand-pull inflation.

Tax Increases   Just as government can use tax cuts to increase consumption spending, it can use tax increases to reduce consumption spending. In the economy in **Figure 13.2**, the government must raise taxes sufficiently to reduce consumption such that the aggregate demand curve will shift leftward from AD_4 to AD_3. That way, the demand-pull inflation will have been controlled.

Because part of any tax increase reduces saving rather than consumption, a tax increase must exceed a decrease in government spending to cause the same leftward shift of the aggregate demand curve. Only the part of the tax increase that lowers consumption spending reduces aggregate demand.

Combined Government Spending Decreases and Tax Increases   The government may choose to combine spending decreases and tax increases in order to reduce aggregate demand and check inflation. Some combination of lower government spending and higher taxes will shift the aggregate demand curve from AD_4 to AD_3.

Built-In Stability

Under normal circumstances, government tax revenues change automatically over the course of the business cycle in ways that stabilize the economy. This automatic response, or built-in stability, constitutes nondiscretionary (or "passive" or "automatic") budgetary policy and results from the makeup of most tax systems. We did not include this built-in stability in our earlier discussion of fiscal policy because we implicitly assumed that the same amount of tax revenue was being collected at each level of GDP. But the actual U.S. tax system is such that *net tax revenues* vary directly with GDP. (*Net taxes* are tax revenues less transfers and subsidies. From here on, we will use the simpler "taxes" to mean "net taxes.")

Virtually any tax will yield more tax revenue as GDP rises. In particular, personal income taxes have progressive rates and thus generate more-than-proportionate increases in tax revenues as GDP expands. Furthermore, as GDP rises and more goods and services are purchased, revenues from corporate income taxes and from sales taxes and excise taxes also increase. And, similarly, revenues from payroll taxes rise as economic expansion creates more jobs. Conversely, when GDP declines, tax receipts from all these sources also decline.

Transfer payments (or "negative taxes") behave in the opposite way from tax revenues. Unemployment compensation and welfare payments decrease during economic expansion and increase during economic contraction.

Automatic or Built-In Stabilizers

A **built-in stabilizer** is anything that increases the government's budget deficit (or reduces its budget surplus) during a recession and increases its budget surplus (or reduces its budget deficit) during inflation without requiring explicit action by policymakers. As **Figure 13.3** reveals, this is precisely what the U.S. tax system does. Government expenditures G are fixed and assumed to be independent of the level of GDP. Congress decides on a particular level of spending, but it does not determine the magnitude of tax revenues. Instead, it establishes tax rates, and the tax revenues then vary directly with the level of GDP that the economy achieves. Line T represents that direct relationship between tax revenues and GDP.

built-in stabilizer
A mechanism that increases government's budget deficit (or reduces its surplus) during a recession and increases government's budget surplus (or reduces its deficit) during expansion without any action by policymakers. The tax system is one such mechanism.

Economic Importance

The economic importance of the direct relationship between tax receipts and GDP becomes apparent when we consider that:

- Taxes reduce spending and aggregate demand.
- Reductions in spending are desirable when the economy is moving toward inflation, whereas increases in spending are desirable when the economy is slumping.

As shown in **Figure 13.3**, tax revenues automatically increase as GDP rises during prosperity, and because taxes reduce household and business spending, they restrain the economic expansion. That is, as the economy moves toward a higher GDP, tax revenues automatically rise and move the budget from deficit toward surplus. In **Figure 13.3**, observe that the high and perhaps inflationary income level GDP_3 automatically generates a contractionary budget surplus.

Conversely, as GDP falls during recession, tax revenues automatically decline, increasing spending by households and businesses and thus cushioning the economic contraction. With a falling GDP, tax receipts decline and move the government's budget from surplus toward deficit. In **Figure 13.3**, the low level of income GDP_1 will automatically yield an expansionary budget deficit.

FIGURE 13.3
Built-in stability. Tax revenues, *T,* vary directly with GDP, and government spending *G* is assumed to be independent of GDP. As GDP falls in a recession, deficits occur automatically and help alleviate the recession. As GDP rises during expansion, surpluses occur automatically and help offset possible inflation.

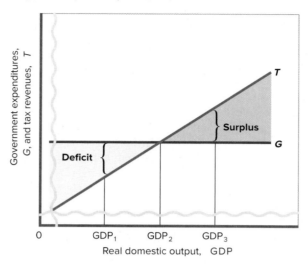

The built-in stability provided by the U.S. tax system has reduced the severity of business fluctuations, perhaps by as much as 8 to 10 percent of the change in GDP that otherwise would have occurred.[1] In recession year 2009, for example, revenues from the individual income tax fell by a staggering 22 percent. This decline helped keep household spending and real GDP from falling even more than they did. But built-in stabilizers can only dampen, not counteract, swings in real GDP. Discretionary fiscal policy (changes in tax rates and expenditures) or monetary policy (central bank–caused changes in interest rates) may be needed to counter a recession or an inflation of any appreciable magnitude.

Evaluating Fiscal Policy

How can we determine whether a government's discretionary fiscal policy is expansionary, neutral, or contractionary? We cannot simply examine the actual budget deficits or surpluses that take place under the current policy because they will necessarily include the automatic changes in tax revenues that accompany every change in GDP. In addition, the expansionary or contractionary strength of any change in discretionary fiscal policy depends not on its absolute size but on how large it is relative to the size of the economy. So, in evaluating the status of fiscal policy, we must adjust deficits and surpluses to eliminate automatic changes in tax revenues and also compare the sizes of the adjusted budget deficits and surpluses to the level of potential GDP.

cyclically adjusted budget
A measure of what the federal budget deficit or budget surplus would be with the existing tax and government spending programs if the economy had achieved full-employment GDP in the year.

Economists use the **cyclically adjusted budget** (or *full-employment budget*) to adjust actual federal budget deficits and surpluses to account for the changes in tax revenues that happen automatically whenever GDP changes. The cyclically adjusted budget measures what the federal budget deficit or surplus would have been under existing tax rates and government spending programs if the economy had achieved its full-employment level of GDP (its potential output). The idea is to compare *actual* government expenditures with the tax revenues *that would have occurred* if the economy

---

[1] Alan J. Auerbach and Daniel Feenberg, "The Significance of Federal Taxes as Automatic Stabilizers," *Journal of Economic Perspectives*, Summer 2000, p. 54.

had achieved full-employment GDP. That procedure removes budget deficits or surpluses that arise simply because of cyclical changes in GDP and thus tells us nothing about whether the government's current discretionary fiscal policy is fundamentally expansionary, contractionary, or neutral.

Consider **Figure 13.4**, where line G represents government expenditures and line T represents tax revenues. In full-employment year 1, government expenditures of $500 billion equal tax revenues of $500 billion, as indicated by the intersection of lines G and T at point a. The actual budget deficit and the cyclically adjusted budget deficit in year 1 are zero—government expenditures equal tax revenues, and government spending equals the tax revenues forthcoming at the full-employment output GDP_1. Obviously, the cyclically adjusted budget deficit *as a percentage of potential GDP* is also zero. The government's fiscal policy is neutral.

Now suppose that a recession occurs and GDP falls from GDP_1 to GDP_2, as shown in **Figure 13.4**. Let's also assume that the government takes no discretionary action, so lines G and T remain as shown in the figure. Tax revenues automatically fall to $450 billion (point c) at GDP_2, while government spending remains unaltered at $500 billion (point b). A $50 billion actual budget deficit (represented by distance bc) arises. But this **cyclical deficit** is simply a by-product of the economy's slide into recession, not the result of discretionary fiscal actions by the government. We would be wrong to conclude from this deficit that the government is engaging in an expansionary fiscal policy. The government's fiscal policy has not changed; it is still neutral.

That fact is highlighted when we consider the cyclically adjusted budget deficit for year 2 in **Figure 13.4**. The $500 billion of government expenditures in year 2 is shown by b on line G. And, as shown by a on line T, $500 billion of tax revenues would have occurred if the economy had achieved its full-employment GDP. Because both b and a represent $500 billion, the cyclically adjusted budget deficit in year 2 is zero, as is this deficit as a percentage of potential GDP. Because the full-employment deficits are zero in both years, we know that government did not change its discretionary fiscal policy, even though a recession occurred and an actual deficit of $50 billion resulted.

cyclical deficit
A federal budget deficit that is caused by a recession and the consequent decline in tax revenues.

FIGURE 13.4
Cyclically adjusted budget deficits. The cyclically adjusted budget deficit is zero at the full-employment output GDP_1. But it is also zero at the recessionary output GDP_2 because the $500 billion of government expenditures at GDP_2 equals the $500 billion of tax revenues that would be forthcoming at the full-employment GDP_1. Here, fiscal policy did not change as the economy slid into recession. The deficit that arose is simply a cyclical deficit.

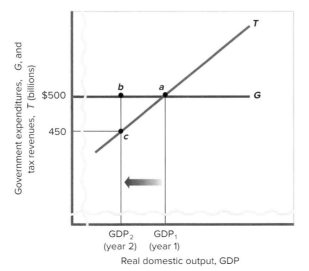

In contrast, if we observed a cyclically adjusted deficit of zero in a specific year, followed by a cyclically adjusted budget surplus in the next, we could conclude that fiscal policy has changed from being neutral to being contractionary. Because the cyclically adjusted budget adjusts for automatic changes in tax revenues, the increase in the cyclically adjusted budget surplus reveals that government either decreased its spending (G) or increased tax rates such that tax revenues (T) increased. In **Figure 13.4**, the government either shifted line G downward or line T upward. These changes in G and T are precisely the discretionary actions that we have identified as elements of a *contractionary* fiscal policy.

APPLYING THE ANALYSIS

Recent U.S. Fiscal Policy

Table 13.1 lists actual federal budget deficits and surpluses (column 2) as a percentage of actual GDP, and cyclically adjusted deficits and surpluses (column 3) as a percentage of potential GDP, between 2000 and 2018. Note that:

- Cyclically adjusted deficits are generally smaller than actual deficits because the actual deficits include cyclical deficits, whereas the cyclically adjusted deficits eliminate them.
- Only cyclically adjusted surpluses and deficits as percentages of potential GDP (column 3) provide the information needed to determine whether fiscal policy is expansionary, contractionary, or neutral.

TABLE 13.1
Federal Deficits (−) and Surpluses (+) as Percentages of GDP, 2000–2018

(1)	(2)	(3)
Year	Actual Deficit − or Surplus +	Cyclically Adjusted Deficit − or Surplus +[*]
2000	+2.4	+1.5
2001	+1.2	+1.1
2002	−1.4	−0.8
2003	−3.3	−2.4
2004	−3.4	−2.9
2005	−2.5	−2.3
2006	−1.8	−1.9
2007	−1.1	−1.3
2008	−3.1	−2.9
2009	−9.3	−7.6
2010	−8.3	−6.4
2011	−8.1	−6.5
2012	−6.6	−5.3
2013	−4.0	−2.8
2014	−2.7	−1.8
2015	−2.4	−1.9
2016	−3.1	−2.7
2017	−3.4	−3.1
2018	−3.9	−3.9

[*]As a percentage of potential GDP.
Source: Congressional Budget Office, www.cbo.gov.

Take a look at the data for the year 2000. The economy was fully employed that year. Tax revenues poured into the Treasury and exceeded government expenditures by 2.4 percent. But not all was well. A bubble in tech stocks burst that spring, and the U.S. economy noticeably slowed during the latter half of the year. In March 2001, the economy slid into a recession.

Congress and the Bush administration responded by cutting taxes by $44 billion in 2001 and scheduling an additional $52 billion of cuts for 2002. These stimulus policies helped boost the economy, offset the recession, and cushion the economic blow delivered by the September 11, 2001, terrorist attacks. In March 2002, Congress passed further tax cuts totaling $122 billion over two years and extended unemployment benefits.

As **Table 13.1** reveals, the cyclically adjusted budget moved from a surplus of 1.5 percent of potential GDP in 2000 to a deficit of −0.8 percent in 2002. Fiscal policy had definitely turned expansionary. Nevertheless, the economy remained sluggish through 2002 and into 2003.

In June 2003, Congress again cut taxes, this time by a much larger $350 billion over several years. The new tax legislation accelerated the reduction of marginal tax rates already scheduled for future years and slashed tax rates on income from dividends and capital gains. It also increased tax breaks for families and small businesses. This tax package increased the cyclically adjusted budget deficit as a percentage of potential GDP to −2.4 percent in 2003. The economy strengthened, and both real output and employment grew between 2003 and 2007. By 2007, full employment had been restored, although a −1.3 percent cyclically adjusted budget deficit still remained.

In the summer of 2007, a crisis in the market for mortgage loans flared up and then quickly exploded through every part of the financial system. Banks went bankrupt, major corporations like General Motors hurtled toward bankruptcy, and the stock market fell almost 50 percent. As the crisis worsened, general pessimism spread beyond the financial markets to the overall economy. Businesses and households curtailed spending, and in December 2007, the economy entered the Great Recession. To stimulate the economy, Congress passed a $152 billion stimulus package in 2008 that focused primarily on sending checks of up to $600 each to taxpayers, veterans, and Social Security recipients.

As a percentage of GDP, the *actual* federal budget deficit jumped from −1.1 percent in 2007 to −3.1 percent in 2008. This increase resulted from an automatic drop-off of tax revenues during the recession, along with the fiscal stimulus checks paid out in 2008. As **Table 13.1** shows, the *cyclically adjusted* budget deficit rose from −1.3 percent of potential GDP in 2007 to −2.9 percent in 2008. This increase in the cyclically adjusted budget deficit reveals that fiscal policy in 2008 was expansionary.

The government hoped that those receiving checks would spend the money and thus boost consumption and aggregate demand. But households either saved the money or used it to pay down credit card loans. Spending remained low and the economy continued to flounder.

In response, Congress enacted the American Recovery and Reinvestment Act of 2009. This gigantic $787 billion program consisted of tax rebates, plus large spending increases on infrastructure, education, and health care. The idea was to flood the economy with additional spending to try to boost aggregate demand and get people back to work.

Unlike the lump-sum stimulus checks of 2008, the 2009 tax rebates showed up as small increases in workers' monthly payroll checks. By giving workers smaller amounts per month rather than a single large check, the government hoped that people would spend rather than save the bulk of their enhanced income.

The recession officially ended during the summer of 2009, but the economy did not rebound vigorously. Unemployment remained elevated and tax collections were low due to a stagnant economy. As a result, policymakers decided to continue with large amounts of fiscal stimulus. Annual actual (not cyclically adjusted) budget deficits amounted to −4.0, −2.7, and −2.4 percent of GDP, respectively, in 2013, 2014, and 2015. The cyclically adjusted budget deficits for those years were, respectively, −2.8, −1.8, and −1.9 percent of potential GDP. Thus, while the intensity of fiscal stimulus was gradually diminishing, it remained substantially expansionary.

More recent years have seen a continued use of fiscal stimulus, as evidenced by the fact that the cyclically adjusted deficit rose above 3 percent in both 2017 and 2018. These were, however, full-employment years. As a result, quite a few economists questioned whether the government should have been applying so much stimulus at a time when the economy's resources were fully employed. In their reckoning, that much stimulus would only lead to inflation. Other economists countered that strong fiscal stimulus was still needed to counter lingering problems in the financial sector.

Inflation was 2.1 percent in 2017 and 2.4 percent in 2018. Both groups of economists claimed that those figures supported their own position. The group worried about inflation pointed out that inflation was above the

Federal Reserve's 2-percent inflation target in both years and, in addition, was rising. To them, this indicated that the economy was overheating and inflation would accelerate. The other group argued that with inflation under 3 percent, overheating was unlikely.

In February 2020, the COVID-19 pandemic diminished inflation concerns as the economy spiraled into recession. Congress responded quickly, passing the Coronavirus Aid, Relief, and Economic Security (CARES) Act in March 2020. This $2.2 trillion fiscal stimulus included sending $1,200 checks ("Economic Impact Payments") to most adults, increasing unemployment benefits, creating the Paycheck Protection Program to encourage small businesses to maintain payrolls, and providing aid for large corporations and support for state and local governments. A second round of smaller stimulus checks was passed in December 2020, and in March 2021, the American Rescue Plan, an additional $1.9 trillion in COVID relief, was proposed by President Biden and passed in Congress.

Predictably, these expansionary fiscal measures increased the size of the government's budget deficit. The deficit reached −14.9 percent of GDP in 2020, a level not seen since World War II, and was projected for 2021 to be −10.3 percent of GDP, the second-largest deficit since 1945.

QUESTION:

Some argue that the fiscal policy response to the COVID-19 pandemic should have only targeted groups in the economy with the most urgent need for assistance; others contend relief was not broad enough. How would you expect the two approaches to differ in their effectiveness at promoting economic recovery and restoring full employment?

Problems, Criticisms, and Complications

Governments may encounter a number of significant problems in enacting and applying fiscal policy.

Problems of Timing

Several problems of timing may arise in connection with fiscal policy:

- **Recognition lag** is the time between the beginning of recession or inflation and the certain awareness that it is actually happening. This lag arises because the economy does not move smoothly through the business cycle. Even during good times, the economy has slow months interspersed with months of rapid growth and expansion. Recognizing a recession is difficult because several slow months will have to happen in succession before people can conclude with any confidence that the good times are over and a recession has begun. The same is true with inflation. Several high-inflation months must come in sequence before people can confidently conclude that inflation has moved to a higher level. Due to recognition lags, the economy is often four to six months into a recession or inflation before the situation is clearly discernible in the relevant statistics. As a result, the economic downturn or inflation may become more serious than it would have if the situation had been identified and acted on sooner.

- **Administrative lag** is the time between when policymakers recognize the need for a fiscal action and when that fiscal action is taken. The wheels of democratic government turn slowly. Following the terrorist attacks of September 11, 2001, the U.S. Congress was stalemated for five months before passing a compromise economic stimulus law in March 2002.

- **Operational lag** is the delay between the time fiscal action is ordered and the time that it actually begins to affect output, employment, or the price level. Tax changes have very short operational lags because they can be lowered instantly and have immediate impacts on household and business spending. By contrast, government spending on public works—new dams, interstate highways, and so on—requires long planning periods and even longer periods of construction. Such spending is of questionable use in offsetting short (e.g., 6- to 12-month) periods of recession. Consequently, discretionary fiscal policy has increasingly relied on tax changes rather than on changes in spending so as to reduce or eliminate the operational lag.

Political Considerations

Fiscal policy is conducted in a political arena. That reality not only may slow the enactment of fiscal policy but also generate situations in which political considerations override economic considerations. Politicians are human—they want to get re-elected. A strong economy at election time will certainly help them. So they may favor large tax cuts under the guise of expansionary fiscal policy even though that policy is economically inappropriate. Similarly, they may rationalize increased government spending on popular items such as farm subsidies, highways, education, and homeland security.

At the extreme, elected officials and political parties might collectively "hijack" fiscal policy for political purposes, cause inappropriate changes in aggregate demand, and thereby cause (rather than avert) economic fluctuations. In short, elected officials may cause so-called **political business cycles**—swings in overall economic activity and real GDP resulting from election-motivated fiscal policy, rather than from a desire to offset volatility in the private sector. Political business cycles are difficult to document and prove, but there is little doubt that political considerations weigh heavily in the formulation of fiscal policy.

political business cycle
The alleged tendency of presidential administrations and Congress to destabilize the economy by reducing taxes and increasing government expenditures before elections and to raise taxes and lower expenditures after elections.

Future Policy Reversals

Fiscal policy may fail to achieve its intended objectives if households expect future reversals of policy. Consider a tax cut, for example. If taxpayers believe the tax reduction is temporary, they may save a large portion of their tax cut, reasoning that rates will return to their previous level in the future. They save more now so that they will be able to draw on their extra savings in the future when taxes rise again. So a tax reduction thought to be temporary may not increase present consumption spending and aggregate demand by as much as our simple model (**Figure 13.1**) suggests.

The opposite may be true for a tax increase. If taxpayers think it is temporary, they may reduce their saving to pay the tax while maintaining their present consumption. They may reason that they can restore their saving when the tax rate again falls. So the tax increase may not reduce current consumption and aggregate demand by as much as policymakers intended.

To the extent that *consumption smoothing* occurs over time, fiscal policy will lose some of its strength.

Offsetting State and Local Finance

The fiscal policies of state and local governments are frequently *pro-cyclical*, meaning that they worsen rather than correct recession or inflation. Unlike the federal government, most state and local governments face constitutional or other legal requirements to balance their budgets. Like households and private businesses, state and local governments increase their expenditures during prosperity and cut them during recession.

During the Great Depression of the 1930s, most of the increase in federal spending was offset by decreases in state and local spending. During and immediately following the recession of 2001, many state and local governments offset lower tax revenues by raising tax rates, imposing new taxes, and reducing spending.

The $787 billion fiscal package of 2009 made a special effort to reduce this problem by giving substantial aid dollars to state governments. Because of the sizable federal aid, the states did not have to increase taxes and reduce expenditures as much as they would have otherwise. Thus, their collective fiscal actions did not offset the federal stimulus by nearly as much as would have been the case if states had not received the aid money.

Crowding-Out Effect

crowding-out effect
A rise in interest rates and a resulting decrease in investment caused by the federal government's increased borrowing to finance budget deficits or debt.

Another potential flaw of fiscal policy is the **crowding-out effect:** An expansionary fiscal policy (deficit spending) may increase the interest rate and reduce investment spending, thereby weakening or canceling the stimulus of the expansionary policy. The rising interest rate might also potentially crowd out interest-sensitive consumption spending (such as purchasing automobiles on credit). But because investment is the most volatile component of GDP, the crowding-out effect focuses its attention on investment and whether the stimulus provided by deficit spending may be partly or even fully neutralized by an offsetting reduction in investment spending.

To see the potential problem, realize that whenever the government borrows money (which it must do to engage in deficit spending), it increases the overall demand for money. If the monetary authorities are holding the money supply constant, this increase in demand will raise the price paid for borrowing money: the interest rate. Because investment spending varies inversely with the interest rate, some investments will be choked off or "crowded out."

Crowding out is likely to be less of a problem when the economy is in recession because investment demand tends to be weak. The reason: Output purchases slow during recessions, and therefore most businesses end up with substantial excess capacity. As a result, they do not have much incentive to add new machinery or build new factories. After all, why should they add capacity when some of the capacity they already have is lying idle?

With investment demand weak during a recession, the crowding-out effect is likely to be very small. Simply put, there isn't much investment for the government to crowd out. Even if deficit spending does increase the interest rate, the effect on investment may be fully offset by the improved investment prospects that businesses expect from the fiscal stimulus.

By contrast, when the economy is operating at or near full capacity, investment demand is likely to be quite strong, and crowding out will probably be a much more serious problem. When the economy is booming, factories will be running at or near full capacity and firms will have investment demand for two reasons. First, equipment running at full capacity wears out fast, so firms will invest substantial amounts to replace worn-out machinery and equipment. Second, the economy is likely to be growing overall, so firms will invest to increase their production capacity and take advantage of the economy's increasing demand for goods and services.

The U.S. Public Debt

public debt
The total amount owed by the federal government to the owners of government securities; equal to the sum of past government budget deficits less government budget surpluses.

The U.S. national debt, or **public debt,** is the accumulation of all past federal deficits and surpluses. The deficits have greatly exceeded the surpluses and have emerged mainly from war financing, recessions, and fiscal policy. As of February 2021, the total public debt was $27.9 trillion—$21.8 trillion held by the public, excluding the Federal Reserve, and $6.1 trillion held by federal agencies and the Federal Reserve.

To provide some historical perspective, the public debt was much smaller prior to the 2007–2009 recession. In 2006, it was $8.5 trillion. It then more than doubled, to $18.2 trillion in 2015, as large budget deficits were run to fight the Great Recession. It continued to rise during the late 2010s despite the economy returning to full employment in 2017. When the COVID-19 pandemic caused a recession in 2020, relief spending added significantly to the total, with the public debt rising roughly $4.5 trillion from February 2020 to February 2021.

The ongoing rise of the public debt, even during times of full employment, has generated a lot of consternation and concern that we will discuss and analyze in this section. As with much else in economics, the public debt brings with it both costs and benefits.

Ownership

The total public debt of nearly $28 trillion represents the total amount of money owed by the federal government to the holders of **U.S. securities:** financial instruments issued by the federal government to borrow money to finance expenditures that exceed tax revenues. U.S. government securities (loan instruments) are of four types: *Treasury bills* (short-term securities), *Treasury notes* (medium-term securities), *Treasury bonds* (long-term securities), and *U.S. savings bonds* (long-term, nonmarketable bonds).

Figure 13.5 shows that the public, not including the Federal Reserve, held 62 percent of the federal debt in 2018 and that federal government agencies and the Federal Reserve held the remaining 38 percent. Foreigners held about 29 percent of the total U.S. public debt in 2018, meaning that most of the U.S. public debt is held internally and not externally. Americans owed 71 percent of the public debt to Americans. Of the $6.2 trillion of debt held by foreigners, China held 21 percent, Japan held 19 percent, and oil-exporting nations held 3 percent.

U.S. securities
Treasury bills, Treasury notes, Treasury bonds, and U.S. savings bonds issued by the federal government to finance expenditures that exceed tax revenues.

FIGURE 13.5

Ownership of the total public debt, 2018. The $21.5 trillion public debt owed by the U.S. federal government in 2018 can be divided into the 62 percent held by the public (excluding the Federal Reserve), and the proportion held by federal agencies and the Federal Reserve System (38 percent). Of the total debt, 29 percent is foreign-owned.

Sources: *Economic Report of the President, 2019*, and *Treasury Bulletin*, March 2019, U.S. Treasury.

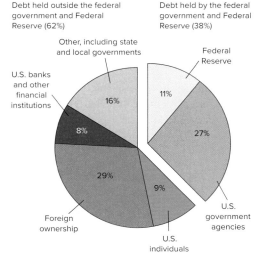

Debt and GDP

A simple statement of the absolute size of the debt ignores the fact that the wealth and productive ability of the U.S. economy are also vast. A wealthy, highly productive nation can incur and carry a large public debt much more easily than a poor nation can. A more meaningful measure of the public debt relates it to an economy's GDP. **Figure 13.6** shows the yearly relative sizes of the U.S. public debt held outside the Federal Reserve and federal agencies. In 2018, the percentage was 76 percent of GDP. The figure also indicates that public debt as a percentage of GDP rose dramatically starting in 2008 because of massive annual budget deficits. The rising percentage indicates that the debt levels of recent years are more burdensome relative to national income than were the debt levels in earlier years.

FIGURE 13.6

Federal debt held by the public, excluding the Federal Reserve, as a percentage of GDP, 1970–2018. As a percentage of GDP, the federal debt held by the public (held outside the Federal Reserve and federal government agencies) increased sharply over the 1980–1995 period and declined significantly between 1995 and 2001. Since 2001, the percentage has gone up again, jumping sharply starting in 2008.

Sources: Federal Reserve Bank of St. Louis and U.S. Office of Management and Budget.

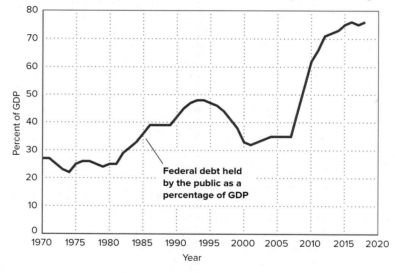

International Comparisons

It is not uncommon for countries to have sizable public debts. As **Global Snapshot 13.1** shows, the public debt as a percentage of real GDP in the United States is neither particularly high nor low relative to such debt percentages in other advanced industrial nations.

GLOBAL SNAPSHOT 13.1

Publicly Held Debt: International Comparisons

Although the United States has the world's largest public debt, a number of other nations have larger debts as percentages of their GDPs.

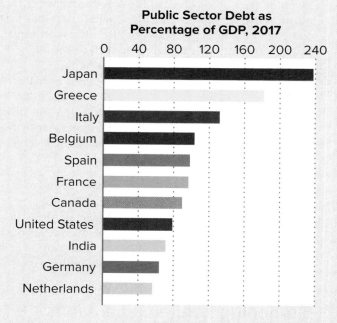

Public Sector Debt as Percentage of GDP, 2017

Source: Central Intelligence Agency

Interest Charges

Many economists conclude that the primary burden of the debt is the annual interest charge accruing on the government notes and bonds sold to finance the debt. In 2018, interest on the total public debt was $371 billion. Although this amount is sizable in absolute terms, it was only 1.8 percent of GDP for 2018. So, the federal government had to collect taxes equal to 1.8 percent of GDP to service the total public debt. This percentage was virtually unchanged from 2000, despite the much higher total public debt, mostly because the Federal Reserve kept interest rates low in the wake of the Great Recession.

False Concerns?

You may wonder if the large public debt might bankrupt the United States or place a tremendous burden on future generations. Fortunately, these are largely false concerns. People were wondering the same things 50 years ago!

Bankruptcy

The large U.S. public debt does not threaten to bankrupt the federal government or leave it unable to meet its financial obligations. There are two main reasons: refinancing and taxation.

Refinancing   As long as lenders view the U.S. public debt as manageable and sustainable, the public debt is easily refinanced. As portions of the debt come due each month, the government does not cut expenditures or raise taxes to provide the funds required. Rather, it refinances the debt by selling new bonds and using the proceeds to pay off the maturing bonds. The new bonds are in strong demand because lenders obtain a tradable security that (unlike other assets such as stocks, corporate debt, and real estate) is considered nearly riskless since there is virtually zero chance that the U.S. government would default on its debt payments.

Of course, refinancing could become an issue with a high enough debt-to-GDP ratio. Some countries, including Greece, have encountered this problem. High and rising ratios in the United States might raise fears that the U.S. government might be unable to pay back loans as they come due. But this is a false concern for the United States, given the U.S. economy's strong long-term growth prospects and how modest the U.S. debt-to-GDP ratio is as compared with those of other countries (see **Global Snapshot 13.1**).

Taxation   Financially distressed private households and corporations cannot extract themselves from their financial difficulties by taxing the public. If their incomes or sales revenues fall short of their expenses, they can indeed go bankrupt. But the federal government *does* have the option to impose new taxes or increase existing tax rates to finance its debt. Such tax hikes may be politically unpopular and may weaken incentives to work and invest, but they *are* a means of raising funds to finance the debt.

Burdening Future Generations

In 2018, public debt per capita was $65,709. Was each child born in 2018 handed a $65,709 bill from the federal government? Not really. The public debt does not impose as much of a burden on future generations because the United States owes a substantial portion of the public debt to itself. U.S. citizens and institutions (banks, businesses, insurance companies, governmental agencies, and trust funds) own about 71 percent of the U.S. government securities. Although that part of the public debt is a liability to Americans (as taxpayers), it is simultaneously an asset to Americans (as holders of Treasury bills, Treasury notes, Treasury bonds, and U.S. savings bonds).

To eliminate the American-owned part of the public debt would require a gigantic transfer payment from Americans to Americans. Taxpayers would pay higher taxes, and holders of the debt would receive an equal amount for their U.S. securities. Purchasing power in the United States would not change. Only the repayment of the 31 percent of the public debt owned by foreigners would negatively impact U.S. purchasing power.

The public debt increased sharply during World War II. But the decision to finance military purchases through the sale of government bonds did not shift the economic burden of the war to future generations. The economic cost of World War II consisted of the civilian goods society had to forgo in shifting scarce resources to war goods production. Regardless of whether society financed this reallocation through higher taxes or through borrowing, the real economic burden of the war would have been the same. That burden was borne almost entirely by those who lived during the war. They were the ones who did without a multitude of consumer goods to enable the United States to arm itself and its allies.

The next generation inherited the debt from World War II, but it also inherited an equal amount of government bonds that would pay them cash in future years. It also inherited the enormous benefits from the victory—namely, preserved political and economic systems at home and the "export" of those systems to Germany, Italy, and Japan. Those outcomes enhanced postwar U.S. economic growth and helped raise the standard of living for future generations of Americans.

Substantive Issues

Although the preceding issues relating to the public debt are false concerns, a number of substantive issues are not. Economists, however, attach varying degrees of importance to them.

Income Distribution

The ownership of government securities is highly uneven. Some people own much more than the $65,709-per-person portion of government securities; other people own less or none at all. In general, the ownership of the public debt is concentrated among wealthier groups. While the overall federal tax system is only slightly progressive, interest payments on the public debt do mildly increase income inequality. Income is transferred from people who, on average, have lower incomes to the higher-income bondholders. If greater income equality is one of society's goals, then this redistribution is undesirable.

Incentives

The current public debt necessitates annual interest payments of $371 billion. With no increase in the size of the debt, that interest charge must be paid out of tax revenues. Higher taxes may dampen incentives to bear risk, to innovate, to invest, and to work. So, in this indirect way, a large public debt may impair economic growth and therefore impose a burden of reduced output (and income) on future generations.

Foreign-Owned Public Debt

The 29 percent of the U.S. debt held by foreign citizens, foreign businesses, and foreign governments *is* an economic burden to Americans. Because we do not owe that portion of the debt "to ourselves," the payment of interest and principal on this **external public debt** enables foreigners to buy some of our output. In return for the benefits derived from the borrowed funds, the United States transfers goods and services to foreign lenders. However, Americans also own debt issued by foreign governments, so payment of principal and interest by those governments transfers some of their goods and services to Americans.

external public debt
Public debt owed to foreign citizens, firms, and institutions.

Crowding-Out Effect Revisited

A potentially more serious problem is the financing (and continual refinancing) of the large public debt, which can transfer a real economic burden to future generations by passing on to them a smaller stock of capital goods. This possibility involves the previously discussed crowding-out effect: the idea that public borrowing drives up real interest rates, thereby reducing private investment spending. If public borrowing only happened during recessions, crowding out would not likely be much of a problem. Because private investment demand tends to be weak during recessions, any increase in interest rates during a recession would at most cause only a small reduction in investment spending.

In contrast, the need to continuously finance a large public debt may be more troublesome. Continuous financing implies having to borrow large amounts of money when the economy is near or at its full-employment output. Because private investment is strong near economic peaks, any increase in interest rates at or near a peak may result in a substantial decline in investment spending. If the amount of current investment crowded out is extensive, future generations will inherit an economy with a smaller production capacity and, other things equal, a lower standard of living.

public investments
Government expenditures on public capital (such as roads, highways, bridges, mass-transit systems, and electric power facilities) and on human capital (such as education, training, and health).

Public Investments and Public–Private Complementarities But even with crowding out, two factors could partly or fully offset the net economic burden shifted to future generations. First, just as private expenditures may involve either consumption or investment, so it is with public goods. Part of the government spending enabled by the public debt is for public investment outlays (e.g., highways, mass transit systems, and electric power facilities) and human capital (e.g., investments in education, job training, and health). Like private expenditures on machinery and equipment, those **public investments** increase the economy's future production capacity by increasing the stock of public capital passed on to future generations. That greater stock of public capital may offset the diminished stock of private capital resulting from the crowding-out effect, leaving overall production capacity unimpaired.

Public–private complementarities may also reduce the crowding-out effect. Some public and private investments are complementary. Thus, a public investment financed through debt could spur some private-sector investment by increasing its expected rate of return. For example, a newly built federal building in a city may encourage private investment in the form of nearby office buildings, shops, and restaurants. Through this complementary effect, government spending on public capital may shift the private investment demand curve to the right. Even if the government borrowing needed to build the new federal building boosts the interest rate, total private investment need not fall. However, the increase in private investment might be smaller than anticipated. If it is, then the crowding-out effect will not be fully offset.

The Long-Run Fiscal Imbalance: Social Security

The percentage of the U.S. population age 62 or older will rise substantially over the next several decades. As a result, fewer workers will be paying taxes into the Social Security system (income during retirement) and the Medicare system (medical care during retirement). Simultaneously, however, the "greying of the population" will result in many more retirees. The number of workers per Social Security and Medicare beneficiary was roughly 5:1 in 1960. Today it is 3:1, and by 2040 it will be only 2:1. As that ratio continues to fall, it will become impossible at current tax rates to fulfill the benefits promised under current law. Either taxes must rise, or benefits must be cut. We will focus our attention on Social Security.

The Social Security Shortfall

Social Security is the major public retirement program in the United States. The program costs $888 billion annually and is financed by a 12.4 percent tax on wage and salary earnings (up to $118,500 in 2016). Half the tax is paid by the worker; the other half by the employer. It is a "pay-as-you-go" plan, meaning that most of the current revenues from the Social Security tax are paid to current Social Security retirees.

Until 2009, annual Social Security tax revenues exceeded annual Social Security retirement payouts. That excess annual inflow was used to buy U.S. Treasury securities that were credited to a government account called the **Social Security trust fund.** But starting in 2009, annual Social Security revenues fell below Social Security payouts, and the system started shifting money from the trust fund to make up the difference. As a result, the trust fund is expected to be exhausted in 2033. For each year thereafter, annual tax revenues will cover only 75 percent of the promised benefits. "Similarly, Medicare has a trust fund, and it is expected to be exhausted by 2024."

Social Security trust fund
A federal fund that saves excessive Social Security tax revenues received in one year to meet Social Security benefit obligations that exceed Social Security tax revenues in some subsequent year.

PHOTO OP

Will Social Security Be There for You?

Social Security is largely a "pay-as-you-go" plan, in which current retirement benefits are paid out of current payroll taxes. But the number of retirees in the United States is growing faster than the number of workers, foretelling a future funding shortfall.

Purestock/SuperStock

Guerilla/Alamy Stock Photo

Policy Options

To restore long-run balance to Social Security, the federal government must either reduce benefits or increase revenues. It's as simple—and as complicated—as that. The Social Security Administration concludes that bringing projected Social Security revenues and payments into balance over the next 75 years would require a 16 percent permanent reduction in Social Security benefits, a 13 percent permanent increase in tax revenues, or some combination of the two.[2]

The options for closing all or part of the Social Security (and Medicare) funding gaps involve difficult economic trade-offs and dangerous political risks. Here are just a few examples:

- Increasing the retirement age for collecting Social Security or Medicare benefits will upset preretirement workers, who will start collecting benefits at older ages.
- Subjecting a larger portion of total earning to the Social Security tax would constitute a gigantic tax increase on the earnings of the country's highest trained and educated individuals. This might reduce the incentive for younger people to obtain education and advance in their careers.
- Disqualifying wealthy individuals from receiving Social Security and Medicare benefits would tilt the program toward welfare and redistribution, rather than insurance programs. This would undermine the broad existing political support for the programs.

[2] Social Security Board of Trustees, "Status of the Social Security and Medicare Programs: A Summary of the 2011 Annual Reports," www.ssa.gov.

- Redirecting legal immigration toward high-skilled, high-earning entrants and away from low-skilled, low-earning immigrants to raise Social Security and Medicare revenues would raise the ire of some native-born high-skilled workers and the proponents of immigration based on family reunification.
- Placing the payroll tax revenues into accounts that individuals, not the government, would own, maintain, and bequeath would transform the Social Security and Medicare programs from guaranteed "defined benefit plans" into much riskier "defined contribution plans." The high short-run volatility of the stock market might leave some unlucky people destitute in old age.

The problem is huge and will not go away. The federal government and American people will eventually have to face up to the overpromising-underfunding problem and find ways to resolve it.

Summary

LO13.1 Identify the purposes, tools, and limitations of fiscal policy.

Fiscal policy consists of deliberate changes in government spending, taxes, or both to promote full employment, price-level stability, and economic growth. Fiscal policy requires increases in government spending, decreases in taxes, or both—a budget deficit—to increase aggregate demand and push an economy from a recession. Decreases in government spending, increases in taxes, or both—a budget surplus—are appropriate fiscal policy for decreasing aggregate demand to try to slow or halt demand-pull inflation.

LO13.2 Explain how built-in stabilizers moderate business cycles.

Built-in stability arises from net tax revenues, which vary directly with the level of GDP. During recession, the federal budget automatically moves toward a stabilizing deficit; during expansion, the budget automatically moves toward an anti-inflationary surplus. Built-in stability lessens, but does not fully correct, undesired changes in real GDP.

LO13.3 Describe how the cyclically adjusted budget reveals the status of U.S. fiscal policy.

Actual federal budget deficits can go up or down because of changes in GDP, changes in fiscal policy, or both. Deficits caused by changes in GDP are called cyclical deficits. The cyclically adjusted budget removes cyclical deficits from the budget and therefore measures the budget deficit or surplus that would occur if the economy operated at its full-employment output throughout the year. Changes in the cyclical budget deficit or surplus provide meaningful information as to whether the government's fiscal policy is expansionary, neutral, or contractionary. Changes in the actual budget deficit or surplus do not, because such deficits or surpluses can include cyclical deficits or surpluses.

In 2001, the Bush administration and Congress chose to reduce marginal tax rates and phase out the federal estate tax. A recession occurred in 2001, and federal spending for the war on terrorism rocketed. The federal budget swung from a surplus of $128 billion in 2001 to a deficit of $158 billion in 2002. In 2003, the Bush administration and Congress accelerated the tax reductions scheduled under the 2001 tax law and cut tax rates on capital gains and dividends. The purposes were to stimulate a sluggish economy. By 2007, the economy had reached its full-employment level of output.

The federal government responded to the severe recession of 2007–2009 by implementing highly expansionary fiscal policy. In 2008, the federal government passed a tax rebate program that sent $600 checks to qualified individuals. This and other programs increased the cyclically adjusted budget deficit from −1.3 percent of potential GDP in 2007 to −2.9 percent in 2008. When the economy continued to plunge, the Obama administration and Congress enacted a massive $787 billion stimulus program to be implemented. The cyclically adjusted budget deficit shot up from −2.9 percent of potential GDP in 2008 to −7.6 percent in 2009, but then decreased to −1.8 percent in 2014 before rising to −3.9 percent in 2018.

The COVID-19 pandemic precipitated recession in 2020, prompting a substantial fiscal policy response. Congress passed the CARES Act in March 2020, sending $1,200 checks to qualified individuals, extending unemployment benefits, and offering relief to businesses. A second round of checks to households was approved in December 2020. This fiscal stimulus ballooned the deficit to −14.9 percent of GDP in 2020, with a projected deficit of −10.3 percent of GDP in 2021.

LO13.4 Discuss the problems that governments may encounter in enacting and applying fiscal policy.

Certain problems complicate the enactment and implementation of fiscal policy. They include (a) timing problems associated with recognition, administrative, and operational lags; (b) the potential for misuse of fiscal policy for political rather than economic purposes; (c) the fact that state and local finances tend to be pro-cyclical; (d) potential ineffectiveness if households expect future policy reversals; and (e) the possibility of fiscal policy crowding out private investment.

LO13.5 Discuss the size, composition, and consequences of the U.S. public debt.

The public debt is the total accumulation of the government's deficits and surpluses. In 2018, the U.S. public debt was $21.5 trillion, or $65,709 per person. The public holds 63 percent of that federal debt; the Federal Reserve and federal agencies hold the other 37 percent. Foreigners hold 29 percent of the federal debt. Interest payments as a percentage of GDP were about 1.8 percent in 2018.

Because of large deficits during the Great Recession and in subsequent years, the total U.S. public debt has more than tripled since 2006, reaching nearly $28.0 trillion in February 2021. The concern that a large public debt may bankrupt the government is generally a false worry because (a) the debt needs only be refinanced rather than refunded and (b) the federal government has the power to increase taxes to make interest payments on the debt.

In general, the public debt is not a vehicle for shifting economic burdens to future generations. Americans inherit not only most of the public debt (a liability) but also most of the U.S. securities (an asset) that finance the debt.

More substantive problems associated with public debt include the following: (a) Payment of interest on the debt may increase income inequality. (b) Interest payments on the debt require higher taxes, which may impair incentives. (c) Paying interest or principal on the portion of the debt held by foreigners means a transfer of real output abroad. (d) Government borrowing to refinance or pay interest on the debt may increase interest rates and crowd out private investment spending, leaving future generations with a smaller stock of capital than they would have otherwise.

The increase in investment in public capital that may result from debt financing may partly or wholly offset the crowding-out effect of the public debt on private investment. Also, the added public investment may stimulate private investment, where the two are complements.

LO13.6 Explain why there is a long-run fiscal imbalance in the Social Security system.

The Social Security system has a significant long-term funding problem. The number of Social Security beneficiaries is projected to significantly rise in future years, and those retirees, on average, are expected to live longer than current retirees. Meanwhile, the number of workers paying Social Security taxes will increase relatively slowly. So a large gap between Social Security revenues and payments will eventually arise. This problem has created calls for various kinds of Social Security reform.

Terms and Concepts

fiscal policy	budget surplus	public debt
Council of Economic Advisers (CEA)	built-in stabilizer	U.S. securities
expansionary fiscal policy	cyclically adjusted budget	external public debt
budget deficit	cyclical deficit	public investments
contractionary fiscal policy	political business cycle	Social Security trust fund
	crowding-out effect	

Questions ![Mc Graw Hill] connect

1. The federal government establishes its budget to decide what programs to provide and how to pay for them. How does fiscal policy differ from this ordinary fiscal activity of budgeting? **(LO1)**

2. What are government's fiscal policy options for moving the economy out of a recession? Speculate on which of these fiscal options might be favored by (a) a person who wants to preserve the size of government and (b) a person who thinks the public sector is too large. How does the "ratchet effect" affect anti-inflationary fiscal policy? **(LO1)**

3. Explain how built-in (or automatic) stabilizers work. What are the differences between proportional, progressive, and regressive tax systems as they relate to an economy's built-in stability? **(LO2)**

4. Define the cyclically adjusted budget, explain its significance, and state why it may differ from the actual budget. Suppose the full-employment, noninflationary level of real output is GDP$_3$ (not GDP$_2$) in the economy depicted in **Figure 13.3**. If the economy is operating at GDP$_2$, instead of GDP$_3$, what is the status of its cyclically adjusted budget? The status of its current fiscal policy? What change in fiscal policy would you recommend? How would you accomplish that in terms of the G and T lines in the figure? **(LO3)**

5. Why did the budget surpluses in 2000 and 2001 give way to a series of budget deficits beginning in 2002? Why did those deficits increase substantially beginning in 2008? **(LO3)**

6. Briefly state and evaluate the problem of time lags in enacting and applying fiscal policy. Explain the idea of the political business cycle. How might expectations of a near-term policy reversal weaken fiscal policy based on changes in tax rates? What is the crowding-out effect, and why might it be relevant to fiscal policy? **(LO4)**

7. How do economists distinguish between the absolute and relative sizes of the public debt? Why is the distinction important? Distinguish between refinancing the debt and retiring the debt. How does an internally held public debt differ from an externally held public debt? Contrast the effects of retiring an internally held debt and retiring an externally held debt. **(LO5)**

8. True or false? If the statement is false, explain why: **(LO5)**

   a. The total public debt is more relevant to an economy than the public debt as a percentage of GDP.

   b. An internally held public debt is like a debt of the left hand owed to the right hand.

   c. The Federal Reserve and federal government agencies hold more than three-fourths of the public debt.

   d. As a percentage of GDP, the total U.S. public debt is the highest such debt among the world's advanced industrial nations.

9. Why might economists be quite concerned if the annual interest payments on the U.S. public debt sharply increase as a percentage of GDP? **(LO5)**

10. Trace the cause-and-effect chain through which financing and refinancing of the public debt might affect real interest rates, private investment, the capital stock, and economic growth. How might investment in public capital and public–private complementarities alter the outcome of the cause–effect chain? **(LO5)**

11. What do economists mean when they say Social Security and Medicare are "pay-as-you-go" plans? What are the Social Security and Medicare trust funds, and how long will they have money left in them? What is the key long-run problem of both Social Security and Medicare? To fix the problem, do you favor increasing taxes or do you prefer reducing benefits? **(LO6)**

Problems

1. Refer back to the table in **Figure 12.7** in the previous chapter. Suppose that aggregate demand increases such that the amount of real output demanded rises by $7 billion at each price level. By what percentage will the price level increase? Will this inflation be demand-pull inflation, or will it be cost-push inflation? If potential real GDP (i.e., full-employment GDP) is $510 billion, what will be the size of the positive GDP gap after the change in aggregate demand? If government wants to use fiscal policy to counter the resulting inflation without changing tax rates, should it increase government spending or decrease it? **(LO1)**

2. Refer to the accompanying table for Waxwania: **(LO2, LO3)**

Government Expenditures, G	Tax Revenues, T	Real GDP
$160	$100	$500
160	120	600
160	140	700
160	160	800
160	180	900

   a. What is the marginal tax rate in Waxwania? The average tax rate? Which of the following describes the tax system: proportional, progressive, regressive?

   b. Suppose that Waxwania is producing $600 of real GDP, whereas the potential real GDP (or full-employment real GDP) is $700. How large is its budget deficit? Its cyclically adjusted budget deficit? Its cyclically adjusted budget deficit as a percentage of potential real GDP? Is Waxwania's fiscal policy expansionary, or is it contractionary?

3. Suppose that a country has no public debt in year 1 but experiences a budget deficit of $40 billion in year 2, a budget surplus of $10 billion in year 3, and a budget deficit of $2 billion in year 4. What is the absolute size of its public debt in year 4? If its real GDP in year 4 is $104 billion, what is this country's public debt as a percentage of real GDP in year 4? **(LO5)**

4. Suppose that the investment demand curve in a certain economy is such that investment declines by $100 billion for every 1 percentage point increase in the real interest rate. Also, suppose that the investment demand curve shifts rightward by $150 billion at each real interest rate for every 1 percentage point increase in the expected rate of return from investment. If stimulus spending (an expansionary fiscal policy) by government increases the real interest rate by 2 percentage points, but also raises the expected rate of return on investment by 1 percentage point, how much investment, if any, will be crowded out? **(LO5)**

CHAPTER FOURTEEN

Money, Banking, and Financial Institutions

Learning Objectives

LO14.1 Explain the functions of money.

LO14.2 Describe the components of the U.S. money supply.

LO14.3 Describe what "backs" the money supply.

LO14.4 Discuss the structure of the Federal Reserve.

LO14.5 Identify the functions and responsibilities of the Federal Reserve.

LO14.6 Explain the main factors that contributed to the financial crisis of 2007–2008.

LO14.7 Describe how banks create money in a "fractional reserve" banking system.

Money is a fascinating aspect of the economy:

> Money bewitches people. They fret for it, and they sweat for it. They devise most ingenious ways to get it, and most ingenious ways to get rid of it. Money is the only commodity that is good for nothing but to be gotten rid of. It will not feed you, clothe you, shelter you, or amuse you unless you spend it or invest it. It imparts value only in parting. People will do almost anything for money, and money will do almost anything for people. Money is a captivating, circulating, masquerading puzzle.[1]

In this chapter and the next, we unmask the critical role of money in the economy. A well-operating monetary system helps the economy achieve both full employment and the efficient use of resources. A malfunctioning monetary system distorts the allocation of resources and creates severe fluctuations in the economy's levels of output, employment, and prices.

[1] Federal Reserve Bank of Philadelphia, "Creeping Inflation," *Business Review*, August 1957, p. 3.

The Functions of Money

There is an old saying that "money *is* what money *does.*" Generally, anything that performs the functions of money *is* money. Here are those functions:

- *Medium of exchange* First and foremost, money is a **medium of exchange** that is usable for buying and selling goods and services. A bakery worker does not want to be paid 200 bagels per week. Nor does the bakery owner want to receive, say, halibut in exchange for bagels. Money is a social invention with which resource suppliers and producers can be paid, and it can be used to buy any item in the marketplace. As a medium of exchange, money allows society to escape the complications of barter. And because it provides a convenient way of exchanging goods, money enables society to gain the advantages of geographic and human specialization.

- *Unit of account* Money is also a **unit of account.** Society uses monetary units—dollars, in the United States—to measure the relative worth of a wide variety of goods, services, and resources. Just as we measure distance in miles or kilometers, we gauge the value of goods in dollars. With money as an acceptable unit of account, the price of each item needs to be stated only in terms of the monetary unit. We need not state the price of cows in terms of corn, crayons, and cranberries. Money aids rational decision making by enabling buyers and sellers to easily compare the relative values of goods, services, and resources by simply examining their respective money prices. It also permits us to define debt obligations, determine taxes owed, and calculate the nation's GDP.

- *Store of value* Money also serves as a **store of value** that enables people to transfer purchasing power from the present to the future. People normally do not spend their entire paychecks on the day they receive them. To buy things later, they store some of their wealth as money. The money you place in a safe or a checking account will still be available to you a few weeks or months from now. When inflation is nonexistent or mild, holding money is a relatively risk-free way to store wealth for later use.

People can choose to hold some or all of their wealth in a wide variety of assets besides money. These include real estate, stocks, bonds, precious metals such as gold, and even collectible items like fine art or comic books. But a key advantage that money has over all other assets is that it has the most *liquidity,* or spendability.

An asset's **liquidity** is the ease with which it can be converted quickly into cash with little or no loss of purchasing power. The more liquid an asset is, the more quickly it can be converted into cash and used to purchase goods, services, and other assets.

Levels of liquidity vary radically. By definition, cash is perfectly liquid. By contrast, a house is highly illiquid for two reasons. First, it may take several months before a willing buyer can be found and a sale negotiated. Second, there is a loss of purchasing power when the house is sold because numerous fees have to be paid to real estate agents and other individuals to complete the sale.

As we are about to discuss, our economy uses several different types of money including cash, coins, checking account deposits, savings account deposits, and more unusual things like deposits in money market mutual funds. As we describe the various forms of money in detail, take the time to compare their relative levels of liquidity—both with each other and as compared to other assets like stocks, bonds, and real estate. Cash is perfectly liquid. Other forms of money are highly liquid, but less liquid than cash.

medium of exchange
Any item sellers generally accept and buyers generally use to pay for a good or service; money; a convenient means of exchanging goods and services without engaging in barter.

unit of account
A standard unit in which prices can be stated and the value of goods and services can be compared; one of the three functions of money.

store of value
An asset set aside for future use; one of the three functions of money.

liquidity
The ease with which an asset can be converted quickly into cash with little or no loss of purchasing power. Money is said to be perfectly liquid, whereas other assets have a lesser degree of liquidity.

The Components of the Money Supply

Money is a "stock" of some item or group of items (unlike income, e.g., which is a "flow"). Societies have used many items as money, including whales' teeth, circular stones, elephant-tail bristles, gold coins, furs, and pieces of paper. Anything that is widely accepted as a medium of exchange can serve as money. In the United States, currency is not the only form of money. As you will see, certain debts of government and financial institutions are also used as money.

Money Definition: *M*1

M1
The most narrowly defined money supply, equal to currency in the hands of the public and the checkable deposits of commercial banks and thrift institutions.

The narrowest definition of the U.S. money supply is called **M1.** It consists of two components:

- Currency (coins and paper money) in the hands of the nonbank public.
- Checkable deposits in commercial banks and "thrift" or savings institutions on which checks of any size can be drawn, at any time and as often as desired.[2]

Government and government agencies supply coins and paper money. Commercial banks ("banks") and savings institutions ("thrifts") provide checkable deposits. **Figure 14.1** shows that *M*1 is about equally divided between the two components.

Federal Reserve Note
Paper money issued by the Federal Reserve Banks.

Currency: Coins + Paper Money   The currency of the United States consists of metal coins and paper money. The coins are issued by the U.S. Treasury, while the paper money consists of **Federal Reserve Notes** issued by the Federal Reserve System (the U.S. central bank). Coins are minted by the U.S. Mint, and paper money is printed by the Bureau of Engraving and Printing. Both the U.S. Mint and the Bureau of Engraving and Printing are part of the U.S. Department of the Treasury.

token money
Bills or coins for which the amount printed on the *currency* bears no relationship to the value of the paper or metal embodied within it; for currency still circulating, money for which the face value exceeds the commodity value.

As with the currencies of other countries, the currency of the United States is **token money.** That is, the face value of any piece of currency is unrelated to its *intrinsic value*—the value of the physical material (metal or paper and ink) from which that currency is constructed. Governments make sure that face values exceed intrinsic values in order to discourage people from deconstructing coins and bills in order to resell the material they are made out of as scrap metal or scrap paper. For instance, if 50-cent pieces each contained 75 cents' worth of metal, then it would be profitable to melt them down and sell the metal. Fifty-cent pieces would disappear from circulation very quickly!

Figure 14.1 shows that coins and paper money (currency) constitute 43 percent of the *M*1 money supply in the United States.

checkable deposit
Any deposit in a commercial bank or thrift institution against which a check may be written.

Checkable Deposits   The safety and convenience of checks have made **checkable deposits** a large component of the *M*1 money supply. You would not think of stuffing $4,896 in bills in an envelope and dropping it in a mailbox to pay a debt. But writing and mailing a check for a large sum is commonplace. The person cashing a check must endorse it (sign it on the reverse side); the writer of the check subsequently receives a record of the cashed check as a receipt. Similarly, you must sign your checks, the theft or loss of your checkbook is not nearly as calamitous as losing a large amount of currency. Finally, it is more convenient to write a check than to transport and count out large sums of currency. For all these reasons, checkable deposits are a large component of the stock of money in the United States. About 57 percent of *M*1 is in the form of checkable deposits, on which checks can be drawn.

---

[2] In the ensuing discussion, we do not discuss several of the quantitatively less significant components of the definitions of money, such as traveler's checks, which are included in the *M*1 money supply. The statistical appendix of any recent *Federal Reserve Bulletin* provides more comprehensive definitions.

FIGURE 14.1
Components of money supply *M*1 and money supply *M*2, in the United States. *M*1 is a narrow definition of the money supply that includes currency (in circulation) and checkable deposits. *M*2 is a broader definition that includes *M*1 along with several other relatively liquid account balances.

* These categories include other, quantitatively smaller components such as traveler's checks.
Source: Board of Governors of the Federal Reserve System.

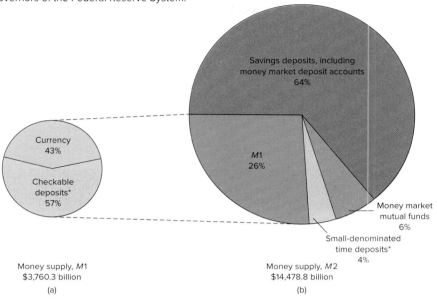

Savings deposits, including money market deposit accounts 64%

*M*1 26%

Money market mutual funds 6%

Small-denominated time deposits* 4%

Currency 43%

Checkable deposits* 57%

Money supply, *M*1
$3,760.3 billion
(a)

Money supply, *M*2
$14,478.8 billion
(b)

It might seem strange that checking account balances are regarded as part of the money supply, but the reason is clear: Checks are simply a way to transfer the ownership of bank deposits, and they are generally acceptable as a medium of exchange. Although checks are less generally accepted than currency for small purchases, most sellers willingly accept checks as payment for major purchases. Moreover, people can convert checkable deposits into paper money and coins on demand; checks drawn on those deposits are thus the equivalent of currency.

To summarize:

$$\text{Money, } M1 = \text{currency} + \text{checkable deposits}$$

Institutions That Offer Checkable Deposits   In the United States, a variety of financial institutions allow customers to write checks in any amount on the funds they have deposited. **Commercial banks** are the primary depository institutions. They accept the deposits of households and businesses, keep the money safe until it is withdrawn via checks, and in the meantime use it to make available a wide variety of loans. Commercial bank loans provide short-term financial capital to businesses, and they finance consumer purchases of automobiles and other durable goods.

Savings and loan associations (S&Ls), mutual savings banks, and credit unions supplement the commercial banks. Collectively, these institutions are called **thrift institutions,** or simply "thrifts." *Savings and loan associations* and *mutual savings banks* accept the deposits of households and businesses and then use the funds to finance housing mortgages and to provide other loans. *Credit unions* accept deposits from and lend to "members," who usually are a group of people who work for the same company.

The checkable deposits of banks and thrifts are known variously as demand deposits, NOW (negotiable order of withdrawal) accounts, ATS (automatic transfer service) accounts, and share draft accounts. Depositors can write checks on all of these accounts whenever, and in whatever amount, they choose.

commercial bank
A firm that engages in the business of banking (accepts deposits, offers checking accounts, and makes loans).

thrift institution
A savings and loan association, mutual savings bank, or credit union.

Two Qualifications   We must qualify our discussion in two important ways. First, currency held by the U.S. Treasury, the Federal Reserve Banks, commercial banks, and thrift institutions is *excluded* from $M1$ and other measures of the money supply. A paper dollar or four quarters in the wallet of, say, Maria Dinero obviously constitutes just $1 of the money supply. But if we counted currency held by banks as part of the money supply, the same $1 would count for $2 of money supply if Maria deposited the currency into her checking account. By excluding currency held by banks when determining the total supply of money, we avoid this problem of double counting.

Also *excluded* from the money supply are any checkable deposits of the government (specifically, the U.S. Treasury) or the Federal Reserve that are held by commercial banks or thrift institutions. This exclusion is designed to enable a better assessment of the amount of money available *to the private sector* for potential spending. The amount of money available to households and businesses is of keen interest to the Federal Reserve in conducting its monetary policy (a topic we cover in the next chapter).

PHOTO OP

Money: Then and Now

Items such as cowry shells were once used as money. Today, bills and coins, along with checkable deposits, constitute the $M1$ money supply.

BSANI/iStock/Getty Images   Index Stock/Alamy   Catherine Jones/Shutterstock

Money Definition: *M2*

near-money
Financial assets, the most important of which are noncheckable savings accounts, time deposits, and U.S. short-term securities and savings bonds, which are not a medium of exchange but can be readily converted into money.

M2
A more broadly defined money supply, equal to $M1$ plus noncheckable savings accounts (including money market deposit accounts), small-denominated time deposits (deposits of less than $100,000), and individual money market mutual fund balances.

A second and broader definition of money includes $M1$ plus several near-monies. **Near-monies** are certain highly liquid financial assets that do not function directly or fully as a medium of exchange but can be readily converted into currency or checkable deposits. The $M2$ definition of money includes three categories of near-monies.

- *Savings deposits, including money market deposit accounts* A depositor can easily withdraw funds from a **savings account** at a bank or thrift or simply transfer the funds from a savings account to a checkable account. A person can also withdraw funds from a **money market deposit account (MMDA),** which is an interest-bearing account containing interest-bearing short-term securities. MMDAs, however, have a minimum-balance requirement and a limit on how often a person can withdraw funds (which is why they are not included in $M1$).

- *Small-denominated (less than $100,000) time deposits* Funds from **time deposits** become available at their maturity. For example, a person can convert a six-month time deposit (certificate of deposit or CD) to currency without penalty six months or more after depositing it. In return for this withdrawal limitation, the financial institution pays a higher interest rate on such deposits than it does on its MMDAs. Also, a person can "cash in" a CD before its maturity but must pay a severe penalty.

- *Money market mutual funds held by individuals* By making a telephone call, using the Internet, or writing a check for $500 or more, a depositor can redeem shares in a **money market mutual fund (MMMF)** offered by a mutual fund company. Such companies combine the funds of individual shareholders to buy interest-bearing short-term credit instruments such as CDs and U.S. government securities. They then can offer interest on the MMMF accounts of the shareholders (depositors) who jointly own those financial assets. The MMMFs in *M*2 only include the MMMF accounts held by individuals; those held by businesses and other institutions are excluded.

All three categories of near-monies possess substantial liquidity. Thus, in equation form,

$$\text{Money, } M2 = M1 + \text{savings deposits, including MMDAs} + \text{small-denominated}$$

(less than $100,000) time deposits + MMMFs

Note that *M*2 is defined such that it encompasses the immediate medium-of-exchange items (currency and checkable deposits) that constitute *M*1 plus certain near-monies that can be easily converted into currency and checkable deposits. *M*2 is, consequently, a measure of the portion of the money supply that is highly spendable.

In **Figure 14.1**, we see that the addition of all these items yields an *M*2 money supply that is almost four times larger than the narrower *M*1 money supply.

What "Backs" the Money Supply?

The money supply in the United States essentially is "backed" (guaranteed) by government's ability to keep the value of money relatively stable. Nothing more! Paper currency and checkable deposits have no intrinsic value. A $5 bill is just an inscribed piece of paper. A checkable deposit is merely a bookkeeping entry. And coins, we know, have less intrinsic value than their face value. Nor will government redeem the paper money you hold for anything tangible, such as gold.

To many people, it seems shady that the government does not back its currency with anything tangible. But the decision not to back the currency with anything tangible was made for a very good reason. If the government backed the currency with something tangible like gold, then the money supply would vary with the availability of gold. By not backing the currency, the government grants itself the freedom to provide as much or as little money as may be needed to best suit the country's economic needs. By choosing not to back the currency, the government gives itself the ability to freely "manage" the nation's money supply. Its monetary authorities are free to provide whatever amount of money is needed to promote full employment, price-level stability, and economic growth.

The Value of Money

So why are currency and checkable deposits money, whereas, say, Monopoly (the game) money is not? What gives a $20 bill or a $100 check its value? The answer to these questions has three parts.

savings account
A deposit that is interest-bearing and that the depositor can normally withdraw at any time.

money market deposit account (MMDA)
An interest-earning account (at a bank or thrift) consisting of short-term securities and on which a limited number of checks may be written each year.

time deposit
An interest-earning deposit in a commercial bank or thrift institution that the depositor can withdraw without penalty after the end of a specified period.

money market mutual fund (MMMF)
An interest-bearing account offered by investment companies, which pool depositors' funds for the purchase of short-term securities. Depositors may write checks in minimum amounts or more against their accounts.

Acceptability   Currency and checkable deposits are money because people accept them as money. By virtue of long-standing business practice, currency and checkable deposits perform the basic function of money: They are acceptable as a medium of exchange. We accept paper money because we are confident that we can exchange it for goods, services, and resources.

legal tender
A legal designation of a nation's official currency (bills and coins). Payment of debts must be accepted in this monetary unit, but creditors can specify the form of payment, for example, "cash only" or "check or credit card only."

Legal Tender   Our confidence in the acceptability of paper money is strengthened because government has designated currency as **legal tender.** Specifically, each bill contains the statement "This note is legal tender for all debts, public and private." In other words, paper money is a valid and legal means of payment of any debt that was contracted in dollars. (However, private firms and government are not mandated to accept cash. It is not illegal for them to specify payment in noncash forms such as checks, cashier's checks, debit card transactions, or money orders.)

The general acceptance of paper currency by society is more important than the government's decree that money is legal tender. This can be understood by the fact that checks function as money despite never having been designated as legal tender by the government. That being said, the Federal Deposit Insurance Corporation (FDIC) and the National Credit Union Administration (NCUA) enhance our willingness to use checks as a medium of exchange by insuring checking account deposits held at commercial banks and thrift.

 ILLUSTRATING THE IDEA

Are Credit Cards Money?

You may wonder why we have ignored credit cards such as Visa and MasterCard in our discussion of the money supply. After all, credit cards are a convenient way to buy things and they account for about 21 percent of the dollar value of all transactions in the United States. The answer is that a credit card is not money. Rather, it is a convenient means of obtaining a short-term loan from the financial institution that issued the card.

What happens when you purchase an item with a credit card? The bank that issued the card will reimburse the seller by making a money payment and charging the establishment a transaction fee, and later you will reimburse the bank for its loan to you by also making a money payment. Rather than reduce your cash or checking account with each purchase, you bunch your payments once a month. You may have to pay an annual fee for the services provided, and if you pay the bank in installments, you will pay a sizable interest charge on the loan. Credit cards are merely a means of deferring or postponing payment for a short period. Your checking account balance used to pay your monthly credit card bill *is* money; the credit card is *not* money.[*]

Although credit cards are not money, they allow individuals and businesses to "economize" in the use of money. Credit cards enable people to hold less currency in their wallets and, prior to payment due dates, fewer checkable deposits in their bank accounts. Credit cards also help people coordinate the timing of their expenditures with their receipt of income.

> QUESTION:
> How might widespread credit card use affect how much of their money people hold in *M*1 form versus the near-money forms of *M*2?

[*]A bank debit card, however, is very similar to a blank check in your checkbook. Unlike a purchase with a credit card, a purchase with a debit card creates a direct "debit" (a subtraction) from your checking account balance. That checking account balance *is* money—it is part of *M*1.

Relative Scarcity The value of money, like the economic value of anything else, depends on its supply and demand. Money derives its value from its scarcity relative to its utility (its want-satisfying power). The utility of money lies in its capacity to be exchanged for goods and services, now or in the future. The economy's demand for money thus depends on the total dollar volume of transactions in any period, plus the amount of money individuals and businesses want to hold for future transactions. With a reasonably constant demand for money, the supply of money provided by the monetary authorities will determine the domestic value or "purchasing power" of the monetary unit (dollar, yen, peso, etc.).

Money and Prices

The purchasing power of money is the amount of goods and services a unit of money will buy.

The Purchasing Power of the Dollar The amount a dollar will buy varies inversely with the price level. That is, a reciprocal relationship exists between the general price level and the dollar's purchasing power. When the Consumer Price Index or "cost-of-living" index goes up, the value of the dollar goes down, and vice versa. Higher prices decrease the dollar's value because people need more dollars to buy a particular amount of goods, services, or resources. For example, if the price level doubles, the value of the dollar declines by one-half, or 50 percent.

Conversely, lower prices increase the dollar's purchasing power because people need fewer dollars to obtain a specific quantity of goods and services. If the price level falls by, say, 50 percent, then the purchasing power of the dollar doubles.

Inflation and Acceptability In **Chapter 11**, we noted situations in which a nation's currency became worthless and unacceptable in exchange. Runaway inflation may significantly decrease the value of money between the time it is received and the time it is spent. Rapid declines in a currency's value may cause people and businesses to reject it as a medium of exchange. They may refuse to accept paper money because they do not want to incur the loss in its value that will occur while it is in their possession.

Without an acceptable domestic medium of exchange, the economy may revert to barter. Alternatively, more stable currencies such as the U.S. dollar or the European euro may come into widespread use. At the extreme, a country may adopt a foreign currency as its own official currency as a way to counter hyperinflation.

Similarly, people will use money as a store of value only as long as inflation does not seriously diminish the value of that money. And an economy can effectively employ money as a unit of account only when its purchasing power is relatively stable. A monetary "yardstick" that no longer measures a "yard" (in terms of purchasing power) does not permit buyers and sellers to establish the terms of trade clearly. When the value of the dollar is declining rapidly, sellers do not know what to charge and buyers do not know what to pay.

The Federal Reserve and the Banking System

In the United States, the "monetary authorities" are the members of the Board of Governors of the **Federal Reserve System** (the "Fed"). As **Figure 14.2** shows, the Board directs the activities of 12 Federal Reserve Banks, which in turn control the lending activity of the nation's banks and thrift institutions. The Fed's major goal is

Federal Reserve System
A central component of the U.S. banking system, consisting of the Board of Governors of the Federal Reserve and 12 regional Federal Reserve Banks.

to control the money supply. Because checkable deposits in banks are such a large part of the money supply, its duties also involve ensuring the stability of the banking system.

FIGURE 14.2

The framework of the Federal Reserve System and its relationship to the public. The Board of Governors makes the basic policy decisions that provide monetary control of the U.S. money and banking system. The 12 Federal Reserve Banks implement these decisions. Both the Board of Governors and the 12 Federal Reserve Banks are aided by the Federal Open Market Committee (FOMC).

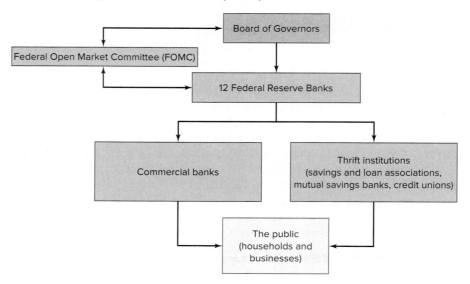

The Board of Governors

Board of Governors
The seven-member group that supervises and controls the money and banking system of the United States; also called the *Board of Governors of the Federal Reserve System* and the *Federal Reserve Board*.

The central authority of the U.S. money and banking system is the **Board of Governors** of the Federal Reserve System. The U.S. president, with the confirmation of the Senate, appoints the seven Board members. Terms are 14 years and staggered so that one member is replaced every 2 years. In addition, new members are appointed when resignations occur. The president selects the chairperson and vice-chairperson of the Board from among the members. Those officers serve four-year terms and can be reappointed to new four-year terms by the president. The long-term appointments provide the Board with continuity, experienced membership, and independence from political pressures that could result in inflation.

The 12 Federal Reserve Banks

Federal Reserve Banks
The 12 banks chartered by the U.S. government to control the money supply and perform other functions.

The 12 **Federal Reserve Banks,** which blend private and public control, collectively serve as the nation's "central bank." These banks also serve as bankers' banks.

Central Banks Most nations have a single central bank—for example, Britain's Bank of England or Japan's Bank of Japan. The U.S. central bank consists of 12 banks whose policies are coordinated by the Fed's Board of Governors. The 12 Federal Reserve Banks accommodate the geographic size and economic diversity of the United States as well as the nation's large number of commercial banks and thrifts that are spread across the country.

Figure 14.3 shows the location of the 12 Federal Reserve Banks and the district that each serves. These banks implement the Board of Governors' basic policies.

FIGURE 14.3

The 12 Federal Reserve Districts. The Federal Reserve System divides the United States into 12 districts, each having one central bank and in some instances one or more branches of the central bank. Hawaii and Alaska are included in the 12th district.

Source: *Federal Reserve Bulletin,* **www.federalreserve.gov/publications/bulletin.htm.**

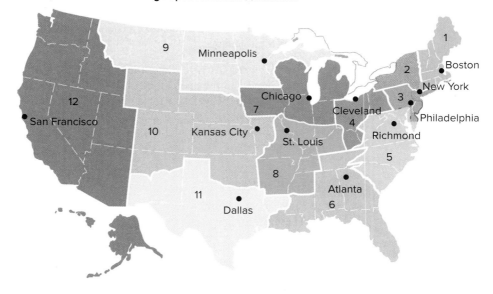

Quasi-Public Banks The 12 Federal Reserve Banks are quasi-public banks that blend private ownership and public control. Each Federal Reserve Bank is owned by the private commercial banks in its district. (Federally chartered commercial banks are required to purchase shares of stock in the Federal Reserve Bank in their district.) But the Board of Governors, a government body, sets the basic policies that the Federal Reserve Banks pursue.

Despite their private ownership, the Federal Reserve Banks are in practice public institutions. Unlike private firms, they are not motivated by profit. The policies they follow are designed by the Board of Governors to promote the well-being of the economy as a whole. Also, the Federal Reserve Banks do not compete with commercial banks. In general, they do not deal with the public. Rather, they interact with the government on the one hand, and commercial banks and thrifts on the other.

Bankers' Banks The Federal Reserve Banks are "bankers' banks." They perform essentially the same functions for banks and thrifts as those institutions perform for the public. Just as banks and thrifts accept the deposits of and make loans to the public, so the central banks accept the deposits of and make loans to banks and thrifts. Normally, these loans average only about $150 million a day, but in emergency circumstances the Federal Reserve Banks become the "lender of last resort" to the banking system and can lend out as much as needed to ensure that banks and thrifts can meet their cash obligations. On the day after terrorists attacked the United States on September 11, 2001, the Fed lent $45 billion to U.S. banks and thrifts. The Fed wanted to make sure that the destruction and disruption in New York City and Washington did not precipitate a nationwide banking crisis.

The Federal Reserve Banks also have a third function, which banks and thrifts do not perform: They issue currency. Congress has authorized the Federal Reserve Banks to put into circulation Federal Reserve Notes, which constitute the economy's paper money supply.

FOMC

Federal Open Market Committee (FOMC)
The 12-member group that determines the purchase and sale policies of the Federal Reserve Banks in the market for U.S. government securities.

The **Federal Open Market Committee (FOMC)** aids the Board of Governors in conducting monetary policy. The FOMC is made up of 12 individuals:

- The seven members of the Board of Governors.
- The president of the New York Federal Reserve Bank.
- Four of the remaining presidents of Federal Reserve Banks, each serving on a one-year rotating basis.

The FOMC meets regularly to direct the purchase and sale of government securities (bills, notes, bonds) in the open market in which such securities are bought and sold on a daily basis. The FOMC also makes decisions about borrowing and lending government securities in the open market. The purpose of these *open-market operations* is to control the nation's money supply and influence interest rates. The Federal Reserve Bank in New York City conducts most of the Fed's open-market operations.

Commercial Banks and Thrifts

There are about 4,600 commercial banks. Roughly three-fourths are *state banks.* These private banks are chartered (authorized) by individual states to operate within their respective borders. One-fourth are private banks chartered by the federal government to operate nationally; these are *national banks.* Some of the U.S. national banks are very large, ranking among the world's largest financial institutions (see **Global Snapshot 14.1**).

GLOBAL SNAPSHOT 14.1

The World's 12 Largest Financial Institutions, 2018

The world's 12 largest private-sector financial institutions are headquartered in just five countries: China, Japan, the United Kingdom, the United States, and France.

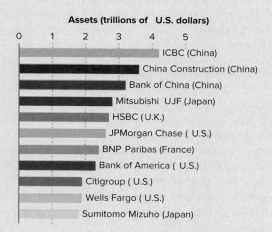

Source: "The World's Largest Public Companies 2018," *Forbes.*

The 7,000 thrift institutions—most of which are credit unions—are regulated by agencies in addition to the Board of Governors and the Federal Reserve Banks. For example, credit unions are regulated and monitored by the National Credit Union Administration. The thrifts are subject to monetary control by the Federal Reserve System. Like banks, thrifts are required to keep a certain percentage of their checkable deposits as "reserves." In **Figure 14.2**, arrows indicate that the thrift institutions are partially subject to the control of the Board of Governors and the central banks. Decisions concerning monetary policy affect the thrifts along with the commercial banks.

Fed Functions and Responsibilities

The Fed performs several functions:

- *Issuing currency* The Federal Reserve Banks issue Federal Reserve Notes, the paper currency used in the United States. (The Federal Reserve Bank that issued a particular bill is identified in black in the upper left of new bills. "A1," e.g., identifies the Boston bank; "B2," the New York bank; and so on.)

- *Setting reserve requirements and holding reserves* The Fed sets reserve requirements, which are the fractions of checking account balances that banks must maintain as currency reserves. The Fed accepts as deposits from the banks and thrifts any portion of their mandated reserves not held as vault cash.

- *Lending money to financial institutions and serving as an emergency lender of last resort* The Fed makes routine short-term loans to banks and thrifts, and charges them an interest rate called the *discount rate.* During financial emergencies, the Fed serves as a *lender of last resort* to critical parts of the financial industry.

- *Providing for check collection* The Fed provides the banking system with a means for collecting on checks. If Ava writes a check on her Miami bank to Julio, who deposits it in his Dallas bank, how does the Dallas bank collect the money represented by the check drawn against the Miami bank? The Fed clears checks by adjusting the reserves (deposits) that the banks hold at the Fed. In this example, the Miami bank's reserves are decreased by the amount of Ava's check while the Dallas bank's reserves are increased by the amount of Ava's check. The Dallas bank can then transfer that money into Julio's account.

- *Acting as fiscal agent* The Fed acts as the fiscal agent (provider of financial services) for the federal government. The government collects huge sums through taxation, spends equally large amounts, and sells and redeems bonds. To carry out these activities, the government uses the Fed.

- *Supervising banks* The Fed supervises the operations of banks. It periodically assesses bank profitability, ensures that banks perform according to the regulations, and seeks to uncover questionable practices or fraud. Following the financial crisis of 2007–2008, Congress expanded the Fed's supervisory powers over banks.

- *Controlling the money supply* The Fed has the ultimate responsibility for regulating the nation's money supply. The Fed's major task under usual economic circumstances is to manage the money supply (and thus interest rates) according to the economy's needs. The Fed's goal is to make an amount of money available that is consistent with high and rising levels of output and employment *and* a relatively stable price level. While most of the Fed's other functions are routine, managing the nation's money supply requires intermittent policy decisions that must be made when and if needed, and tailored as necessary to meet the circumstances. (We discuss those decisions in detail in **Chapter 15**.)

Federal Reserve Independence

Congress purposely established the Fed as an independent agency of government. The objective was to protect the Fed from political pressures so it could effectively control the money supply and maintain price stability. Political pressures on Congress and the executive branch may at times result in inflationary fiscal policies, including tax cuts and special-interest spending. If Congress and the executive branch also controlled the nation's monetary policy, citizens and lobbying groups undoubtedly would pressure elected officials to keep interest rates low even though at times high interest rates are necessary to reduce aggregate demand and thus control inflation. An independent monetary authority (the Fed) can take actions to increase interest rates when higher rates are needed to stem inflation. Studies show that countries that have independent central banks like the Fed have lower rates of inflation, on average, than countries that have little or no central bank independence.

The Financial Crisis of 2007 and 2008

A properly functioning monetary system supports the flows of income and expenditures necessary for an economy to grow, produce near potential output, and enjoy low rates of inflation. In contrast, a malfunctioning monetary system causes major problems in credit markets and can cause severe fluctuations in output, employment, and prices.

"Malfunctioning" is too gentle an adjective to describe the monetary system in late 2007 and 2008, when the U.S. financial system faced its most serious crisis since the Great Depression of the 1930s. We discussed the severe recession of 2007–2009 in previous chapters, and we now want to examine the financial crisis that led up to it. What caused it? And how did it alter the U.S. financial services industry?

Overview

In 2007, a major wave of defaults on home mortgage loans threatened the health of not only mortgage lenders but also the financial institution that had invested in mortgage loans indirectly.

subprime mortgage loans
High-interest-rate loans to home buyers with above-average credit risk.

The majority of these mortgage defaults involved **subprime mortgage loans**. These were mortgage loans extended to home buyers with higher-than-average (subprime) credit risk, meaning loans granted to home buyers who were probably going to have substantial difficulty making their monthly mortgage payments. Several of the biggest investors in these subprime loans were banks, which had loaned money to investment companies that had purchased the right to collect on those mortgages.

When the mortgages started to go bad, many of those investment companies "blew up" and could not repay the money they had borrowed from the banks. To comply with banking regulations, the banks had to "write off" (declare unrecoverable) the loans they had made to the investment companies, but the write-offs reduced their reserves and restricted their ability to lend money to households and businesses. Hundreds of banks, insurance companies, and financial firms either went bankrupt or came very close to going bankrupt. The Fed and the Treasury had to intervene to prevent the entire financial system from imploding.

Prelude

Before the crisis occurred, banks and government regulators had mistakenly believed that an innovation known as the mortgage-backed security had eliminated most of the banks' exposure to mortgage defaults. **Mortgage-backed securities** are bonds backed by mortgage payments. To create them, banks and other mortgage lenders first made mortgage loans. But then instead of holding all of those loans as assets and collecting the monthly mortgage payments, the banks and other mortgage lenders bundled hundreds or thousands of them together and sold them off as bonds—in essence, selling the right to collect all the future mortgage payments. As sellers, the banks obtained one-time cash payments for the bonds. In return, the bond buyers received all future mortgage payments.

From the banks' perspective, this seemed like a smart business decision because it transferred any future mortgage-default risk onto the buyers of the mortgage-backed securities. Unfortunately, the banks created a "circular firing squad" by lending a substantial portion of the money they received from selling the mortgage-backed securities to investment funds that invested in ... mortgage-backed securities! Consequently, the banks were still exposed to mortgage default risk, and they suffered heavy losses when millions of homeowners started defaulting on their mortgages in 2006.

mortgage-backed securities
Bonds that represent claims to all or part of the monthly mortgage payments from the pools of mortgage loans made by lenders to borrowers to help them purchase residential property.

Causes

But what caused the skyrocketing mortgage default rates in the first place? There were many causes, including government programs that subsidized home ownership and the bursting of a large financial bubble in real estate values.

An equally important factor was the bad incentives provided by the mortgage-backed bonds. Because mortgage lenders thought that they were no longer exposed to mortgage default risk, they became lax in their lending practices—so much so that they granted millions of subprime mortgage loans to people who lacked the financial resources to keep current on their monthly mortgage payments.

Some mortgage companies were so eager to sign up new home buyers that they stopped running credit checks and even allowed applicants to claim higher incomes than they were actually earning in order to qualify them for loans. As a result, many people took on "too much mortgage" and were soon failing to make their monthly payments.

Crisis

When the housing bubble burst and home prices began to decline, borrowers who had made relatively small down payments on houses discovered that they owed more on their mortgages than their properties were worth. As the economy slowed, many borrowers fell behind on their monthly mortgage payments. Lenders began to foreclose on many houses, while other borrowers literally handed in their house keys and walked away from their houses *and* their mortgages.

The value of mortgage-backed securities plunged, driving several large financial firms either into bankruptcy or right to the edge of bankruptcy. Merrill Lynch lost more in two years than it had made in the prior decade. Lehman Brothers declared bankruptcy. Goldman Sachs and Morgan Stanley rushed to become "bank holding companies" so they could qualify for emergency loans from the Fed (which under the law could only extend emergency loans to banks and bank holding companies). The nightmarish thought of a total collapse of the U.S. financial system suddenly became a realistic possibility.

Immediate Response

Troubled Asset Relief Program (TARP)
A 2008 federal government program that authorized the U.S. Treasury to loan up to $700 billion to critical financial institutions and other U.S. firms that were in extreme financial trouble and therefore at high risk of failure.

The Treasury Bailout: TARP   In late 2008, Congress passed the **Troubled Asset Relief Program (TARP),** which allocated $700 billion to the U.S. Treasury to make emergency loans to critical financial firms. Most of this "bailout money" was eventually lent out to the likes of Citibank, Bank of America, JPMorgan Chase, and Goldman Sachs. Later, nonfinancial firms such as General Motors and Chrysler also received several billion dollars of TARP loans.

TARP saved several financial institutions whose bankruptcy would have caused a tsunami of secondary effects that would have probably brought down other financial firms and frozen credit throughout the economy. TARP and similar government bailouts were essentially government-provided insurance payouts to financial firms that never had to pay a single cent in insurance premiums for the massive bailouts that they received.

The Fed's Lender-of-Last-Resort Activities   As noted earlier, the Fed serves as the lender of last resort to financial institutions during financial emergencies. The Fed performed this vital function admirably following the 9/11 terrorist attacks. The financial crisis of 2007–2008 presented another, broader-based financial emergency. Under Fed Chair Ben Bernanke, the Fed designed and implemented several highly creative new lender-of-last-resort programs to pump liquidity into the financial system to keep credit flowing.

Total Fed assets rose from $885 billion in February 2008 to $1,903 billion in March 2009. This increase reflected a huge rise in the amount of securities (U.S. securities, mortgage-backed securities, and others) owned by the Fed. In undertaking its lender-of-last-resort functions, the Fed bought these securities from financial institutions. The purpose was to generate liquidity in the financial system by exchanging illiquid bonds (which the firms could not easily sell during the crisis) for cash, the most liquid of all assets.

moral hazard
The possibility that individuals or institutions will change their behavior as the result of a contract or agreement.

Many economists believe that TARP and the Fed's actions helped to avert a second Great Depression. But their policies also intensified the problem of **moral hazard**—a situation where individuals or institutions may change their behavior as the result of a contract or agreement. As it relates to financial investment, moral hazard is the tendency for financial investors and financial services firms to take on greater risks because they assume they are at least partially insured against losses. By greatly limiting losses, the Treasury and the Fed shielded financial firms from the consequences of their own actions. It was feared that this might prompt financial firms to be even more heedless of risk in the future because they would anticipate yet another bailout if things went awry as they had in 2007 and 2008.

Post-Crisis Policy Changes

The financial crisis of 2007–2008 generated much discussion about what went wrong and how to prevent anything like it from happening again. Politicians and financial regulators tightened lending rules to offset the "pass the buck" incentives created by mortgage-backed securities. They also passed legislation to help homeowners who were "underwater" on their mortgages, owing more than their homes were worth. And they acted to prevent companies from issuing loans to people who were probably not going to be able to pay them off.

The single largest policy response to the crisis was the **Wall Street Reform and Consumer Protection Act** that:

- Gave the Federal Reserve broader authority to regulate large financial institutions.
- Created a Financial Stability Oversight Council to watch for risks to the financial system.
- Established a process for the federal government to liquidate (sell off) the assets of large failing nonbank financial institutions, much as the FDIC does with failing banks.
- Required mortgage-backed securities and other derivatives to be federally regulated and traded on public exchanges.
- Required companies selling asset-backed securities to retain a portion of those securities so that they would always share some of the default risks.
- Established a stronger consumer financial protection role for the Fed through creation of the Bureau of Consumer Financial Protection.

Proponents of the law said it would help prevent many of the practices that generated the financial crisis of 2007–2008. They also contended that the law would mitigate the moral hazard problem by sending a strong message to stockholders, bondholders, and executives that they will suffer unavoidable and extremely high personal financial losses if they allowed their firms to ever again get into serious financial trouble.

Skeptics of the new law said that regulators already had all the tools they needed to prevent the financial crisis. They also pointed out that the government's own efforts to promote home ownership had greatly contributed to the financial crisis. Skeptics contended that the law would impose heavy new regulatory costs on the financial industry while doing little to prevent future government bailouts.

Wall Street Reform and Consumer Protection Act of 2010
A law that gave authority to the Federal Reserve to regulate all large financial institutions, created an oversight council to look for growing risk to the financial system, established a process for the federal government to sell off the assets of large failing financial institutions, provided federal regulatory oversight of asset-backed securities, and created a financial consumer protection bureau within the Fed.

The Fractional Reserve System

We have seen that $M1$ and $M2$ include currency (coins and Federal Reserve Notes) and checkable deposits. The U.S. Mint produces the coins and the U.S. Bureau of Engraving creates the Federal Reserve Notes. But who creates the checkable deposits? Surprisingly, it is loan officers!

The United States, like most other countries today, has a **fractional reserve banking system** in which only a portion (fraction) of checkable deposits are backed by reserves of currency in bank vaults or deposits at the central bank. Our goal is to explain how commercial banks can create checkable deposits by issuing loans. Our examples will involve commercial banks, but remember that thrift institutions also provide checkable deposits. So the analysis applies to banks and thrifts alike.

fractional reserve banking system
A banking system in which banks and thrifts are required to hold less than 100 percent of their checkable deposit liabilities as cash reserves.

ILLUSTRATING THE IDEA

The Goldsmiths

Here is the history behind the idea of the fractional reserve system.

When early traders began to use gold in making transactions, they soon realized it was both unsafe and inconvenient to carry gold and to have it weighed and assayed (judged for purity) every time they negotiated a transaction. So by the 16th century they had begun to deposit their gold with goldsmiths, who would store it in vaults for a fee. On receiving a gold deposit, the goldsmith would issue a receipt to the depositor. Soon people were paying for goods with goldsmiths' receipts, which served as one of the first types of paper money.

At this point, the goldsmiths—embryonic bankers—used a 100 percent reserve system, backing their circulating paper money receipts fully with the gold they held "in reserve" in their vaults. But because of the public's acceptance of the goldsmiths' receipts as paper money, the goldsmiths soon realized that owners rarely redeemed the gold they had in storage. In fact, the goldsmiths observed that the amount of gold being deposited with them in any week or month was likely to exceed the amount being withdrawn.

Then, some clever goldsmiths hit on the idea that paper "receipts" could be issued in excess of the amount of gold held. Goldsmiths would put these receipts, which were redeemable in gold, into circulation by making interest-earning loans to merchants, producers, and consumers. A borrower might, for instance, borrow $10,000 worth of gold receipts today with the promise to repay $10,500 worth of gold receipts in one year (a 5 percent interest rate). Borrowers were willing to accept loans in the form of gold receipts because the receipts were accepted as a medium of exchange in the marketplace.

This was the beginning of the fractional reserve system of banking, in which reserves in bank vaults are a fraction of the total money supply. If, for example, the goldsmith issued $1 million in receipts for actual gold in storage and another $1 million in receipts as loans, then the total value of paper money in circulation would be $2 million—twice the value of the gold. Gold reserves would be a fraction (one-half) of outstanding paper money.

QUESTION:

Explain how the gold receipts issued by goldsmiths performed the three major functions of money.

The goldsmith story highlights two significant characteristics of fractional reserve banking. First, banks can create money through lending. In fact, goldsmiths created money when they made loans that were not fully backed by gold reserves. The quantity of such money goldsmiths could create depended on the amount of reserves they deemed prudent to have available. The smaller the amount of reserves thought necessary, the larger the amount of paper money the goldsmiths could create. Today, gold is no longer used as bank reserves. Instead, currency itself serves as bank reserves so that the creation of checkable-deposit money by banks (via their lending) is limited by the amount of *currency reserves* the banks feel obligated, or are required by law, to keep.

A second reality is that banks operating on the basis of fractional reserves are vulnerable to "panics" or "runs." A goldsmith who issued paper money equal to twice the value of their gold reserves would be unable to convert all that paper money into gold in the event that all the holders of that money demanded their gold at the same time. In fact, many European and U.S. banks were once ruined by this unfortunate circumstance. However, a bank panic is highly unlikely if the banker's reserve and lending policies are prudent. Indeed, one reason why banking systems are highly regulated industries is to prevent runs on banks. This is also the reason why the United States has a system of deposit insurance. By guaranteeing deposits, deposit insurance helps to prevent the sort of bank runs that used to happen so often before deposit insurance was available.

A Single Commercial Bank

To illustrate the workings of the modern fractional reserve banking system, we need to examine a commercial bank's balance sheet.

A bank's (or thrift's) balance sheet summarizes the bank's financial position at a particular point in time. The **balance sheet** is a statement of the bank's assets—things owned by the bank or owed to the bank—and claims on those assets. Every balance sheet must balance, which means that the value of *assets* must equal the amount of claims against those assets. The claims shown on a balance sheet are divided into two groups: (1) *liabilities,* which the bank owes to depositors or others, and (2) *net worth,* the claims of the bank's owners against the bank's assets. A balance sheet is balanced because:

balance sheet
A statement of the assets, liabilities, and net worth of a firm or individual at some given time.

$$\text{Assets} = \text{liabilities} + \text{net worth}$$

Every $1 change in assets must be offset by a $1 change in liabilities + net worth. Every $1 change in liabilities + net worth must be offset by a $1 change in assets.

Now let's work through a series of bank transactions involving balance sheets to explain how individual banks can create money.

Transaction 1: Creating a Bank

Suppose some farsighted citizens of the town of Somewhere decide their town needs a new commercial bank to provide banking services for that growing community. Once they have secured a state or national charter for their bank, they turn to the task of selling, say, $250,000 worth of stock (equity shares) to buyers. Their efforts are successful and the Bank of Somewhere comes into existence—at least on paper. What does its balance sheet look like at this stage?

The founders of the bank have sold $250,000 worth of shares of stock in the bank—some to themselves, some to other people. As a result, the bank now has $250,000 in cash on hand and $250,000 worth of stock outstanding. The cash is an asset to the bank. Cash held by a bank is sometimes called *vault cash* or *till money.* The shares of outstanding stock constitute an equal amount of claims that the owners have against the bank's assets. Those shares constitute the net worth of the bank. The bank's balance sheet reads:

Creating a Bank Balance Sheet 1: Somewhere Bank			
Assets		**Liabilities and net worth**	
Cash	$250,000	Stock shares	$250,000

Each item listed in a balance sheet is called an *account.*

Transaction 2: Acquiring Property and Equipment

The board of directors (who represent the bank's owners) must now make the bank a reality. First, property and equipment must be acquired. Suppose the directors, confident of the success of their venture, purchase a building for $220,000 and pay $20,000 for office equipment. This simple transaction changes the composition of the bank's assets. The bank now has $240,000 less in cash and $240,000 of new property assets. Using blue to denote accounts affected by each transaction, we show that the bank's balance sheet at the end of transaction 2 appears as follows:

Acquiring Property and Equipment Balance Sheet 2: Somewhere Bank			
Assets		**Liabilities and net worth**	
Cash	$10,000	Stock shares	$250,000
Property	240,000		

Note that the balance sheet still balances, as it must.

Transaction 3: Accepting Deposits

Commercial banks have two basic functions: to accept deposits of money and to make loans. Now that the bank is operating, suppose that the citizens and businesses of Somewhere decide to deposit $100,000 in the Somewhere bank. What happens to the bank's balance sheet?

The bank receives cash, which is an asset to the bank. Suppose this money is deposited in the bank as checkable deposits (checking account entries), rather than as savings accounts or time deposits. These newly created *checkable deposits* constitute claims that the depositors have against the assets of Somewhere bank. Thus, they are a new liability account. The bank's balance sheet now looks like this:

Accepting Deposits Balance Sheet 3: Somewhere Bank			
Assets		**Liabilities and net worth**	
Cash	$110,000	Checkable deposits	$100,000
Property	240,000	Stock shares	250,000

There has been no change in the economy's total supply of money as a result of transaction 3, but a change has occurred in the composition of the money supply. Bank money, or checkable deposits, has increased by $100,000, and currency held by the public has decreased by $100,000. Currency held by a bank, you will recall, is not part of the economy's money supply.

A withdrawal of cash will reduce the bank's checkable-deposit liabilities and its holdings of cash by the amount of the withdrawal. This withdrawal, too, changes the composition, but not the total supply, of money in the economy.

Transaction 4: Depositing Reserves in a Federal Reserve Bank

required reserves
The funds that banks and thrifts must deposit with the Federal Reserve Bank (or hold as vault cash) to meet the legal reserve requirement; a fixed percentage of the bank's or thrift's checkable deposits.

All commercial banks and thrift institutions that provide checkable deposits must by law keep **required reserves,** which are an amount of funds equal to a specified percentage of the bank's own deposit liabilities. A bank must keep these reserves on deposit with the Federal Reserve Bank in its district or as cash in the bank's vault. To simplify, we suppose the Bank of Somewhere keeps its required reserves entirely as deposits in the Federal Reserve Bank of its district. But remember that vault cash is counted as reserves and that real-world banks keep a significant portion of their own reserves in their vaults.

The specified percentage of checkable-deposit liabilities that a commercial bank must keep as reserves is known as the **reserve ratio**—the ratio of the required reserves the commercial bank must keep to the bank's own outstanding checkable-deposit liabilities:

$$\text{Reserve ratio} = \frac{\text{commercial bank's required reserves}}{\text{commercial bank's checkable-deposit liabilities}}$$

reserve ratio
The specified minimum percentage of its checkable deposits that a bank or thrift must keep on deposit at the Federal Reserve Bank in its district or hold as vault cash.

If the reserve ratio is $\frac{1}{10}$, or 10 percent, the Somewhere bank, having accepted $100,000 in deposits from the public, would have to keep $10,000 as reserves. If the ratio is $\frac{1}{5}$, or 20 percent, $20,000 of reserves would be required.

The Fed has the authority to establish and vary the reserve ratio within limits legislated by Congress. As of 2019, the first $16.3 million of checkable deposits held by a commercial bank or thrift is exempt from reserve requirements. A 3 percent reserve is required on checkable deposits between $16.3 million and $124.2 million. A 10 percent reserve is required on checkable deposits over $142.2 million, although the Fed can vary that percentage between 8 and 14 percent. Also, after consultation with Congress, the Fed for 180 days may impose reserve requirements outside the 8–14 percent range. Beginning in late 2008, the Fed began paying banks interest on their required reserves and on their excess reserves held at the Federal Reserve Banks.

To simplify, let's suppose that the reserve ratio for checkable deposits in commercial banks is $\frac{1}{5}$, or 20 percent. Although 20 percent is higher than the true requirement, the figure is convenient for calculations. The main point is that reserve requirements are fractional, meaning that they are less than 100 percent. This point is critical in our analysis of the banking system's lending ability.

By depositing $20,000 in the Federal Reserve Bank, the Somewhere bank will just be meeting the required 20 percent. We use "reserves" to mean the funds commercial banks deposit in the Federal Reserve Banks to distinguish those funds from the public's deposits in commercial banks.

Suppose the Somewhere bank anticipates that its holdings of checkable deposits will grow in the future. Then, instead of sending just the minimum amount, $20,000, it sends an extra $90,000, for a total of $110,000. In so doing, the bank avoids the inconvenience of sending additional reserves to the Federal Reserve Bank each time its checkable-deposit liabilities increase. And, as you will see, it is these extra reserves that enable banks to lend money and earn interest income from borrowers.

Under normal circumstances, a real-world bank would not deposit *all* its cash in the Federal Reserve Bank. However, because (1) banks as a rule hold vault cash only in the amount of 1.5 or 2 percent of their total assets and because (2) vault cash can be counted as reserves, we assume for simplicity that Somewhere deposits all of its cash in the Federal Reserve Bank.

After the Somewhere bank deposits $110,000 of reserves at the Fed, its balance sheet becomes:

Depositing Reserves at the Fed Balance Sheet 4: Somewhere Bank

Assets		Liabilities and net worth	
Cash	$ 0	Checkable deposits	$100,000
Reserves	110,000	Stock shares	250,000
Property	240,000		

There are three things to note about the last transaction.

excess reserves
The amount by which a bank's or thrift's actual reserves exceed its required reserves; actual reserves minus required reserves.

actual reserves
The funds that a bank has on deposit at the Federal Reserve Bank of its district (plus its vault cash).

Excess Reserves A bank's **excess reserves** are found by subtracting its *required reserves* (or legally required reserves) from its **actual reserves:**

$$\text{Excess reserves} = \text{actual reserves} - \text{required reserves}$$

In this case,

Actual reserves	$ 110,000
Required reserves	−20,000
Excess reserves	$ 90,000

The only reliable way of computing excess reserves is to multiply the bank's checkable-deposit liabilities by the reserve ratio to obtain required reserves ($100,000 × 20 percent = $20,000) and then to subtract the required reserves from the actual reserves listed on the asset side of the bank's balance sheet.

To test your understanding, compute the bank's excess reserves from Balance Sheet 4, assuming that the reserve ratio is (1) 10 percent, (2) 25 percent, and (3) 50 percent.

We will soon demonstrate that the ability of a commercial bank to make loans depends on the existence of excess reserves. Understanding this concept is crucial in seeing how the banking system creates money.

Control You might think the basic purpose of reserves is to enhance a bank's liquidity and to protect commercial bank depositors from losses. Reserves would constitute a ready source of funds from which commercial banks could meet large, unexpected cash withdrawals by depositors.

But this assumption breaks down under scrutiny. Although reserves have been seen historically as a source of liquidity and therefore as protection for depositors, a bank's required reserves are not great enough to meet sudden, massive cash withdrawals. If the banker's nightmare should materialize—everyone with checkable deposits appearing at once to demand those deposits in cash—the reserves held as vault cash or at the Federal Reserve Bank would be insufficient. The banker simply could not satisfy the huge volume of cash that would be demanded during a "bank panic."

So if reserves can't shield against bank panics, what is their function? *Control* is the answer. Required reserves help the Fed control the lending ability of commercial banks. The Fed can take certain actions that either increase or decrease commercial bank reserves and thereby affect banks' ability to grant credit. The objective is to prevent banks from overextending or underextending bank credit. To the degree that these policies successfully influence the volume of commercial bank credit, the Fed can help the economy avoid business fluctuations. Another function of reserves is to facilitate the collection or "clearing" of checks.

Transaction 5: Clearing a Check Drawn Against the Bank

Assume that Razi Fallow, a Somewhere farmer, deposited a substantial portion of the $100,000 in checkable deposits that the Somewhere bank received in transaction 3. Now suppose that Fallow buys $50,000 of farm machinery from the Ajax Farm Implement Company of Elsewhere. Fallow pays for this machinery by writing a $50,000 check against the deposit in the Somewhere bank. Razi gives the check to the Ajax Company. What are the results?

Ajax deposits the check in its account with the Elsewhere bank. The Elsewhere bank increases Ajax's checkable deposits by $50,000 when Ajax deposits the check. Ajax is now paid in full. Fallow is pleased with the new machinery.

Now the Elsewhere bank has Fallow's check. This check is simply a claim against the assets of the Somewhere bank. The Elsewhere bank collects this claim by sending the check (along with checks drawn on other banks) to the regional Federal Reserve Bank. Here a Fed employee will clear, or collect, the check for the Elsewhere bank by increasing Elsewhere's reserve in the Federal Reserve Bank by $50,000 and decreasing the Somewhere bank's reserve by that same amount. The check is "collected" merely by making bookkeeping entries that reduce Somewhere's claim against the Federal Reserve Bank by $50,000 and increase Elsewhere's claim by $50,000.

Finally, the Federal Reserve Bank sends the cleared check back to the Somewhere bank, and for the first time, the Somewhere bank discovers that one of its depositors has drawn a check for $50,000 against his checkable deposit. Accordingly, the Somewhere bank reduces Farrow's checkable deposit by $50,000 and notes that the collection of this check has caused a $50,000 decline in its reserves at the Federal Reserve Bank.

Looking back at these transactions, you will notice that all of the related balance sheets balance: The Somewhere bank has reduced both its assets (reserves) and its liabilities (checkable deposits) by $50,000. The Elsewhere bank has $50,000 more both assets (reserves) and liabilities (checkable deposits). Ownership of reserves at the Federal Reserve Bank has changed—with Somewhere owning $50,000 less and Elsewhere owning $50,000 more—but total reserves stay the same.

If we bring all the other assets and liabilities back into the picture, the Somewhere bank's balance sheet looks like this at the end of transaction 5:

Clearing a Check Balance Sheet 5: Somewhere Bank

Assets		Liabilities and net worth	
Reserves	$ 60,000	Checkable deposits	$ 50,000
Property	240,000	Stock shares	250,000

Verify that with a 20 percent reserve requirement, the bank's excess reserves now stand at $50,000.

Transaction 6: Granting a Loan (Creating Money)

In addition to accepting deposits, commercial banks grant loans to borrowers. What effect does lending by a commercial bank have on its balance sheet?

Suppose the Gristly Meat Packing Company of Somewhere decides it is time to expand its facilities. Suppose, too, that the company needs exactly $50,000—which just happens to be equal to the Somewhere bank's excess reserves—to finance this project.

Gristly goes to the Somewhere bank and requests a loan for this amount. The Somewhere bank knows the Gristly Company's fine reputation and financial soundness and is convinced of its ability to repay the loan. So the loan is granted. In return, the president of Gristly hands a promissory note—a fancy IOU—to the Somewhere bank. Gristly wants the convenience and safety of paying its obligations by check. So, instead of receiving a bushel basket full of currency from the bank, Gristly gets a $50,000 increase in its checkable-deposit account in the Somewhere bank.

The Somewhere bank has acquired an interest-earning asset (the promissory note, which it files under "Loans") and has created checkable deposits (a liability) to "pay" for this asset. Gristly has swapped an IOU for the right to draw an additional $50,000 worth of checks against its checkable deposit in the Somewhere bank. Both parties are pleased.

At the moment the loan is completed, the Somewhere bank's position is shown by balance sheet 6a:

When a Loan Is Negotiated Balance Sheet 6a: Somewhere Bank			
Assets		**Liabilities and net worth**	
Reserves	$ 60,000	Checkable deposits	$ 100,000
Loans	50,000	Stock shares	250,000
Property	240,000		

This balance sheet looks simple enough, but a close examination reveals a startling fact: *When a bank makes loans, it creates money.* The president of Gristly went to the bank with something that is *not* money–an IOU–and walked out with something that *is* money–a checkable deposit.

Contrast transaction 6a with transaction 3, in which checkable deposits were created, but only as a result of currency having been taken out of circulation. In that situation, there was a change in the *composition* of the money supply but no change in the *total supply* of money. By contrast, bank lending creates checkable deposits that *are* money. By extending the loan, the Somewhere bank has "monetized" an IOU. Gristly and the Somewhere bank have created and then swapped claims. The claim created by Gristly and given to the bank is not money; an individual's IOU is not acceptable as a medium of exchange. But the claim created by the bank and given to Gristly *is* money; checks drawn against a checkable deposit are acceptable as a medium of exchange. Checkable deposit money created by loans constitutes about one-half of $M1$ money in the United States and about 10 percent of $M2$.

Certain factors limit a commercial bank's ability to create checkable deposits ("bank money") by lending. The Somewhere bank can expect the newly created checkable deposit of $50,000 to be a very active account. Gristly would not borrow $50,000 at, say, 7, 10, or 12 percent interest for the sheer joy of knowing that funds were available if needed.

Assume that Gristly awards a $50,000 building contract to the Quickbuck Construction Company. Quickbuck, true to its name, completes the expansion promptly and is paid with a check for $50,000 drawn by Gristly against its checkable deposit in the Somewhere bank. Quickbuck does not deposit this check in the Somewhere bank but instead deposits it in the Elsewhere bank. Elsewhere now has a $50,000 claim against the Somewhere bank. The check is collected in the manner described in Balance Sheet 5. As a result, the Somewhere bank loses both reserves and deposits equal to the amount of the check; Elsewhere acquires $50,000 of reserves and deposits.

In summary, assuming a borrower writes a check for the entire amount of the loan ($50,000) and is given to a firm that deposits it in some other bank, the Somewhere bank's balance sheet will read as follows *after the check has been cleared against it:*

After a Check Is Drawn on the Loan Balance Sheet 6b: Somewhere Bank			
Assets		**Liabilities and net worth**	
Reserves	$ 10,000	Checkable deposits	$ 50,000
Loans	50,000	Stock shares	250,000
Property	240,000		

After the check has been collected, the Somewhere bank just meets the required reserve ratio of 20 percent (= $10,000/$50,000). The bank has *no* excess reserves, which poses a question: Could the Somewhere bank have loaned more than

$50,000—an amount greater than its excess reserves—and still have met the 20 percent reserve requirement when a check for the full amount of the loan was cleared against it? The answer is no; the bank is "fully loaned up."

Here is why: Start from Balance Sheet 5 as it looked at the end of transaction 5. That's what Somewhere's balance sheet looked like before any loans were extended. Now suppose the Somewhere bank lends $55,000 to the Gristly company. That would create a "Loans" account worth $55,000 on the left-hand side of Somewhere's balance sheet as well as increasing its checkable deposits account on the right-hand side by $55,000 (to a total of $105,000). If the Gristly company then spends all of that loan money by writing a $55,000 check to Quickbuck Construction, the collection of that check against the Somewhere bank would have lowered the Somewhere bank's reserves to $5,000 (= $60,000 − $55,000), and checkable deposits would once again stand at $50,000 (= $105,000 − $55,000). The ratio of actual reserves to checkable deposits would then be $5,000/$50,000, or 10 percent. But because the reserve requirement is 20 percent, the Somewhere bank could not have legally loaned $55,000.

By experimenting with other amounts over $50,000, you will find that the maximum amount the Somewhere bank could lend starting from Balance Sheet 5 is $50,000. This amount is identical to the amount of excess reserves the bank had available when it negotiated the loan.

A single commercial bank in a multibank banking system can lend only an amount equal to its initial preloan excess reserves. When it lends, the lending bank faces the possibility that checks for the entire amount of the loan will be drawn and cleared against it. If that happens, the lending bank will lose (to other banks) reserves equal to the amount it lends. So, to be safe, it limits its lending to the amount of its excess reserves.

Bank creation of money raises an interesting question: If a bank creates checkable deposit money when it lends its excess reserves, is money destroyed when borrowers pay off loans? The answer is yes. When loans are paid off, the process works in reverse. The bank's checkable deposits decline by the amount of the loan payment.

The Banking System: Multiple-Deposit Expansion

We have seen that a single bank in a banking system can lend one dollar for each dollar of its excess reserves. The situation is different for all commercial banks as a group. Indeed, the commercial banking system can lend—that is, can create money—by a multiple of its excess reserves. This multiple lending is accomplished even though each bank in the system can lend only "dollar for dollar" with its own excess reserves.

How do these seemingly paradoxical results come about? To answer this question succinctly, we will make three simplifying assumptions:

- The reserve ratio for all commercial banks is 20 percent.

- Initially, all banks are meeting this 20 percent reserve requirement exactly. No excess reserves exist; or, in the parlance of banking, the banks are "loaned up" (or "loaned out").

- If any bank can increase its loans as a result of acquiring excess reserves, an amount equal to those excess reserves will be loaned to one borrower, who will write a check for the entire amount of the loan and give it to someone else, who will deposit the check in another bank. This third assumption means that the worst thing possible happens to every lending bank—a check for the entire amount of the loan is drawn and cleared against it in favor of another bank.

The Banking System's Lending Potential

Suppose salvage yard owners find a $100 bill while dismantling a car. They deposit the $100 in bank A, which adds the $100 to its reserves. We will record only *changes* in the balance sheets of the various commercial banks. The deposit changes bank A's balance sheet as shown by entries (a_1):

Multiple-Deposit Expansion Process Balance Sheet: Commercial Bank A			
Assets		**Liabilities and net worth**	
Reserves	$ + 100 (a_1)	Checkable deposits	$ + 100 (a_1)
	− 80 (a_3)		+ 80 (a_2)
Loans	+ 80 (a_2)		− 80 ($a3$)

Recall from transaction 3 that this $100 deposit of currency does not alter the money supply. While $100 of checkable-deposit money comes into being, it is offset by the $100 of currency no longer in the hands of the public (the salvage yard owners). But bank A *has* acquired excess reserves of $80. Of the newly acquired $100 in currency, 20 percent, or $20, must be earmarked for the required reserves on the new $100 checkable deposit, and the remaining $80 goes to excess reserves. Remembering that a single commercial bank can lend only an amount equal to its excess reserves, we conclude that bank A can lend a maximum of $80. When bank A makes a loan for this amount, its loans increase by $80 and the borrower gets an $80 checkable deposit. We add these figures—entries (a_2)—to bank A's balance sheet.

Now we employ our third assumption: The borrower uses the full amount of the loan ($80) to write a check ($80) to someone else, and that person deposits the amount in bank B, a different bank. As we saw in transaction 6, bank A loses both reserves and deposits equal to the amount of the loan, as indicated in entries (a_3). The net result of these transactions is that bank A's reserves now stand at + $20 (= $100 − $80), loans at +$80, and checkable deposits at + $100 (= $100 + $80 − $80). When the dust has settled, bank A is just meeting the 20 percent reserve ratio.

Recalling our previous discussion, we know that bank B acquires both the reserves and the deposits that bank A has lost. Bank B's balance sheet is changed as shown in the entries (b_1) that follow.

Multiple-Deposit Expansion Process Balance Sheet: Commercial Bank B			
Assets		**Liabilities and net worth**	
Reserves	$ + 80 (b_1)	Checkable deposits	$ + 80 (b_1)
	− 64 (b_3)		+ 64 (b_2)
Loans	+ 64 (b_2)		− 64 (b_3)

When the borrower's check is drawn and cleared, bank A loses $80 in reserves and deposits, while bank B gains $80 in reserves and deposits. But 20 percent, or $16, of bank B's new reserves must be kept as required reserves against the new $80 in checkable deposits. Thus, bank B now has $64 (= $80 − $16) in excess reserves. It can therefore lend $64 [entries ($b_2$)]. When the new borrower writes a check for $64 to buy a product, and the seller deposits the check in bank C, the reserves and deposits of bank B both fall by $64 [entries ($b_3$)]. As a result of these transactions, bank B's reserves now stand at + $16 (= $80 − $64), loans at + $64, and checkable deposits at + $80 (= $80 + $64 − $64). Bank B is just meeting the 20 percent reserve requirement.

We could continue this procedure by bringing banks C, D, E, ... , N and so on into the picture. In fact, the process will go on almost indefinitely, for as long as banks farther down the line receive at least one penny in new reserves that they can use to back another round of lending and money creation. We suggest you work through the computations for banks C, D, and E to be sure you understand the procedure.

Table 14.1 summarizes the entire analysis. Data for banks C through N are supplied on their own rows so that you can check your computations. Our conclusion is startling: On the basis of only $80 in excess reserves (acquired by the banking system when someone deposited $100 of currency in bank A), the entire commercial banking system is able to lend $400, the sum of the amounts in column 4. The banking system can lend excess reserves by a multiple of 5 (= $400/$80) when the reserve ratio is 20 percent. Yet each single bank in the banking system is lending only an amount equal to its own excess reserves. What is the explanation? How can the banking system as a whole lend by a multiple of its excess reserves, when each individual bank can lend only dollar for dollar with its excess reserves?

TABLE 14.1
Expansion of the Money Supply by the Commercial Banking System

Bank	(1) Acquired Reserves and Deposits	(2) Required Reserves (Reserve Ratio = .2)	(3) Excess Reserves, (1) − (2)	(4) Amount Bank Can Lend; New Money Created = (3)
Bank A	$100.00 (a_1)	$20.00	**$80.00**	$80.00 (a_2)
Bank B	80.00 (a_3, b_1)	16.00	64.00	64.00 (b_2)
Bank C	64.00	12.80	51.20	51.20
Bank D	51.20	10.24	40.96	40.96
Bank E	40.96	8.19	32.77	32.77
Bank F	32.77	6.55	26.21	26.21
Bank G	26.21	5.24	20.97	20.97
Bank H	20.97	4.20	16.78	16.78
Bank I	16.78	3.36	13.42	13.42
Bank J	13.42	2.68	10.74	10.74
Bank K	10.74	2.15	8.59	8.59
Bank L	8.59	1.72	6.87	6.87
Bank M	6.87	1.37	5.50	5.50
Bank N	5.50	1.10	4.40	4.40
Other banks	21.99	4.40	17.59	17.59
Total amount of money created (sum of the amounts in column 4)				**$400.00**

The answer is that reserves lost by a single bank are not lost to the banking system as a whole. The reserves lost by bank A are acquired by bank B. Those lost by B are gained by C. C loses to D, D to E, E to F, and so forth. Although reserves can be, and are, lost by individual banks in the banking system, there is no loss of reserves for the banking system as a whole.

An individual bank can safely lend only an amount equal to its excess reserves, *but the commercial banking system can lend by a multiple of its collective excess reserves.*

The Monetary Multiplier

monetary multiplier
The multiple of its excess reserves by which the banking system can expand checkable deposits and thus the money supply by making new loans (or buying securities); equal to 1 divided by the reserve requirement.

The **monetary multiplier** (or, less commonly, the *checkable deposit multiplier*) defines the relationship between any new excess reserves in the banking system and the magnified creation of new checkable-deposit money by banks as a group. The monetary multiplier exists because the reserves and deposits lost by one bank become reserves of another bank. It magnifies excess reserves into a larger quantity of checkable-deposit money. The monetary multiplier m is the reciprocal of the required reserve ratio R (the leakage into required reserves that occurs at each step in the lending process). In short,

$$\text{Monetary multiplier} = \frac{1}{\text{required reserve ratio}}$$

or, in symbols,

$$m = \frac{1}{R}$$

In this formula, m represents the maximum amount of new checkable-deposit money that can be created by a single dollar of excess reserves, given the value of R. By multiplying the excess reserves E by m, we can find the maximum amount of new checkable-deposit money, D, that can be created by the banking system. That is,

Maximum checkable-deposit creation = excess reserves × monetary multiplier

or, more simply,

$$D = E \times m$$

In our example in **Table 14.1**, R is .20, so m is 5 (= 1/.20). Thus,

$$D = \$80 \times 5 = \$400$$

Reversibility: The Multiple Destruction of Money

The process we have described is reversible. Just as checkable-deposit money is created when banks make loans, checkable-deposit money is destroyed when loans are paid off. Loan repayment, in effect, sets off a process of multiple destruction of money that is the opposite of the multiple creation process. Because loans are both made and paid off in any period, the total loans, checkable deposits, and money supply in a given period will depend on the net effect of the two processes. If the dollar amount of loans made in some period exceeds the dollar amount of loans paid off, checkable deposits will expand and the money supply will increase. But if the dollar amount of loans made in some period is less than the dollar amount of loans paid off, checkable deposits will contract and the money supply will decline.

Historically, one of the Fed's main ways of influencing the economy was by changing the supply of bank money. But the Fed has other ways, as well, which we explore in the next chapter.

 APPLYING THE ANALYSIS

The Bank Panics of 1930 to 1933

In the early months of the Great Depression, before there was deposit insurance, several financially weak banks went out of business. As word spread that customers of those banks had lost their deposits, a general concern arose that something similar could happen at other banks. Depositors became frightened that their banks did not, in fact, still have all the money they had deposited. This, of course, is a reality in a fractional reserve banking system. Acting on their fears, people en masse tried to "cash out" their bank accounts by withdrawing their money before it was all gone. This "run on the banks" caused many previously financially sound banks to declare bankruptcy. More than 9,000 banks failed within three years.

The massive conversion of checkable deposits to currency during 1930 to 1933 reduced the nation's money supply. This might seem strange because a check written for "cash" reduces checkable-deposit money and increases currency in the hands of the public by the same amount. So how does the money supply decline? Our discussion of the money-creation process provides the answer, but now the story becomes one of money destruction.

Suppose that people collectively cash out $10 billion from their checking accounts. As an immediate result, checkable-deposit money declines by $10 billion, while currency held by the public increases by $10 billion. But here is the catch: Assuming a reserve ratio of 20 percent, the $10 billion of currency in the banks had been supporting $50 billion of deposit money, the $10 billion of deposits plus $40 billion created through loans. The $10 billion withdrawal of currency forces banks to reduce loans (and thus checkable-deposit money) by $40 billion to continue to meet their reserve requirement. In short, a $40 billion destruction of deposit money occurs. This is the scenario that occurred in the early years of the 1930s.

Accompanying this multiple contraction of checkable deposits was the banks' "scramble for liquidity" to try to meet further withdrawals of currency. To obtain more currency, they sold many of their holdings of government securities to the public. A bank's sale of government securities to the public, like a reduction in loans, reduces the money supply. People write checks for the securities, reducing their checkable deposits, and the bank uses the currency it obtains to meet the ongoing bank run. In short, the loss of reserves from the banking system, in conjunction with the scramble for security, reduced the amount of checkable-deposit money by far more than the increase in currency in the hands of the public. Thus, the money supply collapsed.

In 1933, President Franklin Roosevelt ended the bank panic by declaring a "national bank holiday," during which all national banks were shut down for one week so that government inspectors could have time to go over each bank's accounting records. Only healthy banks with plenty of reserves were allowed to reopen. This meant that when the holiday was over, people could trust in any bank that had been allowed to reopen. This identification of healthy banks, along with the initiation of the federal deposit insurance program, reassured depositors and ended the bank panics.

But before these policies could begin to turn things around, the nation's money supply had plummeted by 25–33 percent, depending on how narrowly or broadly the money supply is defined. This was the largest drop in the money supply in U.S. history. This decline contributed substantially to the nation's deepest and longest depression. Simply put, less money meant less spending on goods and services, as well as fewer loans for businesses. Both effects exacerbated the Great Depression.

Today, a multiple contraction of the money supply of the 1930–1933 magnitude is unthinkable. FDIC deposit insurance has kept individual bank failures from becoming general panics. For example, during the financial crisis of 2007–2008, the FDIC increased deposit insurance from $100,000 to $250,000 per account, and the federal government guaranteed the safety of all balances in money market mutual fund accounts. Also, while the Fed stood idly by during the bank panics of 1930 to 1933, in 2007–2008 it took immediate and dramatic actions to maintain the banking system's reserves and the nation's money supply. We discussed these lender-of-last-resort actions earlier. In **Chapter 15**, we will discuss the interest rate policies that the Fed undertook during the crisis.

QUESTION:

Why do fractional reserve banking and deposit insurance closely accompany one another in modern banking systems?

Summary

LO14.1 Explain the functions of money.

Anything that is accepted as (a) a medium of exchange, (b) a unit of monetary account, and (c) a store of value can be used as money.

LO14.2 Describe the components of the U.S. money supply.

There are two major definitions of the money supply. $M1$ consists of currency and checkable deposits; $M2$ consists of $M1$ plus savings deposits, including money market deposit accounts, small-denominated (less than $100,000) time deposits, and money market mutual fund balances held by individuals.

LO14.3 Describe what "backs" the money supply.

The money supply in the United States essentially is "backed" (guaranteed) by the government's ability to keep the value of money relatively stable, which in turn depends on the government's effectiveness in managing the money supply.

LO14.4 Discuss the structure of the Federal Reserve.

The U.S. banking system consists of (a) the Board of Governors of the Federal Reserve System, (b) the 12 Federal Reserve Banks, and (c) some 4,600 commercial banks and 7,000 thrift institutions (mainly credit unions). The Board of Governors is the basic policymaking body for the entire banking system. The directives of the Board and the Federal Open Market Committee (FOMC) are implemented through the 12 Federal Reserve Banks, which are simultaneously (a) central banks, (b) quasi-public banks, and (c) bankers' banks.

LO14.5 Identify the functions and responsibilities of the Federal Reserve.

The major functions of the Fed are to (a) issue Federal Reserve Notes, (b) set reserve requirements and hold reserves deposited by banks and thrifts, (c) lend money to financial institutions and serve as a lender of last resort in national financial emergencies, (d) provide for the rapid collection of checks, (e) act as the fiscal agent for the federal government, (f) supervise the operations of the banks, and (g) regulate the supply of money in the economy's best interests.

The Fed is essentially an independent institution, controlled neither by the president nor by Congress. This independence shields the Fed from political pressure and allows it to raise and lower interest rates (via changes in the money supply) as needed to promote full employment, price stability, and economic growth.

LO14.6 Explain the main factors that contributed to the financial crisis of 2007–2008.

The financial crisis of 2007–2008 was caused by an unprecedented rise in mortgage loan defaults, the collapse or near-collapse of several major financial institutions, and the generalized freezing of credit availability. The crisis resulted from bad mortgage loans together with declining real estate prices. It was facilitated by the securitization of mortgage debt into mortgage-backed securities that ended up in the portfolios of major financial institutions.

Policymakers instituted a number of reforms after the crisis, the most prominent being the Wall Street Reform and Consumer Financial Protection Act, which, among other things, (a) gave the Fed broader powers to regulate financial firms, (b) required asset-backed securities to be regulated and sold on public exchanges, (c) required firms selling asset-backed securities to retain a portion so as to expose them to the same risks that they were selling to others, and (d) created the Consumer Financial Protection Bureau within the Federal Reserve System.

LO14.7 Describe how banks create money in a "fractional reserve" banking system.

Modern banking systems are fractional reserve systems: Only a fraction of checkable deposits is backed by currency. Commercial banks keep required reserves on deposit in a Federal Reserve Bank or as vault cash. These required reserves are equal to a specified percentage of the commercial bank's checkable-deposit liabilities. Excess reserves are equal to actual reserves minus required reserves.

Commercial banks create money—checkable deposits, or checkable-deposit money—when they make loans. The ability of a single commercial bank to create money by lending depends on the size of its excess reserves. Generally, a commercial bank can lend only an amount equal to its excess reserves. Money creation is thus limited because, in all likelihood, checks drawn by borrowers will be deposited in other banks, causing a loss of reserves and deposits to the lending bank equal to the amount of money lent.

The commercial banking system as a whole can lend by a multiple of its excess reserves because the system as a whole cannot lose reserves. Individual banks, however, can lose reserves to other banks in the system. The multiple by which the banking system can lend on the basis of each dollar of excess reserves is the reciprocal of the reserve ratio. This multiple credit expansion process is reversible.

Terms and Concepts

medium of exchange

unit of account

store of value

liquidity

*M*1

Federal Reserve Note

token money

checkable deposit

commercial bank

thrift institution

near-money

*M*2

savings account

money market deposit account (MMDA)

time deposit

money market mutual fund (MMMF)

legal tender

Federal Reserve System

Board of Governors

Federal Reserve Banks

Federal Open Market Committee (FOMC)

subprime mortgage loans

mortgage-backed securities

Troubled Asset Relief Program (TARP)

moral hazard

Wall Street Reform and Consumer Protection Act of 2010

fractional reserve banking system

balance sheet

required reserves

reserve ratio

excess reserves

actual reserves

monetary multiplier

Questions   McGraw Hill connect

1. What are the three basic functions of money? Describe how rapid inflation can undermine money's ability to perform each of the three functions. **(LO1)**

2. Which two of the following financial institutions offer checkable deposits included within the *M*1 money supply: mutual fund companies; insurance companies; commercial banks; securities firms; thrift institutions? Which of the following is *not* included in either *M*1 or *M*2: currency held by the public; checkable deposits; money market mutual fund balances; small-denominated (less than $100,000) time deposits; currency held by banks; savings deposits? **(LO2)**

3. What are the components of the *M*1 money supply? What is the largest component? Which of the components of *M*1 is *legal tender?* Why is the face value of a coin greater than its intrinsic value? What near-monies are included in the *M*2 money supply? **(LO2)**

4. What "backs" the money supply in the United States? What determines the value (domestic purchasing power) of money? How does the purchasing power of the dollar relate to the price level? In the United States, who is responsible for maintaining money's purchasing power? **(LO3)**

5. How is the chairperson of the Federal Reserve System selected? Describe the relationship between the Board of Governors of the Federal Reserve System and the 12 Federal Reserve Banks. What is the purpose of the Federal Open Market Committee (FOMC)? What is its makeup? **(LO4)**

6. What do economists mean when they say that the Federal Reserve Banks are central banks, quasi-public banks, and bankers' banks? **(LO5)**

7. Identify three functions of the Federal Reserve, other than its main role of controlling the supply of money. **(LO5)**

8. How does each of the following relate to the financial crisis of 2007–2008: declines in real estate values, subprime mortgage loans, mortgage-backed securities? **(LO6)**

9. What is TARP and how was it funded? What is meant by the term "lender of last resort" and how does it relate to the financial crisis of 2007–2008? **(LO6)**

10. How did the Wall Street Reform and Consumer Protection Act of 2010 try to address some of the problems that helped cause the financial crisis of 2007–2008? **(LO6)**

11. What is the difference between an asset and a liability on a bank's balance sheet? How does net worth relate to each? Why must a balance sheet always balance? What are the major assets and claims on a commercial bank's balance sheet? **(LO7)**

12. Why does the Federal Reserve require commercial banks to have reserves? Explain why reserves are an asset to commercial banks but a liability to the Federal Reserve Banks. What are excess reserves? How do you calculate the amount of excess reserves held by a bank? What is the significance of excess reserves? **(LO7)**

13. "Whenever currency is deposited in a commercial bank, cash goes out of circulation and, as a result, the supply of money is reduced." Do you agree? Explain why or why not. **(LO7)**

14. Explain why a single commercial bank can safely lend only an amount equal to its excess reserves, but the commercial banking system as a whole can lend by a multiple of its excess reserves. What is the monetary multiplier, and how does it relate to the reserve ratio? **(LO7)**

Problems

1. Assume that the following asset values (in millions of dollars) exist in Ironmania: Federal Reserve Notes in circulation = $700; Money market mutual funds (MMMFs) held by individuals = $400; Corporate bonds = $300; Iron ore deposits = $50; Currency in commercial banks = $100; Savings deposits, including money market deposit accounts (MMDAs) = $140; Checkable deposits = $1,500; Small-denominated (less than $100,000) time deposits = $100; Coins in circulation = $40. **(LO2)**

    a. What is *M*1 in Ironmania?
    b. What is *M*2 in Ironmania?

2. Assume that Jimmy Cash has $2,000 in his checking account at Folsom Bank and uses his checking account debit card to withdraw $200 of cash from the bank's ATM machine. By what dollar amount did the *M*1 money supply change as a result of this single, isolated transaction? **(LO2)**

3. Suppose the price level and value of the U.S. dollar in year 1 are 1 and $1, respectively. If the price level rises to 1.25 in year 2, what is the new value of the dollar? If instead the price level falls to .50, what is the value of the dollar? **(LO3)**

4. Suppose that Lady Gaga goes to Las Vegas to play poker and at the last minute her record company says it will reimburse her for 50 percent of any gambling losses she incurs. Will Lady Gaga probably wager more or less as a result of the reimbursement offer? Explain. **(LO6)**

5. Assume that securitization combined with borrowing and irrational exuberance in Hyperville have driven up the value of existing financial securities at a geometric rate, specifically from $2 to $4 to $8 to $16 to $32 to $64 over a six-year time period. Over the same period, the value of the assets underlying the securities rose at an arithmetic rate from $2 to $3 to $4 to $5 to $6 to $7. If these patterns hold for decreases as well as for increases, by how much would the value of the financial securities decline if the value of the underlying asset suddenly and unexpectedly fell by $5? **(LO6)**

6. Suppose the assets of the Silver Lode Bank are $100,000 higher than on the previous day, and its net worth is up to $20,000. By how much and in what direction must its liabilities have changed from the day before? **(LO7)**

7. Suppose that Serendipity Bank has excess reserves of $8,000 and checkable deposits of $150,000. If the reserve ratio is 20 percent, how much does the bank hold in actual reserves? **(LO7)**

8. Third National Bank has reserves of $20,000 and checkable deposits of $100,000. The reserve ratio is 20 percent. Households deposit $5,000 in currency into the bank, and that currency is added to reserves. What amount of excess reserves does the bank now have? **(LO7)**

9. The following balance sheet is for Big Bucks Bank. The reserve ratio is 20 percent. **(LO7)**

    a. What is the maximum amount of new loans that Big Bucks Bank can make? Show in columns 1 and 1′ how the bank's balance sheet will appear after the bank has loaned this additional amount.
    b. By how much has the supply of money changed?
    c. How will the bank's balance sheet appear after checks drawn for the entire amount of the new loans have been cleared against the bank? Show the new balance sheet in columns 2 and 2′.
    d. Answer questions a, b, and c on the assumption that the reserve ratio is 15 percent.

Assets		(1)	(2)	Liabilities and net worth		(1′)	(2′)
Reserves	$22,000			Checkable deposits	$100,000		
Securities	38,000						
Loans	40,000						

10. Suppose the following simplified consolidated balance sheet is for the entire commercial banking system and that all figures are in billions of dollars. The reserve ratio is 25 percent. **(LO7)**

    a. What is the amount of excess reserves in this commercial banking system? What is the maximum amount the banking system might lend? Show in columns 1 and 1′ how the consolidated balance sheet would look after this amount has been loaned. What is the size of the monetary multiplier?
    b. Answer the questions in part a assuming the reserve ratio is 20 percent. What is the resulting difference in the amount that the commercial banking system can loan?

Assets		(1)	Liabilities and net worth		(1′)
Reserves	$52		Checkable deposits	$200	
Securities	48				
Loans	100				

11. If the required reserve ratio is 10 percent, what is the monetary multiplier? If the monetary multiplier is 4, what is the required reserve ratio? **(LO7)**

CHAPTER FIFTEEN

Interest Rates and Monetary Policy

Learning Objectives

LO15.1 Explain how the equilibrium interest rate is determined.

LO15.2 Explain the goals and tools of monetary policy.

LO15.3 Explain how monetary policy affects real GDP and the price level.

LO15.4 Discuss the effectiveness of monetary policy and its shortcomings.

LO15.5 Describe how the Fed has used monetary policy in recent years to promote macroeconomic stability.

Some newspaper commentators have stated that the chair of the Federal Reserve Board (Jerome Powell in 2021) is the second most powerful person in the United States, after the U.S. president. That statement is an exaggeration. But there is no doubt about the chair's influence, nor about the importance of the Federal Reserve and the monetary policy it conducts. Such policy consists of deliberate changes in the money supply to influence interest rates and thus the total level of spending in the economy. The goal of monetary policy is to achieve and maintain price-level stability, full employment, and economic growth.

Interest Rates

monetary policy
A central bank's changing of the money supply to influence interest rates and assist the economy in achieving price stability, full employment, and economic growth.

Before we examine how the Federal Reserve influences the money supply and interest rates, we need to better understand the market in which interest rates are established. As indicated in **Table 15.1**, there are many different interest rates that vary by purpose, size, risk, maturity, and taxability. (**Global Snapshot 15.1** compares one interest rate—the percentage rate on three-month loans—for several countries in 2020.) For simplicity, however, economists often speak of a single interest rate. As we will see, the interest rate in the economy results from the interaction of money demand and money supply.

TABLE 15.1
Selected U.S. Interest Rates, March 2021

Type of Interest Rate	Annual Percentage
20-year Treasury bond rate (interest rate on federal government security used to finance the public debt)	2.11%
3-month Treasury bill rate (interest rate on federal government security used to finance the public debt)	0.05
Prime interest rate (interest rate used as a reference point for a wide range of bank loans)	3.25
30-year mortgage rate (fixed interest rate on loans for houses)	3.07
4-year automobile loan rate (interest rate for new autos by automobile finance companies for highest credit score customers)	3.24
Inflation-indexed U.S. government savings bond (average interest rate paid on federal government security used to finance the public debt)	−0.03
Federal funds rate (interest rate on overnight loans between banks)	0.07
Consumer credit card rate (average interest rate for brand-new credit cards)	16.12

Sources: Federal Reserve, Bankrate.com, and Creditcards.com.

The Demand for Money

The public wants to hold some of its wealth as money for two main reasons:

- To facilitate purchases (transactions).
- To hold as an asset (store of value).

These two sources of money demand are named, respectively, the transactions demand for money and the asset demand for money. Let's discuss them in sequence.

transactions demand for money
The amount of money people want to hold for use as a medium of exchange (to make payments); varies directly with nominal GDP.

Transactions Demand, D_t People hold money because it is convenient for purchasing goods and services. Households usually are paid once a week, every two weeks, or monthly, but their expenditures are less predictable and typically more frequent. Thus, households must have enough money on hand to buy groceries and to pay mortgage, rent, and utility bills. Businesses, too, need to have money available to pay for labor, materials, and other inputs. The demand for money as a medium of exchange is called the **transactions demand for money.**

Nominal GDP is the main determinant of the amount of money demanded for transactions. The larger the total money value of all goods and services exchanged in the economy, the larger the amount of money needed to facilitate those transactions. The transactions demand for money varies directly with nominal GDP. We specify *nominal* GDP because households and firms will want more money for transactions if prices rise or if real output increases. In both instances, there will be a need for a larger dollar volume to accomplish the desired transactions.

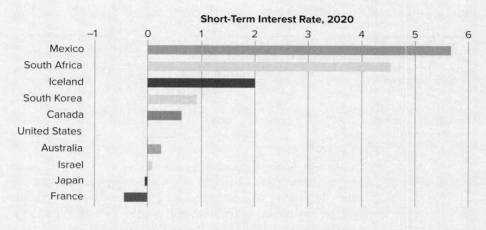

GLOBAL SNAPSHOT 15.1

Short-Term Nominal Interest Rates, Selected Nations

These data show the short-term nominal interest rates (percentage rates on three-month loans) in various countries in 2020. Because these are nominal rates, much of the variation reflects differences in rates of inflation. Differences both in central bank monetary policies and in the risk of default also explain the variations, however.

Short-Term Interest Rate, 2020

Source: Organization for Economic Cooperation and Development, www.oecd.org. Accessed March 2, 2021.

In **Figure 15.1a**, we graph the quantity of money demanded for transactions against the interest rate. For simplicity, let's assume that the quantity demanded depends exclusively on nominal GDP and is therefore independent of the real interest rate. Our simplifying assumption allows us to graph the transactions demand, D_t, as a vertical line. This demand curve is positioned at $100 billion, on the assumption that nominal GDP is $300 billion and each dollar held for transactions purposes is spent an average of three times per year. Thus, the public needs $100 billion (= $300 billion/3) to purchase that amount of nominal GDP.

Asset Demand, D_a The second reason for holding money derives from money's function as a store of value. People may hold their wealth either in tangible assets like real estate or in a variety of financial assets, including stocks, bonds, and money. To the extent they want to hold money as an asset, there is an **asset demand** for money.

asset demand
The amount of money people want to hold as a store of value; this amount varies inversely with the interest rate.

To understand why people have an asset demand for money, you must compare money with other financial assets, such as bonds. Bonds make regular, substantial interest payments, while money earns zero interest (currency) or extremely low interest (checking account deposits). Thus, from that perspective, bonds are a more attractive financial asset.

But that's not the end of the story. Bonds, stocks, and other financial assets are also much riskier than money. Bond prices, for example, sometimes fall, generating capital losses for their owners. By contrast, the value of money is quite steady unless there is a hyperinflation. So while money pays zero interest, it also holds its value much better than bonds and other financial assets under normal circumstances. This gives people a reason to demand money as an asset.

FIGURE 15.1

The demand for money, supply of money, and equilibrium interest rate. The total demand for money, D_m, is determined by horizontally adding the asset demand for money, D_a, to the transactions demand, D_t. The transactions demand is vertical because it is assumed to depend solely on nominal GDP rather than on the interest rate. The asset demand varies inversely with the interest rate because of the opportunity cost involved in holding currency and checkable deposits that pay no interest or very low interest. Combining the money supply, S_m, with the total money demand, D_m, portrays the money market and determines the equilibrium interest rate, i_e.

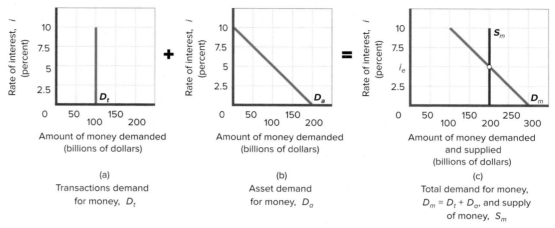

(a)	(b)	(c)
Transactions demand for money, D_t	Asset demand for money, D_a	Total demand for money, $D_m = D_t + D_a$, and supply of money, S_m

A third reason that people demand money as an asset is because money can be used to immediately purchase other assets when opportunities arise. Money will hold its value when the stock market crashes 20 percent; so anyone holding money can jump in and buy stocks at low, post-crash prices. The only way to "buy the dips" is to have money on hand when the prices of other assets decline.

Knowing these advantages and disadvantages, the public must decide how much of its financial assets to hold as money. Their decision depends primarily on the interest rate. When a household or a business holds money, it incurs the opportunity cost of the interest it could have received if it had used that money to purchase bonds. If bonds pay 6 percent interest, for example, then holding $100 as cash or in a noninterest checking account would cost $6 per year of forgone income.

The amount of money demanded as an asset therefore varies inversely with the interest rate (which is the opportunity cost of holding money as an asset). When the interest rate rises, being liquid and avoiding capital losses becomes more costly. So the public reacts by reducing its holdings of money as an asset. By contrast, when the interest rate falls, the cost of being liquid and avoiding capital losses declines. The public therefore increases the amount of financial assets that it wants to hold as money. This inverse relationship just described is shown by D_a in **Figure 15.1b**.

total demand for money
The sum of the transactions demand for money and the asset demand for money.

Total Money Demand, D_m As **Figure 15.1** shows, we find the **total demand for money,** D_m, by horizontally adding the asset demand to the transactions demand. The result is the downward sloping line in **Figure 15.1c**, which represents the total amount of money the public wants to hold, both for transactions and as an asset, at each possible interest rate.

Recall that the transactions demand for money depends on nominal GDP. A change in the nominal GDP will, consequently, shift the total money demand curve by altering the transactions demand for money. Consider an increase in nominal GDP. That will increase the transactions demand for money, and that extra transactions demand will shift the total money demand curve to the right. In contrast, a decline in nominal GDP will shift the total money demand curve to the left. As an example, suppose nominal GDP increases from $300 billion to $450 billion and the average dollar held for transactions is still spent three times per year. Then, the transactions demand curve will shift from $100 billion (= $300 billion/3) to $150 billion (= $450 billion/3). The total money demand curve will then lie $50 billion farther to the right at each possible interest rate.

The Equilibrium Interest Rate

We can combine the demand for money with the supply of money to determine the equilibrium rate of interest. In **Figure 15.1c**, the vertical line, S_m, represents the money supply. It is a vertical line because the monetary authorities and financial institutions have provided the economy with some particular stock of money. Here, it is $200 billion.

Just as in a product market or a resource market, the intersection of demand and supply determines equilibrium price in the **money market**. In **Figure 15.1**, this equilibrium price is the equilibrium interest rate, i_e. At this interest rate, the quantity of money demanded (= $200 billion) equals the quantity of money supplied (= $200 billion).

money market
The market in which the demand for and the supply of money determine the interest rate (or the level of interest rates) in the economy.

As you have just seen, changes in the demand for money, the supply of money, or both can change the equilibrium interest rate. We are, however, most interested in changes in the money supply since the Fed can affect the money supply. To that end, please remember this important generalization: *An increase in the money supply will lower the equilibrium interest rate, while a decrease in the money supply will raise the equilibrium interest rate.*

ILLUSTRATING THE IDEA

That Is Interest

Interest is needed to entice individuals to give up liquidity or sacrifice their present consumption—that is, to let someone else use their money for a period of time. The following story told by economist Irving Fisher (1867–1947) helps illustrate the idea of the "time value of money." The irony is that it was Fisher who had earlier formalized this exact idea in his theory of interest.

> In the process of a massage, a masseur informed Fisher that he was a socialist who believed that "interest is the basis of capitalism and is robbery." Following the massage, Fisher asked, "How much do I owe you?"
>
> The masseur replied, "Thirty dollars."
>
> "Very well," said Fisher, "I will give you a note payable a hundred years hence. I suppose you have no objections to taking this note without any interest. At the end of that time, you, or perhaps your grandchildren, can redeem it."
>
> "But I cannot afford to wait that long," said the masseur.
>
> "I thought you said that interest was robbery. If interest is robbery, you ought to be willing to wait indefinitely for the money. If you are willing to wait ten years, how much would you require?"
>
> "Well, I would have to get more than thirty dollars."
>
> His point now made, Fisher replied, "That is interest."[*]

QUESTION:
Who benefits most from lending at interest: the lender or the borrower?

---

[*]Irving Fisher, as quoted in Irving Norton Fisher, *My Father, Irving Fisher* (New York: Comet, 1956), p. 77.

Tools of Monetary Policy

We can now explore how the Fed can influence the money-creating abilities of the commercial banking system. The Fed has four main tools of monetary control it can use to alter the money supply: open-market operations, the reserve ratio, the discount rate, and interest on excess reserves.

Open-Market Operations

Bond markets are "open" to all buyers and sellers of corporate and government bonds (securities). The Federal Reserve is the largest single holder of U.S. government securities. The U.S. government, not the Fed, issued these Treasury bills (short-term securities), Treasury notes (mid-term securities), and Treasury bonds (long-term securities) to finance past budget deficits. Over the decades, the Fed has purchased these securities from major financial institutions that buy and sell government and corporate securities for themselves and for their customers.

open-market operations
The buying and selling of U.S. government securities by the Federal Reserve Banks for purposes of carrying out monetary policy.

The Fed's **open-market operations** consist of bond market transactions in which the Fed either buys or sells government bonds (U.S. securities) outright, or uses them as collateral on loans of money. Until the mortgage debt crisis of 2008, the Fed's open-market operations consisted solely of outright purchases and sales of government bonds. But in recent years, it has added repos and reverse repos (loans collateralized with government bonds) to its arsenal of open-market operations.

The conduit for the Fed's open-market operations is the trading desk of the New York Federal Reserve Bank. When the Fed buys or sells government bonds, the trading desk interacts exclusively with a group of 23 large financial firms called "primary dealers." Most are major investment banks such as JPMorgan Chase and Goldman Sachs. When the Fed borrows or lends money via *repos* or *reverse repos*, the trading desk interacts with 61 major financial institutions that include major banks, investment management companies, and government-sponsored financial entities such as the Federal National Mortgage Association (Fannie Mae).

Buying Securities   Suppose the Fed directs the Federal Reserve Banks to buy $100 million of government bonds. They can purchase these bonds either from commercial banks or the public. In both cases, the commercial banks' reserves will increase.

When Federal Reserve Banks buy government bonds from commercial banks, those banks send some of their holdings of securities to the Federal Reserve Bank. The Federal Reserve Banks, in paying for these securities, place $100 million worth of newly created reserves in the commercial banks' accounts at the Fed. Because there are no new checkable deposits, the entire $100 million of new reserves in the banking system are excess reserves. This increases the lending ability of the commercial banks.

We know from **Chapter 14** that excess reserves allow the banking system to make loans (expand the money supply) by a multiple of excess reserves. Suppose the reserve requirement is 20 percent, so the monetary multiplier is 5. Then, commercial banks can expand the $100 million of excess reserves to $500 million of new checkable-deposit money. This multiplier effect gives open-market operations a lot of "leverage." A modest change in reserves caused by Fed purchases or sales of government bonds can generate a much larger change in the overall money supply once the money multiplier kicks in.

The effect on commercial bank reserves is much the same when a Federal Reserve Bank purchases securities from the general public through the primary dealers. The Federal Reserve Bank buys the $100 million of securities by issuing checks to the sellers, who deposit the checks in their checking accounts at their commercial banks.

When the checks clear, $100 million of new reserves flow from the Federal Reserve Bank to the commercial banks. Because the banks need only 20 percent of the new reserves for the $100 million of new checkable deposits, the commercial banks have excess reserves of $80 million (= $100 million of actual reserves − $20 million of required reserves). They lend out the excess reserves, expanding checkable deposits by $400 million (= 5 × $80 million). When added to the original checkable deposits of $100 million, the $400 million of loan-created checkable deposits result in a total of $500 million of new money in the economy.

Selling Securities When a Federal Reserve Bank sells government bonds, commercial banks' reserves are reduced. Let's see why.

When a Federal Reserve Bank sells securities in the open market to commercial banks, the Federal Reserve Bank gives up securities that the commercial banks acquire. Commercial banks pay for those securities by drawing checks against their deposits—that is, against their reserves—in Federal Reserve Banks. The Fed collects on those checks by reducing the commercial banks' reserves accordingly. If all excess reserves are already lent out, this decline in commercial bank reserves will decrease the nation's money supply by a multiple amount due to the money multiplier working in reverse.

The outcome is the same when a Federal Reserve Bank sells securities to the public rather than directly to banks. The public pays for the securities with checks drawn on individuals' banks. When the checks clear, the commercial banks send reserves to the Federal Reserve Bank and reduce accordingly the checkable deposits of customers who wrote the checks. The lower reserves mean a multiple contraction of the money supply.

Repos and Reverse Repos In addition to bond purchases and sales, the Fed can also alter the money supply through collateralized loans known as repos and reverse repos.

A money loan is said to be collateralized when an asset (referred to as *collateral*) is pledged by the borrower to reduce the financial harm that will be suffered by the lender if the borrower fails to repay the loan. Consider home mortgages. If Alex takes out a home mortgage, the home he is buying will serve as collateral for his home mortgage loan. If Alex fails to repay the loan, ownership of the home will pass to the lender, who can then sell the home to get back most or all of the money it lent to Alex.

Repos and *reverse repos* are short-hand names for, respectively, repurchase agreements and reverse repurchase agreements.

- When the Fed undertakes a **repo** transaction, it makes a loan of money in exchange for government bonds being posted as collateral. The Fed's repo loans are normally overnight loans, but can last as long as 65 business days. The Fed holds the bonds posted as collateral until the loan is either repaid or goes into default. If the money is repaid on time, the Fed returns the bonds to the borrower. If the money is not repaid on time, the Fed keeps the bonds.

- **Reverse repo** transactions are repos in reverse. Instead of the Fed lending money against bond collateral, it is the Fed that posts government bonds as collateral when borrowing money from financial institutions.

The key point is that repos involve the Fed lending money into the financial system, whereas reverse repos involve the Fed borrowing money out of the financial system. That means repos are like open-market purchases of bonds (because both increase the money supply), while reverse repos are like open-market sales of bonds (because both decrease the supply of money).

repo
A repurchase agreement (or "repo") is a short-term money loan made by a lender to a borrower that is collateralized with *bonds* pledged by the borrower. The name *repo* refers to how the lender would view the transaction. The same transaction when viewed from the perspective of the borrower would be called a *reverse repo*.

reverse repo
A reverse repurchase agreement (or "reverse repo") is a short-term money loan that the borrower obtains by pledging *bonds* as collateral. The name *reverse repo* refers to how the borrower would view the transaction. The same transaction when viewed by the lender would be called a *repo*.

The Reserve Ratio

The Fed can also manipulate the reserve ratio in order to influence the lending ability of commercial banks. Suppose a commercial bank's balance sheet shows that reserves are $5,000 and checkable deposits are $20,000. If the reserve ratio is 20 percent (row 2, **Table 15.2**), the bank's required reserves are $4,000. Because actual reserves are $5,000, this bank's excess reserves are $1,000. On the basis of $1,000 of excess reserves, this one bank can lend $1,000; however, as we saw in **Chapter 14**, the banking system as a whole can create a maximum of $5,000 of new checkable-deposit money over multiple rounds of lending when the reserve ratio is 20 percent (column 7).

Raising the Reserve Ratio Now, what if the Fed raises the reserve ratio from 20 to 25 percent? (See row 3.) Required reserves will jump from $4,000 to $5,000, shrinking excess reserves from $1,000 to $0. This bank's lending ability falls to zero.

Raising the reserve ratio increases the amount of required reserves banks must keep. As a consequence, excess reserves will either shrink to a smaller positive amount, or shrink so far that banks will find themselves holding less reserves than are needed to meet the increased reserve requirement. The first scenario diminishes banks' ability to create money by lending. The second scenario will force banks to shrink checkable deposits and therefore the money supply. In the example in **Table 15.2**, excess reserves are transformed into required reserves, and our single bank's money-creating potential declines from $1,000 to $0 (column 6). Moreover, the banking system's money-creating capacity declines from $5,000 to $0 (column 7).

What if the Fed increases the reserve requirement to 30 percent? (See row 4.) The commercial bank, to protect itself against the prospect of failing to meet this requirement, will be forced to lower its checkable deposits and increase its reserves. To reduce its checkable deposits, the bank could let outstanding loans mature and be repaid without extending new credit. To increase reserves, the bank might also sell some of its bonds, adding the proceeds to the reserves. Both actions will reduce the money supply.

Lowering the Reserve Ratio What will happen if the Fed lowers the reserve ratio from the original 20 percent to 10 percent? (See row 1.) In this case, required reserves will decline from $4,000 to $2,000 and excess reserves will jump from $1,000 to $3,000. The single bank's lending (money-creating) ability will increase from $1,000 to $3,000 (column 6) and the banking system's money-creating potential would expand from $5,000 to $30,000 (column 7). Lowering the reserve ratio transforms required reserves into excess reserves and enhances banks' ability to create new money by lending.

TABLE 15.2
The Effects of Changes in the Reserve Ratio on the Lending Ability of Commercial Banks

(1) Reserve Ratio, %	(2) Checkable Deposits	(3) Actual Reserves	(4) Required Reserves	(5) Excess Reserves, (3)–(4)	(6) Money-Creating Potential of Single Bank, = (5)	(7) Money-Creating Potential of Banking System
(1) 10	$20,000	$5,000	$2,000	$3,000	$3,000	$30,000
(2) 20	20,000	5,000	4,000	1,000	1,000	5,000
(3) 25	20,000	5,000	5,000	0	0	0
(4) 30	20,000	5,000	6,000	−1,000	−1,000	−3,333

The examples in **Table 15.2** show that a change in the reserve ratio affects the money-creating ability of the *banking system* in two ways:

- It changes the amount of excess reserves.
- It changes the size of the monetary multiplier.

For example, when the legal reserve ratio is raised from 10 to 20 percent, excess reserves are reduced from $3,000 to $1,000 and the monetary multiplier is reduced from 10 to 5. The money-creating potential of the banking system declines from $30,000 (= $3,000 × 10) to $5,000 (= $1,000 × 5). Raising the reserve ratio forces banks to reduce the amount of checkable deposits they create through lending.

The Discount Rate

Recall that a central bank is a "lender of last resort." Occasionally, commercial banks have unexpected and immediate needs for additional funds. In such cases, each Federal Reserve Bank will make short-term loans to commercial banks in its district.

When a commercial bank borrows, it gives the Federal Reserve Bank a promissory note (IOU) drawn against itself and secured by acceptable collateral—typically U.S. government securities. Just as commercial banks charge interest on the loans they make to their clients, so too Federal Reserve Banks charge interest on loans they grant to commercial banks. The interest rate they charge is called the **discount rate.**

discount rate
The rate at which banks with excellent credit can borrow from the Federal Reserve.

In providing the loan, the Federal Reserve Bank increases the reserves of the borrowing commercial bank. Since no required reserves need be kept against loans from Federal Reserve Banks, all new reserves acquired by borrowing from Federal Reserve Banks are excess reserves.

From the commercial banks' point of view, the discount rate is a cost of acquiring reserves. This fact allows the Fed to alter the discount rate at its discretion in order to incentivize banks to increase or decrease their reserves and thereby increase or decrease the money supply.

- A *decrease* of the discount rate encourages commercial banks to obtain additional reserves by borrowing from Federal Reserve Banks. When commercial banks lend any of these new reserves, the money supply will increase.

- An *increase* of the discount rate discourages commercial banks from obtaining additional reserves by borrowing from the Federal Reserve Banks. Thus, the Fed may raise the discount rate when it wants to restrict the money supply.

Interest on Reserves

In 2008, federal law was changed to allow the Federal Reserve to pay commercial banks **interest on excess reserves (IOER)** held at the Fed. Before then, any reserves held on deposit at the Federal Reserve were paid zero interest. Thus, before 2008, banks had an incentive to keep their reserves as small as possible because any money kept on reserve at the Fed earned a 0 percent rate of return.

interest on excess reserves (IOER)
Interest rate paid by the *Federal Reserve* on bank *excess reserves.*

The new law allowed the Fed to set positive (above zero) interest rates on excess reserves. The ability to pay interest on reserves gave the Fed a fourth policy tool by which it can either increase or decrease the amount of monetary stimulus in the economy. If the Fed wishes to *reduce* bank lending, it can do so by increasing the IOER rate of interest that it pays on excess reserves held at the Fed. The higher the IOER rate, the more incentive banks will have to reduce their risky commercial lending for car, mortgage, and business loans in order to increase their excess reserves and thereby earn the risk-free IOER.

By contrast, if the Fed wishes to increase the amount of money that banks lend into the economy, the Fed can lower the interest rate it pays on excess reserves. The lower rate makes it less attractive for banks to keep reserves, so banks are incentivized to increase consumer and commercial lending and thereby stimulate the economy.

Relative Importance

Open-market operations are the most important of the four monetary policy tools because they give the Fed the ability to proactively alter the money supply in a way that will have immediate effects on the economy. The Fed can purchase, sell, borrow, or lend government securities in large or small amounts—and the impact on bank reserves is immediate. By contrast, if the Fed lowers the discount rate, banks may or may not come forward to take advantage of it; there may be little to no change in excess reserves.

Changing the reserve ratio has similar problems. If there are plentiful excess reserves in the banking system, as there have been since the Great Recession, then changes in the reserve ratio may have zero effect on lending because even a doubling of the reserve ratio would leave banks with excess reserves and, thus, no strong incentive to reduce lending.

The Fed has, however, shown an eagerness in recent years to alter the rate of interest on excess reserves (IOER) as a way of managing bank reserves and the money supply. After the Great Recession of 2007–2009, the amount of excess reserves in the U.S. banking system peaked at $2.7 trillion in 2014, just as the economy was returning to normalcy. As the unemployment rate fell below 5 percent in 2016, and then under 4 percent in 2018, banks had a choice of keeping excess reserves parked at the Fed or lending them into an economy experiencing increasingly robust growth and a strong demand for loans. By gradually raising the IOER rate from 0.25 percent in January of 2015 to 2.4 percent in April of 2019, the Fed was able to slow the rate at which bank lending was increasing (the higher IOER rate increased the opportunity cost of making new loans). That control, in conjunction with open-market operations, gave the Fed the ability to manage the money supply as it pursued noninflationary increases in real GDP.

As 2019 progressed, the Fed gradually lowered the IOER rate, reaching 1.6 percent in early 2020. In response to the COVID-19 pandemic, the Fed quickly lowered the IOER rate to 0.10 percent in March 2020. It remained at that level for over a year, as the Fed paid almost no interest on excess reserves to encourage bank lending and help the economy recover from the pandemic-induced recession.

Easy Money and Tight Money

Suppose the economy faces recession and unemployment. The Fed decides that an increase in the supply of money is needed to increase aggregate demand so as to employ idle resources. To increase the supply of money, the Fed must increase the excess reserves of commercial banks. How can it do that?

- *Buy or repo securities* By purchasing or loaning against securities in the open market, the Fed can increase commercial bank reserves. When the Fed's checks for the securities are cleared against it, or it issues loans collateralized by the securities, the commercial banks discover that they have more reserves.

- *Lower the reserve ratio* By lowering the reserve ratio, the Fed changes required reserves into excess reserves and increases the size of the monetary multiplier.

- *Lower the discount rate* By lowering the discount rate, the Fed may entice commercial banks to borrow more reserves from the Fed.

- *Lower the interest rate on excess reserves* By lowering the interest rate that the Fed pays on excess reserves, it may encourage commercial banks to lend their excess reserves, rather than keep them in Federal Reserve banks.

These actions are called an **easy money policy** (or *expansionary monetary policy*). Its purpose is to make bank loans less expensive and more available and thereby increase aggregate demand, output, and employment.

Suppose, on the other hand, excessive spending is pushing the economy into an inflationary spiral. Then, the Fed should try to reduce aggregate demand by limiting or contracting the supply of money. That means reducing the reserves of commercial banks. How is that done?

- *Sell or reverse repo securities* By selling or borrowing government bonds in the open market, the Federal Reserve Banks can reduce commercial bank reserves.
- *Increase the reserve ratio* An increase in the reserve ratio will automatically strip commercial banks of their excess reserves and decrease the size of the monetary multiplier.
- *Raise the discount rate* A boost in the discount rate will discourage commercial banks from borrowing from Federal Reserve Banks in order to build up their reserves.
- *Raise the interest rate on excess reserves* Raising the interest rate that the Fed pays on excess reserves may encourage commercial banks to deposit their excess reserves with the Federal Reserve, rather than lend them to consumers and businesses.

These actions are called a **tight money policy** (or *contractionary monetary policy*). The objective is to tighten the supply of money in order to reduce spending and control inflation.

easy money policy
Federal Reserve System actions to increase the money supply to lower interest rates and expand real GDP.

tight money policy
Federal Reserve System actions that contract, or restrict, the growth of the nation's money supply for the purpose of reducing or eliminating inflation.

Monetary Policy, Real GDP, and the Price Level

We have identified and explained the tools of expansionary and contractionary monetary policy. We now want to explain how monetary policy affects investment spending, aggregate demand, real GDP, and the price level.

The Cause-Effect Chain

The three diagrams in **Figure 15.2** will help you understand how monetary policy works toward achieving its goals.

Market for Money **Figure 15.2a** represents the market for money. It brings together the demand curve for money D_m and the three supply curves for money: S_{m1}, S_{m2}, and S_{m3}.

Recall that the total demand for money is made up of the transactions demand for money plus the asset demand for money. Demand curve D_m represents that sum.

Each of the three money supply curves is represented by a vertical line. Each line represents a different amount of money supply determined by the Fed. Since the Fed can set whatever supply of money it wants independently of the interest rate, each money supply curve plots as a vertical line (indicating that the quantity of money is independent of the interest rate).

The equilibrium interest rate is the rate at which the amount of money demanded equals the amount supplied. With money demand D_m in **Figure 15.2a**, if the supply of money is $125 billion ($S_{m1}$), the equilibrium interest rate is 10 percent. With a money supply of $150 billion ($S_{m2}$), the equilibrium interest rate is 8 percent; with a money supply of $175 billion ($S_{m3}$), it is 6 percent.

FIGURE 15.2

Monetary policy and equilibrium GDP. An easy money policy that shifts the money supply curve rightward from S_{m1} to S_{m2} lowers the interest rate from 10 percent to 8 percent. As a result, investment spending increases from $15 billion to $20 billion, shifting the aggregate demand curve rightward from AD_1 to AD_2, so that real output rises from the recessionary level Q_1 to the full-employment level Q_f. A tight money policy that shifts the money supply curve leftward from S_{m3} to S_{m2} increases the interest rate from 6 percent to 8 percent. Investment spending thus falls from $25 billion to $20 billion, and the aggregate demand curve shifts leftward from AD_3 to AD_2, curtailing inflation.

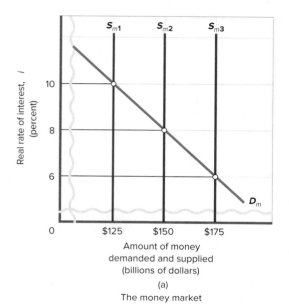

(a)
The money market

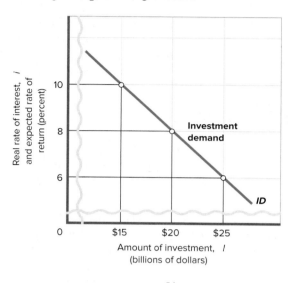

(b)
Investment demand

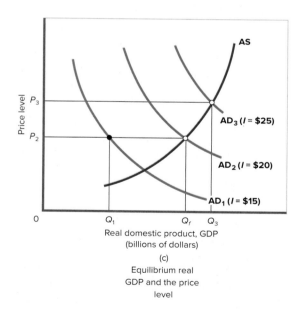

(c)
Equilibrium real
GDP and the price
level

Investment These 10, 8, and 6 percent real interest rates are carried rightward to the investment demand curve in **Figure 15.2b**. This curve shows the inverse relationship between the interest rate—the cost of borrowing to invest—and the amount of investment spending. At the 10 percent interest rate, it will be profitable for the nation's businesses to invest $15 billion; at 8 percent, $20 billion; at 6 percent, $25 billion.

Changes in the interest rate mainly affect the investment component of total spending, although they also affect spending on durable consumer goods (such as autos) that are purchased on credit. Changing interest rates greatly affects investment spending because of the large cost and long-term nature of capital purchases. Capital equipment, factory buildings, and warehouses are tremendously expensive. In absolute terms, interest charges on funds borrowed for these purchases are considerable. So the lower the interest rate, the more firms are willing to invest.

Similarly, the interest cost on a house purchased with a home mortgage is quite large. A 0.5 percent increase in the interest rate could amount to tens of thousands of dollars over the duration of the loan.

In brief, the impact of changing interest rates is mainly on investment (and, through that, on aggregate demand, output, employment, and the price level). Moreover, as **Figure 15.2b** shows, investment spending varies inversely with the interest rate.

Equilibrium GDP **Figure 15.2c** shows the impact that our three interest rates (and their corresponding levels of investment spending) have on aggregate demand. Aggregate demand curve AD_1 is associated with the $15 billion level of investment spending, AD_2 with investment of $20 billion, and AD_3 with investment of $25 billion. Other things equal, higher investment spending shifts the aggregate demand curve to the right.

Suppose the money supply in **Figure 15.2a** is $150 billion ($S_{m2}$), producing an equilibrium interest rate of 8 percent. In **Figure 15.2b**, we see that this 8 percent interest rate will bring about $20 billion of investment spending. This $20 billion of investment spending joins with consumption spending, net exports, and government spending to yield aggregate demand curve AD_2 in **Figure 15.2c**. The equilibrium levels of real output and prices are Q_f and P_2, as determined by the intersection of AD_2 and the aggregate supply curve AS.

To test your understanding of these relationships, explain why each of the other two levels of money supply in **Figure 15.2a** results in a different interest rate, level of investment, aggregate demand curve, and equilibrium real output.

Effects of an Easy Money Policy

Next, suppose that the money supply is $125 billion ($S_{m1}$) in **Figure 15.2a**. Because the resulting real output Q_1 in **Figure 15.2c** is far below the full-employment output, Q_f, the economy will be experiencing recession and substantial unemployment. The Fed therefore should institute an expansionary monetary policy.

To increase the money supply, the Federal Reserve Banks will take some combination of the following actions: (1) Buy or borrow (repo) government securities from banks and the public in the open market, (2) lower the legal reserve ratio, (3) lower the discount rate, or (4) lower the interest rate on excess reserves. The intended outcome will be an increase in bank reserves, which will, in turn, increase bank lending and the money supply. That increase in the money supply will then help to drive down the interest rate, thereby increasing investment, aggregate demand, and equilibrium GDP.

For example, an increase in the money supply from $125 billion to $150 billion ($S_{m1}$ to S_{m2}) will reduce the interest rate from 10 to 8 percent in **Figure 15.2a**, which in turn boosts investment from $15 billion to $20 billion in **Figure 15.2b**. This $5 billion increase in investment shifts the aggregate demand curve rightward, as shown by the shift from AD_1 to AD_2 in **Figure 15.2c**. This rightward shift in the aggregate demand curve will eliminate the negative GDP gap by increasing GDP from Q_1 to the full-employment GDP of Q_f.[1]

Column 1 in **Table 15.3** summarizes the chain of events associated with an easy money policy.

TABLE 15.3
Monetary Policies for Recession and Inflation

(1)	(2)
Easy Money Policy	**Tight Money Policy**
Problem: unemployment and recession	*Problem:* inflation
↓	↓
Federal Reserve buys bonds, lowers reserve ratio, lowers the discount rate, lowers the IOER, or initiates repos	Federal Reserve sells bonds, increases reserve ratio, increases the discount rate, raises the IOER, or initiates reverse repos
↓	↓
Excess reserves increase	Excess reserves decrease
↓	↓
Money supply rises	Money supply falls
↓	↓
Interest rate falls	Interest rate rises
↓	↓
Investment spending increases	Investment spending decreases
↓	↓
Aggregate demand increases	Aggregate demand decreases
↓	↓
Real GDP rises	Inflation declines

Effects of a Tight Money Policy

Next, we consider contractionary monetary policy. Let's assume that the money supply is $175 billion ($S_{m3}$) in **Figure 15.2a**. This results in an interest rate of 6 percent, investment spending of $25 billion, and aggregate demand AD_3. As you can see in **Figure 15.2c**, we have depicted a positive GDP gap of $Q_3 - Q_f$ and demand-pull inflation. Aggregate demand AD_3 is excessive relative to the economy's full-employment level of real output Q_f. To rein in spending, the Fed will institute a tight money policy.

The Federal Reserve Board will direct Federal Reserve Banks to undertake some combination of the following actions: (1) sell or lend (reverse repo) government securities to banks and the public in the open market, (2) increase the legal reserve ratio, (3) increase the discount rate, or (4) increase the interest rate that it pays on excess reserves. The intended outcome is an increase in bank reserves, which will, in turn, decrease bank lending and money creation. That decrease in the money supply will then help to raise the interest rate, thereby decreasing investment, aggregate demand, and equilibrium GDP, restraining demand-pull inflation.

---

[1] For simplicity we assume that the increase in real GDP does not increase the demand for money. In reality, the transactions demand for money would rise, slightly dampening the decline in the interest rate shown in Figure 15.2a. We also assume that the price level was inflexible downward at P_2 when the economy entered the recession. So the easy money policy expands real GDP from Q_1 to Q_f without causing inflation.

If the Fed reduces the money supply from \$175 billion to \$150 billion (S_{m3} to S_{m2} in **Figure 15.2a**), the interest rate will rise from 6 to 8 percent and investment will decline from \$25 billion to \$20 billion (**Figure 15.2b**). This \$5 billion decrease in investment will shift the aggregate demand curve leftward from AD_3 to AD_2 (**Figure 15.2c**). This leftward shift of the aggregate demand curve will eliminate the excessive spending and halt the demand-pull inflation. In the real world, of course, the goal will be to stop inflation—that is, to halt further increases in the price level—rather than to actually drive down the price level, which tends to be inflexible downward.[2] Given the downward inflexibility of prices, reducing the money supply to \$150 billion would push the equilibrium GDP below its full employment level. To stop the inflation and restore output to its full employment level without causing a recession, a smaller monetary contraction would be necessary.

Column 2 in **Table 15.3** summarizes the cause-effect chain of a tight money policy.

Monetary Policy in Action

Monetary policy has become the dominant component of U.S. national stabilization policy. It has two key advantages over fiscal policy:

- Speed and flexibility.
- Isolation from political pressure.

Compared with fiscal policy, monetary policy can be quickly altered. Recall that congressional deliberations may delay the application of fiscal policy for months. In contrast, the Fed is free to update monetary policy on a daily basis if necessary.

Also, because members of the Fed's Board of Governors are appointed and serve 14-year terms, they are relatively isolated from lobbying and need not worry about retaining their popularity with voters. Thus, the Board, more readily than Congress, can engage in politically unpopular policies (such as higher interest rates) that may be necessary for the economy's long-term health. Moreover, monetary policy is subtler and more politically neutral than fiscal policy. Changes in government spending directly affect the allocation of resources, and changes in taxes can have extensive political ramifications. Because monetary policy works more subtly, it is more politically palatable.

dual mandate
The 1977 congressional directive that the Federal Reserve System's highest priorities should be full employment and price level stability. In practice, the Fed aims for the full-employment rate of unemployment and an inflation rate of 2 percent per year.

Fed Targets

The Fed's overall goal is to comply with the dual mandate given to it by Congress in 1977. The **dual mandate** states that the Fed's two highest objectives should be full employment and stable prices. To that end, the Fed has set itself two concrete targets that it pursues simultaneously:

- Achieving the **full-employment rate of unemployment**, currently around 4 to 5 percent.

- Achieving the Fed's **target rate of inflation**, currently set at 2 percent per year.

full-employment rate of unemployment
The unemployment rate at which there is no cyclical unemployment of the labor force; equal to between 4 and 5 percent (rather than 0 percent) in the United States because frictional and structural unemployment are unavoidable.

The Fed's Unemployment Target The full-employment rate of unemployment, or natural rate of unemployment, is the unemployment rate that exists when an economy is producing at its potential output (full employment). Every person who wants a job is employed, so there is zero cyclical unemployment. Structural and frictional unemployment remain, however, as there will still be people either between jobs

target rate of inflation
The publicly announced annual inflation rate that a central bank attempts to achieve through monetary policy actions if it is following an inflation targeting monetary policy.

[2] Again, we assume for simplicity that the decrease in nominal GDP does not feed back to reduce the demand for money and thus the interest rate. In reality, this would occur, slightly dampening the increase in the interest rate shown in Figure 15.2a.

(frictional unemployment) or in need of retraining after their old jobs were eliminated due to changes in consumer preferences, evolving production technologies, or off-shoring (structural unemployment). Thus the full-employment rate of unemployment is not zero, but rather a modest positive number that reflects frictional and structural unemployment.

The full-employment rate of unemployment also reflects government industrial policy and labor force regulations, the size of the labor force growth relative to the growth rate of labor demand, and a wide variety of other factors that affect how much labor is necessary to produce the full-employment level of output, how much labor is available to produce it, and how quickly the frictionally and structurally unemployed return to work. These factors change over time, thereby causing the natural rate of unemployment to change over time, too.

For today's economy, the full employment rate of unemployment is estimated to lie somewhere between 4 and 5 percent. In late 2020, the median estimate made by Federal Reserve Open Market Committee members was 4.1 percent. In practice, this serves as the FOMC's target rate of unemployment:

- If the actual unemployment rate rises appreciably higher than 4.1 percent (say, to 5.0 percent or higher), the Fed will be inclined to pursue an easy money policy to (a) increase bank reserves to boost lending and (b) lower interest rates to increase investment spending.

- Alternatively, if the actual rate of unemployment falls much below 4.1 percent (say to less than 3.8 percent), the Fed will be inclined toward assuming the economy is in danger of a burst of inflation. The Fed will respond with a tight money policy under which the Fed would (a) decrease bank reserves to reduce lending and (b) raise interest rates to decrease investment spending.

The Fed's Inflation Target The unemployment rate cannot by itself determine whether monetary policy should be expansionary, contractionary, or neutral. The Fed must also consider whether inflation is above or below the Fed's target rate of inflation, which has been set at 2 percent since it was first established in 2012.

Why 2 percent? There are multiple reasons:

- ***Compensating for upward measurement bias*** There is a consensus among economists that the Consumer Price Index and other measures of inflation have an upward bias, meaning that they tend to say that inflation is higher than it is (by about 0.5 percent). Setting the target lower than 0.5 percent would increase the risk that the Fed would accidentally cause deflation and put the economy into a recession through overly contractionary monetary policy.

- ***Protecting savers*** On the other hand, the Fed does not want to set an inflation target too high, because it will want to avoid any substantial loss of purchasing power on the part of fixed-income receivers, savers, and creditors who fail to anticipate it. Even an inflation rate of 5 percent would cause noticeable harm to those caught unaware or unable to adjust. The Fed has opted for a 2 percent inflation target as a way of balancing the need to have a target greater than 0.5 percent with the need to not let inflation get uncomfortably high.

Other things equal, the Fed will be more inclined toward a contractionary monetary policy if the actual rate of inflation is above the target rate and more inclined toward an expansionary policy if actual inflation is below the target rate. But it also must consider whether the unemployment rate is above or below the full-employment rate of unemployment. The two parts of the dual mandate must be pursued in tandem.

federal funds rate
The interest rate banks and other depository institutions charge one another on overnight loans made out of their excess reserves.

zero interest rate policy (ZIRP)
A *monetary policy* in which a central bank sets *nominal interest rates* at or near 0 percent per year in order to stimulate the economy.

quantitative easing (QE)
An *open-market operation* in which *bonds* are purchased by a *central bank* in order to increase the quantity of *excess reserves* held by *commercial banks* and thereby (hopefully) stimulate the economy by increasing the amount of lending undertaken by commercial banks; undertaken when interest rates are near zero and, consequently, does not allow the central bank to further stimulate the economy with lower interest rates due to the *zero lower bound problem*.

APPLYING THE ANALYSIS

Recent U.S. Monetary Policy

The Fed has been very busy over the last 20 years.

The mortgage default crisis began during the late summer of 2007 and posed a grave threat to the financial system and the economy. The Fed responded with several actions. In August, it lowered the discount rate by half a percentage point. Then, between September 2007 and April 2008, it lowered the target for the **federal funds rate** (the interest rate banks charge each other on overnight loans) from 5.25 percent to 2 percent. The Fed also took a series of extraordinary actions to prevent the failure of key financial firms.

By late 2008, it was clear that the U.S. economy faced a crisis unequaled since the dark days of the Great Depression of the 1930s. The Fed responded with a series of innovative monetary policy initiatives to stimulate GDP and employment.

The Fed began by moving toward a **zero interest rate policy**, or ZIRP, in December 2008. Under ZIRP, the Fed aimed to keep short-term interest rates near zero to stimulate the economy. It lowered its target for the federal funds rate drastically, down to a targeted range of 0 to 0.25 percent. It also acted aggressively as a lender of last resort, purchasing securities from banks and other financial institutions to provide them with the liquidity they needed to make timely debt payments and avoid bankruptcy.

The immediate crisis was resolved by late 2009, after which the Fed no longer had to act as a lender of last resort. But with the unemployment rate rising toward 10 percent, the Fed had to figure out a way to continue stimulating the economy even though ZIRP meant that short-term interest rates were as low as they would go without violating the *zero lower bound*.

The Fed's solution was to use open-market operations to buy trillions of dollars worth of medium- and long-term financial assets, including mortgage-backed securities and longer-maturing U.S. government bonds. This strategy came to be known as **quantitative easing,** or QE, because the Fed's goal was not to reduce short-term interest rates further (since they were already near the zero lower bound) but to increase the quantity of reserves in the banking system as a way of encouraging lending.

By the close of 2015, the Fed felt that various economic indicators were signaling that monetary stimulus could end. The unemployment rate, in particular, had fallen back to just 5.0 percent after reaching 10.0 percent in 2009. The FOMC decided that the Fed could abandon ZIRP and QE while attempting to raise interest rates back up to normal levels using the mechanisms discussed earlier in this chapter, such as raising the IOER rate. Over the next four years, interest rates gradually increased and the economy continued to improve. By February 2020, the unemployment rate stood at just 3.5 percent and the economy was operating at or slightly above full employment.

With the COVID-19 pandemic shutting down parts of the economy beginning in March 2020, real GDP fell by about a third in the months that followed and the unemployment skyrocketed to 14.8 percent in April. The Fed responded by again pushing short-term interest rates down close to zero, where they remained well into 2021.

QUESTIONS:

What is the current monetary policy stance of the Fed? Has it been increasing interest rates, decreasing them, or leaving them unchanged in recent months? (Answer this question by going to the Federal Reserve's website at www.federalreserve.gov.)

Problems and Complications

U.S. monetary policy faces both limitations and complications.

Recognition and Operational Lags   Recall that fiscal policy is hindered by three delays, or lags—a recognition lag, an administrative lag, and an operational lag. Monetary policy also faces a recognition lag and an operational lag, but because the Fed can implement policy changes within hours, it avoids the long administrative lag that hinders fiscal policy.

Monetary policy is subject to a recognition lag because normal weekly and monthly fluctuations in economic activity and the price level mean that the Fed may not be able to quickly recognize when the economy is truly starting to recede or when inflation is really starting to rise. Once the Fed acts, monetary policy is also subject to an operational lag of three to six months because that much time is typically required for interest-rate changes to have any substantial impacts on investment, aggregate demand, real GDP, and the price level. These recognition and operational lags make it harder for the Fed to precisely target and time monetary policy actions.

Cyclical Asymmetry and the Liquidity Trap   Monetary policy may be highly effective in slowing expansions and controlling inflation, but much less reliable in pulling the economy out of a severe recession. Economists say that monetary policy may suffer from **cyclical asymmetry.** The metaphor of "pushing on a string" is often invoked to capture this problem. Imagine the Fed standing on the left-hand side of **Figure 15.2c**, holding one end of a "monetary-policy string." And imagine that the other end of the monetary-policy string is tied to the AD curve. Because the string would go taut if pulled on, monetary policy may be useful in *pulling* aggregate demand to the left. But because the string would go limp if pushed on, monetary policy will be rather ineffective at *pushing* aggregate demand to the right.

The reason for this asymmetry has to do with the asymmetric way in which people act in response to changes in bank reserves. If pursued vigorously, a restrictive monetary policy can deplete commercial banking reserves to the point where banks are forced to reduce the volume of loans. The result is a contraction of the money supply, higher interest rates, and reduced aggregate demand. Consequently, the Fed can almost certainly achieve a contractionary goal.

By contrast, the Fed cannot be certain of achieving an expansionary goal by adding reserves to the banking system. That's because it may run into the **liquidity trap,** in which adding more reserves to commercial banks' accounts at the Fed has little or no effect on lending, borrowing, investment, or aggregate demand. For example, during the Great Recession, the Fed created billions of dollars of excess reserves that drove down the Federal funds rate to as low as 0.15 percent. Nevertheless, commercial bank lending stalled throughout the first 15 months of the recession and remained weak even after the Fed implemented ZIRP and QE over the following five years. Banks were fearful that loans would not be paid back. So they preserved large reserves over lending.

The liquidity trap scenario demonstrates that the Fed is not omnipotent. An expansionary monetary policy can suffer from a "you can lead a horse to water, but you can't make it drink" problem. The Fed can create excess reserves, but it cannot guarantee that the banks will want to make additional loans. Households and businesses can frustrate the Fed, too, by not wanting to borrow. And when the Fed buys securities from the public, people may choose to pay off existing loans with the money received, rather than increasing their spending on goods and services.

---

cyclical asymmetry
The potential problem of monetary policy successfully controlling inflation during the expansionary phase of the business cycle but failing to expand spending and real GDP during the recessionary phase of the cycle.

liquidity trap
A situation in a severe recession in which the Fed's injection of additional reserves into the banking system has little or no additional positive impact on lending, borrowing, investment, or aggregate demand.

The liquidity trap that occurred during the severe recession was a primary reason why the Congress turned so significantly and forcefully toward fiscal policy in 2009. With monetary policy maxed out, Congress approved the gargantuan American Recovery and Redevelopment Act of 2009, which authorized the infusion of $787 billion of new tax cuts and government spending in 2009 and 2010. This spending helped to ensure stimulus even after interest rates had fallen toward zero and banks were sitting on reserves rather than lending.

APPLYING THE ANALYSIS

Less than Zero

By mid-2016, the Fed planned to raise short-term interest rates back up to historically normal levels. But with that process barely begun, the Fed had to wonder what it might do if the U.S. economy fell into a recession before rates had been returned to normal levels.

One option would be to try another round of quantitative easing, with interest rates low but positive. An entirely different option had, however, already been taken by the European Central Bank (ECB). Starting in 2014, the ECB had dared to plunge below the zero lower bound and set negative interest rates. By March 2016, the ECB had set its version of the Federal funds rate at −0.4 percent for the Eurozone countries. Similar rates in Denmark and Switzerland stood at −0.65 percent and −0.75 percent, respectively.

The ECB had set negative rates in an attempt to force banks to lend more. After all, if banks were set to lose 0.40 percent per year on any unloaned excess reserves, they would be better off lending them out at any interest rate greater than −0.40 percent, including negative rates such as −0.35 percent and −0.12 percent.

Strangely, that is what began to happen. In some countries, home mortgage rates turned negative, so that people were getting paid to borrow money to buy a house. Instead of the borrower mailing in a mortgage payment each month, the bank mailed the borrower a check for the negative interest they were earning by borrowing.

Checking and saving account rates also turned negative. As they did, however, the logic of the zero lower bound began to enforce itself. People began to withdraw money from banks, turning electronic bank balances into physical cash. They did so because they understood opportunity costs. Why get a negative rate on a bank balance when you could hold cash and lose nothing?

With people withdrawing money in the face of negative rates, the various European central banks were in a pickle. Lower (i.e., even more negative) rates would spur banks to lend more of their excess reserves. But the banks would have lower excess reserves to lend out as people withdrew bank balances in favor of cash.

Macroeconomists who had previously worried about the zero lower bound began to speculate about the existence of a "negative lower bound." They conjectured that there was likely a negative interest rate (for instance, −3.0 percent) beyond which any further cuts in interest rates would be counterproductive and fail to stimulate the economy. They reasoned that, below the negative lower bound, withdrawals from the banking system would reduce the total amount lent out by banks more than negative rates helped to increase lending. Negative rates might be stimulatory for a while, but only with diminishing effectiveness and only up until the negative lower bound was reached.

But where is the negative lower bound? How low can central banks go below zero before lower interest rates lose the power to stimulate? One hint comes from looking at the convenience of electronic payments. Many Europeans these days barely use cash. It is simpler to swipe credit and debit cards or wave one's phone to complete a purchase. So a great deal of the reason people leave money in bank accounts is to facilitate electronic transactions. If they switched to cash, they would lose that convenience.

Thus, one way to estimate a possible value for the zero lower bound would be to ask: "How negative could interest rates go before the loss of purchasing power exceeds the convenience that comes from being able to utilize electronic payments?" For some individuals, the tipping point might be −1.0 percent. For others, it might come at −2.5 percent or −4.5 percent. But beyond some point, the loss of purchasing power caused by a negative interest rate will loom larger in people's minds as interest rates decline further into negative territory. The lower the rate, the less people will want to hold electronic bank balances, the more people will convert electronic bank balances into physical cash, and the smaller excess reserves will be.

It is that trade-off that the Fed will have to consider if the United States enters a recession before the Fed has had a chance to normalize short-term interest rates back up to historical levels. If stimulus proves necessary, will the Fed return to quantitative easing, or will it dare to follow the ECB into negative territory? As of March 2021, ECB short-term interest rates were still negative, pushed even lower in response to the pandemic-induced recession.

QUESTIONS:

If interest rates are negative, how does that affect decisions about holding wealth in other financial assets (such as stocks) and real assets (such as houses)? What effect might those decisions have on aggregate demand and real GDP? Explain your reasoning.

Summary

LO15.1 Explain how the equilibrium interest rate is determined.

There is a set of interest rates that vary by loan purpose, size, risk, maturity, and taxability. Nevertheless, economists often speak of a single interest rate in order to simplify their analysis.

The total demand for money consists of the transactions demand and asset demand for money. The amount of money demanded for transactions varies directly with the nominal GDP; the amount of money demanded as an asset varies inversely with the interest rate. The market for money combines the total demand for money with the money supply to determine equilibrium interest rates.

LO15.2 Explain the goals and tools of monetary policy.

The goal of monetary policy is to help the economy achieve price stability, full employment, and economic growth.

The four main instruments of monetary policy are (a) open-market operations, (b) the reserve ratio, (c) the discount rate, and (d) interest on excess reserves.

LO15.3 Explain how monetary policy affects real GDP and the price level.

Monetary policy affects the economy through a complex cause-effect chain: (a) policy decisions affect commercial bank reserves; (b) changes in reserves affect the money supply; (c) changes in the money supply alter the interest rate; (d) changes in the interest rate affect investment; (e) changes in investment affect aggregate demand; and (f) changes in aggregate demand affect real GDP and the price level. **Table 15.3** summarizes all the basic ideas relevant to the use of monetary policy.

LO15.4 Discuss the effectiveness of monetary policy and its shortcomings.

The advantages of monetary policy include its flexibility and political acceptability. In recent years, the Fed has used monetary policy to help stabilize the banking sector in the wake of the mortgage debt crisis and to promote recovery from the Great Recession of 2007–2009. Today, nearly all economists view monetary policy as a significant stabilization tool.

Monetary policy has two major limitations and potential problems: (a) recognition and operational lags complicate the timing of monetary policy; (b) in a severe recession, the reluctance of banks to lend excess reserves and of firms and households to borrow may contribute to a liquidity trap that limits the effectiveness of an expansionary monetary policy.

LO15.5 Describe how the Fed has used monetary policy in recent years to promote macroeconomic stability.

In response to the financial crisis of 2007–2009, the Fed pursued a number of expansionary monetary policies, including lowering the discount rate and Federal funds rate. In December 2008, it embarked on a zero interest rate policy (ZIRP) in an effort to stimulate economic recovery and growth. When lowering interest rates to nearly zero failed to have the desired stimulatory effect, the Fed implemented quantitative easing.

In 2015, the Fed began to take steps to raise interest rates back to historically normal levels, and ZIRP and QE were abandoned. All was well until early 2020, when the Fed again lowered interest rates close to zero in response to the pandemic-induced recession. As of early 2021, interest rates were still near zero, and the economy had not fully reopened or recovered.

Terms and Concepts

monetary policy	discount rate	federal funds rate
transactions demand for money	interest on excess reserves (IOER)	zero interest rate policy (ZIRP)
asset demand		quantitative easing (QE)
total demand for money	easy money policy	cyclical asymmetry
money market	tight money policy	liquidity trap
open-market operations	dual mandate	
repo	full-employment rate of unemployment	
reverse repo	target rate of inflation	

Questions

1. What is the basic determinant of (a) the transactions demand and (b) the asset demand for money? Explain how to combine these two demands graphically to determine total money demand. How is the equilibrium interest rate in the money market determined? Use a graph to show how an increase in the total demand for money affects the equilibrium interest rate (no change in money supply). Use your general knowledge of equilibrium prices to explain why the previous interest rate is no longer sustainable. **(LO1)**

2. What is the basic objective of monetary policy? What are the major strengths of monetary policy? Why is monetary policy easier to conduct than fiscal policy? **(LO2, LO4)**

3. What is the impact of each of the following transactions on commercial bank reserves? **(LO2)**

   a. The New York Federal Reserve Bank purchases government securities from private businesses and consumers.

   b. Commercial banks borrow from Federal Reserve Banks at the discount rate.

   c. The Fed reduces the reserve ratio.

   d. The Fed increases the interest rate on excess reserves.

4. What are the two parts of the Fed's dual mandate? Which of the two targets appears to be more variable? Explain your reasoning. **(LO3)**

5. Suppose you are a member of the Board of Governors of the Federal Reserve System and the economy is experiencing a sharp and prolonged inflationary trend. What changes in (a) the reserve ratio, (b) the discount rate, (c) and open-market operations would you recommend, as well as on (d) the interest rate on excess reserves? Explain in each case how the change you advocate would affect commercial bank reserves, the money supply, interest rates, and aggregate demand. **(LO3)**

6. What do economists mean when they say that monetary policy can exhibit cyclical asymmetry? How does the idea of a liquidity trap relate to cyclical asymmetry? Why is the possibility of a liquidity trap significant to policymakers? **(LO4)**

7. How did the Fed use the main tools of monetary policy to respond to the financial crisis that began in 2007? What additional programs did the Fed create and implement? When was the Fed able to relax these policies? How did the Fed respond to the recession that began in 2020? **(LO5)**

Problems

1. Assume that the following data characterize the hypothetical economy of Trance: money supply = $200 billion; quantity of money demanded for transactions = $150 billion; quantity of money demanded as an asset = $10 billion at 12 percent interest, increasing by $10 billion for each 2-percentage-point fall in the interest rate. **(LO1)**

   a. What is the equilibrium interest rate in Trance?

   b. At the equilibrium interest rate, what are the quantity of money supplied, the total quantity of money demanded, the amount of money demanded for transactions, and the amount of money demanded as an asset in Trance?

2. Refer to **Table 15.2** and assume that the Fed's reserve ratio is 10 percent and the economy is in a severe recession. Also suppose that the commercial banks are hoarding all excess reserves (not lending them out) because they fear loan defaults. Finally, suppose that the Fed is highly concerned that the banks will suddenly lend out these excess reserves and possibly contribute to inflation once the economy begins to recover and confidence is restored. By how many percentage points would the Fed need to increase the reserve ratio to eliminate one-third of the excess reserves? What is the size of the monetary multiplier before and after the change in the reserve ratio? By how much would the

banks' lending potential decline as a result of the increase in the reserve ratio? **(LO2)**

3. Refer to the table for Moola below to answer the following questions. What is the equilibrium interest rate in Moola? What is the level of investment at the equilibrium interest rate? Is there either a recessionary output gap (negative GDP gap) or an inflationary output gap (positive GDP gap) at the equilibrium interest rate and, if either, what is the amount? Given money demand, by how much would the Moola central bank need to change the money supply to close the output gap? What is the expenditure multiplier in Moola? **(LO3)**

Money Supply	Money Demand	Interest Rate	Investment at Interest (Rate Shown)	Potential Real GDP	Actual Real GDP at Interest (Rate Shown)
$500	$800	2%	$50	$350	$390
500	700	3	40	350	370
500	600	4	30	350	350
500	500	5	20	350	330
500	400	6	10	350	310

CHAPTER SIXTEEN

International Trade and Exchange Rates

Learning Objectives

LO16.1 List several key facts about U.S. international trade.

LO16.2 Define comparative advantage and explain how specialization and trade add to a nation's output.

LO16.3 Explain how exchange rates are determined.

LO16.4 Critique the most frequently presented arguments for protectionism.

LO16.5 Explain the objectives of the WTO, EU, NAFTA, and USMCA, and discuss trade adjustment assistance.

Backpackers in the wilderness like to think they are "leaving the world behind," but, like Atlas, they carry the world on their shoulders. Much of their equipment is imported—knives from Switzerland, rain gear from South Korea, cameras from Japan, aluminum pots from England, sleeping bags from China, and compasses from Finland.

International trade and the global economy affect all of us daily, whether we are hiking in the wilderness, driving our cars, buying groceries, or working at our jobs. We cannot "leave the world behind." We are enmeshed in a global web of economic relationships—trading of goods and services, multinational corporations, cooperative ventures among the world's firms, and ties among the world's financial markets.

Trade Facts

The following are important facts relating to international trade:

* U.S. exports and imports have more than doubled as percentages of GDP since 1980.

* A *trade deficit* occurs when imports exceed exports. The United States has a trade deficit in goods. In 2020, U.S. imports of goods exceeded U.S. exports of goods by $916 billion.

* A *trade surplus* occurs when exports exceed imports. The United States has a trade surplus in services (such as air transportation services and financial services). In 2020, U.S. exports of services exceeded U.S. imports of services by $234 billion.

* Principal U.S. exports include chemicals, agricultural products, consumer durables, aircraft, and computer software and services (think Microsoft and Google).

* Principal imports include petroleum, automobiles, metals, household appliances, and computers.

* Like other advanced industrial nations, the United States imports many goods that are in the same categories as the goods that it exports. Examples include automobiles, computers, chemicals, semiconductors, and petroleum.

* Canada is the United States' most important trading partner quantitatively. In 2019, about 18 percent of U.S. exported goods were sold to Canadians, who in turn provided 13 percent of the U.S. imports of goods.

* The United States has a sizable trade deficit in goods with China. In 2019, it was $452 billion.

* Starting in 2012, the hydraulic fracking boom greatly reduced U.S. dependence on foreign oil. In 2018, the United States became a net exporter of oil for the first time in 75 years as well as the largest producer of oil, ahead of Russia and Saudi Arabia.

* The United States leads the world in the combined volume of exports and imports, as measured in dollars.

* China, the United States, Germany, Japan, and the Netherlands (in that order) were the top five exporters by dollars in 2018.

* Currently, the United States provides about 8.5 percent of the world's exports.

* Exports of goods and services make up about 12 percent of total U.S. output. That percentage is much lower than the percentage in many other nations, including Belgium, the Netherlands, Germany, Canada, and the United Kingdom (see **Global Snapshot 16.1**).

* China has become a major international trader, with an estimated $2.7 trillion of exports in 2017. Other Asian economies—including South Korea, Taiwan, and Singapore—are also active in international trade. Their combined exports exceed those of France, Britain, or Italy.

* International trade links the world's economies together. Through trade, changes in economic conditions in one place on the globe can quickly affect other places.

* International trade is often at the center of debates over economic policy, both within the United States and internationally.

🌐 GLOBAL SNAPSHOT 16.1

Exports of Goods as a Percentage of GDP, Selected Countries

Although the United States is the world's second-largest exporter, it ranks relatively low among trading nations in terms of exports as a percentage of GDP.

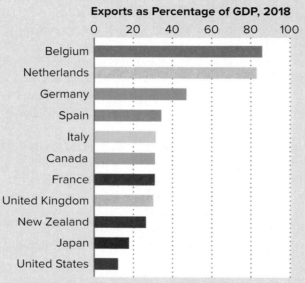

Exports as Percentage of GDP, 2018

Source: Organization for Economic Co-operation and Development (OECD).

With this information in mind, let's turn to the economics of international trade.

The Economic Basis for Trade

The simple answer to the question "Why do nations trade?" is "They trade because it is beneficial." The benefits that emerge relate to three underlying facts:

- The distribution of natural, human, and capital resources among nations is uneven; nations differ in their endowments of economic resources.

- Efficient production of various goods requires different technologies, and not all nations have the same level of technological expertise.

- Products are differentiated as to quality and other attributes, and some people may prefer certain goods imported from abroad rather than similar goods produced domestically.

To understand the interaction of these three facts, think of China, which has an abundance of inexpensive labor. As a result, China can produce efficiently (at low cost of other goods forgone) a variety of *labor-intensive goods*, such as textiles, electronics, and toys. In contrast, Australia has vast amounts of land with which it can inexpensively produce such *land-intensive goods* as beef, wool, and meat. Industrial advanced nations such as Germany that have relatively large amounts of capital can inexpensively produce *capital-intensive goods* such as airplanes, automobiles, and chemicals.

Also, regardless of their resource intensities, nations can develop individual products that are in demand worldwide because of their special qualities. Examples include fashions from Italy, chocolates from Belgium, software from the United States, and watches from Switzerland.

As national economies evolve, the size and quality of their labor force may change, the volume and composition of their capital stocks may shift, new technologies may develop, and even the quality of land and the quantity of natural resources may change. In short, as economists say, comparative advantage can change.

Comparative Advantage and Specialization

In an *open economy* (one with an international sector), a country produces more of certain goods (exports) and fewer of other goods (imports) than it would otherwise. Thus, the country shifts the use of labor and other resources toward export industries and away from import industries. For example, the United States uses more resources to make commercial aircraft and to grow wheat and fewer resources to make television sets and sew clothes. So we ask: Do such shifts of resources make economic sense? Do they enhance U.S. total output and thus the U.S. standard of living?

The answers are affirmative. Specialization and international trade increase the productivity of U.S. resources and allow the United States to obtain greater total output than would otherwise be possible. This idea is not new. Adam Smith had this to say in 1776:

> It is the maxim of every prudent master of a family, never to attempt to make at home what it will cost him more to make than to buy. The taylor does not attempt to make his own shoes, but buys them of the shoemaker. The shoemaker does not attempt to make his own clothes, but employs a taylor. The farmer attempts to make neither the one nor the other, but employs those different artificers. . . .
>
> What is prudence in the conduct of every private family, can scarce be folly in that of a great kingdom. If a foreign country can supply us with a commodity cheaper than we can make it, better buy it of them with some part of the produce of our own industry, employed in a way in which we have some advantage.[1]

Nations specialize and trade for the same reasons that individuals do: Specialization and exchange result in greater overall output and income. In the early 1800s, British economist David Ricardo extended Smith's idea by demonstrating that it is advantageous for a country to specialize and trade with other countries even if it is more productive in *all* economic activities than any other country. The nearby story (**A CPA and a House Painter**) provides a simple, two-person illustration of Ricardo's principle of comparative advantage.

[1] Adam Smith, *The Wealth of Nations* (New York: Modern Library, 1937), p. 424. (Originally published in 1776.)

ILLUSTRATING THE IDEA

A CPA and a House Painter

Consider the certified public accountant (CPA) who is also a skilled house painter. Suppose the CPA is a swifter painter than the professional painter she is thinking of hiring. Also suppose that she can earn $50 per hour as an accountant but would have to pay the painter $25 per hour. In addition, let's say it would take the accountant 30 hours to paint her house but the painter would take 40 hours.

Should the CPA take time from her accounting to paint her own house, or should she hire the painter? The CPA's opportunity cost of painting her house is $1,500 (= 30 hours of sacrificed CPA time × $50 per CPA hour). The cost of hiring the painter is only $1,000 (= 40 hours of painting × $25 per hour of painting). Although the CPA is better at both accounting and painting, she will get her house painted at lower cost by specializing in accounting and using some of her earnings from accounting to hire a house painter.

Similarly, the house painter can reduce his cost of obtaining accounting services by specializing in painting and using some of his income to hire the CPA to prepare his income tax forms. Suppose it would take the painter 10 hours to prepare his tax return, while the CPA could handle the task in 2 hours. The house painter would sacrifice $250 of income (= 10 hours of painting time × $25 per hour) to do something he could hire the CPA to do for $100 (= 2 hours of CPA time × $50 per CPA hour). By specializing in painting and hiring the CPA to prepare his tax return, the painter lowers the cost of getting his tax return prepared.

We will see that what is true for our CPA and house painter is also true for nations. Specializing on the basis of comparative advantage enables nations to reduce the cost of obtaining the goods and services they desire.

> QUESTIONS:
>
> How might the specialization described above change once the CPA retires? What generalization about the permanency of a particular pattern of specialization can you draw from your answer?

Comparative Advantage: Production Possibilities Analysis

Our simple example shows that the reason specialization is economically desirable is that it results in more efficient production. Now let's put specialization into the context of trading nations and use the familiar concept of the production possibilities table for our analysis.

Assumptions and Comparative Costs Suppose the production possibilities for one product in Mexico and for one product in the United States are as shown in **Tables 16.1** and **16.2**. Both tables reflect constant costs. Each country must give up a constant amount of one product to secure a certain increment of the other product. (This assumption simplifies our discussion without impairing the validity of our conclusions. Later, we will allow for increasing costs.)

TABLE 16.1
Mexico's Production Possibilities Table (in Tons)

Product	Production Alternatives				
	A	B	C	D	E
Avocados	0	20	24	40	60
Soybeans	15	10	9	5	0

TABLE 16.2
U.S. Production Possibilities Table (in Tons)

Product	Production Alternatives				
	R	S	T	U	V
Avocados	0	30	33	60	90
Soybeans	30	20	19	10	0

Also, for simplicity, suppose that the labor forces in the United States and Mexico are of equal size. The data then tell us that the United States has an *absolute advantage* in producing both products. If the United States and Mexico use their entire (equal-size) labor forces to produce avocados, the United States can produce 90 tons compared with Mexico's 60 tons. Similarly, the United States can produce 30 tons of soybeans compared to Mexico's 15 tons. There are greater production possibilities in the United States, using the same number of workers as in Mexico. So labor productivity (output per worker) in the United States exceeds that in Mexico in producing both products.

Although the United States has an absolute advantage in producing both goods, gains from specialization and trade are possible. Specialization and trade are mutually beneficial or "profitable" to the two nations if the *comparative costs* of producing the two products within the two nations differ. What are the comparative costs of avocados and soybeans in Mexico? By comparing production alternatives A and B in **Table 16.1**, we see that Mexico must sacrifice 5 tons of soybeans (= 15 − 10) to produce 20 tons of avocados (= 20 − 0). Or, more simply, in Mexico it costs 1 ton of soybeans (S) to produce 4 tons of avocados (A); that is, 1S ≡ 4A. (The "≡" sign simply means "equivalent to.") Because we assumed constant costs, this domestic opportunity cost will not change as Mexico expands the output of either product. This is evident from production possibilities B and C, where we see that 4 more tons of avocados (= 24 − 20) cost 1 unit of soybeans (= 10 − 9).

Similarly, in **Table 16.2**, comparing U.S. production alternatives R and S reveals that in the United States it costs 10 tons of soybeans (= 30 − 20) to obtain 30 tons of avocados (= 30 − 0). That is, the domestic (internal) comparative-cost ratio for the two products in the United States is 1S ≡ 3A. Comparing production alternatives S and T reinforces this conclusion: an extra 3 tons of avocados (= 33 − 30) comes at the sacrifice of 1 ton of soybeans (= 20 − 19).

The comparative costs of the two products within the two nations are obviously different. In this example, the United States has a **comparative advantage** over Mexico in soybeans. The United States must forgo only 3 tons of avocados to get 1 ton of soybeans, but Mexico must forgo 4 tons of avocados to get 1 ton of soybeans. In terms of opportunity costs, soybeans are relatively cheaper in the United States. *A nation has a comparative advantage in some product when it can produce that product at a lower opportunity cost than can a potential trading partner.* Mexico, in contrast, has a comparative advantage in avocados. While 1 ton of avocados costs $\frac{1}{3}$ ton of soybeans in the United States, it costs only $\frac{1}{4}$ ton of soybeans in Mexico. Comparatively speaking, avocados are cheaper in Mexico. We summarize the situation in **Table 16.3**. Be sure to give it a close look.

comparative advantage
A situation in which a person or country can produce a specific product at a lower opportunity cost than some other person or country; the basis for specialization and trade.

TABLE 16.3
Comparative-Advantage Example: A Summary

Soybeans	Avocados
Mexico: Must give up 4 tons of avocados to get 1 ton of soybeans	**Mexico:** Must give up $\frac{1}{4}$ ton of soybeans to get 1 ton of avocados
United States: Must give up 3 tons of avocados to get 1 ton of soybeans	**United States:** Must give up $\frac{1}{3}$ ton of soybeans to get 1 ton of avocados
Comparative advantage: United States	**Comparative advantage:** Mexico

Because of these differences in comparative costs, Mexico should produce avocados and the United States should produce soybeans. If both nations specialize according to their comparative advantages, each can achieve a larger total output with the same total input of resources. Together, they will be using their scarce resources more efficiently.

Terms of Trade   The United States can shift production between soybeans and avocados at the rate of 1S for 3A. Thus, the United States would specialize in soybeans only if it could obtain *more than* 3 tons of avocados for 1 ton of soybeans by trading with Mexico. Similarly, Mexico can shift production at the rate of 4A for 1S. So it would be advantageous to Mexico to specialize in avocados if it could get 1 ton of soybeans for *less than* 4 tons of avocados.

terms of trade
The rate at which units of one product can be exchanged for units of another product; the price of a good or service; the amount of one good or service that must be given up to obtain 1 unit of another good or service.

Suppose that through negotiation the two nations agree on an exchange rate of 1 ton of soybeans for $3\frac{1}{2}$ tons of avocados. These **terms of trade** are mutually beneficial to both countries because each can "do better" through such trade than through domestic production alone. The United States can get $3\frac{1}{2}$ tons of avocados by sending 1 ton of soybeans to Mexico, while it can get only 3 tons of avocados by shifting its own resources domestically from soybeans to avocados. Mexico can obtain 1 ton of soybeans at a lower cost of $3\frac{1}{2}$ tons of avocados through trade with the United States, compared to the cost of 4 tons if Mexico produced the 1 ton of soybeans itself.

Gains from Specialization and Trade   Let's pinpoint the gains in total output from specialization and trade. Suppose that, before specialization and trade, production alternative C in **Table 16.1** and alternative T in **Table 16.2** were the optimal product mixes for the two countries. That is, Mexico preferred 24 tons of avocados and 9 tons of soybeans (**Table 16.1**) and the United States preferred 33 tons of avocados and 19 tons of soybeans (**Table 16.2**) to all other available domestic alternatives. These outputs are shown in column 1 in **Table 16.4**.

TABLE 16.4
Specialization According to Comparative Advantage and the Gains from Trade (in Tons)

Country	(1) Outputs before Specialization	(2) Outputs after Specialization	(3) Amounts Traded	(4) Outputs Available after Trade	(5) Gains from Specialization and Trade (4) − (1)
Mexico	24 avocados	60 avocados	−35 avocados	25 avocados	1 avocados
	9 soybeans	0 soybeans	+10 soybeans	10 soybeans	1 soybeans
United States	33 avocados	0 avocados	+35 avocados	35 avocados	2 avocados
	19 soybeans	30 soybeans	−10 soybeans	20 soybeans	1 soybeans

Now assume that both nations specialize according to their comparative advantages, with Mexico producing 60 tons of avocados and no soybeans (alternative E) and the United States producing no avocados and 30 tons of soybeans (alternative R). These outputs are shown in column 2 in **Table 16.4**. Using our $1S \equiv 3\frac{1}{2}A$ terms of trade, assume that Mexico exchanges 35 tons of avocados for 10 tons of U.S. soybeans. Column 3 in **Table 16.4** shows the quantities exchanged in this trade, with a minus sign indicating exports and a plus sign indicating imports. As shown in column 4, after the trade, Mexico has 25 tons of avocados and 10 tons of soybeans, while the United States has 35 tons of avocados and 20 tons of soybeans. Compared with their optimal product mixes before specialization and trade (column 1), *both* nations now enjoy more avocados and more soybeans! Specifically, Mexico has gained 1 ton of avocados and 1 ton of soybeans. The United States has gained 2 tons of avocados and 1 ton of soybeans. These gains are shown in column 5.

Specialization according to comparative advantage results in a more efficient allocation of world resources, and larger outputs of both products are therefore available to both nations.

Through specialization and international trade, a nation can overcome the production constraints imposed by its domestic production possibilities table and curve. Our discussion of **Tables 16.1**, **16.2**, and **16.4** has shown just how this is done. The domestic production possibilities data (**Tables 16.1** and **16.2**) of the two countries have not changed, meaning that neither nation's production possibilities curve has shifted. But specialization and trade mean that citizens of both countries can enjoy increased consumption (column 5 of **Table 16.4**).

Trade with Increasing Costs

To explain the basic principles underlying international trade, we simplified our analysis in several ways. For example, we limited discussion to two products and two nations. But multiproduct and multinational analysis yields the same conclusions. We also assumed constant opportunity costs, which is a more substantive simplification. Let's consider the effect of allowing increasing opportunity costs to enter the picture.

As before, suppose that comparative advantage indicates that the United States should specialize in soybeans and Mexico in avocados. But now, as the United States begins to expand soybean production, its cost of soybeans will rise. It will eventually have to sacrifice more than 3 tons of avocados to get 1 additional ton of soybeans. Resources are no longer perfectly substitutable between alternative uses, as our constant-cost assumption implied. Resources less and less suitable to soybean production must be allocated to the U.S. soybean industry in expanding soybean output, and that means increasing costs—the sacrifice of larger and larger amounts of avocados for each additional ton of soybeans.

Similarly, Mexico will find that its cost of producing an additional ton of avocados will rise beyond 4 tons of soybeans as it produces more avocados. Resources transferred from soybean to avocado production will eventually be less suitable to avocado production.

At some point, the differing domestic cost ratios that underlie comparative advantage will disappear, and further specialization will become uneconomical. Most importantly, this point of equal cost ratios may be reached while the United States is still producing some avocados along with its soybeans and Mexico is producing some soybeans along with its avocados. The primary effect of increasing opportunity costs is less-than-complete specialization. For this reason, we often find domestically produced products competing directly against identical or similar imported products within a particular economy.

The Fruits of Free Trade*

Because of specialization and exchange, fruits and vegetables from all over the world appear in our grocery stores. For example, apples may be from New Zealand; bananas, from Ecuador; coconuts, from the Philippines; pineapples, from Costa Rica; avocados, from Mexico; plums, from Chile; and potatoes, from Peru.

*This example is from "The Fruits of Free Trade," *2002 Annual Report*, by W. Michael Cox and Richard Alm, p. 3, Federal Reserve Bank of Dallas.

©Pixtal/AGE Fotostock RF

Pixtal RF

The Foreign Exchange Market

Buyers and sellers (whether individuals, firms, or nations) use money to buy products or to pay for the use of resources. Within the domestic economy, prices are stated in terms of the domestic currency, and buyers use that currency to purchase domestic products. In Mexico, for example, buyers have pesos, and that is what sellers want.

International markets are different. Sellers set their prices in terms of their domestic currencies, but buyers often possess entirely different currencies. How many dollars does it take to buy a truckload of Mexican avocados selling for 3,000 pesos, a German automobile selling for 50,000 euros, or a Japanese motorcycle priced at 300,000 yen? Producers in Mexico, Germany, and Japan want payment in pesos, euros, and yen, respectively, so that they can pay their wages, rent, interest, dividends, and taxes.

A **foreign exchange market,** a market in which various national currencies are exchanged for one another, serves this need. The equilibrium prices in such currency markets are called **exchange rates.** An exchange rate is the rate at which the currency of one nation can be exchanged for the currency of another nation. (See **Global Snapshot 16.2**.)

The market price or exchange rate of a nation's currency is an unusual price; it links all domestic prices with all foreign prices. Exchange rates enable consumers in one country to translate prices of foreign goods into units of their own currency: They need only multiply the foreign product price by the exchange rate. If the U.S. dollar–yen exchange rate is $.01 (1 cent) per yen, a Sony television set priced at ¥20,000 will cost $200 (= 20,000 × $.01) in the United States. If the exchange rate rises to $.02 (2 cents) per yen, the television will cost $400 (= 20,000 × $.02) in the United States. Similarly, all other Japanese products would double in price to U.S. buyers in response to the altered exchange rate.

foreign exchange market
A market in which the money (currency) of one nation can be used to purchase (can be exchanged for) the money of another nation.

exchange rate
The rate of exchange of one nation's currency for another nation's currency.

GLOBAL SNAPSHOT 16.2

Exchange Rates: Foreign Currency per U.S. Dollar

The amount of foreign currency that a dollar will buy varies greatly from nation to nation and fluctuates in response to supply and demand changes in the foreign exchange market. The amounts shown here are for March 2021.

$1 Will Buy

73.2 Indian rupees
.72 British pounds
1.27 Canadian dollars
5.69 Brazilian reais
.84 European euros
108 Japanese yen
1.3 Australian dollars
4.1 Malaysian ringgits
6.5 Chinese yuan renminbi
10.99 Botswana pula

PHOTO OP

Foreign Currencies

The world is awash with hundreds of national currencies. Currency markets determine the rates of exchange between them.

Ralf Siemieniec/Shutterstock   Art Vandalay/Getty Images

Exchange Rates

Exchange-rate systems come in two varieties:

* In a *flexible-* or *floating-exchange rate* system, demand and supply determine exchange rates without government interference.

* In a *fixed-exchange rate* system, a government sets the exchange rates for its currency and adjusts monetary and fiscal policy as needed to maintain those rates.

We will focus our attention on flexible exchange rates.

Let's examine the rate, or price, at which U.S. dollars might be exchanged for British pounds. In **Figure 16.1**, we show the demand D_1 and supply S_1 of pounds. Note that both the demand for and supply of pounds are expressed in terms of U.S. dollars. They interact to determine the equilibrium price for pounds, which is expressed in terms of how many dollars are required to purchase 1 pound.

FIGURE 16.1
The market for foreign currency (pounds). The intersection of the demand-for-pounds curve D_1 and the supply-of-pounds curve S_1 determines the equilibrium dollar price of pounds: here, $2. That means that the exchange rate is $2 = £1. Not shown, an increase in demand for pounds or a decrease in the supply of pounds will increase the dollar price of pounds and thus cause the pound to appreciate. Also not shown, a decrease in demand for pounds or an increase in the supply of pounds will reduce the dollar price of pounds, meaning that the pound has depreciated.

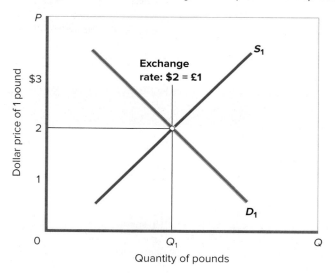

The *demand-for-pounds curve* D_1 slopes downward because all British goods and services will be cheaper to Americans if pounds become less expensive. That is, at lower dollar prices for pounds, Americans can obtain more pounds and therefore more British goods and services per dollar. To buy those cheaper British goods, U.S. consumers will increase the quantity of pounds they demand.

The *supply-of-pounds curve* S_1 slopes upward because the British will purchase more U.S. goods as the dollar price of a pound rises (i.e., as the pound price of a dollar falls). The more dollars the British can get in exchange for £1, the less expensive U.S. products will look to them and hence, the more pounds they will want to supply so as to get the dollars they need to purchase "cheap" U.S. products.

The intersection of the supply curve and the demand curve determine the dollar price of pounds. In **Figure 16.1**, that price (exchange rate) is $2 for £1. At this exchange rate, the quantities of pounds supplied and demanded are equal; neither a shortage nor a surplus of pounds occurs.

Depreciation and Appreciation

An exchange rate determined by market forces can, and often does, change constantly, just as stock and bond prices do.

- When the dollar price of pounds *rises,* for example, from $2 = £1 to $3 = £1, the dollar has *depreciated* relative to the pound (and the pound has appreciated relative to the dollar). **Depreciation** of a currency means that more units of it (dollars) are needed to buy a single unit of some other currency (a pound).

- When the dollar price of pounds *falls,* for example, from $2 = £1 to $1 = £1, the dollar has *appreciated* relative to the pound. **Appreciation** of a currency means that it takes fewer units of it (dollars) to buy a single unit of some other currency (a pound).

depreciation (of a currency)
A decrease in the value of the dollar relative to another currency, so a dollar buys a smaller amount of the foreign currency and therefore of foreign goods.

appreciation (of the dollar)
An increase in the value of the dollar relative to the currency of another nation, so a dollar buys a larger amount of the foreign currency and thus of foreign goods.

Note that a depreciation of the dollar implies an appreciation of the pound, and vice versa. When the dollar price of a pound jumps from $2 = £1 to $3 = £1, the pound has appreciated relative to the dollar because it takes fewer pounds to buy $1. At $2 = £1, it took £1/2 to buy $1; at $3 = £1, it takes only £1/3 to buy $1. Conversely, when the dollar appreciates relative to the pound, the pound depreciates relative to the dollar. More pounds are needed to buy a dollar.

In general, the relevant terminology and relationships between the U.S. dollar and another currency are as follows (where the "≡" sign means "is equivalent to").

- Dollar price of foreign currency increases ≡ dollar depreciates relative to the foreign currency ≡ foreign currency price of dollar decreases ≡ foreign currency appreciates relative to the dollar
- Dollar price of foreign currency decreases ≡ dollar appreciates relative to the foreign currency ≡ foreign currency price of dollar increases ≡ foreign currency depreciates relative to the dollar

Determinants of Exchange Rates

What factors would cause a nation's currency to appreciate or depreciate in the market for foreign exchange? Here are three generalizations:

- If the demand for a nation's currency increases, that currency will appreciate. If the demand declines, that currency will depreciate.
- If the supply of a nation's currency increases, that currency will depreciate. If the supply decreases, that currency will appreciate.
- If a nation's currency appreciates, some foreign currency depreciates relative to it.

With these generalizations in mind, let's examine the determinants of exchange rates—the factors that shift the demand or supply curve for a certain currency. As we do so, keep in mind that the other-things-equal assumption is always in force.

Changes in Tastes   Any change in consumer tastes or preferences for the products of a foreign country may alter the demand for that nation's currency and change its exchange rate. If technological advances in U.S. aircraft make them more attractive to British consumers and businesses, then the British will supply more pounds in the exchange market in order to purchase more U.S. airplanes. The supply-of-pounds curve will shift to the right, causing the pound to depreciate and the dollar to appreciate.

In contrast, the U.S. demand-for-pounds curve will shift to the right if British woolen apparel becomes more fashionable in the United States. The pound will appreciate and the dollar will depreciate.

Relative Income Changes A nation's currency is likely to depreciate if its growth of national income is more rapid than that of other countries. Here's why: A country's imports vary directly with its income level. As total income rises in the United States, Americans will buy both more domestic goods and more foreign goods. If the U.S. economy is expanding rapidly and the British economy is stagnant, U.S. imports of British goods, and therefore U.S. demands for pounds, will increase. The dollar price of pounds will rise, so the dollar will depreciate.

Relative Inflation Rate Changes Other things equal, changes in the relative rates of inflation of two nations change their relative price levels and alter the exchange rate between their currencies. The currency of the nation with the higher inflation rate—the more rapidly rising price level—tends to depreciate. Suppose, for example, that inflation is 0 percent in Great Britain and 5 percent in the United States so that prices, on average, are rising by 5 percent per year in the United States while, on average, remaining unchanged in Great Britain. U.S. consumers will seek out more of the now relatively lower-priced British goods, increasing the demand for pounds. British consumers will purchase less of the now relatively higher-priced U.S. goods, reducing the supply of pounds. This combination of increased demand for pounds and reduced supply of pounds will cause the pound to appreciate and the dollar to depreciate.

Relative Interest Rates Changes in relative interest rates between two countries may alter their exchange rate. Suppose that real interest rates rise in the United States but stay constant in Great Britain. British citizens will then find the United States a more attractive place in which to loan money directly or loan money indirectly by buying bonds. To make these loans, they will have to supply pounds in the foreign exchange market to obtain dollars. The increase in the supply of pounds results in depreciation of the pound and appreciation of the dollar.

Changes in Relative Expected Returns on Stocks, Real Estate, and Production Facilities International investing extends beyond buying foreign bonds. It includes international investments in stocks and real estate, as well as foreign purchases of factories and production facilities. Other things equal, the extent of this foreign investment depends on relative expected returns. To make the investments, investors in one country must sell their own local currency to purchase the foreign currencies needed for the foreign investments.

For instance, suppose that investing in England suddenly becomes more popular due to a more positive outlook regarding expected returns on stocks, real estate, and production facilities. U.S. investors therefore will sell U.S. assets to buy more assets in England. The U.S. assets will be sold for dollars, which will then be brought to the foreign exchange market and exchanged for pounds, which will in turn be used to purchase British assets. The increased demand for pounds in the foreign exchange market will cause the pound to appreciate and the dollar to depreciate relative to the pound.

Speculation Currency speculators buy and sell currencies with an eye toward reselling or repurchasing them at a profit. Suppose speculators expect that the pound will appreciate and the dollar will depreciate. Speculators holding dollars will therefore try to convert them into pounds. This effort will increase the demand for pounds and cause the dollar price of pounds to rise (i.e., cause the dollar to depreciate). A self-fulfilling prophecy occurs: The pound appreciates and the dollar depreciates because speculators act on the belief that these changes will in fact take place. In this way, speculation can cause changes in exchange rates.

Government and Trade

While a nation as a whole gains from trade, trade may harm particular domestic industries and their workers. Those industries might seek to preserve their economic positions by persuading the government to protect them from imports—perhaps through tariffs, import quotas, and other trade barriers.

Indeed, the public may be won over by the apparent plausibility ("Cut imports and prevent domestic unemployment") and the patriotic ring ("Buy American!") of the arguments. The alleged benefits of tariffs are immediate and clear-cut to the public, but the adverse effects cited by economists are obscure and dispersed over the entire economy. When political deal-making is added in—"You back tariffs for the apparel industry in *my* state, and I'll back tariffs for the auto industry in *your* state"—the outcome can be a politically robust network of trade barriers. These impediments to free international trade can take several forms.

Trade Barriers and Export Subsidies

Tariffs are excise taxes or "duties" on imported goods. They may be imposed to obtain revenue or to protect domestic firms. A *revenue tariff* is usually applied to a product that is not being produced domestically, for example, tin, coffee, or bananas in the case of the United States. Revenue tariffs are designed to provide the federal government with revenue, and their rates tend to be modest. A *protective tariff* is implemented to shield domestic producers from foreign competition. These tariffs impede free trade by increasing the prices of imported goods and therefore shifting sales toward domestic producers. Although protective tariffs are usually not high enough to stop the importation of foreign goods, they put foreign producers at a competitive disadvantage. A tariff on imported shoes, for example, would make domestically produced shoes more attractive to consumers.

Import quotas are government-imposed limits on the quantities or total value of specific items that are imported in some period. Once a quota is filled, further imports of that product are prohibited. Import quotas are more effective than tariffs in impeding international trade. With a tariff, a product can go on being imported in large quantities. But with an import quota, all imports are prohibited once the quota is filled.

Nontariff barriers (NTBs) include onerous licensing requirements, unreasonable standards pertaining to product quality, or simply bureaucratic hurdles and delays in customs procedures. Some nations require importers of foreign goods to obtain licenses and then restrict the number of licenses issued. Japan and the European countries frequently require their domestic importers to obtain licenses. By restricting the number of licenses, governments can limit imports.

A **voluntary export restriction (VER)** is a trade barrier by which foreign firms "voluntarily" limit the amount of their exports to a particular country. VERs, have the same effect as import quotas. Exporters agree to them to avoid more stringent trade barriers. In the late 1990s, for example, Canadian producers of softwood lumber (fir, spruce, cedar, pine) agreed to a VER on exports to the United States under the threat of a permanently higher U.S. tariff.

tariff
A tax imposed by a nation on an imported good.

import quota
A limit imposed by a nation on the quantity (or total value) of a good that may be imported during some period of time.

nontariff barriers (NTBs)
All barriers other than protective tariffs that nations erect to impede international trade, including import quotas, licensing requirements, unreasonable product-quality standards, unnecessary bureaucratic detail in customs procedures, and so on.

voluntary export restrictions (VERs)
Voluntary limitations by countries or firms of their exports to a particular foreign nation to avoid enactment of formal trade barriers by that nation.

export subsidies
Government payments to domestic
producers to enable them to reduce
the price of a good or service to foreign buyers.

Export subsidies are government payments to domestic producers of export goods. By reducing production costs, the subsidies enable producers to charge lower prices and thus to sell more exports in world markets. For example, the United States and other nations have subsidized domestic farmers to boost the domestic food supply. These subsidies have artificially lowered the export prices of U.S. agricultural exports.

Economic Impact of Tariffs

Tariffs, quotas, and other trade restrictions have a series of economic effects predicted by supply and demand analysis and observed in reality. These effects vary somewhat by type of trade protection. To keep things simple, we will focus on the effects of tariffs.

Direct Effects   Because tariffs raise the price of goods imported to the United States, U.S. consumption of those goods declines. Higher prices reduce quantity demanded, as indicated by the law of demand. A tariff prompts consumers to buy fewer of the imported goods and reallocate a portion of their expenditures to less desired substitute products. U.S. consumers are clearly injured by the tariff.

U.S. producers—who are not subject to the tariff—receive the higher price (pretariff foreign price + tariff) on the imported product. Because this new price is higher than before, the domestic producers respond by producing more. Higher prices increase quantity supplied, as indicated by the law of supply. Domestic producers thus enjoy both a higher price and expanded sales, which explains why domestic producers lobby for protective tariffs. From a social point of view, however, the greater domestic production means the tariff allows domestic producers to bid resources away from other, more efficient, U.S. industries.

Foreign producers are hurt by tariffs. Although the sales price of the imported good is higher, that higher amount accrues to the U.S. government as tariff revenues, not to foreign producers. The after-tariff price, or the per-unit revenue to foreign producers, remains as before, but the volume of U.S. imports (foreign exports) falls.

Government gains revenue from tariffs. This revenue is a transfer of income from consumers to government and does not represent any net change in the nation's economic well-being. The result is that government gains a portion of what consumers lose by paying more for imported goods.

Indirect Effects   Tariffs have a subtle effect beyond those just mentioned. They also hurt domestic firms that use the protected goods as inputs in their production process. For example, a tariff on imported steel boosts the price of steel girders, thus hurting firms that build bridges and office towers. Also, tariffs reduce competition in the protected industries. With less competition from foreign producers, domestic firms may be slow to design and implement cost-saving production methods and introduce new products.

Because foreigners sell fewer imported goods in the United States, they earn fewer dollars and so must buy fewer U.S. exports. U.S. export industries must then cut production and release resources. These are highly efficient industries, as we know from their comparative advantage and their ability to sell goods in world markets.

Tariffs directly promote the expansion of inefficient industries that do not have a comparative advantage. They also indirectly cause the contraction of relatively efficient industries that do have a comparative advantage. Put bluntly, tariffs shift resources in the wrong direction—and that is not surprising. We know that specialization and world trade lead to more efficient use of world resources and greater world output. But protective tariffs reduce world trade. Therefore, tariffs also reduce efficiency and the world's real output.

Net Costs of Tariffs

Study after study finds that the costs of tariffs to consumers substantially exceed the gains to producers and government. A sizable net cost or efficiency loss to society arises from trade protection. Furthermore, industries employ large amounts of economic resources to influence Congress to pass and maintain protectionist laws. Because these rent-seeking efforts divert resources away from more socially desirable purposes, trade restrictions impose these costs on society as well.

Conclusion: The gains that U.S. trade barriers produce for protected industries and their workers come at the expense of much greater losses for the entire economy. The result is economic inefficiency, reduced consumption, and lower standards of living. Looked at another way, one study suggests that the *elimination* of trade barriers since the World War II has increased the income of the average U.S. household by at least $7,000 and perhaps by as much as $13,000. These income gains are recurring; they happen year after year.[2]

ILLUSTRATING THE IDEA

Buy American?

Will "buying American," as some Americans think, make Americans better off? No, says Dallas Federal Reserve economist W. Michael Cox:

> A common myth is that it is better for Americans to spend their money at home than abroad. The best way to expose the fallacy of this argument is to take it to its logical extreme. If it is better for me to spend my money here than abroad, then it is even better yet to buy in Texas than in New York, better yet to buy in Dallas than in Houston . . . in my own neighborhood . . . within my own family . . . to consume only what I can produce. Alone and poor.[*]

[*]"The Fruits of Free Trade," *2002 Annual Report*, by W. Michael Cox and Richard Alm, p. 16, Federal Reserve Bank of Dallas.

Three Arguments for Protection

Arguments for trade protection are many and diverse. Some—such as tariffs to protect "infant industries" or to create "military self-sufficiency"—have some legitimacy to economists. But other arguments break down under close scrutiny. Three protectionist arguments, in particular, have persisted decade after decade in the United States.

Increased-Domestic-Employment Argument

Arguing for a tariff to "save U.S. jobs" becomes common when the economy encounters a recession. In an economy that engages in international trade, exports involve foreigners spending on domestically produced output and imports reflect domestic residents spending to obtain foreign nations' output. So, according to this argument, reducing imports will divert spending on another nation's output to spending on domestic output. Thus, domestic output and employment will rise.

This "increased domestic employment" argument has several shortcomings. First, while imports may eliminate some U.S. jobs, they create others. While imports may

[2] Scott C. Bradford, Paul L. E. Grieco, and Gary C. Hufbauer, "The Payoff to America from Globalization," *The World Economy*, July 2006, pp. 893–916.

have eliminated the jobs of some U.S. steel and textile workers in recent years, other workers have gained jobs unloading ships, flying imported aircraft, and selling imported electronic equipment. Import restrictions alter the composition of employment, but they may have little or no effect on the overall volume of employment.

Second, nations adversely affected by tariffs and quotas are likely to retaliate, causing a "trade war" that chokes off trade and makes all nations worse off. The **Smoot–Hawley Tariff Act** of 1930 is a classic example. Although that act was meant to reduce imports and stimulate U.S. production, its high tariffs it authorized prompted adversely affected nations to retaliate with their own equally high tariffs. International trade fell, lowering the output and income of all nations. Economic historians generally agree that the Smoot–Hawley Tariff Act contributed to both the length and severity of the Great Depression.

Finally, forcing an excess of exports over imports cannot succeed in raising domestic employment over the long run. It is through U.S. imports that foreign nations earn dollars for buying U.S. exports. In the long run, a nation must import in order to export. The long-run impact of tariffs is not an increase in domestic employment but, at best, a reallocation of workers away from export industries and to protected domestic industries. This shift implies a less efficient allocation of resources.

Smoot–Hawley Tariff Act
Legislation passed in 1930 that established very high tariffs. Its objective was to reduce imports and stimulate the domestic economy, but it resulted only in retaliatory tariffs by other nations.

Cheap-Foreign-Labor Argument

The cheap-foreign-labor argument says that government must shield domestic firms and workers from the ruinous competition of countries where wages are low. If protection is not provided, cheap imports will flood U.S. markets and the prices of U.S. goods—along with the wages of U.S. workers—will be pulled down. That is, the domestic living standards in the United States will be reduced.

The cheap-foreign-labor argument suggests that, to maintain its standard of living, the United States should not trade with low-wage Mexico. But what would actually happen if the United States did not trade with Mexico? Would wages and living standards rise in the United States as a result? No. To obtain avocados, the United States will have to reallocate a portion of its labor from its relatively more efficient soybean industry to its relatively less efficient avocado industry. As a result, the average productivity of U.S. labor will fall, as will real wages and living standards for American workers. Both countries' labor forces will have diminished standards of living because without specialization and trade they will have less output available to them. Compare column 4 with column 1 in **Table 16.4** to confirm this point.

The cheap-foreign-labor argument incorrectly focuses on labor costs *per hour* rather than labor costs *per unit of output produced.* As an example, suppose that a U.S. factory pays its workers $20 per hour while a factory in a developing country pays its workers $4 per hour. Proponents of the cheap-foreign-labor argument look at these numbers and conclude—incorrectly—that it is impossible for the U.S. factory to compete with the factory in the developing country. But this conclusion fails to account for two crucial facts:

- What actually matters is labor costs *per unit of output*, not labor costs *per hour of work.*
- Differences in productivity typically mean that labor costs per unit of output are often nearly identical despite huge differences in hourly wage rates.

To see why these points matter, suppose that in a U.S. factory using more sophisticated technology, better-trained workers, and more capital per worker, one worker in one hour can produce 20 units of output. If U.S. workers get paid $20 per hour, the U.S. factory's labor cost per unit of output is $1. Now suppose the factory in a developing country is much less productive, such that each worker can produce only 4 units per hour. With a foreign wage of $4 per hour, the labor cost per unit of output at the factory in the developing country is also $1. Thus, the lower wage rate per hour at the factory in the developing country does not translate into lower labor costs per unit—meaning that it won't be able to undersell its U.S. competitor just because its workers get paid lower wages per hour.

In short, firms in developing countries only *sometimes* have an advantage in terms of labor costs per unit of output. Whether they do in any specific situation varies by industry and firm and depends on differences in productivity as well as differences in labor costs per hour. For many goods, labor productivity in high-wage countries is so much higher than labor productivity in low-wage countries that it is actually cheaper *per unit of output* to manufacture these goods in high-wage countries. That is why, for instance, Intel still makes microchips in the United States and why most automobiles are still produced in the United States, Japan, and Europe rather than in low-wage countries.

Protection-Against-Dumping Argument

The protection-against-dumping argument contends that tariffs can protect domestic firms from "dumping" by foreign producers. **Dumping** is the sale of a product in a foreign country at prices either below cost or below the prices commonly charged at home. Foreign companies may dump their good to drive their competitors out of business. If that company is a monopoly in the home country, it may dump its good for a lower price in foreign countries in order to achieve the per-unit cost savings associated with large-scale production.

Because dumping is an "unfair trade practice," most nations prohibit it. For example, where dumping is shown to injure U.S. firms, the federal government imposes tariffs called *antidumping duties* on the goods in question. But relatively few documented cases of dumping occur each year, and specific instances of unfair trade do not justify widespread, permanent tariffs. Moreover, antidumping duties can be abused. Often, what appears to be dumping is simply comparative advantage at work.

dumping
The sale of products in a foreign country at prices either below costs or below the prices charged at home.

Trade Adjustment Assistance

A nation's comparative advantage in the production of a certain product is not forever fixed. As national economies evolve, the size and quality of their labor forces may change, the volume and composition of their capital stocks may shift, new technologies may develop, and even the quality of land and the quantity of natural resources may be altered. As these changes take place, the relative efficiency with which a nation can produce specific goods will also change. Also, new trade agreements can suddenly leave formerly protected industries highly vulnerable to major disruption or even collapse.

Shifts in patterns of comparative advantage and removal of trade protection can hurt specific groups of workers. For example, the erosion of the United States' once strong comparative advantage in steel has caused production plant shutdowns and layoffs in the U.S. steel industry. The textile and apparel industries in the United States face similar difficulties. Clearly, not everyone wins from free trade (or freer trade). Some workers lose.

The **Trade Adjustment Assistance Act** of 2002 introduced some innovative policies to help those hurt by shifts in international trade patterns. The law provides cash assistance (beyond unemployment insurance) for up to 78 weeks for workers displaced by imports or plant relocations abroad. To obtain the assistance, workers must participate in job searches, training programs, or remedial education. Also provided are relocation allowances to help displaced workers move to new jobs within the United States. Refundable tax credits for health insurance help workers maintain their

Trade Adjustment Assistance Act
A U.S. law passed in 2002 that provides cash assistance, education and training benefits, health care subsidies, and wage subsidies (for persons age 50 or more) to workers displaced by imports or plant relocations abroad.

insurance coverage during the retraining and job search period. Workers who are 50 years of age or older are eligible for "wage insurance," which replaces some of the difference in pay (if any) between their old and new jobs.

Many economists support trade adjustment assistance because it not only helps workers hurt by international trade but also helps create the political support necessary to reduce trade barriers and export subsidies.

But not all economists favor trade adjustment assistance. Loss of jobs from imports or plant relocations abroad account for only a small fraction (about 4 percent in recent years) of total job losses in the economy each year. Many workers also lose their jobs because of changing patterns of demand, changing technology, bad management, and other dynamic aspects of a market economy. Some critics ask, "What makes losing one's job to international trade worthy of such special treatment, compared to losing one's job to, say, technological change or domestic competition?"

offshoring
The practice of shifting work previously done by American workers to workers located abroad.

APPLYING THE ANALYSIS

Is Offshoring of Jobs Bad?

Some U.S. jobs lost because of international trade are lost because of the ongoing globalization of resource markets, especially the market for labor. In recent years, U.S. firms have found the outsourcing of work abroad to be increasingly profitable. Economists call this business activity **offshoring:** shifting work previously done by U.S. workers to workers located in other nations. Offshoring is not a new practice, but traditionally it involved components for U.S. manufacturing goods. For example, Boeing has long offshored the production of major airplane parts for its "American" aircraft.

Recent advances in computer and communications technology have enabled U.S. firms to offshore service jobs such as data entry, book composition, software coding, call-center operations, medical transcription, and claims processing to countries such as India and the Philippines. Where offshoring occurs, some of the value added in the production process accrues to foreign countries rather than to the United States. Therefore part of the income generated from the production of U.S. goods is paid to foreigners, not to American workers.

Offshoring is a wrenching experience for many Americans who lose their jobs, but it is not necessarily bad for the economy. Offshoring simply reflects growing specialization and international trade in services, or "tasks." As with trade in goods, trade in services reflects comparative advantage and is beneficial to both trading parties. Moreover, the United States has a sizable trade surplus with other nations in services. The United States gains by specializing in high-valued services such as transportation services, accounting services, legal services, and advertising services, where it still has a comparative advantage. It then "trades" to obtain lower-valued services such as call-center and data entry work, for which comparative advantage has gone abroad.

Offshoring also increases the demand for complementary jobs in the United States. Jobs that are close substitutes for existing U.S. jobs are lost, but the number of complementary jobs in the United States grows. For example, the lower price of writing software code in India may mean a lower cost of software sold in the United States and abroad. That lower price, in turn, may create more jobs for U.S.-based workers such as software designers, marketers, and distributors. Moreover, offshoring may encourage domestic investment and the expansion of firms in the United States by reducing their costs and keeping them competitive worldwide. Some observers equate "offshoring jobs" to "importing competitiveness." Entire firms that might otherwise disappear abroad remain profitable in the United States only because they can offshore some of their work.

QUESTION:

What has enabled white-collar labor services to become the world's newest export and import commodity even though such labor itself remains in place?

Multilateral Trade Agreements and Free-Trade Zones

Aware of the detrimental effects of trade wars and the general weaknesses of argument for trade protections, nations have worked to lower tariffs worldwide.

General Agreement on Tariffs and Trade

In 1947, some 23 nations, including the United States, signed the **General Agreement on Tariffs and Trade (GATT)**. GATT was based on three principles: (1) equal, nondiscriminatory trade treatment for all member nations; (2) the reduction of tariffs by multilateral negotiation; and (3) the elimination of import quotas. Basically, GATT provided a forum for the multilateral negotiation of reduced trade barriers.

Since 1947, member nations have completed eight "rounds" of GATT negotiations to reduce trade barriers. The eighth round of negotiations began in Uruguay in 1986. After seven years of complex discussions, in 1993 a new agreement was reached by GATT's 128 member nations. The Uruguay Round agreement took effect on January 1, 1995, and its provisions were phased in through 2005.

Under this agreement, tariffs on thousands of products were eliminated or reduced, with overall tariffs dropping by 33 percent. The agreement also liberalized government rules that in the past impeded a global market for services such as advertising, accounting, legal services, tourist services, and financial services. Quotas on imported textiles and apparel were phased out and replaced with tariffs. Other provisions reduced agricultural subsidies paid to farmers and protected intellectual property (patents, trademarks, and copyrights) against piracy.

General Agreement on Tariffs and Trade (GATT)
The international agreement reached in 1947 in which 23 nations agreed to give equal and nondiscriminatory treatment to one another, to reduce tariff rates by multinational negotiations, and to eliminate import quotas. It now includes most nations and has become the World Trade Organization.

World Trade Organization

The Uruguay Round of 1993 established the **World Trade Organization (WTO)** as GATT's successor. Some 164 nations belonged to the WTO in 2021. The WTO oversees trade agreements and rules on disputes relating to them. It also provides forums for further rounds of trade negotiations. The ninth and latest round of negotiations—the **Doha Round**—was launched in Doha, Qatar, in late 2001. (The trade rounds occur over several years in several venues but are named after the city or country of origination.) The negotiations are aimed at further reducing tariffs and quotas, as well as agricultural subsidies that distort trade.

GATT and the WTO have been positive forces in the trend toward liberalized world trade. The trade rules agreed upon by the member nations provide a strong bulwark against the protectionism called for by the special-interest groups in the various nations.

The WTO is controversial. Critics contend that the rules crafted to expand international trade and investment enable firms to circumvent national laws that protect workers and the environment. Critics ask: What good are minimum-wage laws, worker-safety laws, collective bargaining rights, and environmental laws if firms can easily shift production to nations with weaker laws, or if consumers can buy goods produced in those countries?

Proponents of the WTO respond that labor and environmental protections should be pursued directly by the nations affected, and via international organizations other than the WTO. These issues should not be linked with trade liberalization, which confers widespread benefits across nations. World trade and the free flow of goods and resources raise output and income in developing nations. Historically, such increases in living standards have resulted in stronger, not weaker, protections for the environment and for workers.

World Trade Organization (WTO)
An organization of 164 nations (as of 2017) that oversees the provisions of the current world trade agreement, resolves trade disputes stemming from it, and holds forums for further rounds of trade negotiations.

Doha Round
The latest, uncompleted (as of early 2017) sequence of trade negotiations by members of the World Trade Organization; named after Doha, Qatar, where the set of negotiations began.

European Union

Countries have also sought to reduce tariffs by creating regional *free-trade zones*—also called *trade blocs*. The most prominent example is the **European Union (EU).** Initiated in 1958 as the Common Market, the EU was initially composed of just six European nations. It has since added 22 more for a total of 28 members; however, the 2016 "Brexit" vote in the United Kingdom reduced that number to 27 in January 2020.[3]

The EU has abolished tariffs and import quotas on nearly all products traded among the participating nations and established a common system of tariffs applicable to all goods received from nations outside the EU. It has also liberalized the movement of capital and labor within the EU and has created common policies in other economic matters of joint concern, such as agriculture, transportation, and business practices.

EU integration has achieved for Europe what the U.S. constitutional prohibition on tariffs by individual states has achieved for the United States: increased regional specialization, greater productivity, greater output, and faster economic growth. The free flow of goods and services has created large markets for EU industries. The resulting economies of large-scale production have enabled those industries to achieve much lower costs than they could have achieved in their small, single-nation markets.

One of the most significant accomplishments of the EU was the establishment of the so-called *eurozone* or euro area. As of 2021, 19 members of the 27 EU use the **euro** as a common currency. Economists believe that the adoption of the euro raised the standard of living in eurozone nations. By ending the inconvenience and expense of exchanging currencies, the euro has enhanced the free flow of goods, services, and resources among eurozone members. Companies that previously sold products in only one or two European nations have found it easier to price and sell their products in all 19 eurozone countries. The euro has also allowed consumers and businesses to more easily comparison shop for output and inputs, which has increased competition, reduced prices, and lowered costs.

North American Free Trade Agreement

In 1993, Canada, Mexico, and the United States formed a major trade bloc. The **North American Free Trade Agreement (NAFTA)** established a free-trade zone that has about the same combined output as the EU but encompasses a much larger geographic area. NAFTA eliminated tariffs and other trade barriers between Canada, Mexico, and the United States for most goods and services.

Critics of NAFTA feared that it would cause a massive loss of U.S. jobs as firms moved to Mexico to take advantage of lower wages and weaker regulations on pollution and workplace safety. Also, they were concerned that Japan and South Korea would build plants in Mexico and transport goods tariff-free to the United States, further hurting U.S. firms and workers.

In retrospect, critics were much too pessimistic. Since the passage of NAFTA in 1993, employment in the United States has increased by more than 38 million workers. Increased trade between Canada, Mexico, and the United States has enhanced the standard of living in all three countries.

In late 2018, negotiations were completed for a trade treaty that is the successor to NAFTA. Known as the United States–Mexico–Canada Agreement (or USMCA), the treaty added or modified rules pertaining to a number of areas, including origin requirements, currency manipulation, intellectual property, and e-commerce. It went into effect on July 1, 2020, and is predicted to provide only a modest boost to U.S. GDP and employment.

---

[3] The 27 members are Austria, Belgium, Bulgaria, Croatia, Cyprus, Czechia, Denmark, Estonia, Finland, France, Germany, Greece, Hungary, Ireland, Italy, Latvia, Lithuania, Luxembourg, Malta, the Netherlands, Poland, Portugal, Romania, Slovakia, Slovenia, Spain, and Sweden.

Recent U.S. Trade Deficits

As **Figure 16.2** shows, the United States has experienced large and persistent trade deficits in recent years. These deficits rose rapidly in the early 2000s, with the trade deficit on goods and services peaking at $762 billion in 2006. The trade deficit on goods and services then declined precipitously to just $384 billion in 2009 as consumers and businesses greatly curtailed their purchase of imports during the Great Recession of 2007–2009. As the economy recovered, the trade deficit on goods and services began rising again and reached $550 billion in 2011, before a series of annual deficits that ranged between $461 billion and $679 billion through 2020.

FIGURE 16.2

U.S. trade deficits, 2005–2020. The United States experienced large deficits in *goods* and in *goods and services* between 2005 and 2020. Although reduced significantly by the recession of 2007–2009, large trade deficits are expected to continue for many years to come.

Source: Bureau of Economic Analysis, **www.bea.gov.**

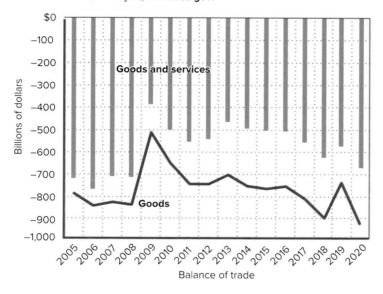

Causes of the Trade Deficits

The large U.S. trade deficits have several causes. First, the U.S. economy expanded more rapidly between 2002 and 2007 than the economies of several U.S. trading partners. The strong U.S. income growth that accompanied that economic growth enabled Americans to greatly increase their purchases of imported products. In contrast, Japan and some European nations suffered recession or experienced relatively slow income growth over that same period. So consumers in those countries increased their purchases of U.S. exports much less rapidly than Americans increased their purchases of foreign imports.

Another factor explaining the large trade deficits is the enormous U.S. trade imbalance with China. In 2017, the United States imported $336 billion more of goods and services than it exported to China. Even in the recession year 2009, the trade deficit with China was nearly $220 billion. The 2017 deficit with China was 74 percent larger than the combined deficits with Mexico ($69 billion), Germany ($67 billion), and Japan ($57 billion). The United States is China's largest export market, and although China has greatly increased its imports from the United States, its standard of living has not yet risen sufficiently for its households to afford large quantities of U.S. products. Adding to the problem, China's government has fixed the exchange rate of its currency, the yuan, to a basket of currencies that includes the U.S. dollar. Therefore, China's large trade surpluses with the United States have not caused the yuan to appreciate much against the U.S. dollar. Greater appreciation of the yuan would have made Chinese goods more expensive in the United States and reduced U.S. imports from China. In China, a stronger yuan would have reduced the dollar price of U.S. goods and increased Chinese purchases of U.S. exports. That combination—reduced U.S. imports from China and increased U.S. exports to China—would have reduced the large U.S. trade imbalance.

A declining U.S. saving rate (= saving/total income) also contributed to the large U.S. trade deficits. Up until the recession of 2007–2009, the U.S. saving rate declined substantially, while its investment rate (= investment/total income) increased. The gap between U.S. investment and U.S. saving was filled by foreign purchases of U.S. real and financial assets. Because foreign savers were willing to finance a large part of U.S. investment, Americans were able to save less and consume more. Part of that added consumption spending was on imported goods.

The COVID-19 pandemic saw a reduction in both exports and imports as global trade overall contracted. By March 2021, U.S. imports had recovered to pre-pandemic levels, but U.S. exports had not.

Implications of U.S. Trade Deficits

The prerecession U.S. trade deficits were the largest ever run by a major industrial nation. Whether the large trade deficits should be of significant concern to the United States and the rest of the world is debatable. Most economists see both benefits and costs to trade deficits.

Increased Current Consumption At the time a trade deficit is occurring, American consumers benefit. A trade deficit means that the United States is receiving more goods and services as imports from abroad than it is sending out as exports. Taken alone, a trade deficit allows the United States to consume outside its production possibilities curve. It augments the domestic standard of living. But there is a catch: The gain in present consumption may come at the expense of reduced future consumption.

Increased U.S. Indebtedness A trade deficit is considered unfavorable because it must be financed by borrowing from the rest of the world, selling off assets, or dipping into foreign currency reserves. Trade deficits are financed primarily by net inpayments of foreign currencies to the United States. When U.S. exports are insufficient to finance U.S. imports, the United States increases both its debt to people abroad and the value of foreign claims against assets in the United States. Financing of the U.S. trade deficit has resulted in a larger foreign accumulation of claims against U.S. financial and real assets than the U.S. claim against foreign assets. In 2017, foreigners owned about $7.8 trillion more of U.S. assets (corporations, land, stocks, bonds, loan notes) than U.S. citizens and institutions owned of foreign assets.

If the United States wants to regain ownership of these domestic assets, at some future time it will have to export more than it imports. At that time, domestic consumption will be lower because the United States will need to send more of its output abroad than it receives as imports. Therefore, the current consumption gains delivered by U.S. current account deficits may mean permanent debt, permanent foreign ownership, or large sacrifices of future consumption.

We say "may mean" here because the foreign lending to U.S. firms and foreign investment in the United States increases the U.S. capital stock. U.S. production capacity might increase more rapidly than otherwise because of a large inflow of funds to offset the trade deficits. Faster increases in production capacity and real GDP enhance the economy's ability to service foreign debt and buy back real capital, if that is desired.

Trade deficits therefore are a mixed blessing. The long-term impacts of the record-high U.S. trade deficits are largely unknown. That unknown worries some economists, who are concerned that foreigners will lose financial confidence in the United States. If that happens, those foreigners will restrict their lending to American households and businesses and also reduce their purchases of U.S. assets. Both actions will decrease the demand for U.S. dollars in the foreign exchange market and cause the U.S. dollar to depreciate. A sudden, large depreciation of the U.S. dollar might disrupt world trade and negatively affect economic growth worldwide. Other economists, however, downplay this scenario. Depreciation of the U.S. dollar will work to correct imbalances by stimulating U.S. exports and reducing U.S. imports, making the overall impact on the American economy relatively small.

Summary

LO16.1 List several key facts about U.S. international trade.

The United States leads the world in the volume of international trade, but trade is much larger as a percentage of GDP in many other nations. The United States' principal exports include chemicals, agricultural products, consumer durables, semiconductors, and aircraft; principal imports include petroleum, automobiles, metals, household appliances, and computers.

LO16.2 Define comparative advantage and explain how specialization and trade add to a nation's output.

Mutually advantageous specialization and trade are possible between any two nations if they have different domestic opportunity-cost ratios for any two products. By specializing on the basis of comparative advantage, nations can obtain larger real incomes with fixed amounts of resources. The terms of trade determine how this increase in world output is shared by the trading nations.

LO16.3 Explain how exchange rates are determined.

Flexible exchange rates between international currencies are determined by the demand for and supply of those currencies. Currencies will depreciate or appreciate as a result of changes in tastes, relative income changes, relative changes in inflation rates, relative changes in interest rates, and currency speculation.

LO16.4 Critique the most frequently presented arguments for protectionism.

The strongest arguments for protectionism are the infant industry and military self-sufficiency arguments. Most other arguments for protectionism are interest-group appeals or reasoning fallacies that emphasize producer interests over consumer interests or stress the immediate effects of trade barriers while ignoring long-run consequences. The cheap-foreign-labor argument for protectionism fails because it focuses on labor costs per hour rather than on what really matters: labor costs per unit of output.

LO16.5 Explain the objectives of the WTO, EU, NAFTA, and USMCA, and discuss trade adjustment assistance.

In 1947, the General Agreement on Tariffs and Trade (GATT) was formed to encourage nondiscriminatory treatment for all member nations, to reduce tariffs, and to eliminate import quotas. The Uruguay Round of GATT negotiations (1993) reduced tariffs and quotas, liberalized trade in services, reduced agricultural subsidies, reduced pirating of intellectual property, and phased out quotas on textiles.

GATT's successor, the World Trade Organization (WTO), had 164 member nations in 2021. It implements WTO agreements, rules on trade disputes between members, and provides forums for continued discussions on trade liberalization. The latest round of trade negotiations—the Doha Development Agenda—began in late 2001 and as of 2021 was still formally in progress.

Free-trade zones liberalize trade within regions. Two examples of free-trade arrangements are the 27-member European Union (EU) and the North American Free Trade Agreement (NAFTA), comprising Canada, Mexico, and the United States. In 2020, the United States–Mexico–Canada Agreement (USMCA) replaced NAFTA. Nineteen EU nations have abandoned their national currencies for a common currency called the euro.

The Trade Adjustment Assistance Act of 2002 recognizes that trade liberalization and increased international trade can create job losses. The Act provides cash assistance, education and training benefits, health care subsidies, and wage subsidies (for persons aged 50 or older) to workers who are displaced by imports or plant relocations abroad. Still, less than 4 percent of all job losses in the United States each year result from imports, plant relocations, or the offshoring of service jobs.

U.S. trade deficits have produced current increases in the living standards of U.S. consumers, but the deficits have also increased U.S. debt to the rest of the world and increased foreign ownership of assets in the United States. This greater foreign investment in the United States, however, has undoubtedly increased U.S. production possibilities.

Terms and Concepts

comparative advantage

terms of trade

foreign exchange market

exchange rate

depreciation

appreciation

tariff

import quota

nontariff barriers (NTBs)

voluntary export restrictions (VERs)

export subsidies

Smoot–Hawley Tariff Act

dumping

Trade Adjustment Assistance Act

offshoring

General Agreement on Tariffs and

Trade (GATT)

World Trade Organization (WTO)

Doha Round

European Union (EU)

euro

North American Free Trade Agreement (NAFTA)

Questions   Mc Graw Hill connect

1. Quantitatively, how important is international trade to the United States relative to the importance of trade to other nations? What country is the United States' most important trading partner, quantitatively? With what country does the United States have the largest trade deficit? **(LO1)**

2. Suppose Big Country can produce 80 units of X by using all its resources to produce X or 60 units of Y by devoting all its resources to Y. Comparable figures for Small Nation are 60 units of X and 60 units of Y. Assuming constant costs, in which product should each nation specialize? Explain why. What are the limits to the terms of trade between these two countries? **(LO2)**

3. Explain why the U.S. demand for Mexican pesos slopes downward and the supply of pesos to Americans slopes upward. Indicate whether each of the following would cause the Mexican peso to appreciate or depreciate, other things equal: **(LO3)**

    a. The United States unilaterally reduces tariffs on Mexican products.

    b. Mexico encounters severe inflation.

    c. Deteriorating political relations reduce American tourism in Mexico.

    d. The U.S. economy moves into a severe recession.

    e. The United States engages in a high-interest-rate monetary policy.

    f. Mexican products become more fashionable to U.S. consumers.

    g. The Mexican government encourages U.S. firms to invest in Mexican oil fields.

    h. The rate of productivity growth in the United States diminishes sharply.

4. Explain why you agree or disagree with the following statements. Assume other things equal: **(LO3)**

    a. A country that grows faster than its major trading partners can expect the international value of its currency to depreciate.

    b. A nation whose interest rate is rising more rapidly than interest rates in other nations can expect the international value of its currency to appreciate.

    c. A country's currency will appreciate if its inflation rate is less than that of the rest of the world.

5. Suppose that a Swiss watchmaker imports watch components from Sweden and exports watches to the United States. Also suppose the dollar depreciates, and the Swedish krona appreciates, relative to the Swiss franc. Speculate as to how each would hurt the Swiss watchmaker. **(LO3)**

6. What measures do governments take to promote exports and restrict imports? Who benefits and who loses from protectionist policies? What is the net outcome for society? **(LO4)**

7. In 2018, manufacturing workers in the United States earned an average compensation of $21.86 per hour. That same year, manufacturing workers in Mexico earned an average

compensation of $3.20 per hour. How can U.S. manufacturers possibly compete? Why isn't all manufacturing done in Mexico and other low-wage countries? **(LO4)**

8. What is offshoring of white-collar service jobs, and how does it relate to international trade? Why has offshoring increased over the past few decades? Give an example (other than that in the text) of how offshoring can eliminate some U.S. jobs while creating other U.S. jobs. **(LO2)**

9. Identify and state the significance of each of the following trade-related entities: (a) the WTO, (b) the EU, (c) the eurozone, and (d) NAFTA. **(LO5)**

Problems

1. Assume that the comparative-cost ratios of two products—baby formula and tuna fish—are as follows in the nations of Canswicki and Tunata:

   Canswicki: 1 can baby formula ≡ 2 cans tuna fish
   Tunata: 1 can baby formula ≡ 4 cans tuna fish

   In what product should each nation specialize? Which of the following terms of trade would be acceptable to both nations: (a) 1 can baby formula ≡ $2\frac{1}{2}$ cans tuna fish; (b) 1 can baby formula ≡ 1 can tuna fish; (c) 1 can baby formula ≡ 5 cans tuna fish? **(LO2)**

2. The accompanying hypothetical production possibilities tables are for New Zealand and Spain. Each country can produce apples and plums. Plot the production possibilities data for each of the two countries separately. Referring to your graphs, answer the following: **(LO2)**

New Zealand's Production Possibilities Table (Millions of Bushels)

Product	Production Alternatives			
	A	B	C	D
Apples	0	20	40	60
Plums	15	10	5	0

Spain's Production Possibilities Table (Millions of Bushels)

Product	Production Alternatives			
	R	S	T	U
Apples	0	20	40	60
Plums	60	40	20	0

a. What is each country's cost ratio of producing plums and apples?

b. Which nation should specialize in which product?

c. Show the trading possibilities lines for each nation if the actual terms of trade are one plum for two apples. (Plot these lines on your graph.)

d. Suppose the optimum product mixes before specialization and trade were alternative B in New Zealand and alternative S in Spain. What would be the gains from specialization and trade?

3. The following hypothetical production possibilities tables are for China and the United States. Assume that before specialization and trade the optimal product mix for China is alternative B and for the United States is alternative U. **(LO2)**

China Production Possibilities						
Product	A	B	C	D	E	F
Apparel (in thousands)	30	24	18	12	6	0
Chemicals (in tons)	0	6	12	18	24	30

U.S. Production Possibilities						
Product	R	S	T	U	V	W
Apparel (in thousands)	10	8	6	4	2	0
Chemicals (in tons)	0	4	8	12	16	20

a. Are comparative-cost conditions such that the two areas should specialize? If so, what product should each produce?

b. What is the total gain in apparel and chemical output that would result from such specialization?

c. What are the limits of the terms of trade? Suppose that the actual terms of trade are 1 unit of apparel for $1\frac{1}{2}$ units of chemicals and that 4 units of apparel are exchanged for 6 units of chemicals. What are the gains from specialization and trade for each nation?

4. Refer to the following table, in which Q_d is the quantity of loonies demanded, P is the dollar price of loonies, Q_s is the quantity of loonies supplied in year 1, and Q_s' is the quantity of loonies supplied in year 2. All quantities are in billions and the dollar-loonie exchange rate is fully flexible. **(LO3)**

Q_d	P	Q_s	Q_s'
10	125	30	20
15	120	25	15
20	115	20	10
25	110	15	5

a. What is the equilibrium dollar price of loonies in year 1?

b. What is the equilibrium dollar price of loonies in year 2?

c. Did the loonie appreciate or did it depreciate relative to the dollar between years 1 and 2?

d. Did the dollar appreciate or did it depreciate relative to the loonie between years 1 and 2?

e. Which one of the following could have caused the change in relative values of the dollar (used in the United States) and the loonie (used in Canada) between years 1 and 2: (1) more rapid inflation in the United States than in Canada, (2) an increase in the real interest rate in the United States but not in Canada, or (3) faster income growth in the United States than in Canada.

5. Suppose that the current Canadian dollar (CAD) to U.S. dollar exchange rate is $0.85 CAD = $1 US and that the U.S. dollar price of an iPhone is $300. What is the Canadian dollar price of an iPhone? Next, suppose that the CAD to U.S. dollar exchange rate moves to $0.96 CAD = $1 US. What is the new Canadian dollar price of an iPhone? Other things equal, would you expect Canada to import more or fewer iPhones at the new exchange rate? Explain. **(LO3)**

PART SEVEN

Resource Markets

CHAPTER SEVENTEEN

Wage Determination

Learning Objectives

LO17.1	Explain why the firm's marginal revenue product curve is its labor demand curve.
LO17.2	List the factors that increase or decrease labor demand.
LO17.3	Discuss the determinants of elasticity of labor demand.
LO17.4	Demonstrate how wage rates are determined in competitive and monopsonistic labor markets.
LO17.5	Discuss how unions increase wage rates and how minimum wage laws affect labor markets.
LO17.6	List the major causes of wage differentials.

We now turn from the pricing and production of *goods and services* to the pricing and employment of *resources.* Although firms come in various sizes and operate under highly different market conditions, each demands productive resources. Firms obtain those resources from households—the direct or indirect owners of land, labor, capital, and entrepreneurial resources, as shown in the circular flow model (**Figure 2.2**).

The basic principles we develop in this chapter apply to land, labor, and capital resources, but we will emphasize the pricing and employment of labor. About 64 percent of all income in the United States flows to households in the form of wages and salaries.

A Focus on Labor

Roughly 150 million Americans go to work each day in the United States. We work at an amazing variety of jobs and receive considerable differences in pay. What determines our hourly wage or annual salary? Why is the salary for a topflight major-league baseball player $30 million or more a year, but the pay for a first-rate schoolteacher is $50,000? Why are starting salaries for college graduates who major in engineering and economics so much higher than those for graduates majoring in English and sociology?

Demand and supply analysis helps us answer these questions. In discussing labor demand, we assume that a firm sells its output in a purely competitive product market and hires labor in a **purely competitive labor market.** In a competitive *product market,* the firm is a "price taker" and can sell as little or as much output as it chooses at the market price. Because the firm is selling such a negligible fraction of total output, its output decisions exert no influence on product price. Similarly, the firm is a "price taker" (or "wage taker") in the competitive *labor market.* It purchases such a negligible fraction of the total supply of labor that its buying (or hiring) decisions do not affect the price of labor.

Workers are also "wage takers" in the competitive labor market. Any individual worker represents a negligible share of the total labor available, and workers in competitive labor markets are assumed to possess identical skills as other workers selling their labor services.

purely competitive labor market
A labor market in which a large number of similarly qualified workers independently offer their labor services to a large number of employers, none of whom can set the wage rate.

Labor Demand

Labor demand is the starting point for any discussion of wages and salaries. Labor demand is a schedule or a curve showing the amounts of labor that buyers are willing and able to purchase at various prices (wages) over some period of time. As with all resources, labor demand is a **derived demand,** meaning that the demand for labor is derived from the demand for the products that labor helps to produce. This is true because labor resources usually do not directly satisfy customer wants but do so indirectly through their use in producing goods and services. Almost nobody wants to directly consume the labor services of a software engineer, but millions of people do want to use the software that the engineer helps create.

derived demand
The demand for a resource that depends on the demand for the products it helps to produce.

Marginal Revenue Product

Because labor demand is derived from product demand, the strength of the demand will depend on two factors:

- The labor's productivity in helping to create a good or service.
- The market value or price of the good or service it helps to produce.

Other things equal, labor that is highly productive in turning out a highly valued commodity will be in great demand. A relatively unproductive resource that is capable of producing only a minimally valued commodity will be in little demand. And no demand whatsoever will exist for a resource that is phenomenally efficient in producing something that no one wants to buy.

Productivity   The table in **Figure 17.1** shows the roles of labor productivity (marginal product) and product price in determining labor demand. Columns 1 and 2 give the number of units of labor employed and the resulting total product (output). Column 3 provides the marginal product (MP), or additional output, resulting from using each additional unit of labor. Columns 1 through 3 remind us that the law of

FIGURE 17.1

The purely competitive seller's demand for labor. The MRP-of-labor curve is the labor demand curve; each of its points relates a particular wage rate (= MRP when profit is maximized) with a corresponding quantity of labor demanded. The downward slope of the D = MRP curve results from the law of diminishing marginal returns.

(1) Units of Labor	(2) Total Product (Output)	(3) Marginal Product (MP)	(4) Product Price	(5) Total Revenue, (2) × (4)	(6) Marginal Revenue Product (MRP)
0	0		$2	$ 0	
		7			$14
1	7		2	14	
		6			12
2	13		2	26	
		5			10
3	18		2	36	
		4			8
4	22		2	44	
		3			6
5	25		2	50	
		2			4
6	27		2	54	
		1			2
7	28		2	56	

diminishing returns applies here, causing the marginal product of labor to fall beyond some point. For simplicity, we assume that these diminishing marginal returns—these declines in marginal product—begin with the second worker hired.

marginal revenue product
The change in a firm's total revenue when it employs 1 additional unit of a resource (the quantity of all other resources employed remaining constant); equal to the change in total revenue divided by the change in the quantity of the resource employed.

Product Price The derived demand for labor depends also on the price of the product it produces. Column 4 in the table in **Figure 17.1** adds this price information. Product price is constant, in this case at $2, because the product market is competitive. The firm is a price taker and cannot therefore sell at any price higher than $2 per unit.

Multiplying column 2 by column 4 provides the total-revenue data of column 5. From these total-revenue data, we can compute the **marginal revenue product (MRP)** of labor—the change in total revenue resulting from the use of each additional unit of labor. In equation form,

$$\text{Marginal revenue product} = \frac{\text{change in total revenue}}{\text{unit change in labor}}$$

The MRPs are listed in column 6 in the table.

Rule for Employing Labor: MRP = MRC

The MRP schedule, shown as columns 1 and 6, is the firm's demand schedule for labor. To understand why, you must first know the rule that guides a profit-seeking firm in hiring any resource: To maximize profit, a firm should hire additional units of a specific resource as long as each successive unit adds more to the firm's total revenue than to the firm's total cost.

Economists use special terms to designate what each additional unit of labor (or other variable resource) adds to total revenue and what it adds to total cost. We have seen that MRP measures how much each successive unit of labor adds to total revenue. The amount that each additional unit of a resource adds to the firm's total (resource) cost is called its **marginal resource cost (MRC).** In equation form,

$$\text{Marginal resource cost} = \frac{\text{change in total (labor) cost}}{\text{unit change in labor}}$$

So we can restate our rule for hiring labor as follows: It will be profitable for a firm to hire additional units of labor up to the point at which labor's MRP is equal to its MRC. If the number of workers a firm is currently hiring is such that the MRP of the last worker exceeds his or her MRC, the firm can profit by hiring more workers. But if the number being hired is such that the MRC of the last worker exceeds his or her MRP, the firm is hiring workers who are not "paying their way" and it can increase its profit by discharging some workers. You may recognize that this **MRP = MRC rule** is similar to the MR = MC profit-maximizing rule employed in our discussion of price and output determination. The rationale of the two rules is the same, but the point of reference is now *inputs* of a resource, not *outputs* of a product.

MRP as Labor Demand Schedule

In a purely competitive labor market, market supply and market demand establish the wage rate. Because each firm hires such a small fraction of the market supply of labor, it cannot influence the market wage rate; it is a wage taker, not a wage maker. Thus, for each additional unit of labor hired, each firm's total labor cost increases by exactly the amount of the constant market wage rate. More specifically, the MRC of labor exactly equals the market wage rate. Thus, resource "price" (the market wage rate) and resource "cost" (marginal resource cost) are equal for a firm that hires labor in a competitive labor market. As a result, the MRP = MRC rule tells us that, in pure competition, the firm will hire units of labor up to the point at which the market *wage rate* (its MRC) is equal to its MRP.

In terms of the data in columns 1 and 6 of **Figure 17.1**'s table, if the market wage rate is, say, $13.95, the firm will hire only one worker. This is the outcome because only the hiring of the first worker results in an increase in profits. To see why, note that for the first worker, MRP (= $14) exceeds MRC (= $13.95). Thus, hiring the first worker is profitable. For each successive worker, however, MRC (= $13.95) exceeds MRP (= $12 or less), indicating that it will not be profitable to hire any of those workers. If the wage rate is $11.95, by the same reasoning we discover that it will pay the firm to hire both the first and second workers. Similarly, if the wage rate is $9.95, three will be hired, and so forth. Here is the key generalization: *The MRP schedule constitutes the firm's demand for labor because each point on this schedule (or curve) indicates the number of workers the firm would hire at each possible wage rate.*

marginal resource cost
The amount the total cost of employing a resource increases when a firm employs 1 additional unit of the resource (the quantity of all other resources employed remaining constant); equal to the change in the total cost of the resource divided by the change in the quantity of the resource employed.

MRP = MRC rule
The principle that to maximize profit, a firm should expand employment until the marginal revenue product (MRP) of labor equals the marginal resource cost (MRC) of labor.

In the graph in **Figure 17.1**, we show the D = MRP curve based on the data in the table. The competitive firm's labor demand curve identifies an inverse relationship between the wage rate and the quantity of labor demanded, other things equal. The curve slopes downward because of diminishing marginal returns.[1]

Market Demand for Labor

The total, or market, demand curve for labor shows the various amounts of labor that firms will purchase or hire at various wages, other things equal. Recall that the total, or market demand curve for a *product* is found by summing horizontally the demand curves of all individual buyers in the market. The market demand curve for *labor* (or any particular *resource*) is derived in essentially the same way—by summing horizontally the individual demand or MRP curves for all firms hiring that type of labor.

Changes in Labor Demand

What will alter the demand for labor (shift the labor demand curve)? The fact that labor demand is derived from *product demand* and depends on *labor productivity* suggests two "resource demand shifters." Also, our analysis of how changes in the prices of other products can shift a product's demand curve (**Chapter 3**) suggests a third factor: changes in the *prices of other resources*.

Changes in Product Demand

Other things equal, an increase in the demand for a product will increase the demand for a resource used in its production, whereas a decrease in product demand will decrease the demand for that resource.

Let's see how this works. Recall that a change in the demand for a product will change its price. In the table in **Figure 17.1**, let's assume that an increase in product demand boosts product price from $2 to $3. You should calculate the new labor demand schedule (columns 1 and 6) that would result, and plot it in the graph to verify that the new labor demand curve lies to the right of the old demand curve. Similarly, a decline in the product demand (and price) will shift the labor demand curve to the left. This effect—labor demand changing along with product demand—demonstrates that labor demand is derived from product demand.

Example: Assuming no offsetting change in supply, a decrease in the demand for new houses will drive down house prices. Those lower prices will decrease the MRP of construction workers, and therefore the demand for construction workers will fall. The labor demand curve will shift to the left.

Changes in Productivity

Other things equal, an increase in the productivity of a resource will increase the demand for the resource, and a decrease in productivity will reduce the demand for the resource. If we doubled the MP data of column 3 in the table in **Figure 17.1**, the MRP data of column 6 also would double, indicating a rightward shift of the labor demand curve in the graph.

---

[1] Note that we plot the points in Figure 17.1 halfway between succeeding numbers of labor units. For example, we plot the MRP of the second unit ($12) not at 1 or 2 but at 1½. This "smoothing" enables us to sketch a continuously downsloping curve rather than one that moves downward in discrete steps as each new unit of labor is hired.

The productivity of labor (or any resource) may be altered over the long run in several ways:

- *Quantities of other resources* The marginal productivity of any resource will vary with the quantities of the other resources used with it. The greater the amount of capital and land resources used with labor, the greater will be labor's marginal productivity and, thus, labor demand.

- *Technological advances* Technological improvements that increase the quality of other resources, such as capital, have the same effect. The better the *quality* of capital, the greater the productivity of labor used with it. Dockworkers employed with a specific amount of capital in the form of unloading cranes are more productive than dockworkers with the same amount of capital embodied in older conveyor-belt systems.

- *Quality of labor* Improvements in the quality of labor will increase its marginal productivity and therefore its demand. In effect, there will be a new demand curve for a different, more skilled, kind of labor.

Changes in the Prices of Other Resources

Changes in the prices of other resources—such as capital—may change the demand for labor. The direction of the change depends on whether labor and capital are substitutes or complements in production.

Substitute Resources Suppose that labor and capital are substitutable in a certain production process. A firm can produce some specific amount of output using a relatively small amount of labor and a relatively large amount of capital, or vice versa. What happens if the price of machinery (capital) falls? The effect on the demand for labor will be the net result of two opposed effects: the substitution effect and the output effect.

- *Substitution effect* The decline in the price of machinery prompts the firm to substitute machinery for labor. This allows the firm to produce its output at lower cost. So at the fixed wage rate, smaller quantities of labor are now employed. This **substitution effect** decreases the demand for labor. More generally, the substitution effect indicates that a firm will purchase more of an input whose relative price has declined. Conversely, it will use less of an input whose relative price has increased.

> **substitution effect**
> The effect of a change in the price of a resource on the quantity of the resource employed by a firm, assuming no change in its output.

- *Output effect* Because the price of machinery has fallen, the costs of producing various outputs also must decline. With lower costs, the firm finds it profitable to produce and sell a greater output. The greater output increases the demand for all resources, including labor. Thus, this **output effect** increases the demand for labor. More generally, the output effect means that the firm will purchase more of one particular input when the price of the other input falls, and less of that particular input when the price of the other input rises.

> **output effect**
> The situation in which an increase in the price of one input will increase a firm's production costs and reduce its level of output, thus reducing the demand for other inputs; conversely for a decrease in the price of the input.

- *Net effect* The substitution and output effects are both present when the price of an input changes, but they work in opposite directions. For a decline in the price of capital, the substitution effect decreases the demand for labor, while the output effect increases it. The net change in labor demand depends on the relative sizes of the two effects: If the substitution effect outweighs the output effect, a decrease in the price of capital decreases the demand for labor. If the output effect exceeds the substitution effect, a decrease in the price of capital increases the demand for labor.

Complementary Resources Recall from **Chapter 3** that certain products, such as computers and software, are complementary goods; they "go together" and are jointly demanded. Resources may also be complementary; an increase in the quantity of one resource used in the production process requires an increase in the amount used of the other resource, and vice versa. Suppose a small design firm does computer-assisted design (CAD) with relatively expensive personal computers as its basic piece of capital equipment. Each computer requires exactly one design engineer to operate it; the machine is not automated—it will not run itself—and a second engineer would have nothing to do.

Now assume that an increase in the supply of these computers substantially reduces their price. There can be no substitution effect because labor and capital must be used in *fixed proportions:* one person for one machine. Capital cannot be substituted for labor. But there *is* an output effect. Other things equal, the reduction in the price of capital goods means lower production costs. Producing a larger output will therefore be profitable. In producing more output, the firm will use both more capital and more labor. When labor and capital are complementary, a decline in the price of capital increases the demand for labor through the output effect.

Now that we have discussed the factors that change labor demand, let's review the effects. Stated in terms of the labor resource, the demand for labor will increase (the labor demand curve will shift rightward) when:

- The demand for (and therefore the price of) the product produced by that labor *increases.*
- The productivity (MP) of labor *increases.*
- The price of a substitute input *decreases,* provided the output effect exceeds the substitution effect.
- The price of a substitute input *increases,* provided the substitution effect exceeds the output effect.
- The price of a complementary input *decreases.*

Be sure that you can "reverse" these effects to explain a *decrease* in labor demand.

PHOTO OP

Substitute Resources versus Complementary Resources

Automatic teller machines (ATMs) and human tellers are substitute resources, whereas construction equipment and their operators are complementary resources.

Onoky/SuperStock RF

Steve Allen/Brand X Pictures/Alamy Stock Photo

APPLYING THE ANALYSIS

Occupational Employment Trends

Changes in labor demand affect wage rates and employment in specific occupations. Increases in labor demand for certain occupational groups result in increases in their employment; decreases in labor demand result in decreases in their employment. Let's look at occupations for which labor demand is growing and then examine occupations for which it is declining.

Table 17.1 lists the 10 fastest-growing and 10 most rapidly declining U.S. occupations (in percentage terms) for 2016–2026, as projected by the Bureau of Labor Statistics. Service occupations dominate the fastest-growing list. In general, the demand for service workers is rapidly outpacing the demand for manufacturing, construction, and mining workers in the United States.

TABLE 17.1

The 10 Fastest-Growing and Most Rapidly Declining U.S. Occupations, in Percentage Terms, 2016–2026

Occupation	Employment, Thousands of Jobs		
	2016	2026	Percentage Change*
Fastest Growing			
Solar photovoltaic installers	11.3	23.1	104.9
Wind turbine service technicians	5.8	11.3	96.3
Home health aides	911.5	1,342.7	47.3
Personal care aides	2,016.1	2,793.8	38.6
Physicians assistants	106.2	145.9	37.3
Nurse practitioners	155.5	211.6	36.1
Statisticians	37.2	49.8	33.8
Physical therapy assistants	88.3	115.8	31.0
Software developers, applications	831.3	1,086.6	30.7
Mathematicians	3.1	4.0	29.7
Most Rapidly Declining			
Locomotive firers	1.2	0.3	−78.6
Respiratory therapy technicians	10.8	4.7	−56.3
Parking enforcement workers	9.4	6.1	−35.3
Word processors and typists	74.9	50.1	−33.1
Watch repairers	1.8	1.2	−29.7
Electronic equipment technicians, motor vehicles	12.1	9.0	−25.6
Foundry mold and coremakers	12.5	9.5	−24.0
Pourers and casters, metal	8.4	6.5	−23.4
Computer operators	51.5	39.7	−22.8
Telephone operators	9.1	7.0	−22.6

* Percentages may not correspond with employment numbers due to rounding of the employment data and the percentages.

Sources: *Thirty Fastest Growing Occupations Projected to Account for 19 Percent of New Jobs from 2016 to 2026*, Bureau of Labor Statistics, 2017; and *Table 1.5, Fastest Declining Occupations, 2016 and Projected 2026*, Bureau of Labor Statistics, 2018.

Of the 10 fastest-growing occupations in percentage terms, 5 are related to health care. The rising demand for these laborers is derived from the growing demand for health services, caused by several factors. The aging of the U.S. population has brought with it more medical problems; rising incomes have led to greater expenditures on health care; and the growing presence of private and public insurance has allowed people to buy more health care than most could afford individually.

Table 17.1 also lists the 10 U.S. occupations with the greatest projected job loss (in percentage terms) between 2016 and 2026. Several of the occupations owe their declines mainly to labor-saving technological change. For example, automated or computerized equipment has greatly reduced the need for parking enforcement workers and telephone operators.

QUESTION:

Name an occupation (other than those listed) that you think will grow in demand over the next decade. Name an occupation that you think will decline in demand. In each case, explain your reasoning.

Elasticity of Labor Demand

The employment changes we have just discussed have resulted from shifts in labor demand curves. Such changes in demand must be distinguished from changes in the quantity of labor demanded caused by a change in the wage rate. Such changes are caused not by a shift of the demand curve but, rather, by a movement from one point to another on a fixed labor demand curve. For example, in **Figure 17.1**, we note that an increase in the wage rate from $5 to $7 will reduce the quantity of labor demanded from 5 units to 4 units. This is a change in the *quantity of labor demanded* as distinct from a *change in the demand for labor*.

elasticity of labor demand
A measure of the responsiveness of labor quality to a change in the wage rate.

The sensitivity of labor quantity to changes in wage rates along a fixed labor demand curve is measured by the **elasticity of labor demand** (or *wage elasticity of demand*). In coefficient form,

$$E_w = \frac{\text{percentage change in labor quantity demanded}}{\text{percentage change in wage rate}}$$

When E_w is greater than 1, labor demand is elastic; when E_w is less than 1, labor demand is inelastic; and when E_w equals 1, labor demand is unit-elastic. Several factors interact to determine the wage elasticity of demand.

Ease of Resource Substitutability

The greater the substitutability of other resources for labor, the more elastic is the demand for labor. For example, the high degree to which computerized voice recognition systems are substitutable for human beings implies that the demand for customer service representatives at call centers is quite elastic. In contrast, good substitutes for physicians are rare, so demand for them is less elastic or even inelastic.

Time can play a role in the input substitution process. For example, a firm's truck drivers may obtain a substantial wage increase with little or no immediate decline in employment. But over time, as the firm's trucks wear out and are replaced, that wage increase may motivate the company to purchase larger trucks so as to deliver the same total output with fewer drivers.

Elasticity of Product Demand

Because the demand for labor is a derived demand, the elasticity of the demand for labor's output will influence the elasticity of the demand for labor. Other things equal, the greater the elasticity of product demand, the greater the elasticity of labor demand. For example, suppose that the wage rate falls. The result is a decline in the cost of producing the product and a drop in the product's price. If the elasticity of product demand is great, the resulting increase in the quantity of the product demanded will be large and thus necessitate a large increase in the quantity of labor demanded, which implies an elastic demand for labor. But if the demand for the product is inelastic, the increase in the amount of the product demanded will be small, and so will the increase in the quantity of labor demanded. Here, the demand for labor is inelastic.

Ratio of Labor Cost to Total Cost

The larger the proportion of total production costs accounted for by labor, the greater is the elasticity of demand for labor. In the extreme, if labor cost is the only production cost, then a 20 percent increase in wage rates will increase marginal cost and average total cost by 20 percent. If product demand is elastic, this substantial increase in costs will cause a relatively large decline in sales and a sharp decline in the amount of labor demanded. So labor demand is highly elastic. But if labor cost is only 50 percent of production cost, then a 20 percent increase in wage rates will increase costs by only 10 percent. With the same elasticity of product demand, this will cause a relatively small decline in sales and therefore in the amount of labor demanded. In this case, the demand for labor is much less elastic.

Market Supply of Labor

On the supply side of a purely competitive labor market, we assume that no union is present and that workers individually compete for available jobs. The supply curve for each type of labor slopes upward, indicating that employers as a group must pay higher wage rates to obtain more workers. Employers must do so to bid workers away from other industries, occupations, and localities. Within limits, workers have alternative job opportunities. For example, they may work in other industries in the same locality, or they may work in their present occupations in different cities or states, or they may work in other occupations.

Firms that want to hire these workers must pay higher wage rates to attract them away from the alternative job opportunities. They also must pay higher wages to induce people who are not currently in the labor force—who are perhaps doing household activities or enjoying leisure—to seek employment. In short, assuming that wages are constant in other labor markets, higher wages in a particular labor market entice more workers to offer their labor services in that market. This fact is expressed graphically by the upward sloping market labor supply curve S in **Figure 17.2a**.

FIGURE 17.2

Labor supply and labor demand is (a) a purely competitive labor market and (b) a single competitive firm. In a purely competitive labor market (a), market labor supply *S* and market labor demand *D* determine the equilibrium wage rate W_c and the equilibrium number of workers Q_c. Each individual competitive firm (b) takes this competitive wage W_c as given. Thus, the individual firm's labor supply curve *s* = MRC is perfectly elastic at the going wage W_c. Its labor demand curve, *d,* is its MRP curve (here labeled *mrp*). The firm maximizes its profit by hiring workers up to the point where MRP = MRC.

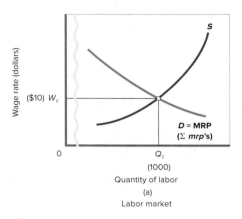 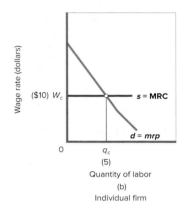

Wage and Employment Determination

What determines the market wage rate and how do firms respond to it? Suppose 200 firms demand a particular type of labor: say, carpenters. These firms need not be in the same industry; industries are defined according to the products they produce and not the resources they employ. Thus, firms producing wood-framed furniture, wood windows and doors, houses and apartment buildings, and wood cabinets will demand carpenters. To find the total, or market, labor demand curve for a particular labor service, we sum horizontally the labor demand curves (the marginal revenue product curves) of the individual firms, as indicated in **Figure 17.2**. The horizontal summing of the 200 labor demand curves like *d* in **Figure 17.2b** yields the market labor demand curve *D* in **Figure 17.2a**.

The intersection of the market labor demand curve and the market labor supply curve determines the equilibrium wage rate and the level of employment in this purely competitive labor market. In **Figure 17.2a**, the equilibrium wage rate is W_c ($10) and the number of workers hired is Q_c (1,000).

To the individual firm (**Figure 17.2b**), the market wage rate W_c is given at $10. Each of the many firms employs such a small fraction of the total available supply of this type of labor that no single firm can influence the wage rate. As shown by the horizontal line *s* in **Figure 17.2b**, the labor supply faced by an individual firm is perfectly elastic. It can hire as many or as few workers as it wants to at the market wage rate. This fact is clarified in **Table 17.2**, where we see that the marginal cost of labor MRC is constant at $10 and is equal to the wage rate. Each additional unit of labor employed adds precisely its own wage rate (here, $10) to the firm's total resource cost.

TABLE 17.2
The Supply of Labor: Pure Competition in the Hiring of Labor

(1) Units of Labor	(2) Wage Rate	(3) Total Labor Cost (Wage Bill)	(4) Marginal Resource (Labor) Cost
0	$10	$ 0	
			$10
1	10	10	
			10
2	10	20	
			10
3	10	30	
			10
4	10	40	
			10
5	10	50	
			10
6	10	60	

Each individual firm will apply the MRP = MRC rule to determine its profit-maximizing level of employment. Thus, the competitive firm maximizes its profit by hiring units of labor to the point at which its wage rate (= MRC) equals MRP. In **Figure 17.2b**, the employer will hire q_c (5) units of labor, paying each worker the market wage rate W_c ($10). The other 199 firms (not shown) that are hiring workers in this labor market will also each employ five workers and pay $10 per hour.

Monopsony

In the purely competitive labor market, each firm can hire as little or as much labor as it needs, but only at the market wage rate, as reflected in its horizontal labor supply curve. The situation is quite different when the labor market is a **monopsony,** a market structure in which there is only a single buyer. A labor market monopsony has the following characteristics:

monopsony
A market structure in which there is only a single buyer of a good, service, or resource.

- There is only a single buyer of a particular type of labor.
- The workers providing this type of labor have few employment options other than working for the monopsony either because they are geographically immobile or because finding alternative employment would mean having to acquire new skills.
- The firm is a "wage maker" because the wage rate it must pay varies directly with the number of workers it employs.

There are various degrees of monopsony power. In *pure* monopsony, such power is at its maximum because only a single employer hires labor in the labor market. The best real-world examples are probably the labor markets in towns that depend almost entirely on one major firm. For example, a Colorado ski resort, a Wisconsin paper mill, or an Alaskan fish processor may provide most of the employment in its geographically isolated locale. In other cases, three or four firms may each hire a large portion of the supply of labor in a certain market and therefore have some monopsony power. Moreover, if they tacitly or openly act in concert in hiring labor, they greatly enhance their monopsony power.

Upward-Sloping Labor Supply to Firm

When a firm hires most of the available supply of a certain type of labor, its decision to employ more or fewer workers affects those workers' wage rates. Specifically, if a firm is large in relation to the size of the labor market, it will have to pay a higher wage rate to attract labor away from other employment or leisure. Suppose there is only one employer of a particular type of labor in a certain geographic area. In this pure monopsony situation, the labor supply curve for the *firm* and the total labor supply curve for the *labor market* are identical. The labor supply curve–represented by curve S in **Figure 17.3**–slopes upward because the monopsonist must pay higher wage rates if it wants to attract and hire additional workers. This same curve is also the monopsonist's average-cost-of-labor curve. Each point on curve S indicates the wage rate (cost) per worker that must be paid to attract the corresponding number of workers. The larger the number of workers, the higher the wage rate.

FIGURE 17.3

Monopsony. In a monopsonistic labor market, the employer's marginal resource (labor) cost curve (MRC) lies above the labor supply curve S. Equating MRC with MRP at point b, the monopsonist hires Q_m workers (compared with Q_c under competition). As indicated by point c on S, it pays only wage rate W_m (compared with the competitive wage W_c).

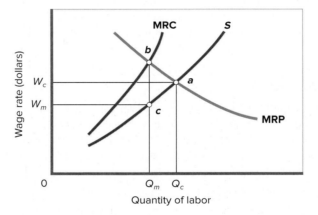

MRC Higher than the Wage Rate

When a monopsonist pays a higher wage to attract an additional worker, it must pay that higher wage not only to the additional worker, but also to all the workers it currently employs at a lower wage. If not, labor morale will deteriorate and the employer will be plagued with labor unrest because of wage-rate differences existing for the same job. Paying a uniform wage to all workers means that the cost of an extra worker–the marginal resource (labor) cost (MRC)–is the sum of that worker's wage rate and the amount necessary to bring the wage rate of all current workers up to the new wage level.

Table 17.3 illustrates this point. One worker can be hired at a wage rate of $6, but hiring a second worker forces the firm to pay a higher wage rate of $7. The marginal resource cost (labor) of the second worker is $8–the $7 paid to the second worker plus a $1 raise for the first worker. From another viewpoint, total labor cost is now $14 (= 2 × $7), up from $6 (= 1 × $6). So the MRC of the second worker is $8 (= $14 − $6), not just the $7 wage rate paid to that worker. Similarly, the marginal labor cost of the third worker is $10–the $8 that must be paid to attract this worker from alternative employment plus $1 raises, from $7 to $8, for the first two workers.

TABLE 17.3
The Supply of Labor: Monopsony in the Hiring of Labor

(1) Units of Labor	(2) Wage Rate	(3) Total Labor Cost (Wage Bill)	(4) Marginal Resource (Labor) Cost
0	$ 5	$ 0	
			$ 6
1	6	6	
			8
2	7	14	
			10
3	8	24	
			12
4	9	36	
			14
5	10	50	
			16
6	11	66	

Here is the key point: Because the monopsonist is the only employer in the labor market, its marginal resource (labor) cost exceeds the wage rate. Graphically, the monopsonist's MRC curve lies above the average-cost-of-labor curve, or labor supply curve *S*, as **Figure 17.3** clearly shows.

Equilibrium Wage and Employment

How many units of labor will the monopsonist hire, and what wage rate will it pay? To maximize profit, the monopsonist will employ the quantity of labor Q_m in **Figure 17.3** because, at that quantity, MRC and MRP are equal (point *b*). The monopsonist next determines how much it must pay to attract these Q_m workers. From the supply curve *S*, specifically point *c*, it seems that it must pay wage rate W_m. Clearly, it need not pay a wage equal to MRP. It can attract and hire exactly the number of workers it wants (Q_m) with wage rate W_m, and that is the wage it will pay.

Contrast these results with those that would prevail in a competitive labor market. With competition in the hiring of labor, the level of employment would be greater (at Q_c) and the wage rate would be higher (at W_c). Other things equal, the monopsonist maximizes its profit by hiring a smaller number of workers and thereby paying a less-than-competitive wage rate. Society obtains a smaller output, and workers get a wage rate that is less by *bc* than their marginal revenue product. Just as a monopolistic seller finds it profitable to restrict product output to realize an above competitive price for its goods, the monopsonistic employer finds it profitable to restrict employment in order to reduce wage rates below competitive wage rates.

APPLYING THE ANALYSIS

Monopsony Power

Monopsonistic labor markets are uncommon in the United States. In most labor markets, several potential employers compete for most workers, particularly for workers who are occupationally and geographically mobile. Also, where monopsony labor market outcomes might have otherwise occurred, unions have often sprung up to counteract that power by forcing firms to negotiate wages. Nevertheless, economists have found some evidence of monopsony power in the markets for nurses, professional athletes, and public school teachers.

In the case of nurses, the major employers in most locales are a relatively small number of hospitals. Further, the highly specialized skills of nurses are not readily transferable to other occupations. Other things equal, the smaller the number of hospitals in a town or city (i.e., the greater the degree of monopsony), the lower the beginning salaries of nurses.

Professional sports leagues also provide a good example of monopsony, particularly as it relates to the pay of first-year players. The National Football League, the National Basketball Association, and Major League Baseball assign first-year players to teams through "player drafts." That device prohibits other teams from competing for a player's services, at least for several years, until the player becomes a "free agent." In this way, each league exercises monopsony power, which results in lower salaries than would occur under competitive conditions.

> QUESTION:
>
> The salaries of star players often increase substantially when they become free agents. How does that fact relate to monopsony power?

Union Models

Thus far we have assumed that workers compete with one another in selling their labor services. In some labor markets, however, workers unionize and sell their labor services collectively. In the United States, about 10 percent of wage and salary workers belong to unions. (As shown in **Global Snapshot 17.1**, this percentage is low relative to some other nations.)

When a union is formed in an otherwise competitive labor market, it usually bargains with a relatively large number of employers. It has many goals, the most important of which is to raise wage rates. It can pursue that objective in several ways.

Demand-Enhancement Model

From the union's viewpoint, increasing the demand for union labor is highly desirable. An increase in the demand for union labor will create both a higher union wage and more jobs.

Unions can increase the demand for their labor by increasing the demand for the goods or services they help produce. Political lobbying is the main tool for increasing the demand for union-produced goods or services. For example, construction unions have lobbied for new highways and stadium projects. Teachers' unions have pushed for more spending on public education. U.S. steel unions have lobbied for tariffs on foreign imports of steel to boost domestic production, employment, and wages.

GLOBAL SNAPSHOT 17.1

Union Density, Selected Nations

The percentage of workers unionized varies considerably across countries, but sometimes this is due to differences in international practices, including some nations' legal restrictions preventing unionization in certain occupations. To adjust for these differences, alternative measures such as "union density," the rate of "actual" to "potential" membership, are used. Compared with most other industrialized nations, the percentage of potential wage and salary earners belonging to unions in the United States is small.

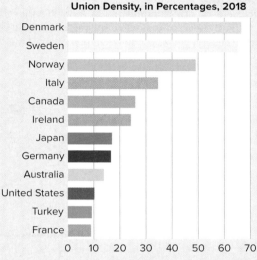

Union Density, in Percentages, 2018

Denmark
Sweden
Norway
Italy
Canada
Ireland
Japan
Germany
Australia
United States
Turkey
France

0 10 20 30 40 50 60 70

Source: Organization for Economic Co-operation and Development, Trade Union Density, retrieved March 2021,.

Unions can also increase the demand for labor by raising the price for potential substitute inputs. For example, even though union members are generally paid significantly more than minimum wage, unions have strongly supported minimum wage increases. This would raise the price of low-wage, nonunion labor that may be substitutable for union labor. A higher minimum wage for nonunion workers will discourage employers from substituting such workers for union workers, thus bolstering demand for union members.

Unions sometimes seek to increase the demand for labor by supporting policies that keep down prices of complementary resources. For example, unions in industries that represent workers who transport fruits and vegetables may support legislation that allows low-wage foreign agricultural workers to temporarily work in the United States. Where union labor and another resource are complementary, a price decrease for the other resource will increase the demand for union labor through the output effect.

The Exclusive or Craft Union Model

Unions can boost wage rates by reducing the supply of labor, and over the years organized labor has favored policies to do just that. For example, labor unions have supported legislation that has (1) restricted permanent immigration, (2) reduced child labor, (3) encouraged compulsory retirement, and (4) enforced a shorter workweek.

exclusive unionism
The practice of a labor union of restricting the supply of skilled union labor to increase the wages received by union members; the policies typically employed by a craft union.

Moreover, certain types of workers have adopted techniques designed to restrict the number of workers who can join their union. This is especially true of *craft unions,* whose members possess a particular skill, such as carpenters, masons, and plumbers. Craft unions have sometimes forced employers to agree to hire only union members, thereby gaining virtually complete control of the labor supply. Then, by following restrictive membership policies—for example, long apprenticeships, very high initiation fees, and limits on the number of new members admitted—they have artificially restricted labor supply. As **Figure 17.4** indicates, such practices result in higher wage rates and constitute what is called **exclusive unionism.** By excluding workers from unions and therefore from the labor supply, craft unions succeed in elevating wage rates.

FIGURE 17.4
Exclusive or craft unionism. By reducing the supply of labor (say, from S_1 to S_2) through the use of restrictive membership policies, exclusive unions achieve higher wage rates (W_c to W_u). However, restriction of the labor supply also reduces the number of workers employed (Q_c to Q_u).

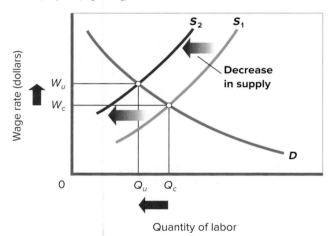

occupational licensing
State and local laws that require a worker to satisfy certain specific requirements and obtain a license from a licensing board before engaging in a particular occupation.

This craft union model applies to many professional organizations, such as the American Medical Association, the National Education Association, and the American Bar Association. These groups often seek to enact laws requiring **occupational licensing.** These laws mandate that some occupational group (e.g., physicians, lawyers, plumbers, cosmetologists, pest controllers) can practice their trade only if they meet certain requirements. Those requirements might include level of education, amount of work experience, and the passing of an examination. Members of the licensed occupation typically dominate the licensing board that administers such laws. The result is self-regulation, which often leads to policies that restrict entry to the occupation and reduce labor supply.

The expressed purpose of licensing is to protect consumers from incompetent practitioners—surely a worthy goal. But such licensing results in above-competitive wages and earnings for those in the licensed occupation (**Figure 17.4**). Moreover, licensing requirements often include a residency requirement, which inhibits the interstate movement of qualified workers. Some 1,100 occupations are now licensed in the United States.

The Inclusive or Industrial Union Model

Instead of trying to limit their membership, however, most unions seek to organize all available workers. This is especially true of the *industrial unions,* such as those of the automobile workers and steelworkers. Such unions seek as members all available unskilled, semiskilled, and skilled workers in an industry. It makes sense for a union to be exclusive when its members are skilled craft workers for whom the employer has few substitutes. But it does not make sense for a union to be exclusive when trying to organize unskilled and semiskilled workers. To break a strike, employers could then easily substitute unskilled or semiskilled nonunion workers for the unskilled or semi-skilled union workers.

By contrast, an industrial union that includes virtually all available workers in its membership can put firms under great pressure to agree to its wage demands. Because of its legal right to strike, such a union can threaten to deprive firms of their entire labor supply—and an actual strike can do just that. Further, with virtually all available workers in the union, it will be difficult in the short run for new nonunion firms to emerge and thereby undermine what the union is demanding from existing firms.

Figure 17.5 illustrates such **inclusive unionism.** Initially, the competitive equilibrium wage rate is W_c and the level of employment is Q_c. Now suppose an industrial union is formed that demands a higher, above-equilibrium wage rate of, say, W_u. That wage rate W_u would create a perfectly elastic labor supply over the range *ae* in **Figure 17.5**. If firms wanted to hire any workers in this range, they would have to pay the union-imposed wage rate. If they decide against meeting this wage demand, the union will call a strike. If firms decide it is better to pay the higher wage rate than to suffer a strike, they will cut back on employment from Q_c to Q_u.

inclusive unionism
The practice of a labor union of including as members all workers employed in an industry.

FIGURE 17.5
Inclusive or industrial unionism. By organizing virtually all available workers in order to control the supply of labor, inclusive industrial unions may impose a wage rate, such as W_u, that is above the competitive wage rate W_c. In effect, this changes the labor supply curve from S to aeS. At wage rate W_u, employers will cut employment from Q_c to Q_u.

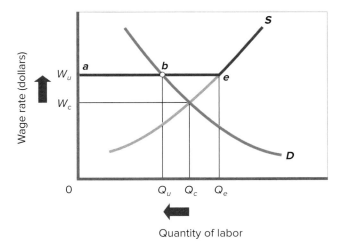

By agreeing to the union's wage demand, individual employers become wage takers at the union wage rate W_u. Because labor supply is perfectly elastic over range *ae,* the marginal resource (labor) cost is equal to the union wage rate W_u over this range. The Q_u level of employment is the result of employers' equating this MRC (now equal to the union wage rate) with MRP, according to our profit-maximizing rule.

Note from point e on labor supply curve S that Q_e workers desire employment at wage W_u. But as indicated by point b on labor demand curve D, only Q_u workers are employed. The result is a surplus of labor of $Q_e - Q_u$ (also shown by distance be). In a purely competitive labor market without the union, the effect of a surplus of unemployed workers would be lower wages. Specifically, the wage rate would fall to the equilibrium level W_c, where the quantity of labor supplied equals the quantity of labor demanded (each, Q_c). But this drop in wages does not happen because workers are acting collectively through their union. Individual workers cannot offer to work for less than W_u, nor can employers pay less than that.

Wage Increases and Job Loss

Evidence suggests that union members, on average, achieve a 15-percent wage advantage over nonunion workers. But when unions are successful in raising wages, their efforts also have another major effect.

As **Figures 17.4** and **17.5** suggest, the wage-raising actions achieved by both exclusive and inclusive unionism reduce employment in unionized firms. Simply put, a union's success in achieving above-equilibrium wage rates thus tends to be accompanied by a decline in the number of workers employed. That result acts as a restraining influence on union wage demands. A union cannot expect to maintain solidarity within its ranks if it seeks a wage rate so high that 20–30 percent of its members lose their jobs.

Wage Differentials

wage differential
The difference between the wage received by one worker or group of workers and that received by another worker or group of workers.

Hourly wage rates and annual salaries differ greatly among occupations. **Table 17.4** lists average annual salaries for a number of occupations to illustrate such **wage differentials.** For example, anesthesiologists on average earn 10 times as much as retail salespersons. In addition, there are large wage differentials within some of the occupations listed. For example, although average wages for retail salespersons are relatively low, some top salespersons selling on commission make several times the average wages listed for their occupation.

TABLE 17.4
Average Annual Wages in Selected Occupations, 2017

Occupation	Average Annual Wages
Anesthesiologists	$265,990
Petroleum engineers	154,780
Financial managers	143,530
Law professors	129,840
Pharmacists	121,710
Civil engineers	91,790
Dental hygienists	74,680
Registered nurses	73,550
Police officers	64,540
Electricians	57,910
Travel agents	40,840
Barbers	30,480
Janitors	27,900
Retail salespersons	25,560
Child care workers	23,760
Fast-food cooks	21,610

Source: *Occupational Employment and Wages*, U.S. Bureau of Labor Statistics, May 2017.

What explains these wage differentials? Once again, the forces of demand and supply are highly revealing. As **Figure 17.6** shows, wage differentials can arise on either the supply or the demand side of labor markets. Panels (a) and (b) in **Figure 17.6** represent labor markets for two occupational groups that have identical *labor supply* curves. Labor market (a) has a relatively high equilibrium wage (W_a) because labor demand is very strong. In labor market (b), the equilibrium wage is relatively low (W_b) because labor demand is weak. Clearly, the wage differential between occupations (a) and (b) results solely from differences in the magnitude of labor demand.

FIGURE 17.6

Labor demand, labor supply, and wage differentials. The wage differential between labor markets (a) and (b) results solely from differences in labor demand. In labor markets (c) and (d), differences in labor supply are the sole cause of the wage differential.

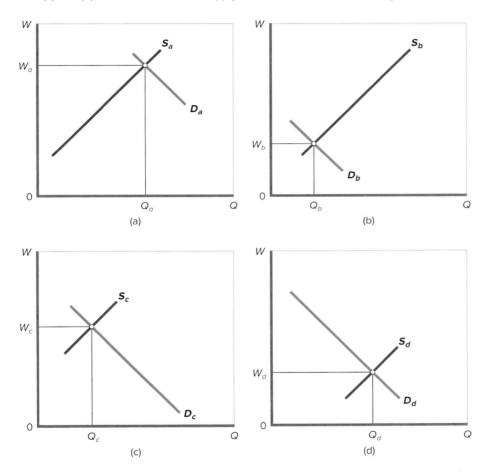

Contrast that situation with panels (c) and (d) in **Figure 17.6**, where the *labor demand* curves are identical. In labor market (c), the equilibrium wage is relatively high (W_c) because labor supply is low. In labor market (d), labor supply is highly abundant, so the equilibrium wage (W_d) is relatively low. The wage differential between (c) and (d) results solely from the differences in the size of labor supply.

Although **Figure 17.6** provides a good starting point for understanding wage differentials, we need to know *why* demand and supply conditions differ in various labor markets. There are several reasons.

Marginal Revenue Productivity

The strength of labor demand—how far rightward the labor demand curve is located—differs greatly among occupations due to differences in how much various occupational groups contribute to their respective employers' revenue. This revenue contribution, in turn, depends on the workers' productivity and the strength of the demand for the products they are helping to produce. Where labor is highly productive and product demand is strong, labor demand also is strong and, other things equal, pay is high. Top professional athletes, for example, are highly productive at producing sports entertainment, for which millions of people are willing to pay billions of dollars over the course of a season. Because the marginal revenue productivity of these players is so high, they are in very high demand by sports teams. This high demand leads to their extremely high salaries (as in **Figure 17.6a**). In contrast, most workers generate much more modest revenue for their employers. The result is much lower demand for their labor and, consequently, much lower wages (as in **Figure 17.6b**).

Noncompeting Groups

On the supply side of the labor market, workers differ in their mental and physical capacities and in their education and training. At any given time, the labor force is made up of many noncompeting groups of workers, each representing several occupations for which the members of that particular group qualify. In some groups, qualified workers are relatively few, whereas in others they are plentiful.

Ability   At any moment in time, only a few workers have the skills or physical attributes to be brain surgeons, concert violinists, top fashion models, research chemists, or professional athletes. Because the supply of these particular types of labor is very small in relation to labor demand, their wages are high (as in **Figure 17.6c**). The members of these and similar groups do not compete with one another or with other skilled or semiskilled workers. The violinist does not compete with the surgeon, nor does the surgeon compete with the violinist or the fashion model.

human capital
The accumulation of knowledge and skills that make a worker productive.

Education and Training   Another source of wage differentials is differing amounts of **human capital,** which is the personal stock of knowledge, know-how, and skills that enables a person to be productive and thus to earn income. Like expenditures on machinery and equipment, productivity-enhancing expenditures on education or training are investments. In both cases, people incur *present costs* with the intention that those expenditures will lead to a greater flow of *future earnings.*

Figure 17.7 indicates that workers who have made greater investments in education achieve higher incomes during their careers. The reason is twofold: (1) There are fewer such workers, so their supply is limited relative to less-educated workers, and (2) more educated workers tend to be more productive and thus in greater demand. **Figure 17.7** also indicates that the incomes of better-educated workers generally rise more rapidly than those of poorly educated workers. Why? Employers provide more on-the-job training to the better-educated workers, boosting their marginal revenue productivity and therefore their earnings.

Although education yields higher incomes, it carries substantial costs. A college education involves not only direct costs (tuition, fees, books) but also indirect or opportunity costs (forgone earnings). Does the higher pay received by better-educated workers compensate for these costs? The answer is yes. Rates of return are estimated to be 10 to 13 percent for investments in secondary education and 8 to 12 percent for investments in college education. Overall, each year of schooling raises a worker's wage by about 8 percent.

FIGURE 17.7

Education levels and average annual income. Annual income by age is higher for workers with more education than less. Investment in education yields a return in the form of earnings differences enjoyed over one's work life.

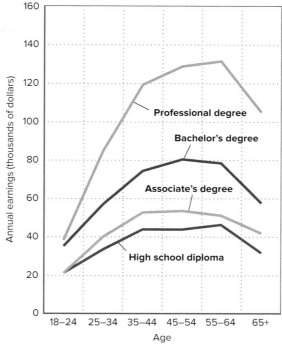

Source: U.S. Bureau of the Census, www.census.gov. Data are for all genders in 2017.

ILLUSTRATING THE IDEA

My Entire Life

For some people, high earnings have little to do with actual hours of work and much to do with their tremendous skill, which reflects their accumulated stock of human capital. The point is demonstrated in the following story: It is said that a tourist once spotted the famous Spanish artist Pablo Picasso (1881–1973) in a Paris café. The tourist asked Picasso if he would do a sketch of his wife for pay. Picasso sketched the wife in a matter of minutes and said, "That will be 10,000 francs [roughly $2,000]." Hearing the high price, the tourist became irritated, saying, "But that took you only a few minutes."

"No," replied Picasso, "it took me my entire life!"

> QUESTION:
>
> In general, how do the skill requirements of the highest-paying occupations in **Table 17.4** compare with the skill requirements of the lowest-paying occupations?

Compensating Differences

compensating differences
Differences in the wages received by workers in different jobs to compensate for nonmonetary differences in the jobs.

In virtually all locales, construction laborers receive much higher wages than sales-clerks. These wage differentials are called **compensating differences** because they must be paid to compensate for nonmonetary differences in various jobs.

The construction job involves dirty hands, a sore back, possible accidents, and irregular employment, both seasonally and during recessions (economy-wide economic slowdowns). The retail sales job means clean clothing, pleasant air-conditioned surroundings, and little fear of injury. Other things equal, it is easy to see why workers would rather process a credit card payment than pick up a shovel. Thus, the amount of labor supplied to construction firms (as in **Figure 17.6c**) is smaller than that supplied to retail shops (as in **Figure 17.6d**).

Compensating differences spring up throughout the economy. Other things equal, jobs having high risk of death or injury pay more than comparable, safer jobs. Jobs lacking employer-paid health insurance, pensions, and vacation time pay more than comparable jobs that provide these benefits. Jobs with flexible hours pay less than jobs with rigid work-hour requirements. Jobs with greater risk of unemployment pay more than comparable jobs with little unemployment risk. Entry-level jobs in occupations that provide very poor prospects for pay advancement pay more than entry-level jobs that have clearly defined "job ladders."

Just as wages vary across an economy, they differ between countries, as shown in **Global Snapshot 17.2**.

APPLYING THE ANALYSIS

The Minimum Wage

Since the passage of the Fair Labor Standards Act in 1938, the United States has had a federal minimum wage. That wage has ranged between 35 and 50 percent of the average wage paid to manufacturing workers and was most recently raised to $7.25 in July 2009. (An attempt to raise it to $15 failed in March 2021.) Numerous states, however, have minimum wages considerably above the federal mandate. For example, in 2019 the minimum wage in the state of Washington was $12 an hour. The purpose of minimum wages is to provide a "wage floor" that will help less-skilled workers earn enough income to escape poverty.

Critics, reasoning in terms of **Figure 17.5**, contend that an above-equilibrium minimum wage (say, W_u) will simply cause employers to hire fewer workers. Downward sloping labor demand curves are a reality. The higher labor costs may even force some firms out of business. Then some of the poor, low-wage workers whom the minimum wage was designed to help will find themselves out of work. Critics point out that workers who are *unemployed* and desperate to find a job at a minimum wage of $7.25 per hour are clearly worse off than they would be if *employed* at a market wage rate of, say, $6.50 per hour.

A second criticism of the minimum wage is that it is "poorly targeted" to reduce household poverty. Critics note that much of the benefit of the minimum wage accrues to workers, including many teenagers, who do not live in impoverished households.

Advocates of the minimum wage say that critics analyze its impact in an unrealistic context, specifically a competitive labor market (**Figure 17.2**). They contend that much of the low-pay labor market is not competitive. They believe the monopsony labor market of **Figure 17.3** is a better model for these markets. There, the minimum wage can increase wage rates without causing significant unemployment. Indeed, a higher minimum wage may even produce more jobs by eliminating the motive that monopsonistic firms have for restricting employment. For example, a minimum-wage floor of W_c in **Figure 17.3** would change the firm's labor supply curve to $W_c aS$ and prompt the firm to increase its employment from Q_m workers to Q_c workers.

Moreover, even if the labor market is competitive, the higher wage rate might prompt firms to find more productive tasks for low-paid workers, thereby raising their productivity. Alternatively, the minimum wage may reduce *labor turnover* (the rate at which workers voluntarily quit). With fewer low-productivity trainees, the *average* productivity of the firm's workers would rise. In either case, the alleged negative employment effects of the minimum wage might not occur.

Which view is correct? Unfortunately, there is no clear answer. All economists agree that firms will not hire workers who cost more per hour than the value of their hourly output—so there is some minimum wage so high that it would severely reduce employment. Consider $30 an hour, as an absurd example. Because the majority of U.S. workers earned barely over $21 per hour in 2017, a minimum wage of $30 per hour would render the majority of U.S. workers unemployable because their employers would have to pay a wage that far exceeds their workers' marginal revenue products.

However, a minimum wage will only cause unemployment in labor markets where the minimum wage exceeds the equilibrium wage. Jobs in these labor markets are typically filled by unskilled or low-skilled workers including teenagers, adults who did not complete high school, and immigrants with low levels of education and poor English language proficiency. For members of such groups, recent research suggests that a 10 percent increase in the minimum wage will reduce employment of unskilled workers by about 1 to 3 percent. However, estimates of the employment effects of minimum wage laws vary from study to study, and significant controversy remains.

The overall effect of the minimum wage is thus uncertain. On the one hand, the employment and unemployment effects of the minimum wage do not appear to be as great as many critics fear. On the other hand, because a large part of its effect is dissipated on nonpoverty families, the minimum wage is not as strong an antipoverty tool as many supporters contend.

Voting patterns and surveys make it clear, however, that the minimum wage has strong political support. Perhaps this stems from two perceptions: (1) More workers are believed to be helped than hurt by the minimum wage, and (2) the minimum wage provides some assurance that employers are not taking undue advantage of vulnerable, low-skilled workers.

QUESTIONS:

Have you ever worked for the minimum wage? If so, for how long? Would you favor increasing the minimum wage by $1? By $2? By $5? Explain your reasoning.

GLOBAL SNAPSHOT 17.2

Hourly Wages of Production Workers, Selected Nations

Wage differences are pronounced worldwide. The data shown here indicate that hourly compensation in the United States is not as high as in some European nations. It is important to note, however, that the prices of goods and services vary greatly among nations, and the process of converting foreign wages into dollars may not accurately reflect such variations.

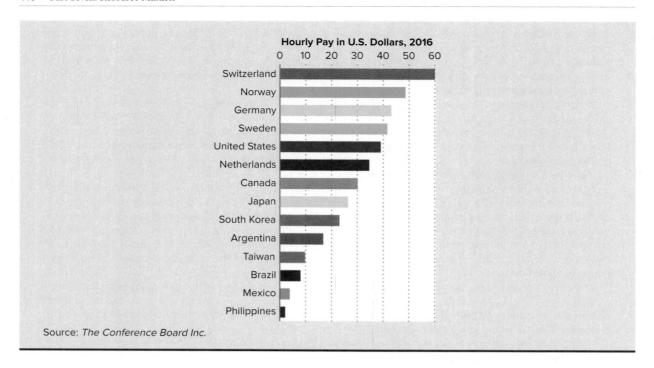

Source: *The Conference Board Inc.*

Summary

LO17.1 Explain why the firm's marginal revenue product curve is its labor demand curve.

The demand for labor is derived from the product it helps produce. The demand for labor depends on its productivity and on the market value (price) of the good it is used to produce.

Marginal revenue product is the extra revenue a firm obtains when it employs 1 more unit of a resource. The marginal revenue product curve for labor is the firm's labor demand curve. Each point on the MRP curve indicates how many labor units the firm will hire at a specific wage rate.

The firm's labor demand curve slopes downward because of the law of diminishing returns. The market demand curve for labor is derived by summing horizontally the demand curves of all the firms hiring that type of labor.

LO17.2 List the factors that increase or decrease labor demand.

The demand curve for labor will shift as the result of (a) a change in the demand for, and therefore the price of, the product the labor is producing; (b) changes in the productivity of labor; and (c) changes in the prices of substitutable and complementary resources.

LO17.3 Discuss the determinants of elasticity of labor demand.

The elasticity of demand for labor measures the responsiveness of producers hiring labor to a change

in the wage rate. The coefficient of the elasticity of labor demand is

$$E_w = \frac{\text{percentage change in labor quantity demanded}}{\text{percentage change in wage rate}}$$

When E_w is greater than 1, labor demand is elastic; when E_w is less than 1, labor demand is inelastic; and when E_w equals 1, labor demand is unit-elastic.

The elasticity of labor demand will be greater (a) the greater the ease of substituting other resources for labor, (b) the greater the elasticity of demand for the product, and (c) the larger the proportion of total production costs attributable to labor.

LO17.4 Demonstrate how wage rates are determined in competitive and monopsonistic labor markets.

Specific wage rates depend on the structure of the particular labor market. In a competitive labor market, the equilibrium wage rate and level of employment are determined at the intersection of the labor supply curve and labor demand curve. For the individual firm, the market wage rate establishes a horizontal labor supply curve, meaning that the wage rate equals the firm's constant marginal resource cost. The firm hires workers to the point where its MRP equals its MRC.

Under monopsony, the marginal resource cost curve lies above the resource supply curve because the monopsonist must bid up the wage rate to hire extra workers and must pay that higher wage rate to all workers. The monopsonist hires fewer workers than are hired under competitive conditions, pays less-than-competitive wage rates (has lower labor costs), and thus obtains greater profit.

LO17.5 Discuss how unions increase wage rates and how minimum wage laws affect labor markets.

A union may raise competitive wage rates by (a) increasing the derived demand for labor, (b) restricting the supply of labor through exclusive unionism, or (c) directly enforcing an above-equilibrium wage rate through inclusive unionism. On average, unionized workers realize wage rates 15 percent higher than those of comparable nonunion workers.

LO17.6 List the major causes of wage differentials.

Wage differentials are largely explainable in terms of (a) marginal revenue productivity of various groups of workers; (b) noncompeting groups arising from differences in the capacities and education of different groups of workers; and (c) compensating wage differences that must be paid to offset nonmonetary differences in jobs.

Economists disagree about the desirability of the minimum wage as an antipoverty mechanism. While it causes unemployment for some low-income workers, it raises the income of those who retain their jobs.

Terms and Concepts

purely competitive labor market	substitution effect	occupational licensing
derived demand	output effect	inclusive unionism
marginal revenue product (MRP)	elasticity of labor demand	wage differential
marginal resource cost (MRC)	monopsony	human capital
MRP = MRC rule	exclusive unionism	compensating differences

Questions   Mc Graw Hill connect

1. Explain the meaning and significance of the fact that the demand for labor is a derived demand. Why do labor demand curves slope downward? **(LO1)**

2. Complete the following labor demand table for a firm that is hiring labor competitively and selling its product in a competitive market. **(LO1)**

   a. How many workers will the firm hire if the market wage rate is $27.95? $19.95? Explain why the firm will not hire a larger or smaller number of units of labor at each of these wage rates.

   b. Show this firm's labor demand curve in schedule form and graphically.

3. In 2018, General Motors (GM) announced that it would reduce employment by 14,000 workers. What does this decision reveal about how GM viewed its marginal revenue product (MRP) and marginal resource cost (MRC)? Why didn't GM reduce employment by more than 14,000 workers or by fewer than 14,000 workers? **(LO2)**

4. What factors determine the elasticity of resource demand? What effect will each of the following have on the elasticity or location of the demand for resource C, which is being used to produce commodity X? Where there is any uncertainty as to the outcome, specify the causes of that uncertainty. **(LO2, LO3)**

Units of Labor	Total Product	Marginal Product	Product Price	Total Revenue	Marginal Revenue Product
0	0		$2	$____	$____
1	17	____	2	____	____
2	31	____	2	____	____
3	43	____	2	____	____
4	53	____	2	____	____
5	60	____	2	____	____
6	65	____	2	____	____

a. An increase in the demand for product X.
b. An increase in the price of substitute resource D.
c. An increase in the number of resources substitutable for C in producing X.
d. A technological improvement in the capital equipment with which resource C is combined.
e. A fall in the price of complementary resource E.
f. A decline in the elasticity of demand for product X due to a decline in the competitiveness of product market X.

5. Florida citrus growers say that the recent crackdown on illegal immigration is increasing the market wage rates necessary to get their oranges picked. Some are turning to $100,000 to $300,000 mechanical harvesters known as "trunk, shake, and catch" pickers, which vigorously shake oranges from the trees. If widely adopted, what will be the effect on the demand for human orange pickers? What does that imply about the relative strengths of the substitution and output effects? **(LO2)**

6. Why is a firm in a purely competitive labor market a *wage taker*? What would happen if it decided to pay less than the going market wage rate? **(LO4)**

7. Contrast the methods used by inclusive unions and exclusive unions to raise union wage rates. **(LO5)**

8. Have you ever worked for the minimum wage? If so, for how long? Would you favor increasing the minimum wage by a dollar? By two dollars? By five dollars? Explain your reasoning. **(LO5)**

9. "Many of the lowest-paid people in society—for example, short-order cooks—also have relatively poor working conditions. Hence, the notion of compensating wage differentials is disproved." Do you agree? Explain. **(LO6)**

10. What is meant by investment in human capital? Use this concept to explain (a) wage differentials and (b) the long-run rise of real wage rates in the United States. **(LO6)**

Problems

1. Suppose that marginal product tripled while product price fell by one-half in the table accompanying **Figure 17.1**. What would be the new MRP values in the table? What would be the net impact on the location of the resource demand curve in **Figure 17.1**? **(LO2)**

2. Complete the following labor supply table for a firm hiring labor competitively: **(LO4)**
    a. Show graphically this firm's labor supply and marginal resource (labor) cost curves. Are the curves the same or different? If they are different, which one is higher?
    b. Plot the labor demand data of question 2 on the graph used in part a above. What are the equilibrium wage rate and level of employment?

Units of Labor	Wage Rate	Total Labor Cost	Marginal Resource (Labor) Cost
0	$14	$_____	$_____
1	14	_____	_____
2	14	_____	_____
3	14	_____	_____
4	14	_____	_____
5	14	_____	_____
6	14	_____	

3. Assume a firm is a monopsonist that can hire its first worker for $6 but must increase the wage rate by $3 to attract each successive worker (so that the second worker must be paid $9, the third $12, and so on). **(LO4)**
    a. Draw the firm's labor supply and marginal resource cost curves. Are the curves the same or different? If they are different, which one is higher?
    b. On the same graph, plot the labor demand data of *question* 2. What are the equilibrium wage rate and level of employment?
    c. Compare these answers with those you found in *problem* 2 above. By how much does the monopsonist reduce wages below the competitive wage? By how much does the monopsonist reduce employment below the competitive level?

4. Suppose that low-skilled workers employed in clearing woodland can each clear one acre per month if they are each equipped with a shovel, a machete, and a chainsaw. Clearing one acre brings in $1,000 in revenue. Each worker's equipment costs the worker's employer $150 per month to rent and each worker toils 40 hours per week for four weeks each month. **(LO5)**

a. What is the marginal revenue product of hiring one low-skilled worker to clear woodland for one month?
b. How much revenue per hour does each worker bring in?
c. If the minimum wage is $11.20, would the revenue per hour in part *b* exceed the minimum wage? If so, by how much per hour?
d. Now consider the employer's total costs.

These include the equipment costs, as well as a normal profit of $50 per acre. If the firm pays workers the minimum wage of $11.20 per hour, what will be the firm's economic profit or loss per acre?
e. At what value would the minimum wage have to be set so that the firm would make zero economic profit from employing an additional low-skilled worker to clear woodland?

CHAPTER EIGHTEEN

Income Inequality and Poverty

Learning Objectives

LO18.1   Explain how income inequality in the United States is measured and described.

LO18.2   Discuss the extent and sources of income inequality.

LO18.3   Demonstrate how income inequality has changed since 1980.

LO18.4   Debate the economic arguments for and against income inequality.

LO18.5   Relate poverty to age, gender, and ethnicity characteristics.

LO18.6   Identify the major components of the U.S. income-maintenance program.

Wide income disparity in the United States is easy to find. In 2017, boxer Floyd Mayweather earned $285 million while celebrity Kylie Jenner earned $167 million. In contrast, the salary of the president of the United States is $400,000, and the typical schoolteacher earns $59,000. A full-time minimum-wage worker at a fast-food restaurant makes about $15,000. Cash welfare payments to a parent with two children average $5,300.

In 2017, about 39.7 million Americans—or 12.3 percent of the population—lived in poverty. An estimated 553,000 people were homeless on any given night. The richest fifth of American households received about 51.5 percent of total income, while the poorest fifth received about 3.1 percent.

What are the sources of income inequality? Is income inequality rising or falling? Is the United States making progress against poverty? These are some of the questions we answer in this chapter.

Facts about Income Inequality

Average household income in the United States is among the highest in the world: In 2017, it was $61,372 per household (one or more persons occupying a housing unit). But that average tells us nothing about income inequality. To learn about that, we must examine how income is distributed around the average.

Distribution by Income Category

One way to measure **income inequality** is to look at the percentages of households in a series of income categories. **Table 18.1** shows that about 21.4 percent of all households had annual before-tax incomes of less than $25,000 in 2017, while 26.2 percent had annual incomes of $100,000 or more. These data suggest a wide dispersion of household income and considerable income inequality in the United States.

income inequality
The unequal distribution of an economy's total income among households or families.

TABLE 18.1
The Distribution of U.S. Income by Households, 2017

(1) Personal Income Category	(2) Percentage of All Households in This Category
Under $15,000	11.6
$15,000–$24,999	9.8
$25,000–$34,999	9.5
$35,000–$49,999	13.0
$50,000–$74,999	17.7
$75,000–$99,999	12.3
$100,000 and above	26.2
	100.0

Source: Household Income: 2017. U.S. Census Bureau.

Distribution by Quintiles (Fifths)

We can also measure income inequality by dividing the total number of individuals, households, or families (two or more persons related by birth, marriage, or adoption) into five numerically equal groups, or *quintiles,* and examining the percentage of total personal (before-tax) income received by each quintile. We graph the relevant numbers for households in **Figure 18.1**, which also provides the upper income limit for each quintile. Any amount of income greater than that listed in each row of column 3 places a household into the next-higher quintile.

The Lorenz Curve and Gini Ratio

We can display the quintile distribution of personal income with a **Lorenz curve. In Figure 18.1**, we plot the cumulative percentage of households on the horizontal axis and the cumulative percentage of income they obtain on the vertical axis. The diagonal line 0e represents a *perfectly equal distribution of income* because each point along that line indicates that a particular percentage of households receive the same percentage of income. That is, points on the diagonal line show values where the percentage of households and the percentage of income are the same: for example, 20 percent of all households receiving 20 percent of total income, 40 percent receiving 40 percent, 60 percent receiving 60 percent, and so on.

Lorenz curve
A curve showing the distribution of income in an economy. The cumulated percentage of families (income receivers) is measured along the horizontal axis, and cumulated percentage of income is measured along the vertical axis.

FIGURE 18.1

The Lorenz curve and Gini ratio. The Lorenz curve is a convenient way to show the degree of income inequality (here, household income by quintile in 2017). The area between the diagonal (the line of perfect equality) and the Lorenz curve represents the degree of inequality in the distribution of total income. This inequality is measured numerically by the Gini ratio—area *A* (shown in blue) divided by area *A* + *B* (the blue + green area). The Gini ratio for the distribution shown is 0.480.

(1) Quintile	(2) Percentage of Total Income	(3) Upper Income Limit
Lowest 20%	3.1	$ 24,625
Second 20%	8.2	47,169
Third 20%	14.3	75,494
Fourth 20%	23.0	121,116
Highest 20%	51.5	No limit
Total	100.0	

Source: Bureau of Labor Statistics.

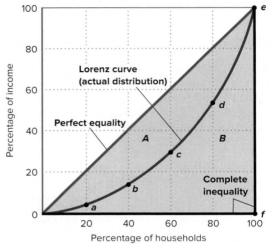

By plotting the quintile data from the table in **Figure 18.1**, we obtain the Lorenz curve for 2017. The bottom 20 percent of all households received 3.1 percent of the income, as shown by point *a*; the bottom 40 percent received 11.3 percent (= 3.1 + 8.2), as shown by point *b*; and so forth. The blue area between the diagonal line and the Lorenz curve indicates the degree of income inequality. If the actual income distribution were perfectly equal, the Lorenz curve and the diagonal would coincide and the blue area would disappear. But if the Lorenz curve sagged well below the diagonal, the blue area would be large, indicating a substantial amount of income inequality. In general, the farther the Lorenz curve sags away from the diagonal, the larger is the blue area and the higher is the degree of income inequality.

The income inequality described by the Lorenz curve can be transformed into a **Gini ratio**—a numerical measure of the overall dispersion of income:

Gini ratio
A numerical measure of the overall dispersion of income among households, families, or individuals; found graphically by dividing the area between the diagonal line and the Lorenz curve by the entire area below the diagonal line.

$$\text{Gini ratio} = \frac{\text{area between Lorenz curve and diagonal}}{\text{total area below the diagonal}}$$

$$= \frac{A \text{ (blue area)}}{A + B \text{ (blue + green area)}}$$

The Gini ratio is 0.482 for the income distribution shown in **Figure 18.1**. Lower Gini ratios denote less inequality; higher ratios indicate more inequality. The Gini ratio for complete income equality is zero and for complete inequality (where all households but one have zero income) is 1. So the higher the Gini coefficient, the more unequal the distribution of income.

Because Gini ratios are numerical, they are easier to use than Lorenz curves for comparing the income distributions of different racial and ethnic groups, and for different countries. For example, in 2017 the Gini ratio of U.S. household income for African Americans was 0.501; for Asians, 0.482; for whites, 0.472; and for Hispanics, 0.460.[1] In 2014, national Gini ratios ranged from a low of 0.241 in the Slovak Republic to a high of 0.623 in South Africa. Examples within this range include Denmark, 0.263; Italy, 0.328; Mexico, 0.459; and China, 0.514.[2]

---

[1] U.S. Census Bureau, *Historical Income Tables*, www.census.gov.
[2] *CIA World Factbook, 2018*, www.cia.gov.

Income Mobility: The Time Dimension

The income data we have examined so far have a major limitation: The income accounting period of one year is too short to be very meaningful. Because the Census Bureau data portray the income distribution in only a single year, they may conceal a more equal distribution over a few years, a decade, or even a lifetime. If Aki earns $1,000 in year 1 and $100,000 in year 2, while Baahir earns $100,000 in year 1 and only $1,000 in year 2, do we have income inequality? The answer depends on the period of measurement. Annual data would produce a Gini coefficient revealing great income inequality between Aki and Baahir, but there would be complete equality if the Gini coefficient were calculated based on their respective cumulative incomes over the two-year period.

This point is important because evidence suggests considerable "churning around" in the income distribution over time. Movement of individuals or households from one income quintile to another over time is called **income mobility.** For most income receivers, income starts at a relatively low level during youth, reaches a peak during middle age, and then declines. Thus, if all people receive exactly the same income stream over their lifetimes, considerable income inequality would still exist in any specific year because of age differences. In any single year, the young and the old would receive low incomes while the middle-aged receive high incomes.

income mobility
The extent to which income receivers move from one part of the income distribution to another over some period of time.

If we change from a "snapshot" view of income distribution in a single year to a "time exposure" portraying incomes over much longer periods, we find considerable movement of income receivers among income classes.

- Looking at the top of the income distribution, 70 percent of the U.S. population will enjoy at least one year between ages 25 and 60 in which their income places them in the top 20 percent of income earners.[3]

- Looking at the bottom of the income distribution, 62 percent of the U.S. population will experience at least one year between ages 25 and 60 in which their income places them in the bottom 20 percent of incomes.[4]

- Duration also matters. Between ages 25 and 60, 15 percent of the U.S. population will encounter five or more consecutive years in which their incomes place them in the bottom 20 percent of income earners.[5]

These facts about individual and household income mobility over time are significant; for many people, "low income" and "high income" are not permanent conditions.

Effect of Government Redistribution

The income data in the table in **Figure 18.1** include wages, salaries, dividends, and interest. They also include all cash transfer payments such as Social Security, unemployment compensation benefits, and welfare assistance to needy households. The data are before-tax data and therefore do not take into account the effects of personal income and payroll (Social Security) taxes that are levied directly on income receivers. Nor do they include government-provided in-kind or **noncash transfers,** which provide specific goods or services rather than cash. Noncash transfers include Medicare, Medicaid, housing subsidies, subsidized school lunches, and food stamps. Such transfers are "income-like" because they enable recipients to "purchase" goods and services.

noncash transfer
A government transfer payment in the form of goods and services rather than money, for example, food stamps, housing assistance, and job training; also called *in-kind transfer.*

---

[3] T.A. Hirschl and M.R. Rank, "The Life Course Dynamics of Affluence," 2015. PLoS ONE. 10(1): e0116370. https://doi.org/10.1371/journal.pone.0116370.

[4] M.R. Rank and T.A. Hirschl, "The Likelihood of Experiencing Relative Poverty over the Life Course," 2015. PLoS ONE. 10(7): e0133513. https://doi.org/10.1371/journal.pone.0133513.

[5] Ibid.

One economic function of government is to redistribute income, if society so desires. **Figure 18.2** and its table reveal that the U.S. government significantly redistributes income from higher- to lower-income households through taxes and transfers. Note that the U.S. distribution of household income before taxes and transfers are taken into account (dark red Lorenz curve) is substantially less equal than the distribution after taxes and transfers (light red Lorenz curve). Without government redistribution, the lowest 20 percent of households in 2015 would have received only 3.7 percent of total income. *With* redistribution, they received 7.3 percent, about twice as much.[6]

FIGURE 18.2

The impact of taxes and transfers on U.S. income inequality. The distribution of income is significantly more equal after taxes and transfers are taken into account than before. Transfers account for most of the lessening of inequality and provide most of the income received by the lowest quintile of households.

| | Percentage of Total Income Received, 2015 | |
| | (1) | (2) |
Quintile	Before Taxes and Transfers	After Taxes and Transfers
Lowest 20 percent	3.7	7.3
Second 20 percent	8.7	11.0
Third 20 percent	13.6	14.7
Fourth 20 percent	20.3	20.3
Highest 20 percent	55.0	48.3

Source: Congressional Budget Office.

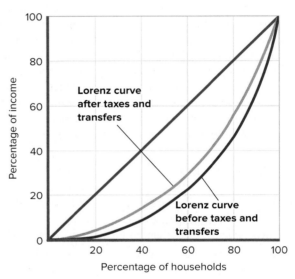

In fact, nearly all the reduction in income inequality is attributable to transfer payments. Together with job opportunities, transfer payments have been the most important means of alleviating poverty in the United States.

Causes of Income Inequality

There are several causes of income inequality in the United States. In general, the market system is permissive of a high degree of income inequality because it rewards individuals on the basis of the contributions that they make, or the resources that they own, in producing society's output.

More specifically, the factors that contribute to income inequality are the following.

Ability

People have different mental and physical abilities.

---

[6] The "before" data in this table differ from the data in the table in Figure 18.1 because the latter include cash transfers. Also, the data in Figure 18.2 are based on a broader concept of income than the data in Figure 18.1.

Some people have a natural ability to quickly learn skills that require strong mental focus, while others have inherited the strength and coordination required for more physically demanding jobs. There are people who are naturally talented in the arts, and others who struggle with cognitive disabilities that hinder their capacity to earn income. These differences in abilities as a whole are a contributing factor to income inequality.

Education and Training

Ability alone rarely produces high income; people must develop and refine their capabilities through education and training. Individuals differ significantly in the amount of education and training they obtain and thus in their capacity to earn income. Such differences may be a matter of choice: For instance, Chin enters the labor force after graduating from high school, while Rodriguez takes a job only after earning a college degree. Other differences may be involuntary: Chin and her parents may simply be unable to finance a college education.

People also receive varying degrees of on-the-job training, which contributes to income inequality. Some workers learn valuable new skills each year on the job and therefore experience significant income growth over time; others receive little or no on-the-job training and earn no more at age 50 than they did at age 30. Moreover, firms tend to select for advanced on-the-job training the workers who have the most formal education. That added training magnifies the education-based income differences between less-educated and better-educated individuals.

Discrimination

Discrimination in education, hiring, training, and promotion undoubtedly causes some income inequality. If discrimination confines certain racial, ethnic, or gender groups to lower-pay occupations, the supply of labor in those occupations will increase relative to demand, and hourly wages and income in those lower-pay jobs will decline. Conversely, labor supply will be artificially reduced in the higher-pay occupations populated by "preferred" workers, raising their wage rates and income. In this way, discrimination can add to income inequality. In fact, economists cannot account for all racial, ethnic, and gender differences in work earnings on the basis of differences in years of education, quality of education, occupations, and annual hours of work. Many economists attribute the unexplained residual to discrimination.

Economists, however, do not see discrimination by race, gender, and ethnicity as a dominant factor explaining income inequality. The income distributions *within* racial or ethnic groups that historically have been targets of discrimination—for example, African Americans—are similar to the income distribution for whites. Other factors besides discrimination are obviously at work, too.

Preferences and Risks

Incomes also differ because of differences in preferences for market work relative to leisure, market work relative to work in the household, and types of occupations. People who choose to stay home with children, work part-time, or retire early usually have less income than those who make the opposite choices. Those who are willing to take arduous, unpleasant jobs (e.g., underground mining or heavy construction), to work long hours with great intensity, or to "moonlight" tend to earn more.

Individuals also differ in their willingness to assume risk. We refer here not only to the race-car driver or the professional boxer but also to the entrepreneur. Although many entrepreneurs fail, many of those who develop successful new products or services realize very substantial incomes. That contributes to income inequality.

Unequal Distribution of Wealth

Income is a *flow;* it represents a stream of wage and salary earnings, along with rent, interest, and profits, as depicted in **Chapter 2**'s circular flow diagram. In contrast, wealth is a *stock,* reflecting at a particular moment the financial and real assets an individual has accumulated over time. A retired person may have very little income and yet own a home, mutual fund shares, and a pension plan that add up to considerable wealth. A new college graduate may be earning a substantial income as an accountant, middle manager, or engineer but has yet to accumulate significant wealth.

The ownership of wealth in the United States is more unequal than the distribution of income. This wealth inequality leads to inequality in rent, interest, and dividends, which in turn contributes to income inequality. Those who own more machinery, real estate, farmland, stocks, and bonds and who have more money in savings accounts receive greater income from that ownership than people with less or no wealth.

Market Power

The ability to "rig the market" in one's own favor also contributes to income inequality. For example, in *resource* markets, certain unions and professional groups have adopted policies that limit the supply of their services, thereby boosting the incomes of those "on the inside." Also, legislation that requires occupational licensing for, say, doctors, dentists, and lawyers can bestow market power that favors the licensed groups. In *product* markets, "rigging the market" means gaining or enhancing monopoly power, which results in greater profit and thus greater income to the firms' owners.

Luck, Connections, and Misfortune

Other forces also play a role in producing income inequality. Luck and "being in the right place at the right time" have helped individuals stumble into fortunes. Discovering oil on a ranch, owning land along a major freeway interchange, and hiring the right press agent have accounted for some high incomes. Personal contacts and political connections are other potential routes to attaining high income.

In contrast, economic misfortunes, such as prolonged illness, serious accident, death of the family's primary wage-earner, or unemployment, may plunge a household into the low range of income. The burden of such misfortune is borne very unevenly by the population and thus contributes to income inequality.

Income inequality of the magnitude we have described is not exclusively an American phenomenon. **Global Snapshot 18.1** compares income inequality in the United States (here by individuals, not by households) with that in several other nations. Income inequality tends to be greatest in South American nations, where land and capital resources are highly concentrated in the hands of a relatively small number of wealthy families.

GLOBAL SNAPSHOT 18.1

Percentage of Total Income Received by the Top One-Tenth of Income Receivers, Selected Nations

The share of income going to the highest 10 percent of income receivers varies widely among nations.

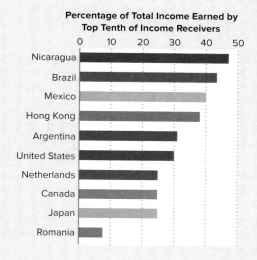

Source: *The World Factbook,* Central Intelligence Agency.

Income Inequality over Time

Over a period of years, economic growth has raised incomes in the United States: In *absolute* dollar amounts, the entire distribution of income has been moving upward. But incomes may move up in *absolute* terms while leaving the *relative* distribution of income less equal, more equal, or unchanged. **Table 18.2** shows how the distribution of household income has changed since 1980. This income is "before tax" and includes cash transfers but not noncash transfers.

TABLE 18.2

Percentage of Total Before-Tax Income Received by Each One-Fifth and by the Top 5 percent of Households, Selected Years*

Quintile	1980	1985	1990	1995	2000	2005	2010	2015
Lowest 20%	4.3	4.0	3.7	3.6	3.4	3.4	3.3	3.1
Second 20%	10.3	9.7	9.1	8.9	8.6	8.6	8.5	8.2
Third 20%	16.9	16.3	15.2	14.8	14.6	14.6	14.6	14.3
Fourth 20%	24.9	24.0	23.3	23.0	23.0	23.0	23.4	23.2
Highest 20%	43.7	46.6	48.7	49.8	50.4	50.4	50.3	51.1
Total	100.0	100.0	100.0	100.0	100.0	100.0	100.0	100.0
Top 5%	15.8	17.0	18.6	21.0	22.1	22.2	22.3	22.1

*Numbers may not add to 100 percent due to rounding.

Source: Income Data Tables. Bureau of the Census, 2018.

Rising Income Inequality since 1980

It is clear from **Table 18.2** that the distribution of income by quintiles has become more unequal since 1980. In 2015, the lowest 20 percent of households received 3.1 percent of total before-tax income, compared with 4.3 in 1980. Meanwhile, the income share received by the highest 20 percent rose from 43.7 in 1980 to 51.1 percent in 2015. The percentage of income received by the top 5 percent of households rose significantly over the 1980–2015 period.

Causes of Growing Inequality

Economists suggest several major explanations for the increase in U.S. income inequality since 1980.

Greater Demand for Highly Skilled Workers Perhaps the most significant contributor to the growing income inequality has been increasing demand for workers who are highly skilled and well educated. Moreover, several industries requiring highly skilled workers have either recently emerged or expanded greatly, such as the computer software, business consulting, biotechnology, health care, and Internet industries. Because highly skilled workers remain relatively scarce, their wages have been bid up. Consequently, the wage differences between them and less-skilled workers have increased.

The rising demand for skill also has shown up in rapidly rising pay for chief executive officers (CEOs), sizable increases in income from stock options, substantial increases in income for professional athletes and entertainers, and huge fortunes for successful entrepreneurs. This growth of "superstar" pay also has contributed to rising income inequality.

Demographic Changes The entrance of large numbers of less-experienced and less-skilled "baby boomers" into the labor force during the 1970s and 1980s may have contributed to greater income inequality in those two decades. Because younger workers tend to earn less income than older workers, their growing numbers contributed to income inequality. There also has been a growing tendency for men and women with high earnings potential to marry each other, thus increasing household income among the highest income quintiles. Finally, the number of households headed by single or divorced women has increased greatly. That trend has increased income inequality because such households lack a second major wage earner and also because the poverty rate for female-headed households is relatively high.

International Trade, Immigration, and Decline in Unionism Other factors are probably at work as well. Stronger international competition from imports has reduced the demand for and employment of less-skilled (but highly paid) workers in such industries as the automobile and steel industries. The decline in such jobs has reduced the average wage for less-skilled workers. It also has swelled the ranks of workers in already low-paying industries, placing further downward pressure on wages there.

Similarly, the transfer of jobs to lower-wage workers in developing countries has exerted downward wage pressure on less-skilled workers in the United States. Also, an upsurge in immigration of unskilled workers has increased the number of low-income households in the United States. Finally, the decline in unionism in the United States has undoubtedly contributed to wage inequality because unions tend to equalize pay within firms and industries.

Two cautions: First, when we note growing income inequality, we are not saying that the "rich are getting richer and the poor are getting poorer" in terms of absolute income. Both the rich and the poor are experiencing rises in real income. Rather, what has happened is that, while incomes have risen in all quintiles, income growth has been fastest in the top quintile. Second, increased income inequality is not solely a U.S. phenomenon. The recent rise of inequality also has occurred in several other industrially advanced nations.

The Lorenz curve can be used to contrast the distribution of income at different points in time. If we plotted **Table 18.2**'s data as Lorenz curves, we would find that the curve shifted away from the diagonal between 1980 and 2015. The Gini ratio rose from 0.403 in 1980 to 0.479 in 2015.

PHOTO OP

The Rich and the Poor in America

Wide disparities of income and wealth exist in the United States.

Franck Boston/123RF

Denis Tangney Jr/Getty Images

Equality versus Efficiency

The main policy issue concerning income inequality is how much is necessary and justified. While there is no general agreement on the justifiable amount, we can gain insight by exploring the economic cases for and against greater equality.

The Case for Equality: Maximizing Total Utility

The basic argument for an equal distribution of income is that income equality maximizes the total consumer satisfaction (utility) from any particular level of output and income. The rationale for this argument is shown in **Figure 18.3**, in which we assume that the money incomes of two individuals, Anderson and Brooks, are subject to the **law of diminishing marginal utility**. In any time period, income receivers spend the first dollars received on the products they value most—products whose marginal utility is high. As their most-pressing wants become satisfied, consumers then spend additional dollars of income on less-important, lower-marginal-utility goods. The identical diminishing curves (MU_A and MU_B) reflect the assumption that Anderson and Brooks have the same capacity to derive utility from income.

law of diminishing marginal utility
The principle that as a consumer increases the consumption of a good or service, the marginal utility obtained from each additional unit of the good or service decreases.

FIGURE 18.3

The utility-maximizing distribution of income. With identical marginal-utility-of-income curves MU$_A$ and MU$_B$, Anderson and Brooks will maximize their combined utility when any amount of income (say, $10,000) is equally distributed. If income is unequally distributed (say, $2,500 to Anderson and $7,500 to Brooks), the marginal utility derived from the last dollar will be greater for Anderson than for Brooks, and a redistribution toward equality will result in a net increase in total utility. The utility gained by equalizing income at $5,000 each, shown by the blue area below curve MU$_A$ in panel (a), exceeds the utility lost, indicated by the red area below curve MU$_B$ in (b).

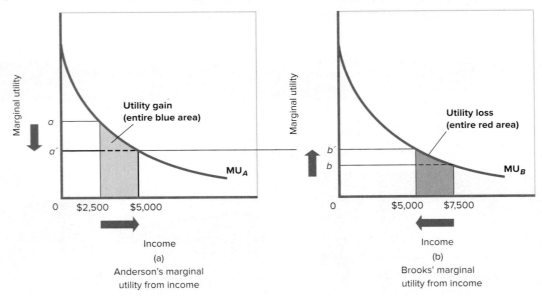

(a)
Anderson's marginal
utility from income

(b)
Brooks' marginal
utility from income

Suppose that there is $10,000 worth of income (output) to be distributed between Anderson and Brooks. According to proponents of income equality, the optimal distribution is an equal distribution, which causes the marginal utility of the last dollar spent to be the same for both persons.

Now assume that the $10,000 of income initially is distributed unequally, with Anderson getting $2,500 and Brooks $7,500. The marginal utility, a, from the last dollar received by Anderson is high, while the marginal utility, b, from Brooks' last dollar of income is low. If a single dollar of income is shifted from Brooks to Anderson—that is, toward greater equality—then Anderson's utility increases by a and Brooks' utility decreases by b. The combined utility then increases by a minus b (Anderson's large gain minus Brooks' small loss). The transfer of a second dollar from Brooks to Anderson again increases their combined utility, this time by a slightly smaller amount. Continued transfer of dollars from Brooks to Anderson increases their combined utility until the income is evenly distributed and both receive $5,000. At that time, their marginal utilities from the last dollar of income are equal (at a' and b'), and any further income redistribution beyond the $2,500 already transferred would begin to create inequality and decrease their combined utility.

The area under the MU curve and to the left of the individual's particular level of income represents the total utility of that income. Therefore, as a result of the $2,500 transfer, Anderson has gained utility represented by the blue area below curve MU$_A$ and Brooks has lost utility represented by the red area below curve MU$_B$. The blue area is greater than the red area, so income equality yields greater combined total utility than income inequality does.

The Case for Inequality: Incentives and Efficiency

Although the logic of the argument for equality might seem solid, critics of income equality say that income equality is both unfair and unwise. They argue that income inequality largely reflects rewards to individuals for supplying their talents and resources to the economy. They conclude that it is not fair to take some of Brooks' income and give it to Anderson. Further, critics note that the proponents of income equality falsely assume that there is some fixed amount of output produced and therefore income to be distributed. These critics argue that the way in which income is distributed is an important determinant of the amount of output or income that is produced and is available for distribution.

Refer again to **Figure 18.3** and assume that Anderson earns $2,500 and Brooks earns $7,500. In moving toward equality, society (the government) must tax away some of Brooks' income and transfer it to Anderson. This tax and transfer process diminishes the income rewards of high-income Brooks and raises the income rewards of low-income Anderson; in so doing, it reduces the incentives of both to earn high incomes. Why should high-income Brooks work hard, save and invest, or undertake entrepreneurial risks when taxation will reduce the rewards from such activities? And why should low-income Anderson be motivated to increase his income through market activities when the government stands ready to transfer income to him? Taxes reduce the rewards from increased productive effort; redistribution through transfers is a reward for diminished effort.

In the extreme, imagine a situation in which the government levies a 100 percent tax on income and distributes the tax revenue equally to its citizenry. Why would anyone work at all? Why would anyone assume business risk? Or why would anyone save (forgo current consumption) in order to invest? The economic incentives to "get ahead" will have been removed, greatly reducing society's total production and income.

The Equality-Efficiency Trade-Off

At the essence of the income equality-inequality debate is a fundamental trade-off between equality and efficiency. In this **equality-efficiency trade-off,** greater income equality (achieved through redistribution of income) comes at the opportunity cost of reduced production and income. And greater production and income (through reduced redistribution) come at the expense of less equality of income. The trade-off obligates society to choose how much redistribution it wants, in view of the costs. If society decides it wants to redistribute income, it needs to determine methods that minimize the adverse effects on fairness, incentives, productivity, and economic efficiency.

equality-efficiency trade-off
The decrease in economic efficiency that may accompany a decrease in income inequality; the presumption that some income inequality is required to achieve economic efficiency.

 ILLUSTRATING THE IDEA

Slicing the Pizza

The equality-efficiency trade-off might better be understood through an analogy. Assume that society's income is a huge pizza, baked year after year, *with the sizes of the pieces going to people on the basis of their contribution to making it.* Now suppose that, for fairness reasons, society decides some people are getting pieces that are too large and others are getting pieces too small. But when society redistributes the pizza to make the sizes more equal, they discover the result is a smaller pizza than before. Why participate in making the pizza if you get a decent-size piece without contributing?

The shrinkage of the pizza represents the efficiency loss—the loss of output and income—caused by the harmful effects of the redistribution on incentives to work, to save and invest, and to accept entrepreneurial risk. The shrinkage also reflects the resources that society must divert to the bureaucracies that administer the redistribution system.

How much pizza shrinkage will society accept while continuing to agree to the redistribution? If redistributing pizza to make it less unequal reduces the size of the pizza, what amount of pizza loss will society tolerate? Is a loss of 10 percent acceptable? 25 percent? 75 percent? This is the basic question in any debate over the ideal size of a nation's income redistribution program.

> QUESTION:
>
> Why might "equality of opportunity" be a more realistic and efficient goal than "equality of income outcome"?

The Economics of Poverty

We now turn from the broader issue of income distribution to the more specific issue of very low income, or poverty. A society with a high degree of income inequality can have a high, moderate, or low amount of poverty. But what exactly is poverty?

Definition of Poverty

Poverty is a condition in which a person or family does not have the means to satisfy basic needs for food, clothing, shelter, and transportation. The means include currently earned income, transfer payments, past savings, and property owned. The basic needs have many determinants, including family size and the health and age of its members.

poverty rate
The percentage of the population with incomes below the official poverty income levels that are established by the federal government.

The federal government has established minimum income thresholds below which a person or a family is "in poverty." In 2017, an unattached individual receiving less than $12,488 per year was said to be living in poverty. For a family of 4, the poverty line was $24,858; for a family of 6, it was $32,753. Based on these thresholds, in 2017 about 39.7 million Americans lived in poverty. In 2017, the **poverty rate**—the percentage of the population living in poverty—was 12.3 percent.

Incidence of Poverty

The poor are heterogeneous: They can be found in all parts of the nation; they are whites and nonwhites, rural and urban, young and old. But as **Figure 18.4** indicates, poverty is far from randomly distributed. For example, the poverty rates for African Americans and Hispanics are above the national average, while the rates for whites and Asians are below the average.

Figure 18.4 shows that female-headed households (no husband present), African Americans, foreign-born noncitizens, Hispanics, and children under 18 years of age have very high incidences of poverty. Marriage and full-time, year-round work are associated with low poverty rates, and, because of the Social Security system, the incidence of poverty among the elderly is less than that for the population as a whole.

FIGURE 18.4

Poverty rates among selected population groups, 2017. Poverty is disproportionately borne by African Americans, Hispanics, children, foreign-born residents who are not citizens, and families headed by women. People who are employed full-time or are married tend to have low poverty rates.

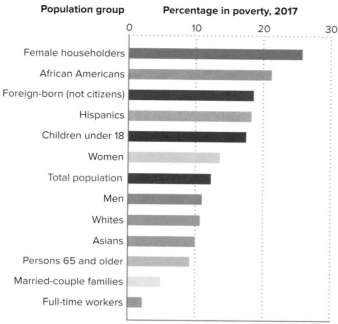

Source: U.S. Census Bureau.

The high poverty rate for children is especially disturbing because poverty tends to be cyclical in nature. Poor children are at greater risk for a range of long-term problems, including poor health and inadequate education, crime, drug use, and teenage pregnancy. Many of today's impoverished children will reach adulthood unhealthy and illiterate and unable to earn above-poverty incomes.

As many as half of people in poverty are poor for only one or two years before climbing out of poverty. But poverty is much more long-lasting among some groups than among others. In particular, African American and Hispanic families, families headed by women, persons with little education and few labor market skills, and people who struggle with addiction or mental illness are more likely than others to remain in poverty. Also, long-lasting poverty is heavily present in economically depressed areas of cities, parts of the Deep South, and some Native American reservations.

Measurement Issues

Poverty data should be interpreted cautiously. The official income thresholds for defining poverty are necessarily arbitrary and therefore may inadequately measure the true extent of poverty in the United States.

Some observers say that the high cost of living in major metropolitan areas means that the official poverty thresholds exclude millions of families whose income is slightly above the poverty level but clearly inadequate to meet basic needs for food, housing, and medical care. These observers use city-by-city studies on "minimal income needs" to argue that poverty in the United States is much more widespread than officially measured and reported.

social insurance programs
Programs that replace a portion of the earnings lost when people retire or are temporarily unemployed, that are financed by payroll taxes, and that are viewed as earned rights (rather than charity).

In contrast, some economists point out that using only income to measure poverty understates the standard of living of many of the people who are officially poor. When individual, household, or family *consumption* is considered rather than family *income,* some of the poverty in the United States disappears. Some low-income families maintain their consumption by drawing down past savings, borrowing against future income, or selling homes. Moreover, many poor households receive substantial noncash benefits, such as food stamps and rent subsidies, that boost their living standards. Such "in-kind" benefits are not included in determining official poverty status. One study found that if in-kind benefits were counted as a form of income, poverty rates would be about 20 percent lower.

The U.S. Income-Maintenance System

public assistance programs
Government programs that pay benefits to those who are unable to earn income (because of permanent disabilities or because they have very low income and dependent children); financed by general tax revenues and viewed as public charity (rather than earned rights).

Helping those who have very low income is a widely accepted goal of public policy. A wide array of antipoverty programs, including education and training programs, subsidized employment, minimum-wage laws, and antidiscrimination policies, are designed to increase the earnings of the poor. In addition, a number of income-maintenance programs have been devised to reduce poverty, the most important of which are listed in **Table 18.3**. These programs involve large expenditures and numerous beneficiaries.

TABLE 18.3
Characteristics of Major Income-Maintenance Programs

Program	Basis of Eligibility	Source of Funds	Form of Aid	Expenditures,* Billions	Beneficiaries, Millions
Social Insurance Programs					
Social Security	Age, disability, or death of parent or spouse; lifetime work earnings	Federal payroll tax on employers and employees	Cash	$911	61
Medicare	Age or disability	Federal payroll tax on employers and employees	Subsidized health insurance	$706	60
Unemployment compensation	Unemployment	State and federal payroll taxes on employers	Cash	$28	5
Public Assistance Programs					
Supplemental Security Income (SSI)	Age or disability; income	Federal revenues	Cash	$55	8
Temporary Assistance for Needy Families (TANF)	Certain families with children; income	Federal-state-local revenues	Cash and services	$14	2
Supplemental Nutrition Assistance Program (SNAP)	Income	Federal revenues	Cash via EBT cards	$61	40
Medicaid	Persons eligible for TANF or SSI and medically indigent	Federal-state-local revenues	Subsidized medical services	$582	63
Earned-income tax credit (EITC)	Low-wage working families	Federal revenues	Refundable tax credit, cash	$63	25

*Expenditures by federal, state, and local governments; excludes administrative expenses.

Source: Social Security Administration, Annual Statistical Supplement, 2017, www.socialsecurity.gov; U.S. Department of Agriculture, www.fns.usda.gov; Internal Revenue Service, www.irs.gov/taxstats; and other government sources. Latest data.

The U.S. income-maintenance system consists of two kinds of programs: (1) social insurance and (2) public assistance or "welfare." Both are known as **entitlement programs** because all eligible persons are legally entitled to receive the benefits set forth in the programs.

Social Insurance Programs

Social insurance programs partially replace earnings that have been lost due to retirement, disability, or temporary unemployment; they also provide health insurance for the elderly. The main social insurance programs are Social Security, unemployment compensation, and Medicare. Benefits are viewed as earned rights and do not carry the stigma of public charity. These programs are financed primarily out of federal payroll taxes. In these programs, the entire population shares the risk of an individual's losing income because of retirement, unemployment, disability, or illness. Workers (and employers) pay a part of their wages to the government while they are working. The workers are then entitled to benefits when they retire or face specified misfortunes.

Social Security and Medicare The major social insurance program known as **Social Security** replaces earnings lost when workers retire, become disabled, or die. This gigantic program ($911 billion in 2016) is financed by compulsory payroll taxes levied on both employers and employees. The retirement age at which a worker can collect full benefits was originally 65 years of age, but it is being gradually increased to age 67. Workers currently may retire at age 66 years and two months and receive full retirement benefits or retire early at age 62 with reduced benefits. When a worker dies, benefits accrue to their family survivors. Special provisions provide benefits for disabled workers.

Social Security covers over 90 percent of the workforce; some 61 million people receive Social Security benefits averaging about $1,360 per month. In 2019, those benefits were financed with a combined Social Security and Medicare payroll tax of 15.3 percent, with the worker and the employer each paying 7.65 percent on the worker's first $132,900 of earnings. The 7.65 percent taxes comprise 6.2 percent for Social Security and 1.45 percent for Medicare. Self-employed workers pay a tax of 15.3 percent.

Medicare provides hospital insurance to those 65 or older and people who are disabled. It is financed by payroll taxes on employers and employees. This 2.9 percent tax is paid on all work income, not just on the first $132,900. Medicare also makes available supplementary low-cost insurance programs that help pay for doctor visits and prescription drugs. In 2016, some 60 million people received Medicare benefits. The benefits paid to recipients totaled $306 billion.

The number of retirees drawing Social Security and Medicare benefits is rapidly rising relative to the number of workers paying payroll taxes. As a result, Social Security and Medicare face serious long-term funding problems. These fiscal imbalances have spawned calls to reform the programs.

Unemployment Compensation All 50 states sponsor unemployment insurance programs called **unemployment compensation,** a federal-state program that makes income available to unemployed workers. This insurance is financed by a relatively small payroll tax, paid by employers, that varies by state and by the size of the firm's payroll. Any insured worker who becomes unemployed can, after a short waiting period, become eligible for benefits payments. The size of the payments and the number of weeks they are made available varies considerably from state to state. Generally, benefits approximate 33 percent of a worker's wages up to a certain maximum weekly payment. In 2018, benefits averaged about $354 weekly.

entitlement programs
Government programs such as social insurance, SNAP, Medicare, and Medicaid that guarantee particular levels of transfer payments or non-cash benefits to all who fit the programs' criteria.

Social Security
The federal program, financed by compulsory payroll taxes, that partially replaces earnings lost when workers retire, become disabled, or die.

Medicare
A federal program that is financed by payroll taxes and provides for (1) compulsory hospital insurance for senior citizens, (2) low-cost voluntary insurance to help older Americans pay physicians' fees, and (3) subsidized insurance to buy prescription drugs.

unemployment compensation
The social insurance program that in the United States is financed by state payroll taxes on employers and makes income available to workers who become unemployed and are unable to find jobs.

The number of beneficiaries and the level of total disbursements vary with economic conditions. Typically, unemployment compensation payments last a maximum of 26 weeks. But during recessions—when unemployment rates soar—Congress often extends the benefits for additional weeks.

Unemployment benefits were temporarily expanded in both amount and duration during the COVID-19 pandemic. Under the CARES Act, unemployed workers received an additional $600 in benefits for each week of unemployment from April through July of 2020, as well as an additional 13 weeks of unemployment benefits for those who had exhausted eligibility. A second round of extended benefits was implemented in December 2020, with unemployed workers provided an additional $300 per week through mid-March 2021. President Biden's "American Rescue Plan," passed in March 2021, extended the $300 per week additional benefit through September 6, 2021.

Public Assistance Programs

Public assistance programs (welfare) provide benefits for those who are unable to earn income because of permanent disabling conditions or have no or very low income and also have dependent children. These programs are financed out of general tax revenues and are regarded as public charity. They include "means tests," that require individuals and families to demonstrate low incomes in order to qualify for aid. The federal government finances about two-thirds of the welfare program expenditures, and states pay for the rest.

Supplemental Security Income (SSI)
A federally financed and administered program that provides a uniform nationwide minimum income for the aged, blind, and disabled who do not qualify for benefits under Social Security in the United States.

Many needy persons who do not qualify for social insurance programs are assisted through the federal government's **Supplemental Security Income (SSI)** program. This is a federal program (financed by general tax revenues) that provides a uniform, nationwide minimum income for people who are aged, blind, and disabled, are unable to work, and do not qualify for Social Security aid. In 2016, the average monthly payment was $735 for individuals and $1,103 for couples with both people eligible. More than half the states provide additional income supplements for people who are aged, blind, and disabled.

Temporary Assistance for Needy Families (TANF)
A state-administered and partly federally funded program in the United States that provides financial aid to poor families; the basic welfare program for low-income families in the United States; contains time limits and work requirements.

Temporary Assistance for Needy Families (TANF) is the basic welfare program for families with low incomes in the United States. The program is financed through general federal tax revenues and consists of lump-sum payments of federal money to states to operate their own welfare and work programs. These lump-sum payments are called TANF funds, and in 2016 about 2.3 million people (including children) received $14 billion of TANF assistance, collectively.

In 1996, TANF replaced the six-decade-old Aid for Families with Dependent Children (AFDC) program. Unlike that welfare program, TANF established work requirements and placed limits on the length of time a family can receive welfare payments. Specifically, the TANF program:

- Set a lifetime limit of five years on receiving TANF benefits and required able-bodied adults to work after receiving assistance for two years.
- Ended food-stamp eligibility for able-bodied persons age 18 to 50 (with no dependent children) who are not working or are engaged in job-training programs.
- Tightened the definition of "disabled children" as it applies to the eligibility of low-income families regarding SSI assistance.
- Established a five-year waiting period on public assistance for new legal immigrants who have not become citizens.

In 1996, about 12.6 million people, or about 4.8 percent of the population, were welfare recipients. By 2000, the number of welfare recipients had fallen to 2.7 million households, or about 2.6 percent of the population. That decline was attributed by proponents of TANF as proof that it had helped people transition from welfare into work. Others countered that the decline was mostly due to the economic boom that had taken place during the late 1990s. The severe 2007–2008 recession caused welfare rolls to swell again. In 2017, 12.3 million households, or about 12.3 percent of U.S. households, were welfare recipients.

The **Supplemental Nutrition Assistance Program (SNAP)** was formerly known as the food-stamp program. SNAP is a federal program (financed through general tax revenues) designed to provide all eligible Americans with low incomes with a nutritionally adequate diet. Under the program, eligible households receive monthly deposits of spendable electronic money on specialized debit cards known as Electronic Benefit Transfer (EBT) cards. The EBT cards are designed so that the deposits can be spent only on food. The amount deposited onto a family's EBT card varies inversely with the family's earned income; the poorer the family, the more they receive.

Medicaid is a federal program (financed through general tax revenues) that provides medical benefits to people covered by the SSI and TANF (basic welfare) programs.

The **earned-income tax credit (EITC)** is a federal wage subsidy provided to low-income wage earners to supplement their families' incomes and encourage work. It is available for working families with low incomes, with or without children. The credit reduces the federal income taxes that such families owe or provides them with cash payments if the credit exceeds their tax liabilities. The purpose of the credit is to offset Social Security taxes paid by low-wage earners and thus keep the federal government from "taxing families into poverty." But the EITC can exceed the amount of Social Security taxes, in some cases by as much as $2 per hour for the lowest-paid workers with families. Under the program, many people owe no income tax and receive direct checks from the federal government once a year. According to the Internal Revenue Service, 25 million taxpayers received $63 billion in payments from the EITC in 2016.

Several other welfare programs are not listed in **Table 18.3**. Some provide help in the form of noncash transfers. Head Start provides education, nutrition, and social services to economically disadvantaged three- and four-year-olds. Housing assistance in the form of rent subsidies and funds for construction is available to families with low incomes. Pell Grants provide assistance to college students who are from families with low incomes. Low-income home energy assistance provides help with home heating bills. Other programs—such as veteran's assistance and black lung benefits—provide cash assistance to those eligible.

Supplemental Nutrition Assistance Program (SNAP)
A government program that provides food money to low-income recipients by depositing electronic money onto special debit cards.

Medicaid
A federal program that helps finance the medical expenses of individuals covered by the Supplemental Security Income (SSI) and Temporary Assistance for Needy Families (TANF) programs.

earned-income tax credit (EITC)
A refundable federal tax credit for low-income working people designed to reduce poverty and encourage labor-force participation.

PHOTO OP

Social Insurance versus Public Assistance Programs

Beneficiaries of social insurance programs such as Social Security have typically paid for at least a portion of that insurance through payroll taxes. Food stamps and other public assistance are funded from general tax revenue and are generally seen as public charity.

Kreinick/123RF

Hero Images/Getty Images

 APPLYING THE ANALYSIS

Universal Basic Income

The idea of a universal basic income, or UBI, is not new. President Nixon wanted to implement one back in the late 1960s but could not muster the votes in Congress. UBI has become a hot topic again in recent years. Specific plans vary, but the basic idea is simple: the government would guarantee a minimum monthly income to every citizen, with the money arriving by automatic deposits into recipients' bank accounts.

Advocates assert a wide variety of benefits, including a reduction in poverty, a reduction in income inequality, and a reduction in income insecurity—the negative effects that come with the fear of becoming unable to support oneself financially. Some advocates urge replacing most or all of our existing government welfare and income maintenance programs with UBI. They argue that it would cost much less for the government to administer a single monthly UBI payment than to administer the large and sometimes confusing array of payment and reimbursement systems currently used to deliver welfare and public assistance. Instead of tax credits, food stamps, disability payments, housing subsidies, unemployment benefits, and cash payments made through EBT cards, the government would only have to administer a single monthly UBI payment.

Detractors cite high costs, unfairness, and unintended consequences as reasons for opposition. With respect to costs, they point out that sending every American a check for $1,000 each month would cost $3.96 trillion, substantially more than the $3.4 trillion that the federal government currently collects each year in taxes. They argue that UBI is politically impossible because voters would not accept the massive tax increase that would be necessary to fund UBI.

With respect to unfairness, opponents point out that it would not make sense to send everyone a UBI check. Most people are employed. Over 60 percent of Americans own homes. Why should financially secure people get a government welfare check each month?

Finally, opponents of UBI argue that giving everybody a guaranteed $1,000 per month would reduce the incentive to work. Many people, they assert, would either work fewer hours or not work at all. Thus, they say, UBI would encourage laziness and freeloading off the people that continue to work and pay taxes.

The evidence that we have with respect to UBI is limited. Several trials involving no more than a few thousand people are under way in a dozen countries. None of them gives money to better-off people. Instead, benefits are being targeted at people with financial need, such as low-income mothers and poor rural villagers. The results will give evidence about whether UBI works and, if so, under what circumstances and for what sorts of beneficiaries.

UBI has attracted supporters from across the political spectrum, including Martin Luther King; economics Nobel laureates Milton Friedman, Friedrich Hayek, and Angus Deaton; liberal Senator Daniel Patrick Moynihan; union leader Andy Stern; and a host of prominent business people, including Elon Musk, Sam Altman, and Mark Zuckerberg.

The experiments under way will help determine whether their enthusiasm is warranted. But even if the experiments indicate net benefits, there still will be a large political fight over how much, for whom, and how to pay for it. A similar political fight doomed President Nixon's attempt at UBI five decades ago.

QUESTION:

Do you think the UBI would increase, decrease, or leave unchanged the total amount of income in the economy? Explain your reasoning.

Summary

LO18.1 Explain how income inequality in the United States is measured and described.

The distribution of income in the United States reflects considerable inequality. The richest 20 percent of families receive 51.5 percent of total income, while the poorest 20 percent receive 3.1 percent.

The Lorenz curve shows the percentage of total income received by each percentage of households. The extent of the gap between the Lorenz curve and a line of total equality illustrates the degree of income inequality.

The Gini ratio measures the overall dispersion of the income distribution. The Gini ratio ranges from 0 to 1; higher ratios signify more income inequality.

LO18.2 Discuss the extent and sources of income inequality.

Recognizing that the positions of individual families in the distribution of income change over time and incorporating the effects of non cash transfers and taxes would reveal less income inequality than do standard annual census data. Government transfers (cash and noncash) greatly lessen the degree of income inequality; taxes also reduce inequality, but not nearly as much as transfers.

Causes of income inequality include differences in abilities, in education and training, and in job tastes, along with discrimination, inequality in the distribution of wealth, and unequal distribution of market power.

LO18.3 Demonstrate how income inequality has changed since 1980.

Census data show that income inequality has increased since 1980. The major cause of recent increases in income inequality is a rising demand for highly skilled workers, which has boosted their earnings significantly.

LO18.4 Debate the economic arguments for and against income inequality.

The basic argument for income equality is that it maximizes consumer satisfaction (total utility) from a particular level of total income. The main argument for income inequality is that it provides the incentives to work, invest, and assume risk and is necessary for the production of output, which, in turn, creates income that is then available for distribution.

LO18.5 Relate poverty to age, gender, and ethnicity characteristics.

Current statistics reveal that 12.3 percent of the U.S. population lives in poverty. Poverty rates are particularly high for female-headed families, young children, African Americans, and Hispanics.

LO18.6 Identify the major components of the U.S. income-maintenance program.

In the United States, the government's income-maintenance program currently consists of social insurance programs (Social Security, Medicare, and unemployment compensation) and public assistance programs (SSI, TANF, SNAP/food stamps, Medicaid, and earned-income tax credit).

Terms and Concepts

income inequality

Lorenz curve

Gini ratio

income mobility

noncash transfer

law of diminishing marginal utility

equality-efficiency trade-off

poverty rate

social insurance programs

public assistance programs

entitlement programs

Social Security

Medicare

unemployment compensation

Supplemental Security Income (SSI)

Temporary Assistance for Needy Families (TANF)

Supplemental Nutrition Assistance Program (SNAP)

Medicaid

earned-income tax credit (EITC)

Questions Mc Graw Hill connect

1. Use quintiles to briefly summarize the degree of income inequality in the United States. How and to what extent does government reduce income inequality? **(LO1)**

2. Assume that Al, Beth, Carol, David, and Ed receive incomes of $500, $250, $125, $75, and $50, respectively. Construct and interpret a Lorenz curve for this five-person economy. What percentages of total income are received by the richest quintile and by the poorest quintile? **(LO1)**

3. How does the Gini ratio relate to the Lorenz curve? Why can't the Gini ratio exceed 1? What is implied about the direction of income inequality if the Gini ratio declines from 0.42 to 0.35? How would one show that change of inequality in the Lorenz diagram? **(LO1)**

4. Why is the lifetime distribution of income more equal than the distribution in any specific year? **(LO2)**

5. Briefly discuss the major causes of income inequality. With respect to income inequality, is there any difference between inheriting property and maintaining a high IQ? Explain. **(LO2)**

6. What factors have contributed to increased income inequality since 1980? **(LO3)**

7. Should a nation's income be distributed to its members according to their contributions to the production of that total income or according to the members' needs? Should society attempt to equalize income or economic opportunities? Are the issues of equity and equality in the distribution of income synonymous? To what degree, if any, is income inequality equitable? **(LO4)**

8. Comment on or explain: **(LO4)**

a. Endowing everyone with equal income will make for very unequal enjoyment and satisfaction.

b. Equality is a "superior good"; the richer we become, the more of it we can afford.

c. The mob goes in search of bread, and the means it employs is generally to wreck the bakeries.

d. Some freedoms may be more important in the long run than freedom from want on the part of every individual.

e. Capitalism and democracy are really the most improbable mixture. Maybe that is why they need each other—to put some rationality into equality and some humanity into efficiency.

f. The incentives created by the attempt to bring about a more equal distribution of income are in conflict with the incentives needed to generate increased income.

9. How could the poverty rate fall while the number of people in poverty rises? Which group in each of the following pairs has the higher poverty rate: (a) children or people age 65 or over? (b) African Americans or foreign-born noncitizens? (c) Asians or Hispanics? **(LO5)**

10. What are the essential differences between social insurance and public assistance programs? Why is Medicare a social insurance program, whereas Medicaid is a public assistance program? Why is the earned-income tax credit considered to be a public assistance program? **(LO6)**

11. What are the main arguments for and against UBI? What is your personal opinion on the probable effects of UBI? **(LO6)**

Problems

1. In 2019, *Forbes* magazine listed Jeff Bezos, the founder of Amazon, as the richest person in the United States. His personal wealth was estimated to be $131 billion. Given that there were about 328 million people living in the United States that year, how much could each person have received if Bezos's wealth had been divided equally among the population of the United States? (*Hint:* A billion is a 1 followed by nine zeroes, while a million is a 1 followed by six zeroes.) **(LO1)**

2. following figure, the Lorenz curve for this two-person economy consists of two line segments. The first runs from the origin to point *a*, while the second runs from point *a* to point *b*. **(LO1)**

   a. Calculate the Gini ratio for this two-person economy using the geometric formulas for the area of a triangle (= ½ × base × height) and the area of a rectangle (= base × height). (*Hint:* The area under the line segment from point *a* to point *b* can be thought of as the sum of the area of a particular triangle and the area of a particular rectangle.)

   b. What would the Gini ratio be if the government taxed $20,000 away from Roger and gave it to Larry? (*Hint:* The figure will change.)

   c. Start again with Larry earning $20,000 per year and Roger earning $80,000 per year. What would the Gini ratio be if both their incomes doubled? How much has the Gini ratio changed from before the doubling in incomes to after the doubling in incomes?

3. In 2018, many unskilled workers in the United States earned the federal minimum wage of $7.25 per hour. By contrast, average earnings in 2018 were about $27 per hour, and certain highly skilled professionals, such as doctors and lawyers, earned $100 or more per hour. **(LO6)**

   a. If we assume that wage differences are caused solely by differences in productivity, how many times more productive was the average worker than a worker being paid the federal minimum wage? How many times more productive was a $100-per-hour lawyer compared to a worker earning minimum wage?

   b. Assume that there are 20 minimum-wage workers in the economy for each $100-per-hour lawyer. Also, assume that both lawyers and minimum-wage workers work the same number of hours per week. If everyone works 40 hours per week, how much does a $100-per-hour lawyer earn a week? How much does a minimum-wage worker earn in a week?

   c. Suppose that the government pairs each $100-per-hour lawyer with 20 nearby minimum-wage workers. If the government taxes 25 percent of each lawyer's income each week and distributes it equally among the 20 minimum-wage workers with whom each lawyer is paired, how much will each of those minimum-wage workers receive each week? If we divide by the number of hours worked each week, how much does each minimum-wage worker's weekly transfer amount to on an hourly basis?

   d. Suppose the government taxes each lawyer 100 percent before dividing the money equally among the 20 minimum-wage workers with whom each lawyer is paired. How much per week will each minimum-wage worker receive? And how much is that on an hourly basis?

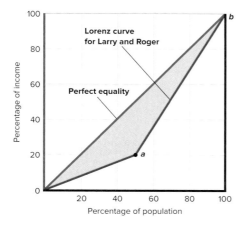

Appendix Tables

Relevant Economic Statistics, United States, 1970–1990

Relevant Economic Statistics, United States, 1991–2011

Relevant Economic Statistics, United States, 2012–2020

Relevant Economic Statistics, United States, 1970–1990

		1970	1971	1972	1973	1974	1975	1976	1977
1.	Gross domestic product (billions of dollars)	1,038.5	1,127.1	1,238.3	1,382.7	1,500.0	1,638.3	1,825.3	2,030.9
2.	Real gross domestic product (billions of 2005 dollars)	4,266.3	4,409.5	4,643.8	4,912.8	4,885.7	4,875.4	5,136.9	5,373.1
3.	Economic growth rate (percent change in real GDP)	0.2	3.4	5.3	5.8	−0.5	−0.2	5.3	4.6
4.	Consumption expenditures (billions of dollars)	648.5	701.9	770.6	852.4	933.4	1,034.4	1,151.9	1,278.6
5.	Gross private domestic investment (billions of dollars)	152.4	178.2	207.6	244.5	249.4	230.2	292.0	361.3
6.	Government purchases (billions of dollars)	233.8	246.5	263.5	281.7	317.9	357.7	383.0	414.1
7.	Rate of inflation (percent change in CPI)	5.7	4.4	3.2	6.2	11.0	9.1	5.8	6.5
8.	Money supply, M1	214.4	228.3	249.1	262.9	274.2	287.1	306.2	330.9
9.	Federal funds interest rate (%)	7.17	4.67	4.44	8.74	10.51	5.82	5.05	5.54
10.	Prime interest rate (%)	7.91	5.73	5.25	8.03	10.81	7.86	6.84	6.83
11.	Population (millions)	205.0	207.7	209.9	211.9	213.8	216.0	218.0	220.2
12.	Immigration (thousands)	373.3	370.5	384.7	400.1	394.9	386.2	398.6	462.3
13.	Labor force (millions)	82.8	84.4	87.0	89.4	91.9	93.8	96.2	99.0
14.	Employment (millions)	78.7	79.4	82.2	85.1	86.8	85.8	88.8	92.0
15.	Unemployment rate (%)	4.9	5.9	5.6	4.9	5.6	8.5	7.7	7.1
16.	Federal budget surplus (+) or deficit (−)	−2.8	−23.0	−23.4	−14.9	−6.1	−53.7	−73.7	−53.7
17.	Public debt (billions of dollars)	380.9	406.2	435.9	466.3	483.9	541.9	629.0	706.4
18.	Price of crude oil (dollars per barrel)	3.39	3.60	2.85	4.75	9.25	12.21	13.10	14.40
19.	Average hourly earnings, private nonagricultural industries (dollars)	3.63	3.90	4.14	4.43	4.73	4.73	5.06	5.44
20.	Average weekly hours, private nonagricultural industries	37.0	36.8	36.9	36.9	36.4	36.0	36.1	35.9
21.	Research and development expenditures (billions of dollars)	28.3	17.8	31.3	20.7	36.4	23.5	43.1	28.9
22.	Net farm income (billions of dollars)	14.4	15.0	19.5	34.4	27.3	25.5	20.2	19.9
23.	Federal minimum wage (dollars per hour)	1.60	1.60	1.60	1.60	2.00	2.10	2.30	2.30
24.	Poverty rate (% of population)	12.6	12.5	11.9	11.1	11.2	12.3	11.8	11.6
25.	Gini ratio for household income distribution**	0.394	0.396	0.401	0.397	0.395	0.397	0.398	0.402
26.	Productivity growth, business sector (%)	2.0	4.1	3.2	3.0	−1.6	3.5	3.1	1.7
27.	Trade surplus (+) or deficit (−) (billions of dollars)	2.3	−1.3	−5.4	1.9	−4.3	12.4	14.8	−27.2

1978	1979	1980	1981	1982	1983	1984	1985	1986	1987	1988	1989	1990
2,294.7	2,563.3	2,789.5	3,128.4	3,255.0	3,536.7	3,933.2	4,220.3	4,462.8	4,739.5	5,103.8	5,484.4	5,803.1
5,672.8	5,850.1	5,834.0	5,982.1	5,865.9	6,130.9	6,571.5	6,843.4	7,080.5	7,307.0	7,607.4	7,879.2	8,027.1
5.6	3.2	−0.2	2.5	−1.9	4.5	7.2	4.1	3.5	3.4	4.1	3.5	1.9
1,428.5	1,592.2	1,757.1	1,941.1	2,077.3	2,290.6	2,503.3	2,720.3	2,899.7	3,100.2	3,353.6	3,598.5	3,839.9
438.0	492.9	479.3	572.4	517.2	564.3	735.6	736.2	746.5	785.0	821.6	874.9	861.0
453.6	500.8	566.2	627.5	680.5	733.5	797.0	879.0	949.3	999.5	1,039.0	1,099.1	1,180.2
7.6	11.3	13.5	10.3	6.2	3.2	4.3	3.6	1.9	3.6	4.1	4.8	5.4
357.3	381.8	408.5	436.7	474.8	521.4	551.6	619.8	724.6	750.2	786.6	792.8	824.8
7.91	11.20	13.35	16.39	12.24	9.09	10.23	8.10	6.80	6.66	7.57	9.21	8.10
9.06	12.67	15.26	18.87	14.85	10.79	12.04	9.93	8.33	8.21	9.32	10.87	10.01
222.6	225.1	227.8	230.0	232.2	234.3	236.3	238.5	240.7	242.8	245.0	247.3	250.1
601.4	460.3	530.6	596.6	594.1	559.8	543.9	570.0	601.7	601.5	643.0	1,091.0	1,536.5
102.3	105.0	106.9	108.7	110.2	111.6	113.5	115.5	117.8	119.9	121.7	123.9	125.8
96.0	98.8	99.3	100.4	99.5	100.8	105.0	107.2	109.6	112.4	115.0	117.3	118.8
6.1	5.8	7.1	7.6	9.7	9.6	7.5	7.2	7.0	6.2	5.5	5.3	5.6
−59.2	−40.7	−73.8	−79.0	−128.0	−207.8	−185.4	−212.3	−221.2	−149.7	−155.2	−152.6	−221.1
776.6	829.5	909.0	994.8	1,137.3	1,371.7	1,564.6	1,817.4	2,120.5	2,346.0	2,601.1	2,867.8	3,206.3
14.95	25.10	37.42	35.75	31.83	29.08	28.75	26.92	14.44	17.75	14.87	18.33	23.19
5.87	6.33	6.84	7.43	7.86	8.19	8.48	8.73	8.92	9.13	9.43	9.80	10.19
35.8	36.6	35.2	35.2	34.7	34.9	35.1	34.9	34.7	34.7	34.6	34.5	34.3
53.5	37.1	69.8	43.2	89	63.7	111.4	82.4	132	90.2	149	99.9	166.4
25.2	27.4	16.1	26.9	23.8	14.3	26.0	28.5	31.1	38.0	39.6	46.5	46.3
2.65	2.90	3.10	3.35	3.35	3.35	3.35	3.35	3.35	3.35	3.35	3.35	3.80
11.4	11.7	13.0	14.0	15.0	15.2	14.4	14.0	13.6	13.4	13.0	12.8	13.5
0.402	0.404	0.403	0.406	0.412	0.414	0.415	0.419	0.425	0.426	0.427	0.431	0.428
1.1	0.0	−0.2	2.1	−0.8	3.6	2.7	2.3	3.0	0.6	1.5	1.0	2.0
−29.8	−24.6	−19.4	−16.2	−24.2	−57.8	−109.1	−121.9	−138.5	−151.7	−114.6	−93.1	−80.9

*Revised definition of this series beginning in 1973.
**Revised definitions have occurred within this series.

Sources: Bureau of Economic Analysis; Bureau of Labor Statistics; *Economic Report of the President, 2021;* U.S. Bureau of the Census; Federal Reserve System; National Science Foundation; U.S. Citizenship and Immigration Services; U.S. Department of Energy.

Relevant Economic Statistics, United States, 1991–2011

		1991	1992	1993	1994	1995	1996	1997	1998	1999
1.	Gross domestic product (billions of dollars)	5,995.9	6,337.7	6,657.4	7,072.2	7,397.9	7,816.9	8,304.3	8,747.0	9,268.4
2.	Real gross domestic product (billions of 2005 dollars)	8,008.3	8,280.0	8,516.2	8,863.1	9,086.0	9,425.8	9,845.9	10,274.7	10,770.7
3.	Economic growth rate (percent change in real GDP)	-0.2	3.3	2.7	4.0	2.5	3.7	4.5	4.2	4.5
4.	Consumption expenditures (billions of dollars)	3,486.1	4,235.3	4,477.9	4,743.3	4,975.8	5,256.8	5,547.4	5,879.5	6,282.5
5.	Gross private domestic investment (billions of dollars)	802.9	864.8	953.4	1,097.1	1,144.0	1,240.3	1,389.8	1,509.1	1,625.7
6.	Government purchases (billions of dollars)	1,234.4	1,271.0	1,291.2	1,325.5	1,369.2	1,416.0	1,468.7	1,518.3	1,620.8
7.	Rate of inflation (percent change in CPI)	4.2	3.0	3.0	2.6	2.8	3.0	2.3	1.6	2.2
8.	Money supply, M1	897.0	1,025.1	1,129.9	1,150.7	1,126.9	1,079.8	1,072.2	1,094.8	1,122.6
9.	Federal funds interest rate (%)	5.69	3.52	3.02	4.21	5.83	5.30	5.46	5.35	4.97
10.	Prime interest rate (%)	8.46	6.25	6.00	7.15	8.83	8.27	8.44	8.35	8.00
11.	Population (millions)	253.5	256.9	260.2	263.4	266.6	269.7	272.9	276.1	279.3
12.	Immigration (thousands)	1,827.2	974.0	904.3	804.4	720.5	915.9	798.4	654.5	646.6
13.	Labor force (millions)	126.3	128.1	129.2	131.1	132.3	133.9	136.3	137.7	139.4
14.	Employment (millions)	117.7	118.5	120.3	123.1	124.9	126.7	129.6	131.5	133.5
15.	Unemployment rate (%)	6.8	7.5	6.9	6.1	5.6	5.4	4.9	4.5	4.2
16.	Federal budget surplus (+) or deficit (-)	-269.3	-290.3	-255.1	-203.2	-164.0	-107.5	-21.9	69.2	125.5
17.	Public debt (billions of dollars)	3,598.2	4,001.8	4,351.0	4,643.3	4,920.6	5,181.6	5,369.2	5,478.2	5,605.5
18.	Price of crude oil (dollars per barrel)	20.20	19.25	16.75	15.66	16.75	20.46	18.64	11.91	16.56
19.	Average hourly earnings, private nonagricultiral industries (dollars)	10.50	10.76	11.03	11.32	11.64	12.03	12.49	13.00	13.47
20.	Average weekly hours, private nonagriculatural industries	34.1	34.2	34.3	34.5	34.3	34.3	34.5	34.5	34.3
21.	Research and development expenditures (billions of dollars)	175	178.7	179.1	182.8	196.7	210.8	225.8	239.6	259
22.	Net farm income (billions of dollars)	40.2	50.7	46.7	52.6	39.8	60.0	51.3	47.1	47.7
23.	Federal minimum wage (dollars per hour)	4.25	4.25	4.25	4.25	4.25	4.75	5.15	5.15	5.15
24.	Poverty rate (% of population)	14.2	14.8	15.1	14.5	13.8	13.7	13.3	12.7	11.8
25.	Gini ratio for household income distribution**	0.428	0.434	0.454	0.456	0.450	0.455	0.459	0.456	0.458
26.	Productivity growth, business sector (%)	1.5	4.3	0.4	1.0	0.2	3.0	1.9	2.8	3.0
27.	Trade surplus (+) or deficit (-) (billions of dollars)	-31.1	-39.1	-70.2	-98.4	-96.3	-104.0	-108.3	-166.1	-265.1

2000	2001	2002	2003	2004	2005	2006	2007	2008	2009	2010	2011
9,817.0	10,128.0	10,469.6	10,960.8	11,685.9	12,433.9	13,194.7	13,841.3	14,291.5	13,973.7	14,498.9	15,075.7
11,216.4	11,337.5	11,543.1	11,836.4	12,246.9	12,623.0	12,958.5	13,206.4	13,161.9	12,757.9	13,063.0	13,299.1
3.7	0.8	1.6	2.5	3.6	3.1	2.9	2.2	-0.3	-3.1	2.4	1.8
6,739.4	7,055.0	7,350.7	7,703.6	8,195.9	8,707.8	9,224.5	9,734.2	9,750.9	9,566.4	9,936.1	10,729.0
1,735.5	1,614.3	1,582.1	1,664.1	1,888.6	2,077.2	2,209.2	2,125.4	2,087.6	1,549.3	1,737.3	1,854.9
1,721.6	1,825.6	1,961.1	2,092.5	2,216.8	2,363.4	2,523.0	2,689.8	2,878.1	2,917.5	3,002.8	3,029.7
3.4	2.8	1.6	2.3	2.7	3.4	3.2	2.8	3.8	-0.3	1.6	3.2
1,087.0	1,182.0	1,219.2	1,306.1	1,376.3	1,374.5	1,367.1	1,375.2	1,606.7	1,697.7	1,840.2	2,167.8
6.24	3.88	1.67	1.13	1.35	3.22	4.97	5.02	1.92	0.16	0.18	0.10
9.23	6.91	4.67	4.12	4.34	6.19	7.96	8.05	5.09	3.25	3.25	3.25
282.4	285.3	288.2	290.9	296.6	296.3	299.2	302.0	304.1	306.8	309.3	311.6
849.8	1,064.3	1,063.7	703.5	957.9	1,122.4	1,266.3	1,052.4	1,107.1	1,130.8	1,042.6	1,062.0
142.6	143.7	144.8	146.5	147.4	149.3	151.4	153.1	154.3	154.1	153.9	153.6
136.9	136.9	136.5	137.8	139.3	141.7	144.4	146.0	145.3	139.9	139.0	139.9
4.0	4.7	5.8	6.0	5.5	5.1	4.6	4.7	5.8	9.3	9.6	8.9
236.2	128.2	-157.8	-377.6	-412.7	-318.3	-248.2	-160.7	-458.5	-1,412.7	-1,293.5	-1,299.6
5,628.7	5,769.9	6,198.4	6,760.0	7,354.7	7,905.3	8,451.4	8,950.7	7,876.3	9,481.1	11,036.3	11,371.7
27.39	23.00	22.81	27.69	37.66	50.04	58.30	64.20	91.48	53.48	71.21	87.04
14.00	14.53	14.95	15.37	15.69	16.13	16.76	17.43	18.08	18.63	19.07	19.44
34.3	34.0	33.9	33.7	33.7	33.8	33.9	33.9	33.6	33.1	33.4	33.6
285	294.5	297.2	310.3	323.9	347.7	373.5	401.5	422.3	415.3	428	450.8
50.7	55.0	40.1	59.7	85.9	77.1	59.0	87.5	89.0	75.6	99.4	134.7
5.15	5.15	5.15	5.15	5.15	5.15	5.15	5.85	6.55	7.25	7.25	7.25
11.3	11.7	12.1	12.5	12.7	12.6	12.3	12.5	13.2	14.3	15.1	15.0
0.462	0.466	0.462	0.464	0.466	0.469	0.470	0.463	0.466	0.468	0.470	0.477
2.8	2.5	4.0	3.8	2.9	2.0	1.0	1.5	0.6	2.9	3.1	0.7
-379.8	-365.1	-423.7	-496.9	-607.7	-711.6	-753.3	-696.7	-698.3	-381.3	-500.0	-559.9

*Revised definition of this series beginning in 1973.
**Revised definitions have occurred within this series.

Sources: Bureau of Economic Analysis; Bureau of Labor Statistics; *Economic Report of the President, 2021;* U.S. Bureau of the Census; Federal Reserve System; National Science Foundation; U.S. Citizenship and Immigration Services; U.S. Department of Energy.

Relevant Economic Statistics, United States, 2012–2020

		2012	2013	2014	2015	2016	2017	2018	2019	2020
1.	Gross domestic product (billions of dollars)	16,197.0	16,784.9	17,527.3	18,224.8	18,745.10	19,543.00	20,611.90	21,433.20	20,936.60
2.	Real GDP (billions of 2012 dollars)	16,197.0	16,495.4	16,912.0	17,403.8	17,730.50	18,144.10	18,687.80	19,091.70	18,426.10
3.	Economic growth rate (percent change in real GDP)	2.2	1.8	2.5	2.9	1.7	2.3	3	2.2	−3.5
4.	Consumption expenditures (billions of dollars)	11,006.8	11,317.2	11,822.8	12,284.3	12,770	13,340.40	13,993.30	14,544.60	14,145.30
5.	Gross private domestic investment (billions of dollars)	2,621.8	2,826.0	3,044.2	3,223.1	3,188.30	3,351.10	3,632.90	3,751.20	3,604.70
6.	Government purchases (billions of dollars)	3,137.0	3,132.4	3,168.0	3,237.3	3,299.30	3,407.00	3,595.20	3,747.90	3,833.8
7.	Rate of inflation (percent change in CPI)	2.1	1.5	1.6	0.1	1.3	2.1	1.9	2.20	1.7
8.	Money supply, M1	2,440.2	2,660.5	2,927.3	3,087.2	3,612.00	3,653.10	3,794.30	3,844.30	12,808.70
9.	Federal funds interest rate (%)	0.14	0.14	0.07	0.37	0.66	1.41	2.40	2.16	0.38
10.	Prime interest rate (%)	3.25	3.25	3.25	3.37	3.64	4.4	5.35	5.29	3.53
11.	Population (millions)	313.9	317.1	319.5	321.7	324	326.1	327.2	330.30	332.6
12.	Immigration (thousands)	1,154	1,036	1,133	1,673	1,281	1,255	1,165	1,137	966
13.	Labor force (millions)	155.0	155.1	156.1	158.3	159.2	160.3	162.1	163.5	160.7
14.	Employment (millions)	142.5	144.7	147.4	150.1	151.4	153.3	155.8	157.5	147.8
15.	Unemployment rate (%)	8.1	6.7	5.6	5.0	4.9	4.4	3.9	3.7	8.1
16.	Federal budget surplus (+) or deficit (−) (billions of dollars)	−1,087.0	−680.0	−485.0	−439.0	−584.7	−665.4	−779.0	−984.4	−3,131.90
17.	Public debt (billions of dollars)	16,050.9	16,738.0	17,824.0	18,151.0	19,976.8	20,492.8	21,974.1	22,493.0	26,098.6
18.	Price of crude oil (dollars per barrel)	94.05	97.98	93.17	48.66	43.29	50.8	65.23	56.99	39.68
19.	Average hourly earnings, private nonagricultural industries (dollars)	19.72	20.13	20.59	21.02	21.54	22.05	22.7	23.51	24.68

	2012	2013	2014	2015	2016	2017	2018	2019	2020***
20. Average weekly hours, private nonagricultural industries	34.4	34.5	34.5	34.5	34.4	34.4	34.5	34.4	34.6
21. Research and development expenditures (billions of dollars)	460.5	481.5	500.8	523.6	549.5	572.1	617.6	669.1	696.6
22. Net farm income (billions of dollars)	109.6	138.2	101.2	88.7	67	79.3	83.8	84.6	119.6
23. Federal minimum wage (dollars per hour)	7.25	7.25	7.25	7.25	7.25	7.25	7.25	7.25	7.25
24. Poverty rate (% of population)	15	14.5	14.8	13.5	12.7	12.3	11.8	10.5	11.4
25. Gini ratio for household income distribution	0.477	0.482	0.48	0.479	0.481	0.482	0.489	0.486	0.484
26. Productivity growth, business sector (%)	0.3	1.5	0.6	0.6	1.3	1.4	1.0	1.7	2.5
27. Trade surplus (+) or deficit (−) (billions of dollars)	-568.6	-490.8	-507.7	-519.8	-512.5	-555.5	-609.5	-610.5	-647.2

***National Income and Product Account data for 2020 and immediately prior years are subject to change because of further government revisions.

Sources: Bureau of Economic Analysis; Bureau of Labor Statistics; Economic Report of the President, 2021; U.S. Bureau of the Census; Federal Reserve System; National Science Foundation; U.S. Citizenship and Immigration Services; U.S. Department of Energy.

Glossary

A

ability-to-pay principle The idea that those who have greater income (or wealth) should pay a greater proportion of it as taxes than those who have less income (or wealth).

absolute advantage The ability to produce a good better, faster, or more quickly than a competitor.

accounting profit The total revenue of a firm less its explicit costs.

actual reserves The funds that a bank has on deposit at the Federal Reserve Bank of its district (plus its vault cash).

advance estimate First estimate of quarterly GDP by the Bureau of Economic Analysis.

aggregate A collection of specific economic units treated as if they were one. For example, all prices of individual goods and services are combined into a price level, or all the units of output are aggregated into gross domestic product.

aggregate demand A schedule or curve that shows the total quantity of goods and services demanded (purchased) at different price levels.

aggregate demand–aggregate supply (AD–AS) model The macroeconomic model that uses aggregate demand and aggregate supply to determine and explain the price level and the real domestic output.

aggregate supply A schedule or curve showing the total quantity of goods and services supplied (produced) at different price levels.

allocative efficiency The apportionment of resources among firms and industries to obtain the production of the products most wanted by society (consumers); the output of each product at which its marginal cost and price or marginal benefit are equal.

appreciation (of the dollar) An increase in the value of the dollar relative to the currency of another nation, so a dollar buys a larger amount of the foreign currency and thus of foreign goods.

asset demand The amount of money people want to hold as a store of value; this amount varies inversely with the interest rate.

average fixed cost (AFC) A firm's total fixed cost divided by output (the quantity of product produced).

average product (AP) The total output produced per unit of a resource employed (total product divided by the quantity of that employed resource).

average revenue (AR) Total revenue from the sale of a product divided by the quantity of the product sold (demanded); equal to the price at which the product is sold when all units of the product are sold at the same price.

average tax rate Total tax paid divided by total (taxable) income, as a percentage.

average total cost (ATC) A firm's total cost divided by output (the quantity of product produced); equal to average fixed cost plus average variable cost.

average variable cost (AVC) A firm's total variable cost divided by output (the quantity of product produced).

B

balance sheet A statement of the assets, liabilities, and net worth of a firm or individual at some given time.

barrier to entry Anything that artificially prevents the entry of firms into an industry.

barter The exchange of one good or service for another good or service.

basic research Research into foundational scientific questions without regard to practical use.

benefits-received principle The idea that those who receive the benefits of goods and services provided by government should pay the taxes required to finance them.

Board of Governors The seven-member group that supervises and controls the money and banking system of the United States; also called the *Board of Governors of the Federal Reserve System* and the *Federal Reserve Board.*

budget deficit The amount by which the expenditures of the federal government exceed its revenues in any year.

budget line A line that shows the different combinations of two products a consumer can purchase with a specific money income, given the products' prices.

budget surplus The amount by which the revenues of the federal government exceed its expenditures in any year.

built-in stabilizer A mechanism that increases government's budget deficit (or reduces its surplus) during a recession and increases government's budget surplus (or reduces its deficit) during expansion without any action by policymakers. The tax system is one such mechanism.

business A firm that purchases resources and provides goods and services to the economy.

business cycles Recurring increases and decreases in the level of economic activity over periods of years; a cycle consists of peak, recession, trough, and expansion phases.

C

capital Human-made resources (buildings, machinery, and equipment) used to produce goods and services; goods that do not directly satisfy human wants; also called *capital goods* and *investment goods.*

capital goods Items that are used to produce other goods and therefore do not directly satisfy consumer wants.

cartel A formal agreement among firms (or countries) in an industry to set the price of a product and establish the outputs of the individual firms (or countries) or to divide the market for the product geographically.

case fatality rate (CFR) The percentage of confirmed cases that result in death.

causative pathogen The viral, bacterial, parasitic, or fungal source of a disease.

change in demand A change in the quantity demanded of a good or service at every price; a shift of the demand curve to the left or right.

change in quantity demanded A movement from one point to another on a demand curve.

change in quantity supplied A movement from one point to another on a fixed supply curve.

change in supply A change in the quantity supplied of a good or service at every price; a shift of the supply curve to the left or right.

checkable deposit Any deposit in a commercial bank or thrift institution against which a check may be written.

circular flow diagram The flow of resources from households to firms and of products from firms to households. These flows are accompanied by reverse flows of money from firms to households and from households to firms.

Coase theorem The idea, first stated by economist Ronald Coase, that externality problems may be resolved through private negotiations of the affected parties.

collusion A situation in which firms act together and in agreement (collude) to fix prices, divide a market, or otherwise restrict competition.

command system A method of organizing an economy in which property resources are publicly owned and government uses central economic planning to direct and coordinate economic activities; command economy; communism.

commercial bank A firm that engages in the business of banking (accepts deposits, offers checking accounts, and makes loans).

community spread Spread that occurs when the source or contact with an infected person is unknown.

comparative advantage A situation in which a person or country can produce a specific product at a lower opportunity cost than some other person or country; the basis for specialization and trade.

comparative advantage The ability to produce a good at a lower opportunity cost of the resources used.

compensating differences Differences in the wages received by workers in different jobs to compensate for nonmonetary differences in the jobs.

competition The presence in a market of independent buyers and sellers competing with one another along with the freedom of buyers and sellers to enter and leave the market.

complementary goods Products and services that are used together. When the price of one falls, the demand for the other increases (and conversely).

constant opportunity cost An opportunity cost that remains the same for each additional unit as a consumer (or society) shifts purchases (production) from one product to another along a straight-line budget line (production possibilities curve).

constant returns to scale No changes in the average total cost of producing a product as the firm expands the size of its operations (output) in the long run.

constant-cost industry An industry in which expansion by the entry of new firms has no effect on the prices firms in the industry must pay for resources and thus no effect on production costs.

consumer goods Products and services that satisfy human wants directly.

Consumer Price Index (CPI) An index that measures the prices of a fixed "market basket" of some 300 goods and services bought by a "typical" consumer.

consumer sovereignty Determination by consumers of the types and quantities of goods and services that will be produced with the scarce resources of the economy; consumers' direction of production through their dollar votes.

contractionary fiscal policy A decrease in government purchases for goods and services, an increase in net taxes, or some combination of the two, for the purpose of decreasing aggregate demand and thus controlling inflation.

cost-benefit analysis A comparison of the marginal costs of a government project or program with the marginal benefits to decide whether or not to employ resources in that project or program and to what extent.

cost-push inflation Increases in the price level (inflation) resulting from an increase in resource costs (e.g., raw-material prices) and hence in per-unit production costs; inflation caused by reductions in aggregate supply.

Council of Economic Advisers (CEA) A group of three persons that advises and assists the president of the United States on economic matters (including the preparation of the annual *Economic Report of the President*).

creative destruction The hypothesis that the creation of new products and production methods simultaneously destroys the market power of existing monopolies.

cross-elasticity of demand The ratio of the percentage change in *quantity demanded* of one good to the percentage change in the price of some other good. A positive coefficient indicates the two products are *substitute goods;* a negative coefficient indicates they are *complementary goods.*

crowding-out effect A rise in interest rates and a resulting decrease in investment caused by the federal government's increased borrowing to finance budget deficits or debt.

cyclical asymmetry The potential problem of monetary policy successfully controlling inflation during the expansionary phase of the business cycle but failing to expand spending and real GDP during the recessionary phase of the cycle.

cyclical deficit A federal budget deficit that is caused by a recession and the consequent decline in tax revenues.

cyclical unemployment A type of unemployment caused by insufficient total spending (or by insufficient aggregate demand).

cyclically adjusted budget A measure of what the federal budget deficit or budget surplus would be with the existing tax and government spending programs if the economy had achieved full-employment GDP in the year.

D

decreasing-cost industry An industry in which expansion through the entry of firms lowers the prices that firms in the industry must pay for resources and therefore decreases their production costs.

deflation A decline in the economy's price level.

demand A schedule or curve that shows the various amounts of a product that consumers are willing and able to purchase at each of a series of possible prices during a specified period of time.

demand curve A curve illustrating demand.

demand shocks Sudden, unexpected change in *aggregate demand*.

demand-pull inflation Increases in the price level (inflation) resulting from an excess of demand over output at the existing price level, caused by an increase in aggregate demand.

demand-side market failures Underallocations of resources that occur when private demand curves understate consumers' full willingness to pay for a good or service.

dependent variable A variable that changes as a consequence of a change in some other (independent) variable; the "effect" or outcome.

depreciation (of a currency) A decrease in the value of the dollar relative to another currency, so a dollar buys a smaller amount of the foreign currency and therefore of foreign goods.

derived demand The demand for a resource that depends on the demand for the products it helps to produce.

determinants of aggregate demand Factors such as consumption spending, investment, government spending, and net exports that, if they change, shift the aggregate demand curve.

determinants of aggregate supply Factors such as input prices, productivity, and the legal-institutional environment that, if they change, shift the aggregate supply curve.

determinants of demand Factors other than price that determine the quantities demanded of a good or service.

determinants of supply Factors other than price that determine the quantities supplied of a good or service.

differentiated oligopoly An oligopoly in which the firms produce a differentiated product.

direct relationship The relationship between two variables that change in the same direction, for example, product price and quantity supplied.

discount rate The interest rate that the Federal Reserve Banks charge on the loans they make to commercial banks and thrift institutions.

diseconomies of scale Increases in the average total cost of producing a product as the firm expands the size of its plant (its output) in the long run.

division of labor The separation of the work required to produce a product into a number of different tasks that are performed by different workers; specialization of workers.

Doha Round The latest, uncompleted (as of early 2017) sequence of trade negotiations by members of the World Trade Organization; named after Doha, Qatar, where the set of negotiations began.

dollar votes The "votes" that consumers and entrepreneurs cast for the production of consumer and capital goods, respectively, when they purchase those goods in product and resource markets.

dumping The sale of products in a foreign country at prices either below costs or below the prices charged at home.

E

earned-income tax credit (EITC) A refundable federal tax credit for low-income working people designed to reduce poverty and encourage labor-force participation.

easy money policy Federal Reserve System actions to increase the money supply to lower interest rates and expand real GDP.

economic cost A payment that must be made to obtain and retain the services of a resource; the income a firm must provide to a resource supplier to attract the resource away from an alternative use; equal to the quantity of other products that cannot be produced when resources are instead used to make a particular product.

economic growth (1) An outward shift in the production possibilities curve that results from an increase in resource supplies or quality or an improvement in technology; (2) an increase of real output (gross domestic product) or real output per capita.

economic perspective A viewpoint that envisions individuals and institutions making rational decisions by comparing the marginal benefits and marginal costs associated with their actions.

economic problem The need for individuals and society to make choices because wants exceed means.

economic profit The total revenue of a firm less its economic costs (which include both explicit costs and implicit costs); also called *pure profit* and *above-normal profit*.

economic resources The land, labor, capital, and entrepreneurial ability that are used in the production of goods and services; productive agents; factors of production.

economic system A particular set of institutional arrangements and a coordinating mechanism for solving the economizing problem; a method of organizing an economy, of which the market system and the command system are the two general types.

economics The study of how people, institutions, and society make economic choices under conditions of scarcity.

economies of scale Reductions in the average total cost of producing a product as the firm expands the size of plant (its output) in the long run; the economies of mass production.

elastic demand Product or resource demand whose price elasticity is greater than 1. This means the resulting change in quantity demanded is greater than the percentage change in price.

elasticity of labor demand A measure of the responsiveness of labor quality to a change in the wage rate.

employment–population ratio The ratio of employment in a country to its population.

entitlement programs Government programs such as social insurance, SNAP, Medicare, and Medicaid that guarantee particular levels of transfer payments or noncash benefits to all who fit the programs' criteria.

entrepreneurial ability The human resource that combines the other resources to produce a product, makes nonroutine decisions, innovates, and bears risks.

epidemic An outbreak that applies to a larger area or population.

equality-efficiency trade-off The decrease in economic efficiency that may accompany a decrease in income inequality; the presumption that some income inequality is required to achieve economic efficiency.

equilibrium price The price in a competitive market at which the quantity demanded and the quantity supplied are equal, there is neither a shortage nor a surplus, and there is no tendency for price to rise or fall.

equilibrium price level The price level at which the aggregate demand curve intersects the aggregate supply curve.

equilibrium quantity (1) The quantity demanded and supplied at the equilibrium price in a competitive market; (2) the profit-maximizing output of a firm.

equilibrium real output The gross domestic product at which the total quantity of final goods and services purchased (aggregate expenditures) is equal to the total quantity of final goods and services produced (the real domestic output); the real domestic output at which the aggregate demand curve intersects the aggregate supply curve.

euro The common currency unit used by 19 European nations as of 2021 (Austria, Belgium, Cyprus, Estonia, Finland, France, Germany, Greece, Ireland, Italy, Latvia, Lithuania, Luxembourg, Malta, the Netherlands, Portugal, Slovakia, Slovenia, and Spain).

European Union (EU) An association of 28 European nations (as of early 2017) that has eliminated tariffs and quotas among them, established common tariffs for imported goods from outside the member nations, eliminated barriers to the free movement of capital, and created other common economic policies.

excess capacity Plant resources that are underused when imperfectly competitive firms produce less output than that associated with achieving minimum average total cost.

excess reserves The amount by which a bank's or thrift's actual reserves exceed its required reserves; actual reserves minus required reserves.

exchange rate The rate of exchange of one nation's currency for another nation's currency.

exclusive unionism The practice of a labor union of restricting the supply of skilled union labor to increase the wages received by union members; the policies typically employed by a craft union.

expansion The phase of the business cycle in which output, income, and business activity rise.

expansionary fiscal policy An increase in government purchases of goods and services, a decrease in net taxes, or some combination of the two, for the purpose of increasing aggregate demand and expanding real output.

explicit cost The monetary payment a firm must make to an outsider to obtain a resource.

export subsidies Government payments to domestic producers to enable them to reduce the price of a good or service to foreign buyers.

external public debt Public debt owed to foreign citizens, firms, and institutions.

extrapolation The mathematical technique of taking present data and extending it to the future.

F

factors of production Economic resources: land, capital, labor, and entrepreneurial ability.

federal funds rate The interest rate banks and other depository institutions charge one another on overnight loans made out of their excess reserves.

federal funds rate The market-determined rate at which banks borrow from one another to meet obligations imposed on it by the Federal Reserve.

Federal Open Market Committee (FOMC) The 12-member group that determines the purchase and sale policies of the Federal Reserve Banks in the market for U.S. government securities.

Federal Reserve Banks The 12 banks chartered by the U.S. government to control the money supply and perform other functions.

Federal Reserve Note Paper money issued by the Federal Reserve Banks.

Federal Reserve System A central component of the U.S. banking system, consisting of the Board of Governors of the Federal Reserve and 12 regional Federal Reserve Banks.

dual mandate The 1977 congressional directive that the Federal Reserve System's highest priorities should be full employment and price level stability. In practice, the Fed aims for the full-employment rate of unemployment and an inflation rate of 2 percent per year.

final goods and services Goods and services that have been purchased for final use and not for resale or further processing or manufacturing.

fiscal policy Changes in government spending and tax collections designed to achieve a full-employment and noninflationary domestic output; also called *discretionary fiscal policy.*

fixed cost Any cost that in total does not change when the firm changes its output; the cost of fixed resources.

foreign exchange market A market in which the money (currency) of one nation can be used to purchase (can be exchanged for) the money of another nation.

fractional reserve banking system A banking system in which banks and thrifts are required to hold less than 100 percent of their checkable deposit liabilities as cash reserves.

free-rider problem The inability of potential providers of an economically desirable good or service to obtain payment from those who benefit because of nonexcludability.

freedom of choice The freedom of owners of property resources to employ or dispose of them as they see fit, of workers to enter any line of work for which they are qualified, and of consumers to spend their incomes in a manner that they think is appropriate.

freedom of enterprise The freedom of firms to obtain economic resources, to use those resources to produce products of the firm's own choosing, and to sell their products in markets of their choice.

frictional unemployment A type of unemployment caused by workers voluntarily changing jobs and by temporary layoffs; unemployed workers between jobs.

full-employment rate of unemployment The unemployment rate at which there is no cyclical unemployment of the labor force; equal to between 4 and 5 percent (rather than 0 percent) in the United States because frictional and structural unemployment are unavoidable.

G

game theory A means of analyzing the business behavior of oligopolists that uses the theory of strategy associated with games such as chess and bridge.

GDP gap Actual gross domestic product minus potential output; may be either a positive amount (a positive GDP gap) or a negative amount (a negative GDP gap).

General Agreement on Tariffs and Trade (GATT) The international agreement reached in 1947 in which 23 nations agreed to give equal and nondiscriminatory treatment to one another, to reduce tariff rates by multinational negotiations, and to eliminate import quotas. It now includes most nations and has become the World Trade Organization.

Gini ratio A numerical measure of the overall dispersion of income among households, families, or individuals; found graphically by dividing the area between the diagonal line and the Lorenz curve by the entire area below the diagonal line.

government purchases Expenditures by government for goods and services that government consumes in providing public goods and for public capital that has a long lifetime; the expenditures of all governments in the economy for those final goods and services.

gross domestic product (GDP) The total market value of all final goods and services produced annually within the boundaries of the United States, whether by U.S.- or foreign-supplied resources.

gross private domestic investment Expenditures for newly produced capital goods (such as machinery, equipment, tools, and buildings) and for additions to inventories.

growth accounting The bookkeeping of the supply-side elements that contribute to changes in real GDP over some specific time period.

H

homogeneous oligopoly An oligopoly in which the firms produce a standardized product.

household An economic unit (of one or more persons) that provides the economy with resources and uses the income received to purchase goods and services that satisfy economic wants.

human capital The accumulation of knowledge and skills that make a worker productive.

I

interest on excess reserves (IOER) Interest rate paid by the *Federal Reserve* on bank *excess reserves*.

immediate-short-run aggregate supply curve An aggregate supply curve for which real output, but not the price level, changes when the aggregate demand curve shifts; a horizontal aggregate supply curve that implies an inflexible price level.

implicit cost The monetary income a firm sacrifices when it uses a resource it owns rather than supplying the resource in the market; equal to what the resource could have earned in the best-paying alternative employment; includes a normal profit.

import quota A limit imposed by a nation on the quantity (or total value) of a good that may be imported during some period of time.

imported cases Cases in travelers returning from an infected region to a previously uninfected region and introducing it to the area.

inclusive unionism The practice of a labor union of including as members all workers employed in an industry.

income elasticity of demand The ratio of the percentage change in the quantity demanded of a good to a percentage change in consumer income; measures the responsiveness of consumer purchases to income changes.

income inequality The unequal distribution of an economy's total income among households or families.

income mobility The extent to which income receivers move from one part of the income distribution to another over some period of time.

increasing returns An increase in a firm's output by a larger percentage than the percentage increase in its inputs.

increasing-cost industry An industry in which expansion through the entry of new firms raises the prices firms in the industry must pay for resources and therefore increases their production costs.

independent variable The variable causing a change in some other (dependent) variable.

inelastic demand Product or resource demand for which the price elasticity of demand is less than 1. This means the resulting percentage change in quantity demanded is less than the percentage change in price.

infection morality rate (IMR) The percentage of confirmed cases that result in death.

inferior good A good or service whose consumption declines as income rises, prices held constant.

inflation A rise in the general level of prices in an economy.

inflexible prices Product prices that remain in place (at least for a while) even though supply or demand has changed; stuck prices or sticky prices.

infodemic The phenomenon where an excess of information in varying levels of accuracy makes it challenging to find dependable sources.

information technology New and more efficient methods of delivering and receiving information through use of computers, fax machines, wireless phones, and the Internet.

infrastructure The capital goods usually provided by the public sector for the use of its citizens and firms (e.g., highways, bridges, transit systems, wastewater treatment facilities, municipal water systems, and airports).

intermediate goods Products that are purchased for resale or further processing or manufacturing.

Interpolation The mathematical technique of filling in data between two known observations.

inverse relationship The relationship between two variables that change in opposite directions, for example, product price and quantity demanded.

investment Spending for the production and accumulation of capital and additions to inventories.

"invisible hand" The tendency of firms and resource suppliers that seek to further their own self-interests in competitive markets to also promote the interest of society.

K

kinked-demand curve The demand curve for a noncollusive oligopolist, which is based on the assumption that rivals will match a price decrease and will ignore a price increase.

L

labor People's physical and mental talents and efforts that are used to help produce goods and services.

labor force Persons 16 years of age and older who are not in institutions and who are employed or are unemployed and seeking work.

labor force participation rate The percentage of the civilian, non-institutionalized population that is either employed or searching for a job.

labor productivity Total output divided by the quantity of labor employed to produce it; the average product of labor or output per hour of work.

labor-force participation rate The percentage of the working-age population that is actually in the labor force.

land Natural resources ("free gifts of nature") used to produce goods and services.

law of demand The principle that, other things equal, an increase in a product's *price* will reduce the quantity of it demanded, and conversely for a decrease in price.

law of diminishing marginal utility The principle that as a consumer increases the consumption of a good or service, the marginal utility obtained from each additional unit of the good or service decreases.

law of diminishing returns The principle that as successive increments of a variable resource are added to a fixed resource, the marginal product of the variable resource will eventually decrease.

law of increasing opportunity costs The principle that as the production of a good increases, the opportunity cost of producing an additional unit rises.

law of supply The principle that, other things equal, an increase in the *price* of a product will increase the quantity of it supplied, and conversely for a price decrease.

learning by doing Achieving greater productivity and lower average total cost through gains in knowledge and skill that accompany repetition of a task; a source of economies of scale.

legal tender A legal designation of a nation's official currency (bills and coins). Payment of debts must be accepted in this monetary unit, but creditors can specify the form of payment, for example, "cash only" or "check or credit card only."

leverage ratio The percentage of all assets considered Tier 1 assets.

liquidity The ease with which an asset can be converted quickly into cash with little or no loss of purchasing power. Money is said to be perfectly liquid, whereas other assets have a lesser degree of liquidity.

liquidity trap A situation in a severe recession in which the Fed's injection of additional reserves into the banking system has little or no additional positive impact on lending, borrowing, investment, or aggregate demand.

liquidity trap A situation where zero or near zero interest rates do not stimulate borrowing.

long run (1) In microeconomics, a period of time long enough to enable producers of a product to change the quantities of all the resources they employ; period in which all resources and costs are variable and no resources or costs are fixed. (2) In macroeconomics, a period sufficiently long for nominal wages and other input prices to change in response to a change in the nation's price level.

long-run aggregate supply curve The aggregate supply curve associated with a time period in which input prices (especially nominal wages) are fully responsive to changes in the price level.

long-run supply curve A curve showing the prices at which a purely competitive industry will make various quantities of the product available in the long run.

Lorenz curve A curve showing the distribution of income in an economy. The cumulated percentage of families (income receivers) is measured along the horizontal axis, and cumulated percentage of income is measured along the vertical axis.

M

M1 The most narrowly defined money supply, equal to currency in the hands of the public and the checkable deposits of commercial banks and thrift institutions.

M2 A more broadly defined money supply, equal to $M1$ plus noncheckable savings accounts (including money market deposit accounts), small-denominated time deposits (deposits of less than \$100,000), and individual money market mutual fund balances.

macroeconomics The part of economics concerned with the economy as a whole; with such major aggregates as the household, business, and government sectors; and with measures of the total economy.

mandatory spending Budget items for which a previously passed law requires that the money be spent.

marginal analysis The comparison of marginal ("extra" or "additional") benefits and marginal costs, usually for decision making.

marginal cost (MC) The extra (additional) cost of producing 1 more unit of output; equal to the change in total cost divided by the change in output (and, in the short run, to the change in total variable cost divided by the change in output).

marginal product (MP) The additional output produced when 1 additional unit of a resource is employed (the quantity of all other resources employed remaining constant); equal to the change in total product divided by the change in the quantity of a resource employed.

marginal resource cost The amount the total cost of employing a resource increases when a firm employs 1 additional unit of the resource (the quantity of all other resources employed remaining constant); equal to the change in the total cost of the resource divided by the change in the quantity of the resource employed.

marginal revenue (MR) The change in total revenue that results from the sale of 1 additional unit of a firm's product; equal to the change in total revenue divided by the change in the quantity of the product sold.

marginal revenue product The change in a firm's total revenue when it employs 1 additional unit of a resource (the quantity of all other resources employed remaining constant); equal to the change in total revenue divided by the change in the quantity of the resource employed.

marginal tax rate The tax rate paid on an additional dollar of income.

mark-to-market An accounting rule that requires banks to revise their balance sheets to reflect the drop in the value of any financial assets they hold.

market Any institution or mechanism that brings together buyers (demanders) and sellers (suppliers) of a particular good or service.

market failure The inability of a market to bring about the allocation of resources that best satisfies the wants of society; in particular, the overallocation or underallocation of resources to the production of a particular good or service because of spillovers or informational problems or because markets do not provide desired public goods.

immediate market period A period in which producers of a product are unable to change the quantity produced in response to a change in its price and in which there is a perfectly inelastic supply.

market system All the product and resource markets of a market economy and the relationships among them; a method that allows the prices determined in those markets to allocate the economy's scarce resources and to communicate and coordinate the decisions made by consumers, firms, and resource suppliers.

Medicaid A federal program that helps finance the medical expenses of individuals covered by the Supplemental Security Income (SSI) and Temporary Assistance for Needy Families (TANF) programs.

Medicare A federal program that is financed by payroll taxes and provides for (1) compulsory hospital insurance for senior citizens, (2) low-cost voluntary insurance to help older Americans pay physicians' fees, and (3) subsidized insurance to buy prescription drugs.

medium of exchange Any item sellers generally accept and buyers generally use to pay for a good or service; money; a conve-

nient means of exchanging goods and services without engaging in barter.

microeconomics The part of economics concerned with such individual units as a household, a firm, or an industry and with individual markets, specific goods and services, and product and resource prices.

minimum efficient scale (MES) The lowest level of output at which a firm can minimize long-run average total cost.

monetary multiplier The multiple of its excess reserves by which the banking system can expand checkable deposits and thus the money supply by making new loans (or buying securities); equal to 1 divided by the reserve requirement.

monetary policy A central bank's changing of the money supply to influence interest rates and assist the economy in achieving price stability, full employment, and economic growth.

monetary transmission mechanism The process by which the use of a monetary policy tool impacts the overall economy.

money Any item that is generally acceptable to sellers in exchange for goods and services.

money market The market in which the demand for and the supply of money determine the interest rate (or the level of interest rates) in the economy.

money market deposit account (MMDA) An interest-earning account (at a bank or thrift) consisting of short-term securities and on which a limited number of checks may be written each year.

money market mutual fund (MMMF) An interest-bearing account offered by investment companies, which pool depositors' funds for the purchase of short-term securities. Depositors may write checks in minimum amounts or more against their accounts.

monopolistic competition A market structure in which many firms sell a differentiated product, into which entry is relatively easy, in which the firm has some control over its product price, and in which there is considerable nonprice competition.

monopsony A market structure in which there is only a single buyer of a good, service, or resource.

moral hazard The possibility that individuals or institutions will change their behavior as the result of a contract or agreement.

mortgage-backed securities Bonds that represent claims to all or part of the monthly mortgage payments from the pools of mortgage loans made by lenders to borrowers to help them purchase residential property.

MR = MC rule The principle that a firm will maximize its profit (or minimize its losses) by producing the output at which marginal revenue and marginal cost are equal, provided product price is equal to or greater than average variable cost.

MRP = MRC rule The principle that to maximize profit, a firm should expand employment until the marginal revenue product (MRP) of labor equals the marginal resource cost (MRC) of labor.

multiplier The ratio of a change in the equilibrium GDP to the change in *investment* or in any other component of aggregate expenditures or *aggregate demand;* the number by which a change in any such component must be multiplied to find the resulting change in the equilibrium GDP.

municipal bond A bond issued by a state, city, or public university.

mutual interdependence A situation in which a change in price strategy (or in some other strategy) by one firm will affect the sales and profits of another firm (or other firms). Any firm that makes such a change can expect the other rivals to react to the change.

N

national income and product accounts (NIPA) The national accounts that measure overall production and income of the economy and other related aggregates for the nation as a whole.

natural monopoly An industry in which economies of scale are so great that a single firm can produce the product at a lower average total cost than would be possible if more than one firm produced the product.

near-money Financial assets, the most important of which are noncheckable savings accounts, time deposits, and U.S. short-term securities and savings bonds, which are not a medium of exchange but can be readily converted into money.

negative externalities Spillover production or consumption costs imposed on third parties without compensation to them.

net exports Exports minus imports.

network effects Increases in the value of a product to each user, including existing users, as the total number of users rises.

nominal GDP Gross domestic product measured in terms of the price level at the time of the measurement; GDP that is unadjusted for inflation.

nominal income The number of dollars received by an individual or group for supplying resources during some period of time; income that is not adjusted for inflation.

nominal interest rate The interest rate expressed in terms of annual amounts currently charged for interest and not adjusted for inflation.

noncash transfer A government transfer payment in the form of goods and services rather than money, for example, food stamps, housing assistance, and job training; also called *in-kind transfer.*

nonprice competition Competition based on distinguishing one's product by means of product differentiation and then advertising the distinguished product to consumers.

nontariff barriers (NTBs) All barriers other than protective tariffs that nations erect to impede international trade, including import quotas, licensing requirements, unreasonable product-quality standards, unnecessary bureaucratic detail in customs procedures, and so on.

normal good A good or service whose consumption increases when income increases and falls when income decreases, price remaining constant.

normal profit The payment made by a firm to obtain and retain entrepreneurial ability; the minimum income entrepreneurial ability must receive to induce it to perform entrepreneurial functions for a firm.

North American Free Trade Agreement (NAFTA) A 1993 agreement establishing, over a 15-year period, a free-trade zone composed of Canada, Mexico, and the United States.

O

occupational licensing State and local laws that require a worker to satisfy certain specific requirements and obtain a license from a licensing board before engaging in a particular occupation.

offshoring The practice of shifting work previously done by American workers to workers located abroad.

oligopoly A market structure in which a few firms sell either a standardized or a differentiated product, into which entry is difficult, in which the firm has limited control over product price because of mutual interdependence (except when there is collusion among firms), and in which there is typically nonprice competition.

open-market operations The buying and selling of U.S. government securities by the Federal Reserve Banks for purposes of carrying out monetary policy.

operations The actual conversion process to transform resources into products.

opportunity cost The value of the good, service, or time forgone to obtain something else.

opportunity cost The forgone alternative of the choice made.

optimal reduction of an externality The reduction of a negative externality such as pollution to a level at which the marginal benefit and marginal cost of reduction are equal.

other-things-equal assumption The assumption that factors other than those being considered are held constant; *ceteris paribus* assumption.

outbreak A sudden increase in the number of cases infecting a limited geographic area.

output effect The situation in which an increase in the price of one input will increase a firm's production costs and reduce its level of output, thus reducing the demand for other inputs; conversely for a decrease in the price of the input.

P

pandemic When spread expands across several countries or continents impacting large populations.

per se violations Collusive actions, such as attempts to fix prices or divide markets, that are violations of the antitrust laws, even if the actions are unsuccessful.

perfectly elastic demand Product or resource demand in which quantity demanded can be of any amount at a particular product price; graphs as a horizontal demand curve.

perfectly inelastic demand Product or resource demand in which price can be of any amount at a particular quantity of the product or resource demanded; quantity demanded does not respond to a change in price; graphs as a vertical demand curve.

personal consumption expenditures The expenditures of households for durable and nondurable consumer goods and services.

personal protective equipment (PPE) Equipment that is used by medical professionals to protect them from infection by patients as well as to protect patients from infection by medical professionals.

Pigovian tax A tax or charge levied on the production of a product that generates *negative externalities*. If set correctly, the tax will precisely offset the overallocation (overproduction) generated by the negative externality.

political business cycle The alleged tendency of presidential administrations and Congress to destabilize the economy by reducing taxes and increasing government expenditures before elections and to raise taxes and lower expenditures after elections.

positive externalities Spillover production or consumption benefits conferred on third parties without compensation from them.

potential output The real output (GDP) an economy can produce when it fully employs its available resources.

poverty rate The percentage of the population with incomes below the official poverty income levels that are established by the federal government.

price ceiling A legally established maximum price for a good or service.

price ceiling Price above which a commodity may not sell.

price discrimination The selling of a product to different buyers at different prices when the price differences are not justified by differences in cost.

price elasticity of demand The ratio of the percentage change in quantity demanded of a product or resource to the percentage change in its price; a measure of the responsiveness of buyers to a change in the price of a product or resource.

price elasticity of supply The ratio of the percentage change in quantity supplied of a product or resource to the percentage change in its price; a measure of the responsiveness of producers to a change in the price of a product or resource.

price floor A legally established minimum price for a good or service.

price gouging The negative term applied to the circumstance when firms raise prices substantially when demand increases unexpectedly.

price leadership An informal method that firms in an oligopoly may employ to set the price of their product: One firm (the leader) is the first to announce a change in price, and the other firms (the followers) soon announce identical or similar changes.

price taker A seller (or buyer) that is unable to affect the price at which a product or resource sells by changing the amount it sells (or buys).

private good A good or service that is individually consumed and that can be profitably provided by privately owned firms because they can exclude nonpayers from receiving the benefits.

private property The right of private persons and firms to obtain, own, control, employ, dispose of, and bequeath land, capital, and other property.

product differentiation A strategy in which one firm's product is distinguished from competing products by means of its design, related services, quality, location, or other attributes (except price).

product market A market in which products are sold by firms and bought by households.

production possibilities curve A curve showing the different combinations of two goods or services that can be produced in a full-employment, full-production economy where the available supplies of resources and technology are fixed.

productive efficiency The production of a good in the least costly way; occurs when production takes place at the output at which average total cost is a minimum and marginal product per dollar's worth of input is the same for all inputs.

productivity A measure of average output or real output per unit of input. For example, the productivity of labor is determined by dividing real output by hours of work.

progressive tax A tax whose average tax rate increases as the taxpayer's income increases and decreases as the taxpayer's income decreases.

proportional tax A tax whose average tax rate remains constant as the taxpayer's income increases or decreases.

public assistance programs Government programs that pay benefits to those who are unable to earn income (because of permanent disabilities or because they have very low income and dependent children); financed by general tax revenues and viewed as public charity (rather than earned rights).

public debt The total amount owed by the federal government to the owners of government securities; equal to the sum of past government budget deficits less government budget surpluses.

public good A good or service that is characterized by nonrivalry and nonexcludability; a good or service with these characteristics provided by government.

public investments Government expenditures on public capital (such as roads, highways, bridges, mass-transit systems, and electric power facilities) and on human capital (such as education, training, and health).

pure competition A market structure in which a very large number of firms sell a standardized product, into which entry is very easy, in which the individual seller has no control over the product price, and in which there is no nonprice competition; a market characterized by a very large number of buyers and sellers.

pure monopoly A market structure in which one firm sells a unique product, into which entry is blocked, in which the single firm has considerable control over product price, and in which nonprice competition may or may not be found.

purely competitive labor market A labor market in which a large number of similarly qualified workers independently offer their labor services to a large number of employers, none of whom can set the wage rate.

purely public good A good with the characteristics if both exclusivity and rivalry.

Q

quantitative easing (QE) An *open-market operation* in which *bonds* are purchased by a *central bank* in order to increase the quantity of *excess reserves* held by *commercial banks* and thereby (hopefully) stimulate the economy by increasing the amount of lending undertaken by commercial banks; undertaken when interest rates are near zero and, consequently, does not allow the central bank to further stimulate the economy with lower interest rates due to the *zero lower bound problem*.

quasi-public good A good or service to which excludability could apply but that has such a large spillover benefit that government sponsors its production to prevent an underallocation of resources.

R

real GDP Gross domestic product measured in terms of the price level in a base period (i.e., GDP that is adjusted for inflation).

real GDP per capita Real output (GDP) divided by population.

real income The amount of goods and services that can be purchased with nominal income during some period of time; nominal income adjusted for inflation.

real interest rate The interest rate expressed in dollars of constant value (adjusted for inflation) and equal to the nominal interest rate less the expected rate of inflation.

recession A period of declining real GDP, accompanied by lower real income and higher unemployment.

regressive tax A tax whose average tax rate decreases as the taxpayer's income increases and increases as the taxpayer's income decreases.

rent-seeking behavior The actions by persons, firms, or unions to gain special benefits from government at the taxpayers' or someone else's expense.

repo A repurchase agreement (or "repo") is a short-term money loan made by a lender to a borrower that is collateralized with *bonds* pledged by the borrower. The name *repo* refers to how the lender would view the transaction. The same transaction when viewed from the perspective of the borrower would be called a *reverse repo*.

required reserves The funds that banks and thrifts must deposit with the Federal Reserve Bank (or hold as vault cash) to meet the legal reserve requirement; a fixed percentage of the bank's or thrift's checkable deposits.

reserve ratio The specified minimum percentage of its checkable deposits that a bank or thrift must keep on deposit at the Federal Reserve Bank in its district or hold as vault cash.

reserve requirement The percentage of every dollar deposited in a checking account that a bank must maintain at a Federal Reserve branch.

resource market A market in which households sell and firms buy resources or the services of resources.

reverse repo A reverse repurchase agreement (or "reverse repo") is a short-term money loan that the borrower obtains by pledging *bonds* as collateral. The name *reverse repo* refers to how the borrower would view the transaction. The same transaction when viewed by the lender would be called a *repo*.

rule of reason The rule stated and applied in the U.S. Steel case that only combinations and contracts unreasonably restraining trade are subject to actions under the antitrust laws and that size and possession of monopoly power are not illegal.

S

savings account A deposit that is interest-bearing and that the depositor can normally withdraw at any time.

scarcity The limits placed on the amounts and types of *goods* and *services* available for consumption as the result of there being only limited *economic resources* from which to produce output; the fundamental economic constraint that creates *opportunity costs* and that necessitates the use of *marginal analysis (cost-benefit analysis)* to make optimal choices.

scientific method The procedure for the systematic pursuit of knowledge involving the observation of facts and the formulation and testing of hypotheses to obtain theories, principles, and laws.

self-interest The most-advantageous outcome as viewed by each firm, property owner, worker, or consumer.

shocks Sudden, unexpected changes in *demand* (or *aggregate demand*) or *supply* (or *aggregate supply*).

short run (1) In microeconomics, a period of time in which producers are able to change the quantities of some but not all of the resources they employ; a period in which some resources (usually plant) are fixed and some are variable. (2) In macroeconomics, a period in which nominal wages and other input prices do not change in response to a change in the price level.

short-run aggregate supply curve An aggregate supply curve relevant to a time period in which input prices (particularly nominal wages) do not change in response to changes in the price level.

short-run supply curve A supply curve that shows the quantity of a product a firm in a purely competitive industry will offer to sell at various prices in the short run; the portion of the firm's short-run marginal cost curve that lies above its average-variable-cost curve.

shortage The amount by which the quantity demanded of a product exceeds the quantity supplied at a particular (below-equilibrium) price.

shortage The condition where firms do not want to sell as many goods as consumers want to buy.

simultaneous consumption A product's ability to satisfy a large number of consumers at the same time.

slope of a straight line The ratio of the vertical change (the rise or fall) to the horizontal change (the run) between any two points on a line.

Smoot–Hawley Tariff Act Legislation passed in 1930 that established very high tariffs. Its objective was to reduce imports and stimulate the domestic economy, but it resulted only in retaliatory tariffs by other nations.

social insurance programs Programs that replace a portion of the earnings lost when people retire or are temporarily unemployed, that are financed by payroll taxes, and that are viewed as earned rights (rather than charity).

Social Security The federal program, financed by compulsory payroll taxes, that partially replaces earnings lost when workers retire, become disabled, or die.

Social Security trust fund A federal fund that saves excessive Social Security tax revenues received in one year to meet Social Security benefit obligations that exceed Social Security tax revenues in some subsequent year.

specialization The use of the resources of an individual, a firm, a region, or a nation to concentrate production on one or a small number of goods and services.

start-up (firm) A new firm focused on creating and introducing a particular new product or employing a specific new production or distribution method.

store of value An asset set aside for future use; one of the three functions of money.

strategic behavior Self-interested economic actions that take into account the expected reactions of others.

structural unemployment Unemployment of workers whose skills are not demanded by employers, who lack sufficient skill to obtain employment, or who cannot easily move to locations where jobs are available.

subprime mortgage loans High-interest-rate loans to home buyers with above-average credit risk.

substitute goods Products or services that can be used in place of each other. When the price of one falls, the demand for the other product falls; conversely, when the price of one product rises, the demand for the other product rises.

substitution effect The effect of a change in the price of a resource on the quantity of the resource employed by a firm, assuming no change in its output.

Supplemental Nutrition Assistance Program (SNAP) A government program that provides food money to low-income recipients by depositing electronic money onto special debit cards.

Supplemental Security Income (SSI) A federally financed and administered program that provides a uniform nationwide minimum income for the aged, blind, and disabled who do not qualify for benefits under Social Security in the United States.

supply A schedule or curve showing the amounts of a product that sellers (or a seller) will offer for sale at each of a series of possible prices during a specific period.

supply chain Processes that facilitate the movement of goods from the manufacturer to their end user (in the case of finished goods) or to another manufacturer (in the case of raw materials or components for work-in-process goods).

supply curve A curve illustrating supply.

supply shocks Sudden, unexpected changes in *aggregate supply.*

supply-side market failures Overallocations of resources that occur when private supply curves understate the full cost of producing a good or service.

surplus The amount by which the quantity supplied of a product exceeds the quantity demanded at a specific (above-equilibrium) price.

T

tariff A tax imposed by a nation on an imported good.

target rate of inflation The publicly announced annual inflation rate that a central bank attempts to achieve through monetary

policy actions if it is following an inflation targeting monetary policy.

Temporary Assistance for Needy Families (TANF) A state-administered and partly federally funded program in the United States that provides financial aid to poor families; the basic welfare program for low-income families in the United States; contains time limits and work requirements.

terms of trade The rate at which units of one product can be exchanged for units of another product; the price of a good or service; the amount of one good or service that must be given up to obtain 1 unit of another good or service.

thrift institution A savings and loan association, mutual savings bank, or credit union.

Tier 1 assets The core capital of a bank.

tight money policy Federal Reserve System actions that contract, or restrict, the growth of the nation's money supply for the purpose of reducing or eliminating inflation.

time deposit An interest-earning deposit in a commercial bank or thrift institution that the depositor can withdraw without penalty after the end of a specified period.

token money Bills or coins for which the amount printed on the *currency* bears no relationship to the value of the paper or metal embodied within it; for currency still circulating, money for which the face value exceeds the commodity value.

total cost The sum of fixed cost and variable cost.

total demand for money The sum of the transactions demand for money and the asset demand for money.

total product (TP) The total output of a particular good or service produced by a firm (or a group of firms or the entire economy).

total revenue (TR) The total number of dollars received by a firm (or firms) from the sale of a product; equal to the total expenditures for the product produced by the firm (or firms); equal to the quantity sold (demanded) multiplied by the price at which it is sold.

total-revenue test A test to determine elasticity of demand between any two prices: Demand is elastic if total revenue moves in the opposite direction from price; it is inelastic when it moves in the same direction as price; and it is of unitary elasticity when it does not change when price changes.

Trade Adjustment Assistance Act A U.S. law passed in 2002 that provides cash assistance, education and training benefits, health care subsidies, and wage subsidies (for persons age 50 or more) to workers displaced by imports or plant relocations abroad.

transactions demand for money The amount of money people want to hold for use as a medium of exchange (to make payments); varies directly with nominal GDP.

translational research Research into practical applications of basic research.

Troubled Asset Relief Program (TARP) A 2008 federal government program that authorized the U.S. Treasury to loan up to $700 billion to critical financial institutions and other U.S. firms that were in extreme financial trouble and therefore at high risk of failure.

U

U.S. securities Treasury bills, Treasury notes, Treasury bonds, and U.S. savings bonds issued by the federal government to finance expenditures that exceed tax revenues.

unemployment compensation The social insurance program that in the United States is financed by state payroll taxes on employers and makes income available to workers who become unemployed and are unable to find jobs.

unemployment rate The percentage of the labor force unemployed at any time.

unit elasticity Demand or supply for which the elasticity coefficient is equal to 1; means that the percentage change in the quantity demanded or supplied is equal to the percentage change in price.

unit of account A standard unit in which prices can be stated and the value of goods and services can be compared; one of the three functions of money.

utility The want-satisfying power of a good or service; the satisfaction or pleasure a consumer obtains from the consumption of a good or service (or from the consumption of a collection of goods and services).

V

variable cost A cost that in total increases when the firm increases its output and decreases when the firm reduces its output.

voluntary export restrictions (VERs) Voluntary limitations by countries or firms of their exports to a particular foreign nation to avoid enactment of formal trade barriers by that nation.

W

wage differential The difference between the wage received by one worker or group of workers and that received by another worker or group of workers.

Wall Street Reform and Consumer Protection Act of 2010 A law that gave authority to the Federal Reserve to regulate all large financial institutions, created an oversight council to look for growing risk to the financial system, established a process for the federal government to sell off the assets of large failing financial institutions, provided federal regulatory oversight of asset-backed securities, and created a financial consumer protection bureau within the Fed.

World Trade Organization (WTO) An organization of 164 nations (as of 2017) that oversees the provisions of the current world trade agreement, resolves trade disputes stemming from it, and holds forums for further rounds of trade negotiations.

X

X-inefficiency The production of output, whatever its level, at higher than the lowest average (and total) cost.

Z

zero interest rate policy (ZIRP) A *monetary policy* in which a central bank sets *nominal interest rates* at or near 0 percent per year in order to stimulate the economy.

Index

Note: Page numbers followed by n refer to notes.

E

H

I

S

X

Y

Z